KU-254-930

FOURTH EDITION

scientific social surveys and research

An Introduction to the Background, Content, Methods, Principles, and Analysis of Social Studies

PAULINE V. YOUNG, PH.D
Research Sociologist and Lecturer-at-large

With chapters on statistics, scaling techniques, graphic presentation, and human ecology by

CALVIN F. SCHMID, PH.D.
University of Washington

PRENTICE-HALL, INC.
Englewood Cliffs, New Jersey

PRENTICE-HALL SOCIOLOGY SERIES
Herbert Blumer, *Editor*

Library of Congress Catalog Card No.: 66-10949
Printed in the United States of America C-79650

Current printing (last digit):

10 9 8 7 6 5 4 3 2 1

PRENTICE-HALL INTERNATIONAL, INC., *London*
PRENTICE-HALL OF AUSTRALIA, PTY. LTD., *Sydney*
PRENTICE-HALL OF CANADA, LTD., *Toronto*
PRENTICE-HALL OF INDIA (PRIVATE) LTD., *New Delhi*
PRENTICE-HALL OF JAPAN, INC., *Tokyo*

to the memory of

ERLE FISKE YOUNG

scholar, poet, inventor

preface to fourth edition

The present fourth edition of *Scientific Social Surveys and Research* begins its twenty-seventh year of existence in the United States and abroad—a situation often disconcerting to an author. Originally this volume was designed to serve the needs of Americans beginning research undertakings. Aware of its wide use in foreign countries and its appearance in translation, the author began to contact teachers abroad who knew the volume intimately. These offered valuable general criticism as to "universals" in scientific procedure, as opposed to needs of particular groups. Such suggestions have been considered in the revision and rewriting of the text.

This text assumes that a beginner's understanding of the basic research procedures which he is to follow—the ways in which he is to use scientific tools and concepts and the theoretical considerations with which he is to approach his research undertakings—can be greatly enhanced by the frequent use of selective illustrative data drawn from varied empirical research studies. Much attention was devoted to this problem.

Chapter 1, "General Overview of a Research Project in Process,"[1] new to the present edition, is one of many illustrations provided to enable the beginner to form a suitable picture of the nature of social research and to perceive the many diverse aspects of the research process. It was found that students can involve themselves with greater interest and less of a "research, oh!" attitude if they can visualize at the outset the essential central steps, the thinking-through process, and the various precautions to be taken in a research study. . . . An "Overview" has an added advantage if commonly used but highly technical terms are explained, at least tentatively—"sample," "pilot study," "statistical data," "analysis," among others.

Much additional material was included in Chapters 2 and 3 in order to highlight the cumulative wisdom of trail blazers and other highly sophisticated researchers who guided their work by careful methodological and theoretical considerations. These studies illustrate not only the broad scope and nature of social research, but provide also a map pointing to many fruitful paths and bypaths that a beginner must explore for himself. The ensuing chapters on scientific attitudes, research design, observation, schedules and questionnaires, interviewing, and case-studies were largely rewritten, enlarged, or condensed as needed.

Dr. Schmid's chapters on "Scaling Techniques," "Graphic Presentation," and "Basic Statistical Concepts and Techniques" have been updated with additional material included on statistical inference; new illustrations have been supplied and old ones eliminated. Large portions of the chapter on "Research Techniques in Human Ecology" have been rewritten and the latest methodological and substantive developments pertinent to this field incorporated. The chapter on "Some Guiding Considerations in the Analysis of Data" has been so completely rewritten that it may be considered a virtually new chapter.

Regretfully, the chapters on "Development of the Social Survey Movement," which appeared in previous editions, have been omitted due to space limitations. However, a number of illustrations drawn from these chapters have been interspersed throughout the present volume.

In writing *Scientific Social Surveys and Research,* the authors and contributors have relied on their varied and continuous experiences as actual field research workers, social scientists, and teachers of research methods at different universities in the United States and abroad. They intended to (1) present a clear, vivid, realistic, and above all, a thoroughgoing and well-balanced discussion of the research essentials—in lucid English; (2) avoid a priori theorizing and ponderous abstractions apt to confuse a beginner; (3) provide logical and systematic treatment of the different techniques of social study and their underlying logic; (4) quote from a variety of sources and disciplines—sociology, psychology, anthropology,

[1] The Project was performed by students at Hong Kong Baptist College and at Chung Chi College, the latter now a part of the Chinese University of Hong Kong.

social work, philosophy, general literature—in order to provide a broad basis for understanding human behavior and social life, its organization and disorganization. (It has been said that understanding is the greatest boon a textbook can bestow on students.) (5) Finally, a consistent attempt has been made to point out the relationship between the research process and human purposes and values in twentieth century group life.

Scientific Social Surveys and Research is both an introductory text and a reference volume for social science and social work students and research organizations. Throughout the years of gathering data and writing the text, an attempt has been made to cultivate in readers a scientific spirit of social inquiry and to enable them to share meaningfully in the thinking and the actual research adventures which aimed to verify, correct, and extend knowledge, and thereby "arm men with their greatest victory—the conquest of themselves."

The University of Hawaii
Honolulu, Hawaii

PAULINE V. YOUNG

editor's note

The vigorous growth of research in social science poses three needs in the instruction and training of students. *First,* students must learn the basic rudiments of careful and systematic inquiry. They must understand the guiding rules and procedures that ensure the setting of proper problems, the collection of relevant data, and the making of meaningful and careful analysis. *Second,* they must comprehend clearly the nature of each of the major techniques of social research. The problems in social science are very diverse and the data needed for their solution vary significantly. This diversity in problems and subject matter has compelled the development of markedly different techniques, each with its own set of steps and its own body of safeguarding rules. *Third,* students should understand both the differences and the relations between these different techniques—when to use one and not another, and how they may be employed in combination.

The present volume is admirably designed to meet these three needs. The author has a thorough knowledge of these matters. She has sought assiduously for many years to find the simplest and most telling ways of communicating this knowledge to beginning students. In this earnest quest she has solicited and gained the assistance of many scholars who, like herself, are expert in given areas and forms of social research. The content and form of the present book bear testimony to the effectiveness of her efforts. The reader will find a decisive, clean-cut, and simple account of the manner in which the basic forms of social research are made, a clear portrayal of the nature of each of the major techniques, and an understandable treatment of their relation to each other.

Modern life is largely group life, intricately interrelated with the social, economic, and cultural forces of the community. Human beings must be studied in their cultural milieu, if we are to attain a realistic and sane view of their activities and their goals. The acceptance of such a view provides us with a catholic as well as an understandable insight into the life and labor of the groups or social institutions under consideration. Furthermore, with such a treatment the relation between the different methods of study becomes clear. The statistical, the case study, the historical, and the ecological methods seem to fit into an integrated arrangement and to aid in securing a natural view and a balanced picture of human life.

Dr. Pauline Young is admirably qualified to develop this approach through the study of community life. She has had an extensive and productive experience in this kind of study and has made notable contributions through her field studies of juvenile delinquency, crime among young adults, labor problems and unemployment, and immigrant group life, notable among which is her study, *Pilgrims of Russian-Town,* in the University of Chicago Sociological Series. Such experience has enabled Dr. Young to write a volume on social surveys and research which is no doctrinaire treatment but which stands close to actual life. Her intimate knowledge of research procedure makes the present discussion vivid and realistic.

University of California
Berkeley, California

HERBERT BLUMER

contents

I
general overview and scope of social research

III

suggestive outlines for the study of: a culture group a social institution an urban and rural community

general overview and scope of social research

I

general overview of a research project in process

1

The scientific value of a fact depends on its connection with other facts, and in this connection the most commonplace facts are often precisely the most valuable ones, while a fact that strikes the imagination or stirs the moral feelings may be either isolated or exceptional, or so simple as to involve hardly any problem.

W. I. THOMAS

In order for the beginning student to form a suitable picture of the nature of social research and to perceive the many diverse aspects of the research process, he might imagine himself starting a research project "from scratch." For this reason we present here an account of an actual research study as it was undertaken by a class of senior students with no previous experience in field research. This account will reveal a number of central steps, the thinking-through process, and certain precautions of which the beginner is not likely to be aware. The account will also provide some appreciation of research procedure as a down-to-earth working enterprise, systematically conducted, instead of as a series of abstract formulations.

Concern over practical problem initiates a scientific inquiry. Some twenty Chinese college seniors (out of a total of fifty) in two introductory courses on methods of social research, in the British Crown Colony of Hong Kong, expressed a deep concern to the writer, serving there as visiting professor of sociology, about "a slow but steady increase in juvenile delinquency in the Colony." Their statements—based chiefly on newspaper accounts, cursory observation, and rumor—may be summarized as follows:

1. There is now comparatively little juvenile delinquency in the Colony as

a whole. Yet, although there is only a slow increase, certain delinquencies present serious problems, "and a study should be made."

2. These delinquencies pertain chiefly to abandonment of babies, for the most part female babies, by mothers ranging in age from sixteen to middle thirties, child begging, auto thefts, picking pockets, "hostessing by youthful dancers in questionable cafés and dance halls." (Ages for most groups of delinquents were not known.)

3. The resident population of Hong Kong in 1963 was rapidly approaching the four million mark. Close to 99 per cent of the Colony's population is Chinese, over two million of them refugees from China since the 1948 Communist Revolution. The population in Hong Kong has almost doubled since 1948.

4. Juveniles under eighteen years of age constitute 51 per cent of the Colony's total population.

5. There is as yet no compulsory school-attendance law in the Colony.

Although these statements were vague and unverified, they bore an air of urgent concern for students in two different colleges, who had comparatively little contact with each other. Also, it was apparent even to the casual observer that no adequate housing, health, school, employment, or recreational facilities were available to the large masses of displaced persons in the Colony.

The students' concern seemed to relate itself largely to two interconnected questions: How can the low incidence of juvenile delinquency be explained, particularly in view of conditions which have prevailed over a period of years? What are the causative factors and the extent of the major delinquencies? An additional question was raised by the writer: Why the concern of the students in the existing problems? This question was examined first, since it could be dealt with directly and immediately by the members of the research course.

Most of the students wanted to "find a solution to growing problems," thus applying pressure to gaining practical knowledge. Only two or three members of the class wanted to "learn scientific procedure and principles of research in general." These few students, it would appear, realized that they could best serve practical purposes by means of the scientific method. These students also advanced the oft-repeated assertion that "there is nothing more practical than a good theory," although not one could explain adequately what is meant by "a good theory." It was pointed out that both of the expressed desires for making the study were logical and "scientifically legitimate."

It is true that a scientific study may prove its usefulness if it is productive of practical results, *provided, however,* that in the pursuit of the study no other goals are kept in mind than those of science.[1] (For further discussion of this point see pp. 92–94.)

As logicians often point out, a scientific inquiry starts with the recognition of a problem: "when something is unsatisfactory; when the facts necessary to solve a problem are unknown; when the traditional beliefs are inadequate in explaining the problem."[2] In this connection the question which is essential to all scientific inquiries was raised: Are the facts which are necessary to explain the problem known or available to science? Divergent views on this point were expressed by the students, but all agreed that much could be learned from scientific literature "in psychology," "also in sociology," "and social work." Thus, all saw the need for what was labeled "library research" and for looking at the problem of human behavior from several standpoints.

Before going further it should be indicated that the following overview is presented in the belief that beginners in social research are able to involve themselves in a vivid report of a research project and in the thinking of others, and thus profit by vicarious experience. Furthermore, the discussion should help the reader substantially in gaining a perspective of a research project as a whole. The overview also points to the way in which abstract propositions were formulated and scientific procedures followed throughout the study. With this discussion, readers may gain a greater appreciation of the many illustrative studies cited in their readings, and of the concepts and techniques used by authors who take for granted the students' "know-how" and ability to see the thinking involved in their studies.

The presentation which follows is not a report of a simulated project. The students enrolled in the course on methods of social research were actually involved in every procedural operation, through either their own field work or class discussion. The present overview, however, is a *simulation* for the reader; that is, this discussion attempts to present a model which will reproduce in writing the social and psychological processes, as well as the physical field work, which entered into the study. This model should help the reader to make certain decisions in the selection and evaluation of his own actual project; help him to

[1]W. J. Goode and Paul K. Hatt, *Methods in Social Research,* pp. 18 ff. McGraw-Hill Book Company, 1952.

[2]F. S. C. Northrop, *The Logic of the Sciences and the Humanities,* p. 17. The Macmillan Company, 1947.

determine the choice of techniques; it may even help him to avoid pitfalls, or, as Guy H. Orcutt maintains,[3] it may enable the trainee "to get some feel of what he would experience in the real situation and some indication of the likely outcome of various actions and responses on his part." But it is best to realize that it is only a model and will need revision and modification as circumstances demand.

THE THINKING-THROUGH PROCESS. In the study of delinquency in Hong Kong the students realized that a research study does not begin by a "search for facts" in "the field." Research demands as a prerequisite careful deliberation, a thinking-through of the issues and problems involved in every step of the research process. This "thinking-through" branched out into several directions and assumed different forms. The students were soon led to the realization that no study should be undertaken on the basis of impressions or rumors. They verified the population figures through the Hong Kong Census Reports. From *The Hong Kong Report for the Year 1963* (official annual report for calendar year, issued by the Hong Kong Government), the following Table was obtained. It is here presented (in condensed form) for the sole purpose of indicating the bases of questions raised in the students' thinking-through process.

Table 1.1

NUMBER OF SERIOUS CRIMES REPORTED AND DETECTED, AND NUMBER OF PERSONS PROSECUTED, 16 YEARS AND OVER, IN THE YEAR 1963 IN HONG KONG

Crime	*Number of Cases Reported*	*Number of Cases Detected*	*Number of Persons Prosecuted*	
			Under 16 years	*16 years and over*
Against Lawful Authority				
1. Against Public Order	5	5	2	21
2. Perjury	111	111	1	94
3. Escape and Rescue	43	35	1	31
4. Unlawful Society	212	212	7	203

[3]"Simulation of Economic Systems," *The American Economic Review,* (1960), 895. For a comprehensive discussion of Simulation, see Harold Guetzkow (Ed.), *Simulation in Social Sciences: Readings,* Prentice-Hall, Inc., 1960.

Crime	Number of Cases Reported	Number of Cases Detected	Number of Persons Prosecuted	
			Under 16 years	16 years and over
5. Other Offences against Lawful Authority	30	27	—	21
Total Class I...	401	390	11	370
Against Public Morality				
6. Rape	3	—	—	—
7. Indecent Assault on Female ...	127	86	13	54
8. Other Sexual Offences	54	54	—	40
9. Unnatural Offences	6	6	—	5
10. Other Offences against Public Morality	3	3	—	2
Total Class II	193	149	13	101
Against the Person				
11. Murder and Manslaughter ...	25	21	—	19
12. Attempted Murder	8	8	—	5
13. Serious Assaults	633	570	66	478
14. Abortion	2	1	—	1
15. Kidnapping	—	—	—	—
16. Criminal Intimidation	13	13	3	8
17. Other Offences against the Person	121	36	—	21
Total Class III	802	649	69	532
Against Property				
18. Robbery with Firearms	1	1	—	1
19. Other Robberies	152	97	46	101
20. Demanding with Menaces	128	113	10	30
21. Burglary	137	66	—	55
22. Housebreaking	377	144	14	86
23. Other Breakings	265	91	12	75
24. Attempted Breaking	21	13	1	9
25. Possession of Housebreaking Implement	28	28	1	11

Crime	*Number of Cases Reported*	*Number of Cases Detected*	*Number of Persons Prosecuted*	
			Under 16 years	*16 years and over*
Against Property—Cont'd				
26. Larceny from Person (S)	419	245	35	147
27. Larceny from Person (P)	505	427	52	259
28. Larceny in Dwelling	735	312	41	173
29. Larceny from Ship and Wharf ...	34	24	—	29
30. Larceny from Vehicle	965	459	72	174
31. Larceny of Bicycle	260	179	35	70
32. Miscellaneous Larcenies	4,949	3,269	443	1,814
33. Embezzlement	290	281	5	46
34. Larceny by Servant	241	228	6	107
35. Obtaining by False Pretences ...	261	239	1	86
36. Larceny by Bailee	74	69	3	32
37. Larceny by Trick	110	69	7	25
38. Fraudulent Conversion	137	126	—	31
39. Obtaining Credit by Fraud ...	49	46	2	24
40. Other Frauds and Cheats	290	288	3	121
41. Receiving Stolen Property ...	111	111	17	58
42. Malicious Injuries to Property ...	155	109	11	80
43. Unlawful Possession	478	478	24	364
44. Possession of Unlawful Instrument	158	158	13	46
45. Loitering and Trespass	387	383	9	343
46. Other Offences against Property	—	—	—	—
Total Class IV	11,717	8,053	863	4,397
Other Serious Crime				
47. Forgery and Coinage	184	174	1	57
48. Bribery and Corruption	75	75	—	27
49. Possession of Arms and Ammunition	15	15	—	16
50. Conspiracy	12	12	—	20
51. Breach of Deportation	45	45	—	37
52. Other Serious Crime	330	329	1	156
Total Class V	661	650	2	313

Crime	*Number of Cases Reported*	*Number of Cases Detected*	*Number of Persons Prosecuted*	
			Under 16 years	*26 years and over*
Narcotics Offences				
53. Manufacturing Dangerous Drugs	10	9	—	29
54. Exporting Dangerous Drugs ...	—	—	—	—
55. Importing Dangerous Drugs ...	13	7	—	9
56. Dealing in Dangerous Drugs ...	70	70	2	101
57. Possession of Dangerous Drugs	43	39	1	42
Total Class VI	136	125	3	181
Grand Total	13,910	10,016	961	5,894

Percentage of Crime Detected in All Cases = 72.00 per cent.

The following questions were raised with respect to Table 1.1: What is meant by a "serious crime"? What is meant by a "case"? Are cases counted by the number of convictions per minor, or by the number of individuals who are convicted by the court, regardless of the number of convictions? How many cases of "persons arrested, sixteen years and over" involve minors? When are persons over sixteen but under twenty-one not minors? In the total number of "miscellaneous larcenies"—5,689, the largest number of offenses listed in any category of Table 1.1—what subclassifications might be included?

Also, such questions as: Does the term "delinquent" invariably involve social or personal disorganization? If not, how valid are comparisons of delinquent and nondelinquent groups?

Frédéric Le Play, a French social scientist of the nineteenth century, referred to the thinking-through process as "vigorous reasoning" and maintained that scientific procedure is established only upon *facts* systematically gathered and upon inferences derived from them through vigorous reasoning.

But what are "facts"? "Facts" and "data" are probably the most frequently referred-to terms in scientific writings, yet these terms are among the most difficult to define. Facts are defined* as "what has really happened." But facts are not limited to the tangible. Thoughts

*See *American College Dictionary*.

and feelings and sentiments are facts in social science. Data are defined as "facts, figures, etc. [*sic*!] known or are available; information." Not a very helpful definition for a researcher.

Facts must be seen as physical, mental, or emotional occurrences or phenomena which can be affirmed with certainty and are accepted as true in a given "world of discourse." Facts expressed in words assume different meanings to different people, depending on their past experience as well as on the many things with which they associate the facts and words. For example, the concept evoked in a person's mind by the word "food" is determined by what he eats, by:

> . . . the normal state of his appetite and digestion, the ease or difficulty with which he secures his daily ration, whether he grows, hunts, or buys it, whether or not he prepares it, whether he has ever been near starvation, and so forth. No two people have exactly the same experience by which to define the same facts and words, and sometimes the resulting difference is immeasurably great. This is the meaning of the saying of the logician that persons attach different meanings to the same words and the same things are in different "universes of discourse," that is, do not talk in the same world.[4]

Data are more than "facts, figures," more than "information," "events," or "experiences," more than memories of a teller of life histories. Data are all the relevant materials, past and present, serving as bases for study and analysis. They are "the living stuff, with all the relevant emotional [and mental] signs attached,"[5] to one's expressions, actions, attitudes and values within his social world.

Perhaps the most important result of the thinking-through process was the realization that: 1) Delinquency is not an isolated phase of behavior. It is intertwined with other patterns and an outgrowth of other modes of life. In order to explain delinquency, it may be necessary to reach into personality traits, family relations, role of the delinquent in the primary groups of which he is a member, influence of community conditions and changes. 2) Also, numerical data do not stand alone. They are involved with human material in general. Numerical data become valuable when they are viewed in a sociological frame of reference. And in this frame of reference the data must be precisely

[4]R. E. Park and H. E. Miller, *Old World Traits Transplanted,* p. 265. Harper & Row, 1921.

[5]John Dollard and Frank Auld, *Scoring Human Motives,* p. 1. Yale University Press, 1959.

measured, as the task is not complete until a high degree of precision is attained.

But here another question could be raised: Since numerical data are translations of real events or traits into numbers, how can be it be determined whether or not the translation was adequately and uniformly carried out for each number among the many in each column of Table 1.1? There is no adequate answer. Furthermore, as C. H. Combs[6] points out, we are tempted to measure something, even if we cannot measure it. "Such . . . compulsiveness defeats our basic objective of remaining maximally faithful to the events which we observe. The proper solution to this dilemma of rigor *vs* faithfulness lies not in abandoning either objective but in reassessing the means by which rigor is attainable, given that a certain sort of event is to be investigated."[7]

Some students were greatly stimulated by the questions raised, particularly since the study was related to social problems in their own community, and "it made them think." It was impressed upon them that many similar problems exist in metropolitan centers throughout the world, and the same methodological procedures they were to follow would apply elsewhere in the same types of studies and objectives. They were referred to the library card catalog for references on each phase of the study.

STRATEGY OF THE STUDY. It was impressed upon the class that strategy means more than planning a study and more than decisions made as to its execution. Strategy refers also to personal values and standards of conduct during an investigation. True, the investigator is intent on obtaining reliable, verifiable, measurable data, but he must do this without embarrassment or harassment to the informants or agencies from which data are secured or by which they are verified.

As Doctor A. T. M. Wilson, of Tavistock Institute in London, has said,

> "It isn't so much that honesty is the best policy; it's the only possible policy." The honest investigator, who knows (or should know) more than the client about consequences for client participation in the

[6]See Combs, "Theory and Methods of Social Measurement," in Leon Fesinger and Daniel Katz, (Eds.), *Research Methods in the Behavioral Sciences,* pp. 471 ff. The Dryden Press, 1953.

[7]T. M. Newcomb, "Interdependence of Social-Psychological Theory and Methods," *ibid.,* p. 10.

> research, must not only not take advantage of his wider knowledge but must actually seek to turn it to the client's advantage. The temporary [imposition] on laboratory subjects does not necessarily violate this concept of honesty, where as sheer thoughtlessness on the part of the investigator who would never think of lying to a client may violate it fundamentally.[8]

The rationalization that "in the interest of science any means is justified" is actually harmful to social science. In the long run, confidence in, and the respect for, the explorer win cooperation and honesty of informants.

Strategy also demands an objective attitude and ability to set aside one's convictions in the face of contrary findings. (See Chapter Five on development of a "Scientific Attitude and Plan of Study.") "The training of a scientist, of course, prepares him to behave in this way, not only by moral injunction but also in practical fashion. It is early learned that falsification or distortion of facts cannot succeed for long. Science is the most pitilessly public activity in which men can engage."[9]

The Research Design

The social researcher, guided either by desire to gain knowledge or by an urgency to solve a problem scientifically, works out a plan of study (see pp. 131–133). At the beginning this plan is generally vague and tentative. It undergoes many modifications and changes, as the study progresses and insights into it deepen. The working out of the plan consists in reality of making certain decisions with respect to:

What the study is about and the types of data that are needed
Why the study is being made
Where the needed data can be found
Where, or in what areas, the study will be carried on
When, or what periods of time, the study will include
How much material or how many cases will be needed
What bases of selection will be used
What techniques of gathering data will be adopted.

Thus, the considerations which enter into making the decisions regarding the what, where, when, how much, by what means, constitute a

[8] *Ibid.,* p. 4.
[9] Goode and Hatt, *op. cit.,* p. 21.

plan of study or a study design. Going somewhat further, it may be said that a study design includes at least the following component parts, which are interdependent and not mutually exclusive: 1) sources of information to be tapped, 2) nature of study, 3) objectives of study, 4) sociocultural context of study, 5) geographical areas to be covered by the study, 6) periods of time to be encompassed, 7) dimensions of the study, 8) the bases for selecting the data, 9) techniques to be used in gathering data.

Sources of information. The research study in Hong Kong began with seeking out a variety of sources: 1) documentary sources —official and unofficial statistics, local newspaper accounts, census publications—from which descriptive materials were derived, often sketchy and generally not comparable. 2) Personal sources were of two kinds. First, they included professional persons in the field who had knowledge and insight into the data desired. One such source was a court worker, from whom it was learned that official statistics were not always reliable for scientific purposes, since the data were supplied by a variety of official personnel with different conceptions of what constituted delinquent acts and how to classify such acts. Second, persons directly involved in the commission of delinquencies were sought out for personal interviews. 3) Library sources supplied knowledge, both practical and theoretical, which guided in the accumulation of pertinent data.

Note-taking (see pp. 143–146) on separate cards or separate sheets of paper slowly became an established habit but not without some reluctance to give up the traditional large notebook. Notes on separate cards or sheets permit their easy arrangement and rearrangement—a matter of great importance in the subsequent classification and analysis of the data.

Nature of study. In discussing the nature of a study some writers refer to a statistical study, or a case study, or a comparative study; others designate experimental study or some combination of these and other types. Here we shall confine ourselves to the nature of the research case.[10] Does this study pertain to one person, as Shaw's *The Jack Roller;* several persons, as "Doc," Mike and Danny in dis-

[10]See Matilda White Riley, *Sociological Research: A Case Approach,* pp. 3–31 and *passim*. Harcourt, Brace & World, Inc., 1963.

cussions of Whyte's *Street Corner Society;* or does the study concentrate on a small group, as in Paul Hare's, *et. al., Small Groups;* or on a very large number of cases, as in Kinsey's studies of sexual behavior? With regard to the delinquency studies in Hong Kong, most of the students referred to "the core of the study," by which some meant behavior, the social situations and norms of a given group in a given district in Hong Kong. Others conceived their study to be confined to fifteen or twenty delinquency cases. One student concentrated on the study of a small predatory gang, while three paid exclusive attention to one or two individual delinquents. Whatever the core of the study, attention was given to the attitudes of the delinquents, the roles they played or thought they played in the group, on the relationships they maintained with other individuals and groups, and the social world which exerted an influence.

With the realization that each research study is complex came the conclusion that the specific nature of the study should be determined early, and precisely, particularly when limited time and energy forbid false starts.

Objectives of research studies. (See index for further discussion of each type.) Objectives differ with nature of studies and goals to be attained. Some research studies aim to gather descriptive data, or explanatory data, or data from which theoretical constructs could be deduced, or data which promote administrative changes or comparisons.

QUASI-EXPLANATORY STUDIES. The objective of the delinquency studies in question was not theory building. To be sure, hypotheses were formulated; that is, certain propositions were provisionally advanced regarding the underlying problems of study. For example, some students believed that there was a relationship between child begging and poverty; others saw a relationship between child begging and ready "handouts" by gullible tourists.

Toward the end of the academic year, most students sought some fundamental explanation of behavior of delinquent groups in general. But it cannot be claimed that beginners in social research are ready to engage in systematic exploratory studies which aim at scientific testing of hypotheses for the sake of analyzing ideas. The beginner's work is rarely more than quaisi-explanatory.

The students were warned against undertaking a correlational study on the mere strength of the number of delinquents known among the poor. True, the correlation showed an existence of an association between poverty and delinquency, but the demonstration ended there. "An index of relationship tells nothing about cause and effect . . . when no sound testimony beyond the correlation itself is available. Further evidence such as that provided by a manipulation study is required to establish cause and effect."[11] It cannot be forgotten that correlation is not synonymous with causation.

Sociocultural context. Every person lives somewhere. This somewhere has its own mode of life to which persons adhere or from which they deviate or even withdraw completely. In order to gain some understanding of behavior patterns—deviant or conforming—local norms have to be ascertained. A girl, for example, may not consider it breaking the law against public morality when she becomes a concubine, if concubinage is within established local norms.

Some students found a number of divergent cultural groupings in small areas (two or three square miles), each group with its own way of life. Other small areas, however, contained a highly homogeneous population that had adhered to the same modes of life for several generations. Most of the cases under study came from heterogeneous urban areas—cases of refugees who had lived in rural areas of mainland China, or Australia, or New Zealand until about the 1950's. A person's habitat is so intimate a part of his life that to ignore it means to carry on a study in a vacuum. In this connection the students found John Dollard and Frank Auld's statement highly appropriate:

> Every science has its ancestors, near or remote, and every [project] has its frame of reference larger than its contents. . . . Human behavior occurs under specific conditions—social conditions. It is unthinkable without such conditions. . . . [People] share a common culture and they are members of a specific social class. . . . Neither culture nor class works with precision effects. The human being can be seen as a kind of "marker" stamped out by culture only if viewed from a great distance; seen close up, we observe that culture stamps quite unevenly. Some part of this unevenness is due to the fact that cultural conditions are not a mechanical form; are not uniform throughout a society; and

[11]E. E. Levitt, *Clinical Research Design and Analysis,* p. 152. Charles C Thomas, 1961.

some great part is also due to the fact that bodies presented to culture for indoctrination are different one from the other.[12]

Each sociocultural area should also be studied in relation to its physical and geographical aspects. All students drew maps of the area of their concern; they took many photographs of the physical conditions in the area; some were able to obtain from agency files or their own homes a few old photographs to enable them to contrast the old and new, the then and now, the before and after.

Sociotemporal context. Strictly speaking, sociotemporal context refers to some definite historical period of a country. We refer to the Stalinist era, or the Victorian era, or the postwar era, and so on. But the Hong Kong cases under consideration seem to have fallen under the influence of a certain short period of time which markedly changed their modes of life. Most of the cases referred to "the time when we still lived in Red China" or "the time when we first arrived in Hong Kong" or "now when we are settled [in Hong Kong]." It was often difficult to explore the influences which operated before and after settlement in the Colony. However, the importance of this variable—at various stages of development and influence—cannot be overstressed. The individual must be seen in the sociotemporal context, that is, in the historical setting of time and place.

Dimensions of study and sampling procedures. (For a discussion of sampling and underlying theory, see Chapter 11.) The ever-recurring question came up: How many cases do I need? Some students proposed "at least one hundred." But when they weighed their desires against available time and energy, they revised the number downward to 15 or 20, or at the most 25. These are practical limitations which cannot be overlooked in students' projects. At this time the problems of sampling were introduced, though briefly. The students were aware that it is neither possible nor advisable to study the whole range of behavior or of social phenomena, called "the universe." It was assumed that the parts chosen from this "universe" or "supply" are capable of supplying valid and reliable information which becomes meaningful when viewed in its sociotemporal and sociocultural contexts. Statistician Margaret Hagood reminds us that this

[12]Dollard and Auld, *op. cit.*, p. 3. Quoted with permission of Yale University Press.

can be a risky assumption. She suggests the following criteria as a guide in the choice of a sample: "1) the sample must represent the universe (that is, it must be unbiased); 2) the sample must be of adequate size to produce reliable results (that is, as measured in terms of specific range of error); 3) the sample must be designed in such a way as to be efficient (that is, in comparison with alternate designs)."[13]

The students concentrated on two major aspects in the problem of sampling: 1) the determination of items in the cases which were to constitute the sample, and 2) the measurement of reliability of the sample data. The first aspect calls to mind John Madge's point that the investigator is placed in the predicament of having to know something about the data which are to be gathered before he can complete plans for carrying out his investigation. Pilot studies (miniature studies in which the procedures to be adopted in a large-scale study are tested in advance) might be of value. Still good exploration must discern variables.

Although the students pooled their cases and attempted to discern variables, these were at first seen darkly. It took considerable contemplation and extended numerical treatment before the variables were seen as more or less definite quantities as well as qualities. Measurement can begin only in an area where the exploratory processes can be properly carried out.[14] It cannot be said that, at first, cases chosen by the students were the result of a systematically selected sample; rather, the choice was guided by expediency. Until they learned the problems and pitfalls of choosing a representative sample, the generalizations of their findings could not be regarded by them as valid. The question of how many cases are needed in a study is difficult to answer even by mature researchers. It depends largely on the degree of reliability that is required for the purpose of research and on the amount of dispersion of the characteristics studied, as will be indicated in a later chapter on "Basic Statistical Concepts and Techniques."

Definition of terms. (See also pp. 133–136.) With greater awareness of the need for precision in research, the students began to see the pitfalls in such expressions as they had formerly used: "There is now comparatively little serious delinquency in the Colony."

[13]Hagood, *Statistics for Sociologists,* p. 272. Holt, Rinehard & Winston, Inc., 1953.

[14]Dollard and Auld, *op. cit.,* p. 2.

They began to question: When is "now"? What is "little"? As "compared" with what? Who is a "juvenile"? Who is a "delinquent"? What area in the "Colony"? What types or groups of "Chinese" are to be included? Virtually every word in the earlier statements came under scrutiny in order to formulate a rigorously defined idea, that is, a concept. Such precise definitions of concepts were especially essential, since the findings were to be funded, compared, and quantitatively analyzed. Each collaborator must have the same understanding of the concepts if the collaborative data are to be similarly classified and the findings pooled and tested, or reproduced. Classification and comparison demand uniform and precise definitions of categories expressed in concepts.

It was also realized that dictionary definitions do not suffice for scientific studies. A dictionary, for example, defines "now" as "at the present time," which explanation is not any clearer or less vague than "now." Various people conceive "now" or "at the present time" in various ways. "Now" may mean to some people this minute, or this hour, or day, or some may refer to the twentieth century as "now." For the sake of definiteness and accuracy and the ability to classify and generalize, periods of time should be definitely indicated, let us say, January 1, 1960, through June 30, 1960, or any other suitable period within the limits and purposes of the study. "Little" should be expressed in terms of number of cases, and so on. Thus, the earlier formulated title projects came under critical review. For example, such a title as "A Study of Juvenile Delinquency in Hong Kong" emerged as "A Case Study of 25 Chinese Refugee Boys, 10 through 15 years of age, Living in Homatin District of Hong Kong, Who Were Prosecuted for Picking Pockets, July 1 through December 30, 1962." (It should be noted that the title of the project indicates "the core of the study," its dimensions, its geographical limits, its sociocultural context, its time limits, its technique of study.)

The following definitions, of persons and phenomena considered equivalent, were adopted for *the purposes of the particular study:*

> *Chinese*—a person who lives in a Chinese community with which he has identified himself and of which he has considered himself a member. (Other Chinese living in the same community but who do not consider themselves members of it may have different behavior patterns, are regarded as unequivalent, and are therefore not included in this definition.)
>
> *Boy*—a male, twelve through sixteen years of age.

Case study—the process of acquiring information, individual by individual, in order to determine behavior patterns, attitudes, and motivations.

Prosecuted—case heard or tried in superior court of the Colony, juvenile or criminal court.

Picking pockets—an act or attempt, successful or unsuccessful, to steal money from someone else's pocket.

Homatin District—an area the boundaries of which are outlined on an official map and designated as Homatin.

1962—calendar year of the Western World, January 1 through December 31, inclusive.

The definitions of such terms as behavior patterns, attitudes, and motivations were adopted from standard sociological texts used in introductory courses.

Working or exploratory hypotheses. (See also pp. 103–111.) From the beginning of their study the students in Hong Kong pondered over what facts would explain: 1) the slow increase of juvenile delinquency in the Colony, and 2) factors which contributed to the problems existing there. In the process of thinking and searching for explanations, a researcher generally falls back on previous, though preliminary, observations, made by himself or others. Aided by these observations and some cursory knowledge he may have about the problem posed, he tries to identify those significant factors which may throw light on his question. By shrewd guess or profound hunch he tries to establish causal relations between various sets of facts at hand. This penetrating hunch, this provisional explanation which becomes the basis for a systematic investigation, is known as a working or exploratory hypothesis.

A large number of hypotheses were suggested by the students as tentative explanations for the existing delinquency situation in Hong Kong. Some linked the low rate of delinquency there with strong family ties among the Chinese, efficient and alert policing systems throughout the Colony, employment of Chinese boys at an early age, heavy home responsibilities assumed willingly by Chinese youth, prevalence of home industries in which Chinese youth participate, lack of delinquency tradition in the Colony, and numerous other factors. These tentative explanations—though unverified and untested—sounded plausible and reasonable; that is, they appeared consistent with the sociocultural situation of the group under study. Finally, these hypotheses could be tested empirically. In other words, they appeared to have the essential requirements of "good" hypotheses—plausibility, consistency, and chance for empirical testing. But, without actual testing, they could neither be accepted as valid nor rejected as invalid.

There are various devices for testing hypotheses. Here we will indicate only that the students used a control group to test their hypotheses. For example, in their assumption that strong family ties do not tend to produce delinquency, they employed a second group of subjects or cases which had equivalent traits with the experimental group except for that trait which was under investigation. Pooling their delinquency cases, they were able to observe about 100 families. Then they obtained a similar number of cases from schools and health agencies, in which there was no delinquency record. (In the choice of the control group a researcher should make certain that he is viewing it within the same frame of reference and is defining the terms in the same manner as he does in the cases under observation.) The students found that in the group of nondelinquent cases there were families with records of desertion, conflicts between husband and wife, parent-child conflicts; in all, about 70 per cent of this group of cases could not be regarded as maintaining strong family ties—a large enough percentage to prove the hypothesis false. Each test confined itself to one proposition at a time. If the test proved the assumption to be false, another assumption was tested, continuing the process until a proposition proved correct.

Many of those who were studying the underlying factors of picking pockets, dancer-hostessing, and abandonment of babies confined themselves at first to testing—one at a time—the propositions that poverty, low intelligence, or emotional instability were the responsible factors in these delinquencies in Hong Kong. With the employment of a control group, they generally found their hypotheses incorrect.

The main benefits the students derived from formulating and testing their hypotheses were the realizations that, to put them in the words of M. R. Cohen and E. Nagel, 1) "the function of a hypothesis is to direct our search for the order among facts. . . . 2) It is of considerable advantage if a systematic inquiry is begun with a suggested explanation or solution of the difficulty which originated it. Such tentative explanations are suggested to us by something in the subject matter and our previous knowledge."[15]

[15]Cohen and Nagel, *An Introduction to Logic and Scientific Method.* Harcourt, Brace & World, 1934.

The main benefits derived from the use of control groups led to the realization that no comparison or measurement of phenomena can take place until it is precisely known what is being compared or measured. A "boy" can be anybody from a newborn male to one past his teens. Attempting to compare undifferentiated boys, even within the same culture, might be the same as attempting to compare oranges and onions. "A concept exhibits its vagueness most sharply when we begin to define the procedures and operations for dealing with it in research."[16]

One of the main assumptions which guided the research project on delinquency was that, by and large, human behavior is not "reducible to fixed cause-and-effect sequences; nor is it the result of a person's being swept along as a neutral and indifferent organism by external influences. The human being is capable of initiating and directing changes in his own actions. Humans build up their conduct by interpreting or defining the situations in which they find themselves."[17]

Soon the pressures to "solve" a practical problem diminished. The students became absorbed in, and saw the necessity for, examining assumptions, defining concepts, and pursuing scientific techniques of study as prerequisites to the understanding of a practical problem. They held firmly to the belief that "theory and scientific techniques are handmaidens to the solution of practical problems." There are no short cuts or substitutes in gaining concrete knowledge about social problems which need fundamental understanding.[18]

Techniques of Study

In their project on juvenile delinquency the students assumed that behavior of delinquents can be observed and studied by the same processes and techniques as other aspects of human behavior. They employed observational techniques, schedules and questionnaires, the interview, statistical and case-study data.

[16]Goode and Hatt, *op. cit.,* p. 35.

[17]Meyer Weinberg and Oscar E. Shabat, *Society and Man,* p. 194. Prentice-Hall, Inc., 1959. At this point the students began reading about the Cambridge-Somerville Youth Study; in Edwin Powers and Helen Witmer, *An Experiment in the Prevention of Delinquency.* Columbia University Press, 1951.

[18]Karl R. Popper, *The Open Society and Its Enemies,* pp. 426 ff. Princeton University Press, 1950.

Observation. (See Chapter 7). Much can be learned about human behavior by observing it, even at a distance. Observation is most meaningful when it is planned in terms of the formulated hypotheses and of the general scheme of the study. But accurate observation is difficult, because: 1) what we observe is complex; 2) we have to keep in mind a number of interrelated factors; 3) our sense organs are not exempt from liability to error; 4) it is necessary to keep fact and inference apart, especially when one is engrossed in the study.

The students went into their chosen districts at first to observe the general social atmosphere. Then they attempted to observe single aspects—the housing of the subjects of study, the cultural groupings that surrounded them, the presence or absence of social institutions, the occupations and modes of earning a living, the noticeable participation of youth in various activities, the interrelations of youth and adults, and a vast variety of other observable phenomena which related to the formulated hypotheses of the studies. Each student then concentrated on the specific group of factors most relevant to the purposes of his study.

It was also helpful to observe concrete details which characterized the factors on which the students concentrated, and to assign meanings to them. If they saw a relationship, for example, between delinquency and "blighted areas," they were to define "blighted" in terms of the specific area observed. Insight is not gained through sweeping generalities and description devoid of detail. Well-defined and uniformly used details are the keynotes in preliminary as well as subsequent attempts to observe and collect data.

The researcher must be steadily on guard against preconceived notions, although he may never be able to rule them out completely. No one comes to work with a blank mind, devoid of previous experience from which he can divorce himself at will. Only steady watchfulness and a genuine attempt to examine the collected data objectively can minimize error. Furthermore, learning to observe behavior in terms of its meaning to the observed will aid in keeping fact and inference and preconceived notions apart. Students whose families had *amahs* (servants) at first viewed household chores performed by youngsters as undue burdens, only to learn from the youngsters themselves that they "liked to help mother with the care of the little ones," or to chop wood and do other tasks.

The students made their observations both during the day and evening, then went back for repeat observations to gain details missed or to check on doubtful ones. Numerous photographs of various aspects of the life of the area were taken, with the consent of the inhabitants.

At first the observations were merely a study through the eye, or nonparticipant observation. Later, through overt personal communication, participant observation was introduced. A few students were able to make arrangements to spend a week end in the homes of families under study; a few obtained permission to live for a few days in a correctional institution for delinquent youth. These students were able to observe at close range the routine of life and the reactions of the inmates, and therefore their reported observations were richer in content and more complete than those of casual observers or ones "on the outside."

In either case the students had to learn to be cautious about difficulties involved in spontaneous mingling with inmates studied, difficulties which minimize detachment and which even seasoned observers find hard to overcome.

The thinking-through of the relationship between what is observed and what is pertinent to one's particular study is not generally an easy or rapid process. Only slow deliberation as to the nature and the purpose of study, steadily kept in the forefront of one's attention, will aid avoidance of irrelevancies, or tendencies to clutter up the study with observations not definitely related to it, interesting as they may be in other respects.

Notes were made on each phase of observation as well as on the difficulties encountered during the observations. In recording the observed phenomena, the students specified those that were unusual or striking. They aimed to get representativeness and specific details which could lend themselves to quantitative expression; in other words, additive data.

Interviews. (See Chapter 9). Most students preferred to conduct personal interviews before presenting a self-administered questionnaire to those subjects of study who could fill it out. A few students saw advantages in introducing the questionnaire first. In either case the informants were not approached until each interviewer had thought through the questions to be raised; what the interview as a whole involved; what pertinent information was needed to validate the formulated hypotheses; what questions might inhibit or embarrass the interviewed person, or cause resentment, or "put him on the spot."

Some experiments with questions were conducted in class to have students gain practice with raising questions which stimulate a flow of information with a minimum of interruptions. Each question was examined as to its clearness or ambiguity to the prospective informant. It required considerable practice and many illustrative examples before the desired goals were reasonably well reached.

The first interview with an informant was recorded verbatim. Some of these reports showed "too much talk" on the part of the interviewer. The subsequent interviews showed too much wishful thinking—what the students had hoped the informants would say.

Although the interviews improved with practice and made interesting, often fascinating, reading, lack of uniformity of the data obtained created problems of classifying them that were not easily overcome. Standardized questions were of considerable aid in the classification of procured information. At best, not all data were usable, either because of ambiguity in meaning or inapplicability to the frame of reference, or incompleteness. Some informants supplied only data relative to their overt activities and gave scant information regarding their attitudes. Some information had to be set aside because it was in sharp contrast to observed and reobserved behavior. Since these students were not ready to study psychic conflicts, some of the data on attitudes had to be set aside. None of the secured information was discarded. It was filed for future reference and possible follow-up use when greater insights on the subject would have been developed, but lack of time prevented its re-examination.

Questionnaires and schedules. (See Chapter 8.) As will be seen later, schedules and questionnaires are of various forms and types, with various goals and ways of administering them. In the study under discussion the students used schedules and questionnaires in an attempt to secure additional information or to verify already obtained data through the personal interview and observation techniques. In other words, schedules and questionnaires were used as supplemental techniques, except in a brief study of public opinion.

As in the interview, the questions to be introduced into the schedule or questionnaire have to be carefully considered as to their meaning to the informant. Does *he* understand what activities are included under "begging" or "thieving" or "running away"? Until such understanding is achieved, the proposed questions may be regarded as floating in a vacuum. Furthermore, as Kinsey maintained, "the point of the question" calls not only for an exact definition but also an indication of the category into which to place the replies given to the question.

Both in the use of schedules and personal interviews, the students learned that often it is more expedient to begin with simple subject matter, of least emotional content, particularly if the informant's ability to handle complexities and disturbing subject matter is not known, or if the mores and class habits of the group have not yet been learned.

Some of the students, who used the interview first, noticed that, after informants were given a schedule or self-administered questionnaire, they indicated a loss of interest and a change in the warm relationship that had previously obtained. Under these conditions, some students reported a marked decrease in respondents' articulateness and a pronounced desire to end the questioning as soon as possible.

On the whole, the information from the questionnaires was not as revealing, though the coverage of various points was greater, as compared with the interview data. (It is regrettable that the whole problem of the priority in the use of questionnaires and interviews was not researched.)

PILOT STUDIES were carried on by few students, and those that were undertaken were of limited scope, chiefly because of lack of time. They understood, however, that in large-scale studies, preliminary pilot studies are essential in order to foresee flaws and handicaps which might be encountered in the full-scale study. Such foreshadowing of difficulties requires utmost care in the execution of the preliminary study. If the pilot study does not succeed in disclosing the significant difficulties which should be guarded against, the full-scale study modeled on it may perpetuate and even augment these difficulties.

REPLICATED STUDIES AND VERIFICATION. Because of fallibility of human judgment and of mechanical instruments which are used more and more for computing data, a scientist does not consider it safe to regard his findings as final. He, or someone else who is thoroughly conversant with his study and its implications, should repeat at least certain aspects of the study, using subject matter and procedures identical to the original study's. But as E. E. Levitt points out:

> There are simply not enough research workers available to repeat every study (thousands are published each year), and few scientists have the necessary facilities to replicate a particular experiment.... There is no really adequate solution available at present. The implicit stand which is currently prevalent is that a study need not be verified

> as long as it is *verifiable*. This means that it must conform to the standards of a scientific experiment in every other way and that it must be reported accurately and in sufficient detail to permit replication.[19]

Strictly speaking, the students in the Hong Kong project did not replicate their studies. However, a few students who worked on the same project and used the same procedures, could—in a measure only—verify each other's findings.

EXPERIMENTAL STUDIES. (See pp. 74–77.) Only to a limited degree were experimental studies made in the introductory course. It was realized that, as John Madge points out, "there is in fact no substitute for experiment, in which the complex of variables is manipulated by control of certain key elements in a system."[20] But by the time the students learned how to gather this complex of variables in a systematic way, the course was over.

Case-study data. (See Chapter 10.) Only one student made a case study of a small community—a village and its role in the surrounding territory. The study touched on all major phases in the life of the people—their mode of earning a living, the processes and attitudes exemplified in their family life, training and schooling the young, their religious life, village organization, historical background, educational background, health and social problems.

The rest of the students compiled life-history data from documents, personal interviews, questionnaires, observation of persons and families. These case studies aimed to discern: 1) the characteristics of the group and its mode of life to which the persons under study conform, or diverge, or clash and conflict; 2) the characteristics which are unique to the individuals and distinguish them from others in the group; 3) types of available resources and types of problems.

Some readers may desire to know something about our findings. Since the study, used here for illustrative purposes only, is still in process, no general conclusions can be drawn. Few hypotheses were fully tested, and therefore conclusions are risky. However, on the basis of present indications, it may be said (tentatively and provisionally) that, for the most part, the Chinese in Hong Kong still live in

[19]Levitt, *Clinical Research Design and Analysis in the Behavioral Sciences,* p. 15. Charles C Thomas, 1961.

[20]Madge, *Origins of Scientific Sociology,* p. 527. The Free Press of Glencoe, Inc., 1962.

primary groups and carry on home industries in which youth are assigned many responsibilities. The young have many opportunities to play adult roles and cooperate, rather than competing or conflicting with their parents. Furthermore, the *Kai Fungs* (mutual-aid organizations) help to emphasize the role of the family, the responsibility of the youth to family groups, the importance of diligent work, and the necessity to obey the law and maintain order among the Chinese in the British Crown Colony of Hong Kong. These factors are probably instrumental in social and personal organization and may account for the low incidence of juvenile delinquency there, at this time, among the older teen-agers. But these assumptions need testing.

Often, work and home responsibilities are assigned to preteen-agers as well. When not at work or school, they find street life and play highly colorful and absorbing. All Hong Kong streets, with the exception of the Peak, are hustling with purposeful activity from morning until late evening, generally until eleven o'clock. There are few or no loafers or loiterers among the Chinese in Hong Kong. Street after street is crowded with diverse stores and shops, fruit and vegetable markets amid money-changing barred counters, cafés, radio and TV shops which blare the latest hits. For lack of store space, a generous sprinkling of bargain counters line the sidewalks, adjacent to fresh and dry fish markets, butcher shops, shoe stores, furniture displays or art objects.

There is a constant flow of rapid and heavy traffic—automobiles and rickshaws, buses, trucks and pickups, human conveyors—with heavy bamboo rods suspended from the shoulders and back—transport anything from heavy loads of vegetables to furniture or parts of heavy machinery.

Many of the urban and rural Chinese live in crowded quarters in back of their business enterprises. In the crowded sections of Hong Kong, and most sections are crowded, street and sidewalk life is indigenous to their mode of existence. The street and the sidewalk are an extension of the home. Frequently, one observes not only children, but entire family groups, who eat, rest, or play in front of their businesses. In spite of the dirt and noise, lack of zoning regulations, mixture of residential, industrial, and business establishments, these areas cannot be regarded as slums. Rather, they might be considered ghettos, where life is warm, intimate, personal. There is a high degree of public opinion, group consciousness, native leadership, and, above all, watchfulness of the welfare of the young, the preteen-agers as well as babes playing on the sidewalks and curbs. The adults may be the youngsters' parents, or relatives, or neighbors, or self-appointed childwatchers. Individually and collectively, they watch and observe, guide and correct, any untoward activity on the spot. If drastic action, a beating or isolation, is needed, it is carried out unceremoniously—in public. Specifically, what the relationship is between watchful interested adult eyes of the streets and ghetto life needs further study. Again, the above are only assumptions, based on cursory observation, which need testing.

Summary and Definition of Social Research

The following discussion may serve both as a summary of the foregoing pages and as a basis for defining social research. The overview was based on the belief that it is best first to grasp the totality of a complex situation, such as the processes involved in a research study, and later to become concerned with its details.

In the study of juvenile delinquency in Hong Kong, as in many other research studies, a concern about a practical problem initiated the actual inquiry. However, the immediate aim was not to find "a way out" or to take action in a problem situation. The aim was to find a causal relation between observable and measurable factors which would explain the problem at hand. To this end it was necessary to study the characteristic ways of behavior of the subjects, their attitudes and values, their modes of conforming and of deviating from group norms, the effects of the sociocultural context upon the personality of members, and the influences and social forces within the group which promote or undermine social and personal organization.

It is obvious that no single scientific technique in gathering and analyzing these complex data would suffice. Research studies generally utilize not only a variety of techniques but approach the subject matter from a variety of viewpoints. This procedure rests on the assumption that no one point of view or scientific discipline can encompass total social reality. Neither should a single technique of study be regarded as sovereign. Each is a complement to others.

The process of a study is best promoted by a research plan or design which aids in achieving optimum reliability and efficiency, with a minimum of bias.

Another illustration of a research study may further illustrate the aims, processes, and procedures involved in social research. The primary interests of Samuel A. Stouffer and his associates in *The Studies of the American Soldier* (see pp. 58–61) were to discover and analyze the soldiers' adjustment processes as a phase of collective behavior, to discern the differential social attitudes these processes foster, and to study the soldier as a personality type. The authors—highly sophisticated social researchers and sociological theorists—at times obtained and explored their subject matter by means of existing scientific techniques or by modifying them to suit their particular purposes. At other times they had to create new scientific tools of study. The choice of the procedure depended upon the nature of the data, the circumstances under which these data could be secured, and the underlying theory of the usefulness and applicability to the data at hand. Often a certain technique was used only after considerable experimentation with each new set of informants and each new set of data. This was especially the case in the authors' use of scaling techniques which they devised for the study (see Chapter 12).

The authors of *The American Soldier* were very cautious in adopting procedures which would yield representative, uniform empirical data that could be compared, tested, and measured, in order to determine the precise relationships among behavior patterns, personal traits of the subjects under study, and the factors in the social environment influencing behavior and shaping personality. This procedure is best used by experienced researchers but can be followed by students in training under good supervision, continued over a considerable period of time.

The research plan used by those authors was more flexible than the one followed in our study of delinquency in Hong Kong. Their study dealt with far greater masses of data than ours, and they tested and devised new techniques of exploration over a period of several years, while we utilized only existing scientific tools. However, both studies were fully in accord with Karl Pearson's statement that "the man who classifies facts of any kind, who sees their mutual relations and describes their sequences, is applying the scientific method and is a man of science. . . . It is not the facts themselves which make science, but the method by which they are dealt with."[21]

Both studies developed suitable hypotheses and concepts, which preceded the gathering of the data and which combined generality with

[21]Pearson, *The Grammar of Science,* pp. 16–17. London: J. M. Dent & Sons, Ltd., 1937.

the power of reaching some concrete conclusions. This idea implies that neither scientific nor practical results can be expected without development of some provisional explanation (a hypothesis) of a class of phenomena or problems. Scientists firmly believe that there is nothing as practical as a good theory, and conversely, practice is a "blessing for the development of a theory."[22]

What is social research? In brief and provisionally, social research may be defined as a scientific undertaking which, by means of logical and systematized techniques, aims to: 1) discover new facts or verify and test old facts; 2) analyze their sequences, interrelationships, and causal explanations which were derived within an appropriate theoretical frame of reference; 3) develop new scientific tools, concepts, and theories which would facilitate reliable and valid study of human behavior. A researcher's primary goal—distant or immediate—is to explore and gain an understanding of human behavior and social life, and thereby gain a greater control over them. Stated in other words, social research is a systematic method of exploring, analyzing, and conceptualizing social life in order to "extend, correct, or verify knowledge, whether that knowledge aid in the construction of a theory or in the practice of an art."[23]

Stating it still differently, social research seeks to find explanations to unexplained social phenomena, to clarify the doubtful, and correct the misconceived facts of social life. Gathering knowledge for knowledge's sake is termed "pure" or "basic" research. Gathering knowledge that could aid in the betterment of human destiny is termed "applied" or "practical" research. In reality, no sharp line of demarcation can be drawn between these two types of research. Each is dependent upon the other for development and verification.

As can be gathered from the illustrative study of juvenile delinquency in Hong Kong, theory is an essential element in research work. A theoretical frame of reference lifts research work progressively and meaningfully to new relevant stages of the work, and spotlights the major research problems involved in the undertaking. It indicates the necessity of establishing "the probability of accuracy, validity, relia-

[22]The above paragraph is based on Kurt Lewin's statements in an article by the Research Center of Group Dynamics at the Massachusettes Institute of Technologgy, *Sociometry,* I, 128–133.

[23]Donald Slessinger and Mary Stevenson, "Social Research," *Encyclopaedia of the Social Sciences,* vol. IX, 330. The Macmillan Company, 1930.

bility of all generalizations or other conclusions that are offered.... Without such a theory it is impossible to find any effective meaning in the research itself."[24]

The research studies presented in this text are generally empirical. That is, they represent: 1) a systematic method of exploring actual persons and groups, focused primarily on their experiences within their social worlds, inclusive of social attitudes and values; 2) the mode of analysis of these experiences which permit stating propositions in the form, "*If* so-and-so is true and correct, *then* it follows...." Empirical social research, like any other type of research, does not aim at persuasion nor at finding ultimate truths.[25] Rather, it aims, through precise demonstration, to understand and clarify the behavior of man, the social world in which he lives, the relationships which he maintains, the influences which are exerted upon him, and the effects these have upon him and, subsequently, upon the social institutions of which he is a part. Research studies aim to gather empirically verifiable and valid data, and data which are meaningful in relation to the formulated hypotheses and the theoretical frame of reference.

A social researcher does not view his facts as isolated phenomena; rather, he sees them as closely intertwined and associated with each other. As M. R. Cohen stated it, facts are not intelligible unless they are related to other facts and are shown to be part of a larger system.[26] And Pavlov cautions: "Do not collect facts for the mere collection of them. Try to penetrate the secret of their occurrence and their relationships. Search persistently for the reasons for their occurrence and their relationships." Obviously, such a search cannot be accomplished without a unified approach of various scientific disciplines. Man lives in a socioeconomic and political world and thrives on its varied relationships. It is inconceivable that a study of bare and isolated events on any one aspect of man's life would yield any meaningful results. Nor can they be derived from haphazard day-by-day experiences in his life. His past, present, and future activities, aspirations, motives, and attitudes influence each other and form a variegated and closely knit pattern of behavior.

[24]Allan W. Eister, "Some Deficiencies in Theory in General Sociology Textbooks," *Social Forces,* XXVIII (Dec. 1949), 186, 187. See also Talcott Parsons, "The Position of Sociological Theory," *American Sociological Review,* Vol. 13.

[25]Cohen and Nagel, *op. cit.,* p. 5.

[26]Goode and Hatt, *op. cit.,* Chapter 2, "Science: Theory and Facts."

Social researchers do not believe that facts and figures speak for themselves. These are often too complex, too subtle, and nebulous not to require interpretation and analysis.

Strict definition of terms aids in the development of a system of classification, and helps to relate various phases of data to each other and compare their significance. Scientific definitions are dependent on the purpose of the study and its theoretical framework. Each unique study has to formulate its own technical definitions.

A scientific study, in the last analysis, is a means to an end; that is, it aims to solve a problem—practical or theoretical or methodological. It aims at discovery, verification, and validation, and finding relationships among the accumulated data. These feats can be accomplished only by means of both scientific method, that is, logical and systematized application of the fundamentals of science to the general and over-all questions of a study, and scientific techniques which provide precise tools, specific procedures and technical, rather than philosophical, means for getting and ordering the data prior to their logical and statistical manipulation.[27]

Research requires also proper personal conduct and values in one's relationships with informants. A researcher needs, in addition to his training and experience in the arts and science of research, a sensitivity to human relations.

The following two chapters on the scope of social research will summarize briefly: 1) the broad range of social research studies since the dawn of the twentieth century, 2) the modes of thought involved in social research, 3) the application of scientific techniques to research studies, and 4) the theories formulated by the authors of these studies. The cumulative wisdom of experienced researchers can contribute much to the beginner in social research. But it should be firmly borne in mind that such wisdom is not a substitute for, rather an addition to, controlled field research procedures. As a matter of fact, many of the earlier scientific ancestors knew little of rigorous measurement and scientific controls. They were highly perceptive and remarkably clear thinkers, guiding their work by sound and profound theoretical frameworks, even though there was little tendency to test either theories or findings. However, many of their assertions were sound, astute, and accurate. These are now being rediscovered and applied to current research.

[27]Goode and Hatt, *op. cit.,* pp. 5–6.

Furthermore, the summaries of the research studies that follow may answer at least some of the questions students and laymen frequently raise regarding the nature and purpose of social research in the modern world.

At many points in the discussion the alert reader should be able to compare his own thinking and field procedures of his research project with those that are summarized here. These studies constitute a map of the road traversed by earlier researchers. This map points to many fruitful paths and bypaths in research undertakings yet to be achieved.

scope of social research: contributions of our scientific ancestors and contemporary trail blazers

There are many rewards to be derived from consulting the maps of previous explorers. . . . We need in sociology a better regard for our past accomplishments.

HARRY ALPERT

2

Some of the questions asked most frequently by students in introductory courses on social research, and at times by intelligent laymen as well, are: In the main, with what do social researchers concern themselves? On what general assumptions do they base their researches? And, tersely stated: Research for what? If a question is added as to what method and techniques researchers use, the whole field of social research has to be unfolded. The field is broad and complex; the unfolding, slow, gradual, and at times uncertain.

Obviously, not all the contributions, even of outstanding researchers, can be included within the confines of two chapters. The selection that was made was based on explorations which: 1) provided new insights into organized society and its social structures (for example, research by Charles H. Cooley, George Herbert Mead, W. I. Thomas and Florian Znaniecki, and others); 2) or charted new horizons in scientific exploration, advanced and tested new principles of procedure, and suggested new concepts. In this field fall, for example, the pioneering work of E. W. Burgess in predicting the relative degree of social adjustment of marriage partners; or his earlier work in predicting the outcome of behavior of offenders on parole. Here also may be included W. I. Thomas' work in adopting new techniques of studying personality, social organization and disorganization; and Clifford R. Shaw's work in which he formulated new theories about the etiology of delinquency, new concepts such as "delinquency areas," "delinquency tradition," and "radial patterns of delinquency." (For references consult Bibliography at end of this volume.)

3) Another field of research interests is exemplified by studies that attempt to test or challenge existing theories, and revise them in the light of new evidence. Margaret Mead,[1] for example, undertook to test G. Stanley Hall's theory that "the storm-and-stress period of adolescent behavior is an inevitable phase of human development," which can be interpreted as a fundamental biological trait of all adolescents. Upon provisional observation, Dr. Mead had reason to suppose that adolescent behavior is conditioned by cultural values and attitudes. In order to test her supposition, she undertook an intensive study of Samoan adolescent girls, members of a simple, homogeneous, primitive group in Samoa, where conflicts and severe tensions were known to be rare. She studied the cultural factors and organization of life of Samoan society which does not sharply set off youth as a separate social class, as is generally the case in Western cultures. She found (and tested her findings) that in a society which provides socially approved means for dealing with sex tensions arising in adolescence, youth could and would develop without a period of "storm and stress."

As Pendleton Herring avers:

> The obvious function of research is to add new knowledge to the existing store, but its power for cleansing our minds of cliches and removing the rubbish of inapplicable theory is equally notable. Scientific research is a cumulative process . . . it is also a rejective process, especially in the social sciences . . . . Understanding can be [advanced] not only by gains in knowledge but also by discarding outworn assumptions.[2]

4) A wide field of interest of social research students lies also in studies which aim at the collection and analysis of data more or less within the existing frame of scientific theory and established techniques of exploration. Among the many illustrations of studies in this category we may cite *Postwar Problems of Migration,*[3] which aimed primarily

[1]See Mead, *Coming of Age in Samoa,* including Appendix II, "Methodology of This Study." William Morrow & Co., 1928.

[2]Herring, *Research for Public Policy,* p. 15. The Brookings Institution, 1961.

[3]A series of research reports presented at the Round Table on Population Problems, 1946 Conference of the Milbank Memorial Fund.

at collection and analysis of factual data on the various aspects of post-war migration in the United States and certain specified countries in other parts of the world, with an analysis of present status of the immigration laws, demographic and economic implications of immigration, personal experience of refugees, and other factors. Although this study concerned itself somewhat with unique techniques of forecasting the population changes of small areas, in the main it did not pretend to formulate new theories regarding social change or human behavior in general; neither did it try to advance new methods of social exploration. It should be remembered, however, that although primarily concerned with a vital social problem the concrete and objective facts of which were little known and understood, this study proceeded on the basis of established theoretical formulations and methodological principles.

Another field of scientific interest to research students embraces studies of an experimental nature in which the systematic study of social life is carried on under conditions of control and experiment, as we shall see later. (The more advanced student could also profit by a careful reading of Ernest Greenwood's *Experimental Sociology: A Study in Method.*)

The field of social research is virtually unlimited, and the materials of research endless. Every group of social phenomena, every phase of social life, every stage of past and present development is material for the social scientist.[4] He seeks a scheme for understanding the complexities of life around him. He is of the belief, as Robin M. Williams, Jr., stated it, that "few things are more necessary in sociology than a thorough-going effort to see the significance of the obvious. It can be taken as a maxim that the commonplaces of social life are never simple or nonproblematic for science, and that things which are most completely taken for granted in society constitute the most fundamental sociological facts."

It should be kept in mind that there is no clear-cut line of demarcation between the various fields of endeavor of social research workers. There are few research studies which do not, at least occasionally, propose new hypotheses or new scientific concepts, even though their primary aim and contribution may lie in a new orientation of, and application to, existing knowledge. Neither should it be assumed that a newly formulated theory always destroys the achievements of the

[4]Karl Pearson, *The Grammar of Science,* p. 16. J. M. Dent and Sons, 1937.

old, or that a new field view of a situation necessarily frees us from old errors and preconceptions. The new theory, as Einstein points out in another connection, shows the merits as well as the limitations of the old and allows us to regain our concepts from a new level which needs scrutiny. "To use a comparison, we could say that creating a new theory is not like destroying an old barn and erecting a new skyscraper in its place. It is rather like climbing a mountain and gaining new and wider views, discovering unexpected connections between our starting point and its rich environment. But the point from which we started out still exists and can be seen, although it appears smaller and forms a tiny part of our broad view gained by the mastery of the obstacles on our adventuresome way up."[5]

It is possible that few of the following illustrations of research will fit a beginner's frame of reference, but he will be stimulated by the "wider views," discovery of "unexpected connections" in his data, and their relation to the "rich environment." He may also gain a "mastery of the obstacles on our adventuresome way" of research. Above all, he will have a glimpse of what has occupied and is occupying the attention of social researchers, especially in sociology, what contributions they have made to the existing store of fruitful ideas, to methodology, and to basic understanding of social life and control of its problems.

Studies of the bases of organized societies; inquiries into the structural aspects of social life. Charles Horton Cooley[6] (1864–1929) was among the first sociologists to devote his attention to the study of the social bases of organized society and social reality. Among a host of things which could be pointed out, we can here stress only a few theoretical conceptions which Cooley had formulated and which research students will find helpful in studies of social life. He held that primary groups in various forms of development are found in all societies the world over, and intimate face-to-face associations and cooperation are universal human experience. Persons are born into a particular family and clan, and belong to them not by arbitrary choice.

[5]Albert Einstein and Leopold Infeld, *The Evolution of Physics: The Growth of Ideas from Early Concepts to Relativity and Quanta,* pp. 158–159. Simon and Schuster, 1938.

[6]See Cooley's famous trilogy—*Human Nature and the Social Order* (1902), *Social Organization: A Study of the Larger Mind* (1915), and *Social Process* (1924); all three published by Charles Scribner's Sons.

Belonging creates a certain fusion of personalities. Intimate interaction within the primary group develops a certain "we-feeling," so that one's very self is the common life and purpose of the group. But uniqueness and individuality do not disappear; neither are they completely submerged. Persons respond to certain internal stimuli—love, hate, fear and other emotions which guide behavior and create unique personalities.

George Herbert Mead (1863–1931), a social philosopher, also saw the self as a reflection of the ideas, values, and norms of the group (which Cooley called "the looking-glass self"). Mead perceived the self as the "generalized other," a broad and varied self which reflects not only current ideas and ideals and the "acknowledged attitudes" of the members of the community but the organized culture pattern of the larger society, with its many-layered cake of custom, its folkways and mores which have meaning to the self and to which it, in turn, responds. However, he pointed out that "every individual self has its peculiar individuality, its own unique pattern, because each individual self . . . reflects in its organized structure a different aspect or perspective of this whole social behavior pattern from that which is reflected in the organised structure of any individual self within that process."[7]

Both Cooley and Mead had penetrating insight and deliberated long and slowly over their observations. They were not empirical research workers. Neither were they armchair philosophers. Essentially, they were thinkers and keen observers rather than doers. Their original insights are now being re-explored and their writings reintroduced into social-science work. Many of the theoretical assumptions which underlie discussions on conformity and nonconformity, group ideals, small groups, socialization of the person, and the social aspects of conscience are based on the writings of Cooley and Mead. Each coined a large number of concepts which seem to flow out of his theoretical considerations. These concepts have found immediate and continued usage in the social sciences. Cooley's "primary-group association," "secondary-group association," "social forces," "social process," "social control," and "the looking-glass self" are basic in any sociological text. Mead's "social communication," "consciousness of meaning," "social stimulation," the "conversation of gestures," "the self," and "the generalized other" provide a rich basis for studying many aspects of personal and social life.

[7]Mead, *Mind, Self and Society*. University of Chicago Press, 1934.

Concrete empirical field studies. William I. Thomas (1863–1947) devoted himself exclusively to concrete empirical field investigations on which he based theoretical propositions. He was the first sociologist to introduce new foundations of scientific thinking by stressing the necessity of objective, detailed field studies, which would concern themselves with total social situations and their basic antecedent elements. His empiricism is an outgrowth of his revolt against speculative armchair philosophy, especially of the kind imported by American scholars who had studied under certain German social scientists.

In his *Source Book of Social Origins* (1909), Thomas undertook to examine the behavior patterns of simple societies, which would throw light on the more intricate behavior patterns and on the development of social institutions in modern, complex societies. He presented a vast array of ethnological materials dealing with varied cultural elements—economic institutions, education, technology and invention, art, religion, government, and the general way of daily life—in order to learn their influences on human personality and social organization. He, like Cooley, was committed to the theory that human nature is a product of social forces, a theory the social researcher cannot overlook.

Thomas gave further impetus to field research through his publication of *The Polish Peasant in Europe and America.* This publication, at first in five volumes (1918) and later in two (1927), was the cooperative effort of more than seven years of arduous research with a Polish sociologist, Florian Znaniecki (1882–1958).

In their field studies, Thomas and Znaniecki paved the way to a clinically scientific approach in sociology and social psychology. They introduced new and unique techniques for the study of personality dynamics: they gathered masses of subjective data on attitudes, sentiments, and emotional life. They used personal documents, that is, first-person accounts, to study concrete experiences and the resulting attitudes and social values. They also accumulated an enormous volume of such personal accounts, as presented in personal letters, diaries, autobiographies, and confessions. They regarded these subjective accounts as objective records available at any time to other interested persons—scientists, psychiatrists, and psychoanalysts. They regarded personal documents as the chief means for securing a cross-section of the entire process of "*social becoming,*" one of the many concepts they coined.

Among their other concepts, which have been in constant use ever since, are: "social attitudes," "social values," "definition of the social situation," "social wishes," "life organization." It is hard to conceive a sociological work—either in its exploratory or explanatory phases—without numerous references to these concepts.

In short, Thomas and Znaniecki stressed the need for: 1) studying the whole life of a given society instead of arbitrarily selecting beforehand certain particular sets of facts and thus wrenching them out of context; 2) comparative method of study, in order to determine the relation between various social phenomena in groups under observation; 3) systematic search for such experiences as may contradict newly formulated generalizations.[8]

The Polish Peasant represents a turning point in the development of social science method. It was the first field study of any magnitude which concerned itself with selective subject matter and with methodology as well. It stressed field research as a method of discovering, specifically and realistically, what actually is, and not what is assumed to be, a method aimed at ascertaining, intimately and concretely, social attitudes, social values, and other forces which motivate the person and the group. Thomas and Znaniecki conceived research as a method of depicting society as an organic social process—a process interwoven with the cultural setting, the social institutions, the community, and the person.

The personal document, especially the diary, autobiography, and the personal letter, assumed considerable significance as a research tool which facilitated the study of the inner life of the family and its members. Life-history documents came into immediate and widespread use in a variety of research studies.

After more than a decade of uncritical acceptance of Thomas and Znaniecki's new theoretical orientation, the Social Science Research Council asked Professor Herbert Blumer (in 1937) to prepare an extensive appraisal of *The Polish Peasant.* This appraisal centered its attention on: 1) the purposes of the study, 2) degree of success achieved, 3) generalizations reached, 4) extent to which these generalizations rest firmly on the concrete materials presented. (These points are of cardinal import to any social-science study.)

In his 82-page *Critique,*[9] Blumer carefully reviewed some of the more

[8]Thomas and Znaniecki, *The Polish Peasant in Europe and America,* pp. 18 ff. Knopf, 1927.

[9]Blumer, *Critique of Research in the Social Sciences: I. An Appraisal of Thomas and Znaniecki's The Polish Peasant in Europe and America,* pp. 81–82. Social Science Research Council, 1939.

important contributions which Thomas and Znaniecki had made to the scientific study of social life:

1. A demonstration of the need of studying the subjective factor in social life.
2. The proposing of human documents particularly the life record, as source material, thus introducing what is known as the life-history technique.
3. A statement of social theory which outlines the framework of a social psychology and the features of sociology . . . . [Elsewhere in the *Critique,* Blumer points out that without such a guiding scheme, social life cannot be adequately studied. The scheme should include the very factors which represent the uniqueness of social life and which logically constitute the facts of social change.][10]
4. A statement of scientific method which has stimulated and reinforced the interest in making sociology a scientific discipline.
5. A number of important theories, such as those of personality, of social control, of disorganization, and that of the four wishes—wish for new experience, for security, for response, and recognition.
6. A variety of concepts which have gained wide acceptance, such as attitude, value, life organization, definition of situation, and the four wishes.
7. A rich content of insight, provocative generalizations, and shrewd observations.
8. An illuminating and telling characterization of Polish peasant society.

What is perhaps of chief importance is the marked stimulation which Thomas's work has given to actual social research.

But Blumer also found some serious limitations (which Thomas and Znaniecki later acknowledged). Blumer repeatedly pointed to materials which readily lent themselves to "forced manipulation on behalf of some theoretical conceptions." Although he found much of the material gathered in a genuine mood of impartial inquiry, the authors of *The Polish Peasant* transcended the data or "ordered the data" to fit theories and conceptions previously established by them in relation to other of their scientific works. Blumer concluded, therefore, that it could not be said that the data under consideration "yield the genuine

[10]*Ibid.,* p. 72.

test necessary to substantiate the validity of the [conceptual] scheme." Blumer recognized the fact that the outstanding obstacle to an unqualified testing of Thomas and Znaniecki's theories is that which "plagues most social scientists, i.e., the absence of definite guides or rules which would enable one to ascertain positively that a given datum is an instance of a given concept and so deserves its application."[11]

The present writer asked Dr. Blumer whether the absence of definite guides and rules still plagued most social scientists in the 1960's? He replied:

> In my judgment the earlier statement still holds true today. In other words, in our field we have not achieved the ability to establish clear-cut relationships between concept and empirical item. Accordingly it is very difficult to make application of major concepts to the empirical world . . . . I would say that any major publication in our field exemplifies this problem . . . . See, for instance, Talcott Parsons' *Toward a General Theory* or his *Social System.*

In his later studies, *Old World Traits Transplanted* (1921)[12] and *The Unadjusted Girl* (1923), Thomas showed how studies of human behavior are carried on within a relevant context. In the first study he was concerned with problems of assimilation within primary-group organization of Old World immigrants and their adjustment to a new and urban culture in the United States. In the second study he examined factors of personal disorganization, individualization of behavior, and the role of the social wishes in secondary-group organizations. In both studies he further elaborated the definitions of social situation, crisis situation, life organization, social roles, subjective experience, as portrayed in personal documents.

Edmund H. Volkart has gathered Thomas' unpublished materials and those no longer in print; he reviewed and analyzed these and others of Thomas' major contributions to sociopsychological theory and method. Volkart concluded that nowhere is Thomas' well-focused, multidimensional approach to the study of behavior more clearly delineated than in his unpublished materials. Particularly challenging are his research suggestions and penetrating theoretical analyses of the relation between personality development and the biolgi-

[11]Personal communication, Apr. 1963. See also Blumer's "What's Wrong With Social Theory?" *American Sociological Review,* XXVIII, 3–10.

[12]Thomas, for personal reasons, had withheld his name from the list of authors of this volume, but he has been acknowledged as the primary author, in association with H. A. Miller and Robert E. Park.

cal, social, and cultural matrix in which it occurs. In the light of Thomas' total work and basic ideas, the following points are brought to the attention of social scientists:

1. How the adjustive efforts of fundamentally similar men have led to so many different cultures;
2. How men with different heredities and constitutions can, within a single group, reveal so many similarities of behavior;
3. How, despite social learning and rewards and punishments, some members of every population deviate from behavior norms;
4. How individuals in any culture can be so similar to each other, and so different at the same time.[13]

Because of the complex social variables involved in human behavior, Thomas insisted that insight can be achieved only through a multidimensional attack upon them, through study of the biological, social, and cultural forces which exert influence on personal and group conduct.

Volkart believes that it may be said unreservedly that there is no single sociologist who has so profoundly influenced American field-research students as has Dr. Thomas. His systematic concern with fundamental problems of personality and culture, his detailed examination of actual behavior patterns, and their interpretation in the light of a coordinated social science system are unexcelled. His fundamental assessment of the contributions of each of the social sciences to the multidisciplinary study of behavior are equally significant. Volkart shares the studied opinion of many other sociologists that "much of the contemporary emphasis on empirical field work, interdisciplinary research, and the close tie between theory and data, stem from Thomas' efforts along those lines."[14] A prominent sociologist, Louis Wirth, pointed out that from the days of the introduction by Thomas and Znaniecki of life- history materials to the present, social scientists have attempted to make such materials amenable to scientific treatment. A long series of scientific treatises which combine the statistical and the case-study methods along with field observation procedures, attest to the progress made in perfecting a method which would be as precise as possible and yet not confine itself to mere externals of human life, but

[13]Volkart, *Social Behavior and Personality: Contributions of W. I. Thomas to Theory and Social Research,* p. 290. Social Science Research Council, 1951.
[14]*Ibid.,* p. 14.

be adequate to the understanding of meaningful conduct and social values.[15] It is of interest that, for the most part, the sociological studies which followed each other in rapid sucession, spurred by Thomas' emphasis on field research, were cooperative undertakings[16] by sociologists, anthropologists, psychologists, political scientists, and economists. Stuart Chase later called these disciplines "The Big Five." (Thomas also stressed the need for the study of historical developments, but there is no indication that he regarded history as a social science discipline.)

Studies of community life: theoretical bases of "milieu sociology." Primarily under the stimulus of W. I. Thomas and Robert Park (1864–1944), sociologists at the University of Chicago formed in 1923 the Local Community Research Committee (later renamed the Social Science Research Committee), which began a series of studies of the changing character of urban life and group relations. These studies were influenced by Dr. Park's varied backgrounds: training in German sociology and social philosophy as well as American journalism. It is generally acknowledged that Park contributed more than any other single sociologist to the origination of milieu and urban sociology. He regarded the city as "a sort of social organism" and departed from the study of social change and social problems as isolated phenomena in a local community. He saw them intertwined with the whole complex of social life. In Park's writings one finds him searching out relationships between complex social problems and social processes. He saw the necessity of inquiring into the structural aspects of social life as a whole, at a given time and place—the sociocultural and sociotemporal contexts.

Hans Gerth[17] sees Park as a journalist who offered rich descriptive techniques, in the tradition of Balzac's realism, which helped conceptualize the changing milieu in the post-World War I United States. Park often told his students at the University of Chicago of his "tramping about the cities," watching the crowds, the public and the person, and listening to them. He was interested in the nature of the "floating population," in the "marginal man," the crowd and the public, in racial

[15]Wirth, *Eleven Twenty-Six,* p. 59. University of Chicago Press, 1940.

[16]See especially Stuart A. Rice, *Methods in Social Science.* University of Chicago Press, 1931.

[17]Gerth "Relevance of History to Sociological Ethos," *Studies on the Left,* p. 10. (Autumn, 1959).

minorities, religious sectarians, immigrants transplanted upon American soil. His graduate students became infected by his broad scientific curiosity and enthusiasm. They began to associate actively with various groups—from the gold coast to the slum—in order to study behavior patterns at close range. Or as Gerth puts it: "Humanity was studied in the raw, and in its own environment"—Russian peasants in their own new communities, hoboes in hobohemia, gangs in gangland, salesladies at Macy's, industrial strikers at the plant. These and others were studied in their respective roles and respective settings. These studies were published in the sociology series of the University of Chicago (1923–1939), but the "conception of sociology was broad enough to include many borderline interests . . . political, economic, or educational problems were dealt with from the point of view of a general conception of human nature in the social order."

Park stimulated his students to read widely. He deeply impressed upon them the importance of such fiction writers as Emile Zola and Victor Hugo on the one hand and, on the other hand, such anthropologists as Franz Boas, Robert Lowie, and such economist-sociologists as Max Weber and Thorstein Veblen.

Park viewed the city as product and process of complex social interaction which needed careful detailed study from a broad perspective. From his observations of city life, he theorized that the city is more than "a congeries of individual men and social conveniences"; more also than a constellation of institutions and administrative devices. The city was viewed rather as "a state of mind, a body of customs and traditions and of organized attitudes and sentiments that inhere in the customs and are transmitted with this tradition."[18] The street plan of the city, the growth of the population, the colonies and segregated areas were viewed from the standpoint of social control, social change, or social crises; the stock exchange was studied from the standpoint of collective behavior and social contagion. This conception of the city was unique and called for new approaches and the combined viewpoints of sociologists, economists, psychologists, and social psychiatrists, as well as city planners. Park, as well as Thomas, thought of research in interdisciplinary terms. Every phase of the city assumed new meanings when viewed from the standpoint of the prevailing culture and the emotional products of the group.

[18]Park, Burgess, and McKenzie, *The City,* p. 1. University of Chicago Press, 1925.

It is evident that Park's theoretical thinking was profound and that it was derived from concrete field techniques. Social anthropologists before Park were long committed to first-hand observations of group life and customs of primitive peoples, but their studies were chiefly descriptive, with little attempt at analysis and methodology. Also, American regional surveyors gave considerable impetus to detailed studies of specific areas, but the surveyors were handicapped, from a scientific standpoint, by the legacy of reform idealism. Although many aimed at valid results, they paid little attention to the development of research techniques and scientific principles.

Forty years after the formation of the Local Community Research Committee in 1923, the indomitable Burgess (jointly with D. J. Bogue) undertook an evaluation of urban sociology from its pioneering research beginning at the University of Chicago. Among a host of papers presented in the volume, *Contributions to Urban Sociology* (1963), the most relevant here are those which elucidate: 1) the theoretical distinction between the community as a territorial unit and the community as a sociocultural unit; 2) collective behavior as a product of social interaction.

Robert and Helen Lynd's *Middletown* (1927) and *Middletown in Transition* (1937) stand as classics in the study of community life. The authors are lauded for their straightforward, honest, and orderly description of complex facts in the life of a small American town. The average American could view himself "like a mirror held up to him—without dramatization or reformistic overtones." The view was so clear that other communities began to clamor for facts in contemporary American society—vivid, fresh, trustworthy facts.

In a concise appendix the Lynds state the field workers' approach:[19]

1. The types of data they gathered, on activities and attitudes relating to: a) getting a living, b) making a home, c) training the young, d) using leisure, e) engaging in religious practices, f) engaging in community activities.
2. The techniques employed in securing the data: a) mingling with and getting to know the people and "entrenching themselves by going around," attending various meetings, watching, talking casually to people and gaining "a feel" of the community before starting b) systematic observation. c) They viewed the town in its true perspective

[19]Lynd and Lynd, *Middletown,* "Note on Method," pp. 505–510, presented above in highly condensed form.

over a period extending from the 1880's to 1925, but actually concentrated on two key dates—1890 and 1924—and on the changes which had occurred between these two dates. d) They examined official and unofficial documents; e) compiled statistical data on wages, standards of employment, industrial accidents, church and club memberships, library circulation, bank deposits and assets, motion picture attendance. f) They used the questionnaire at clubs, high schools, boys' and girls' organizations to get points of view on public issues and questions. g) They used specially planned interviews with people they knew well for their frankness in response. They took notes "on the scene" or immediately after leaving it.

Although the Lynds used a number of basic assumptions (chiefly regarding universality of basic human activities and comparability of data), they conducted their study from a strictly empirical standpoint, almost without an informed theoretical standpoint of their own.

A series of cultural studies (in the 1930's) of immigrant communities—"Little Italy," "Chinatown," "Russian Town," "the Ghetto"—also provided new insights into hitherto little understood groups, their behavior patterns and social traits. The sociological concept of *natural area* proved fruitful as a unit for studying the local community. Previously, the approach to a whole array of problems in a large community could achieve only an inventory rather than an analysis of community situations. With the introduction of the concept of natural area the community came to be viewed as a mosaic of many diverse regions and was broken up into areas of significant cultural traits, or population elements, each with its institutional activities, modes of life, and tradition. Studies of natural areas also began to serve as a basis for districting social agency services; for example, health districts of New York City or tuberculosis service districts of Chicago.

Furthermore, sociological field studies, with their stress on the total cultural pattern of community life rather than on pathological factors alone, gained ground steadily in progressive social studies. Sociologists pointed to the fact that not merely community ills, which tend to give a distorted and unrealistic picture of the general flow of life, but the whole social process, the group relationships and customs, public opinion, social attitudes and values should be taken into account. An understanding of the daily life—its relevant content—as lived by the majority of people, and not as experienced only by a small portion of disorganized groups of persons, was needed to provide rational bases for social reconstruction. As Gunnar Myrdal pointed out: "Even in the large cities with the shocking amount of political corruption, crime and vice, by far the greater part of the population has no more contact with these phenomena than if they lived in another country."[20]

Comparable basic social data.[21] The Local Science Research Committee of the University of Chicago, under the dynamic leadership of Dr. Burgess, also began in the early 1920's a series of urban studies that later resulted in considerable refinement of methods of social exploration. Burgess pointed out that in order to gain reliable, verifiable, and penetrating knowledge of human behavior and social relations under urban conditions of life, it is necessary to secure comparable masses of data, collected from vital and standardized units, by uniform and permanent districts, continuously gathered and uniformly reported over long periods of time. This was no small order, as it called for new strategy not only in the collection and analysis of data but in the approach to the administrative set-up of the city. Burgess—with his farsighted pioneering spirit—proposed: 1) the funding of existing research data, 2) tabulation of census statistics as basic data, 3) working out a scheme for detailed continuous reporting of basic data, 4) preparation of a social-research base map. (On the side: Burgess must have believed that "blessed are the mapmakers, for they are the only people who can draw nations and groups together.")

THE FUNDING OF CURRENT BASIC DATA of community studies in progress or of data existing in the files of social, civic, governmental, and commercial agencies was undertaken in order to classify, summarize, and integrate these findings and place them in a central depository or clearing house, thus making them readily available in the most advantageous way for future studies and comparisons. Since then, an imposing treasury of basic materials has aided in practical as well as in theoretical studies of city life.

Burgess pointed out that such data as those concerning density, distribution, composition, and movements of the population are correlated with so wide a variety of social phenomena that for purposes of social study they can be regarded as basic social data. Mortality, morbidity, vocations, income, and other similar items may also play this role. Traditionally, such data have been secured and published by the

[20]Myrdal, *An American Dilemma,* p. liv. Harper & Row, 1944.

[21]See Burgess, "Basic Social Data," in Smith and White, *Chicago: An Experiment in Social Science Research,* pp. 47–66. Udiversity of Chicago Press, 1929.

Bureau of the Census, but they were issued in such form as to be of little use in local studies. Reports were made on political and administrative areas whose boundaries had little relation to social and cultural phenomena. These boundaries were arbitrarily changed from one census period to the next, and in most instances included areas too large for local survey purposes.

TABULATION OF CENSUS DATA. Burgess undertook tabulation of census data by small permanent districts—census tracts—to gain satisfactory comparisons, by census periods of changes in their population, their composition, status, occupation, religious bodies, number of prison inmates, and many other phenomena. These areas were sufficiently small to make it possible to combine them, in some instances block by block, in various ways. Thus, data on a wide variety of local conditions could be secured. Furthermore, comparisons from one census period to the next were possible. Also this plan provided a flexible and comprehensive system of census tracts for any city in the country, not only for the one specifically studied by Burgess. The U.S. Census Bureau later adopted Burgess's proposal to code by city blocks all population data in the U. S. Census. This procedure provides a unit of basic social data susceptible of almost any possible combination and permutation of city areas deemed essential in such studies.

Students of city life, especially social surveyors, were quick to recognize that, through this device, they could obtain social data for whatever area they required without regard to political or administrative boundary lines, and that continuing studies could be made over a long period of time. The data available in agency records could then be correlated, area by area, with the census data.

The Social Science Research Council has organized, since the 1950 Census, a Committee on Census Monographs. This committee, in collaboration with the Bureau of the Census, explores the most effective means of instituting a useful program for the preparation of analytic monographs to supplement the usual tabular reports of the 1950 Census and those following it.[22]

THE SOCIAL-RESEARCH BASE MAP. From the data of the Chicago Zoning Commission, Dr. Erle F. Young and collaborators developed a land usage map of Chicago. On this economic base they plotted the racial, language, and cultural groupings of the population, and thus

[22]Russell Sage Foundation, *Annual Report,* 1950–1951, p. 37.

developed a social base map. Since this map delimited a series of "natural areas," it became a useful base map upon which to superimpose many varieties of social data. This method makes possible the classification of all such superimposed data in terms of basic socially and culturally differentiated areas, rather than in terms of arbitrarily defined political, administrative, or statistical areas traditionally used. Other bases can and have been used, such as land values, trade zones, travel-time zones, and mobility zones. Later, other cities, such as Seattle, Los Angeles, Minneapolis, and Saint Paul, along with many rural areas, have been similarly analyzed.

The early social surveys made considerable use of maps, but these maps were in terms of administrative or political districts, rather than in terms of cultural or natural areas. The social base map, as originally developed by Dr. Young and collaborators, has proved of continuous usefulness in studying not only distribution of social groupings and their institutions and activities, but also in bringing to light changes and trends in these phenomena.

Studies of race relations: attempts to formulate new bases for rational policy. Ray Stannard Baker, a journalist of note, had made a survey of race relations as far back as 1906, which was regarded as the first authentic account of a race riot (in Atlanta, Georgia, in 1906), and the "first disinterested study of race relations" which lead to such serious social eruption. This study was made for, and later published by, the *American Magazine,* in a separate volume—*Following the Color Line,* which described the events leading up to the catastrophe and the conditions which made such an outbreak of elemental passions possible.

In 1919 another extensive race relations survey was carried out under the auspices of the Chicago Commission on Race Relations. The study—published in 1922 and entitled, *The Negro in Chicago: A Study of Race Relations and a Race Riot*—is believed to be the most painstaking and complete made in this field up to the 1930's. It took into account the biological as well as the economic implications of race conflicts; it sought out the attitudes of conflicting groups and the effects of irritations arising in interracial contacts upon public opinion. It traced the history of the growth of conflicts, of the riots, of extensive Negro migrations from the South. It analyzed the economic and sentimental factors of such migrations and set forth with care the processes of social adjustment and maladjustment of the Negro in a metropolitan center.

In the mid-1930', the Carnegie Foundation, in an effort to avoid biased findings, invited a Swedish scholar, Dr. Gunnar Myrdal, to come to the United States and assume the directorship of an extensive survey of race relations and to prepare a report on the findings and method of study. Dr. Myrdal organized a staff of his own selection and drew upon the materials and experiences of other scholars and experts, both Negro and white, who dealt with the anthropological, economic, educational, and social aspects of the Negro question. This study—the most comprehensive work on American trends in ethnic relations—was the first example of heavily financed and institutionalized research in the social sciences. With certain wartime interruptions, the study was in process for five years. The report, *An American Dilemma: The Negro Problem and Modern Democracy,* was published in 1944, in two large volumes.

As the title of the book suggests, the report refers to the ever raging conflict between high democratic principles in which the average American earnestly believes and his attitudes and actual behavior when confronting the Negro as a neighbor, classmate, or worker. Myrdal found Americans embarrassed by this problem which they could neither settle nor ignore. He placed the problem "squarely on the shoulders of all Americans," as Madge points out and adds that, although Myrdal's "conscientious work broke little fresh ground, except perhaps in his theory of method, [the report—because] of provenance and timeliness . . . was to have a profound influence on American attitudes toward race relations."[23]

Myrdal saw the problem as a threat to the future stability of a democracy. He aimed to lay the foundations, on a scientific basis, for the creation of policies that would promote adequate ethnic relations and would curb racial discrimination. Myrdal studied the Negro problem as it is encompassed in the entire American culture. He proceeded from the general American scene to Negro life and problems, to their trends, specific policies governing race relations, and their final integration into the structure of national policies.

Throughout this far-reaching study Dr. Myrdal set himself two major tasks: a theoretical one which implied an analysis in terms of cause and

[23]Madge, *Origins of Scientific Sociology,* p. 6. The Free Press, 1962.

effect, and a practical one in terms of means and ends and practical conclusions about the race problem. He offered no direct recommendations. Frequently, he indicated trends and outlooks regarding violence, the police system, interracial contacts, and other issues. In Volume I, p. li, of his report, Dr. Myrdal said:

> On the *theoretical* side, the aim of this book is to formulate tentative generalizations on the basis of known facts. A corollary of this scientific task is to indicate gaps in knowledge. . . . As the known and verified facts are rare, a courageous use will be made of the writer's own observations. Their conjectural character will always be made explicit. . . . For the outlining of further research they may serve as the projection of plausible hypotheses. On the *practical* side, the aim of this book is to throw light on the future, and to construct, in a preliminary way, bases for rational policy. This is one reason why theoretical analysis will stress interrelations and trends.

Myrdal carefully delimits his subject matter to the relevant and significant elements in the life, work, race contacts and conflicts of Negroes. He traveled to all major centers of Negro population and Black Belts in urban communities, thus avoiding provincialism and gaining a broad perspective. No appreciation of the author's insight and scientific attitudes can be gained without a first-hand reading of his volumes.

Although Myrdal's study is generally heralded for its originality and comprehensiveness, its brilliant interpretation of data on American race relations, there have also been some vigorous criticisms, particularly regarding his methodology and interpretation of American life and mores. Professor Howard Odum pointed out, among many things, that Myrdal did not adequately treat the historical aspects of the Negro problem; there is no mention of the extensive work of the Chicago Commission on Race Relations; there is almost complete lack of recognition of the whole field of public education. Neither has Myrdal, according to Odum, bridged well the distance between his own theoretical assumptions and practical problems, although he is very critical of American social research.[24]

Professor Cox of Tuskegee Institute points out that "Myrdal does not bring to light the social determinants of this well-known dilemma; he merely recognizes it and rails against its existence." Cox also takes

[24]Odum, "Problems and Methodology in an American Dilemma," *Social Forces,* XXIII, 94–98.

issue with Myrdal's proposal to inform the white man—"who wants to be rational, honest, and well-informed"—of the specific mistakes he is making regarding Negro traits. Cox regards it as "consummate naïveté to assume that the ruling class in the South will permit a free, objective discussion of race relations in its schools or public places."[25]

Professor John Madge, a foremost English sociologist and, on occasion, visiting professor at American universities, finds it "difficult to agree the book is an analytic treatment, because in order to analyze a rather more sophisticated framework is called for. According to Madge, Myrdal did not formulate a satisfactory theory of the sources of intergroup tensions nor of the roots of race prejudice. This lack of a sophisticated conceptual framework may perhaps be explained by the fact that "Myrdal is primarily a social economist, a sociologist at one remove, and a psychologist not at all. Though *The American Dilemma* is an extremely courageous book and a mine of information about the past, present, and possibly future of the American Negro, it does not at the substantive theoretical level provide any important increment to the general corpus of the social sciences."[26]

On the methodological level, Myrdal made some lasting contributions. He contended that since social scientists can rarely achieve complete objectivity, they should attempt to satisfy the following criteria: their value premises should be explicitly stated; throughout their work the premises should be specific and concretized; they should be selected with regard to the aims and purpose of the particular study; they should be regarded as hypothetical, and should never be considered as self-evident or valid. It should be remembered that "society admits incompatible valuations." Therefore, "alternative value premises should be introduced." In brief, selection of value premises should be based on: 1) their relevance; 2) significance, that is, selecting those valuations which are held chiefly by large groups; 3) feasibility; 4) internal consistency. The aim of practical research, in Myrdal's contention, is to "show precisely what should be the practical . . . opinions and plans for action from the point of view of various valuations if their holders also had the more correct and comprehensive factual knowledge which science provides.[27]

[25]Cox, *Caste, Class and Race: A Study in Social Dynamics,* pp. 509, 510, 531. Doubleday & Co., 1948.

[26]Madge, *op. cit.,* pp. 273 and 274.

[27]Myrdal, *op. cit.,* pp. 25–29.

Studies of social attitudes in crisis situations: studies of the unemployed. During the economic depression of the 1930's a number of significant concrete studies were made of the unemployed man and his family. These studies had broad scientific value since they concerned themselves primarily with the sociopsychological aspects of behavior in crises, and the validity of social theories formulated on this subject were scientifically tested.

Studies of the unemployed were not a new enterprise either in the United States or abroad; nor are these studies necessarily confined to periods of economic collapse. Extensive surveys were made in England by Charles Booth before the dawn of the twentieth century, and later by Arthur Bowley; and by Paul Kellogg in America (1914). These and numerous other similar studies portrayed the economic and social consequences of unemployed men during relatively prosperous times and the in midst of plenty. But many of the early studies of unemployment dealt primarily with the numerical data of the problem and only secondarily with the psychological effects associated with idleness and the loss of a livelihood. The newer studies aimed to discover the psychological effects of unemployment and to test the assumptions that morale is diminished, efficiency reduced, and ability to adjust to novel untoward circumstances undermined. These studies focused their attention on the unemployed man's personality, on the mental states during the long periods of enforced idleness, on family organization and the family's reactions toward an idle breadwinner, and on the behavior patterns of the persons facing an economic crisis. (One of the most interesting studies on this last point was made in Germany by a group of well-trained social scientists. Those who understand German will find the report by Marie Lazarsfeld-Jahoda and Hans Zeisl, *The 'Arbeitslosen in Marienthal,* stimulating and worthwhile.)

The Family Encounters the Depression, by Robert Cooley Angell, published in 1936, is a sociological contribution on the social effects of the depression upon family life. Angell viewed the depression as crucial in the interrelationships of family members whose future destiny is to a large extent determined by their ability to meet the shock of loss of income. He primarily wanted to identify and test the factors involved in the adjustment, successful or unsuccessful, to this shock. He, therefore, carefully selected for detailed study fifty families who had agreed to prepare intensive family narratives under supervision.

Dr. Angell found that the crucial factors in family adjustment to the depression were the original degrees of integration and of adaptability of these families. The integrated and highly adaptable families, though economically seriously affected by the depression, were invulnerable to any permanent social disorganization which might result from loss of income. As a matter of fact, his studies showed an increase in family unity and retention of general family structure in troublous times. On the other hand, he found that poorly integrated or maladjusted families could not withstand the added pressure of loss of income. On the whole, the general pattern of family organization before the depression forms the basis for the type of reaction experienced in times of prolonged crises.[28]

Dr. Angell's methodological considerations are of equal importance. He stressed the study of: 1) homogeneous cultural backgrounds as comparable units. These families were homogeneous in several respects: (*a*) parents and children living together; (*b*) American-born parents; (*c*) decrease of at least 25 per cent in real income; (*d*) decrease in income apparently of lasting duration; (*e*) decrease came suddenly; (*f*) no crucial event unconnected with the depression had occurred since the decrease. 2) Uniformity in presentation of data was regarded essential to testing of formulated hypotheses and subsequent analysis of data. 3) Detailed specific family narratives (prepared according to an outline provided by Angell) showed the degree of family unity before and during loss of income and the subsequent shift in roles and family status. These narratives were later used as a source of "hunches" with respect to significant variables, and as a testing ground for discerning whether or not the actual outcomes could be predicted from the variables tentatively chosen. Several hypotheses were formulated and discarded before the final one was validated.

The student will be well repaid by careful reading of Angell's methodological procedures and logical considerations, not omitting a statement of the mistakes made during the study and the processes of rethinking as a result of new ideas gained from others (chiefly Znaniecki). Dr. Angell is very generous in acknowledging his scientific debt to other authors who may have indicated the correct analytical road to travel in this study or who may have stimulated his own thinking. The book is more than a scientific report. It is in some measure a confession of a research scholar.

[28]See Angell, *The Family Encounters the Depression,* pp. 260–263 and 265–307, on the methodology of the study. Charles Scribner's Sons, 1936.

Studies of the social status of the unemployed man. Mirra Komarovsky, a sociologist, in her study, *The Unemployed Man and His Family* (1940), sought to determine the causal relations between loss of authority and unemployment. She was concerned with: 1) whether or not the father had actually lost authority (defined as relative power exercised by one individual over another); 2) what are the processes in the loss of authority; 3) what pre-employment factors are predictive in the process after the father begins work again; 4) what nonemployment factors are associated with the loss of authority. To ascertain the existence or nonexistence of these factors, she selected for study certain families from the rolls of a relief agency in an industrial section of New York. She made an elaborate study of 59 homogeneous families. In all of these cases the members were native-born, Protestant; the father was a skilled or whitecollar worker, unemployed at least one year, and was sole provider before the depression; the home was not broken and had at least one child over ten years of age. The author made a systematic inventory of change, in concrete detail, regarding transformations in attitudes.

This study is an outgrowth of earlier ones (*Studien über Autorität und Familie,* 1936) made under the direction of Max Horkheimer, formerly at the International Institute for Social Research, in Vienna. These studies proceeded from tentative hypotheses and from a methodological point of view aimed to contribute, in the words of Paul Lazarsfeld:

> . . . a more careful analysis of those nonquantitative procedures which very often are left to the laziness of "common sense." An assumption is also made that only quantitative procedures can be communicated, whereas all other procedures (insight, understanding) must be left to the inspiration of the student and the exigencies of the problem at hand. The nonquantitative methods cannot be formulated as explicitly as an arithmetic computation. But these procedures, now clothed in ambiguous terms, still remain to be described and standardized.[29]

In her attempt at systematization, Dr. Komarovsky experimented with certain techniques of collecting evidence, on the basis of detailed case records ranging from 25 to 70 typewritten pages, averaging about 35 pages. She devised detailed interview guides to be used with at least three members of each of the 59 families studied. The factual infor-

[29]Komarovsky, *The Unemployed Man and His Family,* p. ix. The Dryden Press, 1940.

mation supplied through uniform methods of interviewing was subjected to quantitative analysis. Duplicate interviews were used to serve as checks for the validity of data secured earlier and by other interviewers. She said that her procedure to determine the causal relations consisted of the following steps:

> 1. Preliminary checking of evidence to make it more specific and complete.
> 2. Checking the evidence for its consistency with other situations in the life of the respondent and, generally, with human reactions observed in similar situations.
> 3. Testing the possible alternative explanations of the change. The criteria in the third step are once again the relative consistency of one or another explanation with what is known of the life of the respondent and with general knowledge concerning human behavior in similar situations.[30]

Among the significant theoretical formulations are those which are focused on predepression husband-wife relationships: if the wife had admired her husband for his own sake, his authority generally had not changed during unemployment; if family ties were weak before the depression, the unemployed father's authority diminished (in about two thirds of the cases). "Unemployment does not so much change the sentiments of the wife toward the husband, as it makes explicit the unsatisfactory sentiments that already existed prior to the depression."[31]

The two last-mentioned studies of unemployed families are good illustrations of strict scientific procedures. They proceed from the hypothetical formulations to the specific studies of cause-effect relations and sequences, and unemployment as a social process associated with other life patterns. These studies are of signal importance to social workers, since they show that many basic problems of unemployed families lie in the degree of organization of family behavior during crises. The response to crises is determined by previous patterns of organization or disorganization.

In general, studies on unemployment conditions, with few exceptions, are not undertaken at the time of their occurrence. Much of the first-hand data, "ripe" only if caught in the process of occurrence, are lost. This situation is particularly true in the realm of social attitudes and values of the unemployed. For a valid systematic analysis of the

[30] *Ibid.,* pp. 135–136.
[31] *Ibid.,* p. 54.

effects of the depression on social institutions and human behavior, it is necessary to collect data at the appropriate time.

Research studies of military life and personnel: bases for new analysis of empirical data. Social research on an extensive scale entered the American Army during World War II. For the first time a large number of research sociologists were hired for their professional capacities by the U.S. Armed Forces.[32] Hitherto only few units in the Intelligence Division and political propaganda operations had employed sociologists to carry on research. During World War II the War Department's Research Branch, Information and Education Division, sponsored the most extensive research project ever undertaken by the military, in war or peace. Under the general directorship of the late Professor Samuel Stouffer, sociologists and social psychologists began to study—at the war theaters—the direct impact of war on the mental and emotional life of the American soldier. The aim was to learn specifically his thinking and feeling, at home and abroad, during and after combat, on a vast variety of detailed items—from reactions to food and recreation to promotional techniques, disciplinary measures, personal plans for the future, and general problems of morale.

The results were published in 1949, in four large volumes under the general heading: *The American Soldier: Studies in the Social Psychology of World War II.*

The first two volumes (*Adjustment During Army Life* and *Combat and Its Aftermath*) provide a base of factual knowledge which aided the Army Information and Education Division in administrative policies and decisions. The director of this Division says: "Without Research we would have often been in the dark. With Research we knew our course and were able to defend it before Congress and press. Further, we made a remarkable discovery. The Army gave little weight to our personal opinions; but when these were supported by factual studies, the Army took them seriously."[33]

This alone would have been a strong statement by the military about the immediate usefulness of research—with a capital R. But in a critical

[32]See Morris Janowitz, *Society and the Military Establishments.* The Russell Sage Foundation, 1959.

[33]"Foreword" to *Adjustment During Army Life,* p. 1. Princeton University Press, 1950.

estimate of the volumes of *The American Soldier,* General George C. Marshall, Chief of Staff during World War II, said:

> They add enormously to our knowledge of the factors which affect soldier morale. Every serious student of military leadership will find these volumes important criteria by which to judge the validity of previously established theories of morale and the circumstances which modify such theories. . . . In the recent war the Research Branch of the Information and Education Division made available, for the first time in our Army, a current picture of what is on the soldier's mind. Through special monthly reports, this knowledge provides an important supplement to the information which formed the basis for many staff decisions.[34]

The studies of soldier morale have shown what the function of the primary group is in the formal structure of larger groups. Stouffer and his associates found, in numerous instances, that a soldier's direct indentification with the military machine or with the war cause was of relative unimportance as contrasted with the soldier's feelings of strength and security in the military primary group and of the loyalty and moral support of his fighting comrades. The soldier's need to protect the primary group was stronger than his desire to win the war.

On one question or another about a half million American soldiers were contacted through personal interviews, group sessions, various tests, and questionnaires. Numerous conferences were held with the military. The results supplied fresh descriptive and explanatory materials supplemented, at every stage of the study, with statistical analyses. Both the method of the study and the consequent data were used with such caution that they are believed to have laid a basis for a new analysis of empirical materials that push forward on several frontiers of social science, as we shall presently see. (Consult especially a symposium volume, edited by R. K. Merton and P. F. Lazersfeld, *Continuities in Social Research: Studies in the Scope and Method of the American Soldier,* 1950.)

But Stouffer and his associates had more than scientific insight into methodological problems, more than extraordinary skill in framing and executing a piece of complex social research. They had, in addition, unusual sensitivity to administrative needs so essential in successful cooperation between highly diverse units of a large organization and its research staff. Furthermore, Stouffer spoke the language of the high

[34]Letter from General Marshall to Princeton University Press, 1950.

military "brass" as well as the lowly "buck private." For these reasons he could speak of "marriage of honest competent research and statesmanlike policy."

After the war the materials were released for further scientific analysis to a civilian committee—a team of experts chiefly from the universities of Cornell and Columbia—sponsored by the Social Science Research Council and supported by a grant from the Carnegie Foundation. This team worked the material over, integrated it, retabulated it, reanalyzed it, and reconceptualized it. The results—the original and reworked materials—were hailed as an administrative as well as a research success.

The Research Branch survey was the basis for calculating the educational costs of the GI bill and for the routine employment of the psychological inventory in all induction stations in the USA. The point system—one of many achievements of the Branch and undoubtedly the best-known—established the order of discharging the soldiers after the war.[35] Most of the studies were directed at specific local problems, at an analysis of social and psychological factors relating to combat and the soldiers' attitudes to it.

To the social scientist these studies are of signal importance because: 1) they are a mine of scientifically gathered data; 2) they are a concrete demonstration that data so gathered help to clarify methodological procedures in the study of collective behavior and in the measurement of social attitudes; and 3) they help to extend social theory and formulate new working principles regarding human relations. Merton points out that the important fact about the data of *The American Soldier* is that they are *systematic* empirical data in which:

> A major effort was made to find out the distribution of behavior or attitudes in various groups of social categories of men under varying conditions. The incidental observation or revealing statement in an interview was utilized, to be sure, but these anecdotal materials were not confused with systematic materials. The systematic data allow one to establish the differences and similarities among the attitudes and behavior patterns prevailing in diverse groups; certainly one of the primary tasks of a soundly based social science.

The data on sentiments, attitudes, practices, and relationships were obtained from large numbers of soldiers, individual by individual, independently from a cross-section of the membership of a group or of a stratum. Under these conditions there is the possibility of ascer-

[35]See Vol. I, pp. 7 ff., and Vol. II, pp. 520 ff.

taining the *typical* (modal, median, or mean) sentiments, attitudes, practices, or relationships obtaining among various social categories of men. The appropriate arrangement of such data stemming from individuals, then, can provide systematic evidence of the cultural norms and social organization of groups."[36]

Thus, although the first two volumes of the four-volume *American Soldier: Studies in Social Psychology of World War II* were primarily reports of researches conducted for the practical purpose of aiding the military in their administrative policies and decisions, these reports were based largely on a *new analysis* of systematic data designed to indicate the scientific by-products of these applied researches.

The following two special studies deserve more than the passing mention which we can afford here due to space limitations. It is hoped that the reader will devote considerable attention to them.

F. J. Roethlisberger and W. J. Dickson, pioneers in industrial sociology, together with a group of Harvard social scientists, undertook as their task to penetrate deeply into industrial operations and the reactions and thinking of the worker, in the famed Hawthorne experiment. This experiment is described in a large volume, *Management and the Worker*. It was the first extensive research undertaking by a large industrial corporation. This many-faceted research project was carried on right at the plant, where workers could be observed more or less casually and interviewed while their reactions to conflict situations in the plant were still fresh and vivid in their minds. This undertaking demonstrated the much disputed belief that empirical research could be carried on impartially within industry. "The book not only showed that empirical research within industry was possible, but also pointed the way to profound advances in industrial psychology and in the whole field of human relations in industry. . . . Use of experimental design and techniques of both observation and interviewing represent a notable advance," in the opinion of John Madge and H. A. Landsberger. The latter tested the original researchers' findings and techniques of study, and praised them in his publication *Hawthorne Revisited:* "Conceptually also, the convergence onto the industrial situation from three major sciences—social psychology, social anthropology, and sociology—was remarkably fruitful." And Madge, in the 1960's, concludes that "*Management and the Worker* is still the most important

[36]Merton, *op. cit.,* pp. 10, 13.

sociological research, ever done . . . but it is most peculiar that the pioneer research has never been replicated. The pioneers themselves are still in office but the research momentum seems to be exhausted. . . . The build-up of knowledge, and not the least of the knowledge how to carry out research, is an erratic and unpredictable process."[37]

Alfred Kinsey, a professor of zoology and a great statistician, in collaboration with two other zoologists, turned social scientist in their monumental research undertakings and publications of *Sexual Behavior of the Human Male* (1948) and *Sexual Behavior of the Human Female* (1953). For both studies the authors interviewed over 12,000 men and women throughout the nation. Their interviews were long and exhaustive, at times probing deeply into human behavior and at times using "rapid-fire questioning" (see entry in index). Kinsey undertook the study of sexual behavior because he was constantly being asked for advice by students with sex problems. He began his studies by reading in the fields of biology, psychiatry, psychology, and sociology. But he was unimpressed by the studies up to that date, so he enlisted the cooperation of his colleagues and made his own studies.

His interviews, some of which are 30 pages in length, cover 521 different items. He provides a 23-point summary of the technical devices used in the interviews (acting "like a thoughtful host"; privacy without fear of interruptions; showing interest in informant as a person rather than in his account; gradual approach to topics of emotional content; recognition of informant's mental status and conducting the interview accordingly; confidentiality of record made during the interview; systematic coverage of "of a basic minimum of 300 items"; supplementary exploration for clarity and completeness; standardizing "the point of the question"; avoiding bias; direct rather than devious questions; "placing the burden of denial on the subject; avoiding multiple questions; inclusion of rapid-fire questions; cross-checks for accuracy; requesting additional information or rephrasing question to secure correct answers; "denouncing dishonest informants"; avoiding personal identification; avoiding controversial issues; stressing overt activities over attitudes).[38]

The statistical details are no less complete. The authors discarded

[37]Madge, *op. cit.*, pp. 208–209.

[38]For list of 521 items of the interview, see pp. 63–70; for technical devices in interviewing, see pp. 47–59 of *Sexual Behavior in the Human Male*. W. B. Saunders Co., 1948.

randomization as an impossibility in the human sciences. They resorted to "a practical means" to safeguard representativeness by "diversifying each collection which enters into a sample . . . . The cases that are used to represent each ultimate cell in the human population should be drawn from a number of groups, widely distributed geographically, and including as great a diversity as is possible within the limits of the groups." And they used 100 per cent samples of the members of family groups studied.[39] It is believed that no inquiry has demonstrated as great an immediate value of the study of man in society as has Kinsey's work,[40] in spite of the many attacks leveled upon it.

[39] *Ibid.*, p. 93.
[40] Madge, *op. cit.*, p. 376.

Social science laboratories. As early as 1925 a few universities in the United States began to establish social science laboratories—workshops for training on the one hand, and institutionalized research centers on the other. The University of Washington was probably the earliest pioneer in this enterprise. The University of North Carolina, almost simultaneously or shortly thereafter, utilized the laboratory for studies on a local, state, and national basis. The major aim was to compile, test, and analyze masses of data under controlled conditions and derive a fundamental understanding of the changes and trends in community life. Not only students but the intelligent public and social agencies participated in these studies.

The laboratory idea spread to many other universities, and social science laboratories were created under various names. The Bureau of Applied Social Research of Columbia University engages—under the watchful eyes of Merton and Lazarsfeld—in such studies as communication and public opinion, the urban community, population problems and trends, advertising and marketing, labor problems and trends, and training of research workers.

Harvard University's Laboratory of Social Relations lists briefly some examples of the types of projects it has been sponsoring since its organization in 1946:

scope of social research continued

. . . Science is concerned not merely to formulate knowledge but to do something with it. . . . According to some, all facts are potentially of equal worth, and their value lies in their accuracy or their truth rather than in their applicability to the problems of the world. This is a philosophy of empty plenty to which many will find it impossible to subscribe.

JOHN MADGE

3

> The research of the Laboratory has covered a wide spectrum from individual behavior at the one end to social values and social systems at the other end. Many, if not most of the projects fall somewhere in between the two extremes. The range includes such topics as perception and thought, motivation and emotion, learning and memory, personality assessment, individual behavior within small groups, the measurement of attitudes, the social training of the child, language, and analyses of the values and social structures of entire societies and segments thereof. In the course of these investigations contributions have been made not only to theory and to substantive knowledge, but also to research. Sometimes the development of a new or improved technique may be the necessary condition for new advances of knowledge.[1]

The Research Center for Group Dynamics, University of Michigan, has been offering a form of social research concerned with the effects and countereffects of groups in their conferences and meetings—various lines of communication between groups and individual members. Kurt Lewin, who organized the Research Center for Group Dynamics, considered living society as the true laboratory of the social scientist. Three fundamental objectives were set up when the Center was established and these have been maintained as a guide to all policy, even after the untimely death of Professor Lewin in 1948 and subsequent changes in the organization of the Center. Briefly stated the objectives are:

> 1. To advance systematic knowledge and to formulate basic theories about the forces underlying group life, those influencing the relations between groups, as well as those acting on personality development and the adjustment of individuals.
> 2. To reduce the gap between the body knowledge of social science and the practice of social action.
> 3. To provide an educational program in the accumulated knowledge of group dynamics, in skills of research, in techniques of training leaders, in consultation, and in social action.[2]

The University of Chicago, ever since the origin of its Social Science Research Committee, has continued an active and intensive program of research in the social sciences. Research Centers have been emerging all over the world. E. S. Bogardus aptly summarizes the function of sociological laboratories:

[1]Department and Laboratory of Social Relations, Harvard University, *The First Decade,* 1946–1956, p. 86. Harvard University Press, 1956.

[2]Dorwin Cartwright, *The Research Center for Group Dynamics: A Report of Five Years' Activities and a View of Future Needs,* pp. 5–7.

> The sociological laboratory stimulates cooperative research. In fact, there is a strong indirect influence which functions in the direction of a continuous exchange of data, experiences, and ideas. The laboratory effects critical comparisons of methods of research and brings about new experiments in obtaining exactness in scientific procedures. Moreover, the sociological laboratory tends to develop a research feeling and even a fellow feeling among research workers.
>
> The sociological laboratory is a place into which research data are more or less continually being brought by student and staff members and sent by social agencies. It is a place in which these data are being analyzed, classified, interpreted, and made available for use whenever a demand arises. It is a place for processing social data and putting reliable research materials into the form of available knowledge.[3]

The laboratory offers opportunities for experimental research on a scale and degree of precision and efficiency not readily possible when working alone and outside. Although social research, like any other type of research, is an individual concern, the laboratory provides the individual researcher with resources, technical processes, organizational devices, as well as constructive stimulation, and thus enhances individual effort. The laboratory aims to supplement, rather than supplant, individual effort and creativeness.

Any type of cooperative research requires: 1) uniform understanding of goals, scope, and units of study; 2) compatible pursuit of subject matter, of classes and subclasses of data; 3) agreement and coordination of techniques of study and analysis; 4) compatible theoretical framework of all participants.

A laboratory without walls—the Cross-cultural Survey and Human Relations Area File. Stimulated by W. I. Thomas' classroom lectures and his prolific writings, and perhaps even earlier by William Graham Sumner's dream about a laboratory without walls,[4] a group of social scientists under the leadership of Professor George P. Murdock, cultural anthropologist at Yale, began in 1937 to assemble systematic files of source materials, chiefly of primitive cultures and peoples in different parts of the world. The information gathered on each cultural group was uniformly indexed according to a carefully prepared classification guide, published under the title, *Outline of Cultural*

[3]Adapted from personal communication, Dec. 1963.

[4]See A. G. Keller, *Reminiscences of William Graham Sumner,* pp. 16–30. Yale University Press, 1910.

Materials (OCM). "This *Outline,* the product of six months' work by Professor Murdock and his collaborators, is the conceptual cornerstone which made possible, first, the Cross-Cultural Survey (CCS), and later, the Human Relations Area Files (HRAF)." In OCM, revised in 1945 and 1950, all human activity is classified under 707 categories. By consulting the appropriate category, the researcher can go directly to the file where the best available materials on his subject have been reproduced.[5]

Murdock's ultimate objective was to "organize in readily accessible form all available data, on a statistically representative sample, of all known cultures—primitive, historical, contemporary—for the purpose of testing cross-cultural generalizations, revealing deficiencies in the descriptive literature and directing collective field work."[6] After the outbreak of World War II, the CCS concentrated its efforts largely on areas of probable combat operations, especially in the Pacific.

The immediate practical usefulness of these materials was realized by the U.S. Navy as "advanced counsel" to the Marines in their relationship to the natives. Later these materials were converted into handbooks for use by American troops. It is reported that the information on how to respect the native cultural groups and how to do business with them had prevented many costly mistakes and had saved many lives.[7]

No File is ever closed. It grows continually. Materials are added as they become available. Before a new File is opened, there is an intensive period of research on bibliographical data. Several considerations enter into the decision of what should be included in a File:

1. Extensiveness of the bibliography on the culture or area in question;
2. Reliability of the source and the nature of the training of the author;
3. Extent of duplication of already available material in the File;
4. Cost of translating into English if the materials are in a foreign language.[8]

The File on each of the more than 200 different societies and cultures consists of carefully selected pages from both published and unpublished sources which are photographed, reduced to a standard size,

[5]Human Relations Area Files, *A Laboratory For The Study of Man,* p. 13. 1949–1959 Reports.

[6]*Ibid.,* p. xiii.

[7]See *Civil Affairs Handbook Series,* Publications of OP 13–2, Military Government Section.

[8]Human Relations Area Files, *Guide to the Use of the Files,* p. 39.

coded for topical content by trained analysts, printed in multiple copies, and cross-filed under topical categories.[9] A complete copy of every File goes to sixteen member universities.[10] In studies of individual cultures, often over a hundred references are listed.

The Files are regarded as a basic research tool for retrieving and ordering information intended primarily for cross-cultural research. There is a separate File for each distinctive culture or subculture, and likewise for each major historical period. The HRAF duplicates original materials, organizing them topically for each culture group. It thus brings together in the same place widely scattered data for the researcher's ready use. The categories under which these materials are organized are very wide is scope—from food and feeding to language, from soil cultivation to religious ritual, from industry to entertainment.

These Files are intended also to provide data essential to the theorist, the analyst, the synthesizer, and the critic in a variety of fields, all the way from the dramatist to the novelist concerned with culture groups, from the botanist interested in the flora of a country to the anthropologist or sociologist interested in the social structures and functions of kinship groups, or the psychologist who wishes to study or compare the mental and emotional habits of certain culture groups.

The materials assembled are based on the conviction that, despite great diversity, "all human cultures have fundamentally a great deal in common, and that these common aspects are susceptible to scientific analysis."[11]

In the words of Professor Murdock, the CCS and HRAF are:

> . . . designed to contribute in several ways to scientific research in the disciplines concerned with cultural phenomena. [They] can answer specific questions of fact with a minimum of time-wasting labor. [They] can reveal gaps in the ethnographic record and thus suggest what groups should be restudied and what hitherto unreported data

[9]Human Relations Area Files, *A Laboratory for the Study of Man,* p. 4. Yale University Press, 1959.

[10]Printed Files are available at the following Universities: Chicago, Colorado, Cornell, Ecole Pratique des Haute Etudes (Paris), Harvard, Hawaii, Illinois, Indiana, Iowa, State University, Michigan, North Carolina, Oklahoma, Pennsylvania, Princeton, Smithsonian Institution, Southern California, Utah, Washington, and Yale.

[11]George P. Murdock, *Social Structures,* p. 364. The Macmillan Company, 1949.

> should be gathered in the field. [They] can subject existing theoretical hypotheses about collective human behavior to a quantitative test, and can be used to formulate and verify new social science generalizations. In short, [they] should prove helpful in nearly every type of research requiring an organized and classified body of cultural materials.[12]

Arnold Rose regards the CCS as "promising and challenging," but points out that the samples used are nonrepresentative, since they display different social conditions, different motivations, and attitudes. Furthermore, he regards the CCS as too broad. The "universals" these studies claim are not in the form of associations among cultural variables, but "of institutions alleged to be discovered in all cultures without exception."[13]

Studies of social trends—barometers of cultural lag or progression. William F. Ogburn's studies of social trends and his concepts of cultural and institutional lag have had wide application and have contributed new insights and approaches to the study of social phenomena both by social scientists and progressive social surveyors. Ogburn in his studies of social trends[14] saw the importance of abstracting out of a variety of factors those that could be measured and controlled statistically. He devoted particular attention to changes relative to population, production and consumption, employment, labor and social legislation, family life, social institutions, government, and foreign policy. These studies reflect changes and effects of World War I, postwar adjustments, the depression and recovery, the New Deal program, and similar subjects. They aimed to provide a record of facts, selected, analyzed, and ordered, with such generalizations and conclusions as to give some indications of how our culture is changing and in what direction it is moving.

Professor Ogburn's studies were not a mere exposition of the nature and extent of social change; they were also designed to test certain theories and establish certain laws of social change. Furthermore,

[12]Murdock, "The Cross-Cultural Survey," *American Sociological Review,* V, 370.

[13]Rose, "Generalizations in the Social Sciences," *American Journal of Sociology,* LIX, 49.

[14]See special volume published by the *American Journal of Sociology,* under the editorship of Ogburn, on *Social Trends, 1928–1942.* See also his *Social Change with Respect to Culture and Original Nature,* and his (jointly with others) *Technological Trends and National Policy.* See also President Eisenhower's statement on *Recent Social Trends* (our pp. 86–87.)

Ogburn, on the basis of systematic, concrete, comparative data accumulated over a period of years, was able to challenge seriously some existing theories about human progress. For example, it was previously assumed that social institutions progressed only as men's brains progressed in size and complexity. Ogburn could not reconcile this idea with the rapid technological advancements made within a comparatively short span of years. He turned to studies in genetics which pointed to the fact that man's brain had not undergone any appreciable change between the oxcart era and the era of airplanes.

Ogburn's studies also revealed (checked and supported by studies of other scientists) that various culture elements accumulate according to an exponential rate of growth, like compound interest. The larger the number of culture elements, the greater the number of inventions, and the faster the rate of social change. However, Ogburn points out, in spite of these rapid developments and adjustments to new devices and ideologies, there is frequently a cultural lag, that is, a failure on the part of social and economic institutions to maintain an equal rate of development with technological changes.

Ogburn's studies of social change are regarded by social scientists as an important foundation upon which can be based the "formulation of large national policies looking to the next phase of the nation's development."[15]

To the social reformer who desires social changes Ogburn offers the following suggestions:

> The first thing to do is to figure out the social forces which will aid the change, and those which will oppose it; in short, prepare a balance sheet of social forces. The next step is to study carefully three important factors which are bound to affect any but the smallest change, namely: 1) the natural environment; 2) the biological factor, or heredity; 3) the going culture.
>
> Natural environment changes only over long periods; but man can control it to a degree [by his inventive skills]. . . . Human heredity has apparently not changed much since Cro-Magnon man. The best thing we can do now is to reform our diets, especially by the better feeding of babies, and so improve the human stock *during their lifetime*. . . . Culture is difficult to change, but progress . . . can be made if the reformer carefully fits his program into the folkways and allows for cultural lag.[16]

[15] *Recent Social Trends in the United States,* p. xi. McGraw-Hill Book Co., 1934.

[16] The above quotations were taken from "Suggestions from W. F. Ogburn," in Stuart Chase, *The Proper Study of Mankind,* pp. 266–267. Harper & Row, 1948.

Prediction studies. These studies are based on the assumption that we "are *all* engaged constantly in predicting social behavior. Indeed, if we could not do so, the society could not exist at all. We *abstract* various factors from the behavior of other people, and find their behavior understandable. . . . It is true that we cannot predict the unique, but that is true for all sciences."[17]

American sociologists have long been committed to the belief that knowledge becomes valuable from both theoretical and practical standpoints when it enables us to predict the future, and thereby possibly control it. In the early 1920's, sociologists began to develop techniques by which they could reliably predict the outcome of behavior on the basis of current tendencies and past trends. But they were aware that, although the future grows out of the present, it is not an exact duplication of history. Many new factors enter—deliberate choice, inventions, discovery—which are apt to disrupt the continuity of the processes in question. The predictors must constantly repeat: "if present tendencies continue," or "all other things remaining equal," or "judging by current trends," or some such cautionary warning. Yet, they knew that vital statisticians and insurance actuaries had developed the so-called *American Experience Tables* which made it possible to state with accuracy the life expectancy of a person whose age, sex, occupation, medical history, and the like were known. These *Tables* make it possible to compute with precision the insurance premium for such a person although only a minimum of personal data is used. One of the most common prediction methods is to prepare a graph showing a trend line from the known data. If the data cover a reasonably long period up to the present, it is possible by statistical methods to project the curve into the future, at least for a short period of time, and thus determine the most probable future situation. It is never, except by pure chance, an absolutely accurate prediction but is the best guess or the most probable condition to anticipate.

E. W. Burgess[18] was among the first sociologists to prepare prediction (often called prognostic) tables to be used in selecting parolees for the Illinois prisons and reformatories. He examined some 3,000 prison records of recently paroled men and used 22 factors (such as age of offender, type of offense, type of home environment, type of

[17]Goode and P. F. Hatt, *Methods in Social Research,* pp. 2–3. W. J. McGraw-Hill Book Co., 1952.

[18]"Factors Determining Success or Failure on Parole," in A. A. Bruce *et al., Parloe and the Indeterminate Sentence,* pp. 205–249. Illinois Superintendent of Public Documents, 1928.

community, prison conduct record, school grades completed, age at which went to work) to predict the man's behavior on parole. For each of these factors it was possible to set up subclassifications and determine the degree of success on parole for each class of parolees. Thus, over twenty different traits, instead of the few used by insurance computations, were used to compute a score for each parolee.

These and other prediction studies that followed were primarily concerned with persons who were already delinquent or criminal and whose patterns of conduct and records at correctional institutions could serve as a basis for prediction. In the early 1950's Sheldon and Eleanor Glueck—who for nearly three decades have been refining prediction instruments through extensive criminological research—developed what they prefer to call diagnostic tables for purposes of finding the true, that is, persistent, delinquents from among seeming nondelinquents and pseudo-delinquents at an early age. They say that their chief aim was to "distinguish those who are probably headed for criminal careers unless early and adequately treated, from those whose childish peccadilloes will be outgrown along with water pistols and bubble gum."[19]

ATTACKS ON PREDICTION STUDIES. These studies have been assailed on the ground that prediction rests on untested and untestable strata of the past experiences, present intuitions, and future hopes. The predictor cannot separate himself completely from these strata of thought.[20] Robert R. Bowie, a political economist, points out that "seeing the outside world is difficult enough under any circumstances [but] trying to see its future . . . involves many confused matters. . . . But in a period of [social] revolution such as ours, it's even more of a fabulous undertaking to 'see' the outside world in meaningful terms."[21] A study of social trends is more profitable, he concludes.

Gordon Allport maintains that if we wish to study a person's chances, for example, on parole, or probation, or marital adjustment, we must study *him:*

> [Prediction studies are based for the most part on the assumption that if we find certain variables frequently present in certain situations,]

[19]Eleanor T. Glueck, "Predicting Juvenile Delinquency," *The Survey* (May 1952), pp. 206–209.

[20]Philip E. Moseley, "Foreign Policy," in *Research for Public Policy* p. 56. Brookings Institution, 1961.

[21]Panel comment by Bowie, *ibid.,* p. 74.

> then the presence of enough of these variables in a new case will indicate likely success or failure. So long as large numbers of cases are concerned there is no flaw in the reasoning. But a nonsequitur occurs when this logic gets twisted, as it sometimes does, and holds that if 10 per cent of the boys from a certain neighborhood becomes delinquent, then *this* boy who comes from that neighborhood has 10 chances in 100 of becoming delinquent. The truth of the matter would seem to be that from the point of view of a deterministic science the boy has either a 100 per cent certainty of becoming delinquent or 100 per cent certainty of going straight. If all the causes were known we could predict for him perfectly [barring environmental accidents], for his chances are determined by the pattern of his life in his own behavioral environment, and not by the frequencies found in the population at large. *Psychological causation is always personal and not actuarial.*[22]

C. Wright Mills cautions against overemphasis on predictive studies because of "unpredictability of social life." But he adds a proviso that "if we can grasp what John Stuart Mill called 'principia media' of society, if we can grasp its major trends; in brief, if we can understand the structural transformation of our epoch, we might have a basis for prediction. . . . In so far as men have some degree of freedom, what they may do is not readily predictable."[23]

The students of prediction acknowledge that at best it is difficult to read the signs even of overt human behavior, let alone to foresee the probable course that behavior will follow. They also acknowledge that dynamic social changes produce "chain reactions," but they point out that although prediction of human behavior is very difficult, it is not impossible if scientific procedure is followed, particularly since techniques for controlling observation have been developed, experimental studies utilized more and more, means for abstracting adequately and for reducing variability and complexity have become more scientific.[24] Through the work of Stouffer and his associates, who utilized these techniques, prediction studies gained great impetus during World War II. The behavior of the enemy and the ally, as well as the reactions of the local population to the very exigencies of war—food shortages, rationing, bombings in which their kin engaged at the war theaters, psychological warfare, prolonged absence of fathers or sons—was

[22]Allport, *The Use of Personal Documents in Psychological Science,* p. 187. Social Science Research Council, 1942.

[23]Mills, *The Sociological Imagination,* p. 000. Oxford University Press, 1959.

[24]Goode and Hatt, *op. cit.,* p. 3.

carefully observed, tested, and prediction tables prepared. After the war, Stouffer prepared a large technical volume, *Measurement and Prediction,* in which the bases for the attempted and actual predictions are carefully presented.

Predictive devices are now frequently used in the administration of criminal justice, since they provide a more effective means for sentencing or for recommending probation and parole. They are used also in predicting personal adjustment, vocational selection, school success, marriage success.[25] Prediction is regarded as an essential link between theory and practice. It is also a matter of common interest to the scientist, philosopher, and intelligent citizen.[26]

Experimental design in sociological research. The experimental method of the natural scientist has long been the envy of the social scientist and the cause of many invidious comparisons between these two branches of science. Some people maintain that no experimentation by the social scientist is possible because of the complexity and dynamic nature of his subject matter and because of the natural resistance to use human beings as guinea pigs even in a sociological laboratory. F. Stuart Chapin, pioneer and authority on experimental design, some three decades ago took up this challenge and began to make observations under controlled conditions and to use the experimental method of modern science. He realized that by reasoning alone it is rarely possible to solve scientific problems, ascertain appropriateness of techniques, or determine accuracy of the data obtained. These factors can best be learned by experimentation. The following is a brief discussion by Professor Chapin of the problems involved and the method employed in experimental designs in sociological research.[27]

> [*Observation of human relations under controlled conditions.*]
>
> In every complex situation, whether physical or social, many factors operate. If the scientist seeks to describe the single relation of factor A to factor B, then he strives to set up an artificial situation in which

[25]See L. E. Ohlin, *Selection for Parole,* Russell Sage Foundation, 1951. Paul Horst, *Prediction of Personal Adjustment.* Social Science Research Council, 1941.

[26]Znaniecki, "Controversies in Doctrine and Method," *American Journal of Sociology,* L (May 1945), p. 516.

[27]In January 1964, the present writer asked Dr. Chapin to review the above statement on experimental design in sociological research. He replied that no essential changes need to be made in the statement he had prepared in 1952.

all other factors, such as C, D, E, etc., are held constant or controlled. This may be readily accomplished in the physical or biological laboratory, but how can it be achieved in the usual social situation of freely operating community influences wherein interference with human freedoms is frowned upon? The answer often made is negative. While it is a true statement when it means that human beings are not to be physically manipulated in an autocratic or in an arbitrary manner, this does not prevent observation of human relations under conditions of control. Why this is so will be clear when a fundamental and simple characteristic of laboratory experimentation is grasped. This fundamental characteristic is that the test of control of the disturbing variables C, D, E, etc., is met whenever constant measurements or "pointer readings" are obtained on them. The fact that variables C, D, E, etc., may be physically manipulated in the laboratory until constant measurements are obtained, is only incidental to the study of inert matter or lower organisms. Manipulation is not the central feature of the experimental method—control of measurements is! There are two ways in which equal measurements (indicative of control) may be obtained: 1) by physical manipulation; but also 2) by selecting cases that have equal measurements, as in control group studies.

It is this latter procedure which makes experimental study of human relations possible through the device of matching measurements between an experimental group (that receives some social program of treatment) and a control group (denied this program). Variable factors C, D, E, etc., are made constant influences as between the two groups when one group is matched against the other on measures of these factors. Thus by *selecting* from each of these two groups for comparison (concomitant variation) on factor A (the program of treatment) and factor B (a measure of the expected resulting adjustment) *only those individuals* with equal measurements on C, D, E, etc., we have rid the situation of the disturbing influences of C, D, E, etc., upon the single A–B relationship which we wish to observe in relative isolation.

At this point another distinction may be helpful: we use the term "experimental designs" to describe control group studies of human relations, rather than the term "experiment," which term is one that tends to focus attention unduly on physical manipulation out of analogy to laboratory experimentation in the physical sciences.

[*Action programs versus controlled study.*]

Now it is obvious that all programs of social reform or social treatment, such as work relief, unemployment, social insurance, low-rent housing, public health measures, or group work techniques directed to the prevention of juvenile delinquency, do aim to influence individuals and are experiments in the trial- and-error sense of directing the course of events toward certain desired ends. Thus regarded, such "experiments" are trial-and-error programs, *but not to be confused with experimental designs*. Such action programs are the means-ends schemata of our democratic society; they are not passive observation of what happens; but on the contrary are overt efforts to see that something desired does happen. It is the merit of experimental designs that they supply the social scientist with a reliable method by which to observe under conditions of control the degrees to which social action programs achieve their objectives.

In experimental designs we *observe* what happens over a period of time to a group of slum families residing in a low-rent public housing project, meanwhile observing also the changes in a control group of low-income families living in slum dwellings for the same period. To rule out the disturbing effects of differences in family size, income, occupational class, education of parents, etc., these factors are held constant by matching the experimental group of residents against the control group on these factors.[28]

[*Practical difficulties involved in experimental study.*]

In practice, the use of experimental designs in social research is much more complicated than may appear from the foregoing account of the basic logic of the procedure. There are practical difficulties to random sampling, losses of cases and shrinkage in numbers in each group during the period of observation, and limitations connected with applications of probability tests as a means of estimating the significance of the results. Nevertheless and despite these difficulties, experimental designs seem to offer a means for the experimental test of social values, a quest that John Dewey set up as one of the most important goals of social science.

[*Illustrative studies of experimental design.*]

In *Experimental Designs in Sociological Research,* by F. Stuart Chapin, Harper & Row, Publishers, December, 1947, there are described in detail, nine studies in which the effects of social programs to promote personal and social adjustment were measured: the effects of rural hygiene in Syria; and in the United States, low-rent public housing, public housing and juvenile delinquency, relief programs, group activity programs to prevent juvenile delinquency, personal adjustment induced by educational devices, etc. Each study is described in the details of its procedures, its limitations and its results, so that the student may be able to organize similar studies in experimental design

[28]For the most recent authoritative study of housing, with improvements in control group techniques, see Daniel M. Wilner, *The Housing Environment and Family Life: A Longitudinal Study,* Johns Hopkins University Press, 1962.

and utilize with discrimination this newest tool of social research. Inasmuch as social measurement and sociometrics lie at the heart of effective use of experimental designs, a whole chapter is devoted to analysis and description of scores of such sociometric scales (of eleven types) available for both the setting of controls and for the measurement of effects of a social program.[29]

Small-group research. (See also pp. 174–177.) Paul Hare, E. F. Borgotta, and Robert Bales, the editors of *Small Groups: Studies in Social Interaction,* state that "the field of small group research is so new that it has not yet sufficiently recognized even the more important of its ancestors" (p. vii). Brilliant and versatile Kurt Lewin (1890–1947), perhaps stimulated by the early writings of Charles Horton Cooley on primary groups, observed that "the greatest recent progress in methodology has been made in the study of relatively small units; of the single social acts and of face-to-face groups."[30] Some characteristics of group structure and its degree of subgrouping have been the object of laboratory studies which record acts by relatively simple means. (See especially Robert F. Bales, "Small Group Theory and Research," in R. K. Merton *et al., Sociology Today,* pp. 293–305.)

Because of its small size (from two to seven or more persons), the group's interactions can be directly observed, the perceptions of each member toward others can be grasped, and the effects of the interaction ascertained more easily than can the intricacies which prevail in large groups which often elude precision. A large variety of small groups has been studied in detail, and each study dealt with the basic processes of social interaction. Such groups as adolescent gangs, adult cliques, work groups, board members, household groups, and play groups have been the focus of attention. As a result of such studies—both in the laboratory and in the field—much has been learned about group structure, leadership qualities, attempts to meet crises, motivating forces, group dynamics, and similar factors. Since, as F. F. Stephen remarks, "the whole group is composed of individual systems in an active state [of interaction], coupled to each other by the verbal and nonverbal communication process"—(a frown, a shrug, a laugh, a

[29]Statement especially prepared by Dr. F. Stuart Chapin, and revised Jan. 1964. See also his *Experimental Design in Social Research:* Harper & Row, Publishers, rev. ed., 1955.

[30]Lewin, *Field Theory in Social Science,* p. 161. Harper & Row, Publishers, 1951.

stare), each member's degree of participation can be recorded, as we shall see in another connection.

In their study of social life in a modern community, W. Lloyd Warner and Paul S. Lunt deliberately chose a small community, in the belief that it would manifest many of the complexities of modern urban life but, at the same time, lend itself to careful study and observation of intimate group relationships. They assumed also that such a study would provide them with an opportunity for better understanding how men live in all groups, regardless of place or time; how they solve their daily problems and social crises; what role their social institutions play; and the forms of leadership to which they respond:

> The more simple types of communities with their smaller populations, less numerous social institutions, less complex ideational and technical systems provide . . . the social [researcher] with the equivalent of a laboratory wherein to test his ideas and research techniques. By investigation of these simple societies he is able to equip himself better for the analysis of more complex forms of human societies.[31]

It should be remembered, however, that if clear insight into the integration of the larger structure is sought through an understanding of the functioning of the face-to-face group, the latter may not always be representative of the former. Carefully selected samples of studies of the larger group may at times be more appropriate for purposes of scientific study. Also, as Morton Grodzins remarks, "The importance of research is not the [size of the] topic chosen. Good research is done by good researchers, people of intelligence and sensitivity who command the techniques appropriate to the data they are examining and who are committed to advancing understanding."[32]

Research and sample surveys. In search of information which could be obtained easily from large, representative but diverse and widely scattered groups of the population, researchers have resorted to the sample surveys. Studies made only of a fraction of the population, called sample surveys, are based on the assumptions that: 1) they contain within themselves, but on a smaller scale, the same characteristics, phenomena, relationships, and processes which the larger group

[31]Warner and Lunt, *The Social Life of a Modern Community,* p. 3. Yale University Press, 1941.

[32]In panel discussion of Pendleton Herring's article, "Research on Government, Politics, and Administration" in *Research for Public Policy,* p. 35. Brookings Institution, 1961.

does; 2) they afford a more consistent investigation of the fabric of group life, its attitudes, values, and opinions. Sample surveys are generally made by means of the personal interview, the questionnaire, or schedule. (Consult index for sampling.)

Sample surveys vary greatly in their scope, objectives, content, means of approach to the public, and design. Among the best known nationwide surveys in the United States are the Current Population Survey made monthly by the U.S. Census Bureau, on the basis of a 25,000 sample, for information on housing and employment; the Survey of Consumer Finances, conducted annually by the Survey Research Center of the University of Michigan for the Federal Reserve Board, on the basis of a 3,500 sample, to obtain basic economic statistics relative to the distribution of the nation's income, savings, purchases, liquid assets, as well as economic attitudes and motivations.[33] Numerous commercial polling organizations make a vast variety of studies in the United States, but since their findings are generally kept confidential, they are of little value to the researchers at large. A number of regional surveys are also conducted, such as by the Washington Opinion Research Laboratory, supported by the State of Washington and conducted by the two state universities, to obtain information on varied questions of public interest. The Institute of Research in Social Science at the University of North Carolina has as its dominant research theme "regionalism and the achievement of an understanding of the State and the South. . . . In addition to its continuing research program, the Institute has in recent years undertaken contract research—usually multidisciplinary team projects—for such agencies as the U.S. Air Force, Library of Congress, United States Public Health Service, the Veterans' Administration, and others."[34] Numerous studies of individual cities and of territorial groups can be added as illustrations of the sample survey. The Department of Agriculture, as indicated previously, has undoubtedly given impetus to the sample survey, with its strict and narrowed definitions of the units to be studied.

PUBLIC OPINION SURVEYS. A research student is interested in public opinion as a phenomenon of collective behavior and as a barometer

[33]A. A. Campbell and G. Katona, "The Sample Survey: A Technique for Social Research," in Festinger and Katz, *op. cit.,* pp. 16–21.

[34]Adapted from personal communication of Katherine Jocher, July 1963.

of the will, tastes, and beliefs of the general public. This interest stems perhaps from the conviction that one of the functions of a democracy is to take into account the considered judgment of the rank and file—the wisdom at the grass roots—and that such knowledge can aid in replacing much of the wishful thinking and blind guessing about questions of public concern.

Public opinion surveys have become a major tool of industry, commerce, government, as well as of social science. J. Stacy Adams points out:

> Today sample surveys are used in arriving at important decisions—decisions which, to a greater or lesser extent, affect everyone. The fare on television is largely influenced by [sample] public opinion surveys. The package design of a certain brand of cigarettes or the silhouette of a new automobile reflect public expressions obtained in surveys. Farm and crop supports by the government and regulations governing the Federal Reserve System are in part predicated on the findings of survey interviews. . . . The content of broadcasts to Iron Curtain countries is guided by careful interviews with refugees.[35]

SCIENTIFIC STUDIES OF PUBLIC OPINION. Considerable confusion prevails as to the differences between a scientist's study of public opinion and the work of the pollsters on the one hand and the social work survey on the other. Both the scientific student of public opinion and the pollster may be interested in the same issue—continuation of foreign aid or a national health program for the aged, for example. Both may have some features in common, but each has distinct goals. (A discussion of the characteristics and goals of the social survey and practitioner will be discussed at the end of this chapter.)

Social scientists, especially sociologists, view the public as a form of social organization—and as a body of verbalized attitudes in a social group regarding some controversial or undetermined issue. (The following discussion is based on Dr. Herbert Blumer's article, "Public Opinion and Public Opinion Polling."[36]

Such issues most frequently arise in secondary group organizations which characterize dynamic community life. They are in response partly to the vast increase in population and partly as a result of complex cultural differentiation and rapid social change. The sociologist in studying public opinion regarding government support of a national

[35] *Interviewing Procedures: A Manual for Survey Interviewers,* pp. 4–5. Reprinted by permission. University of North Carolina Press, 1958.

[36] *American Sociological Review,* XIII, 542–549.

health insurance program, for example, would concern himself with a number of interrelated factors: 1) *the nature of the various social groups* ("the publics") who have voiced their opinions on the issue (well-established medical men, young medical men in process of becoming established; private citizens in upper, middle, and low economic brackets in urban and rural communities); 2) *the social framework* within which the various groups operate and the channels selected for expressing their views (labor unions, churches, medical associations, farm granges, newspapers, for example; 3) *the nature of the social pressures* which are brought to bear upon functional groups and upon key individuals who influence discussion of issues under consideration and who make crucial decisions on the basis of urgings and desires manifested by the group of which they are members; 4) *the patterns of diverse views and positions* on the issues in question and the balancing of the *pros* and *cons* which resolve uncertainty; 5) *the social processes* which crystallized opinion on the subject. In short, the sociologist views public opinion as a "composite opinion formed out of the thought of several opinions that are held in the public; or better, as the central tendency set by the striving among these separate opinions and, consequently, as being shaped by the relative strength and play of opposition among them."[37] The sociologist is also interested in the collective product as a potential social force which tends to mobilize itself for concerted action on a given issue. It should not be assumed that under such circumstances public opinion is unanimous or that it necessarily represents the views and wishes of the majority group. At times a minority group may exert significant influence in shaping collective opinion (the social welfare groups, for example, had a powerful influence in shaping public opinion with respect to establishment of juvenile courts, protection of women in industry, establishment of hospitals for the insane, inauguration of a social security system, and many other social reforms which were discussed in the preceding edition of this text.)

The work of the pollsters. Their approach to the study of public opinion contrasts with that of the social scientists in many essential respects. The pollsters set out to learn the views of thousands of individuals, and at times of millions, on a certain definite question: "Do you believe that the United Nations as it is now set up is capable of

[37]Herbert Blumer, "Collective Behavior," in Alfred McClung Lee (Ed.), *New Outline of the Principles of Sociology,* p. 191. Barnes and Noble, 1951.

preventing war?" The side-walk interviewers of "we-the-people" frequently record only "yes," "no," and "don't know" verbal responses of selected representatives of the population. At times the respondents are given the opportunity to express themselves more fully regarding the questions posed. Care is taken to include in the polling samples persons of both sexes, of various ages, occupations, geographic areas, and other factors depending on the nature of the study. Attempts are made to eliminate biases which might affect the outcome of the results.

However, the procedure is fraught with many difficulties. Here we can only mention a few. No matter how carefully the sample is chosen, how skillfully the questions posed, how adequately the population represented, how competently the reports tabulated, the very nature of polling precludes a systematic knowledge of the cultural backgrounds and the social settings which motivate the respondents. At best the interviewers' "population" or "universe" is an aggregation of disparate individuals who, although living in the same area or working in the same factory, may not belong to the same *universe of discourse* on general questions and may not voice *public* opinion which is the primary purpose of the poll. The pollster has little opportunity to ascertain whether or not the expressed views were crystallized during a process of discussion when various aspects of the issues were aired and certain elements of the question under debate were accepted and others rejected. In other words, it is almost impossible to distinguish off-hand judgments from seasoned and stable opinions based on rational considerations formulated in group interaction. Although public opinion is a natural group phenomenon and is governed by natural social laws, its complexity and dynamic nature make interpretation and analysis very difficult, even when the various stages in the process are carefully observed and analyzed. Neither is it easy to determine when the expressed views are rooted in personal prejudices and are tinged with vague gropings; when the respondent has only an "academic" interest in the question or when it is a "real" value to him and of such concern that he is likely to give it more than passing judgment. Moreover, public opinion is so highly dynamic that its evanescent character is one of the most important aspects in its study. Public opinion grows, and shifts, and changes in unexpected ways not only because of group discussion but also because of sudden changes in social conditions and "the social weather." (This point was fully demonstrated during the last few days before the 1948 presidential election when the pollsters did not recognize the necessity for last-minute check-ups.)

Polsters are now giving much serious consideration to problems of adequate and representative sampling; of clearly and efficiently constructed questionnaires; of choosing and training conscientious interviewers who have insight, tact, and discretion; and to problems of systematic coding, tabulating, and interpreting of the data. These problems are not unlike those which enter into a study of many other social phenomena. (For a complete discussion of problems of sampling, of schedules and questionnaires, of techniques of interviewing see Chapters 7–9.) Since the spectacular failure to predict the outcome of the 1948 presidential election, the pollsters have begun to scrutinize more carefully the social forces and social changes which shape public opinion. It may be hoped that the newly elected Committee on Analysis of Pre-Election Polls and Forecasts of the Social Science Research Council and the American Association for Public Opinion Research, organized within recent years, which includes specialists from various universities, government, and business organizations, will recognize that improvement in the standards and procedures of public opinion polling can be made only through basic research on all phases of its work. Dr. Daniel Katz points out:

> The social scientist has a dual responsibility with respect to public opinion polls. He should distinguish in his own thinking between basic research in the social sciences and the applied research of the market place. On the other hand, he should take responsibility for raising the standards in applied research . . . of polling organizations. . . . Moreover, as commercial organizations they have problems of trade secrets, immediate profit and loss balances, and the acceptance of their services by the newspapers and magazines to which they sell their services. . . . Real advances cannot be made in social science if the pressures of the market place upon research are not balanced in part by pressures of scientific inquiry.[38]

Stuart Chase,[39] who has made an extensive survey of the work of the polls, also suggests that the American Association for Public Opinion "should appoint a good tough committee on ethics to reduce [fraud and misrepresentation], as the doctors and engineers reduce quacks in their profession."

[38]Katz, "Polling Methods and the 1948 Polling Failure," *International Journal of Opinion and Attitude Research* (Winter 1948–1949), pp. 469–480.

[39]Chase, *The Proper Study of Mankind,* p. 177. See also his Chapters 15–16, "Measuring Public Opinion" and "The Future of the Polls." Harper & Row, Publishers, 1948.

Since the 1930's, and especially since the establishment in 1935 of the American Institute of Public Opinion by Dr. George Gallup, in Princeton, New Jersey, interest in public opinion polls has been steadily rising. The polls had demonstrated that it is possible to ascertain the attitudes and opinions of the public, and their tensions and pressures, and "calls for concerted action."

Many techniques are used in public opinion surveys to check the accuracy of data. Comparisons are made with results of other nationwide polls by researchers using the same sampling techniques. Checks are made with research organizations which conduct field surveys on the same issues. The polling agency's history of prediction is carefully scrutinized.

The Gallup poll samples in units of 1,500. "Since different persons are included in each survey, successive surveys (provided they deal with the same issues) can be combined in any number when larger samples are required."[40] Dr. Gallup has found that only relatively small samples are required for accuracy: " ' the average' or 'probable error,' for a pure random sample of 500 cases, is only two percentage points." This statement is especially remarkable in view of the fact that large numbers of interviewers are drawn—on part-time basis—from varied geographical areas and cultural settings, from varied educational backgrounds, experiences and skills. Controls are often difficult or well-nigh impossible. Moreover, the interviewer in these surveys is often, at one and the same time, fact-finder and analyst.

The American public has gradually become "poll-minded" and "survey ready." Campaigns against "Cooper's snoopers" have not gained public support. In general, the public has become increasingly cooperative in large-scale public opinion polls and in survey studies by scientists who concern themselves with national issues.

The policy sciences. Since the great economic depression in the 1930's and the first rumblings of World War II, a new class in the social sciences has arisen: the policy sciences. (See Daniel Lerner and Harold D. Lasswell, Eds., *The Policy Sciences: Recent Development in Scope and Method,* 1951).

Policy sciences concern themselves with the policies made, or needed to be made, with respect to intergroup conflicts (management and labor,

[40]American Institute of Public Opinion, *How a Public Opinion Poll Is Conducted,* 1960.

minority groups); leadership roles in the democratic process as well as in authoritarian procedures; psychological motives in economic and political behavior; resistance to social change which affects government administration; voting behavior of citizens; the dynamics of social communication through radio, TV, cinema, and newspapers. Some government departments have even used devil's advocates, whose function it is to find and state the case against important decisions and recommendations. "The fortunate fact today is that the literature on the policy sciences has become very abundant since 1950. Many good studies have been made on the relations between science and final decision making, and remarkable advances can be seen in this direction,"[41] says Dr. Lasswell.

Harry Alpert in "Government's Growing Recognition of Social Science" lists, among others, the following spheres to which social science research has contributed substantially: soldier orientation, morale, adjustment, prediction of combat performance, evaluation of wartime morale among the Japanese; estimation of war production requirements, regulation of prices and rationing. "To this list may be added the media of analysis activities of the Office of War Information and the Foreign Broadcast Intelligence Service, the Department of Justice, and various intelligence agencies. . . ." and many others.[42]

Alpert points to five factors which contributed to the "more favored governmental position of social science research: 1) changing congressional attitudes toward research; 2) acceptance of the social sciences at the White House level; 3) inclusion of the social sciences as part of broad definitions of scientific disciplines; 4) the general post-Sputnik interest in American education; and 5) the concern with redressing imbalances in American higher education."

Research for public policy- and decision-making has pervaded not only well-developed democratic governments, but considerable research is also being carried on by American scientists in underdeveloped and newly emerging underindustrialized countries that appear to be eager consumers of social science. Studies are being conducted in certain specialized fields of education, of trade unions, and indigenous leadership. These studies concentrate on the bases on which new social institutions should rest, on the essential relations between government

[41]Personal letter from Prof. Lasswell, May 7, 1964. See also his *The Future of Political Science,* The Atherton Press, 1963.

[42]*Annals of the American Academy of Political and Social Sciences,* CCCXXVII, 61 and 59.

and social groups, or, as Pendelton Herring remarks, "matters that have the sweep and dignity of nation-building. . . . Social science research on government, politics, administration has never been more relevant. In times of rapid change, experience ceases to be a dependable guide, precedents are futile in the face of the unprecedented, and common sense is inadequate for coping with the uncommon."[43] (UNESCO has an enormous research set-up to study international tensions and crises.)

The policy scientists make a multiple contribution: They use research on a continuous systematic basis in accordance with scientific canons, and they regard research as a basic value. The steadily growing support of policy research into government, politics, and administration is evidence of need of scientific inquiry at the most strategic level.

It should not be assumed that the goal of the policy sciences is social action. Researchers in this field, as in other fields, have pulled back from emergency or "crash" programs. Instead, they aim to provide insight into human needs, outline the sources from which knowledge can be drawn, and analyze the factors of the social problems facing the country. They have moved close to the bases underlying decision-making. But they leave social reform to the social reformer and social action to the social actionist. "The pursuit of knowledge concerning government is cherished for what it yields and for what it represents."[44]

The "Final Report" of the Select Committee to Investigate Foundations and Other Organizations, of the 82nd Congress (see House Report No. 2514, January 1953, pp. 9–10), stated: "It is entirely possible that in a time when man's mastery over the physical sciences threatens him with possible extermination, the eventual reward from the social sciences may prove even more important than the accomplishments in the physical sciences." President Eisenhower on January 9, 1959, in his State of the Union message, expressed a need to undertake a systematic study of American values, goals, social trends, comparable to the Hoover Committee study, published 25 years earlier, under the title *Recent Social Trends in the United States*, which—according to Eisenhower—"has stood the test of time and has had a beneficial influence on national development." Such studies, he believes, meet the stern test of practicality as well as "spur us on to our finest efforts"

[43] Herring, *op. cit.*, p. 20.
[44] *Ibid.*, p. 5.

and to concerns with "acceleration of our economy's growth and the living standards of our people, their health and education, their better assurance of life and liberty, and their greater opportunities."

A report of the President's Advisory Committee, on December 27, 1958, concluded that "the advances in social psychology might help to reduce tension and conflict at every level of human intercourse—in our communities, in business and industry, in government, and even among nations."[45]

Alpert lists various government units which have provided generous hospitality to the social sciences: the Army, Navy, and Air Force conduct behavioral research; agricultural research has become world famous in its leadership in agricultural economics and rural sociology; the National Institutes of Health include study sections on behavioral sciences, mental health, nursing research, public health research, in all of which social science research plays a major role, especially in the National Institute of Mental Health's Laboratory of Socio-Environmental Studies. Alpert concludes:

> If the social sciences are to fulfill the general public's expectations of them, they must double, at least, the number of trained practitioners. . . . The bottleneck in the advancement of the social sciences is not lack of research funds, but fellowship and scholarship opportunities for basic and advanced training. . . . Advance in the social sciences will depend most immediately in fact on what social scientists do: how well they teach at the undergraduate level, how well they communicate with the general public, how effectively they respond to calls from industry and government for help in resolving problems, and how much they devote to fundamental research.[46]

Since 1950, the Russell Sage Foundation, in collaboration with university research centers and certain social institutions in various communities throughout the nation, has engaged in a series of studies aimed to throw light on: ethnic factors and their relation to mental stress; the relationship between rival cultural values of the wider community and those of certain ethnic groups within the community; ways and means of improving intergroup relations in public schools. The Foundation has also collaborated with the Cornell Social Science Research Center in an effort to focus available scientific knowledge on

[45] President's Advisory Committee, *Strengthening American Science,* 1958, p. 4.

[46] Alpert, "The Government's Growing Recognition of Social Science," *The Annals of the American Academy of Political and Social Science,* (Jan. 1960), 64–67.

community organization work in intergroup relations and to test the effectiveness of some of the current procedures in this direction. A casebook was also prepared funding useful knowledge—for the training of social technologists, administrators, educators, and others—on the cultures, social institutions, and social behavior, which social scientists have at present at their command. This casebook is designed to present "a range of the types of problems encountered in cross-cultural situations and some principles and techniques of value in analyzing and solving them."[47]

Spread of sociological interest and research into the professional fields. Since the late 1940's, or shortly after World War II, a noticeable spread of sociological interest in the professional fields has been observed. And a prodigious growth of sociological studies in selected fields of professional practice has followed. The Russell Sage Foundation, under the leadership of sociologist Donald Young, has collaborated in the preparation and publication of a series of bulletins. (See particularly John A. Claussen, *Sociology and the Field of Mental Health,* 1956; O. G. Brim, Jr., *Sociology and the Field of Education,* 1958; Lloyd E. Ohlin, *Sociology and the Field of Corrections,* 1956; Morris Janonowitz, *Sociology and the Military Establishment,* 1959; E. A. Suchman, *Sociology and the Field of Public Health,* 1963.)

Each bulletin has, according to Wellman J. Warner of New York University, a three-fold objective, within its special field of application: 1) "a tough-minded appraisal of what sociologists have contributed and what they have failed to contribute"; 2) description of certain specific areas "in which further sociological research might contribute not only toward improved practice but also toward a more systematic and general social theory"; 3) indication of a range "of occupational outlets for a growing number of men and women whose training in sociology is to be carried over into the application of the practitioner, and who may be expected to channel back to the study and the research laboratory tested evaluations of research and theory. Such teamwork must increasingly constitute a growing edge of sociology."[48]

[47]Russell Sage Foundation, *Effective Use of Social Science Research in the Federal Services,* pp. 25–27, 1960.

[48]Warner, "Foreword" to Ohlin's *Sociology and the Field of Corrections,* p. 6.

Interrelation between Social Research and Social Practice

It is often stated that the test of science is its ultimate applicability. Most scientists at present would concede this, as long as they did not have to do the applying. At the time of the *Studies in Social Psychology of World War II,* Samuel Stouffer had reported that the pressures to clarify practical problems were so intense that they became the source of greatest frustration to many members of the research staff "who came from academic groves to what seemed to some a Washington madhouse." To them the insistence on the practical was not only intolerable, but often fatal to the formulation and testing of scientific propositions. Such situations were not uncommon in the 1940's, or at least they were much more common than they are at present writing. Then they provoked such books as *Knowledge for What?* because, Robert S. Lynd felt, "American culture presents acute problems demanding all the intelligence science can muster, and because social research appears to be falling short of meeting this need."[49]

Lynd sharply differentiated between:

> . . . the scholar-scientist and the practical man of affairs. . . . The scholarly bloc among social scientists is placed in jeopardy precisely by that leisurely urbanity upon which it prides itself as it looks out upon the confusions in the midst of which we live. . . . [The scientist] works in a long leisurely world in which the hands of the clock crawl slowly over a vast dial; to him the precise penetration of the unknown seems too grand an enterprise to be hurried. . . . In this time-universe of the scholar-scientist certain supporting assumptions have grown up, such as "impersonal objectivity," "aloofness from strife of rival values," and the self-justifying goodness of "new knowledge" about anything big or little. . . . The practical man of affairs, on the other hand, works by a small time-dial over which the second-hand of immediacy hurries incessantly. "Never mind the long past and the infinite future," insists the clattering little monitor, "but do this, fix this—now."[50]

The scholar-scientist recognizes the urgency and the pressure of acute and often gigantic social and personal problems and their

[49]Lynd, *Knowledge for What?* Princeton University Press, 1939, p. ix–x. Reprinted with permission.

[50]*Ibid.,* pp. 1–2.

intense, steady, and all-pervading nature, but he also recognizes that he deals for the most part with highly complex, often illusive, and dynamic social phenomena that require slow scientific treatment and precautions that come only from testing and retesting. He regards scientific procedure not only essential but economical of time in the "small time-dial" of the practical man of affairs. Any but systematic and sustained study would be a sham in a world beset with continued problems. It is high time to study them thoroughly, systematically, and slowly.

The practical man of affairs would probably not have been so impatient and intolerant of the slow process of the penetrating and sustained studies, if he could derive practical results from them. But the "pay-off" was often disappointing. The findings did not improve social practice. The reasons for this failure are too numerous and complex to deal with adequately here. Suffice it to say that since the middle 1940's the two blocs of workers—the scientists and the technicians, or the practitioners—have been approaching each other more and more. The practitioners admit that they are gaining a better understanding of their complex problems when viewed in the light of social science principles, even though they often fail to get a technique which would help them convert this improved understanding into improved social action.

However, the courtship between the scientists and the practioners continues with promise of a lasting marriage, which started cautiously with *The Scientific Basis of Social Work* by M. J. Karpf (1931); *The Contributions of Research to the Progress of Social Work* by Philip Klein (1948); a symposium edited by Norman A. Polansky, *Social Work Research* (1960), "a compilation of extensive experience and modern thinking in the design and measurement of social work research."[51] The contributors to this symposium are among the leading social workers in the field. They, too, are concerned with social action and early amelioration of the widespread and acute social problems; they, too, seek to learn the relative efficiency of different administrative devices and the extent to which citizen participation can be enlisted in the eradication of community ills. But they resort to scientific procedures, to formulations of hypotheses and their testing. They take time to formulate criteria for good hypotheses, to look for negative results, to redesign an already worked-out study plan, and subject their findings to rigorous

[51]See Polanski, *Social Work Research,* pp. v-vi. The University of Chicago Press, 1960.

analysis.[52] These are the signs of development of research orientation in social work.

On the whole, such orientation, though penetrating slowly and in isolated instances, is making steady progress on social work agency levels. The United Community Funds and Councils of America, Inc., through its Research and Statistics Division, sponsors and encourages research within member organizations. The Family Service Association of America established in the late 1940's a Research Consultation and Information Service whose function it is to collect, examine, and disseminate experiences of member agencies, "to provide leadership and guidance in improving study methods in the interest of sound administration and practice. . . ."[53] Community Research Associates, Inc., organized in 1949, with the aim of developing "more precise scientific procedures for planning health, welfare, and recreation services of American communities . . . represents numerous professional disciplines and knowledge. . . ." [54] Many other examples could be cited.

It is obvious that social practice can and has profited from social science and social research. The reverse is also true. In his "Afterthoughts of a Contributor to the American Soldier," Stouffer saw considerable merit in the insistence on the practical and its value to social research:

> 1. If social science is to be taken seriously and receive large financial support, its "engineering application" must visibly pay off. It is an interesting speculation as to how much of the vast financial support of the "pure" research in so-called natural science would be forthcoming except for the spectacular application in industry, in health, in war. If, for example, social science can help explicitly and visibly to show how a counseling system can be most effective in public schools, the public recognition of the importance of social science would be enhanced.
>
> 2. "Applied" research demands many of the same tools of investigation as "pure" research and stimulates the improvement of known tools and the discovery of better ones . . . social science research benefits from techniques developed by practitioners in applied fields. The first big uses of mental testing were in applied fields, such as the Army of World War I. . . . Public opinion research owes more to the

[52]In *ibid.* see articles by Lilian Ripple, "Problem Identification and Formulation," and by Alfred J. Kahn, "The Design of Research," pp. 24–47 and 48–73.

[53]Ann W. Shyne, excerpts from letter, April, 1954.

[54]See *Social Work Year Book,* p. 680. National Association of Social Workers, 1960.

practitioners who were out to make money than it owes to academicians. The problems the practitioners encounter in questionnaire design, in sampling, and in interviewing have stimulated much of the methodological interest in the improvement of the techniques. . . .

3. "Applied" research can speed up thinking about the kind of basic theory that is needed. . . . Often the pressure to "explain" or interpret a surprising empirical practical finding may lead to a reflection which organizes a good many such findings. In the Research Branch I well remember our puzzlement, which went on for months, over the finding that Northern Negroes in Southern camps, in spite of the fact that they said they wanted to be stationed in the North and that they resented discrimination in Soutnern buses and by Southern police, showed as favorable or more favorable responses to items reflecting personal adjustment in the Army than did those in Northern camps. Some of our analysts were almost in despair at this discrepancy. . . . When eventually it was suggested that the Northern Negro soldier in the South had very great advantages over Negro civilians in the South and that the advantage over Negro civilians in the North were much less, a clue to the paradox appeared. After a number of such experiences, it became evident that some concept like "relative deprivation" might be useful. Armed with that concept we would know how to anticipate such discrepancies better and to build into a study a means of checking up directly. . . .

[In brief], applied research contributes to social science 1) by providing the kind of convincing evidence of the usefulness to society which is necessary to continuing support; 2) by utilizing and developing techniques which can also be made to serve so-called basic research; and 3) by providing data and ideas which may speed up the process of generalization.[55]

DIFFERENTIATION BETWEEN SOCIAL PRACTICE AND SOCIAL RESEARCH. In short, social research and social practice function in unique ways and have unique objectives, but both profit by steady interchange of experiences and discoveries. The attention of the practitioner is generally focused on various aspects of a particular single unit. This attention is demonstrated by his insistence that each case is different. He rarely engages in repetitive exploration and examination of similar subject matter, with a view to accumulating a fund of comparable knowledge from which he can draw general conclusions. Nor are his studies

[55]Stouffer, in Merton and Lazarsfeld, *Continuities in Social Research,* pp. 198–199, and 203. The Free Press 1950. Quoted with permission.

generally concerned with a critical examination of analytic social science concepts.

The social practitioner often makes use of scientific techniques and systematic procedures insofar as he organizes his work logically and consistently; consults his sources impartially and objectively; collects, records, and classifies his data on the immediate problems under study. However, his primary concern is not with the development of new or the refinement of old scientific techniques. He is not concerned with the testing of scientific theory. As a rule he does not formulate hypotheses about the social phenomena under study. He proceeds to gather known facts, that is, data accepted as facts by members of the community or a social agency. He diagnoses, analyzes, and records his material, with the sole purpose of formulating a plan of social action and amelioration.

The social researcher, on the other hand, is not concerned with practical problems per se, nor with immediate social planning, therapeutic measures, or social reform; he is not concerned with administrative changes and refinement of administrative procedures. He does not guide himself by pre-established standards of life and work, efficiency and welfare, and does not measure social phenomena in the light of these standards with a view to improvement.

The social researcher is chiefly interested in the discovery and interpretation of social processes, patterns of behavior, similarities and dissimilarities which apply to typical social phenomena and social groups generally. In other words, he is concerned with types and classes of social situations, persons, or groups of which the unit he is studying at the time is a specimen or an instance. He aims to discover the common characteristics in types of general social situations, persons, or groups. He does not direct his attention in the first place toward practical ends, for it would not yield good scientific results. His facts are differently selected and differently related according to their intrinsic nature and their susceptibility to organization into a system. Although he generally makes some contribution toward practical ends, it is often incidental rather than purposeful. He, like some biological scientists, for example, does not aim to discover a cure but to understand the constitution of the human cell, the laws governing its growth, its susceptibility to health and disease. This search for knowledge has a definite relation to people's basic needs and welfare. The scientist assumes that all knowledge is potentially useful, whether it serves to draw inferences or implement action, to aid in the construction of a theory or in the practice of an art. Theory and practice frequently merge in the long run. As Waldemar Kaempffert points out:

> Franklin engaged in "fundamental" or "theoretical" research when he established the identity of lightning and electricity, but he hardly lowered himself by inventing the lightning rod. . . . It probably required more hard thinking and pertinacity for Edison to produce the first incandescent electric lamp than it did for Franklin to establish the basic fact that lightning and electricity are the same. An Edison is just as rare as a Franklin. Even if this were not so, no sharp line divides "theory" and "practice."[56]

Hence, the saying that theory is the father of practice. Practical application slaughtered many a beautiful theory.

The social researcher has greatly profited by the work of the social practitioner and has drawn a substantial array of data for experimental purposes from the concrete factual materials of social agencies. These materials have vitalized his field work and stimulated classroom instruction. They have revealed unsolved problems, and at times were able to indicate the limitations of theoretical procedures which could not stand the test of logic in the light of actual practice.

The social practitioner also makes a contribution to methodology through graphic, detailed, vital, and realistic descriptions of social problems; through the consistent use he makes of educational techniques in bringing these problems to public attention; through his skillful enlistment of enlightened citizens to provide financial and moral support in the study of social problems.

Obviously, there needs to be a constant and consistent crossfertilization if both social practice and social research are not to lose vitality and eventually run the risk of becoming sterile. Paraphrasing and adopting the words of Booker T. Washington in which he stated his conception of a working relationship of the races of the South, we may say that social practice and social research are as "separate as the fingers" in some respects, but as "united as the hand" in other respects.

Summary. At the request of the present writer, Stuart Chase, famed for his penetrating and lucid presentation of scientific facts, summarized the most important contributions he saw as a result of his book, *The Proper Study of Mankind.* He believes the following recent formulations (since the 1950's) in scientific social research—arrived at

[56]*Should the Government Support Science?* Public Affairs Committee, 1946, p. 6.

through the use of rigorous techniques by social anthropologists, sociologists, social psychologists, economists, and political scientists—to be among the most meaningful and dependable storehouse of scientific knowledge. They can also serve as a summary of many aspects of the preceding chapters:

1. *The culture concept* is regarded as the foundation stone of the social sciences. It offers both a theoretical and practical knowledge about the ways of life and characteristics all men share, whether natives of the Congo, Borneo, or Detroit. Many human needs are similar in nature, but are met by patterns and habits which vary spectacularly. The culture concept enlarges one's perspective; demolishes cherished ideas and dogmas about the superiority of Western civilization; shows how human beings are conditioned by the "cake of custom" in their tastes, thoughts, ideals, language, manners, emotions, skills; even the muscles are developed according to the tools and equipment provided by a given culture.

Students who realize the implications of these findings tend to be tolerant and democratic and wary of their own unconscious assumptions, culturally ingrained as these are in every man's early habits and even in his nervous system. Like relativity in physics, this concept has revolutionized social science; indeed it can be described as the relativity of human nature. It gives us also a convincing demonstration of democracy by showing the adaptability of man to any culture.

2. *The cross-cultural index* [for a fuller discussion see pp. 66–69] is a mine of information about past and present cultures. It was used intensively by the Navy during World War II in the operation of the Marshall Islands, the Marianas, Okinawa, and avoided many costly mistakes and embarrassments when the Marines got ashore.

3. *Public opinion research* is a relatively new technique based on sampling of a section of the population. It is assumed that if the sample is adequate, it will accurately represent the whole population, its attitudes, opinions, tensions, and pressures, as well as its call for concerted action. It is also assumed that reliable knowledge of the will of the people, of the wisdom of "the grass roots" can help public officials, save their resorting to blind guesses, wishful thinking, or giving undue weight to the desires of special interest-groups.

4. *Development of techniques for intercultural education* has kept pace with other research developments in social relations. Students in this field require the broadest possible knowledge of cultural differences, obtained through specific research projects. Cooperative research by teams of social scientists is increasing and helps in assembling needed knowledge as well as improving international relations.

5. *Studies of labor-management relations,* especially through laboratory methods, have thrown new light on complex problems. These methods are being developed and expanded at an unprecedented rate. Beginning on the one hand with the classic Hawthorne experiment directed by Elton Mayo, and on the other hand with studies by Kurt Lewin [see p. 65] much documented evidence has been collected on the motivations and behavior of workers, the hidden energies locked up in small face-to-face groups, the best methods for training employees and supervisors to deal with them. Universities throughout the nation, the National Planning Association, as well as some far-sighted labor leaders have recognized the value of scientific method in the approach to these complex problems.

6. *Studies of social change,* chiefly those by William F. Ogburn, have demonstrated that material culture grows not by evolution but by a conscious collection of tools and know-how, and that this collection grows at an accelerating rate. An exponential curve rises at first slowly, then more and more steeply. Compound interest and unchecked population rise in a biological species are examples of such growth. The results are always sensational. Ogburn analyzes the social effects of various individual inventions (radio, automobile, inventions in medicine, in military warfare, and many others) and shows how all-pervading, powerful, and interrelated these effects are in revolutionizing all aspects of modern life. [For a fuller discussion of Ogburn's studies on social change see pp. 69–70.]

7. *Studies of American communities* show the essential structure, the characteristics of the people, systems of belief, hierarchy of social institutions, tensions, stresses, and changes in modes of living, social problems and their impact on the population. These studies offer a rich fund of useful practical knowledge as well as a theoretical basis for social planners, city managers, and social reformers.[57]

Is Sociology on Trial?

A few articles and booklets have appeared in the early 1960's on the shortcomings of American sociology. (See particularly *Sociology on Trial,* edited by Maurice Stein and Arthur Vidich; *Education of Sociologists* by Elbridge Sibley, especially "Summary of Findings and Recommendations"; and Harry Alpert's "Some Observations on the State of

[57]The above is based on a statement by Stuart Chase, prepared especially for this volume. See also his *Roads to Agreement* and *Power of Words*. Harcourt, Brace & World, 1954.

Sociology," in *Pacific Sociological Review,* Vol. VI, Autumn 1963.) The editors of *Sociology on Trial,* as "substantive sociologists who have primarily devoted themselves to the analysis and understanding of social life," see sociology's task as "the analysis and understanding of the organizational structure and operations of society *and* the basis in values and attitudes on which individual participation in social life rests. The carrying out of this task presupposes sociologists capable of doing the work and a society capable of tolerating the results. There are a number of reasons why neither of these presuppositions is easily achieved."[58]

Some eight essays put American sociologists on trial for their limited vision of "the character of the social knowledge toward which their efforts are directed"; "the ascetic attitude toward theories [which] seem to be based on a mistrust of 'philosophy' or 'metaphysics';" "typical American studies [which] start from questions in nowise connected with those problems which arouse passion [in German sociologists] in everyday political and social struggle. . . . One of the greatest German sociologists, Max Weber, has shown how we can discuss the political *nervus rerum* without making propagandistic judgments of value. . . ."[59]

C. Wright Mills, in a stimulating article, "The Bureaucratic Ethos," one of ten contributions to the above symposium, points out that "bureaucratization of social study is now a general trend." Lack of appreciation of the relevance of history to sociological problems; clinging to a myth-free sociology; lack of profound concern with "what and whither social science" are a few of other "indictments" against American sociology. These are brought to view in an effort "to liberate our [American] students from the intimidation they feel when they confront official tomes . . . recently published . . . like: the progress of a decade, sociology today, theories of society, foundations of sociology. . . ."[60] The editors conclude that "these days, even small amounts of irreverence have exceptional regenerative effect on youthful imaginations. It is clear, however, that criticism has its limits and that sociological imagination must find its own productive enterprises."[61] And the editors devote about a third of their booklet to "Rediscovery

[58]Introduction to *Sociology on Trial,* pp. 1–2. Prentice-Hall, 1963.

[59]Karl Mannheim, "The Ethos of American Sociology," in *ibid.,* pp. 3–10.

[60]Karl Mannheim, "American Sociology," Hans Gerth and Saul Landau, "The Relevance of History to the Sociological Ethos," pp. 3–33, in *Sociology on Trial.*

[61]Mannheim, *ibid.,* p. 2.

of Sociology" and advance articles on "Sociology as an Art Form"; "Social Theory in Field Research," and "The Poetic Metaphors in Sociology." All make stimulating reading.

Alpert, however, concludes that "it is, indeed, impossible to take a hard look at sociology without becoming aware of the evidence of solid growth, accomplishments, and ever-renewing dedication to the pursuit of a better understanding of the nature of society and social processes and structures."[62]

On the basis of the empirical studies presented in our Chapters 2 and 3 the reader will have little difficulty in seeing this solid growth and accomplishment. That social study can become enriched by broad historical perspective, vitalized by the essential link with philosophy, history, logic, no social scientist worthy of his name would deny. The insistence on, and steady references to, these essentials can be readily gained from reading the works of Cooley, Mead, Thomas, Znaniecki, Park, Burgess, the Lynds, Angell, Komarowski, Myrdal, Stouffer, Murdock, Merton, Gordon Allport, Blumer, Bales, Madge. The list of authors can be greatly expanded. The reader will feel highly rewarded if he examines these writings at first hand. The constructive approach to the study of the solid contributions by social scientists should stimulate the reader's sociological imagination and impel him toward greater effort in research. Science in any form, is no panacea, but "it can kill off the infection of factual error, reduce the fever of the irrational, and thus eventually steady the pulse of the irresolute. This is no small service in the world at any time."[63]

[62]Alpert, *op. cit.,* p. 47.
[63]Herring, *op. cit.,* p. 20.

principles

and techniques

of social studies

II

general phases and principles of scientific procedure

4

Crafty men condemn studies and principles thereof. Simple men admire them; and wise men use them.

FRANCIS BACON

James Grier Miller, professor of psychology and psychiatry at the University of Chicago, aptly states that if deficiencies in work occur, they are generally not due to lack of knowledge of scientific procedure but to the fact that, when we are intent on getting tomorrow an answer to today's complex problems, we fail to complete the sequence of steps required in scientific procedure.[1] Such failure results in inability to establish reliable and corroborative facts and to make them intelligible. Facts do not lie around in plain view awaiting an explorer. They are often imbedded in a thick crust of cultural norms and are intertwined with diverse and dynamic social relations. Unraveling them is a slow process.

There are often many trials and errors in discerning the nature and extent of their association with other facts and in selecting those that are meaningful and pertinent to the question under study. Furthermore, facts are not easily put into a pattern. A scientist may try to put facts together, but they do not seem related to each other. He tries again on the basis of new insights, but he may still be in doubt about some; he replaces these with others, and continues the process until he sees a logical connection between his facts. In order to

[1] Miller, *Experiments in Social Process: A Symposium on Social Psychology,* p. 16. McGraw-Hill Book Co., 1950.

arrive at this conclusion, the research scientist adopts a number of steps which are not mutually exclusive.

Precise formulation of the problem in question, as was illustrated in the study presented in Chapter 1 and the studies by numerous researchers discussed in subsequent chapters, is a prerequisite to any study.

Roy G. Francis[2] of the University of Minnesota lists twelve steps in scientific research, warning, however, that although "the temporal order of research is pretty much as given, the fact remains that 'steps in scientific research' is a somewhat idealized account of how the scientist actually does his work." Here we shall only list these steps: selection of problem area, acquaintance with current theory and knowledge in the area, definition of the problem, development of hypotheses, development of the formal argument, delineation of the source of data, creation of instruments (questionnaires, scales, recording devices), writing a "dummy argument," pretest of the instruments and possible revision, formal (systematic) acquisition of data, analysis of the data, formal write-up of conclusions reached.

The reader will readily recognize these procedural steps in our discussion in Chapter 1. Briefly, a discussion of the phases of scientific procedure includes: 1) precise formulation of the problem in question; 2) formulation of a working or exploratory hypothesis; 3) observation and exploration of the problem by a variety of scientific techniques; 4) uniform recording of the data obtained; 5) classification of the data into series and/or sequences; 6) scientific generalizing.

These steps are not mutually exclusive; neither are they separate and distinct. They do not necessarily follow each other in any special order. Some of them may enter into a given piece of research almost simultaneously, or reenter after a preliminary use of them. For example, some preliminary observation is inevitable before an adequate working hypothesis can be formulated. After its formulation, systematic observation is indispensable. Observation is generally coupled with some preliminary grouping of the data. Since our sense organs are easily deceived and we seldom see the whole of any social phenomenon, repeated observations and testing are essential. Ideally, observation should be supplemented by experimentation. By isolating the various elements of a complex social situation and observing each in succession, it is possible to learn, in some measure at least, the existing relations between them. A comprehensive discussion of these techniques and

[2]Francis, "Nature of Scientific Research," in John T. Doby (Ed.), *An Introduction to Social Research,* pp. 12–16. Stackpole Co., 1954.

phases is the object of Chapters 5–16. Here the emphasis will fall primarily on the role working hypotheses and theories play in empirical research.

Hypotheses in social research. As already mentioned in Chapter 1 a researcher must choose from the complexity of observed events those significant and relevant facts which will most adequately explain the problem under study, that is, show the essential relationships which exist between the various elements within the complexity. In his search for the significant facts he may fall back on previous experience, his own or that of others, and single out those factors that are known to have explained similar situations in the past. This experience need not necessarily be related to the field of science and need not necessarily constitute measurable data. It may be observed in the realm of descriptive literature, or speculative philosophy, or in the arts and technics, as long as these fields can provide some insight into the situation under observation. On the basis of these observations, assumptions are built as to the relations of facts. In the illustrations afforded by the study of juvenile delinquency in Hong Kong, it was observed that on the basis of cursory knowledge, certain assumptions were made regarding the causal factors involved in the delinquencies. These assumptions were made on the basis of probabilities, shrewd guesses, and profound hunches. When the penetrating hunch points to a possible, though provisional, explanation to a vital central idea which can become the basis for fruitful investigation, it becomes a working or explanatory hypothesis. In the investigations that follow, the explanation is viewed at the start in terms of probabilities and tentatively observed indications. The conclusively established detailed facts are still lacking or are in process of investigation.

It may be recalled that one of the hypotheses advanced in the study —the low incidence of delinquency in Hong Kong—related to the participation of youth in home industries, in family responsibilities, and thus perceiving themselves in adult roles in closely knit family groups, who for the most part still reside in homogeneous neighborhoods rather than in undifferentiated secondary communities. This is a somewhat complex hypothesis which needs testing and verification.

It is obvious that the usefulness of a hypothesis depends on the researcher's: 1) keen observations, 2) disciplined imagination and creative thinking, which provide at least fractional insight, and 3) some formulated theoretical framework. These processes are in reality the guiding lines in exploration. Without a working hypothesis the explorer would find it very difficult, laborious, and time-consuming to make adequate discriminations in the complex interplay of factors before him. The hypothesis guides him in the selection of pertinent facts needed to explain the problem at hand. It also saves him from becoming lost in a welter of irrelevancies. Thus, the road to discovery which "requires hunch, wit, imagination, and method [may be seen as consisting of] half science and half art. . . . It demands searching, delving, trying, failing, and trying again and coming to a conclusion."[3] The greater the imagination and willingness to experiment, think, observe, think, and think again, the more abundant and meaningful the results. In the end, the reward generally is "a harvest of facts followed closely the blossoming of hypotheses."[4]

IMPORTANCE OF A WORKING HYPOTHESIS. For the sake of emphasis, the cardinal values of a hypothesis are summarized: Formulation of a hypothesis gives definite point to the inquiry, aids in establishing direction in which to proceed, and helps to delimit the field of inquiry by singling out the pertinent facts on which to concentrate and by determining which facts should be set aside, at least for the time being. The use of a hypothesis thus prevents a blind search and indiscriminate gathering of data which may later prove irrelevant to the problem under study. George Lundberg, experienced social researcher and theorist, observes:

> The only difference between gathering data without an hypothesis and gathering them with one is that in the latter case we *deliberately recognize* the limitations of our senses and attempt to reduce their fallibility by limiting our field of investigation so as to permit a greater concentration of attention on the particular aspects which past experience leads us to believe are significant for our purpose.[5]

A researcher should not start out to "prove" the correctness of his hypotheses. He should test them and accept either negative or positive results in true scientific spirit of inquiry. As we have already seen, negative results can be just as important as positive ones. Therefore,

[3]Earl S. Johnson, *Theory and Practice of the Social Sciences,* p. 192. The Macmillan Co., 1956.

[4]Maurice Arthus, *Philosophy of Scientific Investigation,* p. 3. Johns Hopkins University Press, 1943.

[5]Lundberg, *Social Research,* p. 119. Longmans, Green & Co., 1942. Reprinted by permission.

the import of Pasteur's words: "[The public] will tell you to prove you are right; I tell you to try to prove you are wrong." Elizabeth Herzog advises the researcher that since "research investigators are by trade both sleuth and judge, it is his business first to find the evidence and then weigh it suspiciously as if someone else had found it."[6]

Hypotheses should also not be defended even though the newly accumulated data support a conclusion exactly the contrary of one the investigator has originally believed his data would bear out. If a scientist wants to *learn* the facts in a given situation, his hypotheses will not become a vested interest, and his reputation and prestige may even be enhanced, rather than threatened, if the new facts disprove his hypotheses. Science aims at stability of belief by cultivating rather than by suppressing doubt. In constantly asking "Is it so?" it seeks to question all that can possibly be questioned. Such rigid scientific skepticism may avoid the pitfalls of trusting data too implicitly, of accepting sources uncritically, or drawing inferences too readily. Skepticism will lead to questioning not only the data but also every step of the analysis, the views, and assumptions. It is easy to take at face value the neatly arranged figures, for example, of statistical publications. It is well to remember that "while figures don't lie, liars figure." However, the very process of questioning does not by itself remove doubt, unless the questions are logical and penetrate to the heart of relevant factors under study.

We often have "the pathetic spectacle of people who started out as scientists [but have become] evangelists and missionaries, employing the techniques of other fanatics in their attempt to bolster up an hypothesis which is no longer supported by facts."[7]

Fry's advice is to "learn to hold [hypotheses] lightly, to admit alternatives and to treasure exceptions . . . to remember that in most social situations you can easily find what you are looking for. . . . [Do] not merely seek answers to specific queries, rather, questions should be considered only as suggestions for investigating a whole social institution or situation."[8]

A sound hypothesis is generally a simple one; but simple does not

[6]Herzog, *Some Guidelines in Evaluative Research,* U.S. Department of Health, Education and Welfare, 1959.

[7]Lundberg, *op. cit.,* p. 121.

[8]*The Technique of Social Investigation,* pp. 7–8. Harper & Row, Publishers, 1934. See also Sidney and Beatrice Webb, *Methods of Social Study,* Chapter 2. Longmans, Green & Co., 1932.

mean obvious. Simplicity, as an essential requirement of an explanation, demands insight. Presumably, the more insight the researcher has into a problem, the simpler will be his hypothesis about it. As early as the fourteenth century, an English philosopher, William of Occam, stressed that neither more nor more onerous causes are to be assumed than are necessary to account for the phenomena.

Because it is a sharp instrument, which cuts out extraneous or useless hypotheses and explanations, this demand for simplicity is known as *Occam's razor*. The simplicity that characterizes acceptable scientific explanation is:

> . . . systematic simplicity, what the mathematicians like to call "elegance"—that is, discovery depends upon the fewest possible factors. Simple hypotheses are not those that are necessarily clear to the layman. Moreover, popularly simple hypotheses, such as many now advanced in politics and economics, are downright dangerous. As used here, simple hypotheses are those which "do not multiply essences," that do not require singular and unique explanations to account for the apparent discrepancies, that make the least number of demands upon special (*ad hoc*) agencies. They are "stingy." Hence *the law of parsimony.*[9]

TESTING OF HYPOTHESES. Science does not admit anything as valid knowledge until a satisfactory test of its validity has been completed. It is a mistake to consider hypotheses—which are only hunches and provisional ideas—as facts, no matter how cleverly and systematically they have been arrived at. Indeed, very exacting proof and measurement are demanded, often by two or more persons, or by retest.

Considerable thought and ingenuity are required in devising an experiment or in following another empirical procedure which will actually test the validity of the hypotheses expressed in general terms. A scientist cannot rest satisfied even with results in which, after repeated observations, he still finds the same occurrences. In a certain district, for example, delinquency is postulated to be "due to poverty." When an equal or similar rate of delinquency is found in another district—of affluent society—the hypothesis that delinquency in general is due to poverty, is obviously false, since other factors than poverty are operative in the production of delinquency among the wealthy. Undoubtedly the tests in the first district were correct—for that district at that particu-

[9]George R. Geiger, *Philosophy and the Social Order,* p. 132. Houghton Mifflin Co., 1947. Reprinted by permission.

lar time. But delinquency in general cannot be assumed to be "due to poverty" or solely to poverty. In another situation, the following proposition was advanced: the greater the degree of active contacts by Russian Molokan youth in an industrial cosmopolitan environment, the greater their degree of emancipation from the norms of their own culture group. This hypothesis was tested by using a control group of Russian Molokans who had few contacts with their neighbors in urban areas, where most Molokans reside. Another control group was used three years later. Invariably, the hypothesis proved correct; that is, there was always a strong relationship between the postulated facts and the observations.

Cora Du Bois' study, *The People of Alore,* offers an example of testing hypotheses by cooperative efforts. Dr. Du Bois, an ethnologist, collected masses of biographical data among the Alorese. She found, among a great many other things, that social institutions affect personality growth in certain prescribed directions. She administered Rorschach tests to the Alorese, whom she also interviewed at length. Both the interviews and the Rorschach tests confirmed her proposition. She submitted her findings to Dr. Emil Oberholzer, a psychologist, who scored, interpreted, and evaluated the results of the tests in his New York office. Then Dr. Abram Kardiner, a psychiatrist, analyzed the biographical transcripts. The correspondence of the conclusions drawn from these varied sources regarding the basic personality structure and its influences, common to all Alorese, was truly remarkable.[10]

Robert Bales lists the following pertinent questions which should be asked about hypotheses before they are adopted for testing:

1. Are the terms empirically specific, so that the concepts or variables can be distinguished in concrete situations?

2. Is the posited relationship between variables such that it could be verified or nullified by means of empirical operations?

3. Is there any prior evidence as to the truth or falseness of the posited relationship?

4. Can an appropriate study design be devised?

5. Are the variables "context-bound" (e.g., restricted to play group or gang), or could they be equally well applied to other interaction situations (e.g., work group or family)?

6–7. Are the generalizations "culture-bound" (e.g., valid only in the United States or Western Europe), or can they be also applied realistically to other cultures?

[10]Du Bois, *The People of Alore,* p. 8. Harvard University Press, 1960.

8. If other relevant factors are subject to change in the course of the observations, are they adequately specified and enumerated, so that the observers can ascertain whether they have changed during the period of observation?

9. Is the generalization part of a theoretical system from which it could be deduced as well as being verified by the proposed empirical induction?

10. Is the empirical system that is constructed sufficiently precise and articulate to permit predictions in concrete situations?[11]

John Stuart Mill, English philosopher and economist of the nineteenth century, provided us with some foundations of testing procedure which are valuable in eliminating proposed faulty propositions. (However, Mill's techniques of "finding the causes" are open to question.) In his *System of Logic,* Mill advocated two means of arriving at logical conclusions in the testing of hypotheses: 1) "the method of agreement," and 2) "the negative canon of agreement."

The method of agreement may be summarized as follows: If in every or most cases in *A* (in example above—degree of emancipation) is found in relation to *B* (urbanization), it is logical to conclude that there is a causal relationship between *A* and *B*. If, however, it is found that it is not possible to rule out various factors irrelevant to our proposition, or we cannot find *A* in most cases of *B*, or *A* is associated not with *B* but with another factor, the hypothesis must be regarded as false.

In *the negative canon of agreement,* we state an alternative hypothesis: lack of urbanization results in lack of emancipation from primary group norms. Mill maintained that when lack of certain phenomena are always, or nearly always, found with lack of other phenomena, we may conclude that there is a causal relationship between them.

It should not be overlooked that untested generalizations can often be quite plausible and reasonable, especially if the generalizer has had extensive and intimate familiarity with his data, as was the case with Dr. W. I. Thomas, for example. At times, researchers have unusual experience and remarkable ability to draw generalizations accurately. But without being subjected to a test, the findings are always under suspicion.

Neither should it be assumed that a research study must of necessity proceed from a hypothesis. Many scientific studies were begun and successfully carried forward without any particular theory to prove

[11] Bales, *Interaction Process Analysis,* p. 117. Addison-Wesley, 1950. Reprinted by permission.

or disprove. Robert S. and Helen M. Lynd maintained that they made no attempt to substantiate a thesis when contemplating or when writing their final report of the famous study of *Middletown*. Generally, monographic studies such as *Middletown* aim to study and record social data as comprehensively as possible, exploring each significant and related fact as it is uncovered. Absence of a working hypothesis does not mean, however, absence of definitely formulated objectives, or of basic assumptions upon which the study is built. The Lynds had their assumptions and objectives carefully outlined and thus had a starting point.

AN ORIENTED SEARCH FOR FACTS. It can be readily concluded that—with or without a hypothesis as a starting point—an oriented search for facts is imperative. As M. R. Cohen points out:

> Scientific achievements are [rarely] made by those who start with an open mind without any knowledge or anticipation of nature. In order to find something we must look for it. . . . Without any anticipatory idea . . . we do not know what facts to look for and cannot recognize what is relevant to the inquiry. It is not easy to start with observing the facts, for to determine what are the facts is the very object of scientific inquiry.[12]

It should be remembered, however, that chance findings can be very fruitful. Theodore Kopanyi,[13] in a stimulating article on progress in science, points out that some of the most important discoveries in the history of science have been made on the basis of false assumptions or by accident—*serendipity*. (This term was coined by Horace Walpole, a writer of some 200 years past.) Many great scientific successes are often prefaced by seeming failures and chance occurrences which at first glance may appear utterly futile to the problems at hand. However, such devious scientific paths have led to the discovery of the X ray, radium, penicillin—the modern instances of serendipity. Scientists cultivate serendipity by being constantly on the alert for chance occurrences that may lead to new explanations and discoveries. They are guided by the maxim that while discoveries cannot be planned, work must be planned if it is to lead to discoveries.

[12]Cohen, "Method," *The Encyclopaedia of the Social Sciences,* Vol. X, p. 390. The Macmillan Co., 1930.

[13]Kopanyi, "Some Reflections on the Progress of Science and the Magnuson-Kilgore Bill," *Bulletin of the American Association of University Professors,* XXXI (Winter 1945), 685.

Hypotheses and deduction-induction. We refer again to the study of delinquency in Hong Kong for illustrative purposes. When the students proposed a study of the causal factors of at least the delinquencies which were on the increase and which seemed serious to them, they had some general anticipatory idea as to what to observe and what specific facts in the main would be relevant to their inquiry, even though they may not have realized these implications. Then, on the basis of their observations of the behavior and the social world of the subjects of study, the students formulated certain single propositions as to the causal factors of delinquency. That is, they *deduced* from the complexities of observed behavior certain single ideas. In other words, they used a process of reasoning about the whole observed situation in order to arrive at a particular idea. This process of reasoning is called *deduction* or *deductive reasoning.*

However, before stating finally the propositions deduced, it is necessary to test them or compare them with other available propositions and ideas. Only after the ideas are found consistent with the observed facts should ideas or propositions be accepted as generalizations.

Logicians often refer to deduction as logical reasoning and point out that, if we start with sound premises, deduction can serve scientific research and discovery in three ways:

> In the first place, it helps in detecting the questionable assumptions logically involved in what is believed to be the truth, and it multiplies the number of available hypotheses by formulating the possible alternatives to those which have been tacitly assumed. Logical reflection is needed to liberate one from the habit of regarding the familiar as the only possibility. In the second place, the logical deduction of its consequences makes clear the meaning of any hypothesis and thus assists in the process of testing or verifying it. Finally, the process of rigorous deduction is an aid in the attempt to steer clear of irrelevancies, and thus when the right principle is found, it serves as a key to unravel our puzzle.[14]

Induction, on the other hand, is the process of reasoning from particulars to a whole group of ideas, phenomena, or situations. Analytic science begins in terms of particulars to generalities and abstractions. It does not approach an object or event by attempting to grasp or explain it in its entirety. Science begins with selective perception. A scientist adopts this approach not only because of expediency but also because of mental limitations. Even the most astute mind finds it

[14]Cohen, *op. cit.,* p. 391.

difficult to deal with great complexities, involving many subtle situations, many permutations and combinations, and varieties which modern social life presents.

In scientific studies it is necessary to isolate certain elements within the complexities and reconstruct them on a simpler model before they can be adequately examined. While doing so, it is essential to keep in mind their organic unity and interdependence. Otherwise, there is a risk of tearing life into fragments and of misrepresenting "the salient organization and the natural integration . . ."[15]

It is reported that the intellectual world was shocked when, in 1903, Bertrand Russell, English philosopher and writer, stated that "induction was more or less methodical guesswork." The reaction was due to false pride and reluctance to admit that guessing can be part of scientific method. "Scientific guessing is distinguished, however, by its methodical character, by the fact that it is recognized as a guess and that there is an organized way of testing its chances of being true."[16]

The simplest form of induction is that of generalization from specific instances, cases, or units, which are held to be representative of the groups, classes, or categories to which they belong. In human behavior, characterized by great heterogeneity and relatively few uniformities, it is essential to *test* the representativeness rather than assume it. (For discussion of the subject see "sampling," Chapter 11.)

It should be remembered that induction and deduction are inseparable parts of a system of reasoning. In other words, *distinct* processes of inductive and deductive reasoning do not exist. We arrive at a proposition deductively by logical operations from the established, known, or self-evident facts. We arrived at the facts by observing and testing individual cases. Or, as Charles Beard has said, "It would be most interesting to find an assumption or premise that is not in some way entangled with experience and the method of inference from particulars."[17]

Classification of gathered data. It is apparent that the data which the research student seeks are no mere collection of accurate

[15]Gordon Allport, *The Use of Personal Documents in Psychological Science,* pp. 145–149. Social Science Research Council, 1942.

[16]Cohen, *op. cit.,* p. 391.

[17]Beard, "Methods of Study of Political Science as an Aspect of Social Science," in *Essays on Research in the Social Sciences,* p. 52. Brookings Institution, Committee on Training, 1931.

facts. Facts become meaningful when they are logically connected with other relevant facts and are sorted according to their essential nature and to the chain of evidence which mutually explain each other. An orderly compilation of facts without a classification system is no more science than an orderly arrangement of a railroad timetable or an almanac.[18] As the researcher observes and gathers his data, he inevitably adopts some scheme for classifying and coordinating them. The nature of the classification will depend on the nature of the study, the completeness and accuracy of the data, the degree of insight into them, and the extent of sociological sophistication attained by the researcher.

The value of classification lies in its grouping together masses of comparable data into relatively few classes. The decrease in the number of units makes the material more readily manipulatable and its essence more easily grasped.

A study of juvenile delinquents would at first probably center around the nature of delinquent acts committed, such as persistent truancy, running away, petty thefts, and auto thefts. Specific detailed studies of these groups, however, reveal fundamental patterns and attitudes common to many delinquents but not to others. Thus, the researcher, in addition to some common-sense classifications, will begin to sort his data in terms of: 1) essential similarities and dissimilarities in them, 2) clusters of related factors which can be observed repeatedly with consistent regularity, and 3) recurring sequences of events. His aim is to discover the series, sequences, and relationship which will throw light on the uniformities in one group of data and on the differences in another.[19]

There are generally some data which do not fit into any of the major classes within the system devised by the researcher. These data may constitute the "negative case" which necessitates the search for a new explanation; or the classificatory scheme might have to be extended to include an additional category. In any event, it is important not to attempt to force data into the adopted scheme. They should be held in reserve as special material.

It should not be assumed, however, that classification is undertaken only after the data have been gathered. The scientific man is an invincible classifier and organizer. As he gathers the data, he adopts some

[18]Cohen, *op. cit.*, p. 390.

[19]Vivien Palmer, *Field Studies in Sociology*, pp. 11–14. University of Chicago Press, 1928.

scheme for classifying them, rudimentary as that scheme may be. (For further discussion of classification, see Chapter 16.)

Generalizations and formulation of concepts. Scientists are not concerned with isolated phenomena or events, not even with sets of these representing single instances. They deplore attempts to derive knowledge from haphazard experiences or situations. Scientists aim to discover "under the surface layer of diversity the thread of uniformity. Around a discovered uniformity a logical class is constructed; about the class and its observed pattern a descriptive generalization is formulated. Scientists are alert for opportunities for combining comparable classes into a broader class and for formulating a wider and more abstract generalization to comprehend the discrete generalizations thereby embraced."[20] Thus, scientific theories are generated.

Strictly defined, a theory, as used in science, is a coherent set of hypotheses. As R. B. Braithwaite states:

> [These] form a deductive system; that is, which is arranged in such a way that from some of the hypotheses as premises all the other hypotheses follow. The propositions in a deductive system may be considered as being arranged in an order of levels. The hypotheses at the highest level being those which occur only as premises in the system; those at the lowest level being those which occur only as conclusions in the system; and those at intermediate levels being those which occur as conclusions of deductions from higher-level hypotheses and which serve as premises to lower level hypotheses.[21]

The following illustration will clarify Braithwaite's statement: If a person is frustrated, and if he is unable or afraid to express his aggression directly toward the perceived source of his frustration, he will divert his aggression into another channel. (This theory may explain why frustrated youth "take it out" on a teacher instead of their parent.)

A theory in science is not the result of mere speculation. It is the gradual outgrowth of constructive study of the accumulated sorted facts, empirically verified over a period of time, until—from the plausible evidence and demonstrable relations—consistent generalizations or

[20]Ernest Greenwood, "Social Science and Social Work: A Theory of Their Interrelationships," *The Social Service Review*, XXIX (1955), 20.

[21]Braithwaite, *Scientific Explanations: A Study of the Function of Theory, Probability, and Law in Science*. See also S. M. Lipset and N. J. Smelser, *Sociology: The Progress of a Decade.*, Part I, "The Discipline of Sociology." Prentice-Hall, Inc., 1961.

logical principles can be formulated. Arnold Rose defines a theory as "an integrated body of definitions, assumptions, and general propositions covering a given subject matter from which a comprehensive and consistent set of specific and testable [principles] can be deducted logically."[22] He characterizes "a good theory" as "one in which (a) definitions, assumptions, and general propositions are consistent in so far as possible with previous research findings and with careful, though not always systematic, observations; (b) a minimum number of definitions and general propositions are made; (c) deducted hypotheses are in readily testable form."

But it should be remembered that a theory, though supported by considerable demonstrable evidence, is still stated in propositional terms and does not relate to conclusively proven facts which would hold invariably true under given conditions. When, however, these facts have been tested and accepted by scientists as invariably correct under the same conditions, the theory comes to be regarded as a law, in social science as a *social law*. A social law, as Karl Pearson stated, is "a résumé in mental shorthand which replaces for use a lengthy description of the sequences among our sense impressions. Law in the scientific sense is thus essentially a product of the human mind and has no meaning apart from men. It owes its existence to the creative power of man's intellect."[23]

Social laws are difficult to formulate, because social facts are hard to measure. They are hard to measure not only because we lack instruments of precision but also because facts are dynamic and complex. In order to measure a fact, it must be a simple fact, and that fact must be seen to reappear many times in the same outward form. Facts in the behavioral sciences are not simple and do not tend to repeat themselves persistently in the same outward form. Some social phenomena are too unstable to be measured. Furthermore, systematization and orderliness in the arrangement of facts are not easily achieved, but these elements are essential for measurement. Of course, it may be argued that all sciences, even the exact sciences, encounter these difficulties, and their data cannot be regarded as absolutely correct. The astronomer's calculations vary with "even so fortuitous a thing as a cloudy night"; the physicist and chemist allow also for many variations. Precise, measurable, and verifiable facts are not easy to come

[22]Rose, "Generalizations in the Social Sciences," *American Journal of Sociology,* July 1953, p. 52.

[23]Pearson, *The Grammar of Science,* p. 87. J. M. Dent & Sons, Ltd., 1937.

by; they are not easy to present, not even easy to "give away" to others. There is much merit in Mees's concern that budding scientists are not sufficiently warned about the "rocky road" in scientific procedure.

The question frequently arises in the classroom as to the differences between a theory and a hypothesis, and between a theory and a law. These concepts are not always clearly stated even in scientific writings, because the lines of demarcation are not always clear. As we have observed, a hypothesis is generally formulated before the facts are verified; it deals with a comparatively narrow range of facts; it is a preliminary assumption adopted for the explanation of facts which have been observed only in cursory manner. A theory, on the other hand, is a generalization arrived at after verification, and it deals with a broader range of facts. It is often said that a theory "is an elaborate and tested hypothesis."

The assembled facts are translated by the researcher into existing or newly invented constructs. The constructs are in turn assembled into a provisional theory, which is subjected to testing and verification to determine its soundness and validity. If after these rigorous operations the theory is proved to be sound and valid, it is designated as a *scientific theory* and may be allowed to fit into the existing pattern of scientific facts about the issue in question. When a series of scientific facts can be reduced to, or summarized by, a precise statement that may be expressed in mathematical form, it is regarded as a *law*. As already indicated, W. I. Thomas suggested "high degree of probability" as a term more appropriate than social law.

SCIENTIFIC CONCEPTS.[24] The process of organizing the data and drawing generalizations from them go hand in hand with concept formulation. As the researcher perceives relationships between his data, or is able to isolate a definite set of occurrences or behavior patterns and describe their characteristics, he begins to abstract from them a certain significance which is representative of a whole class of events, or patterns, or traits. Each new class of data, isolated from the other classes on the basis of definite characteristics, is a given, a name, a label—in short—a concept. A concept is in reality a definition in shorthand of a class or group of facts. "Truancy," "aggression," "frustration," "attitude," "person," "anxiety" are illustrations of concepts into

[24]The more advanced student can profit by reading Carl G. Hempel, *Fundamentals of Concept in Formation of Empirical Science*. University of Chicago Press, 1952.

which are condensed a number of events or phenomena under one general heading. The purpose is to present in simplified form the thinking about phenomena, events, and processes.

To elaborate somewhat on the brief discussion of concepts introduced in Chapter 1, we may stress that no concepts are easy to define. Even in defining such commonplace objects as books, or tables, or automobiles, we may encounter difficulties, if we aim at precision, although we can point out these objects and take a picture of them. But to present a word picture which would embrace a definition would be difficult because of its variety and complexity. Other concepts, like frustration, aggression, or motivation, are still more difficult to define, because they are constructs; that is, they represent inferences "at a higher level of abstraction from concrete events and their meaning cannot be easily conveyed by pointing to specific objects, individuals, or events."[25] This process of higher level of abstraction that is imposed upon the raw data is called *conceptualization.*

The scientific concepts, particularly in the field of sociology, are often commonly used terms. Sociology, unlike other sciences, notably botany, has avoided (or perhaps has not yet gotten around to) coining an elaborate and special vocabulary of its own. Sociology has used terms in everyday language even for its key concepts and the core of its scientific thinking. "Personality," "culture," "community," "society," "group," "attitude," "value" are only a few illustrations of sociological concepts, the meaning of which differ greatly when used by the sociologist and the man in the street. It is easy to understand that this situation often causes confusion and misinterpretation.

E. E. Levitt[26] calls attention to two types of languages: *metalanguage* and *constructs*. A scientist can use metalanguage of everyday communication to a limited degree. If he speaks of apples or oranges, for example, the metalanguage—with its dictionary definitions—suffices. Although there are different varieties, sizes, qualities of apples and oranges, the variations are relatively unimportant either for theoretical formulations or experimentation, regarding processes of shipping, let us say. Constructs, on the other hand, are complex ("frustration" or "aggression," for example) and imply a condition or a state of an organism whose existence can only be deduced from observable phe-

[25]Claire Selltiz, *Research Methods in Social Relations,* p. 41. Holt, Rinehart, & Winston, Inc., 1959.

[26]Levitt, *Clinical Research Design and Analysis in the Behavioral Sciences,* pp. 17–18. Charles C Thomas, 1961.

nomena, rather than by direct observation. Therefore, they not only need to be defined carefully but are also in need of translation into observable incidents, operations, or some means that will produce data that can be accepted as indicating the concept such as "aggression."

Stuart C. Dodd[27] is chiefly responsible for attempts to introduce into sociology *operational definitions* of constructs, that is, to use a series of words which clearly designate performable and observable acts or operations which can be tested and verified by others. But such clear designations depend on: 1) the existence of standardized patterns of behavior and uniform characteristics of social relations; 2) ability to define social phenomena operationally (because of their intricate complexity and subjective elements). However, the proponents of the use and development of operational definitions in sociology contend that it is possible to construct specific scales or tests (sufficiently refined to include variations and shades of meaning) which would determine objectively and verifiably actual behavior and attitudes. (For methods of constructing such scales, see Chapter 12 by Calvin Schmid in this volume.)

Levitt,[28] however, contends that definitions in the behavioral sciences are rarely more than partial definitions since they "rarely encompass the entire substance of what we want them to encompass." This is particularly true with definitions of such concepts as "motivation" or "struggle for status." The social science laboratory may help in precise observation, but the complexity of the situations is not easily overcome. Furthermore, the very artificial environment of the laboratory may inhibit or alter the responses and thus the usual reaction pattern cannot be adequately operationally defined.

As fundamental as the use of precisely defined concepts is to scientific procedure, the development of scientifically defined terminology has been slow and controversial.

To summarize the role of theory and concepts and their relation to empirical data, we quote a statement prepared by Dr. Blumer.

> The aim of theory in empirical science is to develop analytical schemes of the empirical world with which the given science is concerned. This is done by conceiving the world abstractly, that is in terms of classes of objects and of relations between such classes. Theoretical schemes are essentially proposals as to the nature of such

[27]See Dodd, "Operational Definitions Operationally Defined," *The American Journal of Sociology,* XLVIII.

[28]Levitt, *op. cit.,* p. 18.

classes and of their relations where this nature is problematic or unknown. Such proposals become guides to investigation to see whether they or their implications are true. Thus, theory exercises compelling influence on research—setting problems, staking out objects and leading inquiry into asserted relations. In turn, findings of fact test theories, and in suggesting new problems invite the formulation of new proposals. Theory, inquiry and empirical fact are interwoven in a texture of operation with theory guiding inquiry, inquiry seeking and isolating facts, and facts affecting theory. The fruitfulness of their interplay is the means by which an empirical science develops.[29]

As this statement suggests, the use and development of theory may move in two directions. One is to establish relations between theoretical propositions or concepts; this line of effort seeks to construct a *system* of interpretation marked by logical unity and permitting the derivation of deductive consequences. The other direction is to tie theory to research inquiry. We are concerned here with this second direction.

Although a close interplay between theory and empirical observation should always take place in research, theory may enter in differing ways into the separate steps of the research study. Thus, one may set one's research problem in terms of an existing theory or set it in terms of some commonplace but puzzling observations of what is taking place in the actual life of people. Further, one may use one's research study to test a given pre-established theory or one may instead perform the research to secure an answer to a concrete problem. Finally, one may seek to make one's research findings intelligible by explaining them in terms of an existing body of theory, or one may use the research findings to formulate some new theoretical propositions. These few observations show that there is no fixed or tailor-made way of bringing theory into research procedure.

However, there are several general principles which may be noted. First, a knowledge of the prevailing theory in one's area of research can be of great help in selecting the "variable" of one's study, that is to say, the classes of data which one wishes to collect. Accordingly, one should become familiar with relevant theory without, however, becoming lost in it. Second, one should try to make one's concepts as clear as possible so that one can identify in a reliable and discriminating way the empirical data which are covered or not covered by the concept. Concepts are the central or crucial components of theory and consequently their clarity and faithfulness to empirical facts are essential to the formulation or development of good theory. Third, one

[29]Herbert Blumer, "What is Wrong with Social Theory," *American Sociological Review,* XIX, 4.

should view theories, whether taken from the existing literature or developed by oneself, as hypothetical guides and not as established knowledge. In this way one will be more alert to observations which challenge the theory and thus be better prepared to revise the theory so as to fit the empirical world. Fourth, one should pay close attention to all odd and puzzling observations that arise in one's research, and think about them a great deal, instead of excluding them from one's concern. Such unusual observations offer rich opportunities for stimulating imagination and forming new perspectives; more than anything else they are a source for new theoretical approaches. To sum up, the student in conducting his research should use theory to organize and direct his lines of inquiry, but use his empirical observations to test and refine his theoretical leads.[30]

Integration of research disciplines. The most fruitful results in research are achieved not only through an integration of scientific techniques and method but also through a unified approach of the various scientific disciplines. Since man lives in a world of economic, industrial, political, psychological forces and social attitudes and values, it is self-evident that his responses to, and roles in, these should be studied. As a matter of fact, the Social Science Research Council was organized to promote and integrate the social sciences to each other and to the related useful arts of industry, government, and public welfare; to guard against overspecialization and isolated efforts which might result in distorted vision, especially when a section of man's world is wrenched loose from its context in the process of study.

As we have already indicated in the discussion of social science laboratories, one of the most significant considerations in cooperative research is that it facilitates the study and analysis of the complex web of social-psychological-economic forces, intricately interwoven in modern life. Each collaborator not only may provide a new orientation as to subject matter but also may proceed methodologically in a way which enables him to view certain particular aspects of the functional interrelationship of the various social elements.

Before the outbreak of World War II, Dimitrie Gusti directed large teams of experts (at times reaching sixty members) who engaged in extensive as well as intensive studies of village life in Rumania. Social geographers and economists first mapped out physical and economic conditions. Later a group of historians and social anthropologists

[30]Statement prepared by Herbert Blumer especially for this volume.

joined them. At the start they all received training in general methods of observation and recording facts with particular reference to the common enterprise as well as uniform methods in their immediate fields. By such procedure Gusti aimed to provide a "far-reaching uniformity of outlook which helps to break down the artificial academic departmentalization of knowledge," and promotes functional penetration.[31]

Ideally speaking, cooperative research implies a group of specialists who can coordinate their work in a consistent attempt to keep within common scientific interests rather than to pursue lines of specialist relevance.

Free and open criticism of informed colleagues is essential. A man working alone is often too close to his own ideas to be able to catch flaws in them. Without scrutiny and earnest criticism by others interested in the same problem, a scientist cannot presume to speak with authority. Kellogg observed:

> Even the scientist is a layman in most fields. If he simply uses the special techniques of his own field without undertaking the deeper meaning of the scientific method as applied generally, he may be as blindly dogmatic or as bad a dupe as anyone in other fields. We can ask these questions about a scientist: Has he sincerely and competently followed the scientific method? Is he free to tell the truth as he sees it—free from personal prejudices and from political and social pressure? Has his work been tested by free and open criticism? Has he the respect (not necessarily personal friendship) of competent colleagues in the same field? If the answer to any of these questions is "No," we should be slow to believe him.[32]

Cooperative research may tend to minimize the tendency to lose a scientific and detached attitude, a tendency not uncommon when one field worker closely and over long periods of time identifies himself with a given group or community. Loss of a detached attitude may be recognized by other members of the team who know the actual conditions in the community.

Cooperative work presupposes disciplined, united effort of persons who will not be distracted by self-interests, logic arguments, or jealousies. Of course, cooperative effort of itself does not guarantee scientific research. If the cooperators are not capable of recognizing the

[31]For an account in English of Gusti's work, see P. E. Moseley, "The Sociological School of Dimitrie Gusti," *Sociological Review,* XXVIII, 149–165.

[32]Charles E. Kellogg, "What is Farm Research," in Department of Agriculture, *Science in Farming, The Yearbook of Agriculture, 1943–1947*, p. 22.

essential differences in their goals and points of view, their work may result in "scientific chaos," regardless of their efforts and intentions to cooperate. Cooperative research depends on ability to concentrate on the same "key activities," to reach out for a common goal from the same lookout tower. "In fact, as we see it today more clearly, the social sciences to be truly scientific must stand or fall together. The old individualism is in retreat, and . . . social scientists are becoming socialized."[33]

[33]T. V. Smith and Leonard White (Eds.), *Chicago: An Experiment in Social Science Research*, p. 223. University of Chicago Press, 1929.

scientific attitude and plan of study

5

The pioneer can only press on, sustained by the belief that somewhere in this vast territory there lies hidden the knowledge which will arm man for his greatest victory, the conquest of himself.

RALPH LINTON

A scientific attitude is many things in many situations. It requires consistent thinking, stern pursuit of accurate data, stubborn determination to analyze one's own system of thinking and to take nothing for granted. Evidence, tests, proof are the pillars of a stern court of "evidential confrontation."[1]

A scientific attitude is more than "objective," "dispassionate," "unbiased" devotion to collection and treatment of facts. To be sure, a scientist avoids personal and vested interests. He deliberately looks for facts which may be death to casually formulated theory. He seeks facts which could substantiate theory and give facts new meaning and vitality. He does not tailor his views to fit preconceived notions or preferences of men in the "chairs of the mighty." He is aware that strong emotion is notoriously inimical to clear thinking.

A scientific attitude is based on a complexity of elements. A. B. Wolfe stresses the fact that "it must be firmly borne in upon us that the scientific attitude rests upon one, and only one, fundamental article of faith—faith in the universality of cause and effect. Without this faith, a steady, undaunted pursuit of scientific knowledge as a guide to action may be incontinently flouted whenever it interferes with special interest

[1]Herman Wouk, *This Is My God,* p. 226. Doubleday & Co., 1959.

or prejudices."[2] According to Wolfe, as to most scientists, causation in terms of impersonal, phenomenal correlation and sequence is the essence of scientific inquiry. In other words, science is deterministic. The researcher who does not become a thoroughgoing determinist does not acquire a scientific attitude.

" 'Cause' is our name for the inter-connection among natural processes in their contingent relations," says G. Coghill, naturalist and philosopher. "Cause is inherent in the organization of the total situation. It is not imposed upon it from the outside." To answer the research "why" is to account for the facts by showing or identifying the conditions under which events take place.[3]

Many scientists believe that the chief problem of modern social science relates to causal explanation. A sound foundation in any science is laid through an understanding of the *processes of becoming.* Social science cannot avoid this task. "Social becoming, like natural becoming, must be analyzed into a plurality of facts, each of which represents a succession of cause and effect."[4] (See studies by Robert C. Angell, Shaw, Stouffer, and others cited in Chapters 2 and 3. Also link above discussion on cause with the discussion on hypotheses.)

The characteristics of a scientific attitude, discussed below, may sound like a big order even for a mature scientist. But he is not expected to fulfill this role at all times, nor in its entirety at any time. The young student is not expected to acquire these scientific attitudes at the start of a research project. Many students, however, strive for and do consequently develop a scientific spirit and derive a genuine thrill in the pursuit of scientifically conducted research. One author compares this thrill in science to that resulting from finding a gold nugget after shoveling dirt in a gold field for a long time. "It is worth all the drudgery that preceded it," he adds.[5]

To Sir Francis Galton a scientific attitude meant "an inherent stimulus to climb the path that leads to knowledge with the strength to reach the summit—one which, if hindered and thwarted, will fret and strive until all hindrance is overcome, and it is again free to follow its labor-loving instinct."

[2]Wolfe, *Conservatism, Radicalism, and Scientific Attitude,* p. 203. The Macmillan Company, 1923.

[3]Coghill, *World, Regions and Man,* p. 1. Cheshire Publishing House, 1960.

[4]Thomas and Znaniecki, *The Polish Peasant in Europe and America,* p. 36. Knopf, 1927.

[5]"The Young Scientist," *Fortune,* (June 1954), p. 182.

A scientist may encounter many failures and delays in his search for data or in his attempt to confirm their validity and accuracy. Without losing courage and enthusiasm, he must go on undaunted and undismayed. The basis for success in discovery lies in cultivating an ability to rise from failure with a curiosity and a new sense of inquiry.

To John Dewey a scientific attitude was linked with "an ardent curiosity, fertile imagination, and love of experimental inquiry."[6] He pointed out that "young people who have been trained in all subjects to look for social bearings will also be educated to see the causes of present [problems and phenomena]. They will be equipped from the sheer force of what they have learned to see the possibility and the needs of actualizing them. They will be indoctrinated in its deeper sense without having doctrines forced upon them."[7]

Herbert Blumer—in describing Thomas and Znaniecki as "scientists at work"—saw these characteristics in the eminent authors: ". . . rich experience with human beings, keen sensitivity to the human element in conduct . . . lively curiosity . . . [endless] mulling over [their data], reflecting on them, perceiving many things in them, relating these things to their background and experience, checking these things against one another, and charting all of them into a coherent analytical pattern."[8]

To Allyn A. Young a scientific attitude means the ability to raise significant questions and to formulate fruitful hypotheses: "Successful research calls for industry and command of the appropriate technical methods. But if there is to be more than fact-finding, it calls for imagination, for ability to see a problem, and to devise hypotheses that are worth testing. Industry fortunately is not an uncommon virtue. Techniques may be acquired. But imagination, and especially the kind of imagination that keeps its moorings, is rare."[9]

Indeed, a whole large volume was recently devoted by C. Wright Mills[10] to the necessity of sociological imagination in the study of social life. According to Mills, sociological imagination is that quality of mind which aids students in using "information and developing

[6]Dewey, *How We Think,* p. iii. D. C. Heath and Co., 1933.

[7]Dewey, *Problems of Men,* p. 183. Philosophical Library, 1946.

[8]Blumer, *A Critique of Research in the Social Sciences,* p. 76. Social Science Research Council, 1939.

[9]Young, in Wilson Gee, *Social Science Research Methods,* p. 362. Appleton-Century-Crofts, 1950.

[10]Mills, *The Sociological Imagination.* Oxford University Press, 1959.

reason in order to achieve lucid summation of what is going on in the world and of what may be happening within themselves." He urged fellow sociologists to cultivate in students an imagination not only as an aid in acquiring an orderly knowledge of science but also in coming to grips with the major problems of the day as well as with their personal problems.

Charles Horton Cooley, in characterizing the scientific attitude of his colleague, William Graham Sumner (author of the famous volume, *Folkways*), said: "What distinguishes him and makes the manner of his work a possible source of help to others is something inseparable from his personality—his ardor, his penetration, his faith in social science, his almost incredible power of work, his great caution in maturing and testing ideas before publication." The characteristics of a scientific attitude described here are not necessarily those of eminent scholars alone. Frequently we find these traits in young students who have become interested in a piece of research which has fired their imagination.

Sir Francis Bacon conceived a true scientist to possess both "compassion and understanding, since knowledge without charity could bite with the deadliness of a serpent's venom. And mere power and mere knowledge exalt human nature but do not bless it."[11] He urged the scientist to keep close to reality; to ascertain, in a dedicated manner, facts about the universe and man; to test existing knowledge, and to search for new discoveries. The development of the experimental method alone, Bacon had contended, was the means by which all things else might be discovered.

In short, at present as in generations past, among mature scientists and among students, we find a compelling and what Karl Pearson called a "wonderful restlessness," a lively curiosity, endowed with imagination in the study of man. Social scientists in particular are compelled as if they were charged with a great responsibility, to acquire knowledge of human behavior and social processes.

Dangers to scientific attitude. W. I. Thomas warned us against committing the *particularistic fallacy,* which arises through an inclination to generalize on insufficient or incomplete and unrelated data. When one thus bases his judgment of Negroes' ability in general on one's acquaintance with a group of Negroes in the agricultural

[11]Bacon, *The Advancement of Learning,* pp. 75–100. Oxford University Press, 1868.

districts of the South, we may say that he commits a particularistic error. The error of particularistic thinking lies in overlooking the fact that the mind employs the principle of abstraction—sees general principles behind details—and that the precise details with which the process of abstraction begins cannot in all cases be posited or determined.[12] The scientist guards against the particularistic fallacy by the accumulation of a large body of data and by the employment of comparisons and control groups.

The scientist tries to avoid what Francis Bacon termed *false idols.*

> There are *the idols of the cave,* or errors due to narrow and isolated thinking characteristic of the given person alone, or experiences which one has had that no one else knows anything about. There are *the idols of the forum,* errors due to "the influence of mere words over our minds," and due to putting unjustified reliance upon words, phrases, and language. There are *the idols of the market-place,* or errors arising out of undue reliance on traditions, traditional ways of thinking, and from "received systems of thought." There are *the idols of the tribe,* or errors due to one's human or anthropomorphic ways of looking at things. It is difficult for a person to get outside of a personal viewpoint, or to step outside of his own limited perspective of life.[13]

Few persons ever acquire complete objectivity, especially with regard to social problems. This situation is due to the fact that it takes time to overcome personal and prejudicial attitudes fixed in boys and girls by the social controls which are constantly bearing down upon them. Personal preconceptions and value judgments may not only have a distorting effect on the data but are also highly insidious, because they are so "subtle, so implicit, so deeply rooted that it is difficult for us to discern them in ourselves, or when they are called to our attention, to avoid rationalizing them, instead of examining them objectively."[14]

Although strict objectivity may never perhaps pass beyond the realms of a pious wish, it is possible for discriminating and reflective students of social life to attain a reasonable amount of objectivity which will be consistent with logical and systematic thinking.

[12]Thomas, *Source Book for Social Origins,* pp. 22–26. University of Chicago Press, 1909.

[13]See Bacon, *Novum Organum* (rev. ed), pp. 319 ff. Oxford University Press, 1899.

[14]Clyde W. Hart, "Some Factors Affecting the Organization and Prosecution of Given Research Projects," *American Sociological Review,* XII, 516.

H. A. Cantril says that objectivity, as it is usually conceived, is not only illusory; it is undesirable, because:

> Scientific data may become inert and meaningless without value judgment, and science is reduced to a routine collection of facts. . . . The "objectivity" of science can refer then only to the use of accepted rules of empirical research *after* the problem, the variables, and the experimental design have been decided upon. Here the investigator must use every precaution to see that he does not misinterpret what he sees.[15]

Systematic research often requires meritorious patience and self-control. During any phase of the research process various ideas may crowd the mind; there is often a temptation for the researcher to pursue only the seemingly strong ideas and set aside the obscure or involved ones, appeasing the conscience with a promise to come back and fill in the gaps later. The worker may have the power required for retracing his steps, but in the meantime he may have built on unstable foundations, and his results will be weak and shaky. There is also a tendency to be dazzled by apparent "discoveries." Gripped by too forceful or undisciplined imagination—which at times is strongly tinged with wishful thinking—the research worker may feel compelled to pursue his single track, since he thinks he recognizes the germination of practical applications. And as Maurice Arthus suggests, under such circumstances "the spirit of independence and the spirit of originality are suppressed and sterilized for a long time . . . by the enthusiasts and by the careerists. . . . When it is necessary the experimentalist must be able to oppose a categorical, uncompromising and final *no* to his imagination. He must possess full and entire self-control."[16]

In summary, it might be said that the primary difficulties research workers face in studying social situations arise from several sources: 1) The workers have a large stake in the outcome of the study. That is, their own interests are frequently affected by the results they obtain. Although scientists may have freed themselves from the tendency to justify their findings, they are still apt to have a mode of thinking and a way of life that presuppose that certain facts are "truths." By just so much will the analysis be influenced, perhaps unconsciously. No technique is available either to offset or to avoid such personal factors. Only in the interplay of cooperative research and critical interpretations

[15]Cantril, *The Why of Man's Experiences,* p. 7. The Macmillan Company, 1950.

[16]Cf. Maurice Arthus, *Philosophy of Scientific Investigation,* pp. 25 and 23–25. Johns Hopkins University Press, 1943.

of other scientists can corrections be made. 2) Since social data are of the stuff of daily life, and since most individuals have fairly usable schemes of practical adjustment to life situations, the frequent assumption is that common-sense judgments are correct and sufficient. The folkways and mores of each group are usually accepted as naturally valid and adequate to the scheme of living and thinking, but under rapidly changing conditions, common sense does not suffice, and precedent is insufficient in the face of the unprecedented. 3) Social situations are seldom simple, although they may appear to be so at first glance. Their full significance is not easily grasped at once. 4) The necessity for action may often be regarded as urgent. A plan of action may be instituted on the basis of an immediate reaction to what later may prove to be superficial and incorrect data.

The competent research worker, however, recognizes that wishful thinking will seriously warp his study. He disciplines himself to rule out his own desires as to the outcome of his work and to avoid prejudging the social situations he is studying. It is a major psychological feat to achieve the objectivity required for a scientific study, especially on those frequent occasions when an inquiry is apt to challenge the existing frames of social reference. The scientifically inclined researcher is careful to examine the complexity of the data he is gathering and to see what meaning they have to the group in question. He acknowledges that he has to come by facts laboriously and knows well that there is no short cut in accumulating them.[17] He is convinced that research is at one and the same time "a patient, plodding cumulative process . . . and a breathless break-through," which at times may produce a "harvest of facts" and at other times "turn out to be a gimmick or a gadget that briefly dazzles those who are determined quickly to save the world."[18]

The trained researcher knows that carefully ascertained facts have a greater long-time leverage on formulating scientific principles as well as plans to guide public policy than do hasty procedures and plans. He adopts slower processes of scientific inquiry and is steadily concerned with their significance in, and relationship to, the social contexts which they are to illumine. The use of scientific techniques in

[17]Excerpts from manuscript by the late Professor Erle F. Young. (The manuscript, in collaboration with the present author, was reproduced in the third edition of this volume, 1956, pp. 85–89, from which above three paragraphs were drawn.)

[18]L. A. Kimpton, S"The tate of the University," *Tower Topics,* p. 8. University of Chicago, 1960.

gathering, testing, verifying, generalizing are imperative for the progress of any study. And so are doubting and scrutiny. All these elements are components of scientific attitudes. These elements tend to correct not only factual error but also mental, emotional, and volitional frailties of a research worker. In other words, good research is done by disciplined researchers.

Some Guiding Considerations in the Choice of a Research Topic

In chosing a research topic certain points should be kept in mind: 1) ability to grasp and time to deal with its broad implications which have been mentioned earlier. 2) Resources to carry the study forward may be exceedingly limited if no basic research has been previously done by experienced scientists in the field. At times resources are available, but they are not open to research beginners or they are confidential, as was found in the study of court records in Hong Kong. 3) Applicability of study techniques should be considered for the particular topics chosen. 4) We should also consider degree of accuracy or approximation essential for the demands of a scientifically conducted project. We may know something about frustration or motivation, but not enough. Whole collections of approximations do not suffice. Furthermore, available data may be strongly tinged by emotions. International conflicts, strikes and lockouts, poverty and riches are examples of topics heavily weighted by emotions and should, therefore, be carefully considered from the standpoint of feasibility of obtaining accurate and reliable facts. William Ogburn cites his experiences as conciliator on the first morning of a labor strike. He asked the labor leader how many workers were on strike and was told 15,000; when he asked the employer, he was told 300. Since there was no way of determining at the time who was out because of the strike and who was out for other reasons, the blinding or distorting effects of emotions produced such gross exaggerations as to make available figures utterly worthless. "The distorting influence of wishes is not so great where there is only one hypothesis—for instance, the relation of poverty to delinquency—as it is in studies of very complex phenomena, such as, say, the description of Russia under the Soviets."[19]

[19]Ogburn, "Considerations in Choosing Problems of Research," in Brookings Institution, Committee on Training, pp. 161–171. The Institution, 1931.

Some scientists believe that the initiation is the most crucial part of an inquiry. F. S. C. Northrop, philosopher of science, believes:

> One may have the most rigorous method of investigation, but if a false or superficial beginning is made, rigor later on will never retrieve the situation. It is like a ship leaving port for a distant destination. A very slight erroneous deviation in taking one's bearings at the beginning may result in entirely missing one's mark at the end, regardless of the sturdiness of one's craft or the excellence of one's subsequent seamanship.[20]

Delimitation of scope of inquiry. To avoid confusion and superficiality, and promote clarification, it is necessary to keep research within manageable limits, that is, within the ability of the mind to grasp the implications and to explain them.

The wealth and variety of social reality are well-nigh indescribable. Even a complete study of a segment of this complex reality would entail such an overwhelming mountain of data that it would require more than a student's lifetime to gain a glimpse of the proverbial forest though seeing clearly its trees. A study can be profitably delimited from the standpoint of: 1) aims and interests of the research worker, 2) amount of relevant available material, 3) complexity of sound theoretical assumptions formulated regarding the study, 4) previous valid research in the field having direct bearing on the project under consideration. Keeping these factors in mind, a student in training should generally confine himself to relatively small projects rather than to broad scientific problems.

A beginner is especially inclined to undertake too wide a scope, not suspecting at first the far-reaching and complex implications of his study. Not infrequently, a student may announce that for his term project he plans to make a study of housing conditions in a certain city. A comprehensive study of such a subject would involve a corps of experts from the fields of architecture, engineering, sanitation, economics, city planning, sociology, social work, and other disciplines. Furthermore, housing conditions vary with periods of time, with nationality groups, with the purpose for which the houses are intended, with the locality, with the attitudes of the community, and a host of other factors. A thorough study of housing conditions is even delimited in an extensive social study with a large staff of field workers. Some

[20]Northrop, *The Logic of the Sciences and the Humanities,* p. 1. The Macmillan Co., 1937.

phase of the housing situation within a certain area at a certain period of time would be more appropriate.

The Research Design

As has already been seen in the "General Overview of a Research Study in Process" (Chapter 1), a research design is the logical and systematic planning and directing of a piece of research. The design results from translating a general scientific model into varied research procedures. The design has to be geared to the available time, energy, and money; to the availability of data; to the extent to which it is desirable or possible to impose upon persons and social organizations which might supply the data. E. A. Suchman states that "there is no such thing as a single or 'correct' design. . . . Research design represents a compromise dictated by the many practical considerations that go into social research. . . . [Also] different workers will come up with different designs favoring their own methodological and theoretical predispositions. . . . A research design is not a highly specific plan to be followed without deviations, but rather a series of guideposts to keep one headed in the right direction."[21] In other words, a study design is tentative. As the study progresses, new aspects, new conditions, and new connecting links in the data come to light, and it is necessary to change the plan as circumstances demand. An "exactitude complex" or lack of flexibility and rigid pursuit of a plan where, as Ernest Greenwood states it, "every fact is sanctified because it is a fact," can destroy the usefulness of an entire study.

The most meaningful and revealing studies are those that are conceived from a definite point of view, but the views are modified as necessary in the process of study, as well as those that are dominated by a definite set of scientific interests which can be enlarged or curtailed, as the study in process requires.

Samuel Stouffer, in his studies of the *American Soldier*,[22] had worked out a smoothly operating research pattern—a routine procedure which is at one and the same time practical for administrative purposes in applied research and rigorous as to scientific prescription:

[21]Suchman, "The Principles of Research Design, in John T. Doby *et al.*, *An Introduction to Social Research,* p. 254. The Stackpole Co., 1954.

[22]See also Stouffer, *Social Research to Test Ideas,* The Free Press of Glencoe, Inc., 1962.

1. Prompt attention to problems needing study;
2. Personal contacts and discussion with top executives involved in the problems of study;
3. "Scouting around" in order to observe, inspect, examine, survey in a preliminary and later in a general way the problems and situations of the study;
4. Informal interviews with enlisted men in selected camps;
5. Preliminary, but lengthy, discussions with staff about the data obtained by them;
6. Drafting questionnaires and schedules;
7. Pretesting questionnaires and schedules;
8. Examination of results of pretests to detect and eliminate inconsistencies, obscurities, and vagueness;
9. Drafting revised questionnaires and schedules;
10. Conference with initiator of request for a study to ensure clearness and completeness of proposed study;
11. Drafting final questionnaires and schedules;
12. Outlining field interviews;
13. Analyzing collected data;
14. Drafting of final report.

Social scientists have found varied research designs of value. The most recently published (1963) is the one by Matilda White Riley[23] which appears to be very promising. She concerns herself in her "*Paradigms:* Some Alternatives of Sociological Research" with the following items:

P–I—*Nature of research case:* individual role (in a collectivity); dyad or pair of interrelated group members; subgroup; society; some combination of these;

P–II—*Number of cases:* single case, few selected cases; many selected cases;

P–III—*Socio-temporal context:* cases from a single society in a single period; cases from many societies and/or many periods;

P–IV—*Primary basis for selecting cases* (*sampling*)*:* representational; analytical; both;

[23]Riley, *Sociological Research I: A Case Approach,* pp. 7–29. This text is accompanied by a very useful manual *Sociological Research II: Exercises and Manual.* Harcourt, Brace & World, 1963. Reprinted with permission.

P–V—*The time factor:* static studies (covering single point in time); dynamic studies (covering process or change over time);

P–VI—*Extent of researcher's control over the system under study:* no control; unsystematic control; systematic control;

P–VII—*Basic sources of data:* new data collected by the researcher for the express purpose at hand; available data (as they may be relevant to the research problem);

P–VIII—*Method of gathering data:* observation; questioning; combined observation and questioning; other;

P–IX—*Number of properties used in research:* One; a few; many;

P–X—*Method of handling single properties:* unsystematic description; measurement of variables;

P–XI—*Method of handling relationships among properties:* unsystematic description; systematic analysis;

P–XII—*Treatment of system properties as:* unitary; collective.

(This study design should be compared with the one used in our "General Overview of a Research Project in Process," Chapter 1.)

Operating plans in an extensive research study should include such considerations as: 1) length of time required to produce questionnaires and other similar devices in tested form; 2) manner of selection and training of research personnel and orientation of collaborators in an integrated research project; 3) costs of supplies, equipment, tabulation forms, printing of questionnaires, drafting of charts, graphs, and maps; 4) time needed for consultations and conferences with collaborators and committees; 5) execution of the study in relation to its scope, objectives, resources; 6) coordination with other related studies.

Criterion variables and definition of research units. A unit in science means a single act, or a single social situation, or a person, or phenomenon, viewed as a whole. A unit of study can be small or large, simple or complex, obvious or illusive. The term juvenile delinquency, for example, includes a vast variety of composite problems, acts, and conditions which arise out of many sources. As yet, social science has not devised a sound typology of social or personal problems, or patterns of behavior. Neither is there a satisfactory diagnostic classification, nor a descriptive list covering the numerous acts comprising a given type of behavior which is studied as a unit. A description of a delinquent in terms of his misdemeanors or "serious offenses committed" gives no conception of the degree of waywardness, of the sources of the problem, the accompanying attitudes—factors essential to the study of delinquency with any degree of consistent reality.

Elizabeth Herzog[24] provides an excellent illustration of the critical scrutiny to which a researchable definition should be subjected before it becomes a part of a research design. The illustration pertains to a research study of the degree of adjustment of wards since arriving in a correctional school. Holding in abeyance for the moment such questions as "Type of adjustment to be measured?" "Adjustment *to* what?" "Adjustment *from* what?" "Degree of adjustment to be measured?" we should raise the more immediately pertinent question: "How is adjustment to be determined?" or "Who recognizes adjustment?" Do we depend on the juvenile to tell us what he regards as adjustment or how he recognizes it? Or the teacher who may desire to show improvement in his charges? Or the superintendent who may desire to show adequacy of his school program? Gathering opinions from these persons may not constitute reliable test of adjustment.

Neither could adjustment be reliably measured in terms of the person's conformity or success or failure in the school's training program. The results of such measures depend on the standards employed in determining "success" or "failure," and the techniques used in arriving at the evaluation. What is needed is a definition of adjustment in terms of evident behavioral changes in the person under study. It should be remembered that a behavioral or operational definition carries with it a description of segmental acts which can be scored or weighted according to the degree of activity involved—noticeable improvement in family relations (lack of conflicts, destructive arguments, appearance of loyalty); participation in group activities of own accord; ability to hold employment, and other factors.

If a scalogram were to be prepared to measure degree of change, the following items would have to be considered:

> Anxiety; nervousness, tension; frustration or satisfaction of "natural needs and drives"; insight, awareness; dependency; attitude toward authority; self-control; defensiveness; breadth and depth of interests; maturity; organization of personality; growth and development; perception of reality; response to reality (problems, conflicts, crises);

[24]Herzog, *Some Guide Lines for Evaluative Research,* pp. 15 ff. U.S. Government Printing Office, 1959.

effectiveness, ability to utilize capacities; inner *vs.* other-directedness; autonomy; locus of evaluation.[25]

Dr. Robert I. Watson[26] lists more than a hundred criteria which he has used—singly or in combination—in studies of the effectiveness of psychotherapy. He stresses the fact that he has not covered all the criteria that might be identified in such a study. He adds: "At present we are in the unhappy state of not knowing what are the criteria of effectiveness [of adjustment or other processes]. . . . Research has not yet isolated criteria on which there has been some sort of general agreement concerning their value as indices of change." Because of the variety of criterion variables in any social situation, each situation should be regarded as a "structure built of many pieces of observable behavior."

As already implied in the section on "Definition of Terms" in Chapter 1, and the section on "Scientific Concepts" in Chapter 4, complex aggregates must be broken down into specific simple acts, or definitive characteristics, or concrete circumstances. Aggregates, as such, are too complex to be studied meaningfully, too broad to be observed competently, virtually impossible to be compared and quantified. When broken down into observable, comparable, manageable units, they may lead to the discovery of behavior patterns and characteristics that distinguish groups, acts, or situations from one another.

The unit of designation must be as free as possible from conflicting or varying elements. If we wish to study "young males," we need to specify not only from what to what age, but also whether we are including married men, fathers with children, men of what economic groups, educational levels, and other criteria. In dealing with aggregates, the researcher assumes that all units are equal. In mechanical enumeration of houses, let us say, or men dead of a certain disease, or infants born, discrimination need not be as keenly applied as when discerning and registering distinguishing characteristics of social units.

In short, units of study should be representative, clearly defined in operational terms when possible, uniformly gathered in accord with the specific nature of the whole "universe" of which they are a part. Vague, unstandardized, nonrepresentative, out-of-context units can invalidate all of the findings in an otherwise painstaking study. Also, in order to quantify, compare, and corroborate findings, it is essential

[25]*Ibid.*,p. 18.

[26]Watson, "Measuring the Effectiveness of Psychotherapy: Problems for Investigation," *Journal of Clinical Psychology,* VIII, 60–64.

that all persons involved in the same study use the same terminology in the same manner.

Sources of Information

The sources a student should tap vary with his interests and the type of his study. Generally sources are divided into documentary and field sources. The latter include living persons who have a fund of knowledge about, or have been in intimate contact with, social conditions and changes over a considerable period of time. These people are in a position to describe not only the existing state of affairs but also the observable trends and significant milestones in a social process.[27] These persons are regarded as *personal sources* or *direct sources*. If discretion is used in their selection, various professional and business persons, old residents, and community leaders may be utilized as sources of information. Each person supplying information may often serve as a check on the other until the account is reliably reconstructed.

The documentary sources of information are those which are contained in the published and unpublished documents, reports, statistics, manuscripts, letters, diaries, and so on. These sources are generally divided into *primary* sources, which provide data gathered at first hand, the responsibility for their compilation and promulgation remaining under the same authority that originally gathered them; and *secondary* sources, which provide data that have been transcribed or compiled from original sources, and of which the promulgating authority is different from that which controlled the collection of the data at first hand. The federal census is generally cited as an illustration of the first type, whereas the *World Almanac* and the statistics based on the federal census are illustrations of the second type of data. Either type may be compiled by private or public authority. Data from primary sources may be gathered by participant observation, personal interview, conference, correspondence, questionnaire, and other devices. (For a discussion of these techniques, see Chapters 7–13.)

It is important for scientific workers to scrutinize secondary sources very closely. "Their reliability for research work can be determined only by reference to the primary source which should be cited in notes or bibliography. This will enable anyone who so desires to make him-

[27]V. M. Palmer, *Field Studies in Sociology,* p. 57. University of Chicago Press, 1928.

self responsible for the facts by reference to the original source. Discrepancies appear in different secondary sources which must be settled from the original source."[28] Since not all documents can be consulted, it is best to start a selective process early and ask oneself the following questions: "Do the changing circumstances with the passage of time alter their meaning?" "What useful purpose will they serve in the present study?"

Official documents and statistics (as primary and secondary sources). The following list of reports of official bodies refers for the most part to primary source data. But it should not be taken for granted that official reports always supply primary source materials. These reports, at times, may be based on secondary source materials. The person examining these data should, in each instance, inquire into the source of such data. It should also be noted that the list presented below is not exhaustive; it is rather a suggestive illustration of the more common documents, reports, and statistics published by official bodies —federal, state, and local.

1. The state and federal census.
2. Reports of bureaus of vital statistics.
3. Reports of state, county, and municipal health departments.
4. Reports of police departments, prisons, jails, courts, probation departments.
5. Reports of state and federal departments of labor, state boards and commissions, state employment bureaus, state and federal labor and trade federations.
6. Reports of boards of education and of attendance departments.
7. Reports of church federations.
8. Reports of public welfare agencies.
9. Reports of departments of recreation.
10. Reports of U.S. Department of Health, Education and Welfare, Social Security Administration.
11. Reports of the U.S. Children's Bureau.
12. Reports of the Federal Bureau of Investigation.
13. Reports of state and federal immigration and housing commissions.

[28]R. E. Chaddock, *Principles and Methods of Statistics,* p. 393. Houghton Mifflin Co., 1925.

14. Reports of bureaus of commerce.
15. Reports of U.S. Bureau of Efficiency (guide to original sources for the major statistical activities of the U.S. Government).
16. Legislative sources:
    a. Statutes of the federal government.
    b. General state laws.
    c. Special state laws.
    d. County charters.
    e. County ordinances.
    f. City charters.
    g. City council ordinances.
    h. Ordinances of boards of aldermen.
    i. Police department rules and regulations.
    j. Health board rules and regulations.
17. United Nations monthly bulletins of statistics and yearbooks.

Unofficial documents and statistics. Great care must be exerted in differentiating the primary and secondary source materials of unofficial bodies, as many of them tend to mix these materials much more than official bodies tend to do. Source data of unofficial bodies may be found in the following:

1. Reports of councils of social agencies.
2. Reports of private social welfare agencies.
3. Reports of trade and labor unions.
4. Reports of chambers of commerce.
5. Reports of industrial establishments.
6. Reports of character-building agencies.
7. Reports of private employment bureaus.
8. Reports of foundations, private commissions and investigating agencies.
9. Accounts in newspapers in current numbers, and in back files and clues as to public opinion relative to the events under study.
10. Articles in periodicals and various other magazines which often picture some unique aspects of community life and problems.
11. Miscellaneous manuscripts, and minutes of civic bodies on local problems.

12. Photographs, photostats, microfilms, generally well classified at local libraries.

The "what-do-you-know" barber shops, wherever they still exist, general stores in small towns and rural areas, members of religious organizations, and "go-getters" should not be overlooked.

Use of available documentary materials. As a preliminary to field research, or in conjunction with it, a sustained and high-quality search for data in the library is a most pressing need in the social sciences. Although few research people can aspire to the quality and quantity of work carried on by Thomas Edison, it is inspiring to read his statement on the subject: "When I want to discover something, I begin by reading everything that has been done in the past. . . . I see what has been accomplished at great labor and expense in the past. I gather the data of many thousands of experiments as a starting point, and then make thousands more." The rest of us humans have been content with knowing of a few experiments.

The late Clyde Kluckhohn, an eminent field researcher, maintained that "unless a greater proportion of available source materials are collected and synthesized, field research will suffer materially, for the right questions will not be asked."[29] Pertinent materials are able to: 1) provide general orientation essential in creating insight and asking the right questions. 2) They suggest the use of certain techniques of study, not thought of at the outset. 3) They aid in conceptual thinking and in ways of testing tentative assumptions. 4) They help avoid unnecessary duplication, and may steer one away from a direction unpromising of fruitful results. In short, a review of pertinent works and thinking by others helps to enlarge, enrich, and clarify one's own work and thinking.

Occasionally, some researchers advise ignoring available knowledge as "the big bad words" prevent progress and may cause falling into a rut—"groovology." It takes as much effort, they say, to get out of the grooves as it does to solve a problem independently. There may be some truth in such a point of view, if one remains in a groove. But this point of view completely discredits possession of an open mind, of ability to think critically and to listen to suggestions without destroying reflective thought and discretion. Francis Bacon's lines come to mind:

[29]Kluckhohn, "Personal Documents in Anthropological Science," in Louis Gottschalk *et al., The Use of Personal Documents in History, Anthropology, and Sociology,* p. 146. Social Science Research Council, 1945.

Read not to contradict and confute;
Nor to believe and take for granted;
Not to find talk and discourse;
But to weigh and consider.

Rarely is it expedient for a student in training to launch upon a social study without careful examination of the recorded experiences and funds of information accumulated by scientists that frequently have bearing upon his inquiry. The wealth of existing documentary sources may enrich a researcher's point of view; they may suggest comparisons with, and relation to, other types of data yet to be secured; they may stimulate discriminating analogies which will bring into bold relief types and categories of data to be examined or to be empirically verified; and they may frequently aid in avoiding duplication of work and escaping from pitfalls and difficulties encountered by others. But the choice of facts within the myriads of others to be selected is the very crux of meaningful reading. It is difficult to determine in advance the relative importance of recorded facts and explanations. The broad general view of the research project may be an aid in considering certain of the factors applicable to the project at hand. Notes, carefully captioned as to dominant ideas and classified according to the central ideas, may be of value. (Also, here tentative and broad classification of one's own data may begin. Later more refined classification into groups and subgroups will "flow out" of the nature of the accumulated materials. Order in the data, beginning with the library notes, is one of the earliest and simplest ways of discovering relationships between data.)

So numerous, and often so complex, are government publications that various libraries, journals, and government departments regularly prepare special classified lists, catalogs, bibliographies, guides, indexes, policies of distribution, and publication resolutions. Dorothy Campbell Culver, in her *Methodology of Social Science Research: A Bibliography,* lists in one section 104 different important references to a wide variety of bibliographies, methods, and instructions for using government publications. There is great need for a central office where all official and unofficial documents and statistics are gathered. It should not be assumed that all official statistical reports can be found in a large library. It is often necessary to request these by letter or personal visit directly from the source, or from another library, by means of an interlibrary loan.

Furthermore, consulting pertinent materials is considered so important in furthering knowledge that a number of clearing houses of current research have been established. We may refer again to the *Outlines of Cultural Materials,* to the *Sociological Abstracts,* and *Psychological Abstracts,* to a selected inventory of research by Community Research Associates, and many other guides. The U.S. Children's Bureau in 1960 established a clearing house of current research in child welfare. The data in this clearing house are seen as a "systematic aid to research workers and organizations that wish to keep abreast of research in progress in the field of social, cultural, psychological, and physical aspects of child growth and development."

A number of periodic guides to the use of documents are also prepared. See, for example, Brenda Brimmers, *A Guide to the Use of U.N. Documents* (1962); Social Science Research Council, *Report* (various dates): Peter Lewis, *Literature of the Social Sciences: An Introductory Survey Guide*—under the auspices of the London Library Association (1960); Mary Lee Bundy, *Research Methods in the Social Sciences: A Selected Bibliography* (1959). *International Bibliography of the Social Sciences* lists and classifies all published contributions from all countries, in all languages, and covers sociology, anthropology, political science, and economics. Philip Hauser remarked that "the UNESCO *International Bibliography of the Social Sciences* may do more than any other single tool to rid sociology of its nationalistic manifestations and enable it to transcend national boundaries, as must all science." J. Doris Dart edited *International Index: A Guide to Periodical Literature in the Social Sciences and Humanities,* 1960–1961.

Most social science associations publish abstracts. The best-known besides the *Sociological Abstracts* are the bulletins of *Current Sociological Research, Child Development Abstracts and Bibliography,* and *Index Medicus,* a new monthly which appeared for the first time in 1960, after its quarterly predecessor had suspended publication in 1956. Also, some professional journals are supplemented by yearbooks and periodic reviews of new developments in the field. The Anti-Defamation League of the B'nai B'rith issues *Research Reports,* on intergroup relations. *The Review of Educational Research* has for many years carried special issues on research methodology. *Dissertation Abstracts* on research topics are available in microfilm through the University of Michigan at Ann Arbor. To say the least, the available literature, abstracted and reviewed by sensitive experts, saves a great deal of time in surveying one's field. (See especially S. R. Ranganathan's *Social Science Research and the Library,* 1960.)

Ann Shyne believes that, although it cannot be denied that the researcher in full control of data collection can derive considerable benefit from source data, "the difficulty of obtaining them should not be underestimated . . . nor the wisdom and skill required in analysis of the wealth of material already available to him."[30] Above all, source data should be approached with an open critical mind.

In brief, source data are a fertile spring from which ideas and facts might be drawn; they are an invaluable preliminary to direct observation. Or, as John Madge[31] points out, such data "supplement observation, and participation in retrospect, by broadening the base of experience. But by themselves," he warns, "they tell an incomplete story, and it is clearly unwise to stretch their adoption into contexts in which they can offer neither economy nor satisfaction." R. H. Tawney aptly remarks that "what is needed is not more documents but stronger boots for field exploration."

Development of a Bibliography

As soon as the consultation of available sources is begun, the development of a bibliography—preferably with annotations—should be undertaken. Each reference should appear on a separate card or sheet, with last name of the author first, his initials or given name following, and then the title of the reference, publisher's name, and date of publication. Below is shown the form generally adopted for the listing of books and for articles in periodicals:

Madge, John, *Origins of Scientific Sociology*. Free Press of Glencoe, Inc., 1962.

Bensman, Joseph, and Arthur Vidich, "Social Theory in Field Research," in Maurice Stein and Arthur Vidich (Eds.), *Sociology on Trial*. Prentice-Hall, Inc., 1963.

Kitano, H. H. L., "The Concept of 'Precipitant' in Evaluative Research," *Social Work,* Vol. VIII, No. 4 (Oct. 1963), pp. 34–38.

Uniformity in the listing of bibliographical notes is important and is appreciated by publishers and readers. Note that authors' names are inverted in alphabetized lists, but may be written with first names first in footnotes.

[30]Shyne, "Use of Available Materials," in Norman Polansky, *Social Work Research,* p. 123. University of Chicago Press, 1960.

[31]Madge, *Tools of Social Science,* pp. 115–116. Longmans, Green & Co., 1953.

A brief annotation of each reference retained for the bibliography is useful in learning: 1) its value, 2) the relation it bears to other references and to subjects of study, and 3) the classification it should be given in the sectional bibliographies divided by subject or chapter. The annotation should, therefore, pertain to the nature of materials presented, methods used in the study, point of view of author, purpose of study, and so on.

Recording Source Data

Systematic note taking and note keeping, beginning with the preliminary examination of sources and continuing throughout the process of study, are indispensable instruments to the scientific worker. He should be supplied with a large number of separate sheets of paper or cards, of uniform size and shape, which can stand considerable wear. A large notebook is highly impractical, as it does not afford frequent and necessary rearrangement of notes and does not permit classification of facts according to various themes, topics, or hypotheses independent of the order in which they were secured.

Each separate fact, or idea, or hypothesis—for the purpose of classification and comparison—should be entered on a separate sheet of paper, in as much detail as is necessary for clear comprehension and precision. The source should be shown on a separate line. It may even be advantageous to indicate the method by which the data were secured (interview, observation, or document, for example). Care should be taken not to crowd more than one fact, theme, idea, or hypothesis onto one sheet of paper or card. Moreover, these should be recorded singly for each period of time, for each separate location, and for each source of information. Of utmost significance is the axiom "one sheet—one subject matter . . . one sheet—one event in time and space."

It is important to adhere to a system of note taking not only because it aids in classification and reclassification of data, but also because it enables a worker to break up, isolate, and examine a complex set of ideas in their component parts and later to recombine them into other groupings and relationships in order to discover new coexistences and sequences among them.

> The consideration to be kept in mind in the preliminary task of deciding how to record the facts which constitute the subject matter of the study, is so to place the different items of the record—"the

> what," "the where," "the when," and "the why" of the classification or relationship—that in glancing rapidly through a number of sheets the eye catches automatically each of these aspects of the facts. . . . It is indeed not too much to say that this merely mechanical perfection of note taking may become an instrument in actual discovery.[32]

In studying, for instance, the cultural conflicts of the Russian Molokans, we were confronted by a variety of social organizations in Russia and in the new American milieu, over a period of time dating back to the origin of the sect in the eighteenth century. This variety of social organizations on two continents, in diverse cultural settings, belonging to distinct periods of time, presented a complex variety of functions and ideals, successive waves of thought and influence, varying social and political ties of tangled emotional relationships, rooted in diverse economic, social, and religious systems. An attempt was made to discover and to describe not only each separate social organization as a unit, such as the church of the sect or the communal organization, but also the social forces that gave them birth and enabled them to thrive, develop, and maintain themselves, or the forces that brought about change in these institutions, at various periods of time.

Information on the subject was secured from Russian documentary sources, from records in possession of the group, and from the members in-the-Know. Hundreds of separate notes were taken in the field and in the library. Each new idea, each new fact, each new development in time and place was set down on a separate sheet of five-by-eight paper as soon as possible after it was secured, whether from a person or a document.

It is difficult to convince students, especially those with " 'literary' rather than 'scientific' training, that it is just this use of mechanical devices like the shuffling of sheets and notes that the process of study often becomes fertile in actual discoveries. Most students seem to assume that it is merely the previous stage of making observations and taking notes which is that of discovery."[33]

In large scale studies electric card-sorting and counting machines may be used for tabulating not only information gathered by means of schedules and questionnaires but at times information secured through a large variety of documentary sources. In this way a great

[32]Beatrice Webb, *My Apprenticeship,* p. 430. Longmans, Green & Co., 1935.

[33]Sidney and Beatrice Webb, *Methods of Social Study,* p. 94. Longmans, Green & Co., 1932.

amount of data may be manipulated and sorted into diverse categories in seeking hypotheses even before the field work is begun on a large scale. (For a discussion of standard Hollerith and other mechanical sorting machines see Chapter 2 of F. E. Croxton and D. J. Cowden, *Applied General Statistics*.)

The careful worker may find it expedient to use a color scheme to designate: 1) bibliographical references, 2) excerpts and abstracts, 3) first-hand field observations, 4) information secured through personal interviews, and 5) original comments and suggestions by the worker or student.

Whenever possible, it is expedient to make at least one carbon copy of the notes and to classify them simultaneously under the different headings and subjects which they imply. When this is done, the cross-classifications should be indicated in ink or pencil of a contrasting color.

When the notes relate to excerpts from written sources, the author's name, the title of the book, article, or journal, the date, the publisher's name, and the volume and page number should accompany each quotation. When no direct quotation is used, but the idea developed was stimulated by a published statement, a reference to the source should be made as above, preceded by *Cf.* (meaning *confer* or compare). Every precaution should be taken to avoid even the remotest possibility of the accusation of plagiarism. (The source of the quotation should later appear in a footnote.)

Notes on, and references to, both personal communications and documents may be listed as follows:

Document No. : personal interview with held on at .
Document No. : official report of issued found in .

In some cases it is necessary to withhold the name of the interviewee, either because he requests it or because it is in his best interests. A confidential file should then be established, identifying the number of the document in case further contacts are necessary with the informant.

Dr. Benjamin Paul strongly advises including in the notes on personal contacts anything which will help later to recapture the tone and vividness of the experiences and supply a surer basis for preparing a realistic report. He also suggests inclusion of specifications of attending circumstances, that is, whether or not notes were recorded on the spot, and if not, length of time elapsed before the recording; whether information was offered spontaneously or in response to a question or many questions; whether the informant was alone or with others; if the latter, with whom, and role assumed by third party; any display of emotions that may illuminate the meaning of the remarks interviewee made; the questions that were asked and the replies supplied.[34]

The source data should be examined for: 1) soundness of premises entertained by the original author or informant; 2) representativeness of data obtained and their applicability to the study at hand; 3) rigor in the design of the research pursued by the original author; 4) accuracy and clarity as well as specificity. If conclusions, no matter how tentative, are drawn from source data, an additional question should be raised: "Over what range may these conclusions be generalized?"

Whenever a worker gets new ideas, based either on his own reflective thinking or reading material, and he sees a new relationship between his accumulated facts, he should record these ideas as soon as convenient to do so, no matter how momentary these flashes might be. If he waits until the "muse of writing" visits him, he may have difficulty in recapturing the idea and its relationship to the pertinent data. Inspiration comes to different people in different forms. Some of the best ideas on a subject have come with ease to a worker when he is immersed in a subject not related to the immediate question at hand. He may hit upon a long-searched-for term or a long-awaited formulation. On another occasion, "inspiration" may bring a flood of ideas and a feverish desire to produce.[35]

In conclusion, it might be said that logical formulation of the research problem is an indispensable first step in any research procedure. Therefore, the oft-repeated saying that "a problem well-formulated is a problem half-solved." Whether this is correct or not, the other half of the "solution" must lean heavily on systematic procedure. The process of research should be regarded as a formal matter, with carefully conceived and premeditated planning. Intensive study and painstaking procedure are required throughout the scientific voyage. Careful delimitation of the scope of an inquiry tends to avoid confusion of issues and to bring the study within the available time limits and resources of the worker. The process of outlining a project implies thinking the problem through; it affords orderly and systematic procedure, subject to revi-

[34]Paul, "Interviewing Techniques and Field Relations," In A. L. Kroeber, *Anthropology Today,* pp. 430–451. University of Chicago Press, 1953.

[35]The Committee on Research of the Amos Tuck School of Administration and Finance, Dartmouth College, *Manual on Research and Reports,* p. 59. 1936.

sion as new insights are gained. Research requires critical discrimination. The "seeing" of the project begins with the preliminaries. The successive stages and concrete details clarify it. Adherence to systematic procedure aids in validating it.

6

the use of historical data in social research

Every model of social structure implies a model of socio-historical change; history consists of changes which social structures undergo.

HANS GERTH

. . . The study of all integrational systems must be generic and therefore historically oriented.

ABRAM KARDINER

Why study the past? Historians, philosophers, social psychiatrists, literary men, as well as social scientists, use the historical approach as an aid in visualizing society as a dynamic organism, and its structures and functions as steadily growing and undergoing change and transformation. Social scientists in particular are concerned with social change, since all groups, social institutions, and personalities undergo changes to a lesser or greater degree, and as a consequence, the social roles and forms of organization they assume are also subject to a process of change and transformation.[1]

The logician, A. N. Whitehead, points out that "each emerging is perceived as containing within itself all its past and seeds of its future." Paraphrasing a statement by George Bernard Shaw, "The past is not behind the group; it is within the group." The past, if it can be located, contains the key to the present. Though today is different from yesterday, it was shaped by yesterday. Today and yesterday will probably influence tomorrow. We can hardly conceive of a social situation or a social structure which is not rooted in conditions and forces long in operation. Therefore, historian Arthur Schlesinger warns: "No individual, let alone a social scientist, can wisely ignore the long arm of the past."

[1]See Ely Chinoy, *Society: An Introduction to Sociology,* p. 62. Random House, 1961.

And Charles Langlois, also a historian, advises that, since history enlarges one's range of observed phenomena, affords "a sense of the mutability of institutions, and suggests the conditioning factors in contemporary life," one should not push the problems of time into the background. "Direct observation of social phenomena in a state of rest is not a sufficient foundation [for study]; it gives neither requisite scope nor accuracy. There must be added a study of development of these phenomena in time, that is, in history."[2] Historians, and especially modern historians, are interested in cultural change in time, "but change, not time, is their true historical perspective."

Some social scientists, however, dismiss the merits of historical perspective. Although they acknowledge an indirect influence of the past on human experience, they stress the belief that "behavior depends neither on the past nor on the future but on the present field."[3] (It is conceivable that Kurt Lewin, who stated this belief, was influenced by American psychologists, who, intent on economical use of time and effort, concentrate on the immediate precipitating causes of behavior rather than on the background of these precipitants.)

Among the social scientists who were steadily preoccupied with the connecting links between past experiences and present attitudes and values were W. I. Thomas (noted for his concept of the "process of becoming") and the authors of *Authoritarian Personality*, A.T. Adorno *et al.* The latter saw the roots of prejudice in early family experiences and examined techniques of combating such experiences at the source of origin. Furthermore, the Committee on Historiography of the Social Science Research Council, after considerable study, concluded that the "analysis of 'dynamics,' of change and development, has only recently been recognized again as a problem of the first priority. . . . The element of time can never be a somewhat inconvenient and unmanageable 'fourth dimension' to be introduced almost as an afterthought in the final stages of the analysis. It must be *in* the analysis from the beginning."[4]

A decade after this Committee's report was issued, Paul Webbing, vice-president of the Social Science Research Council, stated that social scientists "have developed a much stronger consciousness of the im-

[2]C. V. Langlois and C. Seignobe, *Introduction to the Study of History,* p. 320. Holt, Rinehart & Winston, 1925.

[3]Lewin, *The Field Theory in Social Science,* pp. 153–154. Harper & Row, 1951.

[4]Committee on Historiography, *The Social Sciences in Historical Perspective,* .24. Social Science Research Council, 1954.

portance and relevance of historical analysis and historical trends than had been true for some time before."[5]

But the research student in training, not convinced of the fact that history and social phenomena are closely interwoven, may question the advisability of using historical data. As a student of contemporary social life, he may ask why he should concern himself with old records, compiled and written long ago by persons of varied interests and points of view. What can traces of past events stored away in dry documents contribute to an understanding of life, generations or centuries later? These questions are in order and difficult to answer, but a review of a research study (that of the Molokan sect, to which we shall henceforth frequently refer for illustrative purposes) will reveal the worth, in part, of historical data in social research.[6]

Historical data and the study of a culture group: an illustrative example. The study of the Russian Molokans was undertaken during a time when there was a great deal of delinquency in the group. The study aimed at ascertaining the causal factors underlying this wayward behavior. Preliminary observation led to the hypothesis that severe culture conflicts between the old and the young were the responsible factors. In order to test this hypothesis, particularly in view of the reports that there was no overt conflict between the generations while in Russia, a comprehensive study had to be undertaken. The researcher was warned by local teachers and law enforcement officers that the Molokans "greatly resent strangers inquiring into the group's affairs." No direct approach to the problem of delinquency was contemplated. Considerable reading on the researcher's part of the history of the group supplied clues to the indirect approach—asking for accounts of the group's mode of life and experiences while in Russia.

It soon became evident that the older members of the group were quite willing and able to provide remarkably vivid and accurate accounts of events and the order in which these events had transpired in tsarist Russia. It was realized that what was needed, in addition to the indispensable account provided by the elders, was insight. Their accounts provided information but not understanding. For the latter,

[5]Adapted from personal communication, Jan. 1964.

[6]Pauline V. Young, *Pilgrims of Russian-Town,* see especially Part III, "Assimilation Processes and Bibliographies." University of Chicago Press, 1931.

"one must discover the ways in which events are interrelated beyond their relation of temporal sequence or coincidence. In particular one must discover how they are related as cause and consequence."[7] This *cause* seemed to be deeply imbedded in the complex cultural history of the group, although the *consequence* was fairly obvious.

The members of the group had frequently alluded to "the Russian Schism," the disunion between Russian Orthodox Church and the State, as being responsible for the origin of the Molokan sect. Again they gave vivid accounts, but this time the accounts were related to the researcher with considerable pride and emotion of the "unforgettable heroic deeds of their forefathers a l-o-n-g time ago"; they dwelled on "the cruel sufferings and untold anguish" of the "imprisoned heroic forefathers who created a new system of belief and religious practices." These "martyrs advised all faithful to depart from the established church" and prevailing norms, and to adhere to the new way of life of their own making.

The oral accounts by the elders were compared and verified by historical documents on the Russian Schism. It was learned that it occurred in the middle of the eighteenth century; it was closely associated with the revolt against serfdom and with religious persecution of dissenters from the established church. In reality it was a socio-religious-economic-political movement against "the church that initiated oppression and the State that sanctioned it." This movement fairly convulsed the Russian Empire at the time. But the more violent the persecutions, the more persistently the dissenters adhered to their new way of life and belief. Throughout decades of persecution, torture, and imprisonment, the official clergy was not able to stem the tide of desertion from the old church. The suffering they endured served to bind the dissenters into a more closely-knit group, with a high degree of solidarity and devotion to the religious principles of their own creation. They received a great deal of attention from sympathizers outside Russia. Historians, anthropologists, theologians, and economists of Western Europe who studied the situation among the dissenters gave them much moral support.

It became apparent that the Molokan sectarians were animated by a set of religious and social principles which were invincible in their nature. It also became clear that the Molokans were a religious sect not solely because—to paraphrase LeBon—they worshiped a divinity,

[7]Committee on Historiography, *op. cit.*, pp. 24–25.

but also because they put all of the resources of their mind into, completely subjected their will to, and placed their whole-souled ardor at the service of, a cause which became the goal and guiding light of their very life and being.[8]

The historical accounts provided a frame of reference, a point of view of the social and cultural soil in which Molokanism as a unique way of life had its inception.

With this knowledge of the sect the *raison d'être* of their activities and beliefs became evident; it was understood why the group is kindled with such a fervent desire to remain within the protective walls of sectarianism; it became clear why the defenses and the struggles of the sect against the American assimilation of the young are so intense and persistent and, in the face of a new world crisis, successful. The nature, sources, and complexity of the social processes making for culture conflicts and for a struggle for control between the "sacred" and "secular" institutions came clearly to light. As the study progressed and tendencies for a cultural revival were discovered, it was understood what laid the groundwork for the new cycle in the life of the sect.

Without a knowledge of the cultural heritages and the historical developments of the social and religious life of the sect, the very life of the group in an urban American environment would have completely escaped the student, and thus the purposes of the study would have been forfeited.

This account may sound too simple to the seasoned research student who traces the historical developments of a culture group, or a religious sect, or a social institution; whereas it may sound exceedingly complex to the beginner. To the latter we may say that social research is slow, painstaking, but absorbing. It has its own compensations, and a few weeks of study and search in historical data and accounts will lead the searcher on, voluntarily and impellingly, to search out the other facts essential to deeper and richer insight. A vast realm of knowledge and of ideas begins to unfold and absorb his interests, attention, and imagination. He will find that research is fascinating as well as stimulating and recreating. The writer could have undoubtedly attained a certain degree of efficient understanding had she consulted fewer historical accounts, but she found these sources so absorbing and stimulating that few other interests and values dominated her life at the time. The "dry bones of the past" shook vigorously and came to

[8]Gustave LeBon, *The Crowd,* p. 82. George Allen & Unwin, 1903.

life with an intensity of action and so invigorated social imagination that they made scientific pursuits a new and enlarged goal in adventurous living. (No wonder Arnold Toynbee prepared a new volume in 1961, *A Study of History: Reconsiderations,* which is in reality a "why of the sociocultural processes and a fascinating account of the bewildering events of our times.")

The seasoned researcher may also want to make an ethnological study of the Molokans and account through ethnological processes for the development of Molokan personality and social institutions. He would want to study culture adhesion, diffusion, parallels, and change, and a vast variety of other processes which the culture of the group has undergone in its evolution. Similarly, the history of economic developments may be traced in detail to understand the emergence of economic forces shaping the group's social institutions. Some scholars may desire a psychoanalytic study of sectarians; others, variously oriented studies.

Social Research and History[9]

From the foregoing account of the value and use of historical data in the study of a culture group, it may be observed that though historical data were read extensively, they were used in a certain unique manner. No attempt was made to revive the past events in all their particularity. Instead of concentrating attention only on unique and particular events—as they had actually occurred at a distinct time and specified place—these accounts were examined for a possible explanation of their processes of social becoming. The question, "What happened at such and such a time and place?" was supplanted by the questions, "Why, did such and such things transpire?" and "What effect did they produce upon the life of the people and the groups most vitally concerned?" Although a specific cultural group was studied comprehensively, it should be remembered that interest was largely centered in Molokans as a *type* of sectarian group which is representative of other similar sectarian groups. The author studied to a limited extent the history of Quakerism and the Amana Society in order to determine the degree of common characteristics typical of other sects. The aim was to discover regularities representative of other groups and events

[9]For a detailed discussion of this subject see Louis Gottschalk *et al., The Use of Personal Documents in History, Anthropology, and Sociology,* pp. 3–75. Social Science Research Council, 1945.

of a given kind. History, however, is concerned with an accurate account of a particular happening, stressing the location and the date. That is, it works out "an accurate record of how, when, and where [the event] started, how it progressed, and how and when it ceased. [The historian] explains the [event] by describing the conditions which led up to it and out of which it grew. In addition, he may indicate some of the important results which have followed as a consequence of the [event]."[10]

On the other hand, in the study of Molokanism an attempt was made to avoid listing meticulously a series of chronological happenings. The concern was with the fundamental complex of causal factors which gave rise to these happenings, the broad sweep of social change, and the general character of their former influences upon the present social structure. The aim was not to produce uncritically and unreflectively a final, reconstructed historical narrative, but to learn its bearings upon present phenomena, social institutions, social problems. For this purpose no study was made of the archives, the original documents since the eighteenth century, and the chronologies of the distant past. Only historical documents which interpreted the events were carefully scrutinized. That is, not history as such but cultural history by later historians, who viewed history in the light of the complex social world, was studied. However, those interpretations of history were used only when written by reputed competent scholars who were known to have been not too far removed from the historical scenes of action.

Historical treatments which concern themselves with an analysis of the social forces and influences which have shaped the present have been called "new history," "analytical history," "synthetic history," or "culture history."

The social survey also makes considerable use of historical data and sources. It too is concerned with an account of social situations, human problems, and the factors which affected their development and not with a mere record of the course of past events. It is interested in reconstructing the past only in order to learn its influence on present social problems, to determine what conditions are in need of correction, and to find a basis for the intelligent formulation for social planning and social betterment. The social survey looks for clues which might indicate the sources and origin of the problem, the degree of influence it has been exerting on the life conditions of the group, on ways and means of controlling these sources and influences.

[10] James A. Quinn, *The Social World,* p. 73. J. B. Lippincott Co., 1937.

Sources of historical data.[11] The social research student generally confines himself to three major sources of historical information: 1) documents and various historical sources to which the historian himself has access; 2) materials of cultural history and of analytical history; 3) personal sources of authentic observers and witnesses. When, how, and under what circumstances to use any or all of these sources depends a great deal upon the discretion of the student, his interests, the scope of his study, and the availability of these sources.

Direct use of documents may be made when the events which they depict have not as yet been analyzed by historians and have not as yet been incorporated into the writings of the broader cultural historical settings. These documents may be used when we wish to verify directly certain events, or when certain aspects of life in which we are interested have not been embodied in the later writings of analytical historians. They may also be used when we need to supply a missing link in our knowledge of a particular social situation. For such purposes even a record of pure chronological events which have no relation to each other may be of utmost value. We may not be able to deduce from it any scientific principles, but it may round out our understanding of the situation without which generalization might be impossible.[12]

It may be maintained that, if one is to gain perspective, documents should not be resorted to until they are at least a few generations old. But contemporary documents may be the only source of information available at the time; also the closer the person is to the time, spirit, and scene of action, the more able he will be to understand the events. Considerable controversy has arisen over these divergent points of view. Undoubtedly there are elements of truth in each contention. The person who consults original documents will have to decide this question for himself, not once but each time he uses them, since his own understanding may vary with the diverse documents he uses, with the diverse facts they depict, and with the purpose of the documents and of his own study. He has to rely upon his discretion.

Howard Becker in his article on "Historical Sociology," maintains:

> Many of the sources indispensable for anything like adequate knowl-

[11]Consult *International Bibliography of Historical Sciences;* Gottschalk *et al., op. cit.,* pp. 10–14; P. H. Furfey, Chapter 19, "The Use of Written Sources," *The Scope and Method of Sociology,* pp. 462–488. Harper & Row, 1953.

[12]Cf. Lundberg, *Social Research,* 1st ed., p. 78. Longmans, Green and Co., 1929.

edge of the present will not become available until this present is the historical past—diaries, memoirs, confessions, autobiographies, secret archives, covert diplomatic agreements, uncoordinated statistical material, under-cover trade agreements, "cold-storaged" inventions, and countless other data vitally affecting this present day and generation are often beyond our present reach."[13]

This is particularly true when the mature scholar studies facts or hypotheses concerning "process-series" or cycles, which must await indefinite future verifications. Documents of the present or of the near past will not supply the essential source data necessary for comparable and generalizable similarities. Often it will be necessary to extract from these contemporary documents whatever facts and social factors will explain the present situation. For many practical purposes, contemporary documents will serve as a fruitful source of information. Just how far and in what manner a person may draw upon these documents is again a difficult question to answer in a general way. The student, before consulting and drawing upon historical documents, will do well to consult a historian, explain the purposes and scope of the study, and get his suggestions as to methods of obtaining and interpreting these sources and, furthermore, as to what sources should be set aside for future reference (sometimes an indefinite future).[14]

When historical documents depict events not of generations but of centuries past, it is generally useful for social research students to utilize the existing secondary data which are an interpretation or an analysis of history. We assume that a social research student of today would be far less competent to analyze original historical documents and to reconstruct and characterize from the facts extracted—in the fashion of a layman—a particular culture better than the analytical historian himself was at the time of occurrence. However, this assumption does not mean implicit faith in the ability of the cultural historian to provide us with facts which we can accept uncritically and unreflectively. There are many historical writings which are composed of series upon series of different data—a patchwork of records of disputable value, pieced together by less reliable ones and many happy guesses. There are, however, few students who are so unsophisticated as not to be able to recognize such unreliable sources. Daniel Webster

[13]In L. L. Bernard, *The Fields and Methods of Sociology,* pp. 32–33. Farrar, Strauss & Giroux, 1934.

[14]See Committee on Historiography, *Theory and Practice in Historical Study.* Social Science Research Council, 1946.

was apparently wrong when he said that "the past is, at least, secure."

Merton, in his critical review and comparison of American and European conceptions of the sociology of knowledge, characterizes the perspectives on historical data (in the field of public opinion and group beliefs) of the two groups:

> [**American and European perspectives on historical data.**]
> The American variant, with its emphasis on empirical confirmation, devotes little attention to the historical past, since the adequacy of the data on public opinion and group beliefs in the past becomes suspect when judged by the criteria applied to comparable data regarding group beliefs today. This may partly account for the American tendency to deal primarily with problems of short-run [periods of time.] . . . The virtual neglect of historical materials is not for want of interest in or recognition of the importance of long-run effects but only because these, it is believed, require data which cannot be obtained.
>
> With their more hospitable attitude toward impressionistic mass data, the European group can indulge their interest in such long-run problems as the movement of political ideologies in relation to shifts in *systems* of class stratification. . . . The historical data of the Europeans typically rest on the assumptions empirically explored for the present by the Americans. Thus, a Max Weber . . . may write on puritan beliefs obtaining widely in the seventeenth century, basing his factual conclusions on the literate few, who set down their beliefs and impressions of others' beliefs in books we can now read. But, of course, this leaves untouched, and untouchable, the independent question of the extent to which these beliefs as set down in books express the beliefs of the larger and, so far as history goes, wholly inarticulate population (to say nothing of the different strata within that population). This relation between what is found in publications and the actual beliefs (or attitudes) of the underlying population which is taken for granted by the European variant, becomes a problem amenable to research by the American variant.[15]

Limitations of Historical Research

Historians themselves generally agree that few narrators of historical events report them without injecting some impressions. The medieval chronicles in particular were not only impressionistic but often propa-

[15]Merton, *Social Theory and Social Structure: Toward Codification of Theory and Research,* pp. 204–205. Free Press, 1949. Quoted with permission.

gandistic. Even some modern historians have consciously or unconsciously become defenders of a principle or a party.

Arthur M. Schlesinger contends:

> The older history was essentially snobbish and exclusive, paying no attention either to the "Unknown Soldier" or the nameless civilian. As Mr. Dooley once put it, 'I know histhry ain't thrue, Hinnessy, because it ain't what I see ivry day on Halsted Sthreet. If any wan comes along with a histhry iv Greece or Rome that'll show me th' people fightin', gettin' drunk, makin' love, gettin' married, owin' th' grocery man and bein' without hardcoal, I'll believe there was a Greece or Rome, but not befure. . . . Th' other kind iv histhry is a post-mortem examination. It tells ye what a country died iv. But I like to know what it lived iv."[16]

So would social scientists.

Snobbishness and exclusiveness are not the only limitations of some historians. Limitations arise also because: 1) Historians cannot write history life-size. 2) Not all happenings in time and space can be known at the time of writing. 3) Personal biases and private interpretations often enter unconsciously, even when honest attempts are made to select pertinent facts, to arrange them consistently, and to place them in a coherent and true frame of reference. Of necessity the historian must resort to selection. Descriptions of numerous complex happenings, occurring in rapid succession, cannot go on indefinitely until all details are exhausted. Historians find it imperative to omit a mass of detail. In the remaining mass that they do not omit, they often interject their own conclusions.

Thus, the reader must learn whether the selected facts are those which are especially representative and typical of the time and cultural setting or whether they portray merely a unique situation, characteristic of a limited time and space. The research student cannot undertake an examination and testing of all historical material which shaped social situations and institutions. At best he can study certain occurrences which are still woven into the beliefs, behavior patterns, and customs of the group under study. This involves a process of sampling, and a determination that the historians upon whom he relies have a broad perspective and concern themselves with relevant complexities of social forces rather than with unique or isolated phenomena.

[16]Quoted in Schlesinger, "History: Mistress and Handmaid," in Brookings Institution, Committee on Training, *Essays on Research in the Social Sciences,* p. 143. 1931.

Few modern historians at present cling to the "great-man theory of history"; few give merely episodic or dramatic fragments of events. Most modern historians present a cross-section of a level of life and events, of similarities and common traits, of the collective life of mankind.[17] In brief, they are interested in the social process as a seamless web. They realize that a collection of historical events about politics, law, economic activities and developments, religion, and other aspects of life would not constitute a history of mankind. The social process as a whole must also be synthesized and explained.[18]

Adequacy of historical data. Historical data may be regarded as reliable and adequate for social research: 1) when they are presented as complexes of social forces; 2) when social phenomena meaningfully depict intricate social processes; and 3) when sets of interrelationships—psychological, economic, educational, political, and religious—contribute to a unified whole, a configuration or complex pattern.

We may conclude with statements from a report of the Committee on Historiography, Social Science Research Council, and with a summary of Arnold Rose's views on the relation between history and social science research:

> That history can be regarded as a social science needs little argument. Historians have long been aware of their responsibility as social scientists. They have consistently affirmed the necessity of analyzing historical data rigorously. For some generations, too, the practice as well as the philosophy of historians has reflected the scientific spirit; historical studies that exhibit modes of thinking directly traceable to social science viewpoints are now common. . . . History in the United States has attained a certain degree of maturity as a social science. The problem that remains is that of making more explicit as a matter of practice the status already recognized in principle—of making investigation more penetrating, analysis more precise, and demonstration more rigorous. This is a problem that history, in company with other sciences, has always to face.[19]

Dr. Arnold M. Rose feels that sociologists have much to learn from the historian's techniques of internal and external criticism and from

[17]See especially Arnold Toynbee, *The Study of History* (one-vol. ed.), for a broad account of the collective life and social forces of mankind. See also Henry Commager and Richard Morris (eds.), *The New American Nation Series*. Harper & Row, 1954–1964.

[18]Schlesinger, *op. cit.,* p. 145.

[19]Committee on Historiography, *op. cit.,* p. 21.

his synthesis of a variety of factors in a given occurrence. Sociologists also have many uses for the content of history which provides:

1\. . . . comparative data with which to test hypotheses. Durkheim's study of suicide and of religious behavior, and Weber's study of capitalism made just this use of historical data. . . .

2\. . . . descriptions of certain occurrences which occasionally can be used as "crucial tests" of certain theories. . . . The kind of diversified observations, under unusual conditions, provided by history could demonstrate the crucial weaknesses of many current sociological theories. . . .

3\. . . . a source of understanding [at times the only source] of what might be considered a unique pattern of nonunique events. For example, we know that the important racist ideology that has dominated and given a special quality to white-Negro relations in the United States was practically nonexistent before the year 1800. To find out how and why it developed we must turn to history. . . . Gordon Allport has made a significant contribution to our recognition of the need for life histories to understand adult personalities and thus provides a case parallel to the recognition of the need to study culture history in order to understand contemporary society.

4\. . . . "a realistic" basis to definitions, assumptions, and indices used to measure factors in formulating and testing social theory. . . . This is the sort of thing that Charles H. Cooley had in mind when he said that a broad acquaintance with history and ethnology was extremely valuable for a sociologist.

5\. . . . aid in the specification of many conditions held constant since history describes the setting in which the experiment takes place. . . .[20]

[20]*Theory and Method in the Social Sciences, op. cit.*, pp. 251–252. (1954.) Reprinted by permission of University of Minnesota Press. In January 1964, Professor Rose wrote the present author that he continued to subscribe to the above statements.

7

field observation in social research

Observation of social behavior is usually of little value if it does not include an adequate description of the character of the social atmosphere or the larger unit of activity within which the specific social act occurs.

KURT LEWIN

A story circulates among journalists regarding an encounter, at the White House, between President Franklin Roosevelt and a hostile young reporter who felt so insecure that he "stumbled and choked through his queries," during the press conference. F. D. R. carefully observed the hostile young man and the tense social atmosphere which the latter had created among the other reporters present. The group, in turn, observed the President and watched him repress his "famed robust ability to demolish opposition quickly." There was no evidence even of his amiable sarcasm, for which he was equally famous. The reporters soon observed a change in the President, a change from righteous indignation to consideration for a nervous opponent. The President even helped this man toward coherence in expressing his hostility. Later the newsmen present remarked: "F. D. R. observed the reporter but perceived him with more than his eye." The "seeing" was both physical and mental. Viewing or observing must be accompanied by perceiving, that is, apprehending with the mind, if the observing is to be fruitful.

Observation may be defined as systematic viewing, coupled with consideration of the seen phenomena. That is, consideration must be given to the larger unit of activity in which the specific observed phenomena occur. Not all phenomena, of course, are open to observation; not all those open to observation find a ready observer at hand. Not all occurrences lend themselves to study by observational techniques. Social processes, social trends, or cross-sections of life processes, or continuities of personal experiences, require interviewing and life-history techniques. But one can hardly think of an empirical study in which some observation had not been made.

Hypotheses and observation. The observing eye "catches" many more things and acts than are pertinent to a given study. The basis for selection is guided by nature, scope, and objectives of the inquiry. Generally, the formulated hypothesis is the guiding element in the immediate observation. For example: we are interested in the causes of highway accidents and have tentatively formulated an exploratory hypothesis that accidents are caused by speeding and not, as generally assumed, by narrow or poor roads. In the time available we focus our observations on our concepts of speeding vehicles and the consequences to them and to other cars. We do not scatter our attention on the variety of passing cars, nor on the complexity of motorways, highway folkways, and road conditions, all of which may be of interest and value, but confusing to the point of inquiry and to the testing of the formulated hypothesis. If the hypothesis is discarded by test, then we formulate another hypothesis, observe the relevant situations not taken into account earlier, and in turn test each selective observation. The goal in observation determines the direction and stresses the facts upon which to concentrate. Much of what is before our eyes we slight or omit, for the moment at least. The seeing is selective in terms of the categories which will give meaning to the testing of our hypothesis.[1] The selective process is logically sound, since the human mind requires limiting to manageable proportions; it is scientifically sound, because accuracy in testing depends on small comparable units.

But it should be remembered again that, in spite of the need for planning and systematization, the observer must be sensitive to wholly unanticipated and chance phenomena which may come to play an important role in the research process—for finding both strategic data and significant hypotheses and theories.

[1]Karl N. Llewelyn, "Legal Tradition and Social Science Method—A Realist's Critique," in Brookings Institution, Committee on Training, *Essays in Research Method in the Social Sciences,* pp. 113–114.

CRITERIA FOR OBSERVATION. When critically reviewing one's own observations or those of others, a number of questions should be raised:

Are there any evidences that the observer formulated definite objectives of study, rather than groping haphazardly without a goal?

Did he observe the larger setting within which specific acts occurred?

Did he adequately describe the character of the social atmosphere of observed situations?

Did he examine his observations within the general context of a particular study, instead of viewing them as uncoordinated elements?

Did he use observation as a carefully planned technique, instead of resorting steadily to chance, random, and inconsistent procedures?

Are there any evidences of bias in the recorded data? Of relying unduly on memory and recall after a risky delay?

Did he use a control group? Did he subject his observations to scientific tests? Did he compare them in a systemized way with those of other discreet and mature observers?

Did he use precision instruments with a view to quantifying his data?

Did he adequately integrate his observational techniques with other suitable exploratory techniques in the research process?

Maxims, no matter how carefully formulated and meticulously followed, will not in themselves provide guidance for the process of observation, nor will they later guide in the analysis of the observed data, unless throughout the study one keeps in mind the types of data required in this study and why these particular data and not others within the same context have been selected as the object of observation.[2]

Types of Observation

Several types of field observation have been found useful in social research. Here we shall discuss noncontrolled and controlled field observation, in their participant and nonparticipant aspects.

The concepts of both participant and nonparticipant observation date back to Professor Eduard Lindeman's publication, *Social Discovery* (1924). He was sharply critical of the naïveté exhibited in studies "based upon schedules of questions for which the investigator found

[2]See R. K. Merton, *Social Theory and Social Structure: Toward Codification of Theory and Research,* pp. 55–59. Columbia University Press, 1949.

answers by making inquiries of persons. Analysis of such schedules revealed that the questions contained premises which implied simple conclusions." Lindeman considered as absurd any attempt to avoid bias by posing questions requiring a simple "yes" or "no" reply in a study which entailed not only "what" of life, but also "why" and "how." Furthermore, "in answering questions [a person] will reply in terms of the objective thing he is really doing. . . . Thus, if you wish to know that he is *really* doing, watch him, don't ask him."[3]

In the United States, Nels Anderson, through his study of *The Hobo* (1923), still remains the most dedicated follower of the principles of participant and nonparticipant observation. He was an intimate participant in the life of the hobo on the road, in "the jungle," in lodging houses, at Chicago's Hobo College. Such dedication over a period of two or three years is exceptionally rare. And as it has been said, it requires not only certain personal qualities and vocational absorption, but also willingness to sacrifice leading a reasonably normal life and shrugging off possible reflections on one's career.

Noncontrolled and nonparticipant field observation: an illustration. The following excerpts from a description of a slum area indicate the nature of noncontrolled and nonparticipant observation—a study of social situations from the "outside."

> Slum district is drab and mean. . . . Many families are living in one or two basement rooms for which they pay less than ten dollars a month. These rooms are stove-heated, and wood is sold on the streets in bundles, and coal in small sacks. The majority of houses, back toward the river, are of wood, and not a few have windows broken out. Smoke, the odor from the gas works, and the smell of dirty alleys is in the air. . . .
>
> Life in the slum is precarious. One reads in the paper of a mother on North Avenue giving away her baby that the rest of her children may live. . . .
>
> Deteriorated store buildings, cheap dance halls and movies, cabarets and doubtful hotels, missions, "flops," pawnshops and second-hand stores, innumerable restaurants, soft-drink parlors and "fellowship" saloons where men sit about and talk, and which are hangouts for criminal gangs that live back in the slum, fence at the pawnshops, and consort with the transient prostitutes. . . .
>
> The slum harbors many sorts of people: the criminal, the radical, the

[3]Lindeman, *Social Discovery,* pp. 178–179, 182–193. Republic Publishing Co., 1925.

bohemian, the migratory worker, the immigrant, the unsuccessful, the queer and unadjusted. . . .[4]

Though the above illustration is an accurate description of a Chicago slum district, it is not devoid of subjective interpretations: "Slum district is drab and mean"; "life in the slum is precarious"; "doubtful hotel"; and like phrases. Subjective interpretation is not the only pitfall of non-controlled observation. There is also the danger that it is likely to give the feeling that we know more about the observed phenomena than we actually do. "The data are so real and vivid, and therefore our feelings about them are so strong, that we sometimes tend to mistake the strength of our emotions for extensiveness of knowledge."[5] There is also the likelihood that casual observers will misread the state of mind or social atmosphere and characterize it in terms of their own values, rather than of those who are immediately involved.

In the above illustration it is obvious that not only the physical aspects of the community were the object of observation, but also the social atmosphere, the symbiosis (living together) of the population, and the effects of such living in such a social world.

Even external and scattered observations, much like a series of snapshots of a busy tourist, often suggest the inner life of a people, their conflicts, and social distances. External observations pave the way for a more systematic study by other techniques.

Some researchers use passive participant observation over long periods of time within the same group of observees, with the hope of obtaining more reliable data. F. J. Roethlisberger and W. J. Dickson, in their pioneering work, *Management and the Worker,* functioned as passive members of work groups within the industrial plant. Although they had a desk—placed at the back of the workroom—they maintained their presence as unobtrusively as possible and did not enter into any conversation with the workers. They kept a record of the verbal and overt behavior of each worker within the group. Spatially and personally, these observers were part of the group; socially, they were isolated participants whose repeated observations became part of the "natural scenery" of the plant.

[4]Harvey W. Zorbaugh, *The Gold Coast and the Slum,* pp. 9–11. University of Chicago Press, 1929. Reprinted by permission.

[5]Jessie Bernard, "The Sources and Methods of Social Psychology," in L. L. Bernard (Ed.), *Fields and Methods of Sociology,* pp. 273–274. Farrar, Straus & Giroux, 1934.

W. L. Warner and P. S. Lunt suggest a variety of social situations which may be studied by what they call inactive observation. These suggestions might prove useful in any comprehensive study of a community:

> Observations included the study of certain factories, retail stores and banks, of the mass activities of a strike, of the meetings associated with the loss of income and unemployment, of sacred and secular rituals such as those on Memorial Day, and of the ceremonies of the churches and associations. The *rites de passage* surrounding marriage, birth, and death were observed. The police desk, with its flow of arrests, convictions, and discharges, was kept under long-term observation and the behavior of such officials as the truant officer and the policeman on the beat was studied. The mayor's office, the health office, the office of the superintendent of schools, with their several systems of behavior, were each observed by one or more field workers. In the schoolhouses and schoolyards the relations of teachers, of pupils, and of each to the other and to the principal were recorded over periods of time by field workers.[6]

Noncontrolled participant observation: illustrations. The participant observer shares, to lesser or greater degree, the life of the observed group. This sharing may be intermittent but active contacts at close proximity afford intimate study of persons. William F. Whyte, for example, in his studies of *Street Corner Society* lived in "Cornerville," boarded with one of the families there, and intimately associated with a number of members in the Cornerville Athletic Association and social clubs into which he was later initiated as a member. Nels Anderson, it will be recalled, participated to the degree of becoming a *bona fide* hobo for the duration of his study. These observers gained a degree of insight into interpersonal relations and motivations of members which would have been well-nigh impossible by other means of study.

Paul Cressey, in his study of *The Taxi-Dance Hall,* abandoned formal interviews in favor of direct participation and observation "from the inside." The observers became as much a part of the social world of the taxi-dance hall as is ethically possible, functioning as casual acquaintances. Cressey believes that he and his associates were able to obtain "much mate[illegible] without encountering inhibitions and resistances" which might [illegible]ve been met in formal interviews with strangers of the taxi-dance hall group.

[6]Warner and Lunt, *The Social Life of a Modern Community,* p. 53. Harvard University Press, 1939. Reprinted by permission.

The degree of participation depends largely on the nature of the study and the practical demands of the situation. Many investigators must of necessity identify themselves closely with groups studied, because the subject matter is so novel that it needs intensive study under close proximity. Conversely, if the subject matter is familiar, the investigator "may perceive it primarily in terms of his own previous life unless he deliberately takes another role to enable him to experience in himself the more subtle differences."[7]

The account below is an excerpt from a description of a Molokan church service, following a funeral of an eighteen-year-old boy whose father was not regarded by the group of Molokan sectarians as a faithful member. This illustration shows the degree of understanding of local norms that is required before observation becomes meaningful.

> The elder, after a final passionate prayer, pronounced the benediction. All rose to their feet. The elder turned to the father, saying in a low but commanding voice: "You are grief-stricken, but this is the Day of Judgment of your son. You have frequently lost your temper and offended some of the elders. It is your duty to repent and ask forgiveness." The father hesitated for a moment, but presently fell to the feet of the elder and, bending his head low, asked his pardon and that of all those whom he might have offended. . . .
>
> A loaf of bread was then placed on the table, a sign of the approaching feast. Long, improvised tables were brought in, and benches placed beside them. . . . In less than thirty minutes, six hundred people were quietly seated in their respective places according to age and sex. . . .
>
> "We are a brotherhood, and sit close together, and eat from common dishes, and use all things in common," a Molokan woman explained to the writer, as she invited her to partake of the feast.
>
> During the meal many songs were sung. The voices rang through the air with zeal and devotion. Once heard, they are not soon forgotten, nor this multitude of men and women all singing in unison from the very depths of their hearts.
>
> "These songs gladden my heart and thrill me through and through," remarked a Molokan woman. "You see, that's all the joy and relaxation our people have. They get together, they grieve together, and they rejoice together. We are one community, and we must be together and do the same things together." . . .
>
> Several elders got up during the meal, reminding the congregation of their duty to each other as a brotherhood and a spiritual community.

[7]Marie Jahoda *et al., Research Methods in Social Relations,* p. 142. The Dryden Press, 1951.

"Here we are together in a body; let us be together in spirit and in deed."

The final prayer was long, tinged with considerable emotion. Again the parents and the relatives of the deceased prostrated themselves before the elders who blessed them fervently. When they rose to their feet again, they bowed low to the congregation who seemed to respond very warmly and many invited the bereaved parents to their homes.[8]

Observation and insight. Sociological observation requires as its first condition that the members of the group be viewed as social values for one another. Such questions as "What does each individual mean socially to each other individual?" "What does the group mean to its members individually?" "What does a member mean to the group collectively?" cannot be fully answered by observational techniques alone, but the groundwork for further study by other techniques may be laid.[9]

To the casual observer not familiar with the norms of the culture group under study, this bit of religious sectarian life described above may be only a matter of curiosity and wonderment, or seem primitive or crude and peculiar behavior. To all intents and purposes, the casual observer is "blind" to the real issues and meanings of the things he carefully observes. He may look intently, but not see the implications of what he is looking at with concern. He needs to learn the socio-cultural context of the observed phenomena. The continuity and meaning of events are the important elements in observation.

In noncontrolled participant observation, no attempt is made to use precision instruments. The major aim of this type of observation is to get a spontaneous and unposed picture of life and persons. It is favored especially because of its tendency to supply naturalness and completeness of behavior, allowing sufficient time for observing it. In controlled observation, on the other hand, we use mechanical instruments as aids to accuracy and standardization. Although controlled observation has a tendency toward formalized and atomized data, it also makes possible introduction of stimuli by means of which behavior can be tested and retested, and provide data upon which generalizations can be built with some degree of assurance. Robert S. Bales

[8]See Pauline V. Young, *Pilgrims of Russian-Town,* pp. 4–6. University of Chicago Press, 1932.

[9]See Florian Znaniecki, *The Method of Sociology,* p. 177. Farrar, Straus & Giroux, 1934.

has even demonstrated that it is possible to penetrate behind the thinking and the reaction patterns of persons and groups, as we shall presently see.

Controlled observation. Within the last three or four decades, stress has been laid on development of precise observation techniques which would yield measurable data of social phenomena. A variety of instruments have come into use—one-way screens and mirrors,[10] movement recorders, sound recorders, motion pictures, rating scales, observation schedules, and others. R. Stuart Mackay[11] describes in considerable detail measuring devices and miniature radio-telemetering transmitters which can be implanted in body cavities or swallowed by man and animal. These devices, he says, "supply inside information about subjects in a relatively normal physiological state, that is, [the subject] has no sensation caused by the instrument and is not likely to be in an apprehensive state."

Stuart Chapin had foreseen, a long time ago, measuring devices which would be in reality precision tools or "observation instruments just as truly as are the thermometer or the stethoscope of the physician."[12]

Controlled observation is generally carried on according to definite prearranged plans which may include considerable experimental procedure. Some of the most intensive studies of this type have been in the field of child behavior. Among the most famous of these are the studies of nursery school children, conducted by Dorothy S. Thomas[13] and her associates at the Yale Institute of Human Relations and later at Columbia Teachers College. The observers—practice teachers in daily attendance—created natural situations in which the observed children felt few or no restraints. The latter continued their activities not only without self-consciousness, characteristic of young children generally, but also without awareness and concern of being observed. Dr. Thomas and her aides were primarily concerned with the social

[10]See Richard T. Morris, *The Two-Way Mirror: National Status in Foreign Student Adjustment*. University of Minnesota Press, 1960.

[11]Mackay, "Radio Telemetering from Within the Body," *Science*, CXXXIV (Oct. 20, 1961), pp. 1196–1202.

[12]Chapin, "New Trends in Social Research," *Journal of Educational Sociology*, XI, 565–566.

[13]Thomas *et al.*, *Observational Studies of Social Behavior*, pp. 381–416. Yale University Press, 1933. In 1964 Dr. Thomas offered no changes.

NUMBER AND ACTIVITY OF EACH OF FIVE NURSERY SCHOOL CHILDREN (GIRLS) 15 MINUTE PERIODS, INDOORS												
	CHILD Group 1	INACTIVE	CRYING	OBSERVING	BLOCKS	DOLLS	SANDPILE	SWING, SLIDE	PICTURE BOOKS	CONTACT OTHER CHILD	CONTACT ATTENDANT	OTHER ACTIVITIES
		Freq.	Freq.	Freq.	Freq.	Freq.	Freq.	Freq.	Freq.	Freq.	Freq.	Freq.
	A											
PERIOD I Just Before Nap	B											
	C											
	D											
	E											
	A											
PERIOD II Just After Nap	B											
	C											
	D											
	E											
	A											
PERIOD III Just Before Meal	B											
	C											
	D											

Figure 7.1 Observation schedule for preferred activities of certain nursery school children.

behavior and reaction patterns of nursery school children to a multiplicity of stimuli encountered in their nursery school contacts, particularly those relating to other persons, to materials, and to self.

Figure 7.1 represents a sample of an observational schedule as an objective recording device which makes possible accumulation of large quantities of concrete details. It is a standardizing device by which uniform and verifiable details can be obtained by several observers.

In filling out this schedule the observer has to keep in mind the frequency of ten different varieties of activities of five different children during three different play periods, which—with a group of lively youngsters—may require several hundred entries, in cases where each child engages or re-engages twice in each activity. Accuracy is of utmost importance, especially if the data are to be quantified.

Note that the observation in this particular situation is inclusive and continuous; that is, it takes in all observational acts and does not allow for gaps. The recording, too, is clear and specific, although it does not delve into reasons for crying, or inactivity, or other behavior.

The work of Charlotte Buhler, a clinical psychologist at Los Angeles General Hospital, may serve as a further illustration of the skillful use of mechanical devices, particularly schedules and charts, in the observation of young school children. Dr. Buhler states that she concerns herself with the whole personality of the child: sense perceptions, social reactions, and mental productivity; i.e., means of reasoning and mental initiative. She records on schedules the degree of the child's strivings toward a specific goal. Like the schedules of Dr. Thomas, those of Dr. Buhler imply a realization that the behavior even of a young child is tremendously complex, and the observations must of necessity be selective.

Figure 7.2 is an observation record—only partially reproduced here—which is used experimentally by Drs. Buhler and Cross in observing children's behavior in certain test situations. (Other activities observed and recorded, but not reproduced here, relate to the child's free drawing—theme, execution, characteristics included when drawing a person—and the child's activities and attitudes when playing with a doll.)[14]

Drs. Buhler and Cross state that this observation schedule has been found to be of use in the following directions:

1. It forms an objective record for the trained examiner, shortening the time needed for writing reports.
2. It serves as a device to train the beginning worker to pinpoint his observations in an orderly and more or less complete way.
3. In the case of children who return for therapy, it gives a yardstick against which progress may be measured.

The record can be most easily used by circling the numbers of significant items as the examination progresses, and checking them in

[14]Data and schedule supplied by Dr. Buhler for special use in present volume. See also her *From Birth to Maturity: An Outline of the Psychological Development of the Child.* Humanities Press, 1954.

OBSERVATION RECORD
OF CHILDREN'S BEHAVIOR IN TEST SITUATIONS

By Charlotte Buhler, Ph. D. & Jean Cross, Ph. D.

Name: No. Age: 4 3/4 yrs. Date: School: Grade:		Adequate	Immature	Dependent	Timid	Withdrawn	Aggressive or Hostile	Disorganized	Other
Behavior in waiting room.									
1. Quiet absorption in play material	1.								
2. Clinging to mother	2.	✓	✓	✓					
3. Restless running around	3.								
Behavior on way to examination room.									
4. Willingly leaving mother	4.								
5. Takes examiner's hand	5.	✓							
6. Lets mother go after starting to use material in examination room	6.	✓		✓					
7. Unable to stay alone with examiner	7.								
8. Initiates conversation with desire to communicate	8.								
9. Initiates conversation with noisy chattering, not waiting for responses	9.	✓						✓	anxious
10. Answers direct questions only	10.								
11. Remains silent, shy	11.								
12. Remains silent, hostile	12.								
Behavior during test.									
13. Enters tasks with pleasure and pursues with interest	13.	✓							short span
14. Accepts tasks as duty	14.								
15. Asks for help and reassurance	15.	✓		✓					
16. Accepts tasks but is easily distracted	16.								
17. Cannot accept tasks for distractability	17.								
18. Rejects some tasks as too hard- "I can't."	18.								
19. Rejects tasks with hostility	19.								
20. Shares responsibility of putting away, cleaning up	20.	✓							over-conforming, anxious
21. Refuses to help	21.								

Figure 7.2 Observation record of children's behavior in test situations.

the appropriate columns later, when the interpretation of the observed behavior is more apparent.

The construction of observation schedules (see also Chapter 8) involves many procedural difficulties. The schedule must be so devised as to provide an optimum of verifiable, quantifiable data and to avoid selective bias and misinterpretation of observed behavior. The units of observation must be simple, minute, and meticulously worded, if they are to lend themselves to precise and uniform recording by several observers at different times.

Dr. Thomas, for example, in her observational studies of social behavior, resorted to repeated trial observations and to talking-moving pictures to enable her to determine which behavior units did or did not lend themselves to accurate observation or to adequate analysis after observation. She also attempted to measure the observational error within reasonably narrow limits. She felt that until she could find 1) comparable, and therefore additive, units of observation, and 2) observational error capable of measurement (see our discussion of statistical error in Chapter 9), she could not arrive at any statistical analysis, no matter how painstaking the work in other respects.[15] The scientific significance of such studies can be realized only by a careful reading of them. The student will find them rewarding because Dr. Thomas describes not only the general theoretical framework and practical techniques of directed planned observation, but also keenly analyzes the degree of reliability and the limitations of her observational studies.

Dr. Thomas through her techniques of observation has largely overcome one of the greatest obstacles to controlled observation—artificiality of the situation and self-consciousness of the subject. Florence Goodenough questions, however, the validity of the results of observation when deliberate attempts are used to break up complicated acts into simple parts for the express purpose of accurate recording.[16] The validity of the representativeness of the sample on the basis of a small group of children has also been questioned.

Obviously, the fragments produced by segmentation of social behavior into minute units must be reconstructed into an integrated whole if we are to interpret the process of behavior. One should be careful not to draw general conclusions from isolated minutiae, but

[15]Thomas, *op. cit.,* p. 105.

[16]Florence Goodenough, "Observation of Children's Behavior as a Method in Social Psychology," *Social Forces,* XV, 476–479.

rather to use them for whatever they could reveal and supplement them by other studies using other techniques.

One of the most comprehensive, systematic, and sophisticated studies involving laboratory-controlled observation, over a period of three years, is reported by Professor Robert F. Bales of Harvard in his *Interaction Process Analysis: A Method for the Study of Small Groups,* 1950.[17] Although the subjects of study were questioned to a very limited degree, Bales' experiments are regarded as nonparticipant. He relied primarily on objective observation of small problem-solving groups, composed of seven to ten members. He was interested in the interaction process itself, the role of each test participant in this process, and the interrelationships among these roles. That is, he wanted to know how the interstimulations were derived by various members of the test group. The observations were not centered on the specific problems which the group were given to solve, rather on the manner of interaction ("relational behavior"), on the roles assumed during the problem-solving process by the group, and on the manner in which different group members contributed to this process.

A theoretician of high caliber, Bales aimed to develop a special method for observing, recording, coding, and analyzing the behavior of small problem-solving groups while in a process of interaction. He approached his study with certain formulated theories. He maintained that any particular phase of "social behavior is always a part of a larger organized system of action and reaction, and certain approximate uniformities of interaction . . . are more or less inherent in the nature of the interaction or communication itself." He conceived interaction as a series of concrete observable and measurable *actions*—verbal and nonverbal—in the observable *situation* in which these actions take place. He believed that these two elements are inherent in, and must be identified in relation to, all generalizations, whether these pertain to personalities, social systems, groups, or cultures.

Bales defined a "small group" not only in terms of numbers but also as ". . . persons engaged in interaction with each other in single face-to-face meetings or series of such meetings, in which each member receives some impression or perception of each other member, distinct enough so that he can, either at the time or in later questioning, give some reaction to each of the others as an individual person, even though it be only to recall that the other was present." This definition is im-

[17]On the discussion of the interaction process see especially pp. 1–35.

portant since it circumscribes the observation and shows the boundaries which exclude persons not specified.

The unit of observation (and later of measurement) in these interaction studies is the meaningful act—consciously or unconsciously performed, verbally or nonverbally expressed—that can be quantitatively determined. The unit of the verbal act can be any expressive word. The nonverbal acts include a laugh, smile, grunt, frown, shrug, nod, yawn, or fidget. Any of these acts can be meaningful in communication and stimulate reactions.

The test persons were especially selected from large groups of students or others who were not related and did not know each other or knew each other only slightly. Putting the group into the social science laboratory to solve certain problems, Bales had intentionally controlled the size and the nature of the group, the goal of their interaction, and the environment in which the experiment took place. In the experimental study each member was observed as an agent of communication, that is, as an originator of verbal or nonverbal acts.

In order to obtain data on patterns of interaction, uniformities in action, and their frequencies, Bales set up a system of categories based on preliminary observations. The following categories were meant to be mutually exclusive (see Bales, Chapter 1):

1. *Shows solidarity,* raises others' status, gives help, reward.
2. *Shows tension release,* jokes, laughs, shows satisfaction.
3. *Agrees,* shows passive acceptance, understands, concurs, complies.
4. *Gives suggestion,* direction, implying autonomy for others.
5. *Gives opinion,* evaluation, analysis, expresses feeling, wish.
6. *Gives orientation,* information, repetition, confirmation.
7. *Asks for orientation,* information, repetition, confirmation.
8. *Asks for opinion,* evaluation, analysis, expression of feeling.
9. *Asks for suggestion,* direction, possible ways out.
10. *Disagrees,* shows passive rejection, formality, withholds help.
11. *Shows tension,* asks for help, withdraws out of field.
12. *Shows antagonism,* deflates others' status, defends or asserts self.

The observers were trained to empathize with the group, but the fashion in which they did so was presumably "drained of content, evaluation and commitment." They were to observe the *social* situation in which the interpersonal relations of the test group could be distinguished, concretely understood, recorded, and even measured. Only such opportunities, Bales maintained, lead to discovery of uniformities in a test situation.

OBSERVATION ROOM AND EQUIPMENT. The observation room—adjoining a meeting room—was equipped with a row of one-way mirrors that gave a direct view of the test group. The group was generally informed of being observed by inaudible, unseen observers. (Bales does not believe that such awareness unduly distracts the group, "possibly because we are all used to being observed in social situations, at least in an informal sense.")

Speakers and recording systems were installed. Microphones were later replaced by wire recorders for high fidelity, and by plastic discs for low fidelity; and still later, three microphones were introduced to provide audio-balance for stereophonic sound output.

Interaction recorders were also used. These have mechanically moving pads which are divided by horizontal lines into twelve bands, corresponding to the twelve categories into which the observers fit their observations. As the pad continues to move from right to left, the observer marks the appropriate category of the observed action. Built into this recorder is a light, flashing once a minute to remind the observer to take note of nonverbal action.

IBM cards, punched for three items of information, have been used since the early beginning of the experiment: 1) the number of the category into which the act is to be classified; 2) the number of the person who initiates the act; and 3) the number of the person to whom the act is directed. (The information punched on these IBM cards could be analyzed either from the standpoint of the entire test group, or separate members of the group on a sequential basis, or act-to-act sequence.)

Bales specified exactly the type of acts to be observed and how each act was to be classified. The observers were kept busy. They had to identify in the group who said what to whom and in what manner, and who reacted to what had been said and done. In other words, the functions of the observers were: seeing and identifying the subject in question; hearing what he had said—noting the beginning, the end, and the intervening aspects of the act; watching the facial expression; translating all observed actions into categories, and recording them accurately. The observer was, at one and the same time, examiner and interpreter of his own observations.

Observation and interpretation took place almost simultaneously. That is, only a few seconds could elapse after the act took place before it was interpreted and recorded, even though "a burst of interaction occurred." (This process of interpretation may be likened to the task of the translators at UN sessions or at conferences attended by a number of delegates without a knowledge of the language of the speaker.)

For purposes of checking the accuracy of the recorded observations, two observers—sitting side by side—recorded simultaneously and independently the same observed phenomena. Reasonable similarity was generally achieved.

The observers had to be versatile, quick in making decisions, skilled in selecting the proper categories to be marked, accurate of perception, and able to take what Bales called "the role of the generalized other," so that by empathy they could identify themselves with the test participants to such an extent that they could project themselves into the minds of the others and thus not only record the bare acts but attach meaning to these acts and to the ensuing reactions which these acts provoked. (Bales' work is so rich in content—from both an exploratory and descriptive standpoint—that only a first-hand reading of it could supply the full import of his stimulating ideas and procedures. His later work, jointly with N. A. Flanders, "Planning an Observation Room and Group Laboratory," *American Sociological Review,* XIX (1954), 771–781, is also worth studying.)

John Madge points out, regarding Bales' method for Interaction Process Analysis, that:

> [It has] spread all over the world and has led to many insights. Outstanding among these is the identification of at least two types of leadership: the instrumental leader is the chief producer of ideas while the expressive leader maintains the cohesion of the group. Although the approach is abstract many concrete applications have already suggested themselves, for example, in relation to committee work, in relation to family roles, and in relation to purposive groups, such as bomber crews.[18]

Aids in field observation. The following aids—which will be discussed at some length and in their various ramifications in the following chapters—are here presented briefly to indicate the number of devices used as aids in field observation and their relationship to other techniques employed in a social study.

[18]Madge, *The Origins of Scientific Sociology,* pp. 9–10. The Free Press of Glencoe, 1962.

DETAILED FIELD NOTES. Where no automatic recorder is available, field notes should be carefully transcribed as soon as possible after observation. As the mere process of recording stamps the details of observed facts on the mind of the field worker, notes serve as an adjunct to the memory in similar observations to be made in the future. The field notes are also an aid to orderly and purposeful study, as well as an aid to the observer in grasping certain relationships of events he notes. (Consult Index for other references to "notes.")

PHOTOGRAPHS. Observers see in terms of their own interests, backgrounds, and insights into a given situation. Assume for purposes of illustration that a forest ranger, a lumber dealer, a botanist, and an artist walk together through a bit of forest. The word-description accounting of what each of these four men saw in the same forest at the same time, even if they held themselves to the rules of scientific description, would undoubtedly vary so widely that a fifth man reading the separate accounts would not be aware that the same forest is being described. Such selectivity can be supplemented by the use of photographs. Photographs tend to present accurately a mass of detail which is apt to escape the human reporter. The photographic "eye" views with authenticity and impartiality. It has no preconceived notions and selective interests.

Facial expression, and particularly the expression of the eyes, is singularly complex and difficult to describe. This fact is especially true when we attempt a word picture of non-Western faces or of faces of any persons under strong emotions. Language breaks down in any attempt to portray in words the planes, angles, and lineaments in such faces and surpasses the skill even of seasoned writers.

Whenever possible, photographs should be introduced in a series which might illustrate various aspects of situations. Photographs enhance their own value if they portray current as well as past conditions which can be adequately compared and used as a basis for judging trends and degrees of change. Photographs viewed singly may be of interest, but when the photographs, for example, of three Molokan generations are compared, we can gain considerable understanding of the degree of cultural change which occurred in the assimilation processes of the groups portrayed, judging at least by outward appearances.

Composite scenes replete with details are shown to advantage by photographs. (Arna Bontemps and Jack Conroy[19] present an interesting

[19]Bontemps and Conroy, *They Seek a City.* Doubleday & Co., 1945.

pictorial social history of Negro life and tensions in the United States.) A series of studies of cities and culture groups have been portrayed through the use of photographs.[20]

The language of words can at times be deficient in expressing emotions. The United Nations has produced a film "Overtures," which, without a word spoken, conveys some of the world's acute problems—tense faces of peasants surveying barren land, hunger of children, despair of refugees, the silent vigil of a miner's family at the site of a collapsed mine. In informal observation the language of faces can supplement inadequate words.

MAPS. (For a discussion of maps and map-making see Chapter 14.) Maps are in some respects much like photographs, since they also give "pictures" of the various situations. Maps and particularly social base maps are more highly selective than photographs, since they give just those spatial relations upon which one wants to concentrate. By using different base maps the data can be reflected against a variety of social backgrounds. Furthermore, the social base maps—showing the relation of topographical aspects of a community to its social organization—will call for further study and observation which probably would have never come to light otherwise.

SCHEDULES. (For a discussion of the use and limitations of schedules see Chapter 8.) A schedule, as a form on which to enter field data in controlled observation, as was the case in Dorothy S. Thomas' work, isolates basic facts from the general mass of impressions and may objectify the observation of complex situations. It aids in standardizing the recording of observed phenomena; it isolates individual elements, and thus facilitates concentration and measurement. Of course, due caution should be taken later not to remove the individual elements from their context and thus invalidate any comparisons with similar items taken from other schedules.

SOCIOMETRIC SCALES. (For a comprehensive discussion see Chapter 12.) Sociometric scales are used in the measurement of social attitudes, morale, status, home environment, social processes of adjustment, participation, and a vast variety of other factors. Sociometric scales are

[20]See Gregory Bateson and Margaret Mead, *Balinese Character: A Photographic Analysis*. New York Academy of Sciences, 1942.

regarded as tools or instruments of observation, with the same function as the physician's stethoscope or thermometer. The unique value of a scale, as of other observational tools, is the increased clarity of the picture the scale affords, as compared with more subjective judgments. This effect is secured by suppression of detail and the summation of many subordinate elements into a single score. In the case of complex situations, however, it may be that such a process disregards significant details and that no single score will tell what is important for us to know. We should keep in mind that well-known statistical principle that oversimplification is apt to become distortion, if not falsification. The more complex the situation, the less significant and useful the single score.

Crucial Points in Participant Observation

Many observations cannot be made on the sidelines. They require deeper penetration into the "inner sanctum" of the group. Standing on the threshold of this sanctum, the observer should be cautious as, at this crucial moment, he is apt to forfeit his own purposes by any misguided step, when every move is carefully watched by his respondents. They may know little or nothing of scientific work or of the ethical practices of an explorer. At times they may be suspicious and fearful of his wide-range curiosity and of his noncommittal attitudes and dispassionate observations of their intimate life and struggles. Not all informants easily comprehend a study of behavior for its own sake. Status in the group cannot be achieved merely on the grounds of objectivity and dispassionate study of their lives. To many of them—used to face-to-face relations—such attitudes are not only incomprehensible but distasteful. At the very least they demand evidence of sympathetic insight.

In the case of the Russian Molokans the present writer was frequently put to test regarding her appreciation of their "whole-souled devotion" and religious ardor which she was observing at various church ceremonies. She was questioned about her church affiliations. She was frankly told that Molokanism is a highly unique cause which guides every thought and action. Until such a time as she could think—and feel—Molokan, she could not understand their way of life nor appreciate the observed rituals and religious ecstasy. Without this understanding, she was told, everything else would be meaningless.

At the beginning of the study, the Molokans guarded against the writer's observations of the behavior of the younger generation, even though their cultural conflicts lay exposed at every turn. She scrupulously avoided direct contacts with Molokan youth until the time that the parents themselves would have greater confidence in her or seek her advice regarding the problems of the young. In other words, the group's privacy was never intentionally invaded. Even when fortuitous opportunities presented themselves while she was visiting public schools or playgrounds, she did not take advantage of them. This attitude in itself won for her much respect by the Molokan elders, the patriarchs of the sectarian group. She came to be regarded as a "scientific guest" who knew her place and at the same time their predicaments. If he is modest and discreet, the observer at this time no longer needs to remain on the threshold of the Colony. He can now pass through the gateway, and is, indeed, frequently invited to do so.

The personal equation factor in observation. Endless comparisons are steadily being made between the tasks of the social and physical sciences. It is pointed out that the problems of the former "lie nearer to the quick of human emotions"; that they are generally more complex; and in many of them the individual variations make themselves felt as they do not in many of the physical sciences. However, it is of interest to note that now:

> The physical scientists [who] are trying to deal with individual electrons rather than with the average conduct of millions of atoms or molecules (there are more atoms in a piece of sodium the size of a pea than there are human beings in the world) have thrown up their hands and are telling us that the law of cause-and-effect no longer applies, and that all they do is to make a more or less probable prediction of the electrons' conduct; that it is to be compared to that of an organism. From being at rest it may suddenly decide to move about like a dog which is tired of inaction.[21]

A. W. Bertrand Russell, famous philosopher and shrewd observer, points out that not even students of the natural sciences are immune to the influences of the personal factor. He cites the observations of students of animal life who tend to project themselves and watch passionately the behavior of their subjects:

> The manner in which animals learn has been much studied in recent years, with a great deal of patient observation and experimentation. . . .

[21]W. F. G. Swann of the Bartol Research Foundation, in a letter to the author, April 1955.

> One may say broadly that all the animals that have been carefully observed have behaved so as to confirm the philosophy in which the observer believed before his observations began. Nay, more, they have all displayed the national characteristics of the observer. Animals studied by Americans rush about frantically, with an incredible display of hustle and pep, and at last achieve the desired result by chance. Animals observed by Germans sit still and think, and at last evolve the solution out of their inner consciousness. To the plain man, such as the present writer, this situation is discouraging. I observe, however, that the type of problem which a man naturally sets to an animal depends upon his own philosophy, and that this probably accounts for the differences in the results.[22]

Let us not forget that there are often sharp differences of opinion among physicians on such matters as interpreting a chest X ray or a laboratory test. Much as a person may try, he may not be able to rule out completely personal factors when concerned with human behavior. Often the success of an experiment depends as much on the imagination and the dynamic personal qualities of the experimenter as on the precision equipment he is using. There is no substitute for disciplined imagination. In the last analysis it is the experimenter who makes the choices and decisions on what, when, and how to use the complicated system of measuring instruments.[23] These decisions are a scientist's evaluation, and therefore there can be no value-free research or value-free observation.

In a provocative article on "Problems of Participant Observation," M. S. and C. G. Schwartz describe what happens during the interval after a social situation has been observed and before it has been recorded:

> [Retrospectively] the investigator recreates, or attempts to recreate, the social field in his imagination, on a perceptual and feeling level. He takes the role of all the other people in the situation and tries to invoke in himself the feelings and thoughts and actions they experienced at the time the event occurred. He assesses the accuracy of his role-taking and then takes his own role, as he was reacting during the event, and examines the effects of his reactions or his perceptions to the situation. Finally, he tries to integrate his own perceptions of the situation with those of the participants and arrives at one or more pictures of

[22]Russell, *Philosophy,* pp. 29–30. W. W. Norton & Co., 1927. Reprinted by permission.

[23]Cf. L. V. Redman and A. H. Mory, *The Romance of Research,* p. 9. Williams & Wilkins Co., 1933.

> the events which are recorded as data. What occurs is a type of reworking of the representation of the phenomena as initially registered. A continuous shuttle process occurs in which the observer moves back and forth in his imagination (either wittingly or unwittingly) from his *recall* of the event as it was initially registered to his *evaluation* of the event at the time of retrospection. What are finally recorded are the end products of evaluation during this retrospective period and the further evaluation made at the time of the . . . recording of the data. In effect, observation is a continuous process of evaluation . . . [and the process continues as long as the recorder thinks about it].[24]

Evaluation of events is never easy. The observer, as he sorts his observations, appraises them and evaluates them as to their pertinence and fitness with regard to his particular project. The sooner he records his data after observation and the more vivid they are in his mind, the more realistic this evaluation might be, all other things considered.

Self-observation. It may be suggested that the observer take stock of himself and discover what prejudices and biases will prevent impartial study and disinterested points of view. At times, emotional reactions are so deeply imbedded and so subtly expressed that they are difficult to detect even by the most conscientious self-critics. Persistent self-observation and criticism by others may ultimately overcome prejudice and biases. Some directors of social studies require the field workers to write their life history and subject it to the most critical scrutiny and thus discover whatever prejudices and emotional reactions they may have. Margaret Mead alluded to the need for training anthropology students "to form an estimate of their own strengths and weaknesses as observers," in order to minimize errors of observation.[25]

Such introspection may have another social value; that is, it sensitizes the observer to the problems of others and creates sympathetic insight which facilitates, at least to some degree, the understanding of people's behavior in similar circumstances and similar cultural contexts. The net result is orientation and the development of hunches that will extend and enrich the observation.

Errors in observation. The observer should constantly keep

[24]*American Journal of Sociology,* LX, 345. Reprinted by permission of the University of Chicago Press.

[25]Mead, "The Training of the Cultural Anthropologist," *American Anthropologist,* LIV, 343–346.

in mind that it is easy to become attracted by the conspicuous, dramatic, and interesting factors. He should safeguard himself against observing merely the unique and the striking fragments, torn from their cultural context and habitual modes of life. Such piecemeal information has a tendency to leave life "floating in the air, or rather leading a flat existence on paper, with the third dimension, that of the actual life, completely lacking," as Bronislaw Malinowski has stated it.

The observer may judge certain outward appearances of a group in the light of the standards of his own culture. The extreme modesty in the home furnishings of certain religious groups, for example, should not be regarded from the standpoint of "poverty" or "unusual frugality" but as a religious principle approving material simplicity and group equality. If one regards the silent periods of Quakers as a sign of inarticulateness, he might be tempted to break "the awkward moment by a lively joke." In each instance, even in the case of what appears to be a familiar situation, the observer should ask himself, "What meaning does the observed group attach to it?" It is necessary to go even further and ascertain the system of values that determine the various cultural experiences and activities of the group. This is the same as saying that the research observer should be interested in social processes and the sequence of events which make up a social system. Unless the observed phenomena are studied in relation to a social process or a particular way of life, they are incapable of explaining reality or of furthering social exploration of other associated elements. Such unrelated fragments are much like the observations of a foreign student who wrote to his native land that the Americans are very dirty because of the numerous bathtubs in their homes; they are lazy because of frequent holidays; and are superstitious because of the abundance of churches.

It becomes obvious from the foregoing that valid observations cannot be hurried. Even when care is exercised and the scientific dictates are scrupulously followed, it is essential to pause and check on: 1) degree of agreement or disagreement between given observations and those made by other observers under similar situations or by the same observer using different techniques of study; 2) degree to which results of observation dovetail with the existing array of findings on related subjects; 3) significance of the data secured in furthering the thinking, or testing the hypotheses, or in solving scientific problems at hand. These are the serious objectives of social exploration.

It is also important to check one's observations for omissions due to oversight or lack of orientation at the beginning of the study.

Frequently the observer "grows" as the study progresses and he gains profounder insight. It is well to discuss one's observations with someone conversant with the field and discover one's own narrowness in viewpoint or unwitting overemphasis.

If the research student becomes accustomed to guard against common errors likely to be made in the earlier aspects of his work, he may gain ground later and enhance the value of his inferences, which in large measure depend on the accuracy and insight into the preliminary aspects of social exploration.

8

questionnaires and schedules as aids in social exploration[1]

A widely broadcast questionnaire is usually unavailable for anything more than obtaining of raw material of the statistician. . . . It may furnish confirmation of hypotheses, but it is very rare that it brings to light facts of structure and function not already within the knowledge of the investigator, or at least definitely suspected by him to exist.

SIDNEY AND BEATRICE WEBB

Both the questionnaire and the schedule are much used—and frequently abused—tools in gathering a variety of data. They have been used for the collection of personal preferences, social attitudes, belief, opinions, behavior patterns, group practices and habits, and much other data. The increasing use of schedules and questionnaires is probably due to increased emphasis by social scientists on quantitative measurement of uniformly accumulated data.

The questionnaire, like the schedule, is designed to collect data from large, diverse, and widely scattered groups of people. The questionnaire is generally sent through the mail to informants to be answered as specified in a covering letter, but otherwise without further assistance from the sender. The schedule, on the other hand, is generally filled out by the research worker or the enumerator, who can interpret the questions when necessary. Webster defines a schedule as "a formal list, a catalog or inventory," and it may be added that it is a counting device, used in

[1]Some of the material in this chapter is based on the chapter "The Questionnaire and Other Reporting Forms as Aids in Field Exploration," prepared by Mrs. Katherine Gordon Capt for the third edition of this text. The chapter was based on the second edition of the text. The present chapter is a revision by PVY of both second and third editions.

formal and standardized inquiries, the sole purpose of which is aiding in the collection of quantitative cross-sectional data.

The U.S. Bureau of the Census distinguishes between the schedule and the questionnaire on the basis of the auspices under which the data are collected. For the regular programs of the Bureau, the usual practice is to call the collection forms schedules; but for special studies—conducted for other governmental agencies or for nonprofit research organizations—the forms are generally referred to as questionnaires. Outside of governmental agencies, however, it is not common to make such rigid distinctions but to refer to the particular types of forms according to the predominent technique used in obtaining the data for enumeration: observation schedules, interview schedules, rating schedules, document schedules, for example. But it should not be assumed that these types are mutually exclusive. The interview schedules, for example, may contain items which demand observation, and likewise for other types.

Schedules and other types of reporting forms. Schedules and questionnaires are beneficial as supplementary and extending devices in observation, in interviews, and in evaluating personal behavior and social situations. They also aid in standardizing and objectifying observations and interviews, and finally they are useful "devices for isolating one element at a time and thus intensifying observation of it."[2] The vast variety of schedules can be classified in various ways. Here we present only a few forms:

OBSERVATION SCHEDULES OR FORMS. The observation form offers the opportunity for uniform classification in recording the activities and social situations of persons or groups being observed. One observer or several may be employed to secure uniformly systematic data in an observation study. (See Chapter seven for discussion of the use made of this type of form in the studies by Dorothy Thomas and Charlotte Buhler.)

An observation schedule usually serves several purposes simultaneously: 1) it is a specific "memory tickler"; 2) it is an objective recording device which makes possible accurate accumulation of large quantities of data; 3) it is a standardizing device; and 4) it aids to delimit

[2]George A. Lundberg, *Social Research,* p. 162. Longmans, Green and Co., 1942.

the scope of the study and to concentrate on the circumscribed elements essential to the analysis.

DOCUMENT SCHEDULES. These are used for recording data obtained from documents, case histories, and other materials. In order to secure measureable data, the items included on this type of form are limited to those that can be uniformly secured from a large number of case histories or other records. For example, a study of criminal records might include such items as type of offense, number and types of previous offenses, age at time left school, age at time started work, amount of education. It is generally necessary, however, to inspect a large number of records before the items that will yield measurable factors appearing on an adequate number of records can be ascertained.

The document schedule should not be considered a tally sheet. A separate schedule should be used to list the pertinent points from each case record. Tabulations are made from these schedules, either by hand tally or by machine tabulation.

INSTITUTIONAL SURVEY FORMS OR EVALUATION SCHEDULES.[3] Schedules of this type are used to visualize the problems faced by or inherent in a given type of institution. The length of such inquiries depends upon the aspects of the given situation under investigation. The "Evaluation Schedule of the American Public Health Association—For Use in the Study and Appraisal of Community Health Programs"[4] is 38 pages long and includes many items of basic information as well as items related to community facilities.

The most famous schedules are those used by the U.S. Bureau of the Census, for the Population and Housing Censuses. These are models of simplicity and contruction considering their length and their use for universal coverage. They seek the following information: 1) *for each person* in continental United States—name and relationship, race, sex, age, marital status, place of birth, labor force status of each person 14 years and over, occupation; 2) *for a 20 per cent sample* (1 in 5)—service in armed forces, country of birth of parents, school attendence (for persons 5–29 years of age), weeks at work, and so on; 3) for *6²/₃ per cent sample* (1 in 15) of persons 14 years of age and over who have

[3]See Elizabeth Herzog, *Some Guide Lines for Evaluative Research.* U.S. Department of Health, Education and Welfare, 1959.

[4]See Gerold Gurin, Joseph Veroff, and Sheila Field, *Americans View Their Mental Health.* Basic Books, 1960.

been married, whether married more than once, years in present marital status, and (for women only) number of children ever borne. (The use of sampling was introduced by the Bureau in the 1940 Census—which used only a 5 per cent sample—as an economy measure, and was continued in the subsequent censuses for the same reason.)

All information calls for replies to be recorded by: 1) written entries such as "Yes," or "No," a number, or code—married (*M*), widowed (*Wd*), and 2) checking a box. The questions to be asked of informants and the instructions to be followed by the enumerators are precise, simple, and definite; each unit of enumeration is carefully indicated, and the definitions are expertly given. (Many of these appear at the top of the schedule.) Such procedure tends to minimize vagueness and to maximize uniformity in response.

These forms have undergone a series of radical changes since 1790, when the first decennial census was taken during the presidency of Thomas Jefferson. Then the count was 3,929,214, and the main purpose of a nationwide tally was to ensure equal representation in Congress as demanded by the Constitution.

With the ensuing decades, with growth of population, expanding economy, and additional reasons of a tally, the census schedules were steadily modified and enlarged.

The 1960 schedule—seventeen censuses after the first one—was an outgrowth of all previous experience and experimentation. The 1960 Census initiated for the first time a self-administered schedule—a simple do-it-yourself form, as a speedy and economical way of gathering masses of data.

All of the filled census schedules contain virtually billions of facts. Before these data could be presented in numerical form in statistical tables, the 1960 schedules were microfilmed—converted into electrical pulses—and fed into a battery of electronic equipment, six Univacs and other electronic aids. Without this equipment it would have required nearly 2,000 workers toiling about 25 years to complete the gigantic task of counting the population of the United States and tabulating its wealth, its characteristics, urban and rural concentration, social structure, its living conditions, social and economic changes, social and family problems, the working force, the standard of living—a mass of data, expected to fill 100,000 pages.

Some 160,000 census takers or enumerators and 10,000 temporary district supervisors in 400 regional areas visited 60,000,000 households in cities, towns, villages and farms in 50 states as well as the

Commonwealth of Puerto Rico, Panama Canal Zone, Guam, American Samoa, in order to gather and check filled-out forms or answer questions pertaining to them. The enumerators visited a variety of dwellings and institutions, ranging from shacks to penthouses, out-of-the way lighthouses, mountain cabins, and even nudist camps. Yet, in this vast and complicated undertaking it is estimated that about 2,000,000 people were missed, either because they were on the move or impossible to reach in their isolation. The 1960 Census listed over 187,000,000 people in the United and States and its territories.

It takes from three to five years to analyze the data.

Questionnaires. There is also a vast variety of questionnaires which can be classified in various ways. Here we confine ourselves to the structured and unstructured questionnaires.

STRUCTURED QUESTIONNAIRES are those which pose definite, concrete, and preordained questions, that is, they are prepared in advance and not constructed on the spot during the questioning period. Additional questions may be used only when need arises to clarify vague or inadequate replies by informants or when more details are needed than those supplied by them. The form of the particular questions may require responses which are either closed or open. *Closed-form* questionnaires are used when categorized data are required, that is, when they need to be put into definite classifications. A simple example of this type of questionnaire may be quoted from the schedule of the U.S. Census of Population and Housing: "How is the housing unit heated?" The informant chooses from a set of provided responses: 1) steam or hot water heat; 2) warm air furnace; 3) floor, wall, or pipeless furnace; 4) built-in electric unit; 5) other means—flue; 6) other means—no flue. The respondent checks those supplied responses which approximate his situation. The *open-end* responses are free and spontaneous expressions on the part of the informant who is not limited in his replies to a particular question posed to him. The open-end responses are used chiefly for intensive studies of a limited number of cases or for preliminary exploration of new problems and situations. At times the respondent is asked to write a descriptive essay and express his viewpoints, describe his relationships, attitudes, indicate his problems, and report on details and events, without restrictions imposed as in the case of closed questions.

Structured questionnaires are used in a wide range of projects, both to initiate a formal inquiry and also to supplement and check data previously accumulated. These may pertain to studies of economic or

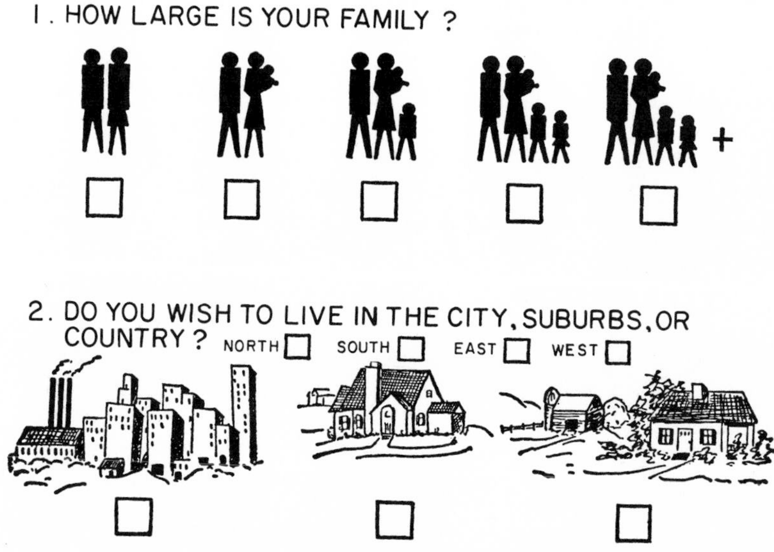

Figure 8.1 Pictorial questionnaire.

social problems, measurement of opinion on public issues or events, studies of administrative policies and changes, studies on the cost of living, consumer expenditures, child welfare, public health, and numerous other issues.

The benefits derived from the open-end question are also its limitations. Since it is nonrestrictive, a wide range of answers is usually given, some articulate and some meaningless, with wide intermediate gradations of response. Obviously nondirected response poses some problem of classification and analysis. The open-end question has been employed successfully where the primary information to be developed is qualitative in nature.

One of the principal values of the open-end question is its use as an exploratory tool before opinion has been solidified or before the research objectives have been clearly defined. The open-end question has been explored very effectively, notably by Lazarsfeld,[5] for determining motivation by several persons.

[5]P. F. Lazarsfeld, "The Art of Asking Why in Marketing Research," *National Marketing Review,* I, 26–38.

Examples of the open form questionnaires include studies conducted by Mirra Komarowsky and Robert Cooley Angell on the factors which affect family integration (see Chapter 2). A number of interesting samples may be cited from studies conducted in England: O. A. Wheeler's inquiry into adolescent religious and friendship experiences, and M. Phillips' research on the development of social, political, and other sentiments.

Generally, the questions posed in this type of questionnaire are sufficiently definite for the responses to be quantified, although much qualitative information is also secured. Both types of information secured may either constitute the basis for a case study or supplement case and statistical data.

PICTORIAL QUESTIONNAIRES. Pictures have been used in some studies solely for the purpose of promoting interest in answering the questions. Figure 8.1 represents some excerpts from a four-page questionnaire used in a housing study by the Veteran's Information Center, Federation of Social Agencies, Pittsburgh, where the pictures were used to increase interest.[6] Pictorial techniques have been used extensively in studies of social attitudes and prejudices in children.[7]

UNSTRUCTURED QUESTIONNAIRES, frequently referred to as interview guides, also aim at precision and contain definite subject matter areas, the coverage of which is required during the interview. The interviewer, however, is free—within limits—to arrange the form and timing of the inquiries. Flexibility is the chief advantage of the unstructured questionnaire. It is designed to obtain viewpoints, opinions, attitudes, and to show relationships and interconnections between data "which might escape notice under more mechanical types of interrogation. The object is to give the respondent maximum opportunity to reveal how he [had arrived at or developed] his world of experience."[8] No check lists with predetermined responses are provided. Rather, free responses are solicited. Questions, for example, regarding gang activities might assume this form: "How would you describe the activities

[6]Reprinted with permission.

[7]See R. E. Horowitz, "Development of Social Attitudes in Children," *Sociometry,* I, 301–338. Also E. L. Hartley and S. Schwartz, *A Pictorial Doll Play Approach for the Study of Children's Intergroup Attitudes* (mimeographed). American Jewish Committee, 1948.

[8]Benjamin D. Paul, "Interviewing Techniques and Field Relationships," in A. L. Kroeber (Ed.), *Anthropology Today,* p. 445. University of Chicago Press, 1953.

in which your group engages?" or "How do you account for the activities of your group?" or "How do such-and-such affect your group?"

This form of questioning assumes insight, articulateness, and possession of facts by the respondents. It is used for intensive studies, but generally for a limited number of selected cases. It has been applied to studies of family group cohesiveness (such as those referred to earlier in the discussion of the studies of the unemployed by Robert Cooley Angel or Mirra Komarowski), to studies of personal experiences, beliefs, and attitudes.

The chief disadvantage of unstructured questionnaires stems from the danger that nonadditive and noncomparable data will be accumulated when no structuring is imposed.

Problems of Communication

Although the content of questionnaires and schedules is governed by the purpose of the study, many problems of communication apply to all surveys regardless of content.

LANGUAGE. Much careful attention and experimentation are needed to produce effectively worded questions. The language should be concise and directed toward producing uniformity of understanding among the respondents. *In evaluating a question, it is more important to ask, "How will the respondent interpret this? than to ask, "What does this question mean?"*[9]

Continued emphasis is being placed upon the study of semantics,[10] and an increasing number of studies are being conducted for the advancement of precision in questionnaire wording.

1. The vocabulary chosen should be simple—within the easy grasp of the least intelligent of the group studied.
2. The syntax should be clear and straightforward. Long, involved sentences that require extended concentration on the part of the respondent defeat their purpose.
3. Phrases and expressions known only in certain sections of the country should be avoided. Professional "jargon" and technical words should be used only if the inquiry is directed to a selected group to

[9] W. Parker Mauldin and Eli S. Marks, "Problems of Response in Enumeration Surveys," *American Sociological Review,* XV, 649–657.

[10] See Alfred Korzybski, *Science and Sanity,* Institute of Semantics, 1958; and Stuart Chase, *Power of Words.* Harcourt, Brace & World, 1954.

whom the language is common. There is some evidence that persons tend to give any answers to questions rather than to state they do not know the meaning of the questions. This point is illustrated in a description of a study conducted by *Fortune*[11] in which the phrases, "initiation fee" and "strict entrance requirements," were used in two questions. The answers were recorded. Later in the interview, the same respondents were asked to restate these two questions in their own words, after having the questions read to them for the second time. Analysis of the consistency of the answers, together with the explanations given of the terms, indicated that only about half the respondents answering the original questions knew what they were about.

4. Questions and statements of a *leading* character—ones that put replies into the mouth of the respondent—are to be guarded against. The wording of the question should not make it easier to say "yes" than to say "no," or vice versa. Presenting a choice to the respondent is acceptable, provided that more than one choice is offered. For example, the question "Is . . . used most of the time?" invites an affirmative answer whereas the question, "Is . . . used most of the time, occasionally, or almost never?" invites no particular answer, and is, therefore, a nonleading question.
5. Units of enumeration should be precisely stated or defined in order to ensure proper orientation of the respondent. It is generally possible to build the unit references into the questions themselves. Take, for example, two apparently uncomplicated characteristics of the population—age and education. Answers to these questions, however, can vary as much as a year or a grade, unless the units of reference are made clear. "How old were you on your last birthday?" is specific in the information wanted; the more frequently used question, "How old are you?" is not so specific, because it leaves the respondent free to report age as of the *nearest* birthday, not necessarily the *last* birthday. The question, "What is the highest grade you completed in school?" makes it clear to the respondent that he is to name the highest grade completed, not attended.

   When the information sought relates to a definite time period, such as a fiscal or calendar year, the specific period should be stated in the question. Phrases such as "this year" and "last year" are not

[11]See Hadley Cantril, *Gauging Public Opinion,* pp. 8–9. Princeton University Press, 1944.

precise enough. In referring to prices, the question should clearly state what kind are involved—retail, wholesale, contract, jobbers', or market prices. Since prices also vary from area to area and with periods of time, the area and year should be specified.

If estimates are sufficient, the questions should so indicate. For example, in the question, "About how many days altogether have you lost from work because of illness during the past twelve months?" the words "about" and "altogether" indicate to the respondent that an exact accounting is not expected. Such phrasing saves time and tends to reduce the resistance often encountered when exactitude is required.

6. Subjective words, such as "bad," "good," "fair," and the like do not lend themselves to quantitative measurement nor qualitative analysis. In a study of housing conditions, for instance, the inclusion of questions on the age of the structure, type of heating and lighting, toilet facilities, and other descriptive facts results in more valuable information than does the use of subjective ratings.

FRAME OF REFERENCE. The respondent's frame of reference will influence his answers. This problem has by no means been solved, but research and experimentation have developed some criteria in constructing effective questions.[12]

1. Complex questions that require the respondent to go through several steps of reasoning before answering are undesirable and have often resulted in misleading information. An illustration of such misunderstanding is given in an article by Bancroft and Welch which describes the results when the respondents answer with a different frame of reference from the one intended. The question, "Did you do any work last week for pay or profit?" used in a study of the labor force conducted by the Bureau of the Census, failed to obtain the total number of persons employed, by the census definition. Persons tended to report their principal activity, and in the case of part-time workers this had the effect of excluding the report of any work performed for pay or profit. The question was revised. A series of questions was then asked which made it possible for a person to classify himself first according to his major activity and then answer questions about full- or part-time work. This change

[12]See Herbert Hyman, *Interviewing in Social Research,* pp. 304–321. University of Chicago Press, 1954.

resulted in a significant increase in the number of employed persons reported.

2. Questions on controversial issues should be broken down into components, so that the tester can determine the respondent's feelings about many aspects of the problem, including those which he refuses to comment upon. A series of specific questions is needed, sometimes referred to as "filter questions," in order to gather adequately the reactions to all sides of the issue.
3. When questions seek to uncover degrees of intensity of feeling or conviction, it is often necessary to find out to what extent the respondent's attitudes have been crystallized toward the subject. It is well to include a series of "why," "what," "when," and "how" questions, the answers to which are analyzed in relation to answers to other specific questions. More precise techniques have been explored, such as the inclusion of questions calling for answers that can be subjected to attitudinal scaling and the use of questions to reveal the intelligence level of the respondent. These techniques are restricted in use because of the specialized skills required for their construction and interpretation.
4. The required answers should be within the informational scope of the respondent. It would be meaningless, for instance, to ask people to report their blood pressure readings, because not enough people would know them. This does not preclude the collection of useful information at the household level about health and illness, as long as the inquiries are limited to events known to the respondents. Several studies conducted recently have collected health information at the household level and validated a sample of the cases through medical and hospital records and through medical examinations and laboratory tests.[13] Such validation studies on a sample of the cases can be designed to provide estimates of the reliability of the health statistics reported through the households.
5. The length of the questions and statements used should be governed by an estimate of the respondent's comprehension level. If a question appears too long, the best way of splitting it should be investigated. For example, the question "Do you have any impairments or handicapping conditions, even though they may not inter-

[13]"The Baltimore Health Survey," conducted by the U.S. Bureau of the Census for the Commission on Chronic Illness and for John Hopkins University, 1953.

fere with your usual activities?" Further investigation and observation indicated that it was not a satisfactory way of eliciting reports of impairments. Either the respondent retained only part of the question or its length confused him. The question was then split into two parts, with the second part—"even though they may not interfere with your usual activities"—asked only if there was an answer of "no" to the first part. The response to the revised question thereby was improved.

ARRANGEMENT OF THE QUESTIONS. The arrangement or ordering of the questions should receive special attention and be pretested with care. Every effort should be made to have the order appear logical to the respondent.

1. The questions placed first on the questionnaire should be those easiest to answer. Factual questions, such as name, relationship, and age, often serve successfully as starters, and also have the desired effect of making it possible for the respondent to participate early in the interview. Sometimes, "interest-catching" questions are used at the beginning of the questionnaire, and this procedure seems to work well, as long as the questions are not controversial in nature.
2. Placing a question early in the questionnaire that can affect answers to later questions on the form should be prevented wherever possible. This defect is not always detectable until several arrangements have been tried out and carefully watched from this standpoint. For example, in a health survey, starting off with a question about chronic illnesses before asking about current illnesses may result in an underreporting of illnesses of all kinds.
3. A time sequence should be observed in the arrangement of questions. If it is necessary to include questions relating to several periods of time on the same form, they should be so grouped that the respondent will not be forced mentally to jump from one time period to another.
4. Subject-matter sequence, likewise, is important, and insofar as possible all questions pertaining to one subject should be grouped together. In fact, if time-sequence and subject-matter sequence conflict and both cannot be observed, it is usually more important to retain the subject-matter sequence.

LENGTH OF THE QUESTIONNAIRE. Much has been said and written about the length of the questionnaire, but the length in itself need not be a guiding factor in the design. The important consideration is that the questionnaire covers the subject and that the techniques used are those which will meet the demands of the study. At the same time, it is wise to make a consistent effort to see that all questions are pertinent to the study and that the form is free of unnecessary repetition. When a complex study calls for a lengthy interview, steps should be taken to provide a successful administration of the questionnaire, rather than to emasculate it by deletions and "short cuts" of important information.

Form of the response. The form in which the responses are to be recorded must, obviously, be integrated with the form of the questions. There should be no hesitancy in using several forms of response on the same questionnaire, since frequently one form is better than another for questions about different aspects of the same subject.

DICHOTOMOUS QUESTIONS. Questions requiring answers of "yes" or "no" lend themselves well to tabulation and are subject to the least bias. They do not always yield sufficient information on the subject under study. When this is the case, other forms of response should be chosen.

MULTIPLE CHOICES INCLUDED IN THE QUESTIONS THEMSELVES AS WELL AS IN THE FORM OF RESPONSE. Questions that present multiple choices to the respondent are effective when the choices are few and easy to follow. For example, in a classification of persons according to marital status, the question "Are you now married, widowed, divorced, separated, or never married?" offers a clear choice for classification. Questions that are more complicated, but still practical, are those that ask the respondent to make certain simple comparisons and then state his position, as in the question "Do you think the traffic regulations here are too strict, fairly strict, not strict enough, or about right?"

When questions are to obtain opinions rather than factual information, additional care should be taken in the ordering of the choices, so that the choice made by the respondent will not reflect merely its position in the question. Sometimes more than one version of the questionnaire is printed in order to distribute any effects the ordering of choices may have upon the groups.

MULTIPLE CHOICES USED IN OTHER DEVICES. When it is desirable to have the respondent select a statement that describes how he feels about an issue or to report a class that best fits him, cards containing all the statements or classes may be shown the respondent. In the case of self-enumeration surveys, the same effect is achieved by printing all of the statements or classes on the questionnaire and providing instruction on how to make and record the selection.

An illustration of this method is found in a health survey[14] where multiple-choice statements were used to obtain the degree to which persons considered themselves limited by illnesses and impairments. The work status of the person had been previously reported, and the interviewer selected the proper card and asked the respondent to read each statement and say which one fitted him best. The card for those persons is as follows:

1. Cannot work at all at the present time.
2. Can work but limited in kind or amount. (For example, needs special working aids, or special rest periods at work, cannot work full time or for long periods of time, cannot do strenuous work, etc.)
3. Can work but limited in kind or amount of outside activities. (For example, sports, clubs, hobbies, visiting, church, etc.)
4. None of the above statements applies.

There are some shortcomings to the use of multiple choices, and these should be recognized and considered carefully. It may be difficult or impossible to cover the whole range of the subject. Attempting to do so may result in too many choices for the respondent to keep in mind. If the goal is to have the respondent make only one choice from several presented, then the choices must be mutually exclusive, and this is sometimes difficult. Another danger lies in the possibility that persons may tend to select the middle positions and avoid the extremes, thus adding another area for investigation and other factors to be taken into account in the analysis.

CHECK LISTS. Check lists are often used as probes to remind the respondent of particular items. Here the respondent is not asked to make a choice, but to respond to each item on the list. There is some evidence that items on a list elicit a higher rate of response than questions that require volunteered replies. Check lists should be used in studies where this effect is not harmful to the findings of the study.

[14]Greater Kansas City Health Survey, conducted by the Bureau of the Census for Community Studies, Inc., Dec. 1954-Dec. 1955.

Arthur Kornhauser[15] prepared a useful check list of points to be considered in formulating questionnaires. (His discussion covers over twenty pages; here we indicate only the barest outline):

QUESTION CONTENT:

Is this question necessary for clear understanding: Just how will it be used?

Are several questions needed on the subject matter of this one question?

Do the respondents have the information necessary to answer the question?

Does the question need to be more concrete, more specific, and more closely related to respondent's experience?

Is the question content sufficiently general and free from spurious concreteness and specificity?

Is the question content biased or loaded in one direction—without accompanying questions to balance the emphasis?

QUESTION WORDING:

Do the questions contain difficult or unclear phraseology tending toward misunderstanding?

Do the questions adequately express the alternatives with respect to choices of responses?

Are the questions misleading by reason of unstated assumptions or unseen implications?

Is the wording biased? Is it emotionally loaded?

Is the question wording likely to be objectionable to the respondents?

Would a more personalized or less personalized wording of the question produce better results?

Can the question be better asked in a more direct or more indirect form?

QUESTION SEQUENCE:

Are the answers to the questions likely to be influenced by the content of the preceding questions?

[15]Kornhauser, "Questionnaire Construction and Interview Procedure," in Claire Selltiz *et al., Research Methods in Social Relations,* pp. 552–574. Holt, Rinehart & Winston, 1959. See also Matilda White Riley, *Sociological Research: II Exercises and Manual,* pp. 15, 17–21. Harcourt, Brace & World, 1963.

Are the questions led up to in a natural way? Are they in correct psychological order?

Do some questions come too early or too late from the point of view of arousing interest and receiving sufficient attention, avoiding resistance and inhibitions?

FIXED MEANING AND FLEXIBLE WORDING. Paul Lazarsfeld departs from the usual procedure of wording questions in such a way that the same reaction from interviewees is assured. He advocates a more flexible type of questionnaire and more liberal handling of questions in which fixed meanings are a more important consideration than fixed wording. When meaning is of paramount importance, then the interviewer holds himself responsible for knowing exactly what he is trying to discover, and he varies the wording in accordance with the interviewee's experience and understanding:

> The resulting margin of error would be greater if a standardized question were to be interpreted in very different ways by different respondents who have their own different experiences in mind. If we get the respondent to interpret to us the determinants of his experience to the best of his knowledge and recollection, our results would be much more homogeneous than in a case where we have flexible words but have not taken any care for ascertaining the meaning placed upon those words by our respondents. . . . By this method we find much easier access to the motives controlling his actions than if we try to compel the respondent to conform to a stereotyped questionnaire which he may not understand in the way we intend.[16]

Some such questions in a questionnaire as "What is most important to you when buying shoes: color . . . price . . . durability . . . style . . . quality . . . fit . . . ?" are ambiguous. The price, color, and style are easily ascertained items at the time of purchase. Quality and durability, on the other hand, are attributes which can be tested only after prolonged wearing of the shoes. At the time of purchase one person may attempt to judge quality by the type of leather, another by the purchase price. If the respondents indicate that they bought according to quality, they had assumed that quality could be determined at the time of purchase. Consequently, the whole group of these responses should be recorded according to the concrete criteria used and not according to a word which implies a tacit assumption unknown to the interviewee.

[16]Lazarsfeld, "The Art of Asking WHY in Marketing Research," *The National Marketing Review* (Summer 1935), pp. 31–32.

Studies of comparative values of mail questionnaires and personal interviews have been made by several competent researchers. (See, for example, the work of Paul Lazarsfeld and Raymond Franzen, by Albert Ellis, by Helen Metzner and Floyd Mann.) Lazarsfeld and Franzen believe that their findings "substantiate several claims that are usually made for mail answers: (a) bias that comes from the respondents' desires to impress or conceal from the interviewer is eliminated; (b) answers to personal questions are more frequently given in an anonymous mail reply; (c) a mail reply is filled out at leisure and thus produces a more thoughful answer."[17]

Other studies point also to the fact that self-administered questionnaires—which remove the physical presence of the interviewer and the possibility of interpersonal involvement—thereby decrease interviewer effect and, consequently, bias. Herbert Hyman, however, believes it is a mistake to assume that the physical absence of interviewer excludes "reactive effect" upon respondents. The latter guide themselves by, anticipate the reactions of, the person who will read the replies. "Thus," Hyman concludes," qualitative data support the notion that there may be present an interviewer effect, even when there is no interviewer. Moreover, the very absence of an interviewer may act as a biasing factor. For in some respects the interviewer might act as a check on tendencies among respondents to distort data in some way that will serve their ego-effects."[18]

Mechanics of the Questionnaire and Schedule

In addition to considering the problems of communication and the form of the response in constructing the question, there are other features that should be considered in the design of schedules and questionnaires.

TO FACILITATE TABULATIONS. Ideally, a complete set of tables should be prepared in advance of the construction of inquiry forms. In actual practice this feat is seldom achieved. However, it is possible to construct and arrange questions with a view toward their forming

[17]Lazarsfeld and Franzen, "The Validity of Mail Questionnaires in Upper Income Groups" (privately distributed). Quoted by Herbert Hyman, *op. cit.*, pp. 142–143.

[18]Hyman, *ibid.*, p. 139.

a logical tabulation scheme, even if the particulars of that scheme are not fully known at the time. Wherever feasible, items should be precoded so as to facilitate punching of tabulation cards directly from the schedules and questionnaires and to avoid the use of an intermediate document such as a transcription sheet. To have the items precoded is also an advantage if the data are to be manually processed. It is recommended that sufficient space be left for coding the entries that have been written in, such as occupation, industry, type of illness or whatever answers may have been required by the open-end inquiries.

If the document is to be processed through special methods, such as the mark-sensing method used in the Current Population Survey conducted each month by the Bureau of the Census, the questionnaire is also the machine card and must be designed accordingly. In special operations of this kind, the initial construction of the questionnaire may present more of a challenge, but this drawback is offset by the integration achieved between the collection methods and the tabulating program.

(Among newest and fastest tabulating equipment in use at the time of writing is the Univac* tabulating machine. Using magnetized tape, it has a speed of the equivalent of 2,000–2,500 80-column punch cards going through the machine per minute. To use the Univac equipment, the inquiry form does not need to be especially designed for that purpose.)

TYPE USED IN THE PRINTING OF INQUIRY FORMS. Agencies that use such printed forms can, of course, vary the size and even the color of the printing used, with advantageous effects. For example, the questions could be printed in bold-face type (or one color) and the instructions and other directions in light-face type (or another color). Such a device would remind the interviewer of the different procedures to be followed and would facilitate understanding of the form by respondents in a self-enumeration study.

KIND OF PAPER. The kind of paper used should depend upon the amount of writing and erasing to be done, the number of copies to be made, the durability and opacity needed. The choice is often affected

*Univac is a contrived name, originating in the 1950's, from the words *Univ*ersal *A*utomatic *C*omputer. The design and construction of the electric equipment is a very dynamic art or science, and faster machines are anticipated.

by the tools to be used, whether pen, pencil, or typewriter. The durability required depends upon whether the form is to have ordinary, routine, or extra handling. It is also important to consider the need for permanency of the record, since paper varies widely in this regard.

MARGINS. In all printed forms, a 3/8-inch margin is necessary on one side and 1/5 or 1/6 inch on all other sides to allow for the grippers of the printing press. If the form is to be bound, margins need to conform to the type of binder used.

SPACING. Forms to be filled out by persons in a self-enumeration study or by interviewers must leave spaces in proportion to the size of the entry to be made, with some allowance for different sizes of writing. If the form is to be filled in by typewriter, it should conform to typewriter spacing.

ITEMS OF THE FORM. Certain items are mandatory for most forms and questionnaires. These are listed below.

1. The identification of the agency or organization collecting the data should appear in a prominent place on the front of the form. If the information is collected by one agency and sponsored by another, the names of both agencies should be shown. If the forms are to be returned by mail, the address to which they are to be sent must be clearly specified.
2. The title of the study or survey should be on the front page of the form and usually it is desirable to have it appear in large print. Printing and spacing devices can both be used for obtaining effective emphasis on the major items of the form.
3. The authority or basis for the collection of the information should be stated. If the inquiry is from a federal agency, a Budget Bureau approval number and an expiration date are required.
4. The confidentialness of the data should be made clear in such a way that the respondent will be assured of protection.
5. The dates of the period covered by the report should be stated in advance, or space should be left for them to be filled in by the respondent or the interviewer.
6. If footnotes are needed, the space for recording them should be clearly identified and the amount of space should be determined by the expected number and type.

7. A place for the date on which the form is filled out should be provided.
8. A place should be provided for the signature of the respondent or the interviewer, unless none is required.
9. It is usually advisable to assign a serial number to each questionnaire in order to identify it easily, and to facilitate the control of interviewing assignments.
10. When a questionnaire contains more than one page, each page should be numbered. If the interviewer is permitted to use extra forms, an item should be inserted for the purpose of identifying each form used; for example: Form ______ of ______ forms.

COVERING LETTERS. Covering letters are used in self-enumeration studies and, to some extent, in personally conducted interviews. In the latter case, they are usually mailed in advance, although they may be left at the household at the conclusion of the interview. Sometimes a letter is mailed in advance and also left at the end of the interview. Brief covering letters are often printed on the form itself, in which case they are usually at the beginning of the form.

The purpose of the questionnaire or the study should be stated in the covering letter, and assurance should be given that the information wanted will be given confidential treatment. The personal appearance of the letter is especially important if the study is launched under auspices not generally recognized by the public. Requests to participate in the study—which may ultimately aid in social improvement—have also been thought to stimulate responses from large numbers of people.

Follow-up letters are used often in surveys where the questionnaires are placed and returned through the mails. Only in some instances are these known to have increased the returns significantly.[19] The specific factors responsible for a large percentage of returns to various types of questionnaires are largely unknown, and further study is needed in this area.

Errors in the Use of Questionnaires

The recognition of the need for measurement of errors present in survey data has developed at an accelerated rate within recent years.

[19]See Carl F. Reuss, "Differences Between Persons Responding and Not Responding to a Mail Questionnaire," *American Sociological Review,* VIII, 433–438.

Actual studies designed to measure errors have not kept pace with the awareness of the need, but such studies have been on the increase in number and have become more comprehensive in scope. As Eckler has pointed out:

> One reason for this increased emphasis is undoubtedly the great expansion in the number and types of sample surveys. . . . A second reason for the increased emphasis upon measuring the accuracy of statistics is to be found in the fact that new and powerful tools are provided for this purpose through recent developments in the sampling field. Except for these developments, the cost of any adequate check of the quality of a survey would still be prohibitively great.[20]

Errors in surveys have been the subject of many studies and experiments in an attempt to learn about their nature and sources. A classification and discussion of such errors appear in a paper by W. E. Deming[21] in which he lists thirteen factors affecting the ultimate usefulness of a survey. These factors include both sampling and nonsampling errors. Among the nonsampling errors are included variability in response and imperfections in the design of the questionnaire.

VARIABILITY IN RESPONSE. In his discussion of variability in response, Deming states: "There are two kinds of variability in response, different descriptions of the same situation, (i) given by the same person at two different times; (ii) given by different persons." This observation is borne out by the results of a study conducted by Gladys Palmer, even when applied to such clearly definable units as age and occupation. In a recanvass of 8,500 persons in Philadelphia, after an interval of 8 to 10 days, 10 per cent of the ages reported differed by one or more years when reported by the same respondents in both canvasses, and 17 per cent were different when reported by different respondents.[22]

CONSISTENT RESPONDENT ERROR. In contrast to variability in response, Marks and Mauldin[23] distinguish consistent respondent error

[20]See A. Ross Eckler and Leon Pritzker, "Measuring the Accuracy of Enumerative Surveys," *Proceedings of the International Statistical Institute,* New Delhi, India, 1951.

[21]Deming, "On Errors in Surveys," *American Sociological Review,* IX, 359–369.

[22]"Factors in the Variability of Response in Enumerative Studies," *Journal of the American Statistical Association,* XXXVIII, 143–152.

[23]Eli S. Marks and W. Parker Mauldin, "Response Errors in Census Research," *Journal of the American Statistical Association,* XLV, 424–438.

(bias) as a contributing factor to errors in surveys. They point out that a "major difficulty with a quality check through reinterviewing is that it does not detect consistent respondent error unless there is a substantial shift in approach." The conditioning effect of the first interview is believed to carry over to the second interview. One example cited in this discussion relates to obtaining the estimated rental value of owned dwelling units. A period of two weeks elapsed between the two interviews, and during the second interview, typical of the response was the following: "I really don't know. We've never rented the place. I told the lady who was here before $50 and that's about the best I can guess."

PRETESTING AND CHECKING SCHEDULES AND QUESTIONNAIRES. Much experimental work has been done in pretesting the qualities of schedules and questionnaires before they are put in circulation. They may need considerable and expensive revision after they have been printed and may be embarrassing after they have been distributed. The questions which do not draw forth consistent or definite responses should be revised unless one is studying individual differences rather than pursuing general conclusions. Indefinite responses invalidate all of the conclusions related to such responses. Pretesting provides not only a test of the clarity of the questions and of the correctness of interpretation put upon them by the respondent, but it also affords the possibility of discovery of new aspects of the problem studied but not anticipated in the planning stage. In short:

> The method of pretesting provides a means of detecting mistakes on procedure before they exact heavy penalties in the form of low proportion of returns or of replies lacking in reliability and validity. Pretesting is essentially a trial and error procedure wherein the successful trials are repeated and the errors are avoided when the final questionnaire is sent to the final group. Through the wider use of pretesting, it may even be possible to appease the critics who have so frequently and justly condemned questionnaires of the past.[24]

RECORD CHECKS. Other tests of the validity of survey data include checks against available records from various public programs. Some types of validations are being done in the health survey field. A subsample of the 1950 and 1960 Population Census statistics was subjected

[24]R. F. Sletto, "Pretesting of Questionnaires," *American Sociological Review*, V, 200.

to the following types of record checks: age against birth certificates; veteran status against files of Veterans Administration; citizenship status against records of the Immigration and Naturalization Service; income and industry classifications against wage and salary reports in the files of the Social Security Administration and tax returns in the Bureau of Internal Revenue. Such checks are valuable but are limited to the extent that the file of records may be incomplete or may cover only certain classes of the population. The matching of the two sets of records is often inconclusive and, again, there is the problem of dealing with the unmatched cases—sometimes these represent a significant number of persons.

Organization of Data from Questionnaires[25]

The ideally planned questionnaire is one that is formulated after the analytical program has been shaped and the final tables to be presented have been specified. The extent to which a questionnaire reflects advance planning in this regard determines the amount and kind of work required to organize the data prior to tabulation. Certain steps, which are independent of the relative efficiency of the questionnaire itself, are essential, however, for organizing questionnaire data. (The ensuing discussion applies equally to data on schedule forms.)

A review of the questionnaire entries, generally referred to as the editing operation, is one essential step. The scope of the edit will vary according to the complexity of the data and the size of the survey. The coding of entries will also be necessary, and this step will involve careful selection of categories that are in line with the principles and concepts of the study. A suitable method for tabulating the data must be selected, preferably in advance of the preparatory work of editing and coding.

If the material from the study is to be tabulated by hand methods of sorting and counting, or if tally sheets are to be used, work sheets for recording the totals of the counts and sorts will need to be designed. Also, a special transcription card may be needed, since a form best suited for field recording may not be easiest for hand sorting and counting. If the material is to be machine-tabulated, a punch card, as well as specifications for the machine runs, must be prepared. If the questionnaire was not designed to make it feasible for punching ma-

[25]Prepared by Mrs. Katherine Gordon Capt.

chine cards directly, a transcription sheet will be needed for transferring information from the questionnaire to a sheet designed in the same manner as the punch card to be used.

EDITING. Editing involves an inspection of the questionnaire for the purpose of detecting omissions and inadequate entries and for making relationship checks for consistency. Inadequate entries are usually found in connection with such descriptive items as the kinds of work people do—subject to occupation and industry coding—or the kinds of illnesses occurring in the population—subject to medical diagnostic coding. Relationship checks are planned when two figures are closely related; for example, total days lost from work on account of illness cannot be greater than total days of illness.

Although editing is set up primarily to *prevent* the tabulation of incorrect information, it is often desirable to use it as a supplement to a machine edit after the data have been transferred to punch cards. A machine edit is designed to identify impossible codes or code combinations and errors in magnitudes and arithmetic resulting from the punch-card operation, as well as inconsistencies not detected in the editing and coding operations.

Editing may be set up as an operation at several different levels. It may be in the field office, the central office, or in both, depending upon the nature of the data and whether the results of editing are to be used as a control of the field work. At each level of editing it is important to have detailed instructions and procedures for carrying out the operation. If a count of errors is to be used for qualifying interviewers, for example, critical and noncritical errors must be specified in advance and the instructions for applying these criteria must be included. Where the major portion of the editing is to be done in the central office, it is still desirable to have at least a minimum field edit to screen out totally unacceptable work in order to facilitate its return to the interviewers for correction.

In large-scale surveys a screening operation, set up as a step prior to editing, can be useful. Such an operation may consist of inspecting all questionnaires or a sample of the work of each interviewer. The purposes of a screening operation are to reject poor work—which is either sent to editing for "repair" or returned to the field for correction—and to speed up the flow of acceptable work to the subsequent operations. For the screening to operate successfully it is necessary to establish a permissible number of errors, which will vary by type of item, so that work passing the screening test is free from major defects.

CODING. Coding consists of setting up classes or categories to be used in presenting the data and then assigning a symbol, usually numerical, to each answer which falls into a predetermined class. When the classes have been agreed upon in advance, it is possible and, for some types of data, desirable to print the codes on the questionnaire. In such cases, the interviewer circles or checks the symbol suitable to the response.

Precoding the questionnaire has some obvious advantages, such as making it possible to eliminate all or major portions of an office-coding operation. It also permits direct punching of the machine cards from the questionnaire. Less easily seen are some disadvantages of precoded questionnaires. These frequently outweigh the advantages. One of the possible dangers is that the categories selected may prove too general for revealing inconsistencies in reporting. Another danger lies in the "catch-all" categories such as "All other" or "Miscellaneous," which may cloak meaningful information unless explained by the interviewers. Because of these and similar reasons, the most prudent practice appears to be a combination of precoded and noncoded items. Those to which the respondent categorized his own answers, such as "yes-no" and multiple-choice questions, are often precoded, while the more complex items are handled in a central coding operation after the data have been collected.

A central-office coding operation may be organized in several different ways. The decision to use each coder for coding all items of information or to divide the work into subject-matter fields and assign different coders to different subjects should depend on the nature of the data and the number of questionnaires involved. It is often feasible to set up a general coding section for handling relatively simple factual items and to organize special coding groups for handling the more complicated items such as occupation and industry, medical information, and attitudinal or opinion statements which require special technical training in applying the codes.

Verification of the coding may be made on a complete basis or on a sample basis.[26] If sample verification is used, the procedure usually

[26]See Joseph F. Daly and Leon Gilford, "Sample Verification and Quality Control Methods in the 1950 Census," in Morris H. Hansen, William N. Hurwitz, and William G. Madow, *Sample Survey Methods and Theory,* Vol. I, pp. 618–625, John Wiley & Sons, 1953.

is to check all work of each coder at first until he reaches a predetermined level of accuracy. After achieving the standard, the coder becomes qualified to have only a portion of his work checked. A qualified coder, then, remains on sample verification as long as his work meets the standard set for the sample that is being verified.

Reliability of the coding is another problem. It may arise from a number of different sources. The judgment of the coder may be unreliable—for example, he may develop certain perspectives in relation to the material which cause him to categorize the data in a biased direction or, on the other hand, he may not be sufficiently deliberate and reflective in judging the responses. Another factor affecting reliability may be that inadequate information appears on the questionnaire, or that inappropriate answers not pertinent to the subject have been reported. Or, the validity of the categories themselves may be in question—they may not be mutually exclusive, or a clear line of demarcation may not have been made between similar classes, making it difficult to distinguish between them. One type of test for reliability in coding, which has been used with some success, is a rotation scheme for independent coding in which the same information is coded by different sets of coders and the analyses are made of the similarities and differences in the application of the codes, using statistical methods for computing reliability.

TRANSCRIPTION SHEETS. In addition to being used as intermediate documents in preparing material from questionnaires prior to tabulations, transcription sheets can be used efficiently for other purposes. By transcription to a document-sensing or mark-sensing card, for example, it is possible to save the costs of manual punching of cards, since punched cards can be reproduced mechanically from the document-sensing or mark-sensing card. When this device is used, the document-sensing or mark-sensing card is set up to follow the columns of a punch card and is, therefore, subject to such limitations of a punch card as the number of columns and the number of digits in any one column. Transcription sheets are also useful for: 1) combining information that has been reported on an individual basis into units representing several persons, such as household or family units, and 2) drawing together related items of information about an individual reported in different sections of a questionnaire. One example of this integrating process is in fertility studies, where a variety of personal characteristics of the individual is analyzed in conjunction with other pertinent data such as size of family, number of children ever born, and similar information.

In summary, the wide use of schedules and questionnaires as independent research tool is a controversial issue. There is more agreement that, if used as a subsidiary research tool, these forms can often be of advantage in a great variety of studies. The disadvantages of schedules and questionnaires stems from: 1) the difficulty of ascertaining the representativeness of the data obtained through these means; and therefore, the generalizations may be said to be based on "unknown" samples. Further difficulties are presented by 2) vague phraseology or questions not readily understood by the masses in all walks of life who are expected to supply data; 3) replies which may have been answered in a perfunctory manner. 4) Uniform questions—a desirable attribute of schedules and questionnaires—do not always "fit" the varied groups, varied cultural patterns, and levels of education of the large numbers of people participating in the study. 5) It is often difficult to learn the meaning to the respondent of the data supplied. Ambiguity, either in wording or meaning of data, is one of the greatest sources of error in surveys. This is especially true in subject matter involving attitudes, estimates, and subjective data which, at best, have a low reliability.

Of prime import in the construction of schedules and questionnaires are: 1) definiteness and concreteness, 2) simplicity of questions, 3) freedom from possibilities of subjective evaluation, 4) care in removing tendencies to put the replies in respondent's mouth. The units of enumeration need to be so precisely defined that they will assure accurate and full information. Everyday language of practical affairs has proved to be the most useful, since it alone can capture the thinking of the public.[27] Questions should be constructed with a view to their forming a logical part of a specific tabulation plan. This procedure points to both superfluous questions and those which have been omitted but need to be included.

Carefully constructed schedules and questionnaires are held to have some advantages over the personal interview. The former provide privacy and leisurely pace, so respondent can reflect on the questions raised and weigh his responses to them. (This opportunity might often be an advantage, but may turn out to be a disadvantage since such

[27] John Madge, *Tools of Social Science,* p. 57. Longmans, Green and Co., 1953.

"second thoughts" with insecure respondents might not always produce reliable answers.)

Schedules and questionnaires are capable of reaching a large number of diverse people relatively speedily and at a fraction of the cost of the personal interview. It is often pointed out that when highly intimate information is sought, the mail questionnaire offers the desired anonymity and thus ensures reliable replies. (Kinsey's experience in gathering sex data through the personal interview would not support this contention.) In spite of their shortcomings—which are being gradually eliminated—schedules and questionnaires are being increasingly used, especially in research surveys.

9

the interview as a tool in field research

Oh, mortal man, be wary how you judge.

DANTE

"I did that," says my memory. "I could not have done that," says my pride, and remains inexorable. Eventually — the memory yields.

NIETZSCHE

"The conversation of gestures."[1] Interviewing is not a simple two-way conversation between an interrogator and informant. Gestures, glances, facial expressions, pauses often reveal subtle feelings. Voice inflections and halting statements can be as much a part of the interplay between conversing persons as their questions and answers. Harry Stack Sullivan, the famous American psychiatrist, points out that as much can be learned from verbal expressions as from vocal, that is, pertaining to the use of sounds. He suggests that we should pay more attention than we now do to tell-tale aspects of "intonation, rate of speech, difficulties in enunciation, and so forth. . . . It is by alertness to the importance of these many things as signs or indicators of meaning, rather than preoccupation only with words spoken, that . . . interviews become practical."[2] Furthermore, not only reactions to a statement but also attitudes can be learned from a blush, nervous laugh, sudden pallor, or undue embarrassment. This behavior is in itself important data for the interviewer.

Philosopher Martin Buber goes even further by saying that "at times, for a conversation to be meaningful, no sign is necessary, not even a

[1]Expression used by George H. Mead.

[2]Sullivan, "The Psychiatric Interview," *Psychiatry: Journal for the Study of Interpersonal Procedures,* XIV (Nov. 1951), 362.

gesture. Speech can denounce all media of sound and still be a speech. . . . Expression and discernment . . . can often be satisfied by a glance; indeed by a mere sharing of a gaze which is rich in inward relations."[3] This is not a statement by a mystic. We all have experienced that penetrating look which pierced innermost thought.

Alfred C. Kinsey, in his famed studies of sexual behavior, reports watching for involuntary reactions which betray a person's emotions:

> A minute change of facial expression, a slight tensing of a muscle, the flick of an eye, a trace of a change in one's voice, a slight inflection or change in emphasis, a slight change in one's rate of speaking, slight hesitancies in putting a question or in following up with the next question, one's choice of words, one's spontaneity in inquiring about items that are off the usual routine, or any of a dozen and one other involuntary reactions . . . [can be noticed even by] unlettered persons or persons of mentally lower levels . . . in ways that may not involve spoken words but which are nonetheless, readily comprehended. . . .[4]

It is evident that the interaction that takes place in an interview is highly complex. What the interviewers hear should be regarded by them as representing merely "the perception of the informant, filtered and modified by his cognitive and emotional reactions and reported through his personal verbal usages [of] the picture of the world as he sees it . . . as he is willing to pass it on to us in *this particular interview situation.* Under other circumstances the moves he reveals to us may be much different."[5] Every interview has its own balance of revelation and of withholding of information. Only under very unusual circumstances is an interview so completely expository that every phrase can be taken at face value.[6]

The personal interview has been variously defined. It may seen as an effective, informal verbal and nonverbal conversation, initiated for specific purposes and focused on certain planned content areas. The objectives of the interview may be exchange of ideas and experiences, eliciting of information pertaining to a wide range of data in which

[3]Buber, *Between Man and Man,* pp. 3–4. Macmillan Company, 1948.

[4]Kinsey *et al., Sexual Behavior of the Human Male,* p. 42. W. B. Saunders Co., 1948. Kinsey, in a very provocative manner, devotes some 30 pages to techniques of interviewing, which are worth studying carefully.

[5]John P. Dean and W. F. Whyte, "How Do You Know If the Informant Is Telling the Truth?" *Human Organization,* XVII, 34.

[6]Mark Benney and Everett C. Hughes, "Of Sociology and the Interview," *American Journal of Sociology,* LXII, 137.

the interviewee may wish to rehearse his past, define his present, and canvass his future possibilities. As the very term implies, *inter*viewing is an interactional process. It is a mutual view of each other.

Every verbal response and nonverbal reaction may be an "eye opener" for a whole new train of thoughts. An answer may not be only a response to a question but also a stimulus to progressive series of other relevant statements about social and personal phenomena which might indicate cause-effect relationships and, at times, may lead to formulation of hypotheses regarding sociopersonal interaction.

Major objectives of the research interview. In modern complex secondary society, experiences are highly varied. Few people share a common lot; their attitudes and values are often quite divergent. Many people can live within a protective wall of anonymity, even though they brush elbows daily. With the growth of urban life, the former more intimate face-to-face contacts are decreasing even in primary social groups, and social distances widen. It becomes the task of the interviewer to penetrate the outer and inner life of persons and groups and learn what T. W. Adorno terms "levels of personality." It is essential, he says "to ascertain opinions, attitudes, values that [are] on the surface; . . . ideological trends that [are] more or less inhibited and reach the surface only in indirect manifestations; and [for psychoanalytically oriented interviewers to explore] personality forces in the subject's unconsciousness."[7]

For purposes of obtaining life history data, that is, an intimate full account of a person's experiences, attitudes, and values during his entire life cycle, it is important to gain "a portrait of human personality" which is broad enough to encompass the social background that governs his present scheme of life, and deep enough to reveal inner strivings, tensions, wishes, and changes in his behavioral relations. In free-flowing accounts, interviewees may suggest explanations of their behavior which may account for their motivations and actions and provide new insights not afforded by other exploratory techniques.

Anthropologist Benjamin D. Paul of Stanford sees the aims of the interview as gathering and relating two sets of data:

> A description of the situation as [the field worker] sees it, looking from the outside in, and a description of a situation as he sees it, look-

[7]Adorno *et al., The Authoritarian Personality,* pp. 11–12. Harper & Row, Publishers, 1950.

ing from the inside out. The first comprises the visible world of objects and actions. . . . [The second], the subjective frame of reference, embraces the world view of the people, the pattern of assumptions that guides their perceptions, the network of meanings that binds their percepts into a semblance of a system, the hierarchy of values animating their actions. He needs also to ascertain . . . the cultural wherefore.[8]

It is hard to visualize an empirical study in which the interview did not play a major role during some aspect of the investigation. Thomas and Znaniecki interviewed many subjects in their studies of personal adjustment of immigrants to new social situations. The Lynds in their study of Middletown interviewed all classes and ranks of society. Kinsey and associates interviewed thousands of people, including children, regarding sex habits and practices. Some of the most sophisticated interview techniques were used in the study of *Authoritarian Personality* by Adorno and associates.[9] The interview was used extensively by Stouffer in the study of *The American Soldier.* Market researchers and public opinion pollsters use the interview steadily. As early as the dawn of the twentieth century, formal sociologists and social anthropologists conceived of interviewing:

Not merely as a sounding of individual minds as with [persons] with attitudes coming from psychology; they used it as a supplement to direct observation in search, like that of the seeker of culture patterns, for the regularities of actual social behavior. [But] they all agree, with other naturalists, that one gets primary data about behavior of even so talkative an animal as man from what he sees men do; they do not feel happy with those psychologists of social science who seem to be interested only in what men say. They concede meanings to be important, but they insist meanings are interpretable only against a background of behavior.[10]

Some Types of Interviews

Interviews may be classified in various ways—according to their function (diagnostic, treatment, research, sample interviews), or ac-

[8]Paul, "Interview Techniques and Field Relations," in A. L. Kroeber (Ed.), *Anthropology Today,* p. 442. University of Chicago Press, 1953. Reprinted by permission.

[9]See Else Frenkel-Brunswick, "The Interviews as an Approach to the Prejudiced Personality," in Adorno *et al., The Authoritarian Personality,* pp. 291–336.

[10]See Conrad Arensberg, "Behavior and Organization," in John H. Rohrer and Muzafer Sherif (Eds), *Social Psychology at the Cross Roads,* pp. 326 ff. Harper & Row, 1951.

cording to number of persons participating (group or individual interviews), or length of contact (short- or long-contact), or type of approach (directive or nondirective, structured or unstructured). Here we are presenting briefly types of interviews based chiefly on the respective roles assumed in them by interviewer and interviewee.

The nondirective interview. This type of interview is also designated as uncontrolled, or unguided, or unstructured. Whatever the designation, interviewers in these types of interviews do not follow a system or list of predetermined questions. Interviewees are encouraged to relate their concrete experiences with no or little direction from interviewer, to dwell on whatever events seem significant to them, to provide their own definitions of their social situations, report their own foci of attention, reveal their attitudes and opinions as they see fit. During a free-flowing interview, the nondirective interviewer at times is at a loss to know how actively he should participate during the course of the discussion. As long as pertinent facts are being related and the informant shows no signs of lack of interest, the interviewer need only round out the discussion by raising additional questions, if need be.[11]

The directive interview. This interview uses a highly standardized technique and a set of predetermined questions. It is especially useful for administrative and market research of various types:

> This routine application of the survey method has led to a very efficient procedure of handling the problems of sampling, question construction, [formal] interviewing, and the analysis of the results. Unfortunately, although the procedures on these points have been reduced to an easily understood set of rules which eliminate the worst errors of handling, they have not led to the development of a method capable of handling but the most simple and superficial of concepts . . . and have contributed little to our knowledge of attitudes, preferences, or behavior.[12]

(The directive interview often takes the form of a questionnaire, the nature, advantages, and limitations of which were discussed in the preceding chapter.)

[11]See R. K. Merton, *Mass Persuasion,* pp. 13–14. Harper & Row, Publishers, 1946.

[12]John Madge, *The Origins of Scientific Sociology,* pp. 533–534. The Free Press of Glencoe, 1962.

The focused interview. This is differentiated from other types of interviews by the following characteristics: 1) it takes place with persons known to have been involved in a particular concrete situation (these persons have seen a particular film, heard a particular broadcast, or have participated in an observed social situation); 2) it refers to situations which have been analyzed prior to the interview; 3) it proceeds on the basis of an interview guide which outlines the major areas of the inquiry and the hypotheses which locate pertinence of data to be secured in the interview; 4) it is focused on the subjective experiences—attitudes and emotional responses regarding the particular concrete situations under study.[13]

Although the whole situation is carefully structured and the major areas of the inquiry mapped out, the interviewee is given considerable freedom to express his definition of a situation that is presented to him. Therefore, the focused interview is regarded is semi-standardized. It may obviate some of the limitations of both the highly directive interview—with its structured battery of questions—and the nondirective, free-flowing clinical type of interview, which is time-consuming and nonstandardized.

The focused interview is based on the assumptions that through it, it is possible to secure precise details of personal reactions, specific emotions called into play, definite mental associations provoked by a certain stimulus, and the like. It is believed that these details are less likely to be distorted or to conceal the actual experiences than in general unfocused interviews of long or short duration. The interviewer, having previously analyzed the situation, is more alert and sensitive to inconsistencies or omission of details which are needed to clarify a given behavior pattern. Furthermore, without these specific, selective, consistent and pertinent details of the total responses, it is not possible to analyze spheres of tensions and their implications.

The focused interview has not yet come into its own. It has not been used as widely as its merits deserve, probably because it requires extreme care in preparation and exceptionally sophisticated handling by skillful interviewers.[14]

[13]R. K. Merton, and Patricia Kendall, "The Focused Interview," *American Journal of Sociology,* LI, 541–542.

[14]Cf. Madge, *op. cit.,* p. 533.

The repeated interview. This type of interview is particularly useful in attempts to trace the specific developments of a social or psychological process, that is, the progressive actions, factors, or attitudes which determine a given behavior pattern or social situation. Paul Lazarsfeld and his associates[15] made extensive use of the repeated interview technique in their study of how the voter makes up his mind in a presidential campaign. These interviews secured the progressive reactions of the voter which chart the specific development of influential factors entering into the choice of a President.

The repeated interview technique is expensive in time, energy, and money, but it offers the advantage of studying the progressive actions and events as they actually occur or of studying attitudes in the process of formation.

The data secured through focused as well as through repeated interviews lend themselves to quantitative interpretation, since they are consistent and specific and they aim at realistic details which can be differentiated, tabulated, and ultimately measured.

The depth interview. Dr. Fay B. Karpf, Rankian-oriented psychotherapist and social psychologist, defines the depth interview as one which:

> Deliberately aims to elicit unconscious as well as other types of material relating especially to personality dynamics and motivations. A depth interview is generally a lengthy procedure designed to encourage free expression of affectively charged information. It may be used in conjuction with special devices, such as free association and projective techniques [see our pages 265–266]. . . . When skillfully and cautiously used by an interviewer having specialized training, the depth interview can reveal important aspects of psycho-social situations which are otherwise not readily available and yet may be crucial for understanding observed behavior and reported opinions and attitudes.[16]

Unless the researcher has specialized training, it is best not to attempt depth interviewing.

[15]See Lazarsfeld *et al., The People's Choice.* Columbia University Press, 1948.

[16]Adapted from a personal communication, Jan. 1964. See also Dr. Karpf's *The Psychology and Pyschotherapy of Otto Rank*. The Philosophical Library, 1953. For an illustration of a lucidly presented and comprehensive account of a case, a cross-section of a life cycle, from an individual psychologist's point of view, see Alfred Adler, *The Case of Miss* R.: *The Interpretation of a Life Story.* Greenberg Publishers, 1929.

John Madge believes it would be prudent to conduct an experimental investigation to determine the differences between the questioning methods of the psychoanalysts and those of attorneys, since these differences are so great, not only in their practical features but also in their implications, as to appear unbridgeable. And yet, both methods have been used to elicit the same kind of facts, often pertaining to highly personal matters. The above suggestion was an outgrowth of Madge's analysis of Kinsey's techniques of interviewing, which the latter pioneered and developed in his studies of sexual behavior. Heretofore it was taken for granted that difficult affect-laden topics would require some form of psychoanalytic penetration into the near-unconscious, and that exceptional interviewing tact would be required to elicit correct answers to such questions as those pertaining to sexual practices. "Then Kinsey came along, using as his model the prosecuting lawyer rather than the psychoanalyst with his couch-side manner, and by all accounts his strict and direct, aggressive technique appeared to work."[17] Furthermore, Kinsey advocated "rapid-fire questioning." He believed that:

> In order to cover the maximum amount of material in a single interview, it is necessary to ask questions as rapidly as the subject can possibly comprehend and reply. This method has the further advantage of forcing the subject to answer spontaneously without too much premeditation. Such rapid-fire questions provide one of the most effective checks on fabrication, as detectives and other law-enforcement officials well know. . . . Looking an individual squarely in the eye, and firing questions at him with maximum speed, are two of the best guarantees against exaggeration.[18]

These techniques have not been tested and, in the hands of inexperienced interviewers, might be hazardous. Yet Kinsey is peculiarly sensitive to the necessity of establishing rapport:

> One is not likely to win the sort of rapport which brings a full and frank expression from a human subject unless he can convince the subject that he is desperately anxious to comprehend what his experience has meant to him. [Personal life] histories often involve a record of things that have hurt, of frustrations, of pain, of unsatisfied longings, of disappointments, of desperately tragic situations, and of complete catastrophes. The subject feels that the investigator who asks merely routine questions has no right to know about such things in another's history. The interviewer who senses what these things can mean, who

[17] Madge, *op. cit.,* pp. 534–535.
[18] Kinsey, *op. cit.,* p. 54.

at least momentarily shares something of the satisfaction, pain, or bewilderment which was the subject's, who shares something of the subject's hope that things will, somehow, work out right, is more effective though he may not be altogether neutral. . . .

[However, the capacity to remain neutral is at times severely tested.] Whatever one's own training and background, each person reaches the limit of things he can understand . . . and the limit of things he can sympathetically admit because he has glimpsed what they have meant to some other people. Beyond that there are always things which seem esthetically repulsive, provokingly petty . . . dishonorable, contemptable, or socially destructive. [Only] gradually one learns to forego judgments on these things, and to accept them merely as facts for the record. If one fails in his acceptance, he will know it by the sudden confusion or sudden tenseness of his subject, and the quick confusion of the story.[19]

Advantages of the interview as a research tool.[20] The research interview is not a separate and independent tool in social exploration. It is supplementary to other techniques. A combination of interviewing, observational, and statistical techniques often yields the best results, but the balance of emphasis shifts with the frame of reference and the objectives of the study. At times, for example, it may be more efficient for the investigator to observe directly a ritual performed by a group than to have it described by its members. Also, as Professor Paul points out, certain rituals, such as those performed at birth and death, rarely come to the attention of a research worker. However, subtle violations of or deviations from customs and mores, or gradual changes in a pattern of life or social organization of a group, may best be secured by asking uniform questions, rather than inferring them from observation alone. But observation may alert the observer to the manner, mood, and arrangement of behavior patterns or organization of life which might escape a field worker, using the personal interview alone.

As previously stated, the interview is a highly flexible tool in the hands of skillful interviewers. It allows a more permissive atmosphere than is the case when using other techniques of investigation. Questions not readily grasped by interviewees can be rephrased, or repeated with proper emphasis and explanations when necessary. Also, the

[19] *Ibid.*, p. 42–44. Reprinted with permission.

[20] For a comprehensive treatise see Herbert Hyman, *Interviewing in Social Research*. University of Chicago Press, 1954.

interviewer has greater opportunity to appraise the accuracy and validity of replies. Contradictory statements can be followed up and possible reasons for contradiction learned. The interviewer might also be able to differentiate on the spot between fact and fiction supplied by informants, their hearsay and impressions, convictions and opinions. In the presence of competent interviewers, interviewees often feel freer to express their fears, complexes, emotionally laden situations, than when filling out a questionnaire.

Only in the study of human beings is it possible for a scientist to talk to his subjects and investigate directly their feeling and thinking processes. The social scientist can secure about the object of his study a degree of intimate and personal knowledge that is denied to the natural scientists. The latter cannot communicate with the subjects despite all the instruments of precision.

Limitations of the interview. In spite of its many advantages, the interview also has many limitations that jeopardize its value, even when it is used as a supplementary research technique. Interviewers, on the one hand, may suffer from a "double dose of subjectivity" and may interject unwarranted interpretations, guesses, impressions into their data and report only informants' "public conduct."[21] On the other hand, interviewers deal frequently with subjects who are not too unsophisticated to modify facts by conscious volition, nor are they too innocent to lie. Interviewees, even though conscientious, may suffer from faulty perception, faulty memory, lack of insight, and inability to articulate. Ralph Berdie[22]—who has made an extensive study of the psychological elements in interviewing—found that, because memory and retention are highly selective processes, interviewees under proper circumstances generally gave accurate and vivid accounts of the most recent or the most intense experiences, or of the situations which they encountered most frequently. Painful or embarrassing experiences were frequently forgotten or consciously avoided. Psychoanalysts may elicit forgotten or repressed experiences by the process of depth interviewing, but few social research workers are qualified by training to use this technique. Therefore, many gaps and distortions may occur in the research data they secure.

[21]See R. L. Schank, *A Study of a Community and Its Groups and Institutions Conceived as Behavior of Individuals*. Psychological Manograph 43, 1932.

[22]Berdie, "Psychological Processes in Interviewing," *Journal of Social Psychology*, XVIII, 3–31.

Herbert Hyman[23] in his study of the interaction processes involved in interviewing, confirms some previously established facts: interviewers often approach their respondents with a prepared set of expectations as to how the latter will answer certain questions, or they develop these expectations in the course of the interview on the basis of early or incomplete responses. This interview bias and a priori thinking may distort and invalidate the results of the whole interview, even though some of the information gained is valid. A certain amount of preliminary thinking on how to approach a difficult or complex situation, however, may often be helpful, provided a number of choices or different views of the situation are developed.

Interviewers and interviewees often live in two different worlds of discourse; they have different social philosophies and may, therefore, ascribe different values and meanings to social phenomena. Neither can account for the other's *apperception mass,* and their minds may never meet. Under such circumstances, their points of view and interests may clash seriously and irreconcilably. What is needed is not so much a proficiency in interviewing as sensitive discretion and social and psychological insight into human nature. Since the interviewer may lack these qualities and since he and the interviewee may lack a common definition of the social situation, the data he secures may be useless for scientific purposes.

Even when both parties are within the same frame of reference, interviewees may consciously or unconsciously sidestep some of their most important experiences, and thus render the particular exploration "lopsided," fragmentary, incomplete, and often irrelevant. At times the interviewer holds rigidly to his objectives and is not sensitive to the value of the bypaths radiating out from the main scheme of his formulated plan. When he drives hard toward his own objectives, he tends to inject his own personal goal and may fail to see that of his subject.

The specialized types of interviews, particularly the structured and unstructured, also come in for their share of criticism. The structured interview, as well as the structured questionnaire, is not believed to yield reliable results, because it imposes selection of topics and thus controls the content of responses; it prescribes length of responses and thus may inhibit full revelations; it indicates form of response and may thereby frustrate even articulate informants in their attempts to relate

[23]Hyman, "Isolation, Measurement, and Control of Interviewer Effect," *Social Science Research Council Items* (June 1949), pp. 15–17. See also Hyman, *Interviewing in Social Research.* University of Chicago Press, 1954.

situations as they see them. Especially in interviews which aim to study characteristics of interviewees, the point is not "getting the subjects' answers to questions but in inducing him to talk freely and display his spontaneous tendencies, in place of cramping them within imposed limits of a question. [The interviewer's role] consists in placing every symptom in a mental context, in place of abstracting it from such a context."[24]

Unstructured interviews, in which neither selection, form, nor length of replies are imposed, may yield unsatisfactory data because of their inadequacy for statistical treatment and their subjective nature.

Social scientists agree, however, that any question is directive, suggestive, and assumptive, whether it is introduced to keep the account flowing, or to minimize irrelevancies and digressions, or to promote a feeling of security in a respondent. (The social and psychological processes involved in interviewing have received but fragmentary attention from social scientists. In spite of criticism leveled by them, little basic research has been completed which would aid in establishing a body of principles governing the process of interviewing. Therefore, interviewing remains largely an art, rather than a science.)

Many limitations ascribed to the interview are not inherent in its general technique or process but are due to faulty perception and ill-defined goals of particular interviewers. H. A. Cantril, who studied the questions that produced unsatisfactory responses to public opinion investigations, found that such questions were generally too vague or too obscure in meaning to permit precise answers. Misunderstandings occurred when the questions involved usage of technical terms or unfamiliar expressions, when the questions concerned themselves only with a portion of the population and were, therefore, meaningless to other people. Inadequate replies were secured when the choices offered were too many or too long for clear understanding, or when the implications of the questions asked were not seen by or not explained to the respondent. Cantril maintains that:

> The extent to which the wording of questions affects the answers obtained depends almost entirely on the degree to which the respondent's mental context is solidly structured. Where people have standards of judgment resulting in stable frames of reference, the same answer is likely to be obtained irrespective of the way questions are asked. . . . Where such standards of judgment are lacking, [people] are highly

[24]Quoted from Jean Piaget by Elton Mayo, *The Problem in Industrial Civilization,* p. 94. Harvard University Press, 1946.

suggestible to the implications of phrases, statements, innuendos or symbols of any kind that may serve as clues to help them make up their minds.[25]

The results obtained through experimentation by the Office of Public Opinion Research sound a clear warning: "Investigators must constantly be on the lookout for possible snags likely to be encountered between the time they themselves have a conception of an issue they want to pose to a sample population and the time they report the opinions of that population on the question they thought they were posing."

These and other criticisms of the interview stimulated efforts, at least in large-scale enterprises, to refine techniques, select more sophisticated interviewers, and devote more attention to their training. Greater informality, a more leisurely and casual approach have been stressed; more attention has been given to development of "complex batteries of questions designed to reveal [uniformly] the many-faceted character of attitudes . . ."[26] It has been recognized that some limitations of the interview can be overcome, at least partially, when interaction and interstimulation processes between respondent and interviewer are better understood by social scientists.

Some Techniques of Interviewing

Any discussion of interviewing techniques is of necessity oversimplified. Even if space permitted, it would not be possible to present the intertwined complexity of feeling tones, variable reactions, reflective thinking processes, symbolic silences, assumed roles, and levels of influence which enter into an interviewing relationship. Not even a continuously recorded transcription could transmit the essential dynamics which spur the interview, or keep it on an even keel, or cause it to deteriorate into a battle of wits, or cease altogether. We can only outline some factors which might, under certain circumstances, enhance satisfying face-to-face relationships, deepen understanding of

[25]Cantril, *Gauging Public Opinion,* pp. 48 and 22. Princeton University Press, 1944.

[26]Herbert Hyman, "Interviewing as a Social Process," in Daniel Lerner and Harold Lasswell, *The Policy Sciences,* p. 207. Stanford University Press, 1951.

the shifting roles, and point out some practical skills found useful by experienced interviewers.

Preparatory thinking. If preparation for an interview accomplishes nothing more than becoming immersed in the subject matter, it serves the purpose well. President Lincoln is reported to have said that, when he was to interview a person, he spent about one third of his time thinking what he would say and about two thirds what his interviewee would say. It is thus easier to approach the person whom "you already know in your imagination." It is possible to plan in advance and keep plan and mind flexible and expectant of new developments.

Convention requires that the interviewer be properly introduced to the interviewee. General letters of introduction "to-whom-it-may-concern" are of little value. The introduction should, if at all possible, be personal or by one who in a sense sponsors the interviewer. The interviewer should, whenever possible, be expected. He needs also to choose a "suitable" time and place in order to be recognized as soon as he gives his name. The most suitable place would be one where it is believed the interviewee will be most at ease.

Some knowledge of the daily routine of the interviewee is essential if a proper time and place are to be chosen. Preoccupation with other immediate interests and interruptions are to be avoided. Interviewers frequently make the mistake of assuming, when dealing with workmen or housewives and other lay persons, that it is not necessary to consider carefully questions of convention and convenience. These people also appreciate a gesture of politeness.

When studying a community or a cultural group it is often wise to interview the leaders first, to enlist their cooperation, and, if they see any justification for the study, to have them recommend the interviewer to others in the group. This is particularly true of an immigrant group. Once the cooperation of the Molokan elders was secured, the author of that study was sought out by a variety of members in the colony—both old and young, presenting a variety of viewpoints, situations, and social problems. The same situation applies to a large extent when making a study of a social organization or institution. The persons in charge should be approached first and their cooperation secured before any attempt is made to interview subordinates or inmates. "Back-door" approaches and encroachments should be avoided.

The approach to the interview. In the initial contact—after friendly greetings are exchanged in accordance with the cultural pattern of the interviewee—the purpose of the interview should be explained. This purpose, however, must be stated in terms of the interviewee's capacity to understand it. He is entitled to know why he is being interviewed, particularly since a considerable expenditure of his time and energy may be involved. Cooperation can be enlisted by asking for help in the study under way. It is frequently assumed that people who did not send for the interviewer and who have nothing to gain from him will not be willing to spare the time and information. In reality such a situation is far from the actual truth. It is often found that when the interviewer is oriented and intelligent about the subject under consideration, when the aim of his work is worthwhile, when he seeks out a convenient time and place and solicits help from interviewees objectively, when they see by his questions and manner that he has no ulterior motives but seeks information for scientific purposes, there is rarely any difficulty in securing it. Such expressions as the following, when sincerely meant and stated, might often start a flow of facts: "There are few persons who have such information as you have"; "What you are telling me is invaluable"; "You are showing me a new angle"; "You have brought many new facts to light"; "As far is I know, you are among the few in a position to supply the information."

A scientific purpose, well explained to the interviewee, and a competent skilled interviewer, with friendly manner, using an informal approach, lend meaning and dignity to an interview. Rapport under such circumstances follows as a matter of course. Kinsey[27] found that even when soliciting data on a tabu subject—sex practices—experienced interviewers were able to obtain frank information with a minimum of defensive reactions. He wrote: "In answer to our request for her [sex] history, a little grey-haired woman at a cabin door, out on the Western plains, epitomized what we had heard from hundreds of people: 'Of all things! In all my years I had never had such a question put to me! But if my experience will help you in your study, I'll give it to you.' " The average person responds to a genuinely scientific attitude and makes an effort to give revealing information. Well-trained interviewers, oriented toward, and interested in, their subject matter, report very few instances of noncooperation.

If the opening topic of conversation is trivial, it may fail to enlist

[27]Kinsey, *op. cit.,* p. 36.

interest. But whatever the opening statement, it should be within the frame of reference of the listener and within his ability to grasp it quickly and initially.

In search of a sympathetic, respectful listener. Experienced interviewers agree that listening is hard work. It requires self-restraint and self-discipline. Also patience and humility. The listener's role, at the moment, is neither that of therapist nor moral judge. Ability to listen with understanding, respect, and curiosity is the gateway to communication. When an interviewee feels that he will not meet with interruptions, denial, contradictions, and other harrassments, he is not likely to resist and withhold information. People are motivated to communicate when the atmosphere is permissive, the attitude non-judgmental; when the listener is so genuinely absorbed in the revelations that he can identify himself, at least vicariously, and gain sympathetic insight into what Robert Redfield called that "little fraction of the human comedy, or drama in which one has become embroiled."

However, mere listening is not sufficient. The listener must steadily reflect on the significance of the account given from the standpoint of: 1) facts; 2) feeling tones; 3) impact of the account on the informant. Thus, the quiet listener must be at the same time an analytic listener. He must watch every turn of a free-flowing account and make mental associations which would aid in checking the consistency of the facts provided. He may temporarily hold in suspense questions on points which need elaboration or verification, but he must avoid, as far as feasible, breaking into critical zones and thus interrupting the flow of the account. At times it may be necessary to jot down unobtrusively the intended questions for later and more timely interrogation.

Sympathetic insight, or ability to enter imaginatively and reflectively into another person's life, is based on the intellectual and rational awareness of another's world of discourse. According to Charles Horton Cooley, "all of the devices of personal communication would fail to win across the void and to bring two beings closer together, were it not for a mutual understanding of each other. A person of definite purpose who comprehends our way of life is sure to exert power over us. He cannot altogether be resisted; because if he understands us, he can make us understand him."[28] On this point Herbert Hyman[29] issues a word of caution: "guard against the over-rapport."

[28]Cooley, *Human Nature and Social Order,* p. 142. Charles Scribner's Sons, 1902.

[29]Hyman, "Interviewing as a Scientific Procedure," *op. cit.,* p. 214.

In short interviews in particular, he believes, a friendly warm approach may make the opening easier but render the interview invalid. The interviewee wants to make an adaptation to his "friend," and too much identification and too much courtesy results in tailoring replies to the image of a "nice interviewer." Note, however, that the stress here falls on "too much . . . ," on "over-rapport." Discretion is the better part of valor in striking a happy medium.

In the early stages of interviewing, the amount of identifying and of directing should be "attuned to the psychological needs of the informant. In the later phases, after rapport has been established [the amount of directing] can be varied according to the informational needs of the interviewer."[30]

It is not too difficult to find persons who are willing to provide considerable material about themselves. Many people are filled with tensions and seek out a "good listening ear." Some hope to find help in analyzing their experiences. Some are stimulated by the sympathetic interest or flattered by the request to help in a study. Others find themselves interesting subjects to talk about. But comparatively few have the ability to make themselves "visible" from the inside out. The very conception of the interview, as a relationship freely and willingly entered into by the informant, suggests an interest, or desire, or need to be "viewed." The implied "promissory element" gives the interviewer confidence and expectance to get cooperation, provided, however, that he in his role shows no compulsion, coercion, or condescension and is able to bite his tongue, if necessary, before interrupting the process of revelation. Some skilled interviewers advise not only undivided attention but personal warmth, "the whole warm human fellowship and not a mere cool sliver of yourself." Rapport is gained most readily with such feelings of friendliness, feelings that an interviewer shares in the interviewee's goal.

"People tell you more when you are looking at them with understanding and sympathy. It is a kind of hypnosis", concluded Edna Ferber,[31] novelist and newspaper reporter. "Looking" here means "a straight look between the eyes," which Kinsey found as highly effective in his interviews. And Robert Bales observed: "Nothing tones up the general harmony of a group like a strong undercurrent of eye contact."

[30]Paul, *op. cit.,* p. 445.

[31]Ferber, *A Peculiar Treasure,* p. 111. Lancer Books, Inc., 1960.

At times we find interviewers who are patient, reserved, sympathetic listeners at the beginning of a free-flowing interview, but their prolonged silence may eventually disarm them. Merton found interviewers who fear a challenge to their status as explorers. They feel impelled to assume a more dynamic overt role and shift the emphasis to the inerview guide. Such untimely emphasis on formal questions may irritate the interviewee who may withdraw or who may feel reluctant to depart from his self-exploration, particularly if he has revealed intimate and personal data to which he has not yet succeeded in giving his own emphasis or interpretation. At this point the interview may even degenerate into "a battle of wits," with interviewer and interviewee struggling to retain their own role. The latter may lose confidence in the former's ability to "understand."

Professor Ferdynand Zweig found that the success of his interviews with London laborers depended primarily on his insight, friendliness, willingness to safeguard the interests of informants, and on what he calls "flow of energy." He says: "When my flow of energy was low or when I was ignorant of the living and labor conditions, the interviews were a failure. Some interviews served only as an introduction to other more complete and satisfactory talks for which I was already prepared."[32] In another connection he states that his research "inquiry was like a fascinating film, a new adventure and experiment in living [in which he] learned more about life in the course of a few months than in many years before, sitting in libraries and lecturing at universities. . . ."[33]

The oft-repeated but always apt remarks from Benjamin Franklin's writings also apply vigorously to the interview. The following embodies within itself a point worthy of our consideration:

> I made it a rule to forbear direct interrogation regarding, and contradiction to, the sentiments of others, and all positive assertions of my own. . . . When another asserted something I thought an error, I denied myself the pleasure of contradicting him abruptly, and of showing immediately some absurdity in his proposition; and in answering I began by observing that in certain circumstances his opinion would be right, but in the present case there *appeared* or *seemed* to appear

[32]Ferdynand Zweig, *Labor, Life, and Poverty,* p. 4. The Ryerson Press, 1948.

[33]*Ibid.,* quoted by Pauline V. Young, "Methods of Studying Society and Culture," in Francis E. Merrill, *Society and Culture: An Introduction to Sociology,* p. 591. Prentice-Hall, Inc., 1961. Reprinted by permission.

> to me some difference. I soon found the advantage of this change in my manner; the conversation I engaged in later went more pleasantly. The modest way in which I proposed my opinions procured them a readier reception and less contradiction.[34]

Denying oneself the pleasure of contradiction and untimely assertions has added advantages: the interviewer is more ready to identify the scope and dimensions of the information revealed in an unhampered manner; he can keep this information in its natural frame of reference without injecting his own viewpoints; he can estimate the breadth of communication barriers which arise spontaneously with the flow of the account. If the interviewer poses contradictions, he is not able to share in the account, he cannot determine the areas of resistance and the barriers he will have to bridge.[35]

RATIONED AND TIMELY QUESTIONS. Some questions are necessary and often unavoidable in a long interview. At times the interview "runs dry" and needs restimulation. Some accounts lack clarity or completeness; some are disconnected, irrelevant assertions. Some interviewees provide a chronological account, devoid of their attitudes and the social matrix in which the events occurred. If, for example, an account is given of mobility merely as a matter of movement through time and space, it is necessary to question how mobility affected personal relations, social status, the roots already established or to be sunk into a new social setting. If interviewees launch upon a long spell of introspection about their feelings, without giving specific experiences, it is necessary to elicit these in order to make the account definite and realistic. Though raising questions informally, there is no attempt to guide the interview. The informant still supplies the essential content, although on occasion the interviewer supplies the form.

Questions must be not only timely and wisely rationed, but they must also be phrased in terms that show concern to the interviewee's problems. Likert cites some interesting examples, drawn from an interview survey of financial situations of families. Such blunt questions as "What is your present income?" or "How much do you have in your savings account?" cause antagonism and withdrawal. In order to secure cooperation, the question should be indirect and imply concern: "Would you say that you people are better or worse off financially

[34]Franklin, *Autobiography,* p. 202. G. P. Putnam's Sons, 1909.

[35]Based on Paul, *op. cit.,* pp. 444–445.

than a year ago?" Then, when a reply is given, the question: "Why do you say so?" or "Are you making as much money as a year ago?" "Why is that?" It may be assumed that if an informant does not supply definite answers to direct questions, the chances are he will do so to indirect questions. Indirection may also be used to resolve resistances.[36] At best, informants who resist giving essential data or are on the defensive are not easy to deal with. To break their resistances and defenses down directly may result in instilling further resistance and destroying rapport. It should be noted that defensive responses are in themselves important data. It may be well to delay getting the planned-for essentials and attempt to ascertain: Why the defenses? What is being defended? What form do the defenses assume? These questions may provide a clue as to how to interview a defensive respondent and to obtain the needed data by phrasing questions differently, by asking them in relation to another aspect of the interview, or asking them in a subsequent interview. Even if some sort of answers are obtained while the informant is in a defensive mood, the data may be worthless, apart from the study of resistances which may not be the immediate purpose of the particular interview.

It should always be kept in mind that the interview period belongs to the interviewee. It is his moment. And it may have been preceded by moments of long, anxious waiting to talk and be listened to. Many interviewees anxiously ask some such question as "Where should I begin?" Obviously this question should be answered by them, and the interviewer should pose a counterquestion: "Where would you like to begin?" Some interviewees prefer to talk about their distant past. They do not feel threatened by it or involved in it. Others prefer to talk about either past or present, simply because they are involved or wish to see a way out or "get it off their chest."

Once the interviewee launches on his account of past or present events, the interviewer must watch every turn for validity and consistency of the account, without "breaking into critical zones" with unwarranted questions. It may take several highly attentive listening-sessions—not all devoid of appropriate questions—before a comprehensive account is obtained. Briefly outlined, such an account or an "own story" should include:

1. The interviewee's point of view and his reactions to his past and

[36]Rensis Likert, "The Sample Interview Survey as a Tool of Research and Policy Formulation," in Lerner and Lasswell, *op. cit.,* pp. 242–243.

present situations (personal attitudes, interests, social roles assumed in group), and his interpretation or definition of his social situation.

2. A picture of the cultural world to which he is responsive and which, in turn, defines his social situation and provides him with a moral code and ideals.
3. The sequence of past events which condition behavior patterns, shape personality and outlook on life, direct hopes and aspirations.

A study of these factors involves both retrospection (an examination of past experiences) and introspection (an "inward look" at one's own thoughts and experiences).[37]

An interviewer at times needlessly introduces a stimulus. Given sufficient time, the interviewee often resumes the account on his own accord. But if the hesitation is too prolonged, harking back to previous topics or reformulating something the latter has said may encourage a renewed flow of conversation. "You said that. . . . Did the same thing ever happen again?" or "You mentioned that. . . .What happened then?"

Direct questions generally elicit replies which serve to satisfy only the interrogator. He often succeeds in ferreting out single unrelated incidents, mistaken for facts. Under such circumstances the data he secures are useless for scientific purposes. Such data are not generally brought into the limelight when the informant is given an opportunity to relate his life as he, and not the interviewer, visualizes it.

When interviewees failed to supply their reactions to related past experiences, Merton and his associates, in their study of mass communication, used such immediate means of re-presenting situations as exhibiting stills from a motion picture or playing back sections of a transcribed radio program. This procedure seeks to "approximate a condition in which subjects virtually *re-experience* the situations to aid their report of significant responses and to have these linked with pertinent aspects of it."[38] Where no such laboratory procedure and equipment can be used in a study and it is essential to re-present the stimulus situation, it is necessary to introduce appropriate questions which will aid in reliving the past: "Under what circumstances did such and such a phenomenon occur?" or "How did you feel about it?" or "What factors were associated with it?" It must be remembered, that

[37]Clifford E. Shaw, *The Jack Roller,* pp. 3–16. University of Chicago Press, 1930.

[38]Merton and Kendall, *op. cit.,* p. 550.

since considerable time may have elapsed since the actual occurrence of the stimulus situation to which we are only now trying to elicit a reaction, the data we secure may suffer from unintentional distortions —new interpretations placed upon the experiences which are at variance with the original meanings of the social situations. Specific questions directed toward the evocative experience and repeated references to it may in a measure reproduce the events and the reactions to them accurately and adequately enough to gain an appreciation of them. Care is needed in conducting such an interview, and great discretion should be used in interpreting the data. Under the best of interviewing conditions, introspection which requires retrospection, or vice versa, is a slow and often hazardous process.

At times interviewees seem to have run their course and pause expectantly, waiting to receive some hint or suggestion which would again start them in a flow of conversation. Under such circumstances it is best to "pick up the cue" and inject brief questions which are related to the data already revealed by them. A brief question and an attitude of expectancy may induce a new flow of material.

Double questions, even those which seem related to each other, should be avoided, as they are often confusing. A question like this one, for example, "When did you first experience tensions and conflicts . . . ?" calls for an account of tensions, which may involve situations and specific details entirely different from those involving conflicts. Even when the double question is not confusing, both parts of the question are rarely answered adequately, as details of one situation are lost while elaborating on another.

Questions tending to bring forth short, unrevealing replies or "Yes" or "No" responses should be avoided. They give the illusion of having covered the ground, while in reality they rarely succeed in gaining specific related information. Instead of asking, "Do you know about . . . ?" the question should be, "What do you know about . . . ?"

After rapport is established and the conversation flows easily, it may, at times, go off on a tangent. Therefore, it may become necessary to control the course of the interview to some extent. Although always on the alert to discover important bypaths, the interviewer may find it essential to check the flow of the story, to hark back to the point of departure and encourage an interviewee to retrace a line of thought. Some interviewers find that when the story begins to drift, they can steer it along channels pertinent to the inquiry by some such remark as: "You know, I was very much interested in what you said a moment ago. That's very important. Could you tell me more about it?" And thus the relevant factors may be reintroduced. Some things are much more difficult to talk about than others. The interviewee may be actually inarticulate at points, unable to express himself, or may know only vulgar terms. The interviewer must then come to the rescue with the required expression, the conventional expression, or technical term, meantime preserving his poise and objective attitude. Thus, as Karen Horney has said: "The silent interviewer is a myth."

The critical points in the interview. There are certain critical points which need special attention in interviewing. When the conversation turns to some intimate subjects, and particularly when it deals with crises in the life of the individual, emotions may be displayed. The interviewee winces when sore spots are touched. The subject may be dropped for the time being and another line of conversation pursued for a time, so that a less direct approach to the subject can be made later. Eventually, protected material may appear with little of its former emotional tone.

Emotional blockage may also occur when the interviewee unsuccessfully attempts to explain a complex situation or an attitude so amorphous that he cannot account for it or cannot even put it into words. Under such circumstances, he may wish to divert the attention from himself and may direct questions to the interviewer: "How do *you* account for it?" "What do *you* think . . . ?" Merton and Kendall found that:

> [Such] attempted reversal of roles is particularly likely to occur at just those points in the interview when continued self-exploration by the subject would be most revealing. . . . It is incumbent upon the interviewer to avoid responding to the nominal meaning of many such questions posed by subjects. . . . In general the interviewer should counter a question with a question, thus converting the implied content of the informant's question into a cue for further discussion. In so doing he indicates that he understands the problem and is sympathetically awaiting further elaboration by the informant. This sort of stimulation is often all that the informant needs to continue his self-exploration.[39]

INCONSISTENCIES. Nearly all interview data reveal some inconsisten-

[39] *Ibid.*, p. 548. The third sentence of the above quotation is italicized by the original authors. The italics are here omitted because they might place a different emphasis on the present context of the material.

cies. These arise from several sources: simple forgetting or overlooking a point, unconscious suppression or rationalization. The interviewee may believe that he has fully revealed the facts, and he may have done so as far as he knows. "What is in his mind may or may not be true, but it is the sum total of his rationalizations upon which his life has proceeded. If he acts upon his rationalizations, they are in so far significant in explaining his behavior."[40] But often there is steady and deliberate cover-up. As soon as the interviewer recognizes it, he may either terminate the interview for the time being by remarking: "We just don't seem to get at significant points today. We might try again another time." An interviewee loses respect if he realizes that he can "fool the interviewer." If the interview is continued, it should be done so as in the case of sore points: Approach the subject from a new point of view. Assume that the misstatement was unintentional. If it was not unintentional, the interviewer has probably proceeded too rapidly, or by his manner he has suggested the need for deception or dissimulation. To catch an interviewee in a deliberate misstatement will inevitably destroy rapport. It requires great tact and mental dexterity to overcome the resulting embarrassment, defensive attitudes, and confusion.

When interviewees take exception or raise objections to something the interviewer says, implies, or stands for, it is best not to defend oneself, particularly if by so doing the interviewer will involve or "show up" the errors of others. He may have to clarify his position in order to avoid misunderstandings, but as little attention as possible should be drawn toward himself. Often, silence and an inconspicuous change of subject matter may be the most effective way of avoiding an argument.

Closing the interview. There is probably a natural closing point to each interview. Best results might be secured if each interview breaks off at a time when the interviewee is still fresh, still has something important to say, and himself proposes another talk. If both have arrived at a stage of physical or nervous strain, or if the story has run its course, there may not be enough momentum to carry over into a second sitting. It is well to share the responsibility of getting a complete account with the interviewee and to ask: "What have we

[40]Eduard C. Lindeman, *Social Discovery,* p. 188. Republic Publishing Co., 1925.

omitted?" or "What have we failed to touch on?" or "What else would you like to tell me?"

There is apt to be a reaction on the part of the interviewee if confessional material has been given. The interviewee may check himself with the statement: "I didn't intend to tell all that." In that case it is very important rapport be re-established before the interview is closed.

Should an interviewee desire his information treated confidentially, as well as anonymously, utmost care must be exercised in respecting his wishes and safeguarding his interests. He is also entitled to know what use will be made of the information secured.

The Interview Guide

A prepared guide, when judiciously used as a suggestive reference, has several advantages that frequently outweigh the disadvantages inherent in any predetermined outline or "map of the road." A guide may aid in: 1) focusing attention on salient points in the study; 2) securing comparable data in different interviews by the same or by various interviewers; 3) gathering the same range of items essential in the analysis of data or in testing the hypotheses formulated; 4) accumulating specific concrete details as a basis for quantitative studies of life histories.

The interview guide serves its best purposes when its various details are reclassified, "digested," by the interviewer who uses them only to fit his particular needs. There is no fixed order in which the various points of the guide should be covered in the interview. It should be remembered at all times that the interview guide is not an oral questionnaire. The guide defeats its own purposes if undue attention is paid to it. Such strict attention to a device—which is supposed to be introduced only as a means to round out the discussion—can become a kind of "interviewing strait jacket," as Merton puts it. When an interview is filled with frequent questions from the guide and is thereby forced into a mold, self-expression vanishes, and so does reality. The interviewer, furthermore, can no longer listen closely and analytically when his attention rests on the guide. He fails to respond to the cues and implications of the interviewee's remarks. However, these limitations apply equally to any scientific tool placed in inexperienced or careless hands. The interview itself—with or without the guide—can be seriously misused by unimaginative and compulsive "inquisitors."

Use of an interview guide does not mean that the interview is of necessity directive. The guide is used only to indicate topics for further conversation when the interviewee seems to have exhausted them. The development of these topics is left to him, however.

The present writer experimented with an *oral* interview guide, which she presented verbally and in the same order to each of over a hundred adult offenders whom she interviewed over a period of two years. (It should be indicated here that these men represented a highly select group, choice of which was determined through a preliminary statistical study of 3,000 court records.)[41]

At the beginning of each interview it was indicated that we proceed on the assumption in our study of adult offenders that there was a series of specific circumstances which led to the commission of offenses. "We would like to know these specific circumstances in your case. We do not desire to ask questions as these may influence your replies." If it was apparent that the interviewee was impatient to start his end of the conversation, he was given full opportunity to talk freely and uninterruptedly until he paused for directions. In all interviews it was suggested that we didn't want just a personal history regarding home, work, school life, but *the meaning* of these experiences and their *effects* upon the interviewee. "We would like to know the situations in detail which made you feel good, or feel bad; the persons who *influenced* you; who *made* you think for yourself; who *made* you go to work or to school. . . ." "What were your *reactions* to these people? How did you *feel* about these situations? Why?" and so on and on.

These preliminary remarks were designed to impress the interviewee that we were not interested in a mere recital of experiences, but in his reactions to them. These remarks were not sufficient to carry the entire interview on their own momentum. Frequently it was necessary to ask, at appropriate pauses, "And how did you feel about it?" or "How do you explain . . . ?" In less than an hour the men generally grasped the desired scope of the inquiry, the stress laid on accounts of social relationships and on the causal factors as these men knew them. These general questions also served to indicate that the self-exploration which the subjects were about to undertake were of a different nature from their brief "own story" which they submitted for official records. These interviewees were assured of their freedom to reveal as much or as little about their intimate lives as they saw fit. Generally such assur-

[41]Pauline V. Young, "Scientific Study of Young, Occasional, Urban Male Offenders," *American Sociological Review,* V, 596–600.

ance strengthened their confidence that they were not being interviewed in an unfriendly or authoritarian setting. The interviewees often reacted by expressing their readiness to "tell everything."

Generally the men talked at great length on one particular phase of their lives, with only occasional brief questions from the interviewer. Little effort was made to control the amount and type of detail they chose to dwell on, until the interviewer felt that she understood the relationships, sequences, and types of experiences they chose to voice. It was necessary, however, to guide interviewees in relating the various phases, types, and roles of such experiences in their lives. Some questions were frequently repeated: "How do you account for such and such acts, ideas, or attitudes?" There was a general tendency at the beginning of the interview to reply with a brief "I don't know myself," or "I just don't understand it." The men were not pressed for a reply, but as they gained insight into their own problems, as they grew and developed with the objective recounting of their experiences and reactions, they were able to explain—and often quite adequately—the factors which may be regarded as contributing to their criminal behavior patterns. Their own explanations at times astonished them but generally convinced them of the desirability of specific, related details. On the whole, the realization of their ability to explain, at least in some measure, certain aspects of their behavior was very stimulating to them, and the idea of a "scientific inquiry" greatly appealed to them. Some of them found "helping in research" to be "a great adventure."

NOTE TAKING. The interviewer often took brief notes during the interview but in such a manner that she did not take her eye off the face of the interviewee. At the end of a prolonged interview, she generally asked the man to help her jot down notes of "all that was covered in the interview." Before each man left and another interview was started, fairly complete notes and catchwords were jotted down on the major details of the life history secured. The same evening the complete life history was either dictated to a stenographer or written out in longhand by the writer. At her leisure, she edited these life histories which vary in length from ten to forty pages. Each interview lasted from three to five hours, generally interrupted by a period of rest away from the office. Such long interviews were held only in cases in which the men requested continuation and showed ability to concentrate and to be absorbed in self-exploration. In these very long interviews more detailed notes were taken during the interview.

Edna Ferber's comments on her experiences with note-taking during her long career as a newspaper reporter find considerable duplication in scientific fields: unobtrusive jotting down of catchword, pencil scrawl unguided, gaze meeting the eye of the person speaking, consciousness of interviewee's concern about a busy pencil traveling over blank paper.[42]

The present author found that reviewing with the informant the topics covered during the interview tends to re-emphasize in the record what he considered important and to minimize omissions, distortions, and other modifications of the data—which might occur in the absence of such a review, especially when the interview is reproduced from sketchy notes after a lapse of time.

Electrical transcriptions[43]—which are being used more and more frequently in various types of interviews—have many obvious advantages over note-taking during or after the interview. Electrical transcriptions, however, also have certain disadvantages. Many interviewees object to or fear "going on record." The use of electrical transcriptions precludes the interviewees' participation in the review of the data supplied. The present author found in her interviews, especially with adults and older teenagers, that the omission of the review often prevented the respondent from seeing his thoughts in broader perspective and thereby gaining greater insight into his situation. Going back over the points of the interview and relating them to a larger context, interviewees often elaborated on certain factors and at times even presented new significant data which might have remained undetected without the new stimulus of seeing experiences in the total setting. At times, however, this new insight caused some interviewees to be concerned about "having revealed too much." Some wished to retrace their steps and "explain" certain occurrences. Such data are valuable, whether they actually present new facts or are mere attempts to rationalize or to defend oneself. It was also found that less than 10 per cent of the interviewees were interested in or capable of *listening* to and comprehending the whole transcribed record when it was "played" back. The most satisfactory results were obtained when the interviewees participated in the review. It served to stimulate a *thinking-through* process and at times produced a new mental catharsis.

[42]Ferber, *op. cit.*, p. 111.

[43]For a discussion of the advantages of electrical transcriptions see E. B. Brody, *et al.*, "Sound Recording and the Problem of Evidence in Psychiatry," *Science,* CXIII (1951), 379–380.

The Process of Validating the Interview

Because of the subjective nature of much of interviewing data and because of unstandardized procedures in the interviewing process, problems of reliability and validity loom large. Inconsistencies, contradictions, coloring of the account by the informant and in the report by the interviewer cannot be lightly dismissed by social scientists intent on reliable analysis of data. Clyde Kluckhohn[44] asserts that, until field investigators deal rigorously with subjective data, their work will be flat and insubstantial, coarse and crude for scientific purposes. He sees the need of a combination of longitudinal and transverse methods. There must be both interviews about the past and about the present. There must also be on-going observational studies as well as "intensive observations of single field season." The full life history can best be, as the Leightons say, illuminated by the detailed cross-section of the moment. Multiple techniques, carried out by observation and analysis are the key to the problem of subjectivity.[45]

Mirra Komarovsky suggests a process of validating, which she calls *discerning*. This process is continued after the completion of the interview since discerning is also indispensable in the process of analyzing the data.

1. The interviewer asks for more detail on important points; the specific nature of these details may serve as a check on other details secured earlier.
2. He cross-checks the statements he may have received from other sources.
3. He seeks out the experienced interconnections between any change in established social relations habitually maintained by the interviewee and a new phenomenon, generally a crisis, which may have evoked new reactions. [In her study of unemployed men Dr. Komarovsky compared the experienced reactions of various members of the family because of changes brought about by the unemployment of the father.]
4. He tests those portions of the interview which show cause-effect relationships in order to determine whether they are situations in which either the supposed cause or effect occurred without the corresponding presence of the other. In her study of the relationship between unemployment [alleged cause] and loss of authority of the father [alleged effect], Dr.

[44]Kluckhohn, "The Use of Personal Documents in Anthropological Science," in Louis Gottschalk *et al., op. cit.*, p. 162.

[45]Alexander and Dorothea Leighton, *The Navaho Door*. pp. 95–134. Harvard University Press, 1944.

Komarovsky tested the alleged causal connections by examining whether the alleged causal factor existed at other times without the result, or the alleged result existed without the alleged causal factor. Finally she examined the interviewing data for other possible plausible explanations which on the surface might appear to be inconsistencies.

Dean and Whyte, in their article "How Do You Know If the Informant Is Telling the Truth," offer further aids in detecting distortion in the personal interview: 1) the important negative check, which points out implausibility, that is, when the account strongly strains our credulity; 2) any knowledge or evidence from other sources which undermine the given account; 3) our knowledge of informant's mental set and understanding of how he might influence his perception and interpretation of events; and 4) the oft-advocated check and comparison of informant's accounts with those by others.[46]

Some sociologists greatly distrust results of interviews; others have considerable confidence. Arnold Rose, for example, states: "Studies have been made to check the validity and completeness of answers secured by competent interviewers on very touchy and personal subjects and it was startling to see how correct the information was."[47]

Kinsey and associates concluded, after having taken more than 12,000 individual case histories, that the validity of these varied "with particular items and for different segments of the population. On the whole the accuracy of the individual history is far greater than might have been expected, with correlation coefficients ranging above 0.7 on most cases, and percents of identical responses ranging between 75 and 99 on particular items." Some low correlations were found but they were regarded as "highly significant because they gave some insight into the factors which are responsible for error and falsification in reporting."[48]

F. J. Roethlisberger and W. J. Dickson,[49] research workers on the

[46]Dean and Whyte, *op. cit.,* pp. 36–37.

[47]Rose, *Theory and Method in the Social Sciences,* p. 298. University of Minnesota Press, 1954.

[48]Kinsey, *op. cit.,* p. 151.

[49]Roethlisberger and Dickson, *Management and the Worker,* pp. 191–194, 286–290, 226–228. Harvard University Press, 1939. Reprinted by permission. Since this work was published over two decades ago, the present writer inquired about "second thoughts" on the subject. Dr. Roethlisberger replied: "I have no serious second thoughts on interviewing. The technique is still an important part of the equipment of the field research worker as well as of all practitioners involved in dyadic relations where the securing of the changes in behavior is the aim." (Personal communication, March 16, 1962.)

sociopsychological implications of industrial management, have for many years studied the conduct of the interview and its effects on interviewees. They summarize their conclusions in the following brief suggestions:

1. The interviewer should treat what is said in an interview as an item in a context.
   A. The interviewer should not pay exclusive attention to the manifest content of the intercourse (but should consider also the latent, hidden content).
   B. The interviewer should not treat everything that is said as either fact or fiction (but remember that some statements may be only partially true; others partially false; and many tinged with emotional overtones).
   C. The interviewer should not treat everything that is said as being on the same psychological level (but consider a variety of levels in the whole psychological context). The interviewer must gauge the level at which the interviewee is responding when he is bored or nervous or joking or desirous to please or searching for the truth.
2. The interviewer should listen not only to what a person wants to say but also to what he does not want to say or cannot say without help. (Silence can mean either desire to avoid rehearsing painful experiences or indifference.)
3. The interviewer should keep the mental contexts described in the preceding rule as indices and seek through them the personal reference that is being revealed. (The responses should be treated as symptoms rather than as realities or facts.)
4. The interviewer should keep the personal reference in its social context. (The expressed sentiments, desires, or interests should be viewed not as things in themselves but as configurations and "end products of a particular historical route," traversed through channels of family, religion, institutional connections, loyalties, community influences, social controls which influence behavior, thinking, and feeling.)
   A. The interviewer should remember that the interview is itself a social situation and therefore the social relation existing between the interviewer and interviewee is in part determining what is said. (Furthermore this social situation tends to change as the interview progresses. As a consequence either more revealing

data may be obtained or withheld; transference or withdrawal may occur; interviewee may regard interviewer as an authority or pay little attention to him. Interviewer needs to watch at what end of the pole he is placed and how the interviewee's reactions affect him.)

A_1. The interviewer should see to it that the speaker's sentiments do not act on his own.

the use of case data in social research

10

Case study deepens our perception and gives us a clearer insight into life . . . It gets at behavior directly and not by an indirect and abstract approach.

CHARLES HORTON COOLEY

Social scientists, in their study of human behavior, strive to obtain a fundamentally real and enlightened record of personal experiences which would reveal in concrete detail a man's inner strivings, tensions, motivations that drive him to action, the barriers that frustrate him or challenge him, the forces that direct him to adopt a certain pattern of behavior and to live according to a certain scheme and philosophy of life.[1] Only some of man's experiences can be learned by observing him in action. To understand his behavior fully and intimately, he must supply a detailed and penetrating account of what he does and has done, what he thinks he does and has done, what he expects to do, and says he ought to do.[2] A fairly exhaustive study of a person or group is called a life or case history.

Social scientists study many culture groups, small social groups (a family, political party, a gang, a leadership group, as indicated in some of the studies in the preceding chapters). They also study large groups as social units (sects, national and racial groups). Social institutions (courts, hospitals, churches, industrial organizations, governmental divisions)

[1]See A. L. Porterfield, *Creative Factors in Social Research,* p. 6. Duke University Press, 1941.

[2]Cf. Clyde Kluckhohn, "The Study of Culture," in Daniel Lerner and Harold Lasswell (Eds.), *The Policy Sciences,* p. 101. University of Chicago Press.

have also been studied comprehensively as social units. Studies of neighborhoods, large and small communities (Russian-Town, Chinatown, the Black Belt, the ghetto, the Gold Coast) have been frequent topics of studies as social units. A comprehensive study of a social unit—be that unit a person, a group, a social institution, a district, or a community—is called a case study. (For such case studies see Chapters 16–19. Below we stress case data of persons.)

Case data may be gathered exhaustively of an entire life cycle of a social unit or a definite section of it. Whether a section or the whole of a life is studied, the aim is to ascertain the *natural history,* that is, an account of the generic development of a person or group, or whatever constitutes the social unit in a particular study, revealing the factors that molded the life of the unit within its cultural setting. Because of its aid in studying behavior in specific, precise detail, Burgess termed the case study method, "the social microscope."[3]

Evolution of the case study method. Frédéric Le Play (1806–1882) is reputed to have introduced the case study method into social science. He used it as a handmaiden to statistics in his studies of family budgets. Herbert Spencer, an English philosophical sociologist (1820–1903), was the first to use case materials in his ethnographic studies. Modern social researchers, however, are dubious about the latter studies because they see in them many "fanciful inferences" and a "predisposition to pigeonhole data under categories" of a sociological system dictated by a particular cast of mind, before testing hypotheses by cases. (This is what Blumer refers to when he says that "theories seem to order the data" rather than having the data mold the theories. See Chapter 3.) "Spencer was notoriously guilty of amassing all favorable cases to prove a point, in utter disregard of negative cases. . . ."[4]

Dr. William Healy, a psychiatrist, was among the first to adopt the case study method in his work with juvenile delinquents. After an intensive statistical study of one thousand delinquents he became convinced that "statistics will never tell the whole story, as they in themselves are but symptoms of unknown causal processes and can

[3]Burgess, "Research Methods in Sociology," in Georges Gurvitch and W. E. Moore (Eds.), *Twentieth Century Sociology,* pp. 25–26. The Philosophical Library, 1949.

[4]Burgess, "Statistics and Case Studies as Methods of Social Research," *Sociology and Social Research,* XII (Nov.-Dec. 1927), 113–114.

serve only as provisional grounds for sociological hypotheses."[5]

Historians, and especially new historians, have used the case method for descriptive accounts of persons, eras, and nations. (See such studies as Arthur S. Link's *Woodrow Wilson and the Progressive Era,* or George E. Mowry's *The Era of Theodore Roosevelt,* or John Gunther's depiction of F. D. R.—*Roosevelt in Retrospect.*)

Anthropologists and ethnologists have utilized the case study method for their detailed descriptions of primitive and modern cultures. (See especially Cora Du Bois' *The People of Alore;* Robert Redfield's *Tepoztlan: A Mexican Village,* or Oscar Lewis' *Life in a Mexican Village: Tepoztlan Restudied.*)

Novelists and wartime correspondents sketched their characters of persons and families by means of the case study method. (See Edna Ferber's *A Peculiar Treasure,* Shalom Ash's *East River,* Robert E. Sherwood's *Roosevelt and Hopkins.*)

In the field of social psychology, some of the most exhaustive case studies have been made by H. A. Murray[6] and his associates at the Harvard Psychological Clinic. Their case studies included preliminary interviews with their subjects; conferences at specified intervals; impromptu conversations; dramatic productions; experimental studies; observations and post-experimental interviews; a wide battery of tests, including hypnotic tests, tests of abilities, aesthetic appreciation, emotional conditioning, social reaction to frustration, imaginal productivity, psychological insight, and a variety of others. The interviews and conferences related to family associations, childhood memories, sexual development, present dilemmas, community contacts, and other subjects.

Dr. Murray obtained also autobiographies from students who were encouraged to view their lives as "temporal series of events which revealed causal relationships between early experiences and later dispositions," as well as future plans and expectations, and desires to achieve certain goals. Along with their aspirations, students revealed their fears and anxieties which showed roots in the past.

Murray maintains that although many memories were without a doubt unconsciously repressed, or consciously withheld and distorted, every autobiography or interview revealed something of importance.

[5]Healy, *The Individual Delinquent,* pp. 15–18. Little, Brown & Co., 1915.

[6]Murray, *Explorations in Personality: A Clinical and Experimental Study of Fifty Men of College Age,* pp. 412, 415, 428. Oxford University Press, 1947. (In April 1962, in a personal communication, Dr. Murray stated that the "excerpts used from the 1947 edition, though they could be enlarged, needed no changes.")

The subject often revealed himself in the interviews, not only in what he said, but in his attitude toward what he had revealed. Murray found most of the subjects "surprisingly frank in writing about their experiences even though it entailed exposure of inferiorities and moral weakness."

The aim of impromptu conversations—ranging in duration from two minutes to two hours or more—was to accumulate those "casual yet contingent words and acts which occurred after, before, or during the more stringent course of something else when the subject temporarily escaped, so to speak, out of the contracted-for bounds . . . and to catch particularly those echoes or repercussions, to record those verbalisms and gestures which emerged as apparent incidentals or as aftermaths of the task itself."

The actual adoption and widespread use of the case study method as systematic sociological field research is attributed to the work of Thomas and Znaniecki, *The Polish Peasant.* As will be recalled, they used extensively personal documents—diaries, letters, autobiographies—and at times combed the files of social agencies, in their search for concrete and specific detail about personal conduct and group behavior within the cultural situation. They wanted to present a continuous picture through time of the person's own interpretation of his experiences and his relations with others. They believed the personal document to be the chief instrument for reaching the actual attitudes and values of people as well as for obtaining a cross-section of the entire process of social becoming. They favored the personal documents for the spontaneity of privacies they reveal regarding personal habits, crises, relationships; for the continuity of experiences they indicate; for the explanations they offer regarding social processes, and for illuminating pesonality structure.[7]

They wrote with considerable emphasis that it is safe to say that "personal life-records, as complete as possible, constitute the *perfect* type of sociological material," since they represent a more enlightening and fundamentally more real record of personal experiences, with a wealth of concrete detail, vivid memories, tensions, anxieties, and multifarious reactions to social situations which escape the attention of most skilled investigators using other techniques.

Thomas and Znaniecki are of the opinion also that if social science has to resort to the use of other than life history data, it is "only because of the practical difficulty of obtaining at the moment a sufficient

[7]Thomas and Znaniecki, *The Polish Peasant.*See especially pp. 1832–1836. Alfred A. Knopf, Inc., 1927.

number of such records to cover the totality of sociological problems and of the enormous amount of work demanded for an adequate analysis of all the personal material necessary to characterize the life of a social group."

Are cases typical? The representativeness and typicalness of cases and life history documents have long been of great concern to social researchers. Life and personal traits are complex and varied. Can we find other Middletowns, other Cornervilles, Elmstowns, other Jackrollers, or "Docs" and Dannys? Are there cases similar enough to those described by the authors of these studies to enable us to say that these cases are representative of their kind? Are we able to say that these data provide bases for generalizations? The answer depends, in some measure at least, on the researchers' wise choice of data, on their ability as impartial observers and accurate recorders.

Those who have had an opportunity to study hundreds of cases (William Healy, Cyril Burt, Alfred Kinsey, Samuel Stouffer, T. W. Adorno, to mention only a few authorities) have found striking similarities and uniformities within large groups of people, studied independently, at different times, in different countries, and under different social conditions. Healy and Burt, for example, found among American and among English juvenile delinquents impressively similar behavior patterns, family organizations, socioeconomic levels.

Thomas and Znaniecki found that "not only single attitudes and values, not only single elementary facts, but more or less complete combinations, series of facts, present a certain similarity." However, "this similarity cannot be assumed to go as far as absolute identity; the identity is always approximate. . . . But the concept of type needs . . . only an approximate identity of individual cases, and a class is supposed to possess only a relative generality."[8]

Anthropologist Franz Boas, on the basis of his famed studies of primitive men, concluded that the organization of the human mind is practically identical among all races of men, and that the modes of thought and action are the same.[9] Even the dynamic changes which groups and communities undergo display a certain degree of similarity and uniformity. Not only do certain personality traits remain constant,

[8] *Ibid.*, pp. 1838–1839.

[9] Boas, *The Mind of the Primitive Man*, p. 102. The Macmillan Company, 1938.

but social change has a certain regularity and consistency in its patterns of recurrence.

These similarities cannot be carried too far, however. Not all aspects of life are comparable. It is the researcher's task to discover *another case* within his subdivision of classes, *a negative case* which does not fit in or defies the adopted classification, or a *marginal case* which does not have full status in, but with certain modifications belongs to, the adopted class.

Life Histories: Their Underlying Assumptions and Criteria

In gathering case data it may be assumed that the identity of human nature persists, by and large, in a variety of circumstances, even though human conduct changes. All human beings share a basic humanity, in spite of unique experiences and personal characteristics. Cora Du Bois, on the basis of her various studies in Southeastern Asia, concludes:

> There are certain experiences and certain physiologically determined tensions, felt subjectively as desires, which no human being escapes, however differently he may seek to satisfy them and however different the level of satisfaction may be. Birth and death, growth and sexual desire, fatigue, laughter, and hunger are among some of these experiences. No groups of people exist among whom these factors—and many others which it would be pointless to enumerate—are known to be congenitally absent. . . . The point is that the basic similarities of human beings the world over are the foundation on which I believe any comparative study of culturally determined personality must rest. This is a basic assumption.[10]

This does not mean that there are no pronounced differences among various cultural groups or persons. Common sense tells that the customs and the way of life of an Indian would make him strikingly different from a Turk, for example. Theoretical sociologists and social philosophers assert that if we accept a law of nature, our very acceptance implies a belief in uniformity. "In establishing a uniformity," they say, "one relates an event to the conditions under which it occurs. This is causation in its broadest and least particularistic sense."[11]

Gordon Allport goes as far as saying that "there are lawful happen-

[10]Du Bois, *The People of Alore,* pp. 2–3. Harvard University Press, 1960.

[11]John C. McKinney, "Methodological Convergence of Mead, Lundberg, and Parsons," *American Journal of Sociology,* LIX, 572.

ings which occur uniquely in human life. . . . Certain statements of tendency in human nature seem *approximately* true for every mortal or for large groups of mortals. There is no reason why some of these tendencies cannot be traced through a comparative study of [personal] documents." All research pertaining to particular individuals (*idiographic research*) is based on the above assumptions.[12]

Another assumption should be stressed here: although much of a person's past may be obscure to him, or out of reach to a research worker, and although the reasons for a subject's responses may seem mysterious, it is possible to find in most persons an underlying reaction system. This system Gardner Murphy terms a *unity thema*. It is the key to the subject's unique nature and can serve as the fundamental basis for the exploration of personality.[13]

Criteria for the life history. John Dollard's[14] discussion of the criteria for the life or case history still remains the most penetrating on the subject. His volume, under the same title, and close to 300 pages, should be read in its entirety. Here we can review in the barest outline some of the main points which serve for judging the adequacy of life history technique as well as to indicate some of the contents of life history data.

1. The subject must be viewed in a cultural series. [That is, even though he is singled out for individual study, he must be regarded as a member of a culture group or community. Community values, standards, and way of life can be studied only through life histories of persons. See, for example, W. L. Warner *et al., Yankee City Series.*]
2. Behavior of individuals must be viewed as socially relevant. [That is, behavior should be seen as arising in response to definite social stimulations.]
3. The family of the subject of study must be viewed in its role of submitting the culture and way of life of the group through its individual members.

[12]Allport, *The Use of Personal Documents in Psychological Science,* p. 147. Social Science Research Council, 1942.

[13]Murphy *et al., Experimental Social Psychology: An Interpretation of Research upon the Socialization of the Individual,* p. 604. Harper & Row, Publishers, 1937.

[14]Dollard, *Criteria for the Life History,* pp. 8–36. Yale University Press, 1935.

4. The specific method of elaboration of organic materials into social behavior must be shown.
5. The *continuous* related character of experience from childhood through adulthood should be stressed.
6. The "social situation" must be studied in order to learn kind and degree of social pressures, social forces, social participation or abstention, exercised by the subject.
7. The life history material must be organized and conceptualized.

It is remarkable that Dollard, strongly psychoanalytically oriented, stressed cultural factors—in five out of seven criteria—as essentials in life history data. He also stressed that case studies of persons should have their starting point not in the life history of that person but in the social situation and group of which he is part. Also, Dollard aptly laid considerable emphasis on "specific series of coordinated, related, continuous, configurated experiences in a complex culture pattern," which motivate social and personal behavior.

His fourth criterion, however—"The specific method of elaboration of organic materials into social behavior must be shown"—needs qualification from a sociological point of view. A score or more theories, before Dollard's publication, have sought to connect the "organic materials" and "social behavior." This very multiplicity of theories indicates well how difficult a task such a connection is and how little success has been attained in doing so. To be sure, occasionally we find a few colorful cases which point to the possibility of establishing some direct connection in human behavior between organic constitution and social situation, but in general, we are still unable to establish specific relationships between them. In fact, the human biological frame of reference is so broad and offers so many potentialities that almost any kind of behavior is possible: witness the variety of languages, customs, mores, ways of life, artifacts, inventions, and the like, to be found in human societies. It would seem that, for practical purposes, the research student needs chiefly to examine the cultural milieu to determine what factors actually account for the particular life pattern under scrutiny. The biological equipment is universal among human beings the world over—with minor variations in skin color, hair texture, and anthropometric measurements. However, the cultural factors are infinitely varied from time to time, group to group, region to region.

The uniformities and differences which the research student seeks, at least in the social sciences, are cultural rather than organic in nature. The permutations and combinations found in the human frame, are, for our purposes, infinite; hence, they are not specific determinants of behavior. Criteria for the life history must take full account of this basic fact. And for this reason it may be quite impossible in any realistic way to show, as Dollard requires, the specific method of elaboration of organic materials into social behavior.[15] (It should be pointed out here that since the publication of his *Criteria for the Life History,* Dollard has modified his own thinking regarding "organic materials" in relation to social behavior. See his, and Neal Miller's, *Social Learning and Imitation.*)

The following brief excerpts from the life history of a young Russian Molokan woman may illustrate the nature of life history data gathered from individual persons who were viewed, according to Dollard's suggestions, as "specimen in a cultural series," from "childhood through adulthood." Their behavior was seen as "socially relevant," and the role of the family in "submitting the culture and a way of life" was stressed; the "social situation" was studied and the "social pressures" taken into account.

> Anna Pavlova, 26 years of age at the time of the study, is a tall, stately appearing person; mentally alert, frank in manner, pleasing personality; has considerable poise; speaks with some insight into her situation. She displays traits generally found among other members of her group. She speaks both Russian and English fluently. (This case is used also in Chapter 15 in which the numbered units are analyzed. Here the numbers may be disregarded.)
>
> I was born in Russia (1), a few months before our trip to the United States (2). My mother says that my birthday is on the first day of the first snow of a late autumn in Southern Russia (3). Just try to figure that out in California (4). My parents, together with a number of other Molokan families, (5) came to Los Angeles (6) in order to escape military service (7) under the tsars during the Russo-Japanese war, as our group, like the Quakers, are conscientious objectors to war (8). . . .
>
> I don't remember much about my first few years of life, except that we were always poor (9). Toiling (10) day and night my father could not make a living (11). In Russia he was a farmer (12). Here he could not get used to dry farming (13). . . .We moved from California to Mexico (14), later to Arizona (15), and back to California (16). I remember that wherever we arrived people looked at us queerly (17). My father had a bushy beard (18); mother wore a shawl on her head, a Russian

[15]Cf. Erle F. Young (manuscript).

dress and a wide, long apron (19), and us kids—six in all—also wore head shawls and dresses to our ankles (20). Oh, we were a sight (21). I was about eight years old (22). I was terribly self-conscious (23). Oh, it was terrible (24) . . . I had made up my mind that as soon as possible I would go to work (25). But I did not get started until I was about eleven (26). A neighbor told me of a cookie manufacturer who would hire me if I told him a "hard-luck story" (27). I did not have to invent one. I just told him our own which was hard enough (28). I went to work a few days later at three dollars a week (29).

Later I heard of a laundry and went to work for a little more money (30). Then I worked in a chocolate factory where the work was not so hard (31). I wanted to appear old, so I stuffed my front out with cotton stockings and told the owner of the factory that I was fourteen (32). He looked at me so queer, but he hired me (33). When I left his office I could still feel his gaze, and no wonder. One of the stockings had slipped down and only one side was padded. I felt weak on my feet (34). . . . I worked there from eight in the morning until six in the evening (35). I used to get terribly worn out (36). . . . I wished that the truant officer would come around and send me to school (37). I worked there for about a year (38). At the age of twelve I went back to work in a laundry (39), for six dollars a week and gave all the money to mother (40). I was laid off several times, but hired again when needed (41). . . .

At fifteen I went to work as a chocolate dipper (42). When I was offered $16 a week I was shocked (43). I told the man I wasn't worth that much (44), but at the end of the week he gave me $16.00 (45). I really took the job on my nerve (46). The Molokan parents say that their children act and work "by their wits," rather than skill and custom (47). But I have been at this job now for eight years (48). Now I make $28.00 a week and work shorter hours (49) and that's more than my poor dad makes (50). Now I don't give all my money to the folks (51).

They don't object to my keeping half of it (52), but they object to what I buy (53). I wore a shawl as long as I could (54). . . . Once I mustered up enough courage to buy a hat (55). When my mother saw it, she carried on something terrible (56): "A hat! What next?" She made me promise that I would not wear it in the Colony (57). To avoid trouble at home (58) I left my hat at a girl friend's house and called for it every morning before going to work, ditching my shawl (59). But when my girl friend moved, I said to my hat: "Well, here we go home together, come what may. My mother said she would burn it (60). I told her frankly I did not want to wear a shawl to work any more (61) and if she burnt my hat, I would buy another one and a better one (62). I got mad (63); she cried that I had no respect for her (64). I felt sorry for her (65). . . . Once a spiritualist told me (66): "Be reasonable with your parents they don't understand your ways (67). You don't try to understand them" (68). I thought it over and felt ashamed of myself (69). I decided to be calm and explain things to them (70). But it is they who don't want to understand us (71). . . .

The next fight was about my buying a new dress (72). I was growing up and comments of my friends made me feel ashamed of the Russian dress (73). I bought a dress, to my knees and not my ankles, and to fit my figure and without a collar and sleeves (74). My mother almost fainted (75) when she saw me in it, and carried on worse than ever (76). "Have you lost all sense of shame?" she cried (77). That's all I heard for days (78). I did try to explain, but it did no good (79). I told the folks I wouldn't wear the American dress to church (80), I would wear it only to work (81), because I have to look decent (82). That was the wrong thing to say. "Decent?" she cried, "If you want to be decent, wear the Russian dress. Only the Russian dress is decent" (83). "Mama," I said: "You want me to compete (84) with American girls at work. How can I when I look so strange to them?" (85). She never saw my point (86). . . .

I'll never forget a trip my sister and I took once to visit some relatives in New Mexico (87). We took our American dresses along (88). They made our trip miserable. The women gossiped about us (89). They really had thought we were a couple of street walkers (90), and would have nothing to do with us . . . (91). One of these relatives had visited us once in California. (I was about twelve or thirteen then), she said then that she wanted me for her daughter-in-law. (92) "But now," she said, "You won't do for my son any more. You're no longer a Russian girl" (93). Again I tried to explain that we live in America now (94); we work with Americans (95) and must look like Americans (96). It was no use, she never saw my point (97). But I continued to wear American clothes (98). . . .

The real fight over clothes started when I was being invited to dances by friends at work (99). I needed some very nice evening clothes (100). I resented giving half of pay envelope to the folks (101). Earlier somehow I was proud that I could help them out (102). The girls at work began calling me a young fool (103). At first I went to dances without my parents' knowledge (104). But they fussed every time I left the house in the evening (105). Once I said: "You might just as well know it. I am going to a dance with an American fellow (106). He is my boss "(107). My mother started crying that I am putting her in the grave alive (108). Until then my father rarely interfered with me (109). He didn't like my actions (110) but left me to my mother (111). But going to dances touched off a storm of protest in him (112). His eyes blazed when he said: "You have lost your soul. You have no conscience any more (113). You dare tell us about going to *dances* with an American fellow" (114).

Well, I was miserable, and cried (115). You get hell if you don't tell the truth and you get hell if you do (116). . . . But it wasn't all joy traveling in high society (117). . . . I didn't know American table manners (118). At home we eat from the family dish (119). . . . I didn't know how to order from a menu (120). . . . At work the girls made fun of me when my father called for me in his rubbish truck (121). I couldn't refuse him (122). The girls asked me: "Who's your sheik? What a nice beard he has" (123). I gave them a dirty look and said proudly: (124): "He is my father. So now" . . . .

My parents wanted me to marry young (125), but I wanted to go back to school (126). My schooling had been so badly interrupted (127). I wanted to quit work and enter grade school (128). At home they thought I had lost my mind (129). They argued that as long as a girl can read and write, she has enough education (130). They tried to convince me that even my boss thought so because he had given me several raises (131). It seemed madness to them to give up a good job for school (132). But I knew they had other motives (133). They were afraid that returning to school would further alienate me from them (134). . . . In the end my parents were proud of my diploma (135), though they were afraid that my sister would follow my footsteps (136). . . .

My folks wanted me to marry young (137), oh at eighteen, I guess. I was regarded as an old maid when I married at twenty-one (138). I was in school for two years after quitting my last job. This business of marrying young is also connected with their notions of remaining "a good Molokan" (139). . . . I often feel sorry for my parents (140). They want to keep us within the faith (141). Their faith satisfies them so completely (142), or maybe they are just used to their ways (143). . . . They have seen so much wickedness in the city (144), that they rather hold on to their own customs (145) than try to take on new ones (145). . . . But the young people can't live like the old folks want them to live (146). But it is sure strange. We can't live like Americans either (147). We aren't even half American and half Molokan (148). At least a third in us is confusion and rebellion (149). . . . My parents say that I am "advanced" (150). By that they mean that I am out of step with my group. I feel that I don't fit in any place (151). . . .[16]

Blumer would probably say that the foregoing document, as most or all human documents, is not useful for validation, but would perhaps admit that it is a rich source of insights and provides a basis for formulation but not for testing of hypotheses. It is true that case data are highly complex, and no adequate technique has yet been devised to unravel the complexity in such a way as to yield strictly uniform and

[16]Document No. 52, secured by present writer during three interviews.

additive data. Although rigorous analysis cannot be applied to case data generally, subtle interpretation of the data does extend and enrich one's understanding of cultural conflicts and the dilemmas of the cultural hybrid. Perspective can also be broadened if we apply the following schedule of questions, suggested by Gordon Allport:

> 1) With what sort of first-person material is the study concerned: comprehensive autobiography, topical autobiography, artistic production, diary, letters, verbatim records—or what? 2) What is the history of the documents employed? Were they written for an audience, on order, or without thought of publication or use? And how were the documents acquired by the psychologist? 3) Does the document (or do the documents) stand alone, or is it supplemented by other material? If the latter, is the supplementary material used for confirmation, contrast, as groundwork for generalization, or for what purpose? 4) Are there attempts to establish either the reliability or the validity of the document? If so, what? 5) What statement does the investigator make about his method, about the value of his material? 6) Does the investigator use the document inductively or as illustration for an hypothesis, theory, or dogma; or does he do both? Are his inferences limited specifically to the case in question, or generalized to apply to "types" or groups of people? 7) What is the bias or frame of reference of the investigator, and how does it seem to influence the interpretation? Do the interpretations seem compulsory, plausible, or strained? Do the investigator's comments clearly draw their meaning and intelligibility from the personal document?[17]

Applying these questions to a critical appraisal of the case materials obtained from Anna Pavlova, they could be answered as follows:

1) The entire study was concerned primarily with comprehensive autobiographies, 2) written for a "sociological audience." 3) They were supplemented by observational, statistical, and historical data which were used at times for contrast, and at times as groundwork for generalizations. 4) Attempts were made to establish reliability of documents by means of a) internal consistency, b) re-interviews, c) interviews with other members of group who knew subject of study well. 5) Only a combination of techniques suffices in getting culturally relevant and scientifically significant data; the study attempted to throw light on several interrelated problems: the bearing of a sectarian brotherhood on the personality of its members, the sources of cultural conflicts, the process of cultural assimilation of a primary group in a highly

[17] Allport, *op. cit.*, p. xiv.

urbanized metropolitan center, and the eventual cultural revival of the group in the face of its high degree of urbanization. 6) The documents were used at times inductively, at times as illustrations for hypotheses; the inferences were not limited to single cases rather than to groups of highly homogeneous persons. 7) The interpretations were regarded by others (Dr. Park, Dr. Bogardus, and Dr. Mangold) as plausible; they also proved reliable in a restudy by another investigator, Miss Ella Hostetter, entitled "A Restudy of the Process of Assimilation as Revealed in Personal Documents," and is on file at University of Southern California Library. (Sufficient material on the study of Russian Molokans has been presented in the present volume to bear out at least six of the above points.)

When gathering case data, the investigator should heed Dr. Thomas' warning: "Be suspicious of striking cases; they may be as surprising to the people among whom they occur as they are to you." Striking facts, especially those that seem abnormal, are frequently far less significant than more commonplace ones, but it should be remembered that there "is no break in continuity between the normal and the abnormal in concrete life."[18] Unusual or rare cases should not be overlooked but should be regarded as exceptions.

The case data, rich in intimate detail, as in the case of Anna Pavlova just cited, supplied not only a portrait of human personality and social situations but also a basis upon which hypotheses relevant to the study can be built. Namely: in the study of culture conflicts between the first and second generation immigrant groups, the following hypotheses were formulated:

1. Life outside the cultural fold demands independence of action and resourcefulness. Yet, it is these traits which bring the person into conflict with the social order of his group.
2. Development of a new scheme of life in accordance with, and attempts to adopt the values of, a new culture do not necessarily ensure acceptance by members of that culture.

In the case of the study of Russian-Town, to which Anna Pavlova contributed one among scores of life histories, these histories were of immense value in formulating theoretical judgments. Without them, such judgments could only have been formulated in a vacuum. "The use of documents offers . . . the opportunity to increase and sharpen

[18]Thomas and Znaniecki, *op. cit.,* Vol. I, pp. 9–10.

[one's] sense of inquiry. Other things being equal, the student who develops through the use of documents an intimate acquaintance with an area of life, will be able to analyze it more fruitfully than would one lacking such an acquaintance."[19] (And this statement comes from Blumer, who is skeptical of the value of personal documents.)

Values of case data. From earliest research usages of case data, their values and limitations have been searchingly analyzed and critically compared with those arising from the use of statistical materials. The statistically committed writers saw an incompatibility between the two techniques, for three principal reasons (as viewed first in the 1920's and 1930's). Later they radically revised their views.

> 1) The case method is not in itself a scientific method at all, but merely a first step in scientific [procedure]; 2) individual cases become of scientific significance only when classified and summarized in such forms as to reveal uniformities, types and patterns of behavior; 3) the statistical method is the best, if not the only, scientific method of classifying and summarizing large numbers of cases. The two methods are not, therefore, under any circumstances opposed to each other, nor is the one a substitute for the other.[20]

Blumer sees both advantages and limitations of personal documents as case data: ". . . Usually the separate documents cannot very well stand evaluation according to the criteria of representativeness, adequacy, and reliability. . . . Yet, to renounce their use in the scientific study of human life would be to commit a fatal blunder, for theoretically they are indispensable and actually they can be of enormous value."[21] Or as someone remarked: "A social psychology without a record of personal experiences would be like a law court without testimony."

The following statement comes from a mathematician: "Science has its firm foundation in the recognition of what the world is like. Nothing but confusion can result when mathematics is used *before* we are quite clear about the sort of things with which we are dealing and what sort of measurement it is useful to make. . . . We have not fully

[19]Blumer, *Critique of Research in the Social Sciences: An Appraisal of Thomas and Znaniecki's 'Polish Peasant'*, p. 80. Social Science Research Council, 1939.

[20]George A. Lundberg, "Casework and the Statistical Method," *Social Forces,* V (1926), p. 61. His later view is found in "Case Studies *vs.* Statistical Method," *Sociometry,* IV, 379–383.

[21]Blumer, *op. cit.,* p. 80.

replaced the sacramental by the instrumental attitude to the use of numbers."[22]

As already stated, Thomas and Znaniecki[23] were thoroughly committed to the value of case data for research purposes and believed them to be "the perfect type of sociological material." They were convinced that if social science has to resort to the use of other than human documents and case data, "it is only because of the practical difficulty of obtaining at the moment a sufficient number of records to cover the totality of sociological problems and of the enormous amount of work demanded for an adequate analysis of all personal materials necessary to characterize the life of a person or a social group."

In spite of their limitations, which will be discussed presently, case data continue to be used widely by clinical psychologists, psychiatrists, industrial psychologists, and anthropologists. (Blumer believes, however, that sociologists in general have not made as extensive use of human documents in the 1950's and 1960's as earlier.[24]) Psychologists "encounter a pragmatic reason why idiographic procedures [i.e., intensive study of an individual case as a personality or social situation] must be admitted to psychological science: practitioners demand them."[25] (Allport's vivid presentation of the need for idiographic knowledge in psychological science should be read in its entirety, pp. 56–59 and 150. Here we reproduce only brief excerpts.)

> Acquaintance with particulars is the beginning of knowledge—scientific or otherwise. In psychology the font and origin of our curiosity in, and knowledge of, human nature lies in our acquaintance with concrete individuals. To know them in their natural complexity is an essential first step. Starting too soon with analysis and classification we run the risk of tearing mental life into fragments and beginning with false cleavages that misrepresent the salient organizations and natural integrations in personal life. In order to avoid such hasty preoccupation with human segments and false abstractions, psychology needs to concern itself with life as it is lived, with significant total processes of the sort revealed in consecutive and complete life documents. . . .
>
> Personal documents are good if they serve the comparison of lives, one with another, leading to statistical generalizations and to an under-

[22]Lancelot Hogben, *Mathematics for the Millions,* pp. 224–225. W. W. Norton Co., 1951.

[23]Thomas and Znaniecki, *op. cit.,* pp. 1832–1833.

[24]Blumer, Personal communication, Jan. 1964.

[25]Allport, *op. cit.,* p. 58.

standing of the uniformities of behavior. But they are good also if standing one by one they provide concrete evidence of the nature of single personal lives from which all psychological science is derived; if they yield evidence of pluralistic causation; if they give clinicians and practitioners a sounder basis for work; if they enhance the understanding, prediction, and control of individual lives which is all that science ultimately demands. . . .

The individual case stands at the gateway and terminus of generalized knowledge. What is more, generalized knowledge is being continually enriched by its interpretation with what is special and concrete.[26]

And the logician adds: "A human mind seeks unity but cannot approach it without paving its way with dichotomies. 'Segmentation' is humanly inevitable, i.e., the problem of causation is . . . merely the wider problem of individuation."[27]

Limitations of case studies. In 1929, a few years after case studies gained considerable prominence in social research, Read Bain vigorously attacked their value as significant scientific material, because they did not provide "impersonal, universal, non-ethical, non-practical, repetitive aspects of phenomena." Instead, he contended, subjects may provide whatever data they think the investigator wants:

The greater the rapport, the more subjective the whole process is. . . . The subject is more likely to be self-justificatory than factual. . . . "The literary itch" . . . results in romantic over- and understatement, convenient forgetting, and inclusion of many things that never happened. . . . It is difficult to apply the usual methods of science [in abstracting uniformities] without destroying the rationale of the life-document method, and the unique value of the personal document will be lost if it is formalized and abstracted [according to the dictates of scientific procedure]. . . . Case situations are seldom comparable . . . in a pluralistic universe of discourse. . . . Since the subject tells his story in his own words, the logical concepts, units of scientific classification, have to be read into it, or out of it, by the investigator.[28]

[26]Allport, *op. cit.,* pp. 56, 59, 150. (In a personal communication, May 1964, Dr. Allport stated that no changes need to be made in above statement of 1942.)

[27]M. R. Cohen, *The Meaning of Human History,* pp. 107–108. Open Court Publishing Co., 1947.

[28]Bain, "The Validity of Life Histories and Diaries," *Journal of Educational Research,* III, 156–161. The above quotation is highly condensed, often giving only topical summaries. Also, in two instances the order of phrases was reversed for clearer meaning in the condensed version.

Since Professor Bain voiced his objections in 1929, it seemed advisable to inquire if he wished to modify his statements, particularly since they have influenced many researchers. The first three paragraphs of the following quotation were prepared by him for inclusion in the 1949 edition of the present text, and the last two paragraphs for the 1956 edition. It is evident from these two statements that Bain saw then many possibilities in the life-history method when it is used by well-trained research students who are methodologically oriented and have insight into the subject matter.

> While the objections made to life history and case study research in 1929 are still valid in general, they are mainly useful as possible warnings to the present-day research worker. Most of the dangers will be avoided as a matter of routine by those who are well-trained in modern methods of collecting such materials and in the scientific techniques of assembling, classifying, and processing data. Such materials are chiefly useful to "pure" research in furnishing clues for further research. They are also useful, if not indispensable, for diagnosis, therapy, and other practical case-by-case problems (applied science). The results of such work may be very useful for the deductively formulated theory. Case studies and life histories are an aspect of ideographic research—natural history, as Robert Park called it—which is a necessary prerequisite for any nomothetic science. The question today is not case study *or* quantitative research; it is rather an "and" relationship.
>
> By case study, in the broadest sense of the term, we get some fruitful hypotheses, as well as some data which may be useful in testing them, without which generalized social science would be seriously handicapped. The logical concepts, units of classification, hypotheses, and conclusions that may be deduced from such data depend upon the competence of the research worker. If errors result, he—not the data and rarely the methods used—must bear the blame.
>
> During [the 1930's and 1940's], there has been a tremendous improvement in the techniques of case studies (controlled interviews, uniform recording, and so on), and the scientific competence of those who use such material has greatly increased. Such persons as Carl Rogers, Elton Mayo, Mirra Komarovsky, Alfred Kinsey, and others, are examples of those who have used the new techniques of collecting, recording, and processing case data. These are "guided" case studies, of course. These, perhaps more than the undirected life histories, can be very useful to competent research workers.[29]
>
> During 1950's and 1960's case studies have shown a steady trend toward formalization, that is, case studies tend to be conducted so that the data can be quantified, processed and analyzed statistically.

[29]Bain, Personal communication, June 1948.

Prethought schedules of questions (structured interviews) are often used; even the answers to open-end questions are analyzed and classified into significant categories amenable to statistical treatment. Kinsey's work, many of the studies reported in the *American Soldier,* and Stuart Dodd's volume on the Revere Project are good illustrations of these techniques.

The accumulation of psychoanalytic, psychiatric, and other casework data is being used increasingly for "pure" science analysis. Case study techniques are indispensable for therapeutic and administrative purposes. The materials thus collected, especially when the social workers are research-minded, can be very useful for "pure" science research. Case study techniques can also be used profitably at present at the data-collecting level in many "pure" research projects. This is also a good example of the reciprocal relation between "pure" and applied science.[30]

Again for the present edition of this volume, Bain's earlier remarks were sent to him for new "second thoughts." In reply he wrote, in 1964:

My remarks in the third edition are substantially sound, but many important problems formerly difficult or impossible for rigorous life history study can now be pursued profitably because still better methodology has been developed in recent years. Presently behavioral scientists pay close attention to collecting of definitive data knowing that good statistical processing cannot improve poor case data. . . . What we are now learning slowly about human behavior, by inadvertence and inference, might be speeded up by good life histories which would include family backgrounds, childhood memories, how and when persons got their "big ideas" and how they worked them out. . . . We can now use biographical and autobiographical data because researchers, properly trained, can find in these data many things which the subjects themselves did not know they were providing. . . . Imaginative workers think of many areas in which life history and case data can be used for rigorous scientific research. It is still true, however, that data which are derived from observing the actual behavior of people is more valuable for rigorous research than asking them what they think, feel, and wish; and in most cases, what they *say* they have done or would do in specified circumstances, especially when taboos and social class norms are involved.[31]

The above quotations from Bain's writings and personal communications, covering a period from 1929 to 1964, typify: 1) the early vociferous objections made by many social scientists; 2) the change in

[30]Bain, Personal communication, Nov. 1954.

[31]Bain, Personal communication, Aug. 1963.

attitude these earlier critics have undergone, a generation later, toward the value of case data; 3) the critics' realization of the wide applicability of the case study method to social research data.

CASEWORK DATA AND CASE DATA IN SOCIAL RESEARCH. Considerable confusion still exists between these two types of data which in reality have quite distinct characteristics. A social case worker gathers specific information pertaining to specific case situations in order ultimately to make a separate differential diagnosis, with a view to putting a plan of treatment into operation. His dictum is "no two cases are alike." Although he has a set of concepts and a workable scheme of diagnosing them, he is rarely concerned with social analysis and with testing the validity of his materials.

The social researcher, on the other hand, seeks *comparable* case data and persistently searches for similarities, for those uniformities that enable him to classify the data and to formulate the law of their occurrence and their relationship. He does not regard specific case situations as a sufficient basis for understanding human behavior. Instead, he seeks *repetitive* and *additive* data within the process of personal, family, or community organization and disorganization in order to generalize on such processes. He is not concerned with therapy as such, although his findings often aid social therapists and community reorganizers. Also, the research scientist regards the cases at hand as possible illustrations of a line of reasoning by which he may develop new concepts or laws or may test the existing schemes of analysis.

Projective techniques. Case data obtained through personal interviews and human documents have, within the last three or four decades, been supplemented by an increasing variety of projective techniques. That is, in addition to direct interrogation and self-reporting, techniques are designed to provide the respondent with a stimulus situation in which he will freely and directly reveal knowledge about himself and his social world. For example, inkblots in the Rorschach test are shown to a respondent and, from his interpretation of them, inferences are drawn regarding his beliefs, feelings, perceptions, and attitudes. Or the respondent is given a list of open-ended questions to which he is to write brief replies. In the study of the *Authoritarian Personality*,[32] for example, some questions as follow were given: "What

[32]See T. W. Adorno, *op. cit.*, pp. 545–578. Harper & Row, 1950.

great people, living or dead, do you admire the most?" "What do you consider the worst crimes a person could commit?" "If you knew you only had six months to live and could do just as you pleased during that period, how would you spend your time?" Expected responses were worked out for each projective technique, and a number of alternatives were given. The responses were preclassified: high, low, and neutral, according to a prepared scoring manual. If such replies to the last question above were given as "I would bring my affairs in order," or "I would prepare myself to meet my Maker," they would be scored as high. Conversely, such replies as "I would try to enjoy life" were scored as low.

Projective techniques are held to be "an economical substitute for the traditional psychoanalytic session, with which it shares the capacity to penetrate to deep-lying layers of personality in a way that leaves the subject unaware of the full implications of his responses."[33] (One of the most exhaustive discussions of projective techniques is found in *An Introduction to Projective Techniques and Other Devices for Understanding the Dynamics of Human Behavior,* edited by the psychologists, Harold H. and Gladys L. Anderson, Prentice-Hall, Inc., 1951.)

Interdependence of Statistical[34] and Case Study Techniques

The statistical and case study techniques frequently supplement each other, since each views a given social situation from different angles and each places a different emphasis on the social factors in the situation. A case study seeks to determine social processes; it reveals the complexity of factors and indicates their sequences and interrelationships. Statistical studies, on the other hand, deal with relatively few factors but are able to provide scope by indicating extent, frequency, trends, and degree of association.

In studies of social change, social adjustment or unadjustment, and other types of human behavior, statistics could confirm or disprove hypotheses, or determine existing correlations, more precisely than can case data. Also, statistics aid in avoiding conclusions based on unusual or exceptional cases and in determining the trends of problems.

Conversely, statistical studies of human behavior can be enriched and seen in broader perspective if supplemented by individual case

[33]Madge, *op. cit.,* p. 408. The Free Press of Glencoe, 1962.

[34]See Chapter 11.

studies. The use of the latter also would reduce the danger which threatens those social investigators who limit themselves to describing behavior in terms of what can be conveniently counted or measured, rather than in terms of what is really useful to know about behavior.[35]

AN ILLUSTRATION OF THE INTERDEPENDENCE OF STATISTICAL STUDY OF INDIVIDUALS AND CASE STUDIES OF INDIVIDUALS, FAMILIES, AND COMMUNITY. This study was made in order to test a hypothesis—formulated on the basis of documentary materials—that there is a direct relationship between the extent of juvenile delinquency and the extent of urban contacts which result in culture conflicts. The study involved 275 Russian Molokan boys, members of 108 Molokan families who lived in an immigrant area. It revealed that 181 boys, or 65.8 per cent, were delinquent and 94 boys, or 34.2 per cent of the total number studied, were their nondelinquent brothers. At the time of this study there were 198 boys between 9 and 19 years of age. (This group we designate as group *A*.) Of this number 155, or 78.3 per cent, were known delinquents. Only 53 boys were between 20 and 24 years of age (group *B*); of this number 25, or 46.2 per cent, were delinquent; and 24 boys (group *C*) were over 25 years of age, of whom only one boy was delinquent.

It would have been impossible to interpret these statistical findings were it not for the use of case data. To some the figures meant that the "Russian Molokan group is rapidly disintegrating"; to others the figures indicated a high degree of psychoses and neuroses. Some persons maintained that the differences in the findings were due primarily to administrative changes in the police and juvenile courts. However, when each of these boys as a unit was studied carefully from many angles[36]—psychological, psychiatric, educational, medical—it was revealed that other factors than those assumed above were operative to explain the high rate of delinquency in group *A* and low rate in group *C*. Furthermore, these case studies revealed that from psychological, psychiatric, and medical standpoints there were no significant differences between the delinquent boys and their nondelinquent brothers, the control group. In addition, other factors were studied statistically, which in other groups are often found to be causal factors in delin-

[35]See John Madge, *op. cit.,* various references to statistical techniques, *passim.*

[36]Pauline V. Young, *Pilgrims of Russian-Town,* Chapter 6 and pp. 17–21, 72–74, 99–100, 162–163, 203–207. University of Chicago Press, 1932.

quency: broken homes, family dependency, housing conditions, occupations of fathers, and other factors. But in this study these factors were practically eliminated, since they were the same for the delinquent and nondelinquent groups of boys, since they were brothers.

When the cultural history of the Molokan colony was scrutinized and when the colony was studied as a case, significant clues to the problem were secured. Following is a brief excerpt from a report presented before the American Sociological Society in Chicago, which will clarify the point:

The Los Angeles Molokan colony has witnessed several stages of social adjustment. Using this fact as a point of reference, we can characterize the three age groups of boys, described above, in terms of their cultural background and contacts with urban American life:

1. The boys in group *C* (25 years and over) were all born in Russia and came to Los Angeles as very young children. Though they have attended American public schools, the majority reached only the fifth or sixth grade, when they were withdrawn and entered into American industries as apprentices, messengers, and helpers of all kinds. They married at an early age, usually at eighteen or nineteen years. Very few of them have broken away from the Molokan church, and a vast majority still attend regularly. On the whole, they have always identified themselves to a large extent with the native institutions of the group and have always been subject to the control of the home and the community, as their life histories indicate. And perhaps most important of all is the fact that when they were children there was no tradition of juvenile delinquency in the group. Everybody was well behaved and under the control of elders. Even as young boys they showed remarkable social stability.
2. The boys in group *B* (20 to 24 years) were born in America. Their parents had been living in the city then for a few years. The contributions of the younger children to the family income were not as urgently needed as previously, and their entry into industries was somewhat delayed. The period of their school attendance was more prolonged, and the time after school unoccupied and unsupervised. These boys were left to their own resources a great deal, and they entered the street life of the district in which they lived. Mingling with other cultural groups became widespread, and participation in a variety of codes and behavior patterns was inevitable. Behavior widely divergent from that of their elders soon appeared, and many clashes within the home arose. The traditional mode of control was no longer fully operative, and home and community influences were greatly undermined. The conflict of cultures began in

earnest with characteristic results well-known to students of social life. Yet careful study of the group shows that as soon as these boys entered industrial life, and their contacts with urban street life terminated, they became stabilized, and their delinquencies ended shortly. They then became once more subject to the control of their elders, and they began to identify themselves in many real ways with the life of the Molokan group. They also married early and they are now, so to speak, Molokans redeemed and reclaimed.

3. The boys in group *A* (9 to 19 years) are also American-born Molokans, but they were born into a situation in which home control was weakened and social disorganization already advancing. They had witnessed the delinquencies of their older brothers, and a delinquency pattern was already set for them. The younger boys were inducted into many delinquencies by the older boys, as the little gangs which they formed nearly all indicated some blood relationship. The cultural conflict seemed (in 1928) to be at its height. Parents generally recognized their utter helplessness in controlling the situation. And as the date for entry into industrial life was delayed and the age of marriage delayed more and more—stabilization of the youth was more uncertain and disintegration more evident. With each year since 1915, not only had the numbers of offenders steadily increased, but the number of offenses per boy had steadily risen, as the data indicate. Evidently, the longer the period of contact with urban conditions and the less the control by native institutions, the greater the opportunities for escape and the greater the rate of recidivism in the group studied. Recidivism thus seems to be a function of urban contacts.

The native institutions apparently had very good control over the children whom the Molokans brought with them to Los Angeles as young boys and girls. These are looked upon by their parents as truly "Russian children," and they identify themselves more completely with the lives, activities, feelings, and sentiments of the older group, while their later-born brothers and sisters identify themselves more with city life and are less responsive to Molokan traditions and religious ideals. These traditional ideals are growing more and more abstract to the American-bred Molokan children. Culture is acquired through contact and participation, and one must literally live it to be affected by it. The American-born Molokan children display remarkable traits of personal initiative and ingenuity and have been constantly brought into contact with situations which demand of them independence of action and ability to make their own decisions. They have thus become individualized at an early age, and under new conditions of living will no longer submit unquestioningly to the traditional control which the elders have so long exercised in the colony. These children have become responsive to a variety of non-Molokan institutions, and have developed new conceptions of their duties and responsibilities.

It might be pointed out here that the control group in this study does not vary in age, race, sex, cultural background, home environment, economic status, and educational facilities. Therefore, to a large extent, the shortcomings of control groups—particularly when a large number of variables is presented in the control and experimental groups—are eliminated. However, this study does not obviate the difficulty of control-group comparisons, since we did not measure the precise degree to which the delinquent behavior was present in the experimental group and absent in the control group. To carry out precise measurements, we would have had to adhere to carefully matching methods in selecting the delinquent and nondelinquent samples in terms of degree of conformity and nonconformity in each group.[37]

In this study the statistical data were analyzed by the case grouping method. This procedure consists largely of trial-and-error grouping, subgrouping, and regrouping of those attributes and simple clusters of traits and happenings which uniformly stand out as relevant to our inquiry.[38] Other patterns and traits rise up as relevant in the process of case grouping. Each case thus steadily expands as we concentrate on, and recognize the number and type of, attributes which characterize and which are uniform among the cases with which it is being grouped. The groupings are at times too complex for simple classification, and it is then necessary to seek out subpatterns and subtraits in the case data. The process of grouping and subgrouping is a crucial one in any scientific procedure, since considerable discretion is needed in determining relevancy of the various factors to the group or subgroup under which they are being classified. Often, rigorous testing is needed before a final grouping is made. Also, in a desire to derive certain conclusions, it is essential to guard against a tendency to "force" certain traits into particular classes, shutting one's eyes to their deviant or marginal nature.

The foregoing discussion serves not only as an illustration of the

[37]The above statement was stimulated by and based on Walter C. Reckless, *The Etiology of Delinquent Behavior: A Planning Report for Research.* Social Science Research Council Bulletin, 1943, pp. 83–84.

[38]This entire paragraph owes much to the ideas expressed by Leonard A. Salters, "Cross-Sectional and Case Grouping Procedures in Research Analysis," *Journal of Farm Economics,* XXXV (Nov. 1942), p. 801.

interdependence of the statistical and case study techniques but shows also the need for establishing independent evidence before an explanation can be offered as to how certain behavior patterns come into being. At the time when the study of the Russian Molokans was first initiated, the present author heard a good many explanations regarding the "causes of delinquency among these Russians: perverse attitudes, poor heredity, low intelligence, emotional instability," and so on. On the basis of the actual study, all of these explanations have to be set aside as invalid. "Explanations of the behavior of an individual in terms of certain personal qualities imputed to him without independent evidence as to how he acquired or developed such qualities do not constitute sound practice, if only for the reason that they cannot be proved or disproved."[39] An analysis of motivational factors in particular requires most rigorous use of evidence.

In conclusion, we may state that much discussion prevails on the relative values and limitations of the case study method as a research tool. Some research workers do not believe that case data, and particularly personal life histories, lend themselves adequately to quantitative expression without which there can be no science. Others contend that case data, when carefully selected from representative members of a given group who are capable of providing concrete categorical experiences of their lives, would typify those of others in their group because they tend to react more or less in characteristic manner to the same stimuli in their culture. Just how far it is possible to select representative cases and typical experiences cannot be finally determined until recourse is had to statistical procedures. Pending statistical tests the research worker can only rely on experience, insight, and sound judgment. This situation is the same, of course, in the social, biological, and physical sciences.

The earliest to the latest proponents of the case study method have pointed out that case data, more so than any other kind or that secured by any other means, are capable of revealing the interests, motives, and inner lives of persons and the meaning the social world assumes in their outlook on, and reactions to, life. Case data tend to represent the natural development of a life-cycle of a person or of an evolving process of a social situation with all complex interrelated factors.

Other scientists have seriously questioned the ability of "case-students" to identify general types, classes, and processes from subjective

[39]Social Science Research Council, *The Social Sciences in Historical Study: A Report of the Committee on Historiography,* Bulletin 64, p. 68. The Council, 1954.

data and to make valid and verifiable generalizations regarding social life. These disputes have stimulated much earnest thought.

The techniques for recording case histories need much serious attention. The raw narrative data are at times a curious admixture of accounts of personal experiences of the narrator and views and biases of the recorder. Devotion to accurate and precise recording of specific situations is a cardinal essential in scientific reports. Writing up a case history should be looked upon as having as much importance as writing up a laboratory experiment. Uniform methods of recording and carefully selected case data may provide a basis for comparison and classification of significant common as well as peculiar differences in given situations, and ultimately serve as a basis for deriving scientific generalizations. This aim can be more easily achieved if the case and statistical methods supplement each other. The feeling is gradually disappearing that these two methods are at variance with each other. As Kimball Young says, many of the problems of the case history method are not unlike those of statistics:

> There is, of course, a recognition of a set of specific and general factors to be studied. The more careful case histories also recognize the problem of sampling, since the aim is to avoid the temptation to generalize from one case. So, too, references are frequently made to typical cases, which is a way of referring to some central tendency. Likewise, attention is given to the divergent instance, which is but an informal way of stating facts about variability. Finally, the worker with these data may compare his findings with those of other samples, and in order to expose dynamic relations he may indicate in qualitative terms covariation or correlation between selected factors and situations.[40]

Although this is not universal procedure among social research workers, it is becoming a more common practice with better trained workers who have a mastery of, and insight into, statistics, sociometry, and case studies.

(With regard to the Molokan colony the question is frequently raised as to "the latest and present developments there." Case studies made during the 1940's and 1950's point to the fact that delinquency has virtually disappeared there. A cultural revival initiated by a large group of young Molokans who, during World War II, began to recognize the advantages of their "brotherhood," has brought about this virtual

[40]Kimball Young, *Personality and Problems of Adjustment,* pp. 250–251. Appleton-Century-Crofts, 1940. Reprinted by permission.

disappearance. However, the case studies also point to the fact that in general there is a far better adjustment to American city life and that the bases for culture conflicts are greatly minimized. Nevertheless, much still remains to be learned.)

basic statistical concepts and techniques[1]

By
CALVIN F. SCHMID
University of Washington

The quantitative expression of social fact is to be preferred for scientific purposes whenever it can be used. It reduces individual bias to a minimum, permits verification by other investigators, reduces and at the same time makes evident the margin of error, and replaces the less exact meanings of descriptive words with the precision of mathematical notation.

STUART A. RICE

11

As the result of an urgent need for more precise and objective methods, statistical techniques have been gaining increasingly wide acceptance among social scientists. It will be found that the development of any science is marked by the extent to which exact quantitative data and techniques have superseded mere speculation and qualitative impressions. Astronomy, physics, and chemistry are frequently referred to as "exact" sciences largely because their data and methodology are relatively precise and quantitative. It seems safe to say that as the social sciences advance from the impressionistic and qualitative stages, statistical methods will become increasingly important. In fact, at the present time, a thorough knowledge of at least the fundamentals of statistics is an indispensable part of the equipment of the research worker in the social science field.[2]

A knowledge of basic statistical concepts and techniques is also neces-

[1]The author is indebted to Dr. Earle H. MacCannell of Portland State College and Dr. Herbert Costner and Mr. Kiyoshi Tagashira of the University of Washington for a critical reading of this chapter and for offering valuable suggestions.

[2]For a more extended but elementary discussion of statistical techniques, see Sanford M. Dornbusch and Calvin F. Schmid, *A Primer of Social Statistics*. McGraw-Hill Book Company, 1955.

sary for an intelligent understanding of current writings in the social sciences. It is generally taken for granted by writers in this field that the reader knows the meaning of such elementary terms as the mean, median, mode, quartiles, standard deviation, correlation, and reliability. The profit which one derives from reading technical studies of this kind is largely in proportion to the understanding of statistical methods.

This chapter is a simple outline of the more common principles and methods used in statistical analysis. The selection and treatment of each topic are based on the author's judgment of what he considers most significant and fundamental for a concise and simple discussion of this kind. Every effort has been made to present the material as clearly and simply as possible without resorting to the more advanced and theoretical techniques. Only a minimum amount of mathematics is required to understand the topics discussed. It is assumed that the reader has a knowledge of arithmetic and the simplest rudiments of algebra. It will be observed that practical application of statistical techniques to concrete problems has been stressed, and all the illustrative examples are based on actual data. Because of the limited space available, emphasis has been placed on computational skills but not to the exclusion of interpretation. The beginner must not get the impression that statistics is a type of mechanical jugglery. A critical judgment and insight as well as a fertile and constructive imagination are perhaps more important than mere computational skills in statistical work.

Statistical Units

Any kind of statistical work presupposes the existence of units. The units are expressed in quantitative form. They are totaled, multiplied, divided, and manipulated in other ways and are of basic importance in the collection, analysis, and interpretation of statistical data. It is imperative that each type of unit be defined accurately and unmistakably. Results of a study may be entirely vitiated by units that are vague and ambiguous.

A satisfactory statistical unit should possess the following qualities: 1) appropriateness, 2) clarity, 3) measurability, and 4) comparability.[3] The appropriateness of a unit is determined by the purpose of

[3]George A. Lundberg, *Social Research,* pp. 93–104. Longmans, Green Co., 1942.

a study. A unit appropriate for one study may not be so for another. The criterion of clarity implies precision and simplicity of definition. The definition of a unit should be readily understandable and should possess the same meaning for all people concerned. Satisfactory statistical units should fulfill the requirement of measurability in the broadest sense of that term. Units must be expressed in objective and quantitative form since they are used for counting and measuring. In planning a statistical study an effort should be made to define the units in such a way as to make them comparable with units of similar studies.

To emphasize the significance and importance of defining statistical units with clarity and precision, the problem of determining college and university enrollment may be cited for illustrative purposes. Superficially, one might consider this problem extremely simple, but in actuality this is not the case. Obviously, the basic statistical unit in measuring enrollment is "student." In practice, however, the term "student" does not possess a precise and consistent meaning. There are "full-time" students and "part-time" students; there are students attending classes during the day and others in the evening; there are students attending campus classes, others at branches and extension centers; undergraduate students and graduate students, while in community colleges there are "vocational" as well as academic students. The United States Office of Education uses the concept "degree-credit" student, which excludes virtually all vocational "students" and others who are taking courses which are not creditable toward a baccalaureate or other type of academic degree.

In an effort to attain reliability and comparability in measuring college and university enrollment, the present author developed the following units and definitions: First, the concept of the individual student taking course work for credit which includes 1) "full-time" student, a student registered for 12 or more credit-hours and 2) "part-time" student, a student registered for less than 12 credit-hours. Second, the concept of "full-time student—equivalent credit-hour load index," which does not represent "live bodies," but rather an index derived from the total number of registered student credit-hours divided by the constant 15. Third, students who do not receive course credit, including auditors and those registered in adult education and vocational classes. Obviously, most of the registrants in such courses are not strictly speaking college students. Nevertheless, if the total service-load of an institution of higher learning is to be determined this category should not be disregarded. Certainly, however, they should be included in a distinct category entirely separate from regular academic students taking work creditable toward a degree.[4]

Tabulating Statistical Data

In the preceding chapters various methods of gathering statistical and other kinds of data were discussed at some length. When a mass of data has been assembled, it is necessary to arrange the material in some kind of concise and logical order. This procedure is referred to as tabulation. The assembled data may be on schedules used by enumerators in a field survey, on questionnaires which have been answered and mailed in by informants, or on forms taken from the files of some private organization or governmental agency.

The first step in tabulating statistical data is to work out a detailed system of classification. Classification is fundamental to any kind of scientific analysis. The general scheme of classification is commonly determined before the data are gathered but is seldom actually completed until all the data have been collected. The basis of any statistical classification is determined by the problem at hand as well as by the characteristic features of the data. In actual practice it will be found that one or more of the following criteria are almost invariably used in statistical classification: 1) geographical, 2) chronological or temporal, 3) qualitative or attributive, and 4) quantitative. If the geographical criterion is chosen as a basis of classification, the data will be organized in terms of some such geographical division as a state, region, city, county, ward, or census tract. Some unit of time such as a day, week, month, or year may serve as the basis of classification for certain kinds of statistical data. Certain qualities or attributes such as sex, color, nativity, occupation, and marital status are also frequently used in statistical classifications. A quantitative criterion as expressed by size or magnitude is a particularly common basis of classification in statistical work. The frequency distribution which will be discussed is an excellent illustration of this type of classification.

After the classification has been determined, the individual cases or items in the assembled data are sorted and counted according to the various categories in the classification. The sorting and counting process

[4]For a more detailed discussion of these concepts see, Calvin F. Schmid, *et al., Enrollment Statistics, Colleges and Universities, State of Washington: Fall Term, 1963,* Seattle: Washington State Census Board, 1964, *passim.*

can be done either by hand or by machinery, depending upon the number of cases or items to be tabulated, as well as upon the staff and money that are available. If the number of cases is relatively small, the tabulating work can be done by hand. In case the data are on cards or small sheets they can be sorted into piles and counted directly. This system was the one generally used for larger-scale projects before the days of mechanical tabulation. Another common method is to enter each case in the appropriate compartment of a tally sheet by means of a line, check, dot, or other mark. The tally sheet is a blank table with properly labeled columns and rows. Figure 11.1 is an example of a

WEIGHT	TABULATION	FRE-QUENCY
90- 99	/	1
100-109	/	1
110-119	~~////~~ ////	9
120-129	~~////~~ ~~////~~ ~~////~~ ~~////~~ ~~////~~ ~~////~~	30
130-139	~~////~~ ~~////~~ ~~////~~ ~~////~~ ~~////~~ ~~////~~ ~~////~~ ~~////~~ //	42
140-149	~~////~~ ~~////~~ ~~////~~ ~~////~~ ~~////~~ ~~////~~ ~~////~~ ~~////~~ ~~////~~ ~~////~~ ~~////~~ ~~////~~ ~~////~~ /	66
150-159	~~////~~ ~~////~~ ~~////~~ ~~////~~ ~~////~~ ~~////~~ ~~////~~ ~~////~~ ~~////~~ //	47
160-169	~~////~~ ~~////~~ ~~////~~ ~~////~~ ~~////~~ ~~////~~ ~~////~~ ////	39
170-179	~~////~~ ~~////~~ ~~////~~	15
180-189	~~////~~ ~~////~~ /	11
190-199	/	1
200-209	///	3
TOTAL NUMBER OF CASES		265

Figure 11.1 Tabular work sheet for a frequency distribution. Data represent weights of 265 freshmen at the University of Washington.

tally sheet for a frequency distribution. It shows the distribution by weight of 265 Freshman students of the University of Washington. If there is a large number of items or cases, or if many detailed tabular forms are contemplated, hand tabulation may be found so laborious and expensive that mechanical tabulation will have to be used. In mechanical tabulation the data on the original forms are transferred to cards by punching holes for each item. The punching of the cards is based on a coding system. After the cards are punched they are first run through a sorting machine and then through a tabulating machine. With modern tabulating equipment it is possible to tabulate tens of thousands of items in a workday.

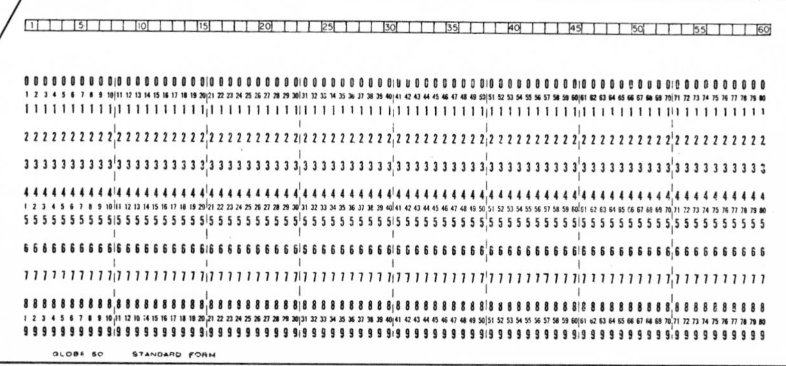

Punched card on which enrollment data for community colleges in the state of Washington have been recorded (reduced size).

Code Sheet for Accompanying IBM Card

Column	Variable or Category
1-2	College code number (from 01 to 14).
3-11	Social Security Number.
12-13	Academic Credit-Hours.
14-15	Vocational Credit-Hours.
16-17	Adult Education Credit-Hours.
18-19	Community Service Student (represented by code 00).
20-21	Total number of registered hours.
22	Sex (1 for male; 2 for female).
23-24	Year of birth.
25	Resident of Washington State (1 for yes; 2 for no).
26-27	Distance one way daily travel (only the first two numbers of the category, i.e., 00 to 0.9 would be 00).
28-34	High School last attended.
35	High School graduate (1 for yes; 2 for no).
36-37	Year of high school graduation.
38	First time in any college (1 for yes; 2 for no).
39	First time in this college (1 for yes; 2 for no).
40	Plan to enter a four-year college (1 for yes; 2 for no).
41-42	College last attended.
43	Student Status: 1 for academic only; 2 for academic with some vocational; 3 for vocation only; 4 for vocational with some academic; 5 for vocational with some adult education; 6 for adult education; 7 for community service.
44	Full-time and part-time (1 for part-time; 2 for full-time).
45-46	State of foreign country (State code same as number by alphabet; foreign country 90).
47-48	County of Washington code.

Variables

A variable is any quantity or characteristic which may possess different numerical values or categories. Time, age, wages, prices, scores on intelligence tests, political party preference, and sex are examples of variables. Some variables can be differentiated according to the number of units of some measure which they possess. Time and age are of this type since they are differentiated according to the number of years, days, months, or some other time units which are associated with them. Other variables can be differentiated only according to a described characteristic. Political preference is not divided into units of political preference, but is differentiated on the basis of Republican, Democrat, Socialist, and other political groupings. Sex is not variable in terms of numbers of units of sex, but in terms of the categories male and female. Variables which have a certain number of defined units, such as years, dollars, inches, or pounds can be manipulated by the rules of mathematics and are called cardinally defined quantitative variables. Some variables do not have countable units associated with them, but can be differentiated according to some less precise definition of quantity. If each of several cakes at a county fair is judged to be best, second best, etc., down to poorest in the group, no number of units of "goodness" is indicated, but some loosely defined amount of "goodness" is implied in the differentiation. Variables which are ordered on a continuum according to some variable characteristic are said to be ordinally defined quantitative variables. Some variables cannot be differentiated according to either implied or explicitly stated units. These are designated as qualitatively defined variables.

Variate values refer to the values indicated by a variable. When considered in the aggregate they constitute a *series*. Qualitatively defined variables are considered to have "all or nothing" variate values.

A distinction is usually made between quantitatively defined variables which are *continuous* and those which are *discrete*. A continuous variable has an unlimited number of possible values ranging between the lowest and highest, with no gaps or breaks except at a limited number of specified values. It is said to be discontinuous at those points. A discrete variable is defined only for a series of specified values with no possibility of variate values between those points. A continuous variable is capable of indefinite refinement, but the discrete variable is not subject to such refinement. Each value of a discrete variable is distinct and separate, whereas the values of a continuous variable merge into one another by minute gradations. Age, weight, and temperature are examples of continuous variables; people, houses and automobiles are examples of discrete variables. In practice all variables are treated as discrete units, the continuous type variables being refined to some specified discrete unit size according to the needs of the particular situation and the precision of the measuring instrument. Although length is subject to indefinite refinement in theory and can be considered to be continuous, in actual practice, length is described in discrete units of inches, hundredths of inches, milimicrons or some other specified length unit. The difference between discrete variables and the specified units used in describing a continuous variable becomes extremely important in connection with class boundaries and class limits in frequency distributions.

Frequency Distribution

Variables that are classified according to magnitude or size are very often arranged in the form of a frequency distribution. Figure 11.1 is a simple illustration of a frequency distribution. It will be observed that the class-intervals expressed in pounds are indicated on the left and the number of cases or frequencies in each interval are shown on the right.

In constructing a frequency distribution it is necessary at the very beginning to determine 1) the number of class-intervals to be used, 2) the size of the class-intervals, and 3) the designation of the class-intervals.

1. Ordinarily there should be not less than 8 or 10 and not more than 18 or 20 class-intervals, depending on the nature of the data and on the number of cases being studied. In order to obtain a clear understanding of the original data the individual items are frequently arranged in either ascending or descending order of magnitude. Such a classification is known as an *array*. After noting the highest and lowest values as well as the characteristic features of the data, the number of intervals can be determined more easily.
2. For many types of data it is extremely important to have intervals of uniform size. The intervals should not be so small as to lose the advantages of summarization or so large as to conceal the more important characteristics of the distribution. Moreover, if the class-intervals are too small, vacant or blank intervals might occur. If comparisons are to be made between similar data, it is advisable to

select class-intervals of the same size for all the distributions. Whenever possible the class-intervals should represent common and convenient numerical divisions such as 5 or 10, rather than odd divisions such as 3 or 7.

3. After the size of the class-intervals has been determined, it is important that they be clearly designated in the frequency table. Each interval must have definite lower and upper limits, and must be expressed in such a way as to obviate any possibility of misinterpretation or confusion. The class-intervals are generally indicated by the first and last numbers of the interval. Thus, for example, 20 to 24 represents an interval of five; 10 to 19, an interval of ten; 2 to 3, an interval of two; and 9 to 11, an interval of three. A distinction should be made between the expressed limits and the actual limits of a class-interval. The actual separation between the intervals depends upon the precision of measurement in the original data. If the measures are carried to two decimal places then the actüal upper limits, say of an interval of ten, would be 0 to 9.99. As will be observed from Figure 11.2 it is a commonly accepted practice in statistics to express the upper limits of class-intervals as integral numbers. In a discrete series the class-intervals are self-evident since a single unit determines the limits of the class-intervals.

Every class-interval has a midpoint which is midway between the upper and lower limits. Figure 11.2 illustrates the midpoints of an even and of an odd interval. It will be observed that the midpoint of

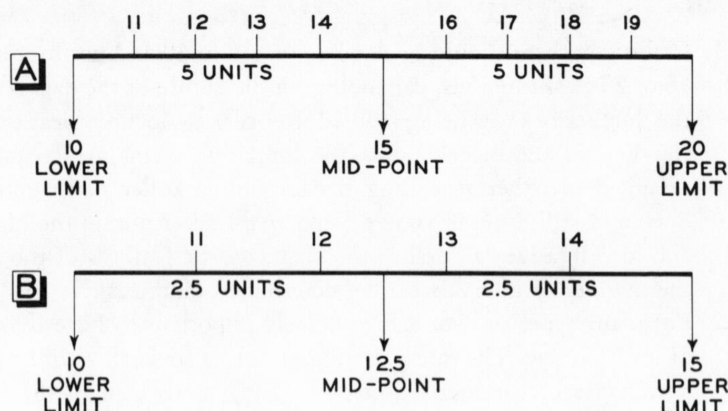

Figure 11.2 Class-intervals and midpoints. A represents an even class-interval, and B represents an odd class-interval.

the interval 10 to 19 is 15 and that of the interval 10 to 14 is 12.5. After the class-intervals have been determined, it is a relatively simple matter to count the number of cases that fall in each interval.

Statistical Tables

After the data have been tabulated, the next step is to arrange at least part of them in statistical tables. Statistical tables have been referred to as the "shorthand of statistics." No matter what type of statistical problem one is investigating, there will almost invariably be a need for tables. It is therefore of extreme importance for the student of social research to have a thorough understanding of table construction. The advantages of presenting statistical data in tabular form are so obvious as to make extended comment unnecessary. It might, however, be pointed out that: 1) statistical tables conserve space and reduce explanatory and descriptive statements to a minimum; 2) the visualization of relations and the process of comparison is greatly facilitated by tables; 3) tabulated data can be more easily remembered than data which are not tabulated; 4) a tabular arrangement facilitates the summation of items and the detection of errors and omissions; and 5) statistical tables provide a basis for computations.[5]

In any discussion of the rules and practices which should be followed in the construction of statistical tables, it is important to make a distinction between the general purpose table and the special purpose table. The first type of table is also known as an original, primary, or reference table, and the latter type has been variously referred to as an analytical, summary, interpretative, derivative, or secondary table. The general purpose table is designed to include large amounts of source data in convenient and accessible form, whereas the special purpose table aims to illustrate or demonstrate certain points in a statistical analysis or to emphasize significant relationships in the data. The difference between the general purpose and the special purpose tables is well illustrated by the many published reports of the United States Bureau of the Census. Virtually all of the tables in the reports

[5]Some useful manuals on statistical tabulation are: Ray Ovid Hall, *Handbook of Tabular Presentation.* The Ronald Press, 1943; H. M. Walker and W. N. Durost, *Statistical Tables, Their Structure and Use,* Teachers College Bureau of Publications, Columbia University, 1936; Bruce L. Jenkinson, *Bureau of the Census Manual of Tabular Presentation.* Government Printing Office, 1949; Hans Zeisel, *Say It with Figures.* Harper & Row, Publishers, 1957.

on population, vital statistics, agriculture, manufacturing, and other subjects are of the general purpose type. They represent extensive repositories of statistical information. Examples of the special purpose table are to be found in monographs and articles in which the table is fundamentally an instrument of analysis. The purpose of such tables is to reveal significant relations among the data or to emphasize certain facts. In the present discussion our main interest is in the special purpose table.

The rules and procedures in constructing statistical tables are not entirely standardized, but there are certain generally accepted principles and usages which should be adhered to closely.

1. Every table should have a title. The title should represent a succinct description of the contents of the table, and should make the table intelligible without reference to the text. The title should be clear, concise, and adequate and should answer the questions *what? where?* and *when?* The title should always be placed above the body of the table.
2. Every table should be identified by a number to facilitate easy reference. The number may be either arabic or roman, and it can be centered above the title or placed on the first line of the title.
3. The captions or column headings and the stubs or row headings of the table should be clear and brief.
4. Any explanatory footnotes concerning the table itself are placed directly beneath the table, and in order to obviate any possible confusion with the textual footnotes such reference symbols as the asterisk (*), dagger (†), double dagger (‡), and section mark (§) should be used.
5. If the data in a series of tables have been obtained from different sources, it is ordinarily advisable to indicate the specific sources in an inconspicuous place just below the table.
6. In order to emphasize the relative significance of certain categories, different kinds of type, spacing, and indentation can be used.
7. Leaders are generally used to guide the eye from the stubs to the first column, except where the column is set so closely that no guide is required.
8. It is important that all column figures be properly aligned. Decimal points and plus-minus signs also should be in perfect alignment.
9. Usually the columns are separated from one another by lines. Lines of this kind bring out the relations of the data more clearly and make the table more readable and attractive. Lines are always

drawn at the top and bottom of the table and below the captions. It is not at all necessary to draw lines along the sides of the table.

10. Sometimes the columns are numbered to facilitate reference.
11. Miscellaneous and exceptional items are generally placed in the last row of the table.
12. Since it may be found very confusing to read a long table when all the rows or lines are single spaced it is a common practice to group the stubs, as these sideheads are called. Generally, grouping of stubs by fives or fours is very satisfactory.
13. Abbreviations should be avoided whenever possible and ditto marks should not be used in a statistical table.
14. The actual arrangement of the major classes in the table depends on the facts and relationships that are to be emphasized. It should always be kept in mind, however, that a statistical table should be made as logical, clear, accurate, and simple as possible.
15. Columns and rows which are to be compared with one another should be brought close together.
16. Totals can be placed either at the top or at the bottom. It might be pointed out in this connection that the most conspicuous part of a table is the upper left-hand corner.
17. The arrangement of the categories in a table may be chronological, geographical, alphabetical, or according to magnitude. Chronological series may read from top to bottom or from bottom to top, or left to right or right to left, depending on the emphasis or importance of the data in the series. With the exception of time series, categories as a rule should be arranged according to magnitude. If the order of importance has no particular significance, geographical order may be employed. Alphabetical arrangement is used much more frequently in general purpose than in special purpose tables.

Graphic Presentation of Frequency Distributions

In analyzing or reporting the data of frequency distributions it is often desirable to use some form of graphic presentation. There are three kinds of graphs which are used for presenting frequency distributions: 1) the histogram or column diagram, 2) the frequency polygon, and 3) the smoothed frequency curve. These graphs are all drawn on rectangular coordinates. The X-axis or axis of abscissae represents the class-intervals and the Y-axis or axis of ordinates represents the frequencies. The horizontal axis reads from left to right and the vertical axis from bottom to top.[6]

1. **Histograms.** The typical histogram is constructed by erecting vertical lines at the limits of the class-intervals and forming a series of contiguous rectangles or columns. The area of each rectangle represents the respective class frequencies. If the histogram is constructed over equal class intervals, the heights of the rectangles will be proportional to the areas. In such cases the heights will represent the class frequencies. Figure 11.3 is an illustration of the histogram.

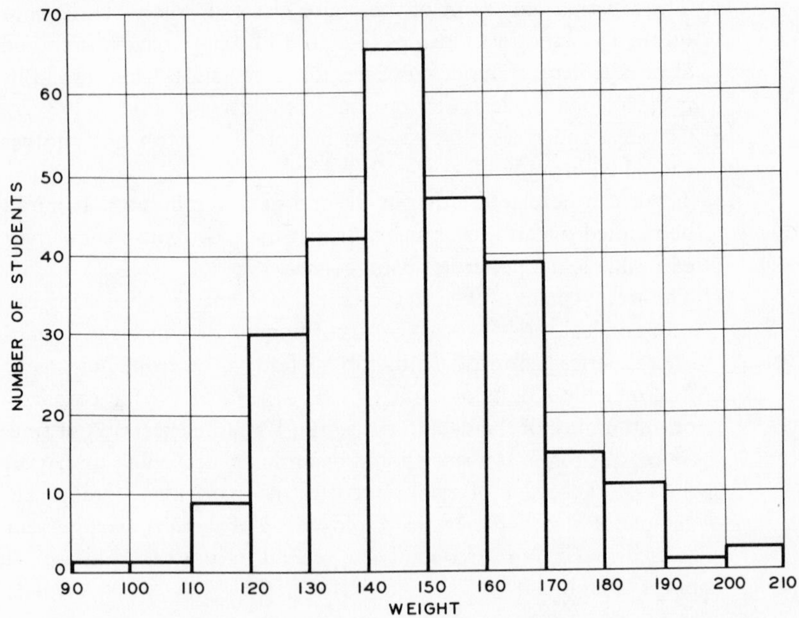

Figure 11.3 Histogram based on the data in Table 11.1, p. 291.

2. **Frequency polygons.** In laying out a frequency polygon the appropriate frequency of each class is located at the midpoint of the interval and the plotting points are then connected by straight lines. If two or more series are shown on the same graph, the curves

[6]For a more detailed discussion of the principles of graphic presentation see Chapter 13.

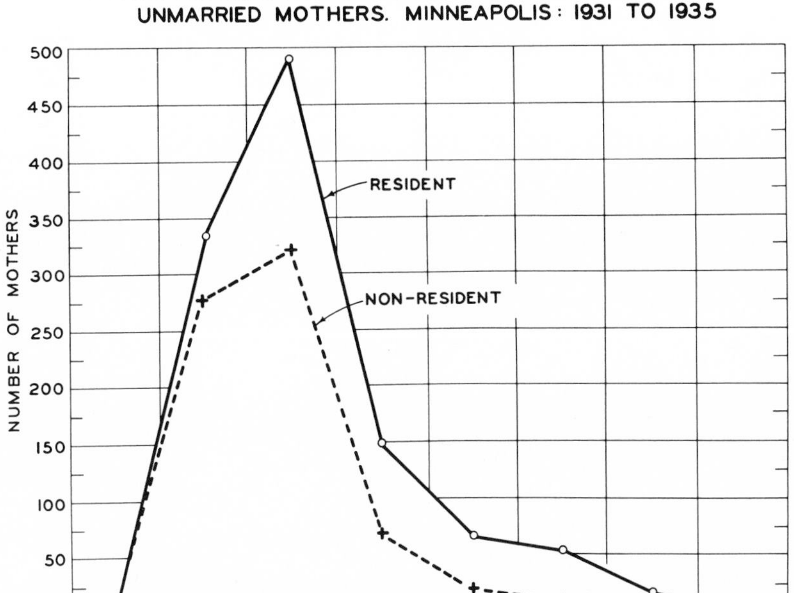

Figure 11.4 Frequency polygons based on original data. From Calvin F. Schmid, *Mortality Trends in the State of Minnesota,* pp. 273–275.

can be made with different kinds of ruling. In Figure 11.4 it will be observed that one polygon is shown by a full line and one by a dashed line. If the total number of cases in the two series is of different size, the frequencies are often reduced to percentages. In this type of chart the vertical scale represents percentages rather than absolute frequencies. The frequency polygon is particularly appropriate for portraying continuous series.

3. **Smoothed frequency curves.** Since many frequency distributions are based on relatively small samples, it is sometimes desirable to portray the data by means of a smoothed curve rather than a polygon. In smoothing a frequency curve it is assumed that the minor fluctuations in the distribution are due to the relatively small number of cases under observation.

If the number of cases in the sample is increased, the irregularities tend to disappear and the real nature of the distribution becomes more apparent. Theoretically, in the same manner, the smoothed curve is supposed to represent more truthfully the general characteristics of the original data. It cannot be emphasized too strongly, however, that the beginner should be very cautious and discriminating in the smoothing of frequency distributions.

Of the many different techniques used for the smoothing of frequency curves, the following simple graphic method will be found satisfactory for most practical purposes.[7]

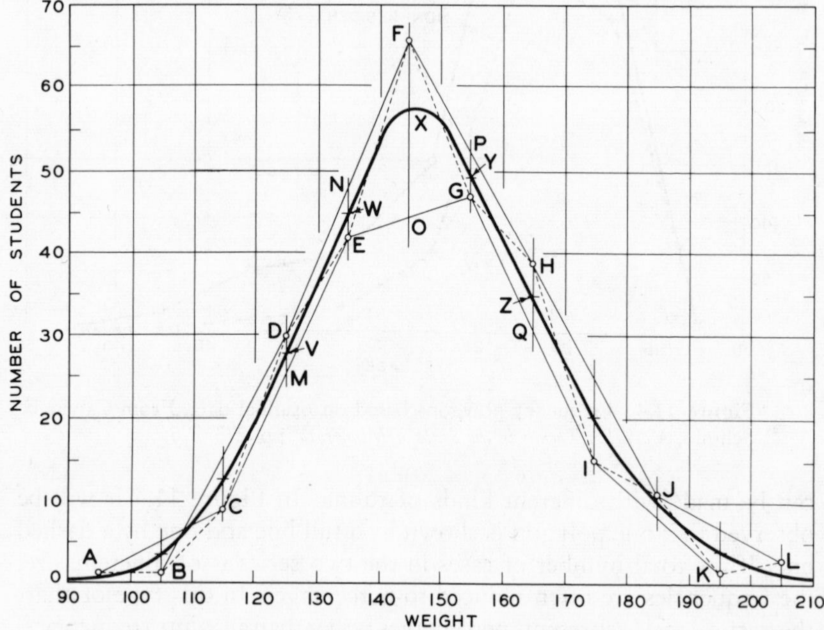

Figure 11.5 Smoothing a frequency distribution. Based on the data in Table 11.1.

1. The first step is to draw a frequency polygon of the data. In Figure 11.5 the original frequency polygon is shown by a light dashed line. The plotting points are represented by small circles and are designated by the letters *A* to *L* inclusive.
2. Every other plotting point is connected by a straight line. That is,

[7] L. L. Thurstone, *The Fundamentals of Statistics*, pp. 39–44. The Macmillan Company, 1938.

the points A and C, B and D, C and E, D and F, and so on in Figure 11.5 are joined by straight lines.

3. Vertical lines are drawn through each of the original plotting points intersecting the connecting lines AC, BD, CE, DF, and so on.
4. The midpoints of the distance between the plotting points and the connecting lines AC, BD, CE, DF, and so on are determined by inspection. As an illustration of this step, observe the vertical lines

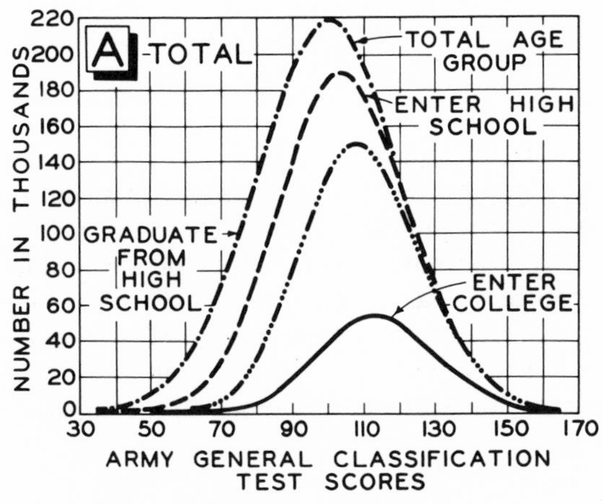

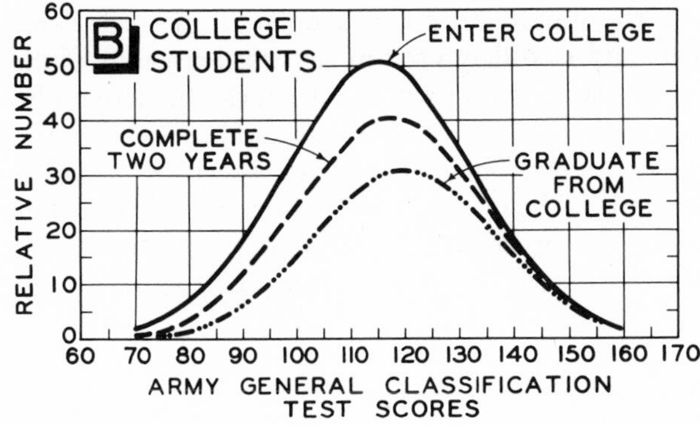

Figure 11.6 Examples of smoothed frequency curves portraying scores on an army classification test. A shows all members in an age group of those reaching three educational levels indicated on the chart. B shows college students in terms of three performance categories. Redrawn from Dael Wolfle, *America's Resources of Specialized Talent.* New York: Harper and Row, Publishers, 1954, pp. 144–145. Reproduced by permission of publisher.

DM, *NE*, *FO*, *PG*, and *HQ* in Figure 11.5 .The midpoints of these respective lines are designated *V*, *W*, *X*, *Y*, and *Z*.

5. The final step is to connect the consecutive midpoints, such as *V*, *W*, *X*, *Y*, and *Z* of the vertical lines by a smooth curve.

Figure 11.6 illustrates a series of smoothed frequency curves representing scores on an army classification test for different educational categories.

Measures of Typical Size—Averages

Frequency distributions are extremely valuable for summarizing large masses of data, but the process of summarization can be carried much further by compressing the characteristics of an entire series into one or at most a few significant figures. These figures are known as averages and they represent typical values of a variable. Averages hold a very important place in all types of statistical work. In fact, statistics has been referred to as "the science of averages." There are many different kinds of averages, but we shall consider only three, namely 1) the mean or arithmetic average, 2) the median, and 3) the mode.

1. Arithmetic mean. Perhaps the most familiar of all the averages is the simple arithmetic average or mean. It is relatively easy to calculate and is widely used in statistical research. If the measure of each item in a series is known, the mean can be derived by adding the measures together and dividing by the number of items. If five students receive grades of 60, 75, 86, 88, and 96 respectively, on an examination, the mean grade is the quotient of the sum of the grades divided by five: $405/5 = 81$. The procedure in calculating the mean from ungrouped data can be expressed in algebraic terms by the following formula:

$$\overline{X} = \frac{\Sigma m}{N}$$

$\overline{X}$ is the mean.

Σ (Greek capital *S* or sigma) is the conventional summation sign. It does not represent a separate quantity but indicates the "sum of" whatever follows.

m is the measures or sizes of the separate items or cases.

N is the total number of items or cases.

If there are relatively few cases, say less than 25 or 30, it is not very difficult to treat the items individually and compute the mean according to the above formula. If there are many more than 30 cases, and when other measures of central tendency and of dispersion are to be computed later, it is generally easier to arrange the data in a frequency distribution and calculate the mean in that way. There are two common methods of computing the mean from a frequency distribution: 1) the long method, and 2) the assumed-mean or short-cut method. Since the assumed-mean, arbitrary origin, or short-cut method is so far superior to the long method and also since the same general method is used in calculating the standard deviation and the Pearsonian coefficient of correlation, it will be the only one considered in the present discussion.

Table 11.1

CALCULATION OF THE MEAN ($\overline{X}$) FROM A FREQUENCY DISTRIBUTION. DATA REPRESENT WEIGHTS OF 265 MALE FRESHMAN STUDENTS AT THE UNIVERSITY OF WASHINGTON.

Class-Interval (Weight)	f	d	fd	
90— 99.	1	−5	− 5	$\overline{X} = g + \frac{\Sigma fd}{N}(i)$
100—109.	1	−4	− 4	
110—119.	9	−3	−27	
120—129.	30	−2	−60	
130—139.	42	−1	−42	$= 145 + \left(\frac{99}{265}\right)(10)$
140—149.	66	0	0	
				$= 145 + (.3736)(10)$
150—159.	47	1	47	
160—169.	39	2	78	
170—179.	15	3	45	$= 145 + 3.74$
180—189.	11	4	44	
190—199.	1	5	5	
200—209.	3	6	18	$= 148.74$

$N = 265$

$\Sigma fd = 237—138$

$= 99$

The steps in the process of calculating the mean from a frequency distribution according to the short-cut method are as follows:

1. Arrange the data in a frequency distribution and ascertain the number of cases. From the illustrative problem in Table 11.1 it will be seen that the class-intervals, representing the weights of 265 University of Washington students, comprise the first column and the frequencies the second column.
2. By mere inspection, estimate the interval in the distribution which is most likely to contain the mean. As far as the final results are concerned, any interval will do, but in order to keep the size of the numbers in the computation process to a minimum, care should be taken to select a class-interval as close as possible to the one that contains the mean, so far as one can judge. The midpoint of the assumed mean interval will be designated g in the formula. In the problem in Table 11.1 the interval 140 to 149 was assumed to contain the mean, and therefore $g = 145$.
3. In the third column the deviations (d) from the assumed mean are marked off consecutively in steps or intervals. Those that are above the assumed mean in value are designated plus (+) and those below, minus (—).
4. The next operation is to multiply each frequency (f) by its corresponding deviation (d). The products are written in the fourth column (fd). Of course, care should be taken to observe signs.
5. Find the algebraic sum (Σ) of the fd's. In Table 11.1 $\Sigma fd_{neg} = -138$ and $\Sigma fd_{pos} = +237$. Therefore, the algebraic sum of the figures in the fd column is $\Sigma fd = +99$.
6. Divide Σfd by N. In the problem we have $99/265 = .3736$ or, dropping the fourth decimal place as not significant, .374. The quotient obtained by this operation gives the correction in terms of the class-interval. Sometimes $\Sigma fd/N$ will be positive and sometimes negative, depending on the position of the assumed mean.
7. In order to obtain the correction in terms of the actual units in the distribution, multiply $\Sigma fd/N$ by the size of the class-interval (i). In the problem in Table 11.1, .374 is multiplied by 10. The result is 3.74.
8. The final step in the process is to add algebraically g and $(N/\Sigma fd)(i)$. In the problem $g = 145$ and $(\Sigma fd/N)(i) = +3.74$, and the mean of the distribution, therefore, is 148.74 pounds.

2. Median. The median is another simple average or measure of central tendency. Many statisticians define the median as the *size* of the middle item when the items are arranged in their order of magnitude. This means, of course, that there are as many items above or larger than the middle one as there are below or smaller than it. If the number of items in the series is even, the median is taken as the arithmetic mean of the middle items. This concept which we are discussing should not be considered as a genuine median but rather as the *value* of the mid-item or mid-case. The concept "median" should be reserved for frequency distributions and not simple arrays. If such a distinction is made, then the median may be defined as that point on the scale of the variable (the point on the X-scale in a frequency graph) which divides the distribution into two equal parts.

Table 11.2

CALCULATION OF THE MEDIAN ($\dot{X}$). DATA REPRESENT WEIGHTS OF 265 MALE FRESHMAN STUDENTS AT THE UNIVERSITY OF WASHINGTON.

Class-Interval (Weight)	f	*Cumulative f "Less than"*
90— 99.	1	1
100—109.	1	2
110—119.	9	11
120—129.	30	41
130—139.	42	83
140—149.	66	149
150—159.	47	196
160—169.	39	235
170—179.	15	250
180—189.	11	261
190—199.	1	262
200—209.	3	265

$$N = 265$$

$$\frac{N}{2} = \frac{265}{2} = 132.5$$

$$\dot{X} = l + \left(\frac{w}{f}\right)(i)$$

$$= 140 + \left(\frac{132.5 - 83}{66}\right)(10)$$

$$= 140 + \left(\frac{49.5}{66}\right)(10)$$

$$= 140 + (.750)\ (10)$$

$$= 140 + 7.50$$

$$= 147.5$$

In a frequency distribution the median is derived by interpolation in one of the classes of the distribution. There are two methods of interpolation: 1) the arithmetic and 2) the graphic. The arithmetic method is the one ordinarily used. However, the graphic method will be considered also since it will assist the beginner in grasping more clearly the significance of the concept.

First, let us summarize the steps that are followed in deriving the median ($\dot{X}$) according to the arithmetic method.

1. The first and second columns in Table 11.2 are identical with those in Table 11.1.
2. The third column represents a cumulative frequency distribution. The frequencies in this column are accumulated from the top of the distribution. The cumulative frequency of any particular class-interval represents the sum of the frequencies of this and all the preceding class-intervals.
3. In order to determine the interval in which the median lies, the next step is to divide N by 2, ($N/2$). In Table 11.2, $N/2 = 265/2 = 132.5$. It will be observed that 132.5 falls in the class-interval 140 to 149.
4. Determine how many cases are required in this particular interval to reach $N/2$ or 132.5. This is accomplished by subtracting the number of cases below the median interval from $N/2$. By substituting in the present illustration we have $132.5 - 83 = 49.5$. This number has been designated w in the formula.
5. Divide w by the number of cases (f) in the median class-interval. In the illustration the frequency of the class-interval in which the median lies is 66. Therefore $49.5/66 = .750$.
6. Multiply this quotient by the size of the class-interval (i). In the problem, (i) is 10 and $10 \times .750 = 7.50$.
7. Add this product to the lower limit (l) of the median interval. It will be observed that 140 is the lower limit of the median interval in the illustrative problem and $140 + 7.50 = 147.5$.

In order to derive a median by graphic interpolation it is necessary to construct either a "less than" or "more than" type (or both) of summation curve or ogive. The data for the "less than" type are accumulated from the top of the frequency distribution and the "more than" from the bottom of the distribution. The X-scale of the cumulative frequency graph is the same as that of the simple frequency graph, but the Y-scale is different in that the values must include a much wider range. In plotting the cumulative frequencies for the various classes the mid-points of the intervals are never used. For the "less than" type of curve the upper limits of the class-intervals are used and for the "more than" type, the lower limits. As will be seen from Figure 11.7 the typical smoothed ogive has the general characteristic of an elongated *S*.

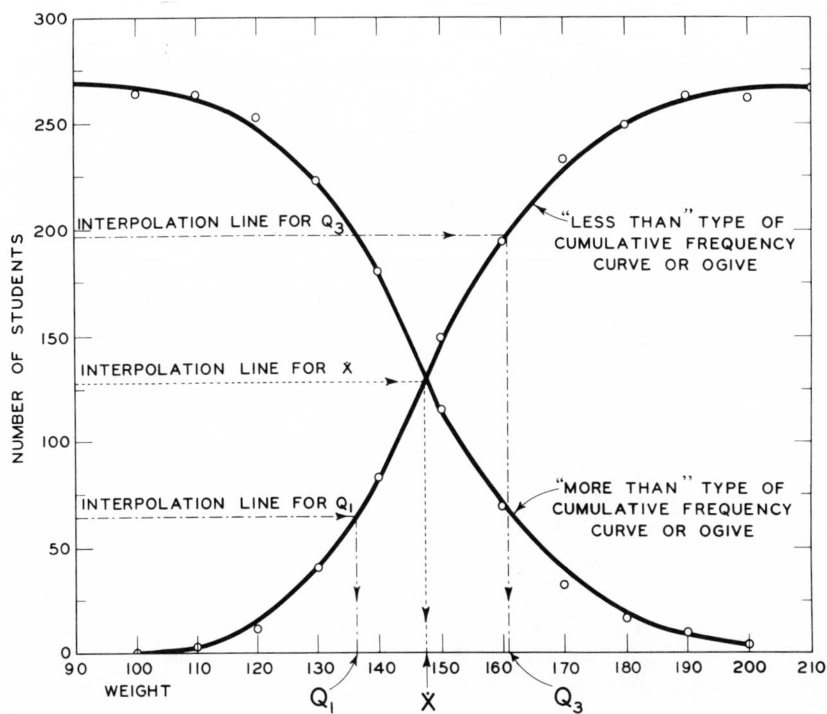

Figure 11.7 Cumulative frequency curves or ogives illustrating the graphic technique of interpolation for median and quartiles. Based on data in table 11.1.

To calculate the median for any distribution, $N/2$ is first located on the vertical axis of the graph and an interpolation line parallel to the horizontal axis is drawn intersecting the curves. A perpendicular line is dropped from this intersection to the X-scale. The point where the perpendicular line cuts the X-scale is the median. It will be observed from Figure 11.7 that the two ogives intersect at a point which divides the distribution into two equal parts. This point, of course, is the same one through which the interpolation line is drawn.

3. Quartiles. Since the techniques for calculating quartiles are so very similar to those used in deriving the median, there is much justification for discussing quartiles at this point. It should be understood, however, that quartiles are not measures of central tendency. Quartiles, deciles, percentiles, and other measures of this kind would more logically be included under the heading of variability.

It will be recalled that the median divides the frequency distribution into two equal parts. The quartiles, on the other hand, divide a frequency distribution into four equal parts. The quartiles, like the median, represent points on the scale of the variable. One of the three points is the median which actually can be designated Q_2, or the second quartile. The quartiles can be computed by either algebraic or graphic procedure.

The steps in calculating the quartiles according to the algebraic method are as follows:

1. The arrangement of the class-intervals, the simple frequencies, and the cumulative frequencies are the same as in Table 11.2.
2. In order to locate the intervals which contain the three quartiles, N is first divided by 4. $N/4$ locates Q_1 (the first quartile); $(N/4)$ times (2) locates Q_2 (the second quartile or median); and $(N/4)$ times (3) locates Q_3 (the third quartile).
3. After the class-intervals containing the quartiles have been located, the same formula used in interpolating for the median is applied. As an illustration let us compute Q_1 for the data in Table 11.2. First, $N/4 = 265/4 = 66.25$. We observe, therefore, that Q_1 lies in the interval 130 to 139. Substituting in the formula $Q_1 = l + (w/f)(i)$ we have $Q_1 = 130 + (25.25/42)(10) = 130 + 6.01 = 136.01$.

Figure 11.7 illustrates the graphic method of calculating quartiles from summation curves. In order to derive Q_1, for example, the value $N/4$ is plotted on the vertical scale of the chart and a horizontal interpolation line is drawn through the "less than" ogive. A perpendicular line is then dropped from the intersection of the interpolation line and the ogive. It will be seen from Figure 11.7 that Q_1 is approximately 136.0.

4. Mode. In a simple series the mode is the *size* of the measurement that occurs most frequently. In the following series of values: 15, 17, 18, 22, 24, 25, 25, 25, 27, 28, 28, 30, and 31, the mode is 25, because 25 occurs more often than any other measure. In a frequency distribution the mode is that point on the scale of the variable where the frequency is greatest. The beginner should never forget that in a frequency distribution the mean, median, and mode are values on the scale of the variable. In a frequency curve they will be represented by points on the X-scale.

Table 11.3

CALCULATION OF THE MODE ($\hat{X}$). DATA REPRESENT WEIGHTS OF 265 FRESHMAN STUDENTS AT THE UNIVERSITY OF WASHINGTON.

Class-Interval (Weight)	f	
90— 99	1	$\hat{X} = l + \left(\frac{f_2}{f_2 + f_1}\right)(i)$
100—109	1	
110—119	9	$= 140 + \left(\frac{47}{47 + 42}\right)(10)$
120—129	30	
130—139	42	
140—149	66	
150—159	47	$= 140 + \left(\frac{47}{89}\right)(10)$
160—169	39	
170—179	15	
180—189	11	$= 140 + 5.3$
190—199	1	
200—209	3	$= 145.3$

In practice it will be found that frequency distributions often have more than one mode. Distributions which have one mode are referred to as being *unimodal.* Those with two modes are described as *bimodal,* those with three, *trimodal* or more generally, *multimodal.*

There are several methods which can be used in deriving the mode in a frequency distribution, but none is entirely satisfactory or universally accepted. We shall mention only two methods in the present discussion. First, there is the method based on inspection, by which the modal class is ascertained and the midpoint of the interval is considered the mode. This mode is frequently referred to as the *inspectional* or *crude mode.* The second method is based on interpolation. After the modal class has been selected, the exact location of the mode within the class is determined by means of interpolation. This procedure is most reliable when it is applied to continuous variables in which the distribution is fairly normal. The formula is based on the assumption that the exact location of the mode within the modal class is determined by the frequencies of the two adjacent classes. If the respective frequencies of the adjacent classes are identical, then the mode is the midpoint of the modal class-interval. If the frequencies of the adjacent classes are different, then the mode is pulled in the direction of the larger frequency away from the midpoint of the modal class.

The steps in the derivation of the mode by this method are as follows:

1. Find the modal class by inspection.[8]
2. The next step is to ascertain the lower limit of the modal class. In the problem in Table 11.3 it is 140.
3. Divide the frequency of the adjacent class above the modal class (f_2) by the sum of the frequencies of both adjacent classes ($f_2 + f_1$). In the problem, $(f_2/f_2 + f_1) = (47/47 + 42) = (47/89) = .53$.
4. Multiply the quotient thus derived (.53) by the size of the class-interval (i). In the problem, .53 is multiplied by 10 and the product is 5.3.
5. The last step is to add (l) and the derived figure from $(f_2/f_2 + f_1)(i)$. Therefore, in the problem, $\hat{X} = 140 + 5.3 = 145.3$ pounds.

Application and Characteristic Features of Mean, Median, and Mode

What are the merits and the defects of the different averages and when should each be used? A satisfactory average should be 1) definite and rigorously defined, 2) simple and concrete, 3) easily calculated, 4) readily comprehended, 5) susceptible of algebraic treatment and 6) suitable for the degree of precision of the measurement of the variables. Judging in terms of these criteria, the mean is no doubt superior to either the median or the mode, but in the final analysis the

[8]Sometimes it is difficult to locate the modal class by mere observation since the frequencies of several classes may be so nearly alike. In that case the modal class can be determined by a process of grouping and re-grouping the class-intervals of the distribution. The intervals are first grouped by two's, beginning at the top of the distribution. The next step is to drop down one interval and repeat the process. The intervals are next grouped by three's, beginning as before at the top of the distribution. After shifting down one interval each time, the intervals are then grouped by four's and the process repeated. By this procedure of grouping and re-grouping it will be found that one interval will tend to appear in the modal class more often than any of the others.

nature of the data and the purpose at hand should really determine the particular average that is chosen. No average can be considered the *best* under all circumstances. Furthermore, too great dependence should not be placed on a single value. An adequate description of a frequency distribution ordinarily requires the computation of two or more averages as well as other types of statistical measurements.

Let us briefly summarize some of the more important characteristics of the mean, the median, and the mode.[9]

Mean

1. The mean is the best known and most frequently used average. Oftentimes it may be advantageous to use the mean merely because it is so well understood.
2. The mean is affected by the value of every case in the series. As a result, undue weight sometimes may be given to extreme and erratic items. For example, the mean wage of a group may actually be misleading if there are extreme and atypical items at either end of the scale.
3. From an algebraic standpoint the mean is superior to either the median or the mode.

Median

1. The median is not influenced by the size of extreme items. It is based on the values lying immediately on either side of it. The median can be used very effectively when extreme items are likely to have an unduly disproportionate influence on the mean.
2. The median is easily calculated.
3. The median is generally less reliable than the mean and is not so well adapted to algebraic manipulation.

Mode

1. The mode, like the median, is a position average and is not affected by extreme items. It is therefore useful in those cases in which it is desirable to eliminate the effects of extreme variations.

[9]G. Udny Yule and M. G. Kendall, *An Introduction to the Theory of Statistics,* 14th ed. London: Charles Griffin, 1950, pp. 102–118; Frederick Cecil Mills, *Statistical Methods.* New York: Holt, Rinehart, & Winston, Inc., 1938, pp. 143–146.

2. The mode is frequently very difficult to locate.
3. The mode possesses little significance unless there is a distinct central tendency and unless it is applied to a relatively large sample.
4. The mode is not susceptible to algebraic manipulation.

Variability

Another important concept in statistics is variability.[10] The mean, median, and mode give only one essential characteristic of a frequency distribution—its typical size or central tendency. To say, for example, that the mean or median value of the residential structures in a particular city is $10,000 does not give a very adequate picture of property values. In addition, it is essential to know how the values vary above and below the mean or median. Some structures may be valued at only $1,500, whereas others may be worth $50,000 or more. Furthermore, it is possible for several distributions to have the same average yet be markedly different in variability. In some distributions the cases may cluster very closely around the average, and in others they may be widely scattered. It is, therefore, very important to determine the spread of the individual values on either side of their central tendency.

In the present discussion consideration will be given to the following measures of variability: 1) the range, 2) the mean deviation, 3) the standard deviation, and 4) the semi-interquartile range.

1. Range. The range of an ungrouped set of measures is merely the difference between the size of the largest and smallest items. For example, the range of the series, 10, 11, 13, 16, 17, and 19 is 9, for $19 - 10 = 9$. Sometimes the range is expressed in terms of the size of the extreme values, such as "a range of 10 to 19" in the foregoing illustration. The range is a very crude and unstable measure of variability since it depends entirely on the two extreme items in the series and indicates virtually nothing about the general form or profile of the series. Moreover, it cannot be used very effectively in a frequency distribution since the exact range cannot ordinarily be determined. If only the total scatter of the items of a series is desired, or if the data are too scanty to warrant the computation of a more reliable measure of variability, the range may be used.

[10]This concept also has been variously designated "dispersion," "scatteration," "spread," or "deviation."

2. Mean deviation. The mean deviation, or average deviation as it is frequently called, is the mean of the sum of the deviations (irrespective of signs) from some measure of central tendency. The mean is usually taken as the standard although the median or mode is sometimes used. Care should always be taken to specify the particular average that is chosen for computing the mean deviation. To illustrate the calculation of the mean deviation let us consider the following simple series of values:

m, series of values:	2, 3, 5, 7, 10, 11, 12, 13, 14, 16, 17
d, the deviation from the mean:	8, 7, 5, 3, 0, 1, 2, 3, 4, 6, 7

$$\bar{X}_m = \frac{110}{11} = 10$$

$$\bar{X}_d = \frac{46}{11} = 4.18$$

It will be observed that the mean of the series was first derived by adding the numbers together and dividing by 11. The deviations of each value from the mean of the series ($\bar{X}_m = 10$) are indicated in the second line. The mean deviation is the sum of these deviations (disregarding signs) from the mean divided by the number of cases in the series, or $46/11 = 4.18$.

When the mean deviation is calculated from a frequency distribution the following procedure can be followed:

1. Compute the measure of central tendency that is to be used as a standard.
2. Indicate in a separate column the midpoint of each class-interval in the distribution.
3. In the next column tabulate the deviations (*d*) from the standard that has been selected to the midpoints of the several class-intervals.
4. In the last column tabulate the products of the frequencies of each class-interval times the deviation (*fd*).
5. Add the figures in the *fd* column, disregarding signs (Σfd).
6. Divide Σfd by the number of cases in the distribution.

$$A.\,D. = \frac{\Sigma fd}{N}.$$

In actual practice it will be found that the mean deviation is of little value and very seldom used in social research. The main justification, therefore, in devoting so much space to the mean deviation is to assist the student in obtaining a clearer understanding of the concept of variability and especially the standard deviation, which is much more widely used and is far superior in every way to the mean deviation.

3. Standard deviation. The standard deviation, like the mean deviation, represents a mean of deviation items. It is different, however, from the mean deviation in that the deviations are squared before being summed, the sum of the squared deviations is divided by the total number of observations (cases) in the distribution, and the square root is extracted from this quotient. The standard deviation is always computed from the mean, whereas the mean deviation may be computed from the mean, the median, or sometimes the mode. Algebraically these steps may be represented by the following formula:

$$\sigma = \sqrt{\frac{\Sigma fd}{N}}$$

Table 11.4

CALCULATION OF THE STANDARD DEVIATION (σ). DATA REPRESENT WEIGHTS OF 265 MALE FRESHMAN STUDENTS AT THE UNIVERSITY OF WASHINGTON.

Class-Interval (Weight)	f	d	fd	fd^2
90— 99......	1	−5	−5	25
100—109......	1	−4	−4	16
110—119......	9	−3	−27	81
120—129......	30	−2	−60	120
130—139......	42	−1	−42	42
140—149......	66	0	0	0
150—159......	47	1	47	47
160—169......	39	2	78	156
170—179......	15	3	45	135
180—189......	11	4	44	176
190—199......	1	5	5	25
200—209......	3	6	18	108
$N = 265$		$\Sigma fd = 99$		$\Sigma fd^2 = 931$

$$\sigma = \left(\sqrt{\frac{\Sigma fd^2}{N} - \left(\frac{\Sigma fd}{N}\right)^2}\right)(i)$$

$$= \left(\sqrt{\frac{931}{265} - \left(\frac{99}{265}\right)^2}\right)(10)$$

$$= (\sqrt{3.5132 - .1396})\ (10)$$

$$= (\sqrt{3.3736})\ (10)$$

$$= (1.8367)\ (10)$$

$$= 18.37 \text{ or } 18.4$$

The standard deviation provides a more refined and statistically important measure of variability than the mean deviation.

The standard deviation squared is another useful statistical measure, called *variance*.

The standard deviation is symbolized by the abbreviation *S. D.*, but much more frequently by σ, the small Greek letter *s*.

In computing the standard deviation from a frequency distribution, the following procedure is the one most generally used. It is known as the short method.

1. It will be observed from the illustrative problem in Table 11.4 that the first column contains the class-intervals and the second column, the frequencies. The total number of cases (N) is 265.
2. Select as an arbitrary origin the interval in which the mean is most likely to occur, and mark off the deviations in terms of intervals above (plus) and below (minus) the assumed mean. The interval 140 to 149 was chosen as the zero interval.
3. Multiply the frequency of each class by its corresponding deviation (fd) and enter the products in the fourth column. Find Σfd. The procedure thus far is identical with that followed in computing the mean.
4. In the fifth column tabulate the products of $(fd)(d)$, that is, the fd^2 values.
5. Obtain Σfd^2. It will be observed that there are never any minus quantities in the fd^2 column. In the problem, $\Sigma fd^2 = 931$.
6. The correction (c), which is $\Sigma fd/N$, is squared. In the problem,

   $$\frac{\Sigma fd}{N} = \frac{99}{265} = .374 \text{ and } (.374)^2 = .1399$$

   It will be observed that c is expressed in terms of the class-interval and not in the original scale unit.
7. The next step is to make the proper substitutions in the complete formula of the standard deviation.

$$\sigma = \sqrt{\frac{\Sigma fd^2}{N} - c^2}\ (i)$$

It will be observed that c^2 is always subtracted. After the calculations have been made under the radical sign, the square root is extracted and the results multiplied by the size of the class-interval (i). In the illustration in Table 11.4 the standard deviation is 18.4. In order to check the accuracy of the calculations a different guessed mean can be chosen and the problem recomputed accordingly.

4. Semi-interquartile range. The semi-interquartile range or quartile deviation is one-half the distance from the third quartile (Q_3) and the first quartile (Q_1). The semi-interquartile range is commonly symbolized by Q. The formula for the semi-interquartile range is:

$$Q = \frac{Q_3 - Q_1}{2}$$

The semi-interquartile range for the distribution in Table 11.1, therefore, is:

$$Q = \frac{160.71 - 136.01}{2}$$

$$= \frac{24.70}{2}$$

$$= 12.35$$

Unlike the mean deviation and the standard deviation, the semi-interquartile range is not measured from any central standard. It will be recalled that the quartiles divide the distribution into four equal parts. Q_1 is a point on the scale of the variable below which there are 25 per cent and above which there are 75 per cent of the cases, and Q_3 is located so that 25 per cent of the cases are above it and 75 per cent below it. If the frequency distribution is perfectly symmetrical and bell-shaped, Q_1 and Q_3 are equidistant from $\dot{X}$. In an asymmetrical distribution this relationship does not hold. The semi-interquartile range is not as satisfactory a measure of variability as the standard deviation since only a portion of the distribution is taken into consideration and the remainder disregarded, and for certain types of distributions the quartiles become indeterminate and unrepresentative.

Relationship Between the Mean Deviation, Standard Deviation, and Semi-Interquartile Range

It will be recalled that the mean, median, and mode represent points or values on the X-scale, and that the average deviation, standard deviation, and semi-interquartile range represent distances on the X-scale. In a normal frequency distribution, 1) what proportion of the area or the cases is included within the limits of the respective measures of valiability? and 2) what is the relationship between the average deviation, the standard deviation, and the semi-interquartile range? In a perfectly normal distribution the *A.D.* ($\bar{X}$ or $\dot{X} \pm A.D.$) defines the limits of the middle 57.5 per cent of the cases; the σ ($\bar{X} \pm \sigma$) marks the range of the middle 68.26 per cent of the cases; and the Q ($\dot{X} \pm Q$) indicates the middle 50 per cent of the items.

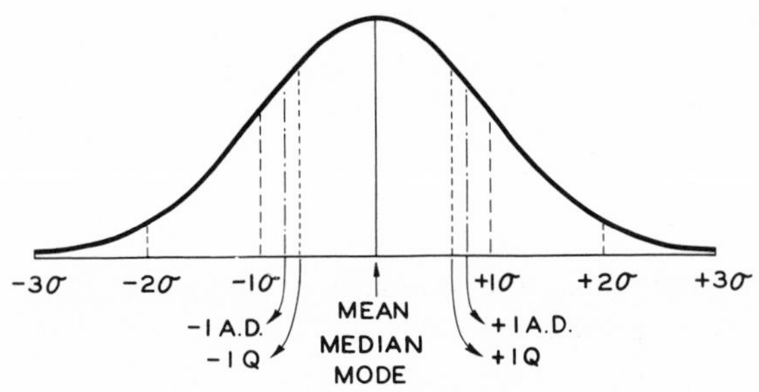

Figure 11.8 Normal curve showing the relationship of measures of variability.

It will be observed from Figure 11.8 that in a perfectly symmetrical distribution, or in a distribution that varies from this type only moderately, the mean deviation is approximately four-fifths of the standard deviation and the semi-interquartile range is about two-thirds of the standard deviation.

Table 11.5 presents more exactly the relationship between these three measures of variability.

As an illustration for interpreting a measure of variability let us take the standard deviation of the distribution in Table 11.4.

Table 11.5

RELATIONSHIP BETWEEN THE MEAN DEVIATION, STANDARD DEVIATION, AND SEMI-INTERQUARTILE RANGE AS FOUND IN NORMAL FREQUENCY DISTRIBUTIONS.

Measure	*Relationship*
σ =	1.2533 *A.D.*
σ =	1.4825 Q
A.D. =	.7979 σ
A.D. =	1.1843 Q
Q =	.6745 σ
Q =	.8453 *A.D.*

The standard deviation was found to be 18.4. In a perfectly normal distribution the standard deviation, when measured off above and below the mean, includes within this range approximately 68.26 per cent of the cases in the distribution. This fact is also approximately true for distributions which are almost normal.

In the problem one standard deviation below the mean (148.7) would be 130.3 and one standard deviation above would extend to 167.1 on the scale; and it could be said, therefore, that approximately two-thirds (68.26 per cent if the distribution were normal) of the students in this sample weigh between 130.3 pounds and 167.1 pounds.

Coefficient of Variation

The mean deviation, the standard deviation, and the semi-interquartile range represent measures of absolute variability. It is also frequently necessary to measure the relative variability of two or more frequency distributions. In Table 11.6 are listed the respective mean ages, standard deviations, and coefficients of variation of four groups of women who gave birth to one or more children in Minneapolis during the five-year period 1931 to 1935.

Table 11.6

MEANS, STANDARD DEVIATIONS, AND COEFFICIENTS OF VARIATION OF THE AGE DISTRIBUTIONS OF FOUR GROUPS OF MOTHERS WHO GAVE BIRTH TO ONE OR MORE CHILDREN IN THE CITY OF MINNEAPOLIS: 1931 TO 1935.*

Classification	$\bar{X}$	σ	*C.V.*
Resident married	28.2	6.0	21.3
Non-resident married	29.5	6.0	20.3
Resident unmarried	23.4	5.8	24.8
Non-resident unmarried	21.7	3.7	17.1

**Data taken from Calvin F. Schmid,* Mortality Trends in the State of Minnesota, *pp. 273–275.*

Which group shows the relatively highest degree of variability and which the least? By merely examining the standard deviations it would be impossible to say. When, however, the standard deviations of the several distributions are related to their corresponding means, it is possible to determine the relative amount of variability of a number of frequency distributions. Karl Pearson has worked out a simple measure of relative variability which is generally known as the coefficient of variation.

$$C.V. \text{ or } V = \frac{\sigma}{\bar{X}}\left(\frac{100}{1}\right)$$

In Table 11.6 it will be seen that the non-resident unmarried mothers show the least relative variability (17.1) in age and the resident unmarried, the highest (24.8). The coefficient of variation for the problem in Table 11.4 is:

$$C.V. = \left(\frac{18.367}{148.736}\right)\left(\frac{100}{1}\right) = 12.3 \text{ per cent}$$

Skewness

In actual practice, frequency distributions are rarely symmetrical; rather they show varying degrees of asymmetry or skewness. In a perfectly symmetrical distribution the mean, median, and mode coincide, whereas this is not the case in a distribution that is asymmetrical or skewed. Figure 11.9 presents illustrations of curves that are notice-

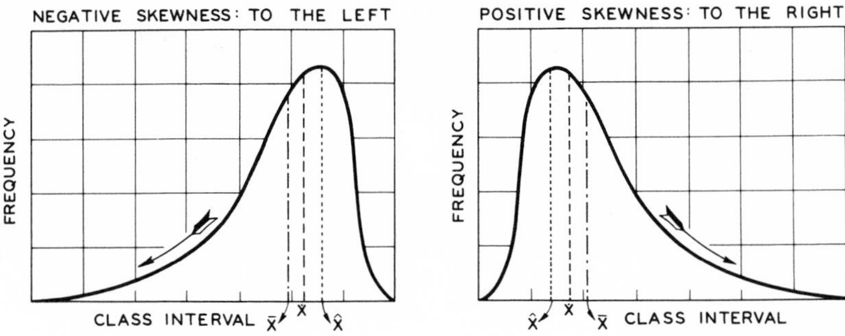

Figure 11.9 Frequency curves showing negative and positive skewness.

ably skewed. The one on the left is skewed negatively and the one on the right is skewed positively. It will be observed that in the curve with negative skewness the mean is less than the mode, whereas in the curve with positive skewness the mean is greater than the mode. The mode is not affected by either the size or the number of extreme items in a frequency distribution, but the mean is.

Coefficients of skewness have been devised which measure the direction of the skewness as well as the degree, either absolutely or relatively. A commonly used but only rough measure of skewness is merely the difference between the mean and the mode ($\bar{X} - \hat{X}$). The sign indicates the direction of skewness and the difference, the amount. The distribution of the weights of 265 university students shows a slight positive skewness for $\bar{X} = 148.74$ and $\hat{X} = 145.28$ and $148.74 - 145.28 = +3.46$.

A more satisfactory measure of skewness in which the degree of variability is given due weight is:

$$Sk = \frac{\bar{X} - \hat{X}}{\sigma}$$

Since the true mode is frequently difficult to determine, another formula developed by Karl Pearson for indicating skewness can be applied, especially if the series is only moderately skewed. According to this formula:

$$Sk = \frac{3\,(\bar{X} - \dot{X})}{\sigma}$$

The frequency distributions which have been considered thus far have been the common type in which the frequencies are relatively low at the ends and high toward the middle. In addition to this type there are frequency curves which show a tendency constantly to increase or decrease. These curves possess the general characteristics of a capital "J" and are known as J-shaped curves. There is also another type of irregular distribution in which the frequencies are relatively high at the two ends and low toward the middle. This type is referred to as U-shaped curves. Both the J-shaped and the U-shaped types of frequency distribution do not occur nearly so often as the bell-shaped type.

Correlation

In popular speech the idea of correlation is frequently expressed but generally in a qualitative and inarticulate manner. Comments are made concerning the relationship between criminality and feeble-mindedness, suicide and mental diseases, poor housing and morbidity, juvenile delinquency and the broken home, divorce and the business cycle, and between many other phenomena. As students of social research we would naturally be interested in these problems, and should we attempt to study one of them, some type of statistical correlation probably would be utilized. In order to measure the relationship between only two variables, some type of simple correlation would be selected. For simple correlation a selection would be made from the following formulae depending upon the characteristics of the data and the problem at hand: 1) Pearsonian or product-moment, 2) rank-difference or rank-order, 3) contingency, and 4) curvilinear. If, on the other hand, the relationship among several variables was to be measured, partial or multiple correlation techniques or factor analysis would be applied.

The present discussion will be devoted largely to the Pearsonian or product-moment type of correlation, since it is the basic type of correlation and the one most commonly used. The product-moment coefficient of correlation (r) is a pure number and ranges in value from positive one (+ 1.0) down through zero (0.0) to negative one (− 1.0). That is, correlation may be direct or positive or it may be inverse or negative according to the direction of change, the size of the coefficient indicating the degree of relationship. When one variable increases (or decreases) and the other changes by constant or nearly constant amounts in the same direction, the relation of the two series is positive; but if the changes in the two variables are in opposite directions, the correlation between the two series is negative. For example, the height and weight of human beings are positively correlated since taller people on the average weigh more than shorter people. On the other hand, in this country there is a negative or inverse relationship between socio-economic status and fertility. Families with the larger income have relatively fewer children than families with smaller incomes.

It should be pointed out that the product-moment coefficient of correlation is based on assumptions that the data are derived from normal populations and that the association, if any, is linear. If there is considerable deviation from these assumptions, some other measure of association such as the Spearman rank-difference coefficient should be used.

In order to elucidate further the concept of correlation let us take the problem of measuring the relationship between the height and weight of college students. The data that will be analyzed have been derived from the freshman medical examination records of a sample of 265 men students at the University of Washington.

1. The first step in computing a coefficient of correlation is to con-

struct a scatter diagram. The scatter diagram portrays in graphic form the degree and type of relationship or covariation in the two series of data. Moreover, if the data are on a scatter diagram they can easily be transferred to the correlation chart for computation. In making a scatter diagram the first step is to select suitable class-intervals for the respective variables so that each will have from approximately 8 to 15 groupings. This procedure is similar to that followed in constructing a frequency distribution. In fact, the scatter diagram is a two-way frequency distribution.

HEIGHT (INCHES)

WEIGHT (POUNDS)

Y \ X	61	62	63	64	65	66	67	68	69	70	71	72	73	74	75	76	77	f
200-209									/		/			/				3
190-199											/							1
180-189									/	//		/	////	///				11
170-179							/		///	///	//	//	/	//	/			15
160-169								////	𝍸	𝍸 //	𝍸 ///	𝍸 ////	///	//			/	39
150-159				/	//	////	𝍸 /	////	𝍸 𝍸 /	𝍸 ////	///	////	///					47
140-149					/	𝍸	//	𝍸 𝍸 𝍸 𝍸	𝍸 ///	𝍸 𝍸 //	𝍸 ////	////	////		/			66
130-139					//	𝍸	𝍸 𝍸 //	𝍸 //	𝍸 //	𝍸	///	/						42
120-129	/		///	////	////	𝍸	////	////	////			/						30
110-119			/	/	/		//	///	/									9
100-109					/													1
90-99	/																	1
f	2	0	4	6	11	19	27	42	41	38	27	22	15	8	2	0	1	265

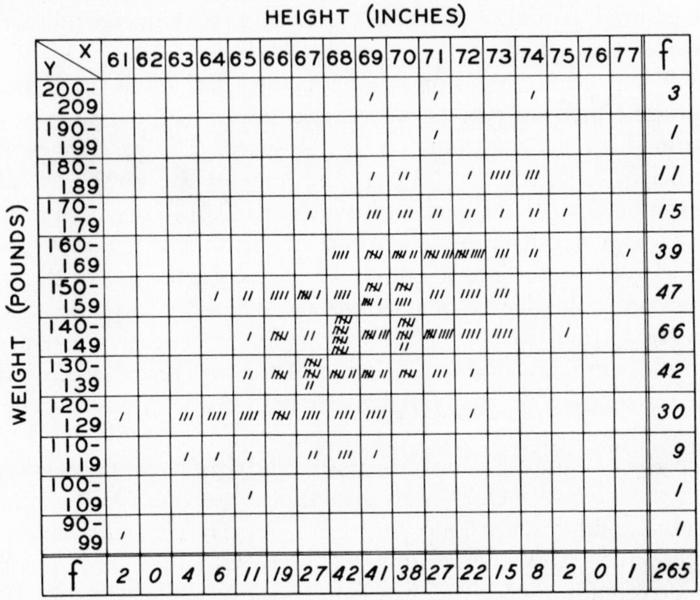

Figure 11.10 Scatter diagram showing the relationship between heights and weights of 265 University of Washington freshmen.

From Figure 11.10 it will be observed that intervals of 10 have been chosen for the series representing weight and intervals of 1 for the series representing height. The class-intervals for the X-variable read from left to right, and unlike the conventional frequency distribution, the intervals of the Y-variable read from bottom to top.

2. Each entry in the field of the chart always represents two numerical values. In the illustrative problem one value will represent height

and the other, weight. For example, the first case (student) chosen from our sample happens to be 66 inches in stature and 145 pounds in weight. The value for height would of course be placed in the column representing the class-interval 66. The exact cell is located by selecting the appropriate row, which would include the corresponding value for weight. For the above illustration a weight of 145 pounds would be included in the row designated by the interval 140 to 149. The paired values for each case are plotted according to this procedure.

3. It will be observed that the dots show a tendency to cluster in a wide band running from the lower left-hand corner to the upper right-hand corner of the diagram, indicating that the correlation is positive. If, on the other hand, the cases were distributed along a band extending from the upper left-hand corner to the lower right-hand corner the correlation would be negative.

After the scatter diagram has been completed, and the distribution has been judged to be rectilinear, the data are then transferred to some standard product-moment correlation chart. It is much cheaper, quicker, and more reliable to use a printed correlation chart than it is to lay one out by hand. The correlation chart that will be used in the present discussion was devised by Professor F. Stuart Chapin, formerly of the University of Minnesota.[11]

The following instructions summarize the various steps to be observed in computing a coefficient of correlation with this type of chart.

1. The class-intervals for both the X- and Y-variables should be written in the spaces at the top and the left-hand side of the correlation chart and the number of cases recorded in the proper cells. The frequencies for the two variables should also be entered on the chart. This operation involves merely a transferral of the essential data from the scatter diagram to the correlation chart. In selecting the zero-intervals for the two variables an attempt should be made to choose intervals in which the means of the respective distribu-

[11] All of the printed forms for computing the coefficient of correlation are very similar. A few of the better known charts are: 1) Thurstone (published by C. H. Stoelting Company, Chicago); 2) Otis (World Book Company, New York); 3) Cureton and Dunlop (Psychological Corporation, New York); 4) Tryon (University of California); 5) Ruch-Stoddard (University of Iowa); 6) Holzinger (University of Chicago); 7) Dvorak (Longmans, Green, New York); 8) Kelley (World Book Company, New York); and 9) Durost-Walker (World Book Company).

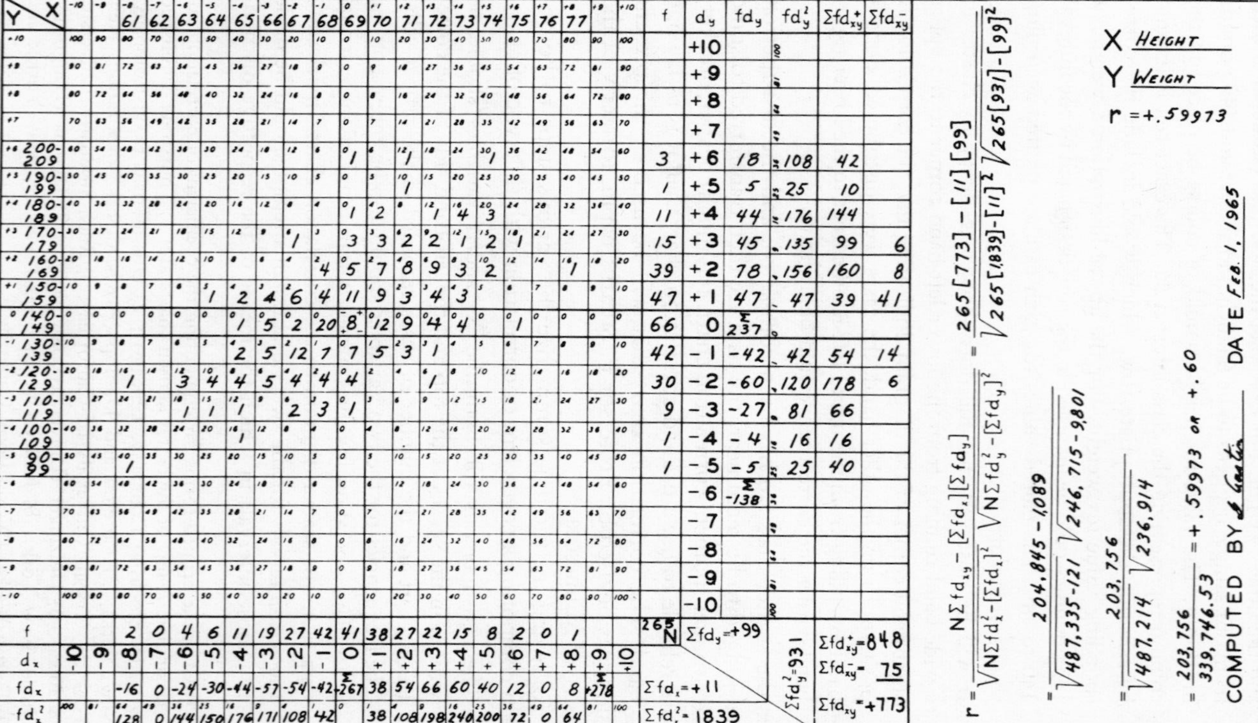

Figure 11.11 Correlation chart developed by F. Stuart Chapin, formerly of the University of Minnesota, and redrawn by Calvin F. Schmid.

tions are most likely to occur. In this problem 69 was chosen to represent the zero-interval for the X-variable and 140 to 149 for the Y-variable.

2. For the X-variable determine the products of (f) (d_x) and record them in the fd_x row. Multiply (f) (d_y) for the Y-variable and enter in the fd_y column. Care should be taken to observe signs. Determine the algebraic sums of the fd_x row and the fd_y column. In Figure 11.11 it will be observed that $\Sigma fd_x = +11$ and $\Sigma fd_y = +99$.
3. The respective values of fd_x^2 are next obtained, as are also the values of fd_y^2, and recorded on the chart. Add the fd_x^2 row and the fd_y^2 column. In the problem, $\Sigma fd_x^2 = 1{,}839$ and $\Sigma fd_y^2 = 931$. It will be recalled that the second and third steps are identical with those used in computing the standard deviation.
4. The fourth operation is different from anything that has thus far been discussed. First, note the small figures printed in the upper left-hand corner of each cell. Second, observe the signs for each of the quadrants indicated in the center of the field of the chart. The lower left-hand quadrant and the upper right-hand quadrant are plus (+) and the other two are minus (—). Multiply the number of cases in each cell by the corresponding printed figure in the cell, observing signs. The products are entered in either the $\Sigma fd_{xy} +$ or the $\Sigma fd_{xy} -$ column, depending on the sign. Let us illustrate this step by performing the computations in the row 130 to 139 in Figure 11.11. Multiply each of the frequencies in the row designated by the class-interval 130 to 139 by the small printed figures in each of the corresponding cells. The products for the numbers located in the plus quadrant are as follows: (4) (2) = 8; (3) (5) = 15; (2) (12) = 24; and (1) (7) = 7. The sum of these products, which is 54, is entered in the $\Sigma fd_{xy} +$ column. The products of the numbers for this row that are located in the minus quadrant are: (3) (1) = —3; (2) (3) = —6; and (1) (5) = —5. By adding these products together we have —14, which is recorded in the $\Sigma fd_{xy} -$ column. The figures in each of the columns are added and entered on the chart. The next step is to determine the algebraic sum of $\Sigma fd_{xy}+$ and $\Sigma fd_{xy}-$. In the problem the figures are: 848 — 75 = 773.
5. This completes all the preliminary computations on the chart. The final step is to substitute in the formula on the right side of the chart and proceed with the calculations. It will be observed from Figure 11.11 that the proper substitutions have been made in the formula and the coefficient of correlation has been computed for

the illustrative problem. The coefficient of correlation between height and weight for this sample of 265 men students is $r = +.60$.

Calculation of Pearsonian or product-moment coefficient of correlation (r) from ungrouped data. If there are no more than 100 or possibly 150 cases, it is generally easier to calculate r by the ungrouped method. This statement is made on the assumption that a good calculating machine is available.

As will be observed from Table 11.7, the procedure in calculating r by this method is very simple. The problem in Table 11.7 is to determine the relationship between cancer mortality and a cultural index for the United States Death Registration Area.

Table 11.7

CALCULATION OF PRODUCT-MOMENT COEFFICIENT OF CORRELATION (r) BY UNGROUPED METHOD. THE RELATIONSHIP BETWEEN MORTALITY FROM CANCER AND OTHER MALIGNANT TUMORS AND STATE QUARTILE DISTRIBUTION IN 152 CULTURAL ITEMS.*

State	*Cancer Rate* X	*Cultural Index* Y	*Rate Times Index* XY	*Rate Squared* X^2	*Index Squared* Y^2
Alabama	60.8	13	790.4	3,696.64	169
Arizona	65.0	41	2,665.0	4,225.00	1,681
Arkansas	46.9	10	469.0	2,199.61	100
California	91.1	93	8,472.3	8,299.21	8,649
Colorado	80.1	34	2,723.4	6,416.01	1,156
Connecticut	96.1	72	6,919.2	9,235.21	5,184
(*In order to conserve space detailed data for only 10 states are included in this table.*)					
Washington	83.1	54	4,487.4	6,905.61	2,916
West Virginia	63.0	19	1,197.0	3,969.00	361
Wisconsin	89.6	38	3,404.8	8,028.16	1,444
Wyoming	62.9	50	3,145.0	3,956.41	2,500
Totals (Σ)	3,586.6	1,740	142,016.3	283,886.98	83,664

**For more details concerning the interpretation of the correlation between cancer mortality and the cultural index in this table see Calvin F. Schmid,* Mortality Trends in the State of Minnesota, *pp. 191–193.*

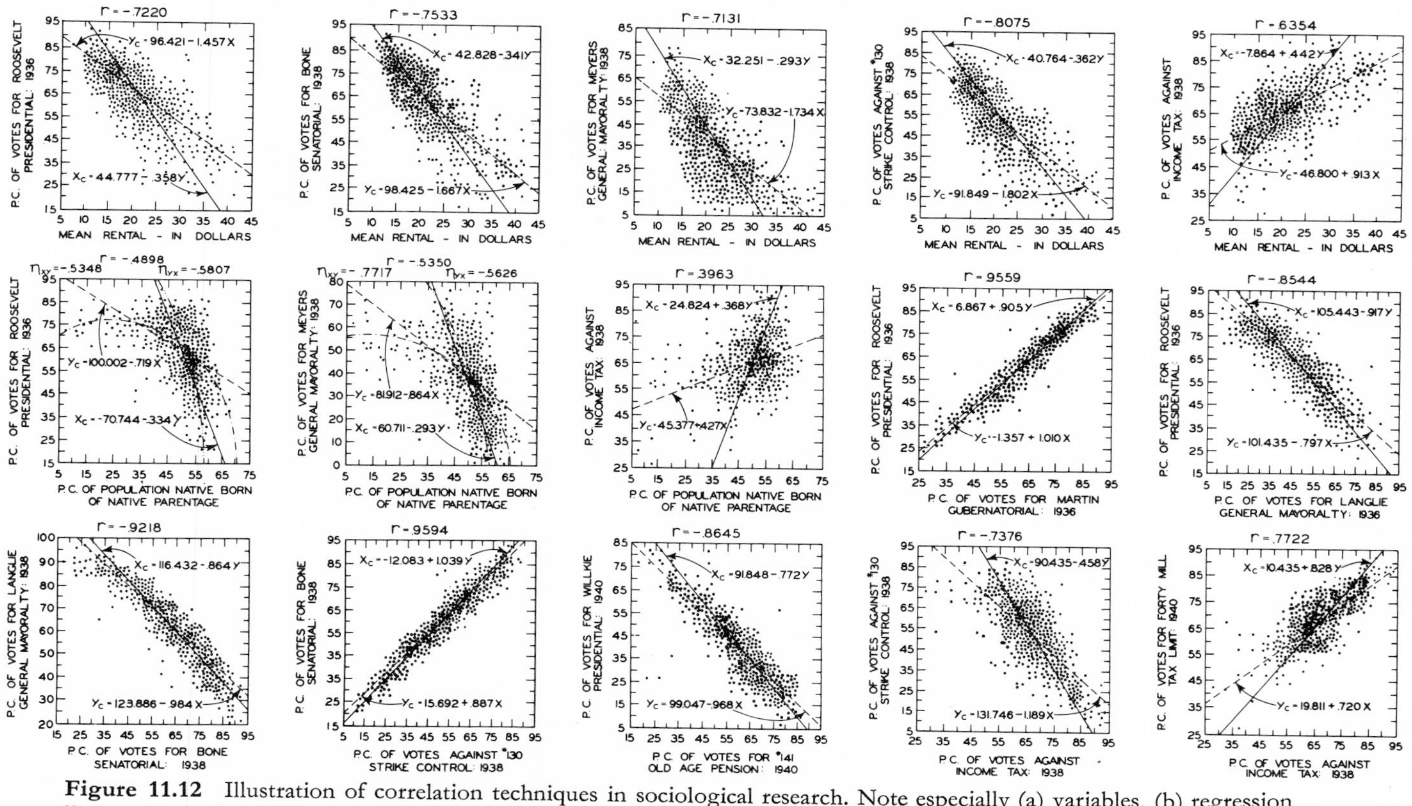

Figure 11.12 Illustration of correlation techniques in sociological research. Note especially (a) variables, (b) regression lines and equations, (c) rectilinear coefficients of correlation, and (d) curvilinear coefficients of correlation. Taken from Calvin F. Schmid, *Social Trends in Seattle,* p. 274.

1. The first column contains the names of the states, the second column the respective cancer rates (X), and the third column, the corresponding cultural index values (Y).
2. The fourth column represents the XY products.
3. The fifth column contains the X^2 values and the sixth column the Y^2 values.

$$r = \frac{N\Sigma XY - (\Sigma X)(\Sigma Y)}{\sqrt{[N\Sigma X^2 - (\Sigma X)^2][N\Sigma Y^2 - (\Sigma Y)^2]}}$$

$$= \frac{47\,(142{,}016.3) - (3586.6)\,(1740)}{\sqrt{[47\,(283{,}886.98) - (12{,}863{,}699.56)]\,[47\,(83{,}664) - (3{,}027{,}600)]}}$$

$$= \frac{6{,}674{,}766.1 - 6{,}240{,}684}{\sqrt{(13{,}342{,}688.06 - 12{,}863{,}699.56)\,(3{,}932{,}208 - 3{,}027{,}600)}}$$

$$= \frac{434{,}082.1}{\sqrt{433{,}296{,}829{,}008}}$$

$$= \frac{434{,}082.1}{658{,}252.8}$$

$$= .659445884 = .66$$

4. The sums of the figures in each of the columns are next determined.
5. Proper substitutions are made in the formula and the coefficient of correlation computed. In the illustrative problem, $r = +.66$.

Interpretation of the coefficient of correlation. In interpreting a coefficient of correlation the size of the coefficient is not the only consideration. Just as important as the absolute size of the coefficient are the relative size of the sample and the nature of the data. To say that a coefficient of correlation of .75 (plus or minus) is "high" may turn out to be very misleading if the standard error or probable error is relatively large. Or again, to say that a coefficient of .40 is always to be considered "low" may be erroneous for certain types of data. In judging the size of a particular coefficient, consideration should be given to other coefficients that have been derived from the same kind of data. It might be found, for example, that the coefficients of correlation for certain variables have been consistently less than .20 so that a coefficient of .40 would be considered relatively high for this particular type of data.

However, in order that the reader may have a few more definite facts which can be used for interpreting the size of the coefficient of correlation, if the sample is large with 100 or more cases, the following general and tentative classification might be found to be of some assistance: 1) a coefficient of .70 to 1.00 (plus or minus) signifies that there is a *high* degree of association between the series; 2) if the coefficient is greater than .40 but less than .70, there is a *substantial* relationship; 3) if the coefficient is greater than .20 but less than .40, there is a *low* correlation, and 4) if the coefficient is less than .20, there is a *negligible* relationship.

The fact that two variables show a "high" correlation is no evidence *per se* of a causal relationship. A coefficient of correlation shows only the degree of association between two sets of phenomena. Whether or not the two phenomena are causally related is a matter of interpretation. There are at least three possible inferences which might be drawn in a case where two variables evidence a pronounced degree of correlation: 1) one might be the "cause" of the other; 2) they both might be related by one or more common "causes"; and 3) the correlation may have occurred by mere chance.

Rank-difference method of correlation. The rank-difference method of correlation may be found useful for relatively small samples —usually less than 30 cases—or where the ranks of the items of the two variables are the only information available. From a mathematical standpoint the rank-difference method is decidedly less satisfactory than the product-moment method. For this reason the product-moment method should generally be preferred to the rank-difference method whenever the assumptions underlying the product-moment method are warranted. Although less precise and sensitive, the rank-difference method is independent of the distribution of the populations and therefore is not limited by the restrictions of normality and linearity which are imposed on the product-moment method.

In describing the procedure for computing a coefficient of correlation (ρ, Greek letter rho) by the rank-difference method, the problem in Table 11.8 may be considered by way of illustration.

1. The problem in Table 11.8 is to determine the relationship between the incidence of suicide and mobility of population in 25 large cities of the United States. In the first column are listed 25 cities and in the second and third columns, respectively, suicide rates, and a mobility index.
2. The relative rankings of the various cities for each of the variables are recorded in the fourth and fifth columns. Ranking merely involves the numbering of the variate values according to the positions they occupy when arranged in order of magnitude. The

highest variate value is given the rank of 1, the next highest, 2, and so on. In case of ties in rank, one of two methods can be followed, the "bracket-rank" method or the "mid-rank" method. In the "bracket-rank" method the items with the same value are assigned the same rank, and the next item after the ties is given the rank it would have had in case there had been no ties. In the "mid-rank" method the tied items are also given the same ranking, but the ranking represents the mean rank of the tied items. The latter method is generally preferable and is the one followed in Table 11.8. It will be observed that for suicide, New York and Milwaukee have a rank of 13.5, Cleveland has a rank of 12, and Baltimore, 15. Since both New York and Milwaukee have rates of 19.3 their rank is merely $(13 + 14)/2$, or 13.5. By the "bracket-rank" method both New York and Milwaukee would be given the rank of 13, and the rankings of Cleveland and Baltimore would still be the same as in the "mid-rank" method.

3. The next step is to find the differences in the rankings $(R_x - R_y)$ for each of the items.
4. The differences in the rankings are next squared and the figures are recorded in the seventh column.
5. The sum of the seventh column $(R_x - R_y)^2$ is obtained and the proper substitutions are made in the formula in Table 11.8. It will be observed that $\rho = +.54$.

The rank-difference coefficient of correlation (ρ) and the product-moment coefficient of correlation (r) are not identical, but they are similar in value. For example, in the illustrative problem $\rho = +.54$; the approximate equivalent of $r = +.558$. Pearson has devised a correction formula which can be used to translate ρ into r or *vice versa*.

Association between qualitatively defined variables. It is frequently desirable in the social sciences to study the degree of association between attributes, or qualitatively defined variables. Although the problem of association is basically that of correlation, it does not seem likely that any measure of association between attributes will lend itself to mathematical manipulation and precision such as has been found in quantitative measures of correlation. Measures of association between attributes are limited to comparisons of predictability of a variable when its association with another variable is taken into account, as compared with its predictability when no association is utilized. A coefficient that performs this function may be considered to be a qualitative correlation coefficient, but more precisely should be called a coefficient of relative predictability.

Table 11.8

CALCULATION OF THE RANK-DIFFERENCE COEFFICIENT OF CORRELATION (ρ). RELATIONSHIP BETWEEN SUICIDE AND MOBILITY OF POPULATION FOR TWENTY-FIVE LARGE AMERICAN CITIES.

City	*Variables*		*Ranks*		$R_x - R_y$	$(R_x - R_y)^2$
	Suicide Rate	*Mobility Index*	*Suicide*	*Mobility*		
	X	Y	R_x	R_y		
New York	19.3	54.3	13.5	11	+ 2.5	6.25
Chicago	17.0	51.5	19	8	+11	121.00
Philadelphia	17.5	64.6	16	17	− 1	1.00
Detroit	16.5	42.5	21	5	+16	256.00
Los Angeles	23.8	20.3	7.5	1	+ 6.5	42.25
Cleveland	20.1	52.2	12	10	+ 2	4.00
St. Louis	24.8	62.4	4	16	−12	144.00
Baltimore	18.0	72.0	15	23	− 8	64.00
Boston	14.8	59.4	23	14	+ 9	81.00
Pittsburgh	14.9	70.0	22	22	0	0.00
San Francisco	40.0	43.8	1	6	− 5	25.00
Milwaukee	19.3	66.2	13.5	19	− 5.5	30.25
Buffalo	13.8	67.6	24	20	+ 4	16.00
Washington, D. C. .	22.5	37.1	9	4	+ 5	25.00
Minneapolis	23.8	56.3	7.5	12	+ 4.5	20.25
New Orleans	17.2	82.9	17.5	25	+ 7.5	56.25
Cincinnati	23.9	62.2	6	15	− 9	81.00
Newark	21.4	51.9	10	9	+ 1	1.00
Kansas City	24.5	49.4	5	7	− 2	4.00
Seattle	31.7	30.7	2	2	0	0.00
Indianapolis	21.0	66.1	11	18	− 7	49.00
Rochester	17.2	68.0	17.5	21	+ 3.5	12.25
Jersey City........	10.1	56.5	25	13	+12	144.00
Louisville	16.6	78.7	20	24	− 4	16.00
Portland	29.3	33.2	3	3	0	0.00

$$\Sigma(R_x - R_y)^2 = 1199.50$$

$$\begin{aligned}\rho &= 1 - \frac{6\Sigma(R_x - R_y)^2}{N(N^2 - 1)}\\ &= 1 - \frac{6\,(1199.50)}{25\,(625 - 1)}\\ &= 1 - .461\\ &= +.539\end{aligned}$$

An attribute is classified into sub-categories to which members of a population are assigned in terms of whether or not they possess the characteristic which defines the category. The attribute "political preference" is classified into the sub-categories: Republican, Democrat, Socialist, etc. Members of a population may then be assigned to these categories in terms of their political preference however such preference is defined.

If the distribution of the attribute throughout a population is known, the best estimate for any member of the population taken at random is that he belongs to the sub-category in which the largest numbers are known to belong. If in a given population it is known that 45 per cent are Republicans, 40 per cent Democrats, and 15 per cent others, the number of errors would be at a minimum if each member chosen at random were predicted to be a Republican. By this choice 55 per cent of the predictions would be errors, but any other method would result in more than 55 per cent errors. For example, if the predictions were divided into the same proportions as the known categories, 61.5 per cent error would be expected. If all were predicted to be Democrats, there would be 60 per cent errors.

If the distribution of a second variable, such as place of residence, is also known for the members of the population, and if the two attributes are associated with each other, the error in prediction can be reduced. For example, it may be known that 60 per cent of the population are urban and 40 per cent are rural. Thirty per cent of the population are urban members and Democrats, 20 per cent are urbanites and Republicans, 10 per cent are urbanites and belong to other sub-categories. Ten per cent of the population are rural members and Democrats, 25

Table 11.9

RELATIONSHIP BETWEEN POLITICAL PREFERENCE AND PLACE OF RESIDENCE.

Class	*Democrats*	*Republicans*	*Others*	*Total*
Urban	△ 30	20	10	60
Rural	10	△ 25	5	40
Total	40	△ 45	15	100

per cent are rural members and Republicans, 5 per cent are rural and belong to other sub-categories. The joint contingency of the two variables can be shown in a table (Table 11.9).

Under these conditions when residence is known, urban members should be predicted to be Democrats, and rural members should be predicted to be Republicans. This additional information about place of residence makes it possible to reduce the total error of prediction from 55 per cent errors—when only the distribution of political preference was known—to 45 per cent when the additional information was taken into account. (The 45 per cent error is made up of predicting Democrats for the 20 per cent Republicans and Democrats for the 10 per cent others in the urban group, and predicting Republicans for the 10 per cent Democrats and Republicans for the 5 per cent others in the rural group.)

The coefficient of relative predictability is defined as the ratio of difference between the original error and the error after a second attribute is taken into account, divided by the original error. If E_1 is the original error and E_2 is the error taking into account the associated variable, the coefficient C can be expressed as:

$$\text{R.P.} = \frac{E_1 - E_2}{E_1}$$

Referring to Table 11.9, the original error, E_1 is the sum of non-modal categories for the first attribute—political preference. That is, the marginal categories 40 plus 15, or 55 per cent. The error under the second condition, E_2, is the sum of all the non-modal, or error, cells in the contingency Table 11.9; that is, 20 plus 10, plus 10 plus 5, or 45 per cent. The improvement in prediction is 10 per cent and the coefficient of relative predictability is 10 divided by 55 or 0.189.

Since directionality is not defined for attributes—they are either present or absent—the coefficient can never be negative. If the amount of error under the second condition is equal to the original error, the coefficient is zero and it can be said that the attributes are not related. Table 11.10 has been constructed according to random probability so that the distribution within the table is exactly the chance distribution.

E_1 for this table is 40 plus 15 or 55 per cent and E_2 is 24 plus 9, plus 16 plus 6, also 55 per cent.

$$\text{R.P.} = \frac{55 - 55}{55} = 0$$

Table 11.10

RELATIONSHIP BETWEEN POLITICAL PREFERENCE AND PLACE OF RESIDENCE.

Class	*Democrats*	*Republicans*	*Others*	*Total*
Urban	24	△ 27	9	60
Rural	16	△ 18	6	40
Total	40	△ 45	15	100

Table 11.11

RELATIONSHIP BETWEEN POLITICAL PREFERENCE AND PLACE OF RESIDENCE.

Class	*Democrats*	*Republicans*	*Others*	*Total*
Urban	△ 45	0	0	45
Rural	0	△ 55	0	55
Total	45	△ 55	0	100

If the attributes are related perfectly so that no error in prediction is found, the coefficient is one. Table 11.11 shows perfect predictability. E_1 for this table is 45 plus zero or 45 per cent, E_2 is zero, and R.P. $= 45 - 0/45 = 1$. The coefficient of relative predictability ranges between zero and one. The coefficient of 0.189 for the two attributes shown in Table 11.9 indicates some correlation between these attributes and a corresponding improvement in prediction if one of the attributes can be identified for each member of the population.

Other measures of association between attributes have been proposed. Most of the better known measures are based on some application of *chi square* as a test of the null hypothesis of no association. Many of them are restricted to fourfold tables and may have other underlying assumptions or restrictions to their general usefulness.

Yule has proposed a coefficient usually designated as "Q" which measures association in a fourfold table. Q is found by computing the ratio between the difference and the sum of the cross products of the diagonal cells. That is, if the cells of the fourfold table are designated as in the figure below,

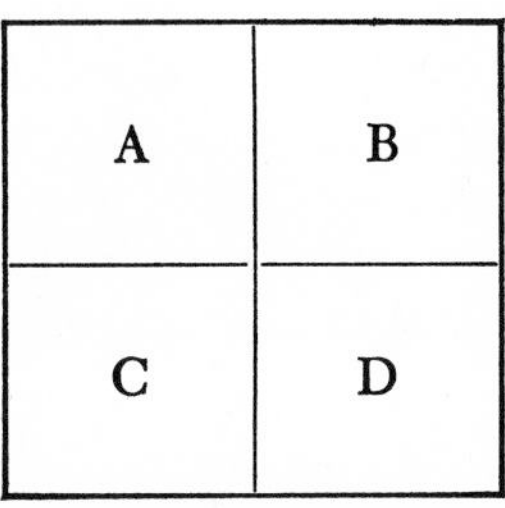

$$Q = \frac{AD - BC}{AD + BC}$$

Q varies between minus one and plus one as BC is less than or greater than AD. The sign of Q is determined by the arrangement of the cells. Frequently this arrangement is arbitrary with no meaningful interpretation in the problem. If AD = BC it can be assumed that there is no association between the variables and Q = 0. If either AD or BC is zero, the association is complete—that is, the correlation is perfect —and Q = ±1.

Other measures of contingency include ϕ which is defined as: $\phi = \sqrt{\chi^2/N}$, and C which is related directly to ϕ and is defined as

$$C = \sqrt{\frac{\frac{\chi^2}{N}}{1 + \frac{\chi^2}{N}}} \quad \text{or} \quad C = \sqrt{\frac{\phi^2}{1 + \phi^2}}$$

an equivalent formula. Tschuprow attempted to refine these contingency measures which are based on *chi square* to take into account the number of categories involved in the cross classification. Tschuprow's T is defined by the formula

$$T^2 = \frac{\chi^2}{N\sqrt{(s-1)(t-1)}}$$

where s is the number of rows and t is the number of columns in the contingency table. All of these measures have serious limitations due to their dependence on assumptions, restrictions to the use of *chi square,* and the dependence of the results on the proper definition of units of classification of the variables. A thorough knowledge and understanding of these concepts and assumptions is essential to the proper application of measures of contingency which are based on distribution statistics such as *chi square.*

Curvilinear correlation. As was already indicated, the Pearsonian or product-moment coefficient of correlation is based on the assumption that the relationship between the two variables is rectilinear. When the data are non-linear (curvilinear), r does not accurately measure the amount of correlation between the variables. The constancy of the ratio of change of the two variables determines whether the correlation is rectilinear or curvilinear. If the amount of change in the two variables bears a constant ratio, the correlation is rectilinear, but if it does not, then the relationship is curvilinear. For example, the relationship between the strength and age of human beings is curvilinear since strength does not bear a constant ratio to age throughout the entire span of life. Facts of this kind can be brought out clearly by plotting the data on a scatter diagram. There are also formulae which can be applied as tests for linearity of regression.[12]

Partial and multiple correlation. Since the social scientist is frequently concerned with a large number of factors and their interrelations, simple correlation techniques may be found to be definitely inadequate for certain problems. Simple correlation does not measure separately the relationship between two variables in such a way that the effects of other related variables are eliminated, nor does simple correlation reliably determine the relationship between any one variable and the combined effect of several related variables. The two problems of correlation as thus stated can be more satisfactorily dealt with by the methods of partial and multiple correlation.

Partial correlation analysis is a statistical technique for measuring the degree of relationship between two variables when the effects of certain other specified variables with which they are related are eliminated. Partial correlation has certain characteristics of the experimental method in that it is possible to study the relation between two factors

[12]For further discussion, see John H. Mueller and Karl F. Schuessler, *Statistical Reasoning in Sociology,* pp. 315–324. Houghton Mifflin Co., 1961; Margaret J. Hagood and Daniel O. Price, *Statistics for Sociologists,* pp. 449–456. Holt, Rinehart & Winston, Inc., 1952.

when several other factors are held constant. In the social sciences it is extraordinarily difficult to conduct controlled experiments in the same manner that the physicist or chemist does in the laboratory. However, partial correlation offers to the social scientist one of the most satisfactory substitutes for controlled experimentation.

Multiple correlation analysis is a statistical technique for measuring the correlation between one variable (dependent variable) and the combined effect of a number of other variables (independent variables).[13]

Sampling[14]

One of the most important as well as most difficult problems in social research is the problem of sampling. Instead of studying every case which might logically be included in an investigation, only a small portion is selected for analysis from which to draw conclusions. Most statistical studies are based on samples and not on complete enumerations of all the relevant data. A statistical sample is a miniature picture or cross-section of the entire group or aggregate from which the sample is taken. The entire group from which a sample is chosen is known as the "population," "universe," or "supply."

The term "population" is not necessarily synonymous with a population of people. A statistical population or universe may consist of attributes, qualities, or behavior of people, the behavior of inanimate objects such as dice or coins, cities or city blocks, households or dwelling structures, the day's output of a factory, or opinions of the electorate of an entire nation.

From an ideal standpoint a complete count of all the relevant cases would probably be considered preferable to a sample. However, it may be found impossible or impractical to include more than a small

[13]For a more complete treatment of partial and multiple correlation see Hubert M. Blalock, Jr., *Social Statistics,* pp. 326–358. McGraw-Hill Book Company, 1960.

[14]See the following papers on the history and development of sampling techniques: F. Yates, "A Review of Recent Statistical Developments in Sampling and Sampling Surveys," *Journal of the Royal Statistical Society,* CIX, 12–30, discussion, 31–42; Frederick F. Stephan, "History of the Uses of Modern Sampling Procedures," *Journal of the American Statistical Association,* XLIII, 12–39; for a relatively simple and practical discussion of sampling see William G. Cochran *et al., Statistical Problems of the Kinsey Report,* pp. 309–331. American Statistical Association, 1954.

portion of the total number of cases. The factors of time and cost are usually important considerations in social research. It is more economical and efficient to base studies on samples, and for most practical purposes the conclusions drawn from a sample can be just as valid as conclusions drawn from the analysis of the entire universe of cases.

There are two basic aspects to the problem of statistical sampling —first, the actual selection of the items that are to make up the sample, and second, the measurement of the reliability of the sample. The present section will be devoted primarily to the principles and procedures of selecting a sample.

Generally speaking, the same mathematical laws of chance or probability should govern statistical sampling in the same way that they do in the flipping of evenly balanced coins, the rolling of well-formed dice, or the drawing of colored symmetrical balls of uniform size from an urn. Obviously the most important consideration in selecting a sample is to see that it is closely representative of the universe. The size of a sample is no necessary insurance of its representativeness. Relatively small samples properly selected may be much more reliable than large samples poorly selected. The actual selection of a sample should be so arranged that every item in the universe under consideration must have the same chance for inclusion in the sample.

A good sample must be representative of the universe or population. A good sample also must be adequate in size in order to be reliable.

A sample that is not representative is known as a biased sample.

> Bias may be due to imperfect instruments, the personal qualities of the observer, defective technique, or other causes. Like experimental error, it is difficult to eliminate entirely, but usually may be reduced to relatively small dimensions by taking proper care. . . . Experience has, in fact, shown that the human being is an extremely poor instrument for the conduct of a random selection. Wherever there is any scope for personal choice or judgment on the part of the observer, bias is almost certain to creep in.[15]

There are many studies in the social sciences bearing the more superficial earmarks of erudition and authority that are intrinsically worthless and misleading because they are based on unrepresentative samples. To illustrate biased samples in social research one might readily cite several studies based on data obtained from incomplete and

[15] G. Udny Yule and M. G. Kendall, *An Introduction to the Theory of Statistics*, *op. cit.*, pp. 371–373.

distorted returns from mailed questionnaires. Although the original mailing list of prospective respondents may be a representative sample, the operation of selective factors on the questionnaires actually returned may result in an extremely biased sample.

The *Literary Digest* public opinion poll of the 1936 presidential election is a dramatic example of the consequences of a biased sample. It would be considered extraordinarily large, but the goodness of a statistical sample is not dependent merely on size. The *Fortune* poll on the other hand, with a sample of 4,500 cases predicted the outcome of the total popular vote for Roosevelt with an error of 1.0 per cent.

From the point of view of sampling technique, what were some of the factors that explain the débacle of the *Literary Digest's* 1936 presidential poll? 1) The mailing lists of the *Literary Digest* were taken largely from telephone directories and automobile registration lists which tended to overweight the proportion of cases in the upper socio-economic classes. 2) The *Literary Digest* sent all its ballots by mail. People in the higher income brackets are more likely to return their ballots than those in the lower income brackets; besides other selective factors such as "protest" voting against the incumbent administration were also operative. 3) In 1932, and especially in 1936, there were definite shifts in political alignments drawn very sharply along economic interests. The wage earners and those on relief voted solidly for Roosevelt, and farmers, Negroes, and other groups returned large majorities for him. With these new alignments the biased sample of the *Literary Digest* assumed major proportions in the 1936 poll.[16]

It must not be inferred that the only errors in social research are due to biased sampling. Other sources of error, as has already been indicated from time to time arise in the interview process, in imperfections in the design of the questionnaire and tabulation plans, in processing the material, and so on.

An adequate sample is one that contains enough cases to insure reliable results. But the question that immediately comes to mind is how many cases, or what proportion of a particular universe should be selected in order to obtain an adequate sample?

> If there is one question asked a consulting statistician more frequently than any other, it is, "How large a sample should I take?" Often one hears such glib answers as, "Never less than 100," or "500,"

[16]Daniel Katz and Hadley Cantril, "Public Opinion Polls," *Sociometry,* I, 155–178; C. E. Robinson, *Straw Votes, A Study of Political Prediction, passim.* Columbia University Press, 1932.

or "At least 5 per cent." However, the question is actually unanswerable until the following items of information are given: the designation of the parameters which one wishes to estimate, the range of unreliability permissible in estimates, and a rough estimate of the dispersion of the investigated characteristic. . . .

Such methods, with adaptations and extensions to take into account the design of the sample, are the only way of answering correctly the question of how large a sample should be. The answer always depends on what degree of reliability is required for the purpose of the research and on the amount of dispersion in the distribution of the characteristic studied if it is quantitative, or on the proportion of incidence if it is nonquantitative. If the universe is very homogeneous with respect to a certain quantitative characteristic, a quite small sample may yield more reliable results in the estimation of the parameters describing this distribution than a much larger sample of another universe which is very heterogeneous with respect to the characteristic studied. Therefore, rule of thumb answers of arbitrary numbers or percentages are misleading, and one should insist on being given the information required, even if in the form of extremely rough estimates, before attempting to answer the question.[17]

In constructing a sampling design there are several criteria which should be kept in mind. First, it is important that measurable or known probability sampling techniques be used:

Methods of sample selection and estimation are available for which the risk of errors in the sample estimate can be measured and controlled. As the size of the sample is increased, the expected discrepancies between the estimated value from the sample and the true value (*i.e.,* the value that would be obtained from a complete census) will decrease if such methods are used. With such methods one can know the risk taken that the error due to sampling will exceed a specified amount. . . .

The use of methods yielding results whose sampling errors can be measured has these advantages: we can indicate to the users of our data the degree of confidence they can place in the published figures; we can make use of an objective criterion for choosing the "best" from among alternative designs; and we can determine in advance of draw-

[17]Margaret J. Hagood and Daniel O. Price, *Statistics for Sociologists,* pp. 279–282. Holt, Rinehart & Winston, Inc., 1952. Reproduced by permission of the publisher. Also see W. G. Cochran, *Sampling Techniques.* John Wiley & Sons, Inc., 1953.

> ing the sample whether resources are available to get results from the sample with the reliability required, and so we may be able to prevent useless sample surveys from being carried forward.[18]

For a number of years, nationally known polling agencies utilized almost exclusively "quota sampling" or "stratified non-random sampling," a procedure which does violence to sound principles of statistical sampling. In quota sampling, interviewers themselves select, in a more or less hit-and-miss fashion, a requisite quota of individuals according to certain predetermined characteristics such as sex, age, education, and occupation. In a procedure of this kind, it is impossible to assess the reliability of the results. At the present time, quota sampling has been largely abandoned, and is used only in combination with other techniques, such as area sampling.[19]

In terms of scientific standards, sampling procedures which do not provide a sound basis for estimating sampling error should be sedulously avoided.

> When the respondents are picked up by quota selection or expert selection of "representative" counties, farms, or firms, too frequently no useful limits of bias can be assigned: the information furnished is then of unknown quality and may lead to extremely embarrassing questions of interpretation. Unless biases can be removed satisfactorily, a method of collection that appears to be cheap is too often cheap only in the sense of providing a lot of schedules per dollar, but may

[18]Morris H. Hansen, William N. Hurwitz, and Margaret Gurney, "Problems and Methods of the Sample Survey of Business," *Journal of the American Statistical Association,* XLI, 173–189.

[19]In this connection the controversy concerning the respective merits of quota and area sampling not only possesses historical interest but also provides insights into the logic of sampling techniques. The proponents of quota sampling point out that quota sampling 1) is cheaper and 2) requires less time. Those who consider area sampling superior argue that in area sampling 1) there is no necessity of estimating the composition of the universe and of establishing quotas; 2) the dangers of bias from interview selection are virtually non-existent; and 3) it is possible to measure the reliability of the data. See, *e.g.,* Joseph R. Hochstim and Dilman M. K. Smith, "Area Sampling or Quota Control?—Three Sampling Experiments," *Public Opinion Quarterly,* XII, 73–80; Norman C. Meier and Cletus J. Burke, "Laboratory Tests of Sampling Techniques," *Public Opinion Quarterly,* II, 586–593. For an excellent, comprehensive presentation of sampling techniques in public opinion polling and other types of surveys, see Frederick F. Stephan and Philip J. McCarthy, *Sampling Opinions.* John Wiley & Sons, Inc., 1963.

actually be very costly when measured in the amount of useful information per dollar or the damage done through misinformation.[20]

Second, one should be careful to use simple, straightforward, workable methods properly adapted to available facilities and personnel. Unduly elaborate and complicated techniques should be avoided. Since the actual work of gathering and tabulating data is usually done by enumerators and clerks, it is important to utilize procedures that are practicable and readily understandable.

Third, every attempt should be made to achieve maximum reliability of results for every dollar spent. It takes experience, thought, and sometimes real ingenuity to work out an optimal balance between expenditures and a maximum of reliable information. For example,

> The statistician does not take chances with sampling errors; he has them under control and knows how much it will cost to reduce them to any desired degree. He knows that precision beyond what can actually be utilized in formulating action on the basis of the data is sheer waste of money. His guiding philosophy is a very practical one, namely, to minimize, in the long run, the net losses arising from two kinds of mistakes—
>
> i. Trying to cut corners by taking too small a sample, or a sample not of the best possible design, too often running into sample errors that are troublesome.
>
> ii. Being too sure, by taking too big a sample, and too often getting more precision than needed, thus wasting funds and slowing up the work, running into the errors and biases that so often beset large operations.[21]

In general, there are four basic procedures that can be followed in the selection of items for statistical samples. These procedures are 1) simple random sampling, 2) stratified random sampling, 3) sampling by regular intervals, and 4) area sampling. It should be clearly pointed out that these four types of sampling procedure are not mutually exclusive, but overlap to a greater or less degree. Moreover, in actual practice a sampling design may include two or more of these procedures.

1. Simple random sampling. Reference has been made to the importance of random selection in statistical sampling. "Random" as used in this connection does not mean haphazard, careless, un-

[20] W. Edwards Deming, "On Training in Sampling," *Journal of the American Statistical Association,* XL (June, 1945), pp. 307–316.

[21] *Ibid.*

planned, or hit-and-miss. Rather, according to accepted standards of statistical sampling, every effort should be made to control the choice of items so that every item in the universe shall have the same probability of being included in the sample. If the extent of the universe is known, each case can be numbered on a slip of paper or cardboard disc, placed in a suitable container, and thoroughly shuffled, after which the individual items to be included in the sample are drawn from the container. Each time before a case is drawn the slips or discs should be thoroughly mixed or "randomized." After a proper notation of the chosen item is made it is replaced in the container. This procedure of mixing the slips or discs in the universe, selecting one item at a time, making a record of the selected item, and then re-inserting it in the container is continued until the entire sample is obtained. It is obvious that there may be serious practical difficulties in this procedure if the universe is very large. In addition, this procedure would be theoretically inapplicable if the universe is not finite.

A less cumbersome and equally valid technique of securing a random sample is to employ a table of random numbers. According to this procedure the items in the universe are numbered systematically, and each item selected for the sample is made in accordance with the listing of random numbers. Lists of random sampling numbers are readily available in published form.[22]

2. Stratified random sampling. If the composition of the universe is known, it is possible to select a sample by taking sub-samples—usually proportional to the size of the significant elements of subdivisions in the universe. After the relative size of each sub-sample has been determined, the individual items are actually chosen either by random selection or according to regular intervals. For example, if such information as sex, college or school, class and fraternity affiliation is known about a student body, sub-samples will be selected on the basis of these different categories, the size of each sub-sample being determined usually by the number of cases in each classification.

The main objective in stratification is to secure a more reliable sample. Sometimes the gains in stratification may be very high and at other times very trivial. If the various strata are so chosen that the variable under consideration is relatively homogeneous within the strata and heterogeneous between strata, variance will be reduced. If, however, the variable is randomly distributed throughout all the

[22]L. H. C. Tippett, *Random Sampling Numbers*. Cambridge University Press, 1927; and R. A. Fisher and F. Yates, *Statistical Tables for Biological, Agricultural and Medical Research,* (Table XXXIII). Oliver and Boyd, 1949.

strata, little or no improvement will take place through stratification. Sampling variance can also be reduced by increasing the number of cases. Frequently, gains of a stratified sample are not justified by the additional costs.

It should be pointed out that the sampling ratios in a stratified sample are not always proportional to the number of cases in the various sub-groups. In fact, where the standard deviations of the sub-groups are comparatively large, higher sampling ratios should be taken.

3. Sampling by regular intervals. Another procedure is to select the cases at regular intervals from a series, alphabetical list, or any other arbitrary arrangement. For example, in selecting the sample of 265 students which has been used for illustrative purposes in the present chapter, every fifth case was taken from the files of freshman male students for the school year 1937–1938. The 265 cases thus selected represent a 20 per cent sample. Instead of taking every fifth case, every third, tenth, twentieth, or twenty-fifth case could have been chosen, depending on the desired number of cases to be included in the sample.

This procedure has been used for many years and from experience has proved satisfactory both from mathematical and practical points of view. It is obvious that this technique can be used only on finite universes where complete listings are available. In selecting items at regular intervals from a file or list it should be made certain that there is no periodicity or other distortions in the arrangement of items that would tend to bias the sample.

4. Area sampling.[23] Since World War II, the United States Bureaus of the Census and of Agricultural Economics have not only made extensive use of techniques of area sampling, but also have made very substantial contributions to our knowledge in this field. In sampling of this kind small areas are designated as sampling units, and the

[23]This section on area sampling is based largely on lectures by Morris H. Hansen, University of Washington, July, 1948, and on the following publications: Sampling Staff, Bureau of the Census, *A Chapter in Population Sampling, passim;* Hansen and Hauser, "Area Sampling—Some Principles of Sample Design," *Public Opinion Quarterly,* IX, 183–193; Howard G. Brunsman, "The Sample Census of Congested Production Areas," *Journal of the American Statistical Association,* XXXIX, 303–310; Morris H. Hansen, "Census to Sample Population Growth," *Domestic Commerce,* 1–2; also, see Morris H. Hansen, William N. Hurwitz, and William G. Madow, *Sample Survey Methods and Theory.* John Wiley & Sons, Inc., 1953 (2 volumes).

households interviewed include all or a specified fraction of those found in a canvass of these designated small areas.

The basic sampling units or segments chosen may be relatively large or relatively small depending on such factors as the type of area being studied, population distribution, the availability of suitable maps and other information, and the nature and desired accuracy of the data being collected. For example, in open country and predominantly farm areas, highway maps, aerial photographs, and other sources of information are used to delineate the sample segments. In the "Master Sample of Agriculture,"[24] the main factors taken into account in defining sampling segments in open country areas are: 1) identifiable boundaries, 2) specified size mainly in terms of the number of farms, 3) comparability of segments with other sampling segments, and 4) suitability of segments in sampling all types of dwellings, including farms. In unincorporated territory with a much higher density of population, smaller sampling segments are used with proper consideration being given to the sampling of non-farm as well as farm units. In cities and towns the segments may be census tracts, enumeration districts, precincts, blocks, or parts of blocks.

It can be demonstrated mathematically that the variance of a sample is decreased by choosing widely scattered blocks rather than a few concentrated clusters. Furthermore, results of analyses indicate that for most population and housing items large sampling units are considerably less efficient than small ones.[25] Accordingly, blocks or parts of blocks rather than larger units such as census tracts and precincts should be used in larger cities. To increase the efficiency of the sampling design further sub-sampling of addresses or dwelling units are chosen from selected blocks. Detailed Sanborn Insurance maps and directories of dwelling units provide excellent sources for defining sampling units.

In the sampling design for the 1948 Greater Seattle Housing Market Survey, for example, the Sanborn maps were used as the basic source

[24]A. J. King and R. J. Jessen, "Master Sample of Agriculture," *Journal of the American Statistical Association,* XL, 38–56; R. J. Jessen, "The Master Sample Project and Its Use in Agricultural Economics," *Journal of Farm Economics,* XXIX, 531–540; Earl E. Houseman and T. J. Reed, *Application of Probability Area Sampling to Farm Surveys,* U. S. Department of Agriculture, Handbook No. 67, (May, 1954).

[25]Hansen and Hurwitz, "On the Theory of Sampling from Finite Populations," *The Annals of Mathematical Statistics,* XIV, 333–362; "Relative Efficiencies of Various Sampling Units in Population Inquiries," *Journal of the American Statistical Association,* XXXVIII, 89–94.

of information within the corporate city and for certain contiguous areas where detailed up-to-date map coverage was available. Attention was given only to the structures in the Sanborn maps which could reasonably be assured to contain dwelling units; warehouses, piers, factories, filling stations, and so on were ignored. The structures with dwelling units were classified into two groups: I), structures which appeared to contain not more than five dwelling units and II), structures which appeared to contain more than five dwelling units. The sampling procedure for the structures in group I were selected from Sanborn maps in the following manner:

> Count the addresses of these structures, starting at the upper left-hand corner of the page and proceeding systematically around each block. Carry over the count from one block to the next, and from one page to the next, for at least 100 pages at a time if possible. Write down on a special form the address of the 21st structure in this count, and every 50th structure thereafter; *i.e.,* the address of the 21st, 71st, 121st, etc. Be sure that these addresses are complete enough that an enumerator can find them in the field. This list of selected group I addresses will form the major part of the sample.[26]

Since the maps were not completely up to date, supplementary listings were made on the basis of a systematic selection of blocks. For the addresses of the dwelling structures in group II (those that appeared to contain more than five dwelling units) a field prelisting was made and the 9th, 59th, 109th, etc. lines were selected for inclusion in the sample.

Measures of Reliability and Significance

A "true" measure of a distribution, such as the arithmetic mean, would be based on all the cases in the universe. The universe value of a summarizing measure of this kind is known as a *parameter*. If the true mean weight or parameter of the male freshman students at the University of Washington were to be computed, every male student

[26]Abstracted from a letter to Nathanael H. Engle, Director of Bureau of Business Research, University of Washington from Morris H. Hansen, Assistant Director for Statistical Standards, U. S. Bureau of the Census, dated February 27, 1948.

registered would have to be included. It will be recalled that the mean weight of 148.74 pounds was based on a sample of 265 cases, or approximately 20 per cent of the universe. This mean of 148.74 pounds is only a probable value. The value of a summarizing measure based on a sample is known as a *statistic*. If another sample of 265 cases were selected, the mean weight would not be identical to the one derived from the first sample, but it would probably be very similar. Moreover, neither the mean of the first sample nor that of the second sample would probably coincide exactly with the true mean based on the entire universe. In other words, measures based on samples are generally larger or smaller than their corresponding parameters.

Since most statistical studies are based on samples, it is therefore important to know how closely the measures based on samples represent the parameters, and also how much variation one may expect if other samples are analyzed. The so-called measures of reliability and significance may be found of great assistance in clarifying these problems.

Measures of reliability are concerned only with fluctuations due to random sampling. Obviously, they have nothing to do with observational or computational errors. Moreover, whenever a measure of reliability is computed, it is understood that the sample is adequate and has been selected according to a rigorously scientific procedure.

According to large sample theory, the reliability of a measure, such as the arithmetic mean, depends upon 1) the number of cases in the sample and 2) the variability of the values in the sample. It is no more than common sense that the reliability of a measure is related to the size of the sample. We would naturally have more confidence in the trustworthiness of a sample that is relatively large than in one that is very small.

The degree of variability of the cases in a sample also has an important influence on the reliability of the measures computed from the sample. If the cases in the sample show a pronounced scatter, a greater chance fluctuation in the measures would naturally be expected. The relationship between the size of the sample and the variability of the items is clearly indicated by the formula for the standard error of the mean. The standard error is a measure of reliability:

$$\sigma_{\bar{x}} = \frac{\sigma}{\sqrt{N-1}}$$

The standard error of the mean weight for the sample of 265 University of Washington freshmen is:

$$\sigma_{\bar{x}} = \frac{18.37}{\sqrt{265 - 1}}$$

$$= \frac{18.37}{16.25}$$

$$= 1.13$$

What does this figure of 1.13 (pounds) signify, or more generally, what is the "meaning" of a standard error? In order to follow the steps in the reasoning process leading to the concept of standard error, and in order to make precise probability statements, it is necessary to reason as follows:

1. If an infinite number of samples each consisting of 265 male freshmen were drawn, about 68 per cent of the samples would have means falling within the range $\mu \pm 1.13$ pounds (where μ is the universe mean).
2. If the mean weight of all university freshman males were in fact known, the probability would be approximately .68 (about two chances out of three) that the mean weight of any random sample of 265 freshman males drawn from among all freshmen would lie within 1.13 pounds of the universe parameter or universe mean.

The same principles apply to other measures of standard error. The formulas for the standard error of the standard deviation and for the standard error of the median are:

$$\sigma_{\sigma} = \frac{\sigma}{\sqrt{2N - 1}}$$

$$\sigma_{\dot{x}} = 1.2533 \frac{\sigma}{\sqrt{N - 1}}$$

Because of the difficulty in stating verbally the precise meaning of statistical concepts it should be pointed out that the foregoing interpretation contains certain inaccuracies. For example, the standard error of the mean (1.13 pounds) has been used as if it were based on a complete knowledge of the universe of college freshmen, whereas it was actually based on only one sample of 265 men. If further samples were taken, it is probable that this figure would be slightly different.

While every statistical measure has its own reliability formula, it should be emphasized that each such formula is subject to special qualifications, limitations, and conditions. For example, the statements made above are reasonably accurate only for samples of more than 30 cases drawn from a universe which is normally distributed.

One form of the standard error of the Pearsonian coefficient of correlation is:

$$\sigma_r = \frac{1}{\sqrt{N - 1}}$$

This formula should be used only for correlation problems involving 30 or more cases, and for testing whether a given correlation coefficient is significantly different from zero.

In the illustrative problem in which the coefficient of correlation for height and weight is computed,

$$\sigma_r = \frac{1}{\sqrt{265 - 1}}$$

$$= \frac{1}{16.25}$$

$$= .0615 \text{ or } .06$$

The classical or traditional techniques of estimating sampling errors as sketched in the preceding paragraphs are frequently referred to as large sample theory. There is another theory of samples known as small sample theory. In small sample theory

> It will no longer be open to us to assume (*a*) that the random sampling distribution of a parameter is approximately normal, or even single-humped, or (*b*) that values given by the data are sufficiently close to the universe values for us to be able to use them in gauging the precision of our estimates.[27]

A "small sample" generally refers to one of less than 30 to 40 cases, although in actual practice it is difficult to draw a sharp distinction between a large sample and a small sample. As a rule, the techniques of small samples are applicable to large sampling without modification, but the reverse does not hold.

In working with small samples, the distributions of the variables become extremely important and tests of significance must be related

[27] Yule and Kendall, *op. cit.*, p. 482.

much more carefully to the proper distributions. Normal approximations no longer result in reasonable tests. Since variables may assume a number of different distributions under different conditions, the mathematics and assumptions underlying the more common of these distributions should be familiar to the researcher. Any variable which is distributed according to a "success or failure" determination, such as heads or tails on a coin, true or false on a test, or occurrence or non-occurrence of any behavior will form a binomial distribution. The ratio of squared difference between observed and theoretical frequencies to the theoretical frequency is distributed according to *chi square*. There are of course other distributions, one of the most significant of which is the *"t" distribution.*

Statistical Inference

The most important development in modern statistics is the logic and techniques which make it possible to use small samples with confidence. These procedures are commonly referred to as statistical inference. Statistical inference is concerned with decision making. Unlike the informal, hit-or-miss practices of daily living, the rules and techniques in statistical inference are clearly specified. Providing that there is agreement concerning rules, two or more statisticians will arrive at the same decision. The rules and techniques of statistical inference are so designed that it is not possible to be certain about the correctness of any particular decision, but in the long run the proportion of correct decisions is known in advance. There is no insurance that one will not make an incorrect decision concerning a population parameter from a statistic based on a sample.

There are several types of errors which may occur in statistical inference: *Type I error* refers to rejection of a hypothesis when it should not be rejected. In statistical inference, the proportion of Type I errors one is willing to make is usually stated in advance. If, for example, there is an extremely low probability (say .002) that a certain characteristic is inferred about the parameter from a measure (statistic) derived from a sample, it may be decided to reject the hypothesis that the sample occurred by chance, and the probability of being in error by rejecting this hypothesis is .002. If a hypothesis is never rejected, a Type I error will never be made. Such a practice, however, will result in Type II errors. *Type II errors* occur when a hypothesis is accepted, when it should be rejected. In actual practice it is not possible to determine whether the rejection of a hypothesis is correct or incorrect. Generally, statisticians are willing to make a Type I error 5 per cent of the time. Under these circumstances the probability of making a Type I error is .05. Thus, on the average 1 time in 20, or 5 times in every 100, the rejection of a particular hypothesis will be a mistake.

The probability with which a Type I error is risked is known as level of significance. In the preceding example, the level of significance is .05. Other common levels of significance are .01 and .001. A *statistical hypothesis* is a hypothesis with a possibility of rejection at some level of significance. The *null hypothesis* is the most widely used type of statistical hypothesis. The rejection of a null hypothesis proceeds as the basis of determining whether the discrepancy between the observed value and the population parameter is so large that it is unlikely to be the result of chance. Such a decision is made within the context of Type I and Type II errors as gauged by the *level of significance*. For example, if there is a probability greater than .05 that a null hypothesis is correct we may fail to reject the null hypothesis. Frequently, it is desirable that level of significance be .01 or .001 before failing to reject the null hypothesis.

Another type of hypothesis is concerned with the testing of the difference between statistics from two samples. The problem arises when a difference in some measure (statistic) occurs between two samples. The probability of such a difference is computed from the sampling distribution of the difference between this particular measure. If, for example, the difference in the two measures would occur less than .05 of the time, the hypothesis that the two samples came from the same population would be rejected.

Another type of problem in statistical inference is to find *confidence limits* for particular measures. For example, if the mean income of a sample is $5,000, it may be desirable to know the interval in which the mean income of the parameter probably lies. This is expressed in terms of *confidence limits*. The 95 per cent confidence limits, for example, does not imply that there is 95 per cent confidence that the population mean lies within a specified interval. Rather, if the process of determining such limits were repeated hundreds of times, the confidence interval would contain the parameter 95 per cent of the time. The 99 per cent confidence limits implies that in one time in 100 the parameter would be between the limits, but, of course, the limits would be wider. The less willing we are to be wrong, the less precise must be the estimate of the interval containing the parameter.

Statistical inference never produces certainty. We do not know whether we are right or wrong in a decision to reject or not to reject a hypothesis, but we do know how often we shall be wrong in rejecting when we make a series of such decisions. Some people may object that they want certainty, not probability. Such a demand is reasonable, but impossible of realization. Even in the physical sciences as a consequence of an increasing awareness of the limitations of measurement, the emphasis on the relativity and probability of scientific conclusions has supplanted the certainties of an earlier generation.

This is merely a brief, simple, nontechnical discussion of a few basic concepts, logic, procedures, and applications of statistical inference. The ability to utilize the principles of statistical inference with proficiency, of course, demands considerably more knowledge than is contained in this section. It is strongly recommended that the student carefully examine the chapters on the statistical inference in a few up-to-date textbooks.[28]

Distribution-Free, or Nonparametric, Methods of Statistical Inference

The dependence of so much of statistical inference upon the normal distribution is somewhat justified since nonnormal distributions usually can be transformed into a normal distribution. Some data are already distributed according to known mathematical functions and are subject to analysis within these functions. However, a large part of the data with which social scientists must deal is not distributed according to known mathematical functions, and assumptions as to normality, uniformity, or some other regularity are at best open to severe criticism. During the past few decades there has been a marked development in techniques for estimating parameters and testing hypotheses which require no assumption about the form of the distribution of the population. These distribution-free, or nonparametric methods are largely based on the principle of "order statistics." By "order statistics" we mean statistics that depend only on the sequence or array of the elements of the variable and are not concerned with any distance between the first and second, second and third units, etc. The fact that the distribution between any two successive observations

[28]This discussion on statistical inference is based on Sanford M. Dornbusch and Calvin F. Schmid, *Primer of Social Statistics, op. cit.*, pp. 124–131.

in an array is independent of the form of the population from which the sample is drawn underlies all of the principles of distribution-free methods of inference.

In distribution analysis the mean and standard deviation are the central concepts of position and dispersion. In distribution-free statistics the median is the measure of central tendency and dispersion is measured in terms of various ranges, such as the interquartile or the decile range. A distribution-free measure of association is the Spearman ρ, or rank difference coefficient of correlation discussed above.

Basic to distribution-free methods is the use of the binomial distribution. By using the simple techniques of array, counting, and probabilities under the binomial distribution, tests of position and range, confidence intervals, and many hypotheses are available which do not in any way depend upon assumptions regarding the distribution of the parent population. In the future the theory and derived techniques of distribution-free statistics will gain in emphasis. The student, especially in the social sciences, should familiarize himself with the various distribution-free methods of analysis and their wide application to small samples and relatively poorly defined variables, so that these more general methods might be substituted when assumptions necessary for more precise statistics, such as the product-moment coefficient of correlation, standard deviation, etc., can not be reasonably inferred.[29]

Time Series

In many types of problems in social research it is frequently necessary to study changes over a period of time. For some of these problems relatively simple tabular and graphic techniques will be found very satisfactory. The vertical bar chart, the rectangular coordinate graph, and the semi-logarithmic chart represent the basic graphic forms for presenting time series. A detailed discussion of these charts will be found in Chapter 13.

Sometimes, however, it may be necessary to use more refined mathe-

[29]For students with somewhat greater mathematical maturity a good discussion of distribution-free methods can be found in Alexander McFarlane Mood, *Introduction to the Theory of Statistics,* pp. 403–425. McGraw-Hill Book Company, 1963. For comprehensive treatises on this subject, see Sidney Siegel, *Nonparametric Statistics for the Behavioral Sciences.* McGraw-Hill Book Co., 1956; John E. Walsh, *Handbook of Nonparametric Statistics.* D. Van Nostrand Company, 1962.

matical techniques to analyze certain types of temporal series adequately. Because of the limitation of space, only a very few of the most elementary techniques can be included in the hope that the student may acquire some appreciation of the problems involved in the analysis of data of this kind. In actual practice it will be found that the movements in time series may assume a number of forms. The length of the period in which the movement completes its course, the general characteristics or configuration of the movements, and the degree of regularity of the movements may evidence many variations. With reference to these points, movements may be described as:[30]

1. Secular or long-time trend. Social phenomena often exhibit a definite or persistent tendency to increase or decrease over a considerable period of time.

2. Periodic fluctuations. Perhaps the most common type is illustrated by the seasonal variation of social phenomena with more or less regularly recurrent maxima and minima. There also may be diurnal or weekly cycles characterized by a marked periodicity.

3. Undulatory or cyclical movements. These movements are wavelike in character but not definitely periodic. The so-called business cycle with its alternating periods of depression and prosperity is a good example of this type of movement.

4. Irregular variations. These irregular movements may be episodic or they may be fortuitous or accidental. The episodic changes may be caused by such factors as strikes, lockouts, conflagrations, earthquakes, or some other type of disaster or natural cataclysm. Episodic changes result in sharp and pronounced breaks in the variable and show no apparent tendency toward recurrence at stated intervals. Fortuitous or accidental movements are generally less pronounced than episodic changes and are not ordinarily due to some easily determined cause.

In order to illustrate a few of the more elementary techniques for

[30]Edmund E. Day, *Statistical Analysis,* pp. 235 ff. The Macmillan Company, 1925. Cf. William Addison Neiswanger, *Elementary Statistical Methods,* pp. 477–584. The Macmillan Company, 1956; Frederick E. Croxton and Dudley J. Cowden, *Practical Business Statistics*, pp. 417–486. Prentice-Hall, Inc., 1960.

analyzing time series let us consider the data in Table 11.12. A cursory examination of these data will reveal that there has been a definite upward trend in mortality from diabetes in the state of Washington during the thirty-one year period, 1920 to 1950. This fact can be brought out more clearly by plotting the data on a chart. Three basic procedures can be used in determining the secular trend of a series of this kind: 1) by drawing freehand a line of best fit, 2) by the method of moving averages, and 3) by the method of mathematical curve fitting. The freehand method is a crude and uncertain procedure for determining the secular trend of a series since it is based merely on a general visual impression. Ordinarily this procedure should not be used except for preliminary work. The method of moving averages is superior to the freehand method but it also possesses definite limitations. The moving average is obtained by averaging consecutive groups in the series; each time one year is omitted and another year is added. For example, if a three-year moving average were calculated for the series in Table 11.12, the first step would be to obtain the mean rate for the first three years: $(66.4 + 55.5 + 61.7)/3 = 61.2$. The derived mean would be recorded for the year 1921, since it is the midpoint of the first three-year period. In order to obtain similar values for the succeeding years one rate is added and one is dropped. To obtain the second moving average in Table 11.12 the rate for 1920 is omitted and the rate for 1923 added: $(55.5 + 61.7 + 56.5)/3 = 57.9$. The mean, 57.9, is recorded opposite the year 1922, the midpoint of the second three-year period. This procedure is continued throughout the entire series. Moving averages can be based on intervals of varying length, depending on the original data. It is not always easy, however, to determine the optimum interval. Since the means must be centered, it is advantageous to use if possible an odd number of years for the interval.

In determining a trend line mathematically, a choice has to be made of the form of line to be fitted. The line may be straight or curvilinear. Curvilinear lines may be expressed by a parabola, hyperbola, compound-interest curve, or a figure of more complicated form. For the series in Table 11.12 a straight line would seem to be the most satisfactory type. In practice it will be found that the most common type of trend is a straight line.

In Figure 11.13 a straight line of least squares has been fitted to the series of mortality rates. This type of trend line is also known as a first-degree parabola. In computing a straight line of least squares one or two common methods can be followed.

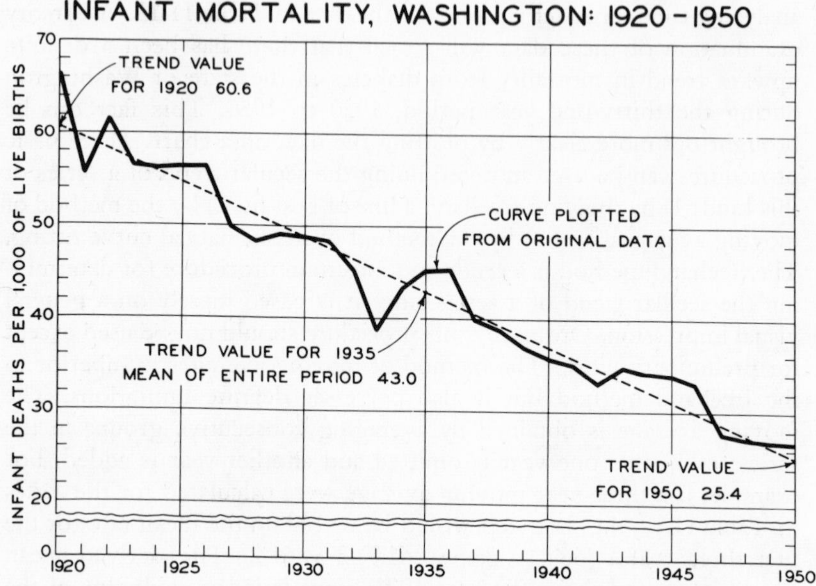

Figure 11.13 Fitting a straight-line trend by the method of least-squares.

1. It will be observed from Table 11.12 that the years and the corresponding rates in the series are listed in the first and second columns.
2. The midpoint of the series is located and deviations are marked off negatively for the earlier years and positively for the later years. In the problem in Table 11.12 the year 1935 is the mid-year or point of origin.
3. The y-values are multiplied by the corresponding deviations and the products are entered in the fourth column (dy).
4. The deviations are squared and recorded in the fifth column (d^2).
5. The value for the mid-year (intercept a) is obtained by computing the mean of the values of the y-column. In the problem, $\Sigma y/N = 1334.2/31 = 43.039$.
6. In order to determine the slope (b) of the line of least squares it is necessary to substitute in the following formula: $b = \Sigma dy/\Sigma d^2$. In the problem, $b = -2907.9/2480 = -1.173$. It will be seen that b may be either plus or minus, depending on whether the line of least squares shows an upward or downward movement.
7. The ordinate for any year in the series can be obtained by the formula $y = a + bx$. It will be recalled that a represents the mean of the y-column and is the ordinate for the mid-year of the series. In the problem, $a = 43.039$. In plotting a straight line of least

Table 11.12

DETERMINATION OF STRAIGHT-LINE TREND BY METHOD OF LEAST SQUARES. DATA REPRESENT INFANT MORTALITY RATES PER 1,000 LIVE BIRTHS FOR THE STATE OF WASHINGTON: 1920 TO 1950.

Year	*Rate* y	*Deviation from Mid-point* d	*Deviation times Rate* dy	*Deviation Squared* d^2	$b = \frac{\Sigma dy}{\Sigma d^2}$ $= \frac{-2907.9}{2480}$
1920....	66.4	−15	−996.0	225	
1921....	55.5	−14	−777.0	196	
1922....	61.7	−13	−802.1	169	$= -1.173$
1923....	56.5	−12	−678.0	144	
1924....	56.2	−11	−618.2	121	
1925....	56.4	−10	−564.0	100	
1926....	56.4	− 9	−507.6	81	
1927....	49.8	− 8	−398.4	64	Trend Values for:
1928....	48.1	− 7	−336.7	49	(1) 1935 (*mid-point*)
1929....	49.0	− 6	−294.0	36	
1930....	48.7	− 5	−243.5	25	$a = \frac{\Sigma y}{N}$
1931....	48.3	− 4	−193.2	16	
1932....	45.2	− 3	−135.6	9	$= \frac{1334.2}{31}$
1933....	38.8	− 2	− 77.6	4	
1934....	43.2	− 1	− 43.2	1	
1935....	45.2	0	0	0	$= 43.039$
1936....	45.4	1	45.4	1	(2) 1920
1937....	39.9	2	79.8	4	$= 43.039 + (-15)\ (b)$
1938....	38.7	3	116.1	9	$= 43.039 + (-15)\ (-1.173)$
1939....	36.8	4	147.2	16	$= 43.039 + (17.595)$
1940....	35.7	5	178.5	25	$= 60.634$
1941....	35.0	6	210.0	36	
1942....	33.1	7	231.7	49	(3) 1950
1943....	34.9	8	279.2	64	$= 43.039 + (+15)\ (b)$
1944....	34.1	9	306.9	81	$= 43.039 + (+15)\ (-1.173)$
1945....	33.9	10	339.0	100	$= 43.039 + (-17.595)$
1946....	33.0	11	363.0	121	$= 25.444$
1947....	27.7	12	332.4	144	
1948....	27.1	13	352.3	169	
1949....	26.8	14	375.2	196	
1950....	26.7	15	400.5	225	

squares on a graph it is not necessary to calculate the ordinates for each year in the series. Two ordinates, relatively widely separated, are all that are required. Let us, therefore, compute the ordinates for the first and last years in the series. For 1920, $Y = 43.039 + (-15)(-1.173) = 60.634$ and for 1950, $Y = 43.039 + (+15)(-1.173) = 25.444$. In Figure 11.13 the ordinates for 1920 and 1950 were plotted on the graph and then connected by a straight line.

Statistical Errors

To be really proficient in statistical work a thorough knowledge of the various techniques is, of course, indispensable, but in addition such qualities as common sense, good judgment, a healthy scepticism, objectivity, experience, and a broad understanding of the field of study are also essential. Many of the more serious errors in statistical work are of a non-mathematical character. This fact is often overlooked by the beginner who has acquired some acquaintance with statistical formulae and techniques. Statistical analysis is not a mere perfunctory mechanical process of applying formulae and operating a calculating machine. Statistical work requires good judgment, a critical attitude, and careful thought.

In order to guard against the common pitfalls of statistical work let us summarize some of the more typical sources of error: 1) inadequate and inaccurate data, 2) mechanical mistakes, and 3) unsound interpretations.

Under the heading of inadequate and inaccurate data the following sources of error might be mentioned: 1) insufficient data, 2) unrepresentative samples, 3) data that have been deliberately falsified by informants, 4) inaccurate data resulting from poor observation and carelessness, and 5) unreliable standards and units of measurement.

Mechanical errors include: 1) mistakes in arithmetic and other mathematical processes, 2) application of wrong formulae, and 3) errors in copying.

The more common fallacies in interpretation are: 1) failing to consider all significant factors, 2) ignoring negative evidence, 3) mistaking correlation for causation, 4) comparing non-comparable data, 5) generalizing from too few cases, and 6) distorting interpretations to fit preconceptions and prejudices.

Anyone who aspires to do statistical research should be thoroughly familiar with the four simple rules of statistical procedure which

Adolph Quételet formulated: 1) Never have preconceived ideas as to what the figures are to prove. 2) Never reject a number that seems contrary to what you might expect merely because it departs a good deal from the apparent average. 3) Be careful to weigh and record all the possible causes of an event, and do not attribute to one what is really the result of the combination of several. 4) Never compare data which are not fully comparable.

scaling techniques in sociological research[1]

By
CALVIN F. SCHMID
University of Washington

There has come an increasing demand for evaluations and measures which shall be impersonal and shall have the general validity and objectivity of measures in the physical sciences, in business, and in industry.

GEORGE A. LUNDBERG

12

An important trend in sociology during the past few decades has been an increasing emphasis on the development of measuring instruments. Such instruments are commonly referred to as scales. Although much of the work in this field is still in a pioneer stage, nevertheless it can be said that as sociology matures as a science, existing measuring instruments and techniques will be improved and new and more precise measuring devices will be developed.

Sociologists have given their attention largely to two types of scales: 1) those concerned with social behavior and personality, and 2) those used to measure certain other aspects of the cultural and social environment. The first type includes the well-known attitude scales, morale scales, character tests, social participation scales, and psychoneurotic inventories. The second type is illustrated by scales used to study socioeconomic status, communities, housing conditions, and social institutions.

Even a cursory examination of recent writings in the field will reveal an extraordinary number and diversity of scales designed by research workers in sociology, psychology,

[1]Acknowledgment is made to Drs. Julius A. Jahn and Clarence C. Schrag for a critical reading of this chapter and for offering valuable suggestions.

education, psychiatry, ethics, institutional administration, and other fields.[2]

Fundamentally, scaling methodology is much the same in all fields. The differences that do exist are differences largely of content and emphasis. The sociologist, for example, is much more concerned with the development of instruments to measure institutions and other cultural phenomena than is the psychologist and psychiatrist. On the other hand, both psychologists and sociologists manifest a very great interest in attitude scales. In this introduction we shall limit our discussion mainly to scales designed to measure attitudes, socio-economic status, quality of housing, and home environment.

Several attempts have been made to work out classifications of scales, but these classifications emphasize form and content rather than the basic statistical theory and techniques underlying the various scales.

In terms of statistical methodology, scales of all kinds—including so-called intelligence, personality, attitude, social status, institutional, and other types of scales—can be subsumed under the following headings: 1) arbitrary scales, 2) scales in which the items, scale values, and other characteristics are largely determined by a panel of judges, 3) scales based on item analysis, 4) scales constructed in accordance with the "scale analysis" techniques devised by Louis Guttman and his co-workers, and 5) "projective tests". In addition, of course, scales may represent a combination of two or more of the five basic types included in the above classification.[3]

[2]See Percival M. Symonds, *Psychological Diagnosis and Social Adjustment*. American Book Company, 1934; Edward B. Greene, *Measurements of Human Behavior*. Odyssey Press, 1952; Raymond B. Cattell, *Description and Measurement of Personality*. World Book Company, 1946; Anne Anastasi, *Psychological Testing*. The Macmillan Company, 1961; Leona E. Tyler, *Tests and Measurements*. Prentice-Hall, Inc., 1963.

[3]Scales also can be classified according to their function. Some scales are designed to arrange data in such fashion as to maximize their power to predict an external criterion. Aptitude tests, predictions of adjustment on parole or probation, and predictions of marital adjustment are some of the most common examples of this type of scale. Other scales are designed to arrange sets of data in such fashion that if the researcher is given a single score, he can reproduce all the items in the scale. Louis Guttman seems to have worked out the most efficient scales of this type. In some cases the functions of *predictability* and *reproducibility* are so confused that the student will find it difficult to ascertain the purpose for which the scale was constructed.

In the following discussion of attitude scales, for example, the Thurstone scale of equal-appearing intervals is a "judgment scale" as is Bogardus' social distance scale. The second type of attitude scale discussed is commonly called the Likert technique and is a scale based on item analysis. The third type of attitude scale considered is the Cornell technique of scale analysis devised by Louis Guttman.

There is a great variety of "arbitrary scales," but in this discussion only cursory consideration will be given them. In this connection McNemar observes that

> The early efforts at attitude or opinion measuring usually involved a questionnaire or battery of questions which were selected on an *a priori* basis. Numerical values were assigned arbitrarily to the item or question responses and these values were summed to secure scores which were then interpreted as indicating the attitude of the respondents. There was nothing about the procedure to guarantee that any one item tapped the same attitudes as the other items. Little thought was given to the number of dimensions—that more than one was frequently involved seems obvious. Reliability was occasionally determined, but validity was seldom mentioned.[4]

Unfortunately, even at the present time many journalists, teachers, and popular writers, not to mention a few sociologists and psychologists, resort to such crude methods. This is particularly true in attempting to construct attitude scales as well as so-called rating scales. The scientist who uses scaling techniques should make every effort to keep abreast of the latest developments in the field and follow the best methods available. The degree of precision or refinement of a measuring instrument should naturally bear some relationship to the problem under consideration. Occasionally for certain purposes a less precise technique may be adequate, but under no circumstances should a scale be used that has not been carefully tested for validity and reliability. A scale should measure what it purports to measure and should yield consistent results when applied under the same conditions.

Attitude Scales

Few problems in sociology and social psychology have commanded more attention than the study of attitudes.[5] An extensive number of

[4]Quinn McNemar, "Opinion-Attitude Methodology," *Psychological Bulletin*, XLIII, 289–374.

[5]Writing on "The Historical Background of Modern Social Psychology" in 1954, Gordon W. Allport states that "the attitude unit has been the primary

monographs, articles, and shorter discussions clearly reflect the importance of this problem. In spite of the extraordinary amount of effort devoted to this subject, "attitude" as a concept in sociology and social psychology possesses no unanimity of meaning. To be sure many verbal definitions have been formulated, but generally speaking they lack clarity and precision. Moreover, such definitions have been given only scant consideration in attitude measurement.

The typical attitude scale consists of a series of short but carefully formulated statements or propositions dealing with several selected aspects or many appropriate aspects of issues, institutions, or groups of people under consideration. The individual reacts verbally with expressions of approval or disapproval, agreement or disagreement to the items on the scale. These reactions purport to "measure" a person's position on controversial issues or problems or the degree to which existing social institutions are approved. Scales have been constructed to measure attitudes toward war, birth control, communism, the church, evolution, God, censorship, Sunday observance, capital punishment, the Negro, Chinese, Japanese and so on.[6]

Technique of equal-appearing intervals. One of the most important methodological contributions to attitude scale construction, as well as perhaps the most widely used procedure of attitude measurement, is L. L. Thurstone's technique of equal-appearing intervals. Thurstone attempted to devise a method that would represent the

---

building stone in the edifice of social psychology. . . . Without some such concept, social psychologists could not work in the fields of public opinion, national character, or institutional behavior—to mention only a few areas; nor could they characterize the mental organization of social man."—Gardner Lindzey, (ed.) *Handbook of Social Psychology,* Vol. I, p. 45. In recent years, however, the interest of both psychologists and sociologists in attitude measurement has waned. "Attitude" has been defined as "a mental and neural state of readiness organized through experience, exerting a directive or dynamic influence upon the individual response to all objects and situations with which it is related."—Gordon W. Allport, "Attitudes" in Carl Murchison, *Handbook of Social Psychology,* Chap. XVII. A more recent definition is as follows: "An enduring system of positive or negative evaluations, emotional feelings, and pro or con action tendencies with respect to a social object." —David Krech, Richard S. Crutchfield, and Egerton L. Ballachey, *Individual in Society,* p. 177. McGraw-Hill Book Company, 1962.

[6]The following are relatively brief and clear discussions of attitude measurement techniques: Allen L. Edwards, *Techniques of Attitude-Scale Construction.* Appleton-Century-Crofts, 1957; Bert F. Green, "Attitude Measurement" in Gardner Lindzey, *op. cit.,* Chap. 9.

attitudes of a group on a specified issue in the form of a frequency distribution, the base line indicating the whole range of attitude gradation from the most favorable at one end to the least favorable at the other with a neutral zone in between. The various opinions or items on a scale are allocated to different positions in accordance with the attitudes they express.[7]

The various steps in constructing a Thurstone attitude scale are as follows:

1. Brief statements expressing attitudes about a particular issue are gathered from current literature or are especially prepared for this purpose. The statements should cover the entire range of attitudes from extremely favorable to extremely unfavorable, including an adequate number of neutral statements. There is no absolutely set number of statements. In constructing an attitude scale about the church, for example, Thurstone began with 130 statements. The statements should be brief, unambiguous, and relevant and in such form that they can be indorsed or rejected in terms of a definitely expressed attitude.[8]
2. After being carefully edited, the statements are given an arbitrary number for identification and mimeographed in such form that they can be cut into fairly uniform individual slips of paper. Complete sets of the statements are given to a large number of judges with clear, simple instructions to sort them into several piles, usually 7 or 11, so that the various piles represent a graduated series of attitudes from extremely favorable to extremely unfavorable. Accordingly, each judge places each statement in one of the 7 or 11 piles, depending on the degree of favorableness or unfavorableness indicated by the statement in the judge's opinion.

   This is perhaps the most important, as well as the most vulnerable, step in the construction of the Thurstone scale. It should be emphasized that the judges are not supposed to express their own attitudes about an issue but attempt to arrange the statements as

[7]L. L. Thurstone and E. J. Chave, *The Measurement of Attitudes, passim.* University of Chicago Press, 1929.

[8]Wang mentions sixteen criteria which should be considered in the preparation of statements for attitude scales. These criteria would apply generally to all types of attitude scales. See Charles K. A. Wang, "Suggested Criteria for Writing Attitude Statements," *Journal of Social Psychology,* III, 367–373.

objectively as possible in terms of the various positions on the scale. If the judges are careless or for some other reason fail to follow instructions, the resulting scale-values might be distorted. In this connection it is significant to point out that the attitudes which the judges hold do not seem to influence their ratings of statements.[9]

3. After all the judges have sorted the statements, a complete tabulation is made of the sortings so that it is possible to determine the number of times each statement is included in the several piles.
4. The scale values for each statement are determined graphically. The accumulated proportions of each statement are plotted in the form of an ogive or cumulative frequency curve. Table 12.1 and Figure 12.1 show the manner in which the data are tabulated as well as the construction of the ogive. By means of simple interpolation the median and quartile values can readily be determined. The median value so obtained represents the scale value of the statement. If a statement is ambiguous the difference between Q_1 and Q_2 will be large. This difference is known as the Q-value or coefficient of ambiguity. Figure 12.1 portrays the ogives for four statements along with the medians and Q-values. For example, statement No. 4, "I believe that membership in a good church increases one's self-respect and usefulness" has a median value of 2.7 and a coefficient of ambiguity of 1.5, which indicates a strongly favorable attitude with a low degree of ambiguity. For comparison the three other statements on the chart give markedly different values.

In addition to being unambiguous each statement should be relevant. This is determined by plotting the responses of each item

[9]E. D. Hinckley, "The Influence of Individual Opinion on Construction of an Attitude Scale," *Journal of Social Psychology,* III, 283–296; Leonard W. Ferguson, "The Influence of Individual Attitudes on Construction of an Attitude Scale," *Journal of Social Psychology,* VI, 115–117; H. J. Eysenck and S. Crown, "An Experimental Study in Opinion-attitude Methodology," *International Journal of Opinion and Attitude Research,* III, 47–86. Also in this connection compare the conclusions in the following papers: C. I. Hovland and M. Sherif, "Judgmental Phenomena and Scales of Attitude Measurement: Item Displacement in Thurstone Scales," *Journal of Abnormal and Social Psychology,* XLVII, 822–832; H. H. Kelley *et. al.,* "The Influence of Judges' Attitudes in Three Methods of Attitude Scaling," *Journal of Social Psychology,* XLII, 147–158.

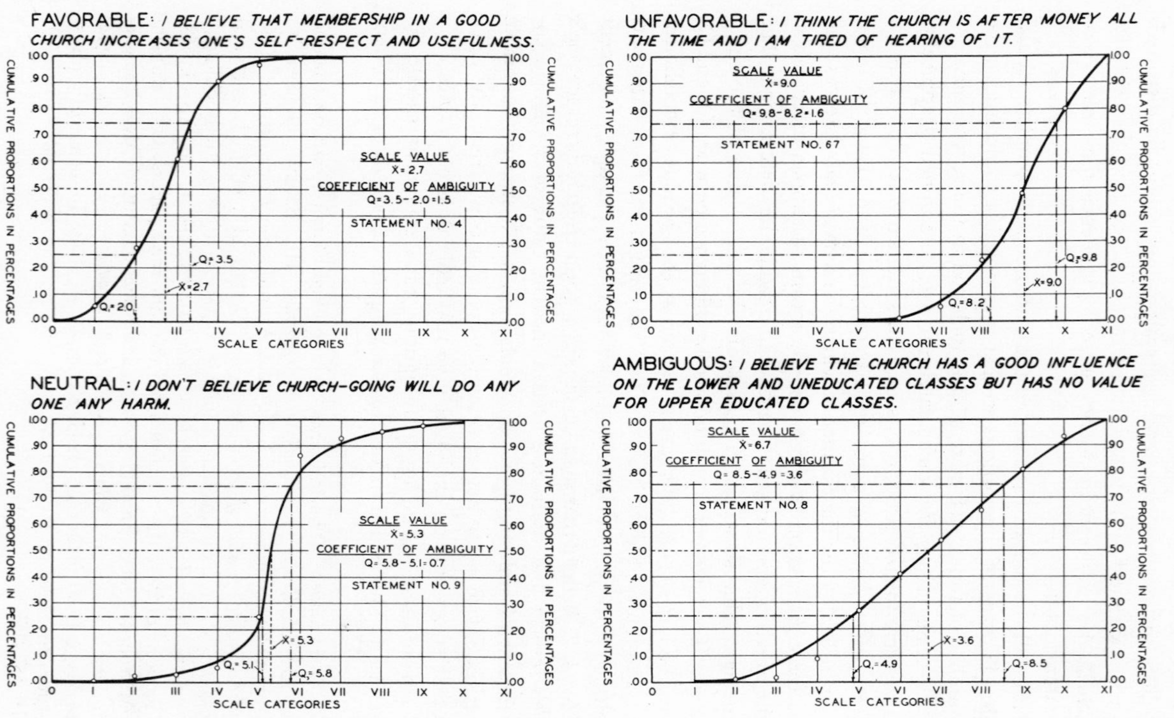

Figure 12.1 Cumulative frequency curves illustrating derivation of scale-value and coefficient of ambiguity according to the Thurstone technique of attitude scale construction. Chart constructed from original data in L. L. Thurstone and E. J. Chave, *The Measurement of Attitudes*, pp. 22–35.

against all other items. Normally, respondents will tend to be consistent in their reactions to the various items in a scale. For example, if several persons indorse items with scale-values around 2.0, they will not indorse items that evidence a marked deviation from this value, say items with scale-values of 6.0 or 7.0. Where it is found that the responses to a particular item are markedly inconsistent, that item is classed as irrevelant and should be eliminated from the scale.

5. The final scale is made up of a selection of 15 to 20 comparatively unambiguous, relevant statements arranged in random order, representing a graded series of values from extremely favorable to extremely unfavorable. The scale is now ready to be administered to a sample of the population whose attitudes are to be measured. Two alternative scoring procedures have been used which give substantially the same results: the score for a subject filling out an attitude scale may be either 1) the arithmetic mean of the scale-values of the statements that are indorsed or 2) the median value of the indorsed statements, indicated by either a single or double check.

Social distance technique. Bogardus' social distance scale like Thurstone's scale of equal-appearing intervals depends to a large extent on the ratings of a panel of judges in determining scale gradations. In constructing certain scales Bogardus has used his own experience and judgment, and in others he has selected a large number of judges for determining degrees of social distance.[10] The following description prepared especially for this volume by Dr. Bogardus embodies very clearly his technique of measuring social distance.

In preparing a social distance scale for measuring highly subjective attitudes, the first problem was to obtain an evenly spaced series of social distance items. A large number of types of social relationships were formulated, and in accordance with the Thurstone method a hundred persons judged them in terms of an increasing degree of social farness or of decreasing social nearness. Seven of these items evenly spaced according to the judges' ratings of increasing social farness were

[10]According to the fivefold classification described above, a scale based on the judgment of one individual should be considered an "arbitrary scale."

selected. These items were given arbitrary numbers from 1 to 7, respectively, representing increasing farness in this proportion.[11]

Table 12.1

SUMMARY OF SORTING OF FOUR SELECTED STATEMENTS FROM ORIGINAL LIST OF 130 USED BY THURSTONE IN CONSTRUCTING A SCALE FOR MEASURING ATTITUDES TOWARD THE CHURCH.

	Statement No. 4 Favorable*		*Statement No. 67* Unfavorable*		*Statement No. 9* Neutral*		*Statement No. 8* Ambiguous*	
Category	*Cumulative Frequency*	*Cumulative Proportion*	*Cumulative Frequency*	*Cumulative Proportion*	*Cumulative Frequency*	*Cumulative Proportion*	*Cumulative Frequency*	*Cumulative Proportion*
I	18	.06	—	.00	3	.01	—	.00
II	78	.26	—	.00	6	.02	3	.01
III	180	.60	—	.00	9	.03	6	.02
IV	273	.91	—	.00	18	.06	27	.09
V	284	.98	—	.00	75	.25	81	.27
VI	287	.99	3	.01	261	.87	123	.41
VII	300	1.00	18	.06	279	.93	162	.54
VIII	—	1.00	66	.22	288	.96	201	.67
IX	—	1.00	144	.48	294	.98	243	.81
X	—	1.00	240	.80	300	1.00	279	.93
XI	—	1.00	300	1.00	—	1.00	300	1.00

**For complete statement see Figure 12.1.*

In formulating each of the 7 evenly-spaced relationships it is not easy to select the best few words in each case that will be understood similarly by all who check the scale. A list of races, religions, occupations, and so on is arranged in the left-hand column of the scale for use in discovering a person's reactions or his attitudes.

[11]Stuart C. Dodd used a combination of the Thurstone and Bogardus techniques in constructing a social distance scale. See his paper entitled, "A Social Distance Test in the Near East," *American Journal of Sociology,* XLI, 194–204.

RACIAL DISTANCE SCALE

(Race is defined here largely as a cultural group.)

1. Remember to give your *first feeling reactions* in every case.
2. Give your reactions to each race as a *group*. Do not give your reactions to the best or to the worst members that you have known, but think of the picture or stereotype that you have of the whole race.
3. Put a cross after each race in as many of the seven rows as your feelings dictate.

In assigning numbers to each of the seven scale items, only *positive values* were used. It is assumed that social distance attitudes are always of positive degree.[12]

The subject is asked to give his *first feeling reactions* and not to rationalize. The assumption is that first feeling reactions reveal atti-

Category	*Armenians*	*Americans (Native White U.S.)*	*Bulgarians*	*Canadians*	*Chinese*
1. Would marry					
2. Would have as regular friends					
3. Would work beside in an office					
4. Would live in same neighborhood					
5. Would have merely as speaking acquaintances					
6. Would debar from my neighborhood					
7. Would debar from my country					

[12]The small degrees of distance are commonly called nearness and the large degrees represent farness. There is no clear-cut dividing line between nearness and farness. In fact, it would vary with different persons and in different social situations.

tudes better than anything else, barring behavior itself over a period of time. Although long-term behavior is the best test of a person's attitudes, the social distance scale is devised to give predictions while waiting for long-term behavior to reveal attitudes. Behavior over a short period may indicate pseudo-attitudes, not real ones. It may measure attitudes that are "faked" in order to gain certain ends.

It is assumed that the first feeling reactions without rationalization are significant in revealing how a person would act if he were to face suddenly the situations which are cited in the scale. Another type of attitude is the rationalized one which may be regarded as an opinion, and it should be measured by a different scale.

In checking the social distance scale the subject is asked to react in line with his first feeling reactions, but to what? To the *stereotype* which arises as soon as each item in the right-hand column is seen. In other words, he is not to react to the best or to the poorest samples of each item. Here is a real problem, for many subjects report that in seeking a stereotype in each instance the thinking processes are unduly stimulated and the first feeling reactions are obscured.

For purposes of illustration we cite only a small portion of the racial distance scale, which will indicate some of the problems in connection with the measurement of social distance attitudes.[13]

Technique of summated ratings. The second type of attitude scale shall be referred to as the "technique of summated ratings," although it is frequently labeled the "Likert technique," and "the method of internal consistency." This technique is similar to the Thurstone technique of equal-appearing intervals. In fact, the only important difference is in the determination of scale values. The basic procedure of attitude scale construction which is associated with Likert had been used previously in constructing personality scales and as early as 1916 was applied by Lewis Terman in his work on intelligence tests. Besides being the first one to apply the method of internal consistency to attitude measurement, Likert also emphasized the importance of each item as a scale in itself, made comparisons of the sigma and arbitrary methods of scoring, and compared the summated rating method

[13]For further details and illustration of Bogardus' social distance scales see the following papers by Dr. Bogardus: "A Social Distance Scale," *Sociology and Social Research,* XVII, 265–271; "Social Distance and Its Practical Implications," *ibid.,* XXII, 462–476; "Scales in Social Research," *ibid.,* XXIV, 69–75.

with the Thurstone method. The technique of summated ratings avoids the somewhat cumbersome procedure of having a group of judges sort the statements for the purpose of determining scale-values. It is alleged that the technique of summated ratings requires less labor and at the same time gives equally reliable, if not more reliable results, since the subjective influence of judges is eliminated.[14]

The basic steps in constructing an attitude scale according to the technique of summated ratings are as follows:[15]

1. Like the Thurstone technique a series of propositions expressive of a wide range of attitudes from extremely positive to extremely negative and concerning a particular question are compiled and carefully edited. In selecting the statements emphasis is placed on values rather than on facts. Moreover, the statements are so constructed as to indicate clearly a position for or against the point at issue.[16]
2. Each proposition usually calls for a response by checking or underlining one of five words such as *strongly approve, approve, undecided, disapprove, strongly disapprove.* Frequently the expressions *strongly agree, agree, undecided, disagree,* and *strongly disagree* are used and *almost always, frequently, occasionally, rarely, almost never* may be applicable for certain purposes. It should be pointed out that the wording or order of response categories may affect the response. Although a five-point continuum is most common, a three-, four-, or six-point continuum is occasionally used. In the five-point continuum, for example, weights of 1, 2, 3, 4, 5, or 5, 4, 3, 2, 1 are assigned in proper order to the several expressions, the direction of weighting being determined by the favorableness or unfavorableness of the statement.

   Two statements taken from an attitude study on the American-born Japanese conducted during the 1940's illustrate how numerical values are assigned to the scale continuum.

It is all right for American-born Japanese to run for political office.
definitely agree (5) *agree* (4) *undecided*(3) *disagree*(2) *definitely disagree*(1).

[14]Rundquist and Sletto, *op. cit.,* pp. 4–6. For a comparative discussion of the Thurstone and Likert techniques see Allen L. Edwards and Kathryn Claire Kenny, "A Comparison of the Thurstone and Likert Techniques of Attitude Scale Construction," *Journal of Applied Psychology,* XXX, 72–83.

[15]Rensis Likert, "A Technique for the Measurement of Attitudes," *Archives of Psychology,* No. 140, 5–55.

[16]See Charles K. A. Wang, *op. cit.*

American-born Japanese should find friends within their own group and not mix with whites.
definitely agree(1) *agree*(2) *undecided*(3) *disagree*(4) *definitely disagree*(5)[17].

3. A large number of subjects are requested to check their attitudes on the original list of statements in accordance with the scheme described in the preceding paragraph. In preparing an attitude scale on the American-born Japanese for example, 99 statements were included in the preliminary list which was filled out by approximately 500 subjects.[18]
4. A total score for each subject taking the test is obtained by summing the value of each item that is checked.
5. As a basis for determining the selection of items for the final scale the discriminative value of each item is computed. This is done by obtaining the difference between the average scores for each item when the total scores are arranged in quartiles. The procedure in computing discriminative values is illustrated in Table 12.2.

Table 12.2

CALCULATION OF ITEM SCALE-VALUE DIFFERENCE AND CRITICAL RATIO.[19]

Item 13: The Future Looks Very Black
N = 28 in each quartile

Response	*Weight*	*Highest Quartile*			*Lowest Quartile*		
	x	f	fx	fx^2	f	fx	fx^2
Strongly agree	5	3	15	75	0	0	0
Agree	4	4	16	64	0	0	0
Undecided	3	10	30	90	1	3	9
Disagree.............	2	11	22	44	19	38	76
Strongly disagree	1	0	0	0	8	8	8
Total	—	28	83	273	28	49	93
Mean	—		2.96			1.75	

Item Scale Value Difference: 2.96 — 1.75 = 1.21

[17]Statements taken from unpublished study by Calvin F. Schmid and Manzer John Griswold.

[18]*Ibid.*

[19]Sletto, *Construction of Personality Scales by the Criterion of Internal Consistency*, p. 3. Sociological Press, 1937.

$$\text{Critical ratio} = \frac{\Sigma fx_1 - \Sigma fx_2}{\sqrt{\Sigma fd_1^2 + \Sigma fd_2^2}} \quad \text{where } \Sigma fd_1^2 = \Sigma fx_1^2 - N(M_1^2)$$

$$\text{Critical ratio} = \frac{83 - 49}{\sqrt{273 - 28\,(2.96^2) + 93 - 28\,(1.75^2)}}$$

$$= \frac{34}{\sqrt{273 + 93 - 28\,(2.96^2 - 1.75^2)}}$$

$$= \frac{34}{\sqrt{34.9252}}$$

$$= 5.75$$

The scale-value difference for each item is arranged in rank order. The items selected for the final draft of the scale should have relatively high discriminative values.

The following statements with their respective scale-value differences were taken from a scale on anti-Semitism:

No one can be a Jew without having Jewish blood in his veins. Scale-value difference = 2.76.

Jews have contributed a great deal to American life and culture. Scale-value difference = .98.[20]

6. In this type of scale two methods of scoring have been used. They are the "arbitrary" method and the "sigma" method. The arbitrary method is generally preferred because it involves less work and is just as reliable as the sigma method. The arbitrary method merely requires adding the values of the expressions for each statement that is checked.

Scale analysis. During World War II Louis Guttman and his co-workers in the Research Branch, Information and Education Divisions of the War Department, developed a technique known as "scale analysis" that represents a very substantial methodological contribution. "Scale analysis" is based upon certain general principles that can be briefly formulated as follows:[21]

DEFINITION OF A SCALE. "For a given population of objects, the multivariate frequency distribution of a universe of attributes will be called a *scale* if it is possible to derive from the distribution a quantitative variable with which to characterize the objects such that each

[20]Paul K. Hatt, "Social Attitudes in Anti-Semitism" (Unpublished Master's Thesis, University of Washington, 1940), pp. 92–94.

[21]Louis Guttman, "A Basis for Scaling Qualitative Data," *American Sociological Review,* IX, 139–150.

attribute is a simple function of the quantitative variable." In this definition, the "population of objects" refers to a class of objects, such as individuals living in a certain city, that are defined as the subjects of an investigation. The "universe of attributes" refers to a class of qualitative variables associated with these objects that is defined for study, for example, statements about "attitudes toward Negroes." These variables may be any type of qualitatively recorded observations, not necessarily restricted to attitudes. The quantitative variable that is derived in this manner is called a "scale score." The degree to which a particular distribution corresponds to this definition of a "scale" is measured by a "coefficient of reproducibility." This coefficient is defined as the relative frequency with which the classification of the individuals with respect to the variables in the defined universe can be "reproduced" correctly from their "scale scores." In practice, complete reproducibility is not expected or obtained, and a coefficient of reproducibility of .90 or more has become a criterion for stating that a particular universe of attributes forms a scale for a defined population.

PURPOSES OF SCALING. Assuming that a defined universe of attributes forms a scale for a defined population of individuals, the "scale scores" possess the following properties: 1) the recorded observations on a large number of variables in the defined universe can be summarized by a single score which will reproduce the original records with a specified degree of reproducibility; 2) individuals can be arranged in a rank order on the scale score in a manner that will be consistent with their rank order on any or all of the variables in the defined universe of attributes; 3) the scale score can be used *to predict any outside variable or criterion whatsoever* with a degree of accuracy as high as can be attained by the direct use of all of the variables in the defined universe, as in a multiple regression equation with the external criterion as the dependent variable.

Guttman and his colleagues developed four specific techniques of scale analysis, all of which produce essentially the same results but differ in the mechanics involved.[22] The best-known and most generally

[22]Guttman's first effort of this kind was published in 1941. See "The Quantification of a Class of Attributes: A Theory and Method of Scale Construction," in Paul Horst *et al., The Prediction of Personal Adjustment,* pp. 319–348. Social Science Research Council, 1941. See also Ward H. Goodenough, "A Technique for Scale Analysis," *Educational and Psychological Measurement,* IV, 179–190.

useful as well as the simplest to apply is commonly referred to by Guttman as the "Cornell" technique.[23]

In testing for scalability according to the Cornell technique the following steps are involved.[24]

The area of content is first defined. This is determined largely in terms of the problem at hand. The problem, for example, may be concerned with 1) attitudes toward some minority racial group, 2) opinions about a particular textbook, 3) students' expressions of adjustment to college life, or 4) students' reactions to the teaching process in some course. Ten or twelve statements are selected which are assumed to be representative of a particular area. The selection of items depends on the definition of the area studied. For example, in developing a scale on attitudes toward the Negro, statements such as the following were used:

I would go out on a date with a Negro.

Strongly agree	Agree	Undecided	Disagree	Strongly disagree
4	3	2	1	0

When possible, I would avoid sitting next to a Negro.

Strongly agree	Agree	Undecided	Disagree	Strongly disagree[25]
0	1	2	3	4

In attempting to ascertain how students in a certain class in race relations regarded one of the texts, *A Nation of Nations* by Louis Adamic, Guttman used the following statements:[26]

[23]Louis Guttman, "The Cornell Technique for Scale and Intensity Analysis," *Educational and Psychological Measurement,* VII, 247–279. Republished in C. West Churchman *et al., Measurement of Consumer Interest,* pp. 60–84, University of Pennsylvania Press, 1947. Samuel A. Stouffer *et al., Studies in Social Psychology in World War II: Measurement and Prediction,* Vol. IV, Chaps. 1–9, Princeton University Press, 1950. Matilda White Riley *et al., Sociological Studies in Scale Analysis, passim.* Rutgers University Press, 1954.

[24]The material for this discussion has been abstracted and summarized from Guttman's articles cited in the present chapter.

[25]Keith S. Griffiths, *The Construction of a Scale to Measure Attitudes Toward Defined Racial and Religious Groups* (Unpublished Master's Thesis, University of Washington, 1949).

[26]Interesting applications of "scale analysis" techniques to the fields of family and industrial relations can be found in Charles E. Bowerman, "The Measurement of Areas of Adjustment in Marriage," (Unpublished Doctoral Dissertation, University of Chicago, 1948); and E. William Noland, "An Application of Scaling to an Industrial Problem," *American Sociological Review,* X, 631–648.

A Nation of Nations does a good job of analyzing the ethnic groups in this country.

Strongly agree	Agree	Undecided	Disagree	Strongly disagree
4	3	2	1	0

Adamic organizes and presents his material very well.

Strongly agree	Agree	Undecided	Disagree	Strongly disagree
4	3	1	1	0

The statements are usually arranged in the form of a three- or five-point scale so that subjects can indicate the intensity of their attitudes for each item. Weights are assigned to the several categories, for each item the least favorable response usually representing the lowest value.

Ten or twelve items are submitted to a sample of 100 or more respondents who check the items in terms of the different intensity categories. This step is designed to determine the scalability of the items.

As was pointed out earlier, the universe of items is scalable for a population if it is possible to rank the people from high to low in such a fashion that from a person's rank alone one is able to reproduce his response to each of the items.

After the total score is obtained for each person by adding up the weights of the categories that are checked, the questionnaires are arranged in rank order from high to low according to total scores. A table or "scalogram" is prepared from the data on the questionnaires. The table is arranged so that it is possible to record separately for each person in the sample the responses to each of the categories of the several statements in the questionnaire. This is done by providing a column for each response category and a row for each person. The responses of each person are indicated by X's in the appropriate columns. The frequencies of response for each category are recorded at the bottom of the table. The sum of the frequencies of the five categories in each question is, of course, always equal to the total number of people in the sample.

If the universe under consideration is scalable, then the pattern of the responses (X's in the tabulation or scalogram) must be of a distinctive type. If, for example, the items are perfectly reproducible, the pattern of X's must be such that no person with a lower total score ranks higher on any item than any person with a higher total score. Frequently, the data are not sufficiently reproducible in the initial tabulation. In order to minimize the error of reproducibility a combination of the response categories is frequently necessary. This is especially true if the pattern of X's in the scalogram indicates an overlapping tendency. Successive combinations of response categories may be continued until the error of reproducibility is minimized. When combinations are made, the categories are re-weighted and a revised scalogram is prepared. In computing a coefficient of reproducibility it is necessary to establish cutting points for each response category for the several items of the scale. Cutting points indicate the approximate position in the rank order of persons where there is a separation or drift from one response category to the next. Sometimes there may be more than one cutting point for a statement. Responses between cutting points should fall in the same category. If not, these responses are classed as errors. The coefficient of reproducibility is the total number of non-errors divided by the total number of responses. If a universe has a coefficient 90 per cent or higher, it is said to be scalable.

The percentage of reproducibility alone is not sufficient to lead to the conclusion that the universe of content is scalable. The frequency of responses to each separate item must be properly evaluated, since the degree of reproducibility may be artificially increased because one category in each item has a very high frequency. The pattern of errors and the number of items in the scale also should be taken into consideration in judging the scalability of a universe of content.

Scales are relative to time and to population. A universe may be scalable at one time but not at another, or it may be scalable at two periods of time but with different orderings of objects and categories. Similarly, a universe may be scalable for one population but not for another, or it may be scalable for two populations but with different orderings of objects and categories.[27]

Samuel A. Stouffer and his colleagues in the Harvard Laboratory of Social Relations recently have developed a procedure designed to in-

[27]The student should also examine Leon Festinger, "The Treatment of Qualitative Data by 'Scale Analysis,' " *Psychological Bulletin,* XLIV, 149–161; Louis Guttman, "On Festinger's Evaluation of Scale Analysis," *Psychological Bulletin,* XLIV, 451–465; Allen L. Edwards, "On Guttman's Scale Analysis," *Educational and Psychological Measurement,* VIII, 313–318; Louis Guttman and Edward A. Suchman, "Intensity and a Zero Point for Attitude Analysis," *American Sociological Review,* XII, 57–67; Louis Guttman, "Questions and Answers About Scale Analysis," (mimeographed memorandum), July 24, 1945; Allen L. Edwards and Franklin P. Kilpatrick, "A Technique for the Construction of Attitude Scales," *Journal of Applied Psychology,* XXXII, 374–384; Samuel A. Stouffer *et al., op. cit.;* Matilda White Riley *et al., op cit.*

crease the precision of cumulative scales. This procedure is known as the H-technique. The objective of the H-technique is to maximize the information available from the basic data, and hence to strengthen confidence in the scalability of the area under consideration and the generality of the dimension which the scale is defining, and to improve the ranking of individuals through reduction of scale error. This is accomplished by establishing stronger or more discriminative cutting points. Instead of using one item to determine a given cutting point on the scale, the H-technique uses two or more items.[28]

Closely related to the theory and practice of scale analysis is latent structure analysis developed by Paul F. Lazarsfeld of Columbia University. The approach is a generalization of the Spearman-Thurstone factor analysis. Like Guttman's scale analysis, latent structure techniques are especially adaptable to qualitative data. Up to the present time, latent structure analysis has had only limited application in actual research problems.[29]

Scales for Measuring Social Status

In addition to attitude scales sociologists have devoted much attention to scales for measuring social status. The measurement of social status is of basic importance since one's position in the social hierarchy is correlated with economic, political, and other attitudes, school-achievement, child-rearing practices, emotional stability, aggressiveness and dominance, verbal behavior, and many other phenomena.[30] These

[28]See Samuel A. Stouffer *et al.,* "A Technique for Improving Cumulative Scales," *The Public Opinion Quarterly,* XVI, 273–291; Allen L. Edwards, "A Technique for Increasing the Reproducibility of Cumulative Attitude Scales," *Journal of Applied Psychology,* XL, 263–265.

[29]For further discussions of latent structure analysis theory and techniques, see Samuel A. Stouffer *et al., Studies in Social Psychology in World War II: Measurement and Prediction,* Chapters 1, 10, and 11; Paul F. Lazarsfeld, ed., *Mathematical Thinking in the Social Sciences,* Chap. 7. The Free Press of Glencoe, Inc., 1954.

[30]See for example, Harrison G. Gough, "A New Dimension of Status: I. Development of a Personality Scale," *American Sociological Review,* XIII, 401–409; Milton M. Gordon, "The Logic of Socio-Economic Status Scales," *Sociometry,* XV, 342–353; and Pitirim A. Sorokin, *Society, Culture, and Personality: Their Structure and Dynamics,* pp. 443–444. Harper & Row, Publishers, 1947.

facts clearly emphasize that research problems involving relationships between social status and economic, psychological, biological, educational, and other correlates are dependent on quantitative measures of social status. From a more utilitarian and practical point of view, standardized scales of social status provide numerical descriptions of family and home conditions which can be used in such problems as child placement, juvenile delinquency, and the development of various kinds of community programs.[31]

Since Chapin's scale has been so widely used by sociologists and also since it embodies the major features of scales of this kind[32] it is reproduced on the following pages.

In his original scale constructed in 1928, Chapin defines socio-economic status as "the position an individual or a family occupies with reference to the prevailing average standards of cultural possessions, effective income, material possessions, and participation in the group activities of the community."[33]

[31]William H. Sewell, *The Construction and Standardization of a Scale for the Measurement of the Socio-Economic Status of Oklahoma Farm Families,* Oklahoma Agricultural and Mechanical College, Agricultural Experiment Station, Bulletin 9, 1940, pp. 50–53.

[32]The first multiple-factor measuring device bearing on social status dates back to 1908 when John R. Commons published his Dwelling House Score Card. See John R. Commons, "Standardization of Housing Investigations," *Journal of the American Statistical Association,* XI, 319–326. In chronological order other examples of scales of social status include the following: Clarence A. Perry, "A Measure of the Manner of Living," *Quarterly Publications of the American Statistical Association,* XIII, 398–403; C. E. Holley, *The Relationship Between Persistence in School and Home Conditions,* p. 119. University of Chicago Press, 1916; J. H. Williams, *A Scale for Grading Neighboring Conditions and A Guide to the Grading of Homes.* Whittier State School, Bulletin 7, 1918; J. Crosby Chapman and V. M. Sims, "The Quantitative Measurement of Certain Aspects of Socio-Economic Status," *Journal of Educational Psychology,* XVI, 380–390; J. D. Heilman, "A Revision of the Chapman-Sims Socio-Economic Scale," *Journal of Educational Research,* XVIII, 117–126; Mary J. McCormick, *A Scale for Measuring Social Adequacy,* National Catholic School of Social Service, 1930; Alice Leahy Shea, *The Measurement of Urban Home Environment.* University of Minnesota Press, 1936; William H. Sewell, *op. cit.;* and American Public Health Association, *An Appraisal Method for Measuring the Quality of Housing.* American Public Health Association, 1950.

[33]Chapin, "A Quantitative Scale for Rating the Home and Social Environment of Middle Class Families in an Urban Environment: A First Approximation to the Measurement of Socio-Economic Status," *Journal of Educational Psychology,* XIX, 99–111.

The Social Status Scale*

Revised, 1952

VISITOR'S NAME ....

SCHEDULE NUMBER ....DATE ....

FAMILY NAME ....

STREET ADDRESS ....

TOWN AND STATE..

RACE ....

DIRECTIONS TO VISITOR

1. The following list of items is for the guidance of the recorder. Not all the features listed may be found in any one home. Entries on the schedules should, however, follow the order and numbering indicated. Weights appear (in parentheses) after the names of the items. Disregard these weights in recording. Only when the list is finally checked should the individual items be multiplied by these weights and the sum of the weighted scores be computed, and then only after leaving the home. All information is confidential.
2. Where the family has no real living room, but uses the room at night as a bedroom, or during the day as a kitchen or as a dining room, or as both, in addition to using the room as the chief gathering place of the family, please note this fact clearly and describe for what purposes the room is used. Scores corrected for these uses are as follows: (1) used as dining room, deduct 6; (2) used as kitchen, deduct 9; (3) used as bedroom *or* dining room and kitchen combined, deduct 12; (4) used as bedroom, dining room, and kitchen combined, deduct 15.
3. If the item you are scoring is present, enter the figure 1 on the *dotted* part of the line. If more than one item is present, write 2, 3, 4, etc., as the case may be. If the item is not present, enter a zero. Each division of each of the twenty items should have a number (0, 1, 2, 3, 4, etc.) entered opposite it. *Be sure that each item gets some number*. Leave no dotted line blank. A blank line means an oversight on your part.
4. Disregard figures in parentheses until all schedules are finished.
5. Always enter color of each family (white or Negro; specify if any other) below town and state.
6. Descriptions of items in Parts I and II.
   (1) Hardwood floors are usually made of narrow boards. Verify your own judgment by asking the occupant.
   (2) A large rug is one covering the entire floor area except a border of about 12 inches. (Usually a 9 × 12-foot rug.)
   (3) A drape is a covering over a window or windows (with or without curtains). The drape may be either at the side of the window or across the top. Each draped window gets one point. Where the drape covers more than one window, give the question as many points as there are windows covered by the drape.
   (4) Only a real fireplace (one in which a coal, wood, or other fire, including gas, can be built) gets a number.
   (6) A library table is any table not used for serving meals. (Exclude such small tables as end tables, card tables, etc.) If a library table is used as a personal-social desk, number it either as a library table or a personal desk, *but not as both*.
   (7) Armchairs include rocking chairs with arms.
   (8) Piano bench: a chair or stool does not get a point.

*Reprinted, with revisions, from F. Stuart Chapin, *The Measurement of Social Status*. Minneapolis: University of Minnesota Press, 1936.

(9) See No. 6. A personal-social desk is a writing desk.
(10) If no bookcase is seen, be sure to ask if there is one in another room. Be sure to record any bookcase, whether in living room or in any other room, except professional library of doctor, lawyer, clergyman, teacher.
(11) Sewing machine must be in living room in order to be marked minus two points. If outside living room, mark zero.
(13) Alarm clock: same as No. 11.
(14) Number of different periodicals *regularly bought* or *subscribed* to. Always get answer to this question by asking.
(15) Newspapers: same as No. 14.
(16) Telephone: to be recorded whether in living room or in some other room. Always ask concerning the telephone if you do not see one.
(17) Radio: to be recorded whether in living room or in some other room. Always ask regarding the radio.
(18) It is possible for a room to be both (a) spotted or stained and (b) dusty. In this case each gets *one* check.
(20) "In good repair" means in good condition and not obviously patched up; therefore only one of the parts (a, b, or c) gets a check.
(21) Only one of the parts (a, b, or c) gets a check.

Part I. Material Equipment and Cultural Expression of the Living Room of the Home

1. Floor, softwood (6) ....
   hardwood (10) ....
2. Large rug (8) ....
3. Windows with drapes (each window 2) ....
4. Fireplace with 3 or more utensils (8) ..
5. Artificial light, electric (8) ....
   kerosene (−2) ....
6. Library table (8) ....
7. Armchairs (8 each) ....
8. Piano bench (4) ....
9. Desk: personal-social (8) ....
10. Bookcases with books (8 each) ......
11. Sewing machine (—2) ....
12. Couch pillows (2 each) ....
13. Alarm clock (—2) ....
14. Periodicals (8 each) ....
15. Newspapers (8 each) ....
16. Telephone (8) ....
17. Radio (2); Television (6); both (8) ....

Score on Part I ....

Part II. Condition of Articles in Living Room

To provide some objective rating of qualitative attributes of the living room, such as "aesthetic atmosphere" or "general impression," the following additional items may be noted. The visitor should check the words that seem to describe the situation. Some of the weights are of minus sign, and so operate as penalties to reduce the total score of the home.

(*Social Status Scale—Continued*)

18. Cleanliness of room and furnishings
    a. Spotted or stained (−4) ....
    b. Dusty (−2) ....
    c. Spotless and dustless (+2) ....
19. Orderliness of room and furnishings
    a. Articles strewn about in disorder (−2) ....
    b. Articles in place or in usable order (+2) ....
20. Condition of repair of articles and furnishings
    a. Broken, scratched, frayed, ripped, or torn (−4) ....
    b. Articles or furnishings patched up (−2) ....

c. Articles or furnishings in good repair and well kept (+2) ....

21. Record your general impression of good taste
 a. Bizarre, clashing, inharmonious, or offensive (−4) ....
 b. Drab, monotonous, neutral, inoffensive (−2) ....
 c. Attractive in a positive way, harmonious, quiet and restful (+2) ....
 Score on Part II........ Total score,* Parts I and II........

*With penalties deducted.

These four attributes of socio-economic status were then measured by four scales. (1) Cultural equipment was measured by a list of articles of household equipment to which were assigned arbitrary numerical weights that represented in each case the agreement of two independent judges; (2) effective income was measured by the Sydenstricker-King scale in *ammains*[34] (3) material possessions were measured by household equipment articles weighted as in the first series; and (4) participation was measured by a weight of 1 for each membership, 2 for each group attended, 3 for each group financially supported, 4 for each committee membership and 5 for each officership of the parents.[35]

Chapin found after several investigations that the totals of the weights given to living room equipment were found to correlate so highly with the combined weights of the four indices that the equipment of the living room could be taken as a fair index of socio-economic status.

Accordingly, it will be observed from the revised scale that material possessions in the living room as well as the condition of the possessions are the indices used to differentiate families in terms of socio-economic status. This scale has been tested for validity and reliability under varying circumstances and tentative norms have been established for interpretation of scores.

Revised Tentative Norms of Chapin's Social Status Scale: 1942[36]

Class		*Ranges in Scores*	*Examples*
Upper:	1. Upper part	250 and over	Professional, physician
	2. Lower part	200—249	Small town banker
Middle:	1. Upper part	150—199	Factory manager
	2. Lower part	100—149	Skilled trades
Lower:	1. Upper part	50—99	Unemployed semi-skilled
	2. Lower part	0—49	Unemployed unskilled

[34]E. Sydenstricker and W. I. King, "The Measurement of Relative Economic Status of Families," *Journal of the American Statistical Association,* XVI, 842–859.

[35]Chapin, *Contemporary American Institutions,* pp. 374–375. Harper & Row, Publishers, 1935.

[36]See Chapin, *Experimental Designs in Sociological Research, op. cit.,* pp. 269–272, and *Contemporary American Institutions, op. cit.,* p. 378. Also see George A. Lundberg, "The Measurement of Socioeconomic Status," *American Sociological Review,* V, 29–39.

Louis Guttman has worked out by means of factor analysis a new weighting of the item scores.[37] A serious defect of most rating scales[38] is the arbitrary and impressionistic weighting of items. Guttman's attempt to derive a more rational and objective basis for determining item weights is a significant contribution. Sound scale construction demands careful item analysis in order to establish proper weightings as well as to eliminate extraneous factors. The following comparisons illustrate the differences as well as certain similarities between the arbitrary weights of Chapin and those derived mathematically by Guttman:

Item	*Old Weight (Chapin)*	*New Weight (Guttman)*[39]
4. Fireplace with 3 or more utensils	8	34.6
6. Library table	8	−1.0
9. Desk: personal-social	8	2.3
16. Telephone	8	24.4
17. Radio	8	8.0

Perhaps the student has detected a fundamental difference between the typical attitude scale and the typical sociometric rating scale. The first type of scale is concerned mainly with the measurement of attitudes and opinions, whereas the second type is a scoring device for measuring more "observable" and "tangible" phenomena. The first type of scale represents attitude or opinion responses to a list of statements. The second type of scale on the other hand generally presupposes definite criteria and information which can be examined and evaluated. The most objective rating scales involve merely a checking or listing of clear-cut and definitive indices.[40]

[37]"A Revision of Chapin's Social Status Scale," *American Sociological Review*, VII, 362–369.

[38]For an excellent review of rating scales developed by psychologists see J. P. Guilford, *Psychometric Methods*, Chap. II. McGraw-Hill Book Company, 1954. It will be observed that many of the scales discussed are extremely crude. Needless to say, such scales should not be used for any serious research or administrative purpose.

[39]One obvious limitation of Guttman's analysis is the fact that it is based on merely 67 Negro families rather than a larger and more representative sample.

[40]A discussion of scales in a research manual for sociologists and social workers would not be complete without referring to *Appraisal Method for Measuring the Quality of Housing* which was prepared by the Committee on the

General principles and techniques in the construction of sociometric scales. In constructing a sociometric scale it is essential to pay strict attention to the best principles and standards that have been evolved by students in this field. A few of the more important principles may be summarized as follows:

1. At the very beginning of an undertaking it is important to determine as far as possible what is to be measured. The analysis and identification of the conditions, traits, or characteristics to be measured should be made before the construction of the scale is begun.
2. Extreme care should be taken in the selection of the elements or criteria to be used as a basis for rating or measurement.
3. Each factor or criterion chosen should be weighted in accordance with some well defined and objective technique.
4. Every effort should be made to construct as simple a scale as possible; an elaborate, complicated, and over-refined scale may turn out to be unduly cumbersome, costly, or even useless.
5. A scale must possess a high degree of validity; that is, it must measure in some demonstrable manner that which it is supposed to measure.
6. A scale must be reliable, that is, produce consistent results.
7. A scale should be easily administered; it should contain proper

---

Hygiene of Housing of the American Public Health Association. This report is printed in three parts: I. *Nature and Uses of the Method,* II. *Appraisal of Dwelling Conditions,* and III. *Appraisal of Neighborhood Environment.* In developing a new appraisal method, the Committee on the Hygiene of Housing has attempted to overcome the limitations and to consolidate the merits of earlier systems of evaluation. For a detailed description of these techniques see, Part I. *Nature and Uses of Method,* and Allan A. Twichell, "An Appraisal Method for Measuring the Quality of Housing," *American Sociological Review,* XIII, 278–287.

The student should also acquaint himself with the American Public Health Association's *Appraisal Form for Local Health Work,* (1938). This publication is an outgrowth of more than a decade of experimentation in evaluating the health services of a community as evidenced by certain typical sample activities. The idea in rating has been to measure actual accomplishment as indicated by the extent to which vaccinations are performed, infants are under medical supervision, cases of tuberculosis are hospitalized, vital statistics are properly recorded, etc. The major categories in the Appraisal Form with their respective weights are: Vital statistics 40; Communicable disease control 160; Syphilis and gonorrhea control 90; Tuberculosis control 90; Maternity hygiene 90; Infant and preschool hygiene 170; School hygiene 140; Sanitation 90; Food and milk control 80; and Bonus for balanced program 50. It will be observed that there is a possible perfect total of 1,000 points.

instructions; it should be easily understood, conveniently arranged for filling out; and where necessary, it should be acceptable to the informant or the institution being studied.

8. A scale should be quantitatively expressed and so formulated that the data are readily susceptible to statistical analysis.
9. A scale should be tried out under varying conditions and revised where necessary.

AN ILLUSTRATION OF THE CONSTRUCTION OF A SOCIOMETRIC SCALE. In order to illustrate the general principles and techniques in constructing rating scales, let us consider very briefly the actual procedure which Alice Leahy Shea followed in formulating her home environment scale.[41] Her purpose was to measure home environment in terms of certain objective elements which are presumed to influence the behavior and development of the child.

There were three main steps in the actual construction of the scale: 1) the definition and selection of various factors or criteria that differentiate living conditions; 2) the determination of the differentiating power of each of the factors; and 3) the incorporation of the most discriminating factors into a scale that may be readily and efficiently administered.[42]

After careful planning in developing schedules and in selecting a sample, comprehensive data on the home environment were obtained from personal interviews with both adult and child members of 600

[41]See A. L. Shea, *The Measurement of Urban Home Environment, op. cit.* In constructing his Farm Family Socio-Economic Status Scale, William H. Sewell followed very closely Dr. Shea's methods. The student is urged to examine Dr. Sewell's monograph and papers on this subject: *The Construction and Standardization of a Scale for the Measurement of the Socio-Economic Status of Oklahoma Farm Families,* Oklahoma Agricultural and Mechanical College, Technical Bulletin No. 9, (April, 1940); "The Development of a Sociometric Scale," *Sociometry,* V, 279–297; "A Scale for the Measurement of Farm Family Socio-Economic Status," *Southwestern Social Science Quarterly,* XXI, 125–137; "The Restandardization of a Sociometric Scale," *Social Forces,* XXI, 302–311; "A Short Form of the Farm Family Socio-Economic Status Scale," *Rural Sociology,* VIII, 161–170. Also, John C. Belcher and Emmet F. Sharp, *A Short Scale for Measuring Farm Family Living: A Modification of Sewell's Socio-Economic Scale,* Oklahoma Agricultural Experiment Station, 1952. For another important contribution to the construction and application of sociometric scales see Stuart C. Dodd, *A Controlled Experiment on Rural Hygiene in Syria, passim.* Beirut, Lebanon: American University Press, 1934.

[42]Shea, *ibid.,* p. 22.

white families representing different socio-economic status, and having one or more children from five to fourteen years of age. A long list of objective elements in the environment was compiled from data collected in this manner. In addition all published scales of this type were carefully examined, and many other items which might prove of value were added to the list. The final list comprised a total of 84 environmental items or factors.

The next step was to determine the differentiating power of each of the 84 factors. In the absence of any outside criteria two statistical tests are commonly used: 1) determination of the correlation of each item with the total of all others, and 2) the criterion of internal consistency in which a comparison is made of the frequency of occurrence of each item in relationship to the total score in selected segments of the distribution. The latter test was chosen by Dr. Shea.[43] It will be recalled that this technique has been used in the construction of attitude scales and various types of psychometric tests.[44] The criterion of internal consistency purports to test the ability of an item to differentiate between extremes of the distribution of the total scores. In the list of 84 items, for example, the purpose of the criterion of internal consistency was to determine the degree to which each item differentiates between rich and poor homes as defined by the factors included in the list. After each of the 84 items was validated in this manner, many of them were not found sufficiently discriminating or reliable and hence were eliminated. For example, the ownership of a radio and Sunday School attendance by the child were excluded because they did not possess adequate differentiating power between the various income levels.[45]

After the items had been selected, the next step was to arrange them in proper order in the scale. In arranging the items such considerations

[43]*Ibid.*, pp. 23–26.

[44]In this connection see Sletto, *Construction of Personality Scales by the Criterion of Internal Consistency, op. cit., passim.*

[45]Guttman criticizes the use of the criterion of internal consistency because of its ambiguity and shifting reference. He suggests that where an external criterion is available, multiple regression coefficients may be used for maximizing the predictive power of the items in the scale. When there is no external criterion, "scale analysis" may be used to determine the degree of reproducibility of the items. Much confusion in scaling techniques results from a failure to take into account the difference between predictive and reproductive functions. See Guttman, "The Quantitative Prediction of a Qualitative Variate" (Part III) and "The Quantitative Prediction of a Qualitative Variate" (Part IV), in Paul Horst *et al., op. cit.*, pp. 271–297. Also see references to Guttman on "scale analysis."

as the facility in administering the scale and the coherence of related items were kept in mind. Moreover, in order not to embarrass the informant the least personal questions were placed first. The various items in the final *Home Status Index* were submitted under the following captions: I. Children's Facilities (11 items), II. Economic Status (13 items), III. Cultural Status (11 items), IV. Sociality (13 items), V. Occupational Status (7 divisions), and VI. Educational Status (12 divisions). An introductory section includes instructions for administering the scale and general informational questions pertaining to the home and the family studied.

In scoring the various items in a scale, one of three methods can be followed: 1) the "simple method," 2) the "difference method," and 3) the "sigma method."[46] In the simple method arbitrary values are assigned to the various items. For example, if a certain factor is present, it is given a value of 1, and if it is absent, it is assigned a value of 0. In cases where the factor is graduated into levels or steps, an arbitrary value is assigned to each level. The scale-values in the "difference method" are based on the reliability of the percentage differences of possession existing between subclasses of the entire population. The score assigned to each item is the average of the ratios of the differences to their standard errors.[47] In the "sigma method" the weight given an item is in relation to its frequency in the total population. Items which occur infrequently are assigned the greatest weight, and the absence or non-possession of an item is also given a value.

Measures of reliability and validity of sociometric scales. In developing a sociometric scale it is very important to test both its reliability and its validity.[48] A reliable scale "agrees with itself" and measures consistently that which it is supposed to measure. The reli-

[46]Shea, *op. cit.*

[47]For a further explanation of the "difference method" see *ibid.*, pp. 41–42.

[48]The sources of unreliability are manifold. For attitude scales in particular the following may be mentioned: 1) complex and ambiguous items, 2) items that are inconsistent with one another, 3) mechanical errors in reading, marking, and scoring items, 4) inadequate and non-uniform instructions, and 5) variable and disruptive factors in the measurement situation. In the case of rating scales unreliability may be attributed to such factors as 1) deficiencies in the structure of the rating scale, 2) complexity of variable to be rated, 3) non-comparability of rating among judges, 4) "halo" tendency in rating, 5) inadequate and incomparable data, and 6) ignorance of respondents with respect to certain issues and problems. David Krech, Richard S. Crutchfield and Egerton L. Ballachey, *Individual in Society, op. cit.*, pp. 157–167 and pp. 172–177; also see the discussion on rating scales in J. P. Guilford, *Psychometric Methods, op. cit.*

ability of a scale may be tested in three different ways: 1) the "test-retest" method where the rating of a particular factor, group, or institution is repeated after an interval of time and the scores obtained in the two operations are correlated with each other; 2) "simultaneous rating" of the same institution or condition by two or more competent investigators and then correlation of the results, and 3) the "split-half" technique where after a scale is administered to a sample, the scores on equal halves of the scale are correlated with each other. The Spearman-Brown formula is usually applied to correct for attenuation in the "split-half" technique.[49] In all three methods the size of the coefficient of correlation is indicative of the reliability of the scale.

Scales may be found to be reliable but not necessarily valid according to one or more of these criteria. Validity implies a predictive power beyond the immediate range of the factors in the scale. A valid scale measures that which it is supposed to measure, such as social status, health conditions, or the efficiency of some type of institution. To say that a scale is valid in the absolute sense is, of course, impossible.

In actual practice one will find it difficult to determine the validity of sociometric scales: first, satisfactory criteria of the phenomena being measured are seldom available, and second, the techniques for determining validity are ill developed and poorly standardized. Three methods commonly used in testing the validity[50] of sociometric scales are: 1) The oldest and least satisfactory is referred to as the "logical test of validity." Essentially it merely indicates in a more or less impressionistic way that the scale is logically compatible with an accepted theory and the results of its application do not violate this theory. 2) The second method is more pragmatic in that the scores of the scale must conform to common-sense observation and experience. 3) The third method is by far the most acceptable and objective. The scores of the scale are correlated with one or more independent criteria of the phenomena being measured.[51] An effort is also made to compare scores of a scale for widely different and for similar classes, insti-

[49]The "split-half" technique is a much less satisfactory method of measuring reliability than the "test-retest" and "simultaneous rating" techniques. For an excellent discussion of this point see Louis Guttman, "A Basis for Analyzing Test-Retest Reliability," *Psychometrika,* X, 255–282.

[50]Louis Guttman re-defines validity in terms of the coefficient of reproducibility. See references, *supra.*

[51]William H. Sewell, "The Development of a Sociometric Scale," *Sociometry,* V, 279–297.

tutions, and conditions. A valid scale will clearly and consistently differentiate various groups or conditions from one another.

In constructing his Farm Family Socio-Economic Status Scale, Sewell used the second and third methods discussed in the foregoing paragraph. In the common-sense test he computed mean scores for a sample of 1,190 farm families in terms of tenure status. The test scores differentiated very decisively the owner, tenant, and labor classes in his sample. In the second test validity coefficients were computed for two samples of Oklahoma farm families by correlating the scale scores with various external criteria of farm family socio-economic status. The results are summarized in the tabulation below.

In conclusion, scaling techniques represent one of the more useful and significant methodological achievements of modern sociological and psychological science. The importance of scales as an instrument of scientific investigation is increasing and every well-trained sociologist should be conversant with the more basic and up-to-date methods in this field. It must not be overlooked that existing techniques possess certain limitations and inadequacies; but with the many psychologists and sociologists who are devoting their efforts to scaling problems, steady improvements are being made.

Table 12.3

VALIDITY COEFFICIENTS OF SEWELL'S FARM FAMILY SOCIO-ECONOMIC STATUS SCALE.[52]

Scale Scores Correlated with:	257 *Family Sample*	800 *Family Sample*
Chapin, S.S.S. 1933	0.80	*
Dickins' revision of Chapin's scale	0.82	*
Clark Rural Home Equipment Scale	0.71	*
Experimental scale	0.97	0.96
Cash income per *ammain*	0.37	0.63
Net wealth per family	0.57	0.55
Expenditures for living per family	0.52	0.63
Total money value of living per *ammain*	0.51	0.67

**Scores on these scales were not available for this sample.*

[52] *Ibid.*

Other measures of socio-economic status. Although the Chapin Living Room Scale as well as other similar scales developed during the 1930's and 1940's are sound methodological contributions, their application at the present time is limited because they are out of date. Modern items and a revised weighting system are essential steps for making these scales more usable and up-to-date.[53]

In recent years, students of social stratification have been inclined to select simpler and more readily available measures of socio-economic status. One of the most popular measures is occupational ranking. Occupational ranking may be used separately or in combination with education and/or income, or other indexes.

Perhaps the best-known occupational scale, representing a single-item index, is that of Alba M. Edwards. Edwards devised an occupational classification system in which specific occupations could be subsumed under broad categories arranged in hierarchial order. The highest is "professional" followed in rank order by "proprietors, managers and officials," "clerks and kindred workers," "skilled workers," "semiskilled workers," and "unskilled workers." Edwards' scheme was used first in the 1940 decennial census and later, with certain modifications, in the 1950 and 1960 censuses.[54]

Another type of occupational index is based on evaluations people make of different occupations. The best known scheme of this type is the North-Hatt index based on data from a national public opinion poll conducted by the National Opinion Research Center in 1946. The purpose of the study was to rank ninety different occupational titles in terms of relative prestige and/or desirability.

In the interviewing procedure each respondent was handed a card with the following instructions: "For each job mentioned, please pick out the statement that best gives *your own personal opinion* of the *general standing* that such a job has.

1. *Excellent* standing
2. *Good* standing
3. *Average* standing
4. *Somewhat below average* standing
5. *Poor* standing

[53]For a more specific evaluation of the "living room" type of scale, see Leonard Reissman, *Class in American Society,* pp. 117–125. The Free Press, of Glencoe, Inc., 1959.

[54]Alba M. Edwards, *A Social-Economic Grouping of the Gainful Workers of the United States,* 1930. U.S.G.P.O., 1938.

x. I don't know where to place that one"

The list of 90 occupational titles was then read so that the respondent could indicate his reactions on the basis of the instructions on the card. According to the findings of the answers, the top ranking occupations are U.S. Supreme Court justice (1), physician (2), mayor of a large city (6), college professor (7), and banker (10) while the lowest ranking occupations are restaurant waiter (79), dock worker (81), night watchman (81), janitor (85), and shoe shiner (90).

Albert J. Reiss remarks that

> Few empirical studies have achieved a place in the scientific literature of sociology comparable to that of the NORC—North-Hatt investigation. Given the predilection of American social scientists for social-status scales, the North-Hatt ranking of occupations has been widely accepted as affirming a rank-structure of the prestige status of occupations.[55]

In addition to occupational status, other criteria such as "style of life," "self-identification," "institutional membership," "status reputation," education, amount of income, source of income, dwelling area, and housing type have been used as indicators of socio-economic status.

W. Lloyd Warner, August B. Hollingshead, and others have incorporated several of these criteria in the techniques they have developed in determining class rankings.[56]

For example, in his "Index of Status Characteristics" (I.S.C.),

[55]Albert J. Reiss *et al., Occupations and Social Status,* p. 7 and p. 19. The Free Press of Glencoe, Inc., 1961. This is the most comprehensive book in print on the subject of occupations and social status. Also, see Leonard Reissman, *op. cit.,* pp. 144–164.

[56]W. Lloyd Warner and Paul S. Lunt, *The Social Life of a Modern Community,* New Haven: Yale University Press, 1941; W. Lloyd Warner *et al., Social Class in America: A Manual for Procedure for the Measurement of Social Status.* Science Research Associates, 1949; August B. Hollingshead, *Elmstown's Youth.* John Wiley & Sons, Inc., 1949. In this connection see Harold W. Pfautz and Otis D. Duncan, "A Critical Evaluation of Warner's Work in Community Stratification," *American Sociological Review,* XV, 205–15 and Robert A. Ellis, W. Clayton Lane, and Virginia Oleson, "The Index of Class Position: An Improved Intercommunity Measure of Stratification," *American Sociological Review,* XXVIII, 272–277. For an excellent discussion of indexes of socio-economic status, including a good bibliography see Joseph A. Kahl and James A. Davis, "A Comparison of Indexes of Socio-Economic Status," *American Sociological Review,* XX, 317–25.

Warner incorporated six of these indices—amount of income, source of income, occupation, house type, location of residence, and education.

Another example of a multiple item index of socio-economic status was developed by Charles B. Nam. The Nam index is a weighted scheme derived from Census Bureau data on education, occupation, and income.[57]

Sociometry[58]

The basic principles and techniques of sociometry were initially embodied in a volume by J. L. Moreno entitled *Who Shall Survive?* first published in 1934.[59] An enlarged revision of this book covering the history, theory, terminology, techniques, bibliography and applications of sociometry was published in 1953. Sociometric techniques have been widely utilized by sociologists, psychologists, and psychiatrists in the study of group structure, social status, and personality traits. Sociometry helps to make more explicit and precise the configuration of group relationships, the characteristics and composition of cliques and other elements in a larger group, the social position of individual members in a group, and the streams and points of influence within and among groups. The value of sociometry as a research tool has been clearly demonstrated by the wide variety of useful studies that have been made. Sociometric

[57]Charles B. Nam, *Methodology and Scores of Socio-Economic Status,* Washington, D. C.: United States Bureau of the Census, Working Paper No. 15, (1963). An application of the technique developed by Nam will be found in a paper by Calvin F. Schmid and Charles E. Nobbe, "Socio-Economic Differentials Among Non-White Races in the State of Washington," *Demography,* Vol. II, No. 2, 1965. (In press)

[58]Prepared by Calvin F. Schmid with the assistance of Lenore Dickson and Douglas Yamamura.

[59]Cf. J. L. Moreno, "Contributions of Sociometry to Research Methodology in Sociology," *American Sociological Review,* XII, 287–292; Gardner Lindzey and Edgar F. Borgatta, "Sociometric Measurement," in Gardner Lindzey, ed., *Handbook of Social Psychology, op. cit.,* Vol. I, Chap. 11; J. L. Moreno *et al., The Sociometry Reader*. The Free Press of Glencoe, Inc., 1960; Mary L. Northway, *A Primer of Sociometry*. University of Toronto Press, 1952; Helen Hall Jennings, *Sociometry in Group Relations*. American Council on Education, 1959.

studies have been made of entire communities,[60] fraternities,[61] grade schools,[62] high schools,[63] college student bodies,[64] camps,[65] armed forces,[66] and factories.[67] Other studies have been made with special emphasis on such problems and processes as leadership,[68] morale,[69]

[60]Charles P. Loomis, "Informal Groupings in a Spanish-American Village," *Sociometry,* IV, 36–51; George A. Lundberg and Mary Steele, "Social Attraction Patterns in a Village," *Sociometry,* I, 375–419; Frank Steward, "Sociometric Study of Influence in Southtown," *Sociometry,* X, 11–31; T. Wilson Longmore, "A Matrix Approach to the Analysis of Rank and Status in a Community in Peru," *Sociometry,* XI, 192–206.

[61]F. M. Vreeland, "Social Relations in a College Fraternity," *Sociometry,* V, 151–162.

[62]Joan Henning Criswell, "A Sociometric Study of Race Cleavage in the Classroom," *Archives of Psychology,* XXXIII, 5-82; M. E. Bonney, "Personality Traits of Socially Successful and Socially Unsuccessful Children," *Journal of Educational Psychology,* XXXIV, 449–472; Norman E. Gronlund, *Sociometry in the Classroom, passim.* Harper & Row, Publishers, 1959. This book contains excellent bibliographies. K. M. Evans, *Sociometry and Education, passim.* Routledge and Kegan Paul, 1962. In this connection the Syracuse Scales of Social Relations might be found useful. They were developed by E. F. Gardner and G. G. Thompson. Harcourt, Brace & World, Inc., 1959.

[63]Mapheus Smith, "Some Factors on Friendship Selections of High School Students," *Sociometry,* VII, 303–310.

[64]Raymond E. Bassett, "Cliques in a Student Body of Stable Membership," *Sociometry,* VII, 290–302; John W. Kidd, "An Analysis of Social Rejection in a College Men's Residence Hall," *Sociometry,* XIV, 226–236; M. E. Bonney *et al.,* "A Study of Some Factors Related to Sociometric Status in a Men's Dormitory," *Sociometry,* XVI, 287–301.

[65]W. I. Newstetter, M. J. Feldstein, and T. M. Newcomb, *Group Adjustment: A Study in Experimental Sociology, passim.* Western Reserve University Press, 1938; M. L. Northway, *Appraisal of the Social Development of Children at a Summer Camp,* University of Toronto Press, 1941, *passim.*

[66]Leslie D. Zeleny, "Selection of Compatible Flying Partners," in J. L. Moreno *et al., The Sociometry Reader, op. cit.,* pp. 534–547.

[67]J. H. Jacobs, "The Application of Sociometry to Industry," *Sociometry,* VIII, 181–198; John T. Gullahorn, "Distance and Friendship as Factors in the Gross Interaction Matrix," in J. L. Moreno *et. al., The Sociometry Reader, op. cit.,* pp. 506–517; B. J. Speroff, "Job Satisfaction and Interpersonal Desirability Values," *ibid.,* pp. 518–521.

[68]Charles L. Howell, "Measurement of Leadership," *Sociometry,* V, 151–162; Helen H. Jennings, *Leadership and Isolation, passim.* Longmans, Green and Co., 1950; Cecil A. Gibb, "The Sociometry of Leadership in Temporary Groups," *Sociometry,* XIII, 226–243.

[69]L. D. Zeleny, "Sociometry of Morale," *American Sociological Review,* IV, 799–808.

social adjustment,[70] race relations,[71] political cleavages,[72] and public opinion polling.[73] In addition, sociometry has proved of value in the development of therapeutic techniques, especially in psychiatry.[74]

Sociometry has been defined as "a method for discovering, describing, and evaluating social status, structure, and development through measuring the extent of acceptance or rejection between individuals in groups."[75] Another typical definition states that sociometry is "a method used for the discovery and manipulation of social configurations by measuring the attractions and repulsions between individuals in a group."[76]

The basic technique in sociometry is the "sociometric test." The "sociometric test" consists in having each member of a group choose from all other members those with whom he prefers to associate in specific situations.[77] Moreno first applied the "sociometric test" to groupings in a public school, and shortly after used it in a study of the State Training School for Girls at Hudson, New York. This institution is a closed community of approximately 500 girls living in 16 cottages. Each girl was asked to list the 5 girls she would most like to have as a housemate, work companion, and table mate and the 5 girls she would

---

[70]Nahum E. Shoobs, "Sociometry in the Class Room," *Sociometry,* X, 154–164; F. M. McClelland and John A. Ratliff, "The Use of Sociometry as an Aid in Promoting Social Adjustment in a Ninth Grade Home-Room," *Sociometry,* X, 147–153. Also see other studies in the May, 1947 issue of *Sociometry.*

[71]Joan H. Criswell, "Racial Cleavage in Negro-White Groups," *Sociometry,* VIII, 64–75; George A. Lundberg and Lenore Dickson, "Selective Association Among Ethnic Groups," *American Journal of Sociology,* XVIII, 1–10.

[72]Charles P. Loomis, "Political and Occupational Cleavages in a Hanoverian Village, Germany," *Sociometry,* IX, 316–333.

[73]Stuart C. Dodd, "On Reliability in Polling: A Sociometric Study of Errors of Polling in War Zones," *Sociometry,* VII, 265–282.

[74]J. L. Moreno, *Who Shall Survive?, op. cit., passim;* "Inter-Personal Therapy and the Psychopathology of Inter-Personal Relations," *Sociometry,* I, 9–76; "Psychodramatic Shock Therapy—A Sociometric Approach to the Problem of Mental Disorders," *Sociometry,* II, 1–30.

[75]Urie Bronfenbrenner, "A Constant Frame of Reference for Sociometric Research," *Sociometry,* VI, 363–372; Also see Ake Bjerstedt, *Definitions of Sociometry,* Sociometry Monographs, No. 39. Beacon House, 1958.

[76]J. G. Franz, "Survey of Sociometric Techniques with an Annotated Bibliography," *Sociometry,* II, 76–90.

[77]Ester B. Frankel and Reva Potashin, "A Survey of Sociometric and Pre-Sociometric Literature on Friendship and Social Acceptance Among Children," *Sociometry,* VII, 422–431.

least like to have in these relationships. Preferences and rejections are always indicated and evaluated in terms of particular criteria around which the group is organized—such as rooming together, eating to-

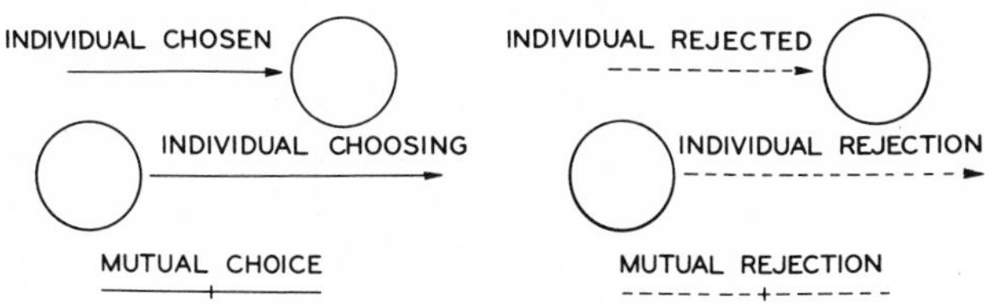

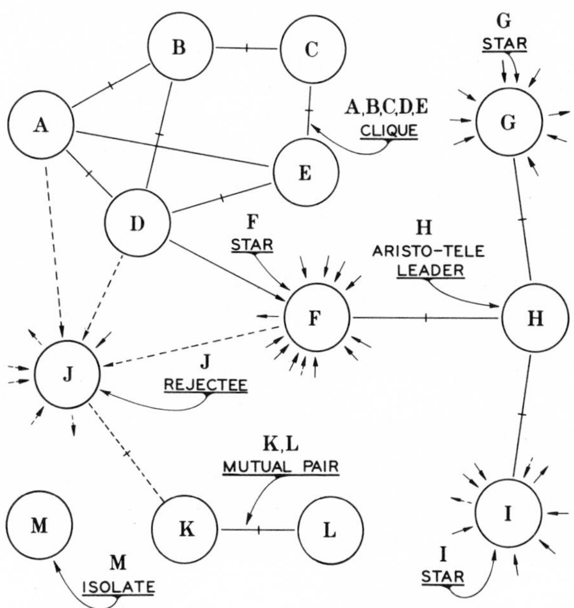

Figure 12.2 Techniques for a sociogram.

gether, working together, or otherwise associating with persons in specified situations. Sociometric studies reveal that certain persons are chosen for all situations, but frequently entirely different individuals are preferred for each type of activity. The initial steps in sociometric procedure then involve first, ascertaining the fundamental criteria around which group activities take place and second, testing for the attraction-repulsion patterns in terms of these criteria.

Sometimes the results of the sociometric tests are augmented by personal interviews. This was the procedure originally followed by Moreno in his study of the girls' training school. In the interview each girl was questioned as to her attitude toward those choosing or rejecting her for each criterion. Did she like, dislike, or feel indifferent toward those indicating attraction or repulsion toward her? Motivation for attraction and rejection was also investigated in the interview in order to obtain a clearer picture of each girl's position in the social structure. A technique which gave a clear picture of the relationships between different girls was that of psycho-drama in which each girl acted in a real-life situation opposite those choosing or rejecting her or chosen or rejected by her. The scenes were acted out on a small stage while a stenographer recorded the time intervals, general mood, facial expressions, and actual conversation. By means of this technique it was possible to discover whether the dominant relationship was one of sympathy, fear, anger, jealousy, or some other emotion. Psychodrama has been found very fruitful in the field of psychiatry and sociatry, but is too complicated a technique to be used extensively in sociometry proper.

The difficulty of securing reliable information from sociometric tests has been clearly recognized. This problem, however, is not basically different from those occurring in attitude scales, case techniques, and questionnaires. Sociometric techniques have to be used with discrimination and carefully adapted to each situation. Recognizing the possibility of antagonizing the residents of a Vermont village by probing into repulsion patterns, Lundberg confined his questioning to friendship patterns.[78]

In discussing the application of sociometry to industry, Jacobs points out that

> personal feelings are generally very closely guarded by individuals and the utmost confidence is needed on the part of the interviewers if they hope to get accurate answers. A great weakness of self-analysis tests lies in the fact that if the confidence of the person being interviewed is not obtained, the person will answer the questions in the way they feel they will benefit most in the light of personal advancement.[79]

[78] Lundberg and Steele, *op. cit.*

[79] J. H. Jacobs, *op. cit.*

Another technique for portraying and analyzing sociometric data is the matrix. The typical matrix is a simple cross-tabulation of $N \times N$ dimensions corresponding to the group of N individuals—the various entries, frequently represented by symbols, indicating each person's feeling toward every other member of the group. Stuart C. Dodd lists the following advantages of the matrix: 1) its inclusiveness—the relationship between every single pair is specifically recorded; 2) joint relationships between pairs are recorded; 3) only one interrelation (criterion) is recorded on each matrix and is thus isolated for scientific study; and 4) matrices may be combined and compared.[80]

In other words, the matrix is especially valuable in mathematical analysis and synthesis. As a graphic device it is inferior to the sociogram; it is also inferior as a tool for detecting and analyzing cliques, mutual choices, and other aspects of group structure. In this connection Moreno makes the following comment:

> Up to now sociogram and sociomatrix each offered certain advantages. They supplement each other. In teaching sociometry the sociogram is more plastic and offers an interrelated whole of the group structure to the eye of the student. He has it all before him instead of having to look for the bits in a matrix and piecing them together in his mind. In research work they should be used jointly. However, I believe that a synthesis between sociogram and sociomatrix is possible. Technicians of the matrix should try more and more to put into it what is missing but available in the sociogram.[81]

A review of the writings in the field of sociometry clearly shows extensive applications of various types of statistical techniques.[82] Among the more distinctive as well as useful statistical techniques to be found in sociometric studies are indexes and scoring devices.

[80]Dodd, "The Interrelation Matrix," *Sociometry,* III, 91–101; "Analysis of the Interrelation Matrix by Its Surface and Structure," *Sociometry,* III, 133–143; Elaine Forsyth and Leo Katz, "A Matrix Approach to the Analysis of Sociometric Data: Preliminary Report," *Sociometry,* IX, 340–347; Corlin O. Beum and Everett Brundage, "A Method for Analyzing the Sociomatrix," *Sociometry,* XIII, 141–145; Leon Festinger, "The Analysis of Sociograms Using Matrix Algebra," in J. L. Moreno *et al., The Sociometry Reader, op. cit.,* pp. 238–244.

[81]Moreno, "Sociogram and Sociomatrix," *Sociometry,* IX, 348–349.

[82]For recent, comprehensive discussions of various methods and techniques in sociometric research see, J. L. Moreno *et al. The Sociometry Reader, op. cit.,* pp. 133–398.

Criswell in her study of race cleavages suggests the index of self preference, based on the actual ratio between in-group and out-group choices, and the expected ratio, based on the total number in each group.[83] Moreno and Jennings have proposed such indexes as the ratio of interest and the ratio of attraction.[84]

Zeleny's indexes of sociation, social status, and morale have been used in sociometric studies.[85] Lundberg and Steele have developed indexes of interaction and of cohesion.[86]

[83] J. H. Criswell, "Sociometric Methods of Measuring Group Preferences," *Sociometry,* VI, 398–408.

[84] J. L. Moreno and Helen H. Jennings, "Statistics of Social Configuration," *Sociometry,* I, 342–374.

[85] L. D. Zeleny, "Measurement of Sociation," *American Sociological Review,* VI, 173–188; L. D. Zeleny, "Status: Its Measurement and Control in Education," in J. L. Moreno *et. al., The Sociometry Reader, op. cit.,* pp. 261–271.

[86] Lundberg and Steele, "Social Attraction-Patterns in a Village," *Sociometry,* I, 375–419.

graphic presentation[1]

By
CALVIN F. SCHMID
University of Washington

If it were more generally realized how much depends upon the method of presenting facts, as compared to the facts themselves, there would be a great increase in the use of the graphic methods of presentation.

WILLARD C. BRINTON

13

For anyone seriously interested in social research, a knowledge of the principles of constructing graphs and charts is indispensable. The average research worker may never actually draw many charts for publication, but he is frequently required to plan them, and most certainly to utilize and interpret charts made by other people.

Graphs and charts are especially valuable in rendering large masses of statistical data clear and comprehensible. The meaning of series of figures in textual or tabular form may be difficult for the mind to grasp or retain. Properly constructed graphs and charts relieve the mind of burdensome details by portraying facts concisely, logically, and simply. Graphs and charts, by emphasizing new and significant relationships, also may be of immense service in discovering new facts and in developing hypotheses.

Like all social research techniques, graphic presentation must be used with much care and discrimination. Poorly constructed charts not only may seriously cheapen an otherwise good report, but they may actually misrepresent or distort the facts. Besides possessing a thorough mastery of the techniques of graphic

[1]For a comprehensive and practical manual on the theory and technique of charting statistics, the student is referred to Calvin F. Schmid, *Handbook of Graphic Presentation.* Ronald Press, 1954.

presentation, it is also important to be extremely thorough and meticulous in the actual construction of the drawings. One cannot afford to be slovenly or careless in work of this kind. Accuracy is just as important in constructing graphs and charts as it is in other types of research work.

Since the main objective of graphic presentation is to clarify data, it is important not to make charts complicated or crowded with too many facts and thus cause confusion. Extreme care must always be taken in selecting the method of graphic presentation that is most appropriate to the problem at hand. There should be a very good reason for preferring a graph or chart to some other form of presentation. After one has decided to use some form of graphic presentation, a choice of the particular type of chart has to be made. Of course, some types are more appropriate than others.

After having studied the basic data very carefully, such questions as the following will have to be answered: What is the purpose of the diagram? What facts are to be emphasized? What is the educational level of the audience? How much time is available for the preparation of the chart? What type of chart has the greatest psychological appeal? What kind of chart will portray the data most clearly and accurately? Let us consider in some detail a few of the more important types of graphs and charts used in social research.

Rectangular Coordinate Graphs

One of the most useful forms of graphic presentation used in social research is the well-known line graph. Figure 13.1 is an illustration of this type of graph. In statistical work it is called a *rectangular, rectilinear,* or *Cartesian coordinate graph*. The basic form of this type of graph is derived by plotting figures in relation to two lines or axes.

As in Figure 13.1, these lines are drawn at right angles, the horizontal being called the *abscissal* or *X*-axis and the vertical, the *ordinal* or *Y*-axis. These two lines divide the region of the plane into four compartments called *quadrants,* which are numbered counter-clockwise. The point of intersection (*O*) of the two axes is referred to as the origin of coordinates. Measurements to the right and above *O* are positive (plus), and measurements to the left and below *O* are negative (minus). To locate any point in the plane of the two axes, measurements are made in terms of the two axes. The point *P* in Figure 13.1 has been

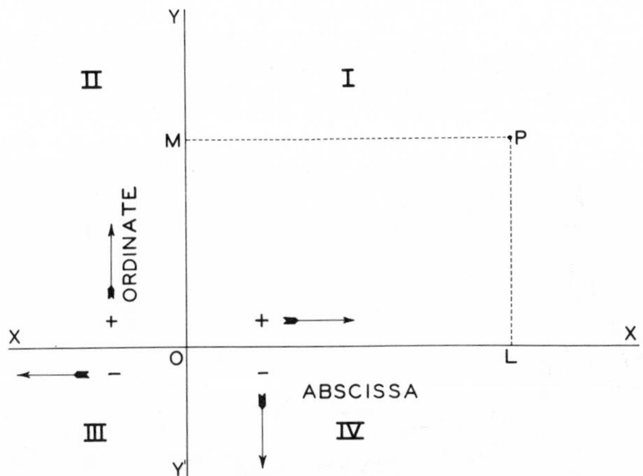

Figure 13.1 Rectangular coordinates.

located by taking a certain distance from the axis of ordinates and the axis of abscissae. The two axes can be marked off according to any desired unit beginning with the point of origin *O* as zero. In ordinary graphic presentation, quadrant *I* is the only one used. Sometimes, however, quadrant *IV* may be used to show such facts as immigration and emigration, profits and losses, and imports and exports.

Figure 13.2 shows the characteristic features of the rectangular coordinate graph as well as certain general rules for graphic presentation. It will be observed that time is represented by the *X*-axis, or axis of abscissae, and the other variable by the *Y*-axis, or axis of ordinates. The distance chosen to represent the units on the scales of the two axes is largely a matter of experimentation and judgment, but such factors as the following are always taken into consideration: 1) characteristics of the data, 2) purpose of the chart, 3) pleasing proportions, and 4) accuracy of presentation.

It will be observed further from Figure 13.2 that:[2]

1. The chart has a title, which has been placed directly above the grid. The title of the chart should be clear, concise, and simple and should generally answer the questions *what? where?* and *when?* The

[2]Several of the statements in the following summary have been taken from *Time-Series Charts: A Manual of Design and Construction,* prepared by The Committee on Standards for Graphic Presentation, The American Society of Mechanical Engineers, New York, 1938.

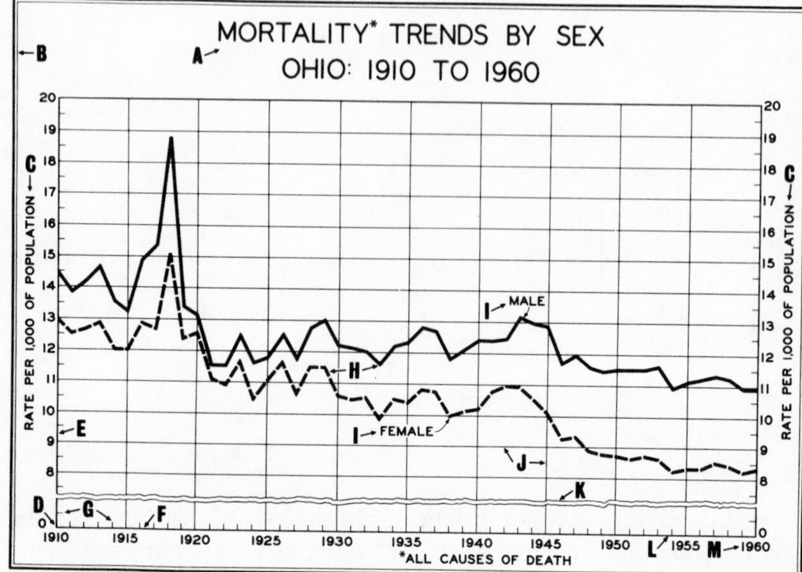

Figure 13.2 Sample chart showing essential characteristics and rules for graphic presentation. A: Title at top. B: Border—optional. C: Scale legend for Y-axis. D: Origin. E: Axis of ordinates or Y-axis. F: X-axis or axis of abscissae. G: Scale points. H: Curves differentiated—solid and dashed. I: Contiguous legend for curves. J: Grid or coordinate lines—no more should be shown than are necessary to guide the eye in reading the diagram. K: Broken line—scale not complete. L: Zero line heavier than other coordinate lines. M: Lettering reads horizontally whenever possible.

title may be drawn as part of the chart or set in type by the printer.

2. The *Y*- or ordinal axis is designated by the arrow marked with the letter *E*. The scale reads from bottom to top.
3. The arrow marked with the letter *C* refers to the scale legend. The scale legend for the ordinal axis can be placed to the left or at the top of the scale. If the chart is relatively wide, the scale legend may be placed on the right side as well, but this is not absolutely essential. Of course, the scale legend should be clear and specific.
4. The letter *G* on the chart refers to scale points for both axes. No more coordinate lines should be shown than are necessary to guide the eye in reading the diagram.

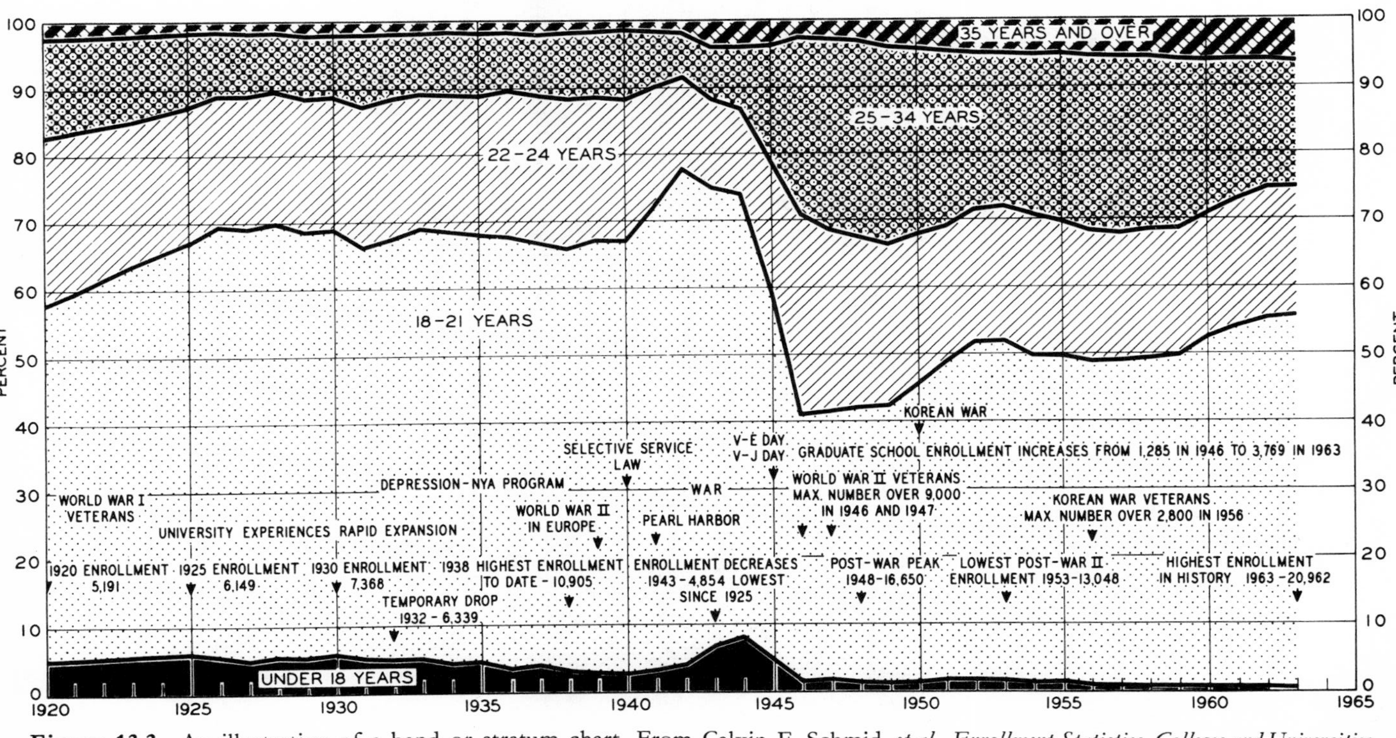

Figure 13.3 An illustration of a band or stratum chart. From Calvin F. Schmid, *et al.*, *Enrollment Statistics, Colleges and Universities, State of Washington, Fall Term:* 1963. Seattle: Washington State Census Board, 1964, p. 60.

5. The curves on the chart should be sharply distinguished from other lines on the chart. If there are more than one they should be clearly differentiated from one another by carefully drawn and distinct patterns. On Figure 13.2 one curve is shown by a full-line and the other by a dashed line. In order to avoid confusion, too many curves should not be superimposed on one grid. The size of the chart as well as the distribution of the curves in the field would naturally influence the number that might be portrayed properly.
6. Each curve on the chart should be unmistakably labeled. Generally, the most satisfactory method is to place the designation or legend contiguous to the curve. Sometimes the legend may be boxed off in one corner of the grid.
7. It is frequently desirable to indicate the plotting points on which the curves are based.
8. In every rectangular coordinate chart it is essential for the vertical zero to be placed in the field of the chart. If, however, the zero line of the vertical scale will not normally appear on the chart, the zero line should be shown by the use of a horizontal break in the grid. The break will prevent any misconceptions that might otherwise result concerning the size of the scale and also will permit larger calibrations on the scale.
9. The arrow marked with the letter *D* indicates the point of origin which was described in connection with Figure 13.1.
10. The zero lines of the scale of a chart should be distinguished from the other coordinate lines by being made a little heavier.
11. The lettering should be of sufficient size to be read clearly and should be made to read horizontally whenever possible.
12. The grid or coordinate lines are indicated by the letter *J*. Grid lines should be drawn relatively lightly and kept to a minimum. No definite rule can be specified as to the optimum number of lines, since the size and other features of the chart must be taken into consideration.
13. Figure 13.2 has a border drawn around the entire chart including the title. Whether or not a diagram should have a border is largely a matter of preference. Charts with and without borders are included in this chapter.
14. The arrow marked with the letter *L* refers to the abscissal or *X*-axis.

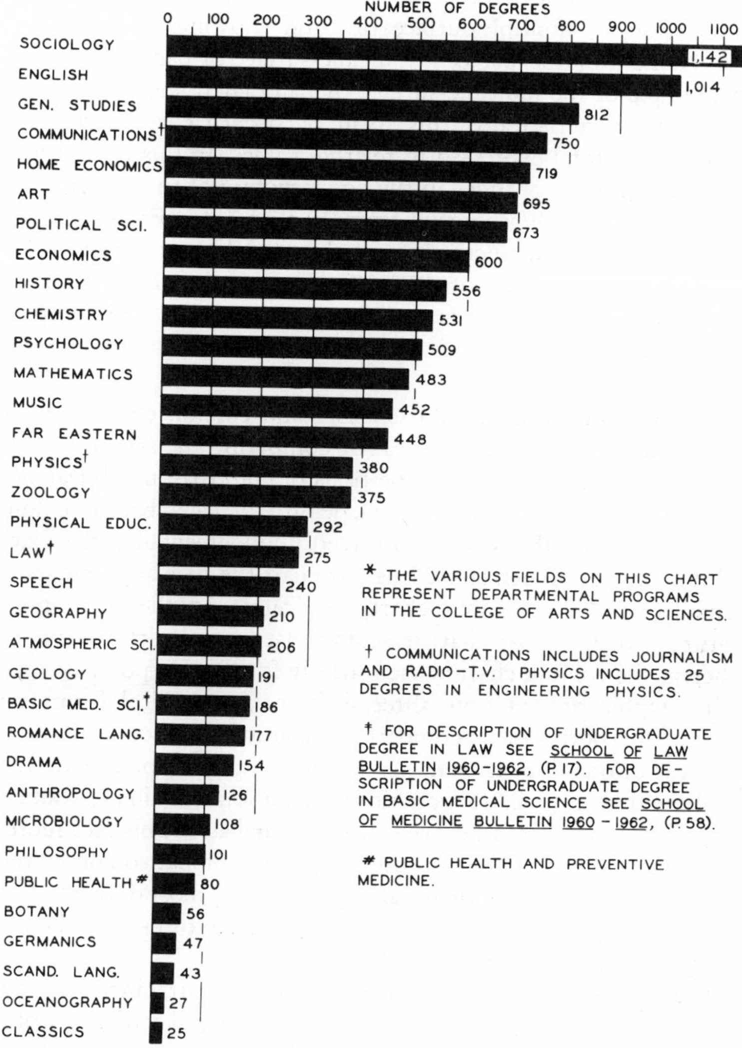

Figure 13.4 An illustration of a simple bar chart. The number of degrees is indicated not only by a scale, but also by figures placed at the end of each bar. From Calvin F. Schmid, *et al., Temporal Analysis of Institutional Patterns, University of Washington:* 1930 *to* 1970. Seattle: University of Washington, 1963, Chapter V.

Surface or band chart. Another common form of the rectilinear coordinate graph is the band, surface, or stratum chart. There are four basic forms of this type of chart: 1) single-surface or silhouette, 2) staircase, 3) multiple-surface or band showing numerical values, and 4) one hundred per cent multiple-surface or band.[3] Figure 13.3 is an example of the multiple-surface or band chart showing percentage values. Characteristically, this form of surface chart portrays components of a total expressed in relative values. In this illustration, the basic data portray changes in the age-structure of the student body at the University of Washington from 1920 to 1963. Each age-group is represented by a distinctively cross-hatched band or stratum on the chart. A special feature of this chart is numerous explanatory notes interpreting specific trends and fluctuations in the age composition of the student body.

Bar and column charts. Bar and column charts are simple, flexible, and effective techniques for comparing the size of coordinate values or of parts of a total. The basis of comparison is linear or one-dimensional. This means that the length of each bar or column is proportional to the value portrayed. Fundamentally, the bar and column are very much alike. In a bar chart the bars are arranged horizontally and in a column chart, vertically. Another distinguishing feature is that the bar chart is seldom used for depicting time series, whereas the column chart is used mainly for that purpose.

In graphic presentation, three different geometrical forms can be utilized for purposes of comparing magnitudes of coordinate items: 1) linear or one-dimensional, 2) areal or two-dimensional, and 3) cubic or three-dimensional. In graphic presentation the simplest and most exact comparisons can be made on a linear basis. This fact represents the real advantage of bar and column charts. Comparison of the relative sizes of areas is more difficult and of volumes, most difficult. Accordingly, where possible the use of areal and cubic forms should be avoided in graphic presentation.

There are several kinds of bar and column charts, including simple, subdivided, bilateral, step, area, as well as special variations of these types. All have one thing in common, namely, the length of the bar or column is proportional to the size or magnitude portrayed. The most widely used bar and column chart is the simple type. The simple

[3]Calvin F. Schmid, *Handbook of Graphic Presentation, op. cit.,* pp. 69–72.

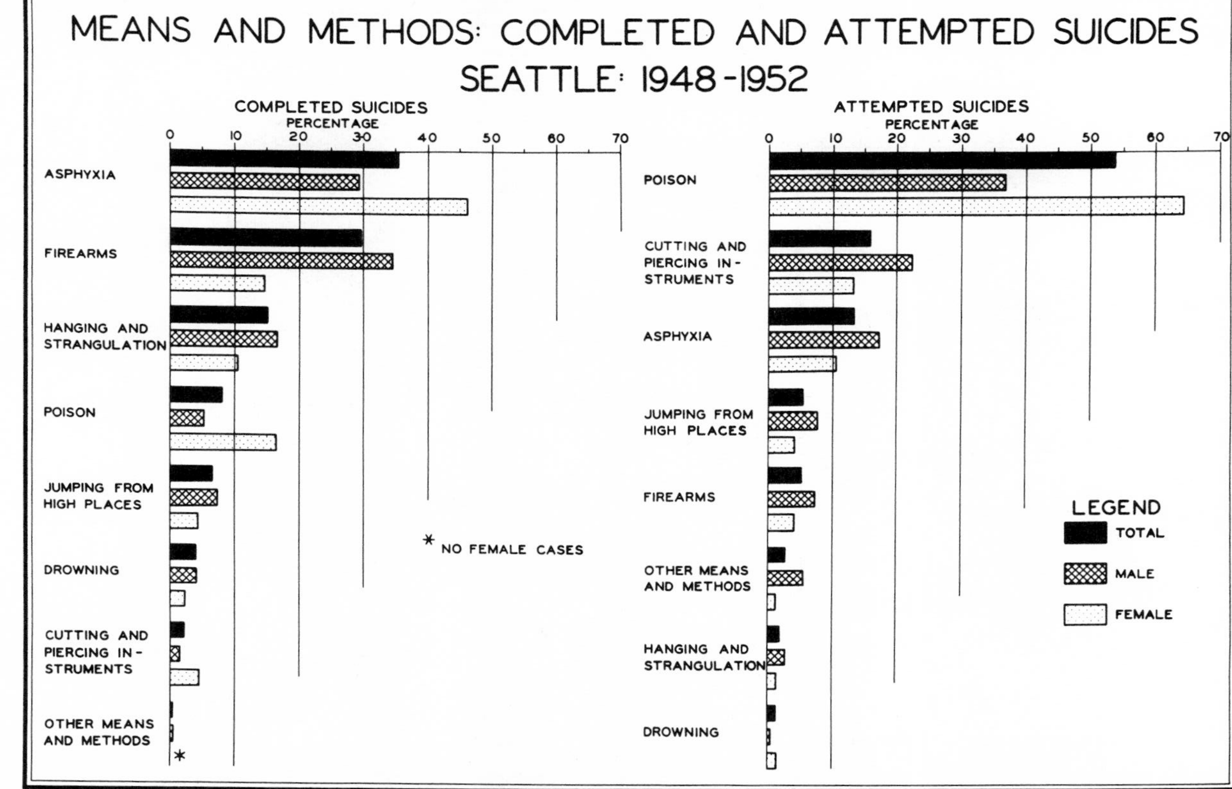

Figure 13.5 An example of the grouped bar chart. From Calvin F. Schmid and Maurice D. Van Arsdol, "Completed and Attempted Suicides: A Comparative Analysis," *American Sociological Review,* XX,273–283.

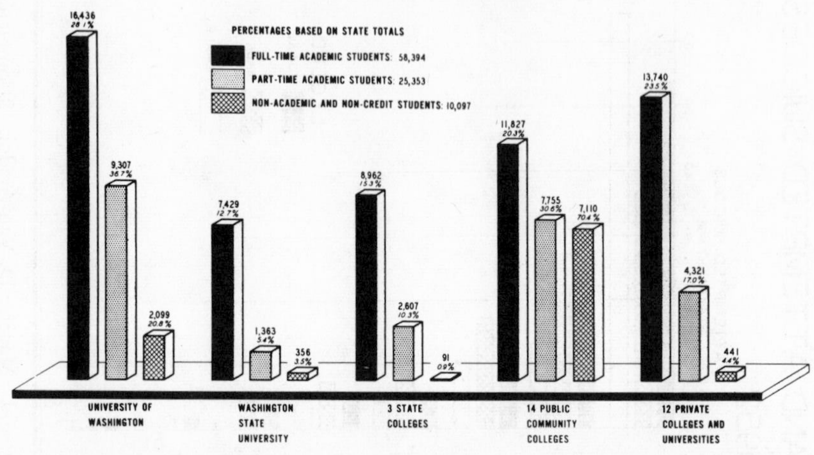

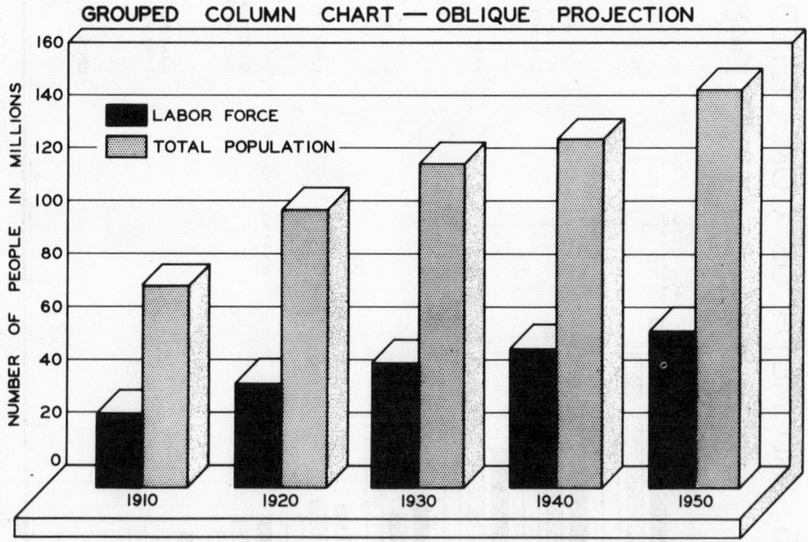

Figure 13.6 Illustration of a grouped column chart. The chart at the top is drawn in conventional form, while the one below is drawn in oblique projection, giving an illusion of three dimensions. Charts drawn in some form of projection—axonometric, oblique, or perspective—reflect depth and other picturelike qualities which possess popular appeal. From Calvin F. Schmid, "What Price Pictorial Charts?" *Esdatistica,* XIV, 12–25.

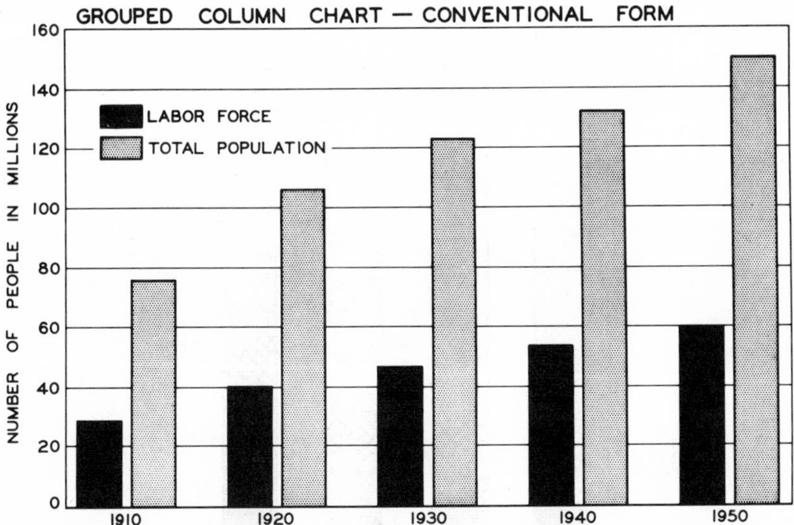

Figure 13.7 Another illustration of a grouped column chart drawn in oblique projection. Note hatching scheme and legend for differentiating categories. From Calvin F. Schmid, *et al., Enrollment Statistics, College and Universities, State of Washington, Fall Term:* 1963. Seattle: Washington State Census Board, 1964, p. 10.

bar chart is illustrated by Figure 13.4 and the grouped bar chart, by Figure 13.5.

Subdivided bar and column charts not only show variations in total values but also components of the respective totals. This breakdown is accomplished by subdividing the bars and columns and differentiating the component parts by cross-hatching patterns (Figure 13.8). Another type is the bilateral or two-way bar or column chart. Bars or columns extend in two directions from a zero or base line. They may show positive and negative values or the comparison of two related categories (Figure 13.9). Limitation of space precludes a more detailed discussion of other more specialized types of bar and column charts.

In constructing bar and column charts careful consideration should be given to the following standards and principles of design:

1. The bars should be arranged in some systematic order usually according to magnitude, starting with the largest. In a column chart, where a time series is portrayed, the columns, of course, should be in chronological order.
2. The width of the bars and columns as well as the spacing between

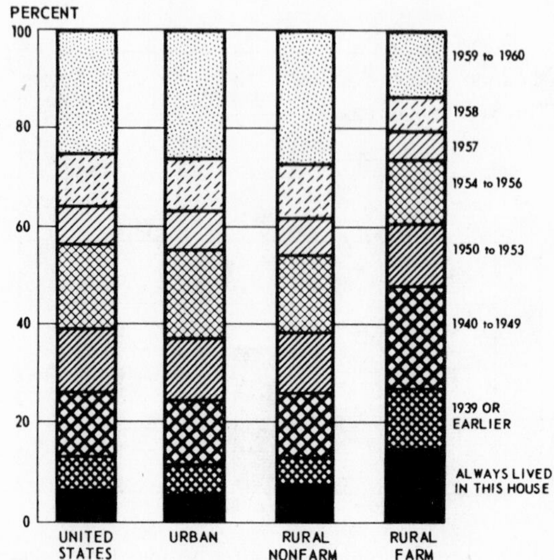

Figure 13.8 Hundred per cent column chart. From United States Bureau of the Census, 1960 Census of Population, *Characteristics of the Population,* United States Summary, Part 1 (Washington, D. C.: U. S. G. P. O., 1963), p. S-45.

them possess no special significance. Needless to say, for any particular chart the bars and columns should be of uniform width and properly adapted to the over-all size, proportion, and other features of the chart. More specifically, in a bar chart the width of the bars should be determined by a) the amount of space available, b) the number of bars, and c) pleasing proportions. The spacing between the bars should be from one-half to three-fourths of the width of a bar. Frequently, in a column chart the spacing between columns may be much wider than between the bars in a bar chart.

3. Customarily the bars and columns are blacked in although hatching or stippling may be used.
4. As a general practice a scale should be included in every bar or column chart. The number of intervals on the scale should be adequate for measuring distances but not too numerous to cause confusion. The intervals should be indicated in round numbers, preferably in such units as 5's, 10's, 25's, 50's and 100's. The scale of bar and column charts always should begin with zero, and never

be broken. There are, of course, scale lines, scale points, scale numerals, and a scale legend.

5. Bar and column charts like other charts, should have titles. The title for a bar or column chart should be placed at the top and conform to the same standards indicated in connection with the discussion of rectangular coordinate charts.
6. The stubs or designations for the various categories of a bar chart should be clearly indicated to the left of the vertical base line.

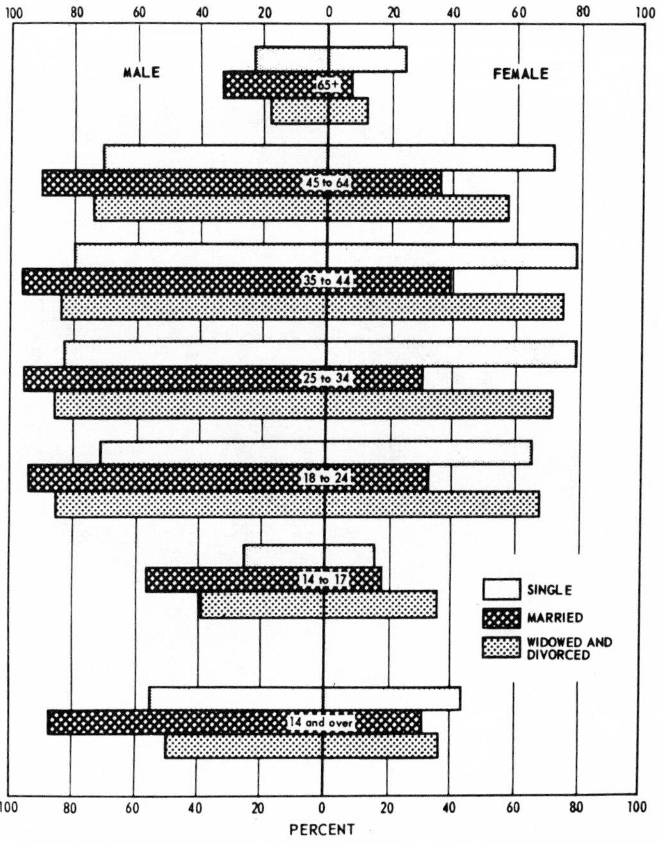

Figure 13.9 An example of a bilateral bar chart. From the United States Bureau of the Census, 1960 Census of Population, *Characteristics of the Population,* United States Summary, Part 1 (Washington, D. C.: U. S. G. P. O., 1963), p. S-57.

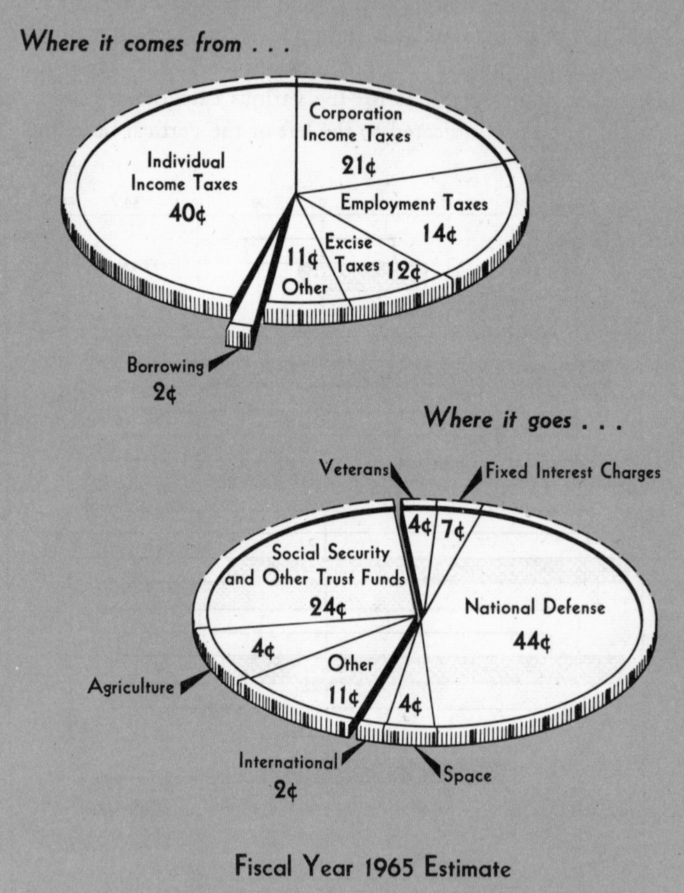

Figure 13.10 Three different graphic forms for comparing components of a total. A: Pie chart. B: One hundred per cent bar chart. C: Simple bar chart. Data represent number of children among a total of 5,553 divorces granted in the state of Iowa in 1952. Chart prepared from data in *1952 Annual Report* of Division of Vital Statistics, Iowa State Department of Health.

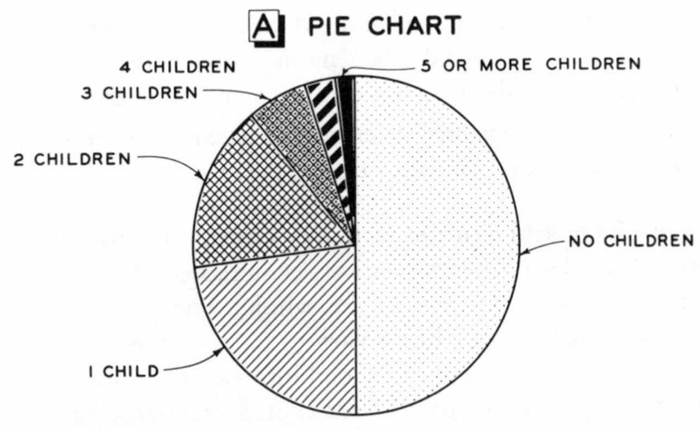

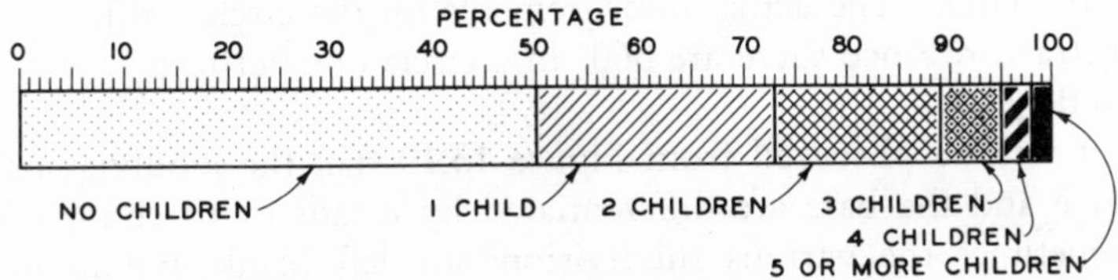

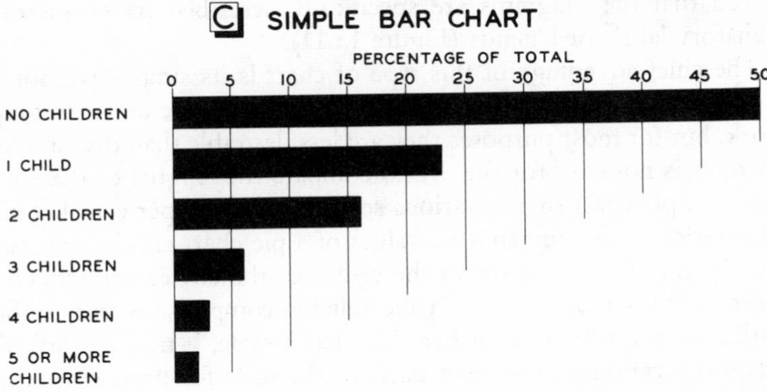

Figure 13.11 Pie chart drawn in axonometric projection in order to emphasize the three dimensional character of the dollar symbol. From United States Bureau of Budget, *The Budget in Brief,* 1964 (Washington, D. C.: U. S. G. P. O., 1963).

7. Sometimes the numerical data upon which a bar or column chart is based are shown on the chart. As a general practice, however, it is much better to include the data in a table entirely separated from the chart in order to avoid confusion and misinterpretation.
8. Whenever explanatory statements or legends are necessary they can be placed to the side of, or below, the main body of the chart.

Pie chart and component bar chart. In both the pie and component bar charts the emphasis is centered on the subdivisions of a geometric form in relation to the whole. The pie chart is a circle divided into sectors representing various parts of the whole. Similarly, the component bar chart is subdivided into two or more parts to show proportions of the whole or 100 per cent. In constructing a pie chart the first step is to convert the data for the various categories into percentages. The next step is to multiply the percentages for each component by 3.6 in order to derive the number of degrees for each sector of the circle. The actual measurements on the circle are made with a protractor. Since there are 360° in a circle one per cent = 360/100 = 3.6 degrees.

It will be observed from Figure 13.10 that the subdivisions of the circle and the bars are differentiated by means of hatching schemes. Sometimes the various subdivisions are left blank, but in order to avoid optical illusions as well as confusion in interpretation, it is more satisfactory to cross-hatch or shade the diagrams. It will also be observed that the diagrams are specifically described by means of explanatory labels or legends (Figure 13.11).

The chief advantage of this type of chart is its simplicity. Both the pie chart and the 100 per cent bar chart possess some utility in graphic work, but for most purposes they are less desirable than the simple bar chart. It is not easy for the eye to compare the lengths of the various arcs of a pie chart or the various sections of a 100 per cent bar chart. Theoretically the comparative values of a pie chart are the arcs cut on the circle by the angles from the center of the circle, but actually the areas of the sectors tend to make reliable comparisons very difficult. Although the 100 per cent bar chart has a scale, it may be difficult to relate the various component parts to the scale for precise interpretation, such as can be done with a simple bar chart where the separate bars extend from a common base line.

It also will be observed from Figure 13.10 that the simple bar chart can be used to depict component relations. In fact, because of its

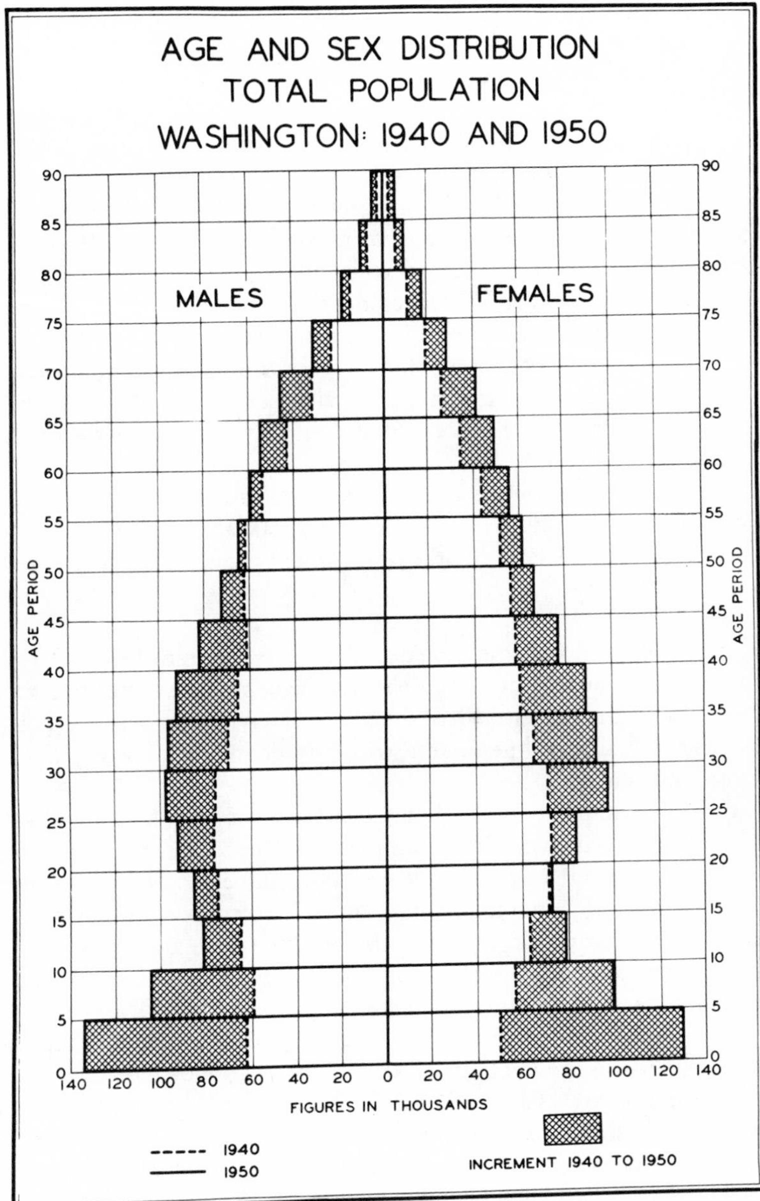

Figure 13.12 An age and sex pyramid. Chart prepared from original data published by the United States Bureau of the Census.

emphasis on one-dimensional comparisons and because of its common base line, it is superior for many purposes to either the pie chart or the one hundred per cent bar chart.

Age and sex pyramid. Another type of chart similar to the bar chart is the age and sex pyramid or triangle. The age and sex pyramid is actually a double histogram with the bars arranged horizontally instead of vertically. A common base line extends vertically through the center of the chart for both sets of bars. The vertical axis always represents age. Wherever possible, equal intervals should be used. The horizontal axis represents the number or percentage of the total population in each age interval according to sex. The male sex is usually placed on the left and the female sex on the right of the center line. The figures on the horizontal axis may indicate percentages or absolute numbers.

Figure 13.12 shows the age and sex composition of the population of the state of Washington for 1940 and 1950. Increases in population between 1940 and 1950 for the various age groups are represented by a shading scheme.

Area and volume charts. As a rule, diagrams involving areal and cubic comparisons should be avoided, because instead of simplifying the comparison desired, they are likely to confuse it. It is extremely difficult to differentiate with any degree of accuracy the sizes of areas or cubes.

Figure 13.13 presents a comparison of lines or bars, areas, and solids. The lines or bars vary in one dimension only (length), areas in two dimensions (length and breadth), and volumes in three dimensions (length, breadth, and thickness). In each form the smaller figure is one-half the larger. From this simple illustration it is apparent that the relative numerical values of lines or bars can be more reliably estimated than those of either a surface or a solid.

Sometimes comparisons of areas and solids are further complicated when the forms are irregular in shape. Such is the case of certain types of pictorial charts. Charts of this type are frequently used in popular articles on social and economic questions and for propagandistic purposes. In comparing the sizes of two standing armies, for example, pictures of soldiers have been used. If the standing army of one country is twice that of another, how large should the respective symbols be? Are the comparisons to be made on the basis of height or area? If the first symbol is two inches high, should the second be twice as large or twice as high? In order to keep the symbols in proper proportion, a doubling of the height would mean a doubling of the width as well, so that the area of the second symbol would actually be four times that of the first, and the volume of the second would be eight times that of the first. In order to maintain the one-dimensional basis of comparison, the width of the second symbol could be kept the same as the first and only the height doubled, but this would result in a grotesquely elongated and unrealistic soldier. Under the circumstances, in order to avoid distortion or misrepresentation, it might be assumed that the proper solution of a problem of this kind is to reconstruct the symbols on the basis of a more consistent and comparable criterion, such as area or volume. This solution would be logically correct, but from the standpoint of visual impression, comparisons of pictorial symbols on the basis either of area or of volume would be quite incomprehensible. The best advice is to avoid pictorial charts involving areal or cubic comparisons.

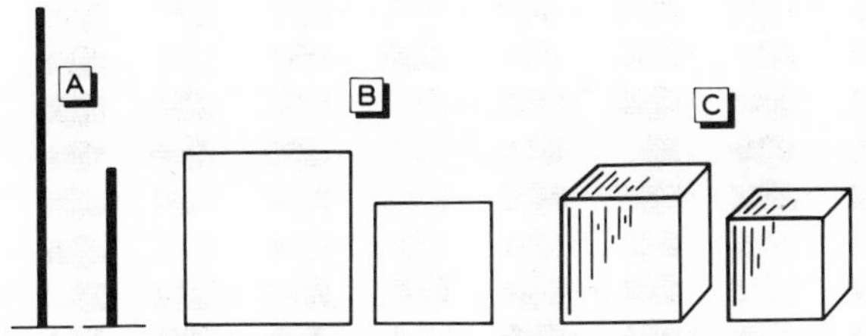

Figure 13.13 The use of geometric forms for comparing sizes. A: lines. B: areas. C: volumes.

Pictorial unit charts. On the other hand, pictorial charts of the one-dimensional type, if used with care and discrimination, are effective and acceptable for social science reports, especially where popular appeal is to be made. Pictorial charts of this type have had wide acceptance and deserve an important place in the field of graphic presentation. Beginning in the early 1920's in Vienna, Dr. Otto Neurath has been largely responsible for the development of this newer type of pictorial statistics. During the latter 1920's and early 1930's Dr. Neurath was director of the *Gesellschafts und Wirtschaftsmuseum* in Vienna

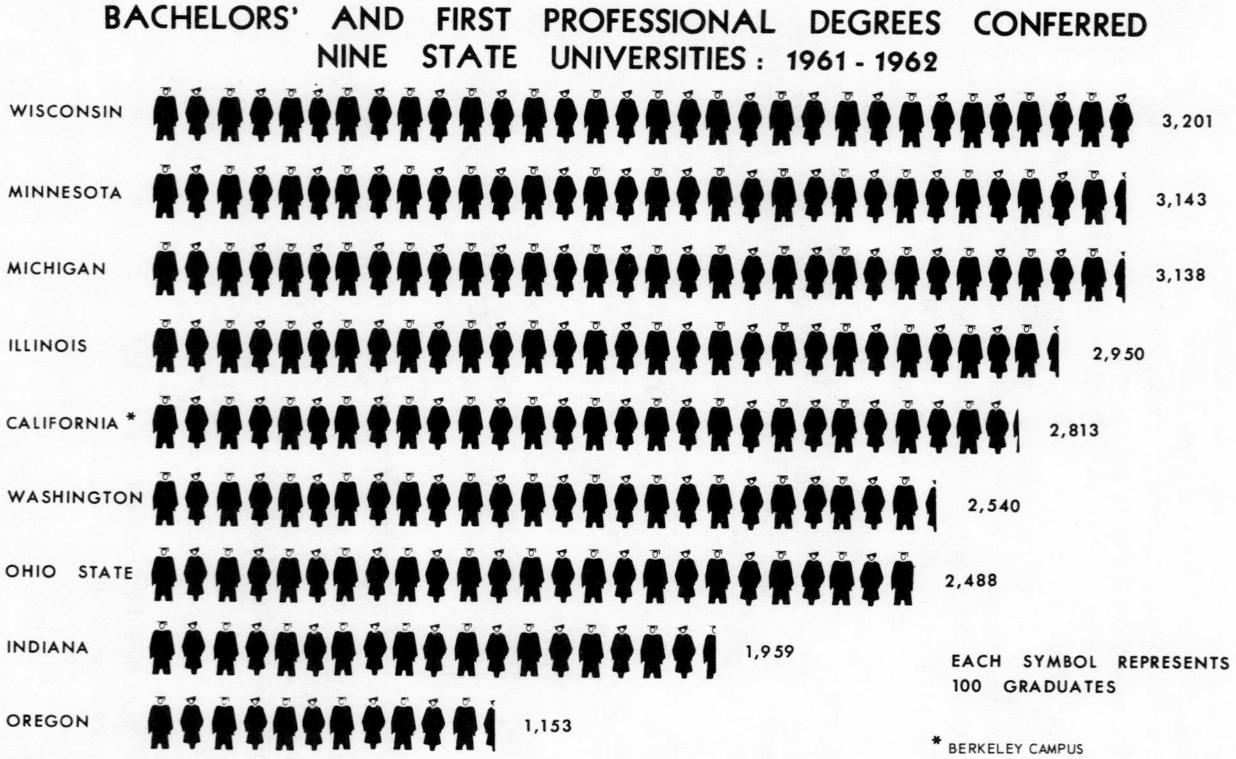

Figure 13.14 An illustration of a pictorial unit chart. Each symbol indicates one hundred graduates. The basic graphic form represented by this illustration is the simple bar chart. Chart prepared from original data published by the United States Office of Education.

where he developed many pictographic techniques as well as the ideas of a universal "visual language."

The basic type of pictorial charts developed by Neurath and others is very much like the simple bar graph already discussed, but the units are represented by pictorial symbols instead of points on a scale. Each pictorial unit represents a certain value in the same way that a division on the scale of a bar chart represents a given value. Comparisons in both instances are in terms of one dimension only—length. Of course, there are many variations of this basic type of chart as well as combinations with other geometric forms (Figure 13.14).

In developing a pictorial unit chart the following basic rules should be observed:

1. The symbols should be self-explanatory. If the chart is concerned with ships, the symbol should be an outline of a ship.
2. All the symbols on the chart should represent a definite unit of value. Each symbol usually represents a convenient sum of individuals.
3. The chart should be made as simple and clear as possible. The number of facts presented should be kept at a minimum.
4. Pictographs should give only an over-all picture; they should not show minute details.
5. Only comparisons should be charted. Isolated facts in themselves cannot be effectively presented by this method.
6. There are many facts that by their very nature cannot be shown pictorially. This is true of large bodies of data that require more refined and elaborate techniques of analysis.[4]

Organization and flow charts. Unlike the other forms of graphic presentation discussed in this chapter, the typical organization chart is not used to analyze or interpret statistical facts. Nevertheless, this type of chart possesses definite utility for certain kinds of research and administrative problems. Characteristically the organization chart is used to present structural forms and relationships. An example of the organization chart is shown in Figure 13.15. This chart presents in simple graphic form a considerable body of information relating to

[4]See Rudolph Modley, *How to Use Pictorial Statistics,* pp. 12–17. Harper & Row, Publishers, 1937; Rudolph Modley, Dyno Lowenstein, *et al., Pictographs and Graphs,* pp. 24–28. Harper & Row, Publishers, 1952.

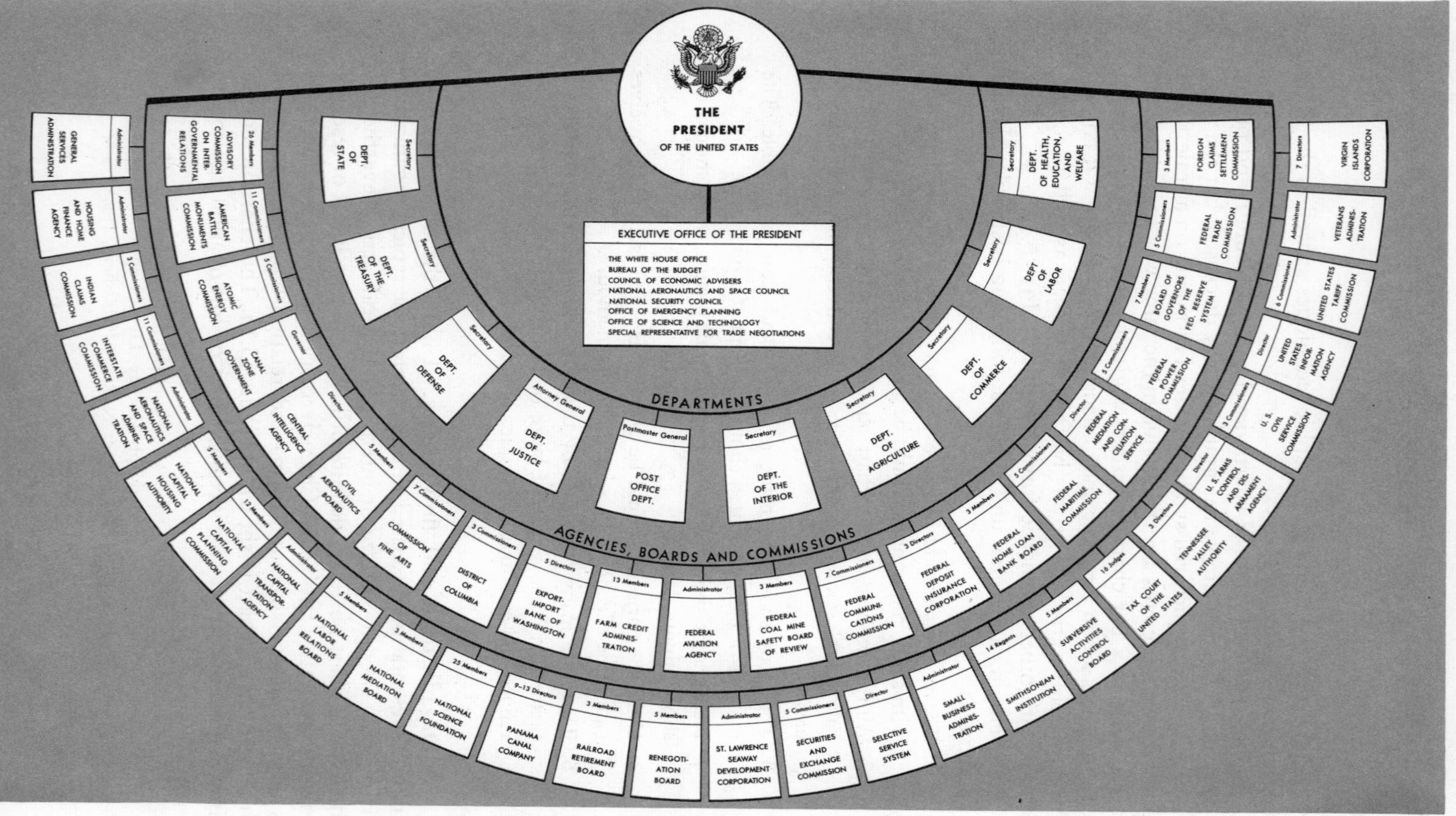

Figure 13.15 Organization Chart. From United States Bureau of the Budget, *The Budget in Brief, 1964* (Washington, D. C.: U. S. G. P. O., 1963)

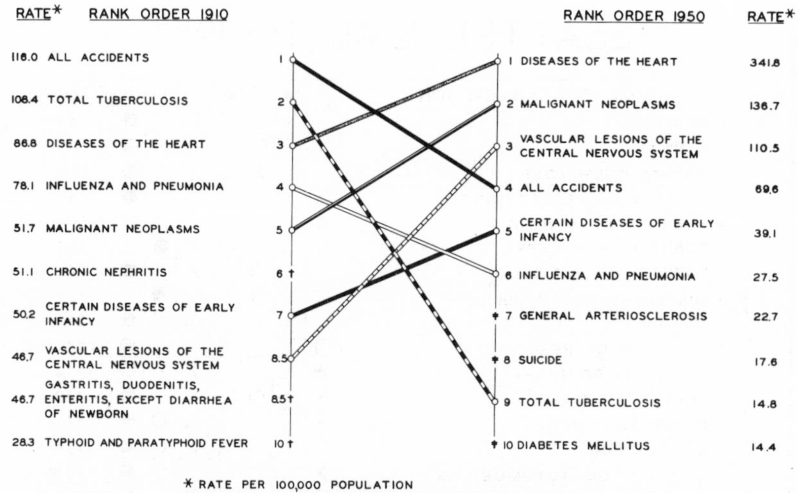

Figure 13.16 A ranking chart. From Calvin F. Schmid, *et al.*, *Mortality Trends in the State of Washington* (Seattle: Washington State Census Board, 1955), p. 42.

bureaus, departments, boards, and commissions comprising the executive branch of the United States Government as well as their organizational relationships.

The flow chart emphasizes process or movement rather than mere structure or organization. Flow charts are used to present both statistical and non-statistical data.

Ranking charts. The purpose of ranking charts is to portray the position of certain items or categories, usually on the basis of magnitude or frequency. Emphasis is placed on rank-order or rating of various items, rather than on their values. Figure 13.16 shows the ranking of the ten major causes of death in the state of Washington in 1910 and in 1950. Figure 13.17 portrays the daily rank-order of 33 different crimes in the city of Seattle for the three-year period, 1949–51.

DAILY DISTRIBUTION OF CRIME OFFENSES KNOWN TO POLICE SEATTLE: 1949 TO 1951

CRIME CLASSIFICATION	S	M	T	W	T	F	S	TOTAL
1 MURDER		\		◎	X		●	44
2 RAPE	\		◎			X	●	73
3 CARNAL KNOWLEDGE			X	◎		\	●	115
4 ROBBERY OF PEDESTRIANS	X	\	◎				●	146
5 ROBBERY IN A VEHICLE	X	\				◎	●	684
6 ROBBERY OF BUSINESS (ALL TYPES)	\	◎		◎	X	●		387
7 ROBBERY OF RESIDENCE		\	◎		X		●	201
8 MISCELLANEOUS ROBBERIES	X	\	◎			●		121
9 ASSAULT		\			◎	X	●	383
10 BURGLARY OF RESIDENCE	◎	\		X			●	3,841
11 BURGLARY OF NON-RESIDENCE	●	\			X		◎	4,659
12 POCKET PICKING	\	X	◎				●	329
13 PURSE SNATCHING	X				\	◎	●	271
14 SHOPLIFTING	\			X		◎	●	934
15 THEFT FROM AUTOMOBILES	X	\				◎	●	3,783
16 THEFT OF AUTOMOBILE ACCESSORIES	◎	\			X		●	3,059
17 BICYCLE THEFT	\		X			●	◎	2,046
18 MISCELLANEOUS LARCENIES	\			◎		X	●	4,738*
19 THEFT FROM PERSONS		\	X			◎	●	478
20 AUTOMOBILE THEFT		\	X			◎	●	4,080
21 DRAWING DANGEROUS WEAPONS	X	\		◎	\		●	129
22 ALL OTHER ASSAULTS	X	\		X		◎	●	1,030
23 BUNCO, CONFIDENCE, SWINDLING	\	●				◎	X	144
24 CHECK FRAUDS	\				X	◎	●	3,020
25 EMBEZZLEMENT	X	\			●		◎	42
26 FALSE IMPERSONATION	\			●	X		◎	436
27 UNSPECIFIED FRAUDS	\	\	\	●	\	◎	◎	59
28 PEEPING TOM	X	◎	X	\	●	●	X	70
29 ANNOYING WOMEN AND CHILDREN		\	●	X			◎	243
30 SODOMY	\	X				●	◎	146
31 OBSCENE PHONE CALLS	\		◎	●			X	65
32 OTHER PERVERSIONS	X			\	●		◎	121
33 INDECENT LIBERTIES		◎		\	X		●	190

* TWO-YEAR PERIOD ONLY

FREQUENCY

\ LOWEST
X SECOND LOWEST
● HIGHEST
◎ SECOND HIGHEST

Figure 13.17 Another illustration of a ranking chart. From Calvin F. Schmid, *Major Crimes in Seattle* (Unpublished ms.).

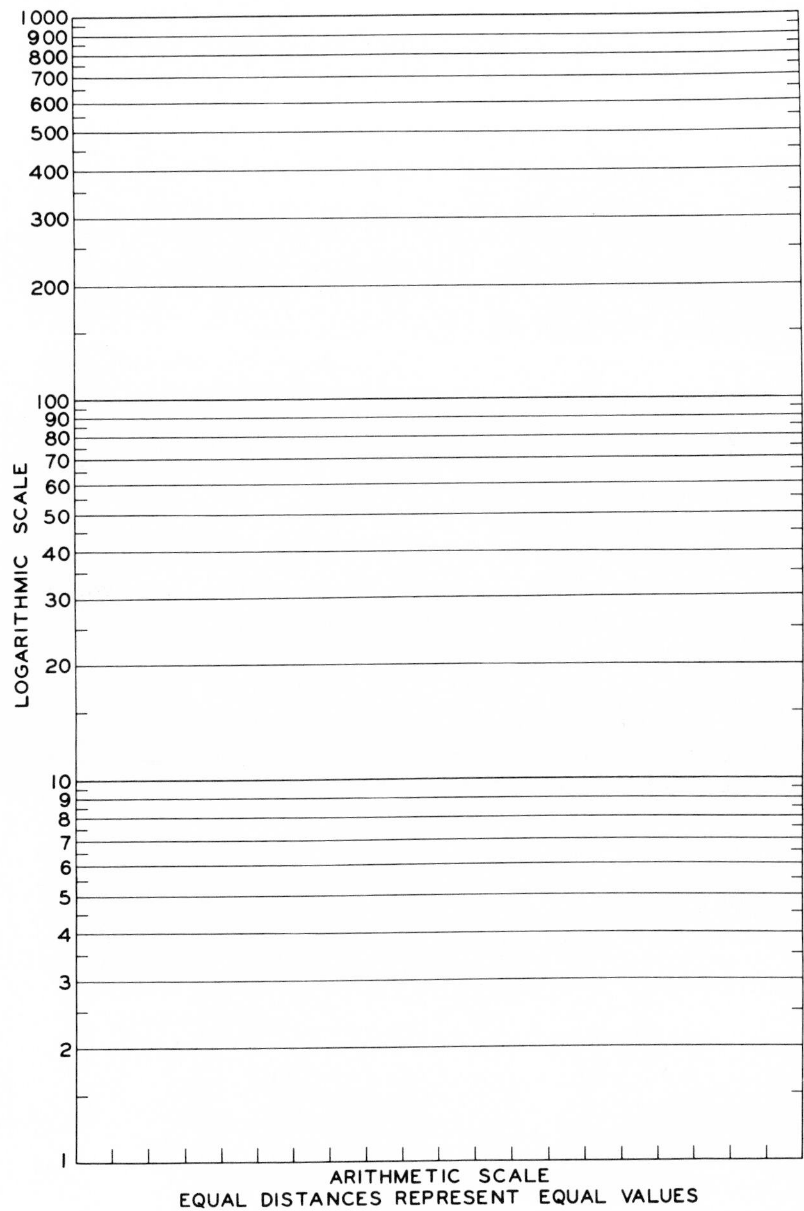

Figure 13.18 Semilogarithmic ruling.

Semilogarithmic charts. Because of its simplicity, accuracy, and adaptability, the semilogarithmic chart is of the greatest importance in social research.[5] In general the semilogarithmic scale is superior to either the natural or the percentage scale, for it can show very clearly both relative and absolute changes. In fact, it combines the advantages of both the natural and percentage scales without the disadvantages of either.

To the beginning student the term "logarithmic" may sound formidable, but a knowledge of logarithms is not essential in order to understand and use this type of chart. Semilogarithmic paper may be purchased already ruled. With a little practice this type of chart can be used effectively. The principles of constructing and interpreting these charts are relatively easy to understand.

The essential features of the semilogarithmic chart are a logarithmic vertical scale and an arithmetic horizontal scale (or *vice versa*). Therefore the chart is called semilogarithmic or sometimes arith-log. In the arithmetic scale equal spaces indicate equal values and the divisions are determined accordingly. The logarithmic scale, on the other hand, is ruled entirely differently, since the divisions are based on logarithms. Figure 13.18 shows a three-cycle semilogarithmic chart.

1. The vertical axis consists of one or more sets of rulings graduated in accordance with series of logarithmic values of 1 to 10.
2. Each complete set of rulings is referred to as a deck or a cycle. Theoretically a chart may have an indefinite number of decks or cycles. Figure 13.18 has three cycles. In practice more than five cycles are seldom used.
3. The rulings for each deck are the same but the scale values change from one to the other. For example, if the first cycle runs from 1 to 10, the adjacent deck above will vary from 10 to 100, the third from 100 to 1,000, the fourth from 1,000 to 10,000, the fifth from 10,000 to 100,000, and so forth. On the other hand, the adjacent cycle below the one from 1 to 10 would vary from .1 to 1.0. The logarithmic scale can thus be extended either upward or downward indefinitely.
4. No matter how far the logarithmic scale is extended downward, zero is never reached. There is no zero line on a semilogarithmic scale.

[5]For a more detailed discussion of semilogarithmic charts, see Calvin F. Schmid, *Handbook of Graphic Presentation, op. cit.*, pp. 109–132.

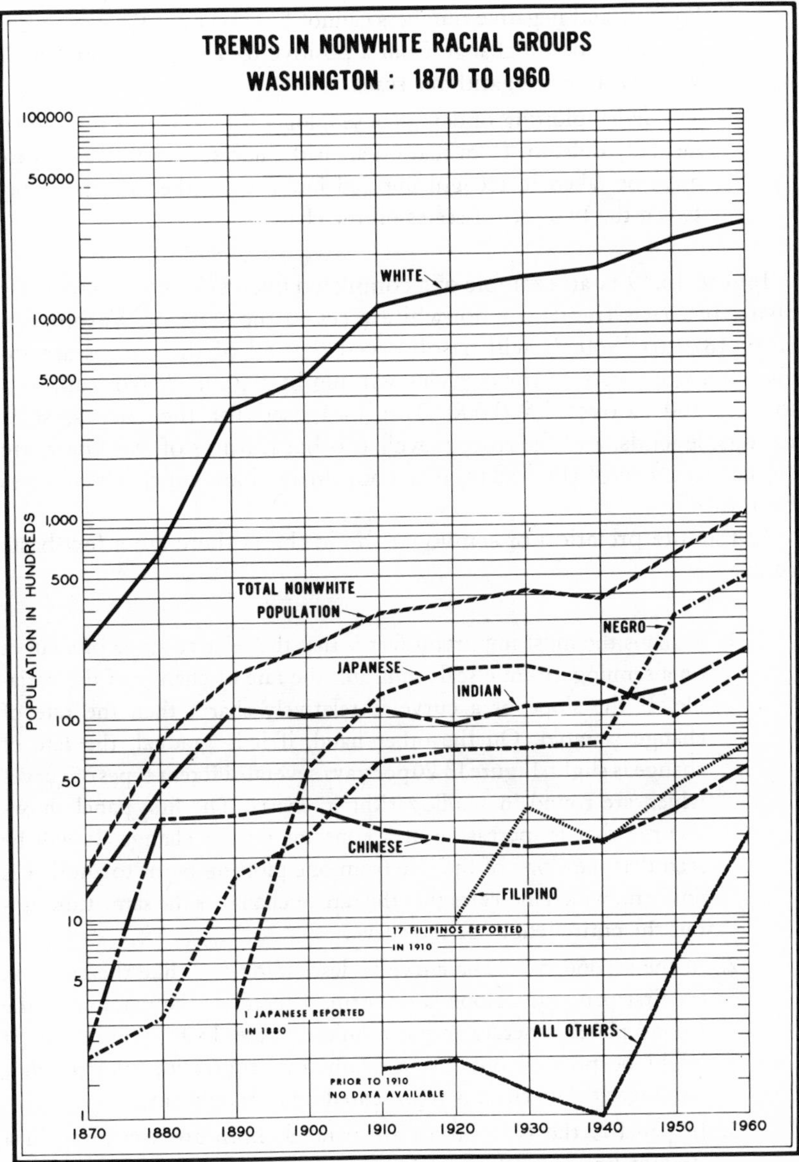

Figure 13.19 Illustration of semilogarithmic chart. Note especially range of values. The eight curves are differentiated from one another by distinctive patterns. From Calvin F. Schmid and Charles E. Nobbe, "Socio-economic Differentials among Nonwhite Races in the State of Washington," *Demography,* II, 549–566.

5. Positive and negative numbers cannot be shown on the same grid. There can be no change from a positive to a negative number or vice versa on a logarithmic scale.
6. The actual plotting of data on a semilogarithmic chart is not fundamentally different from that on an arithmetic scale. Of course, care must be taken in recognizing and interpreting the differences between the two sets of scales on the chart.

Figure 13.19 is an example of a completed five-cycle semilogarithmic chart. It shows trends for nonwhite races in the state of Washington from 1870 to 1960. It will be observed that all of the curves are included within two or three cycles varying in magnitude from approximately 100 to over 2,500,000. The lines used for the curves, scale rulings, legends, and the title, as well as other features of this chart, are similar to those of the rectangular coordinate chart which already has been discussed.

In the interpretation of semilogarithmic charts there are a few basic rules:

1. Perhaps the most important fact is that the relative slope of a curve on a semilogarithmic scale indicates the rate of change of the variable. If the slope of a curve is relatively sharp, then the rate of change is rapid. On the other hand, if it is gradual, the rate of change is slight. Figure 13.20 portrays several different types of curves which are found in semilogarithmic charts. The first panel shows a curve that is increasing at a constant rate of change. It will be seen that the slope of the line from one plotting point to another is uniform, which indicates that the rate of change is the same throughout the entire length of the curve.
2. In the second panel the curve is descending and, like the curve in the first panel, the slope is uniform. Therefore, the variable in the second panel is decreasing at a uniform rate. In this connection it might be pointed out that a geometric progression plotted on a semilogarithmic chart is represented by a straight line.
3. In panel *C* the two curves are parallel. Both are ascending in a straight line. The slope of both is identical. This means that both variables are increasing at the same rate of change.
4. The curve in panel *D* is increasing at a decreasing rate of change. The curve moves upward from left to right, but the relative slope

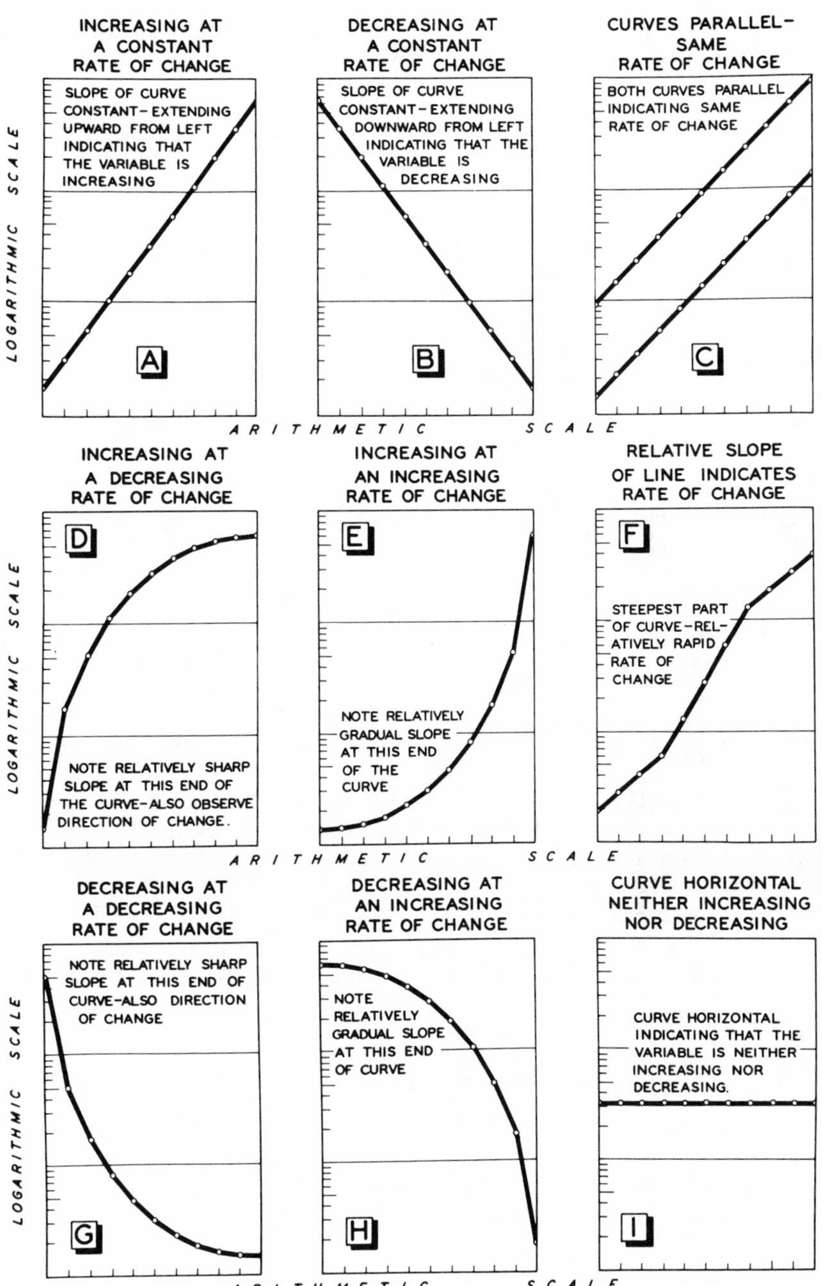

Figure 13.20 Curves illustrating the interpretation of semilogarithmic charts.

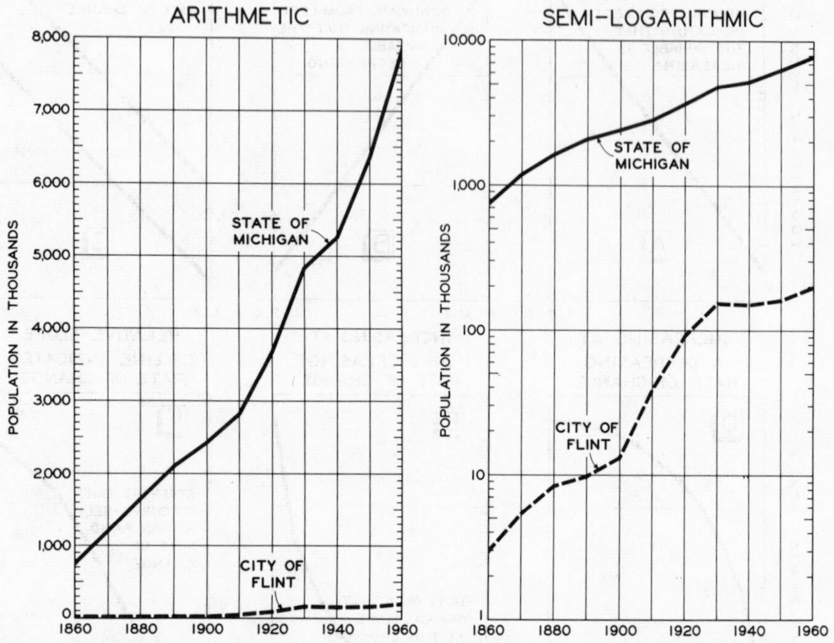

Figure 13.21 Arithmetic and semilogarithmic scales compared. Based on original data from published reports of the United States Bureau of the Census.

of the line tends to diminish toward the upper limit. This fact is apparent when the angle of the curve for the first two plotting points is compared with the angle of the curve for the last two plotting points.

5. The curve in the next panel is increasing at an increasing rate of change. Again, the comparative steepness of different portions of the curve reflects the comparative rates of increase.
6. The curve in panel *F* emphasizes more clearly and simply what has already been said: that the slope of the curve is indicative of the rate of change. The middle portion of this curve shows the most pronounced ratio of increase.
7. The curve in panel *G* is decreasing at a decreasing rate, which can be seen very clearly by the angles of different portions of the curve.
8. The curve in the next panel is decreasing, but at an increasing rate.
9. When a curve is parallel to the base line, it is neither increasing nor decreasing.

The interpretation and significance of the semilogarithmic chart can be further elucidated by comparison with the rectilinear coordinate chart. Figure 13.21 illustrates the differences between the rectilinear and the semilogarithmic graphs as well as the superiority of the latter. The curves in both panels represent the growth of populations of the city of Flint and the entire state of Michigan.

An examination of both sets of curves clearly shows that the rectilinear scale conceals and distorts the rate of change of these two series. The conclusion one naturally draws from the arithmetic chart is that the rate of growth is greater for the state than for the city. The slope of the curve for the state is very sharp and definite, whereas the slope of the curve for the city of Flint is very gradual. Since, however, the figures for the entire state are relatively so large, the changes are greatly exaggerated on the arithmetic scale. By contrast, the semilogarithmic chart reliably indicates rates of change regardless of the absolute size of the figures. Actually the overall rate of population growth from 1860 to 1960 has been noticeably greater for the city of Flint than for the entire state of Michigan. Moreover, the relative ratio of change from one census to another for each of the curves is clearly shown on the semilogarithmic chart.

Maps

A very important tool in social research is the map. The utility of the map is not limited merely to the graphic portrayal of facts. Maps are often indispensable in locating problems, verifying hypotheses, analyzing data, and discovering hidden facts and relationships.

Our primary interest in discussing maps is to describe their functions and applications as well as their limitations in social research. Very little space will be devoted to the actual mechanics of drawing maps. The present survey will be confined largely to the following fundamental types: 1) base map, 2) spot map, 3) cross-hatched map, and 4) maps with one or more types of graphic forms superimposed, such as bars, columns, curves, flow diagrams, or pictorial symbols. (Isoline maps will be discussed in a subsequent chapter, "Research Techniques in Human Ecology.") All of these fundamental types are capable of wide variation and adaptation for special purposes.

Base maps. Of the several types of maps used in social research the base map is perhaps the most useful. The main distinguishing characteristic is the underlying facts of the physical and social environment which it portrays. Maps of this kind provide an important background or framework for primary data which are superimposed upon it, and in this way greatly elucidate as well as facilitate analysis of the spatial patterning of social phenomena.[6] In the construction of a base map a careful selection is made of the features of the physical and man-made environment which are of fundamental importance in conditioning the spatial distribution of social phenomena. These facts are then clearly indicated on the base maps by means of coloring, cross-hatching, or some other suitable technique. Characteristics of the physical environment which are often included on maps of this kind are rivers, lakes, ravines, prominent hills, and other topographical features. Some of the factors of the cultural environment which possess special ecological significance are railroads, railway yards, canals, boulevards, industrial areas, commercial sections, vacant property, heavily traveled thoroughfares, parks, schools, and cemeteries.

In actual practice it may be necessary to forego a detailed presentation of all of these characteristics, unless the base map is drawn to a very large scale and its use is limited entirely to research purposes. Maps to be published usually have to be reduced to such a small scale that only a relatively few details can be included. This fact should be kept in mind in connection with other types of maps.

In planning a base map for an urban community that is not to be used for publication, a blue-line or black-line street map varying in scale from 500 to 1,000 feet to the inch—depending upon the area of the city—should be procured from the city engineer or city planning commission. If, in addition, access can be had to a complete, accurate, and up-to-date land utilization map, very little field or laboratory work will be required to compile the basic data for the base map. With the appropriate kinds of colored inks or cross-hatching, it is a relatively simple task to transpose certain of the data from the land utilization map to the sociological base map. It is very important to discriminate between the essential and non-essential factors in the physical and cultural environment. A map cluttered up with too many inconsequential details is confusing and misleading. In constructing a map of this kind it is important not to make the basic features too heavy, since they may visually overshadow the primary data which later may be superimposed. If colors are used, it is generally most satisfactory to use pastel shades or tints of water colors or diluted drawing ink. If hatching is used, the scheme should be simple and the lines drawn very lightly.

[6]Cf. E. F. Young, "The Social Base Map," *Journal of Applied Sociology*, IX, 202–206.

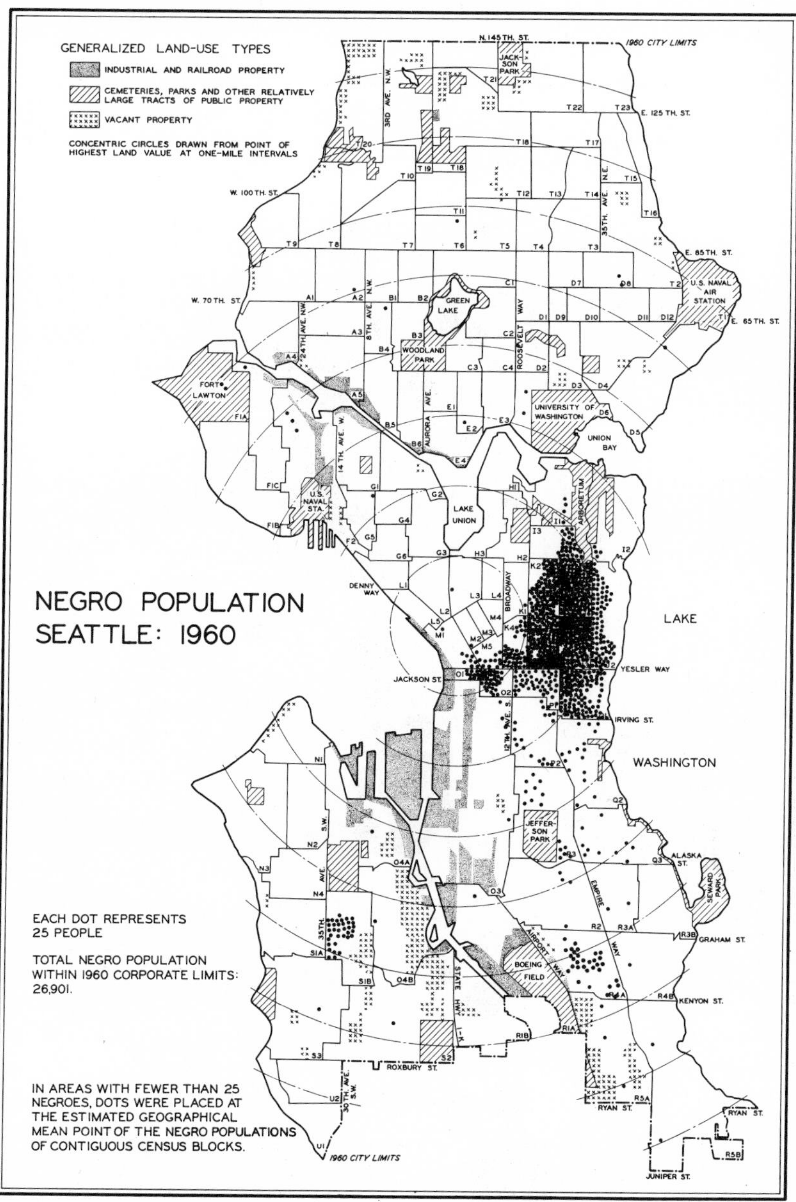

Figure 13.22 Spot map in which density of dot distribution is the basic criterion. From Calvin F. Schmid and Wayne W. McVey, *Growth and Distribution of Minority Races in Seattle, Washington.* Seattle: Seattle Public Schools, 1964, p. 9.

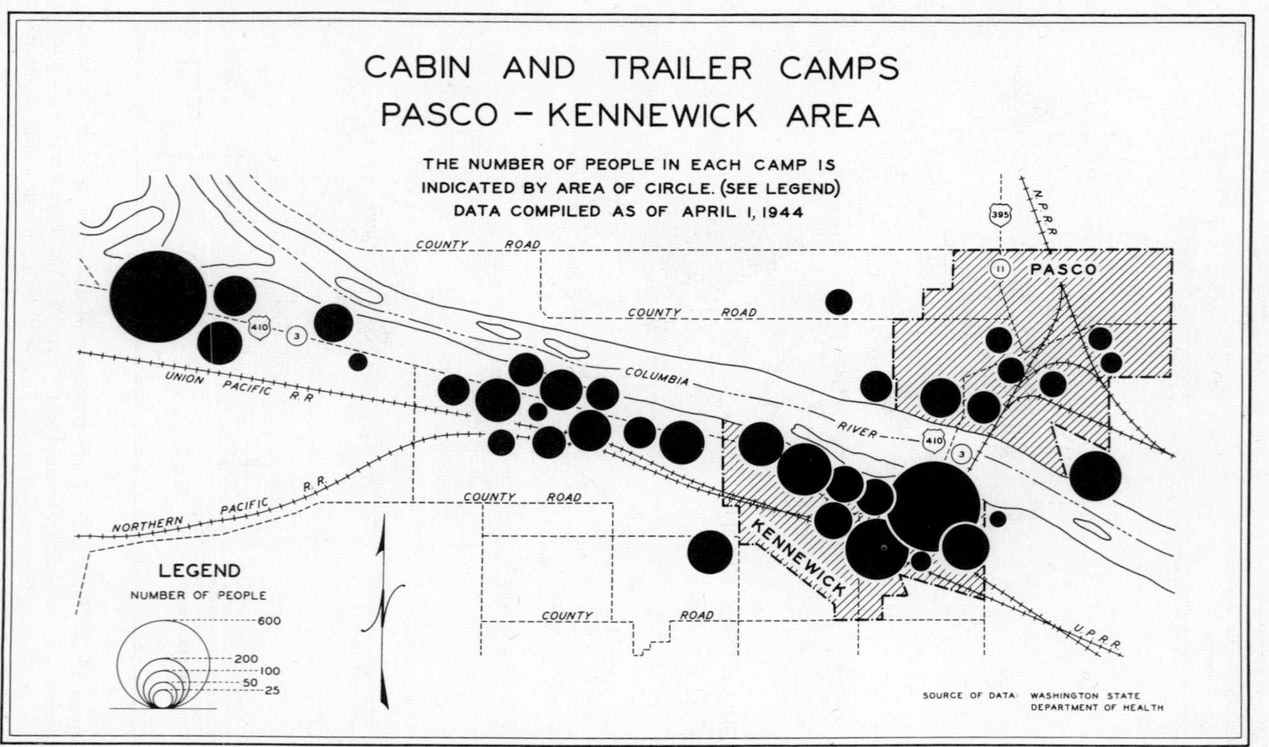

Figure 13.23 An example of a map with a two-dimensional symbol. From Calvin F. Schmid, *Report of Washington State Census Board*, p. 19.

As will be seen in Figure 13.22, only the broader and more significant aspects of the physical and cultural environments can be included on a chart that has been reproduced on a small scale. The size of the original drawing of Figure 13.22 is approximately 24 inches by 30 inches, and, of course, all the lines were drawn in black India ink. It will be observed that the larger bodies of water, parks, cemeteries, railroad and industrial property, vacant land, and census tract boundaries and numbers have been indicated on the map. The primary data on this map—the Negro population of the city of Seattle in 1960—are shown by means of dots.

Spot maps. A very commonly used technique of portraying the geographic location or frequency of social phenomena is by means of dots, discs, squares, spheres, or other symbols. Maps of this general type are frequently referred to as "spot" or "point symbol" maps. There are five different types of "spot" maps. Although in actual practice these types tend to overlap, there is nevertheless in any particular case an emphasis on the 1) size, 2) number, 3) density, 4) shade, or 5) form of the dots or other kinds of point symbols.

In the first type of spot map mentioned, the size of each symbol is proportional to the number or frequency represented. The symbol employed may be either two- or three-dimensional (plane or solid). If a circle is used, then the area is made in proportion to the magnitude or frequency that is to be represented. If on the other hand a sphere is used, the volume indicates the magnitude or frequency portrayed.

Figure 13.23 is an example of a map with two-dimensional symbols. The areas of the symbols indicate the number of people in cabins and trailer camps located in the Pasco-Kennewick area in 1944.

Figures 13.24 and 13.25 present applications of the three-dimensional symbol. For example, it will be observed from Figure 13.24 that the volume of each circle represents the relative size of the populations of the towns and cities in the Seattle-Tacoma area.

It was pointed out earlier in the chapter that the beginner should be very careful in using areal or volume charts. As a general rule, charts of this type should be avoided because of the difficulties of visualizing area or volume and making reliable evaluations and comparisons. In spite of their limitations, charts of this type do have their functions for certain purposes.

In the second type of spot map the basic criterion is not *size*, but

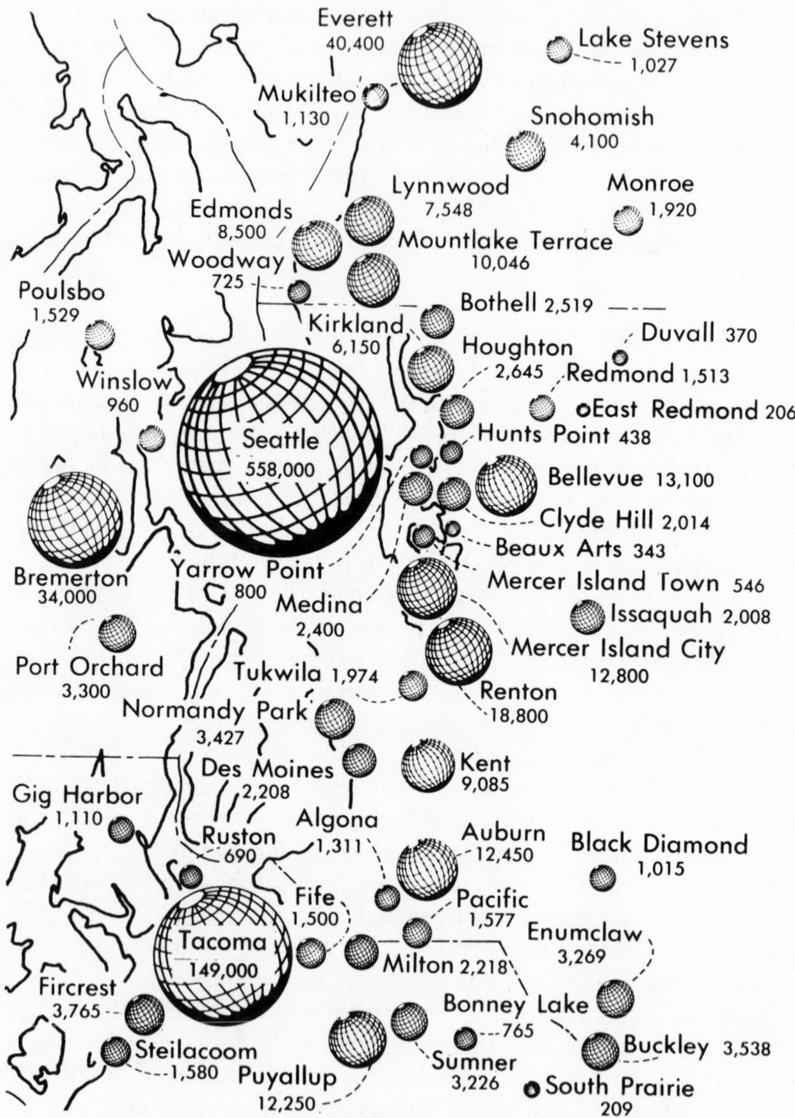

Figure 13.24 Spot map with three-dimensional symbols. The volume of the symbol is the basic criterion in maps of this kind. From Calvin F. Schmid, "Population of Towns and Cities, Washington: April 1, 1961" (map) (Seattle: Washington State Census Board, 1961).

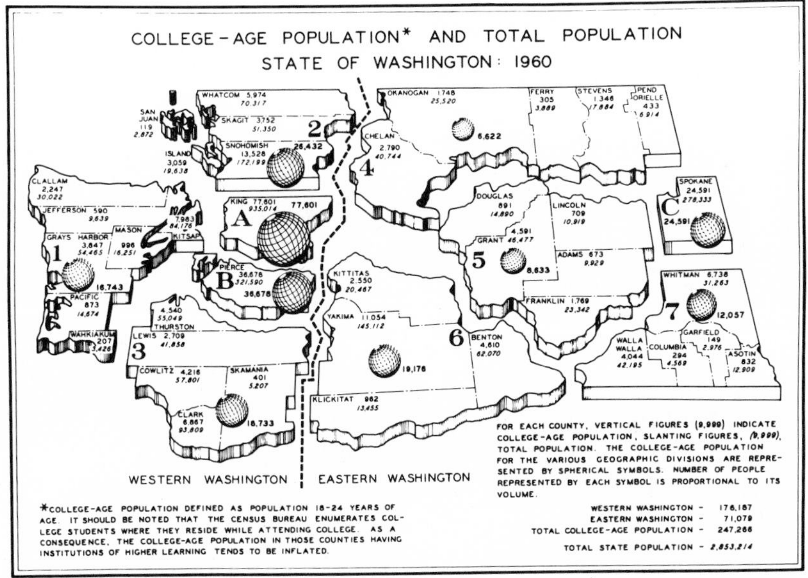

Figure 13.25 Distribution map with spherical symbols superimposed on three-dimensional base map. From Calvin F. Schmid, *et al.*, *Temporal Analysis of Institutional Patterns, University of Washington; 1930 to 1970*. Seattle: University of Washington, 1963, Chapter IX.

rather *number* or *frequency*. All the dots which are of uniform size have a definite value assigned to them. The purpose of this type of map is to show countable frequencies for a given area. With a well constructed map of this kind it is possible to ascertain at a glance whether one geographic area contains more or fewer dots than another, and if one desires to make exact comparisons between two or more areas, it is very easy to count the dots and compare results. As a general rule the smallest geographical area on the map will determine the size of the dot and the number of units of frequency to be represented by each dot. The size of the dot chosen as well as the arrangement on the map should facilitate fairly accurate estimates of the total number of cases.

The purpose of the third type of "spot" map is to portray comparative *densities* of distribution. Like the map just discussed it is of the multiple dot variety, but the emphasis is on the density of the dots rather than on the actual number of dots. Very frequently densities or

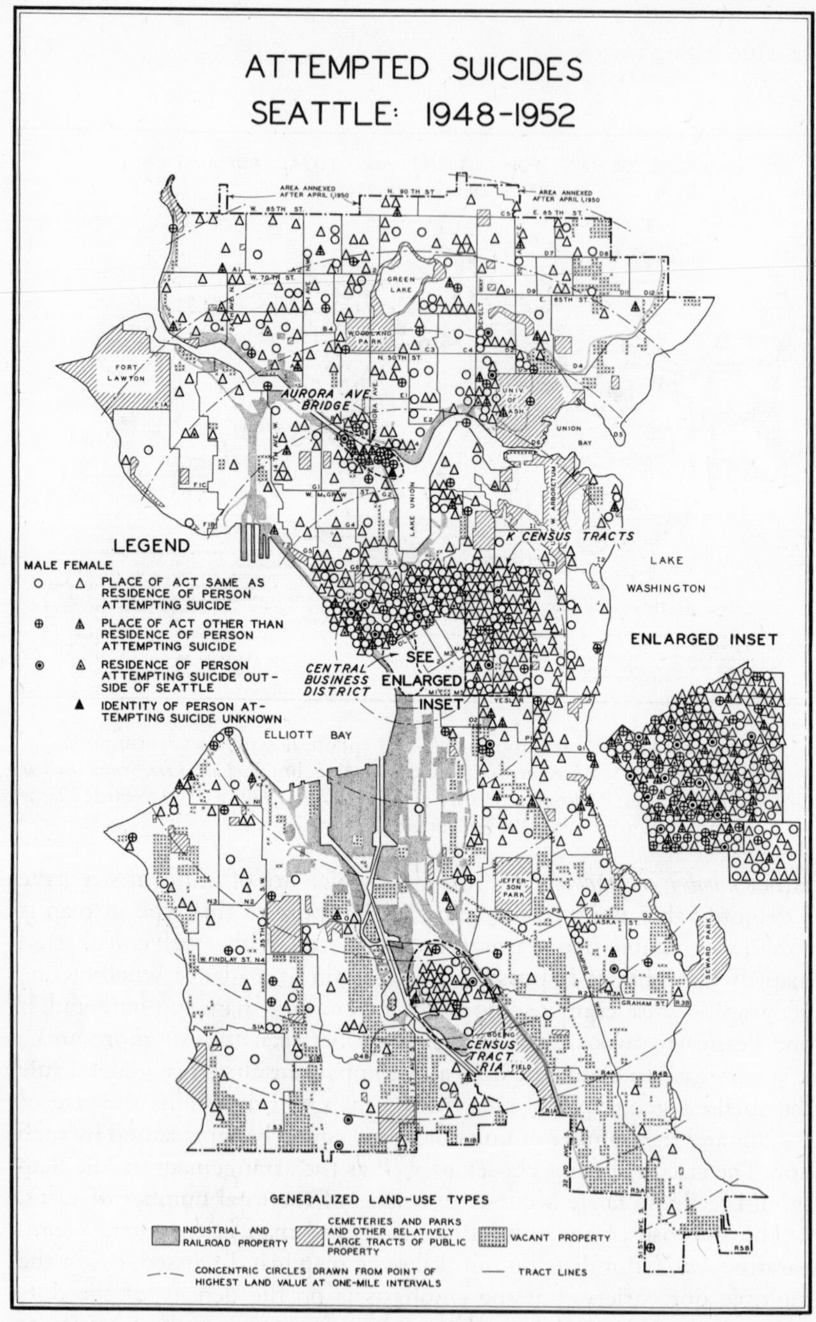

Figure 13.26 Spot map in which the form of the symbol is the basic criterion. From Calvin F. Schmid and Maurice D. Van Arsdol, "Completed and Attempted Suicides: A Comparative Analysis," *American Sociological Review,* XX, 273–283.

degrees of concentration are much more important than actual numbers. The symbol used for this type of map is invariably uniform black dots of relatively small size.

The density of the dots indicates the relative distribution over the entire area. In certain areas very pronounced clusterings of dots may give the impression of almost solid black, whereas in other sections there may be a complete absence of dots. Maps of this type are useful in showing population densities and the distribution of various population groups. Figure 13.22 is an example of this type of map. A single glance gives a clear impression of the population distribution.

The main criterion of the fourth type of spot map is *shading* and not *size, number,* or *density*. The amount of shading within each symbol indicates different values. The most common form is based on a quarter-section shading scheme. The largest frequency or magnitude is represented by a solid symbol, three-quarter, one-half, one-quarter, and possibly other divisions indicating smaller amounts.

The main criterion of the fifth type of spot map is the *form* of the symbol. This type of map is primarily qualitative in contrast to the other types of spot maps which are fundamentally quantitative. The attributes of the data determine the form of the symbols. If, for example, a distinction is to be made on the basis of sex, one symbol will indicate males and another females. If several different kinds of institutions, such as schools, churches, libraries, settlement houses, and hospitals are plotted on the same map, each type of institution will be represented by a different symbol.

Although this type of spot map is essentially illustrative, it has many possibilities as a method of social analysis. As part of five ecological analyses of suicide, multiple-variable spot maps of this type were used with much success.[7] Figure 13.26 is an example of one of the maps used in these studies. It will be seen from the legend that the basic criteria of the classification are the sex and residence of attempted suicides. The males are indicated by circles, the females by triangles; the plain circles and triangles show that the place of attempted self-destruction was the same as the residence of the attempted suicide; the crosses in the circles and triangles indicate residents of Seattle who attempted suicide in some place other than their domicile; the symbols with the solid center designate nonresident cases; and the

[7]E.g., Schmid, *Social Trends in Seattle, op. cit.,* pp. 203–215; Calvin F. Schmid and Maurice D. Van Arsdol, "Completed and Attempted Suicide: A Comparative Analysis," *American Sociological Review,* XX, 273–283.

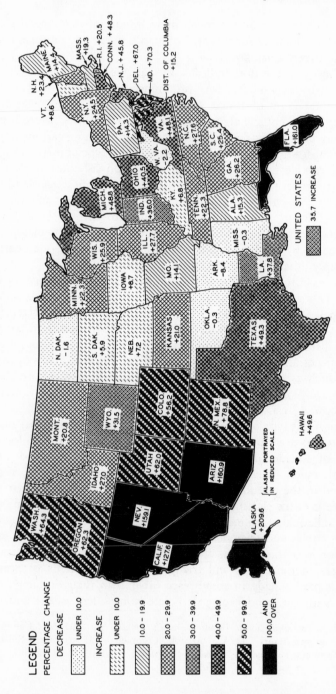

Figure 13.27 Cross-hatched map showing percentage changes in the total population of each of the fifty states during the twenty-year period, 1940 to 1960. From Calvin F. Schmid, *et al., Enrollment Forecasts, State of Washington: 1963 to 1970*. Seattle: Washington State Census Board, 1962, p. 3.

symbols that are entirely black indicate that the identity of the attempted suicide is unknown. Of course, this type of map can be used profitably for other kinds of data. For example, in a study of juvenile delinquency the cases were classified according to sex and offense committed.[8]

Cross-hatched or shaded map. In social research many of the data are expressed in the form of rates and ratios. By far the best technique of portraying data of this kind is the cross-hatched or shaded map. In the case of spot maps the emphasis is placed largely on absolute frequencies and densities, whereas in cross-hatched maps the emphasis is on relative frequencies and rates. In constructing a cross-hatched map the rates or ratios for various geographical units are grouped into a small number of classes, each represented by an appropriate type of cross-hatching.

The fundamental principle underlying the cross-hatching technique is to arrange the density of lines or stippling in such a way as to give an optical effect from light to dark in intensity of tone or pattern. At the same time the shadings should be sufficiently different to be easily identified from a legend on the chart. The smallest values are usually represented by light hatching or stippling; the highest values are represented by full black; and the hatchings for the intervening values are graduated accordingly (Figure 13.27).[9]

The first step in constructing a cross-hatched map is to make an array or frequency distribution with relatively small, equal class-intervals. From this preliminary tabulation it is possible to group the data into a relatively few class-intervals so as to bring out the essential features of the data. In actual practice there usually should not be less than four or more than eight class-intervals for a cross-hatched map. If it is possible, equal class-intervals are to be preferred to those of unequal size. However, spatial distributions are very frequently heterogeneous and do not seem to reflect any law of variation, so that it may be necessary to use class-intervals that are not of uniform size. The hatching scheme should be chosen with great care so that the shading is graduated from light to dark and each interval can be easily distinguished from the others. It should always be kept in mind that in

[8]Schmid, *Social Saga of Two Cities,* pp. 356–357. Minneapolis Council of Social Agencies, 1937.

[9]For a discussion of certain problems of cross-hatching of maps, see Schmid, *Handbook of Graphic Presentation, op. cit.,* pp. 187–198.

this type of map the cross-hatchings are to represent clear-cut variations in magnitudes.[10]

The cross-hatched map is very serviceable in showing variations of social problems, changes in rates of activities from one part of the city or country to another, and changes in the spatial patterning of social phenomena. The relative growth and decline of population according to certain specified geographical divisions can also be effectively shown by the cross-hatching technique. A type of cross-hatched map that is not based on rates or percentages but on divisions of a frequency distribution has been used successfully in showing shifts in land values and shifts in political alignment.

The land value map is used for illustrative purposes since the principle is identical with the one on political behavior. The problem was to devise a method of analyzing the changes in land values in the central business district of Minneapolis during the 40-year period from 1890 to 1930. Since the methods of real estate assessment had changed so frequently, it was out of the question to compare the absolute valuations. However, in order to make the data comparable, frequency distributions were made of the assessed valuation of each piece of property in the central business district in 1890, 1910, and 1930, and deciles were computed for each distribution. The lots that fell in the lowest decile for each period represented the least expensive property whereas the lots that were included in the highest decile were the most expensive, and of course the intermediate values fell in between the two extreme deciles.

The relative land values as expressed in deciles were represented on maps for 1890, 1910, and 1930 by a hatching scheme. As the result of this analysis it was found that in 1890 the sites of greatest value were located in and around the present "Hobohemia" of Minneapolis, and during the past 40 years there has been a shift southward. Much of

[10]The cross-hatched areal map is usually deficient in at least two respects. First, an entire areal unit representing a single class-interval is cross-hatched uniformly regardless of the great differences which may exist within the unit itself. Moreover, as a result, one may infer that changes from one area to another are abrupt and definitive. Second, the amount of cross-hatching is determined solely on the basis of geographical area and not by the number of cases which a district contains. Visually many districts seem very important merely because of the relatively large area which they comprise, but actually, in terms of the number of cases included, they may be very unimportant. For a further discussion and illustrations of the last point, see Schmid, *Social Saga of Two Cities, op. cit.*, pp. 381–383.

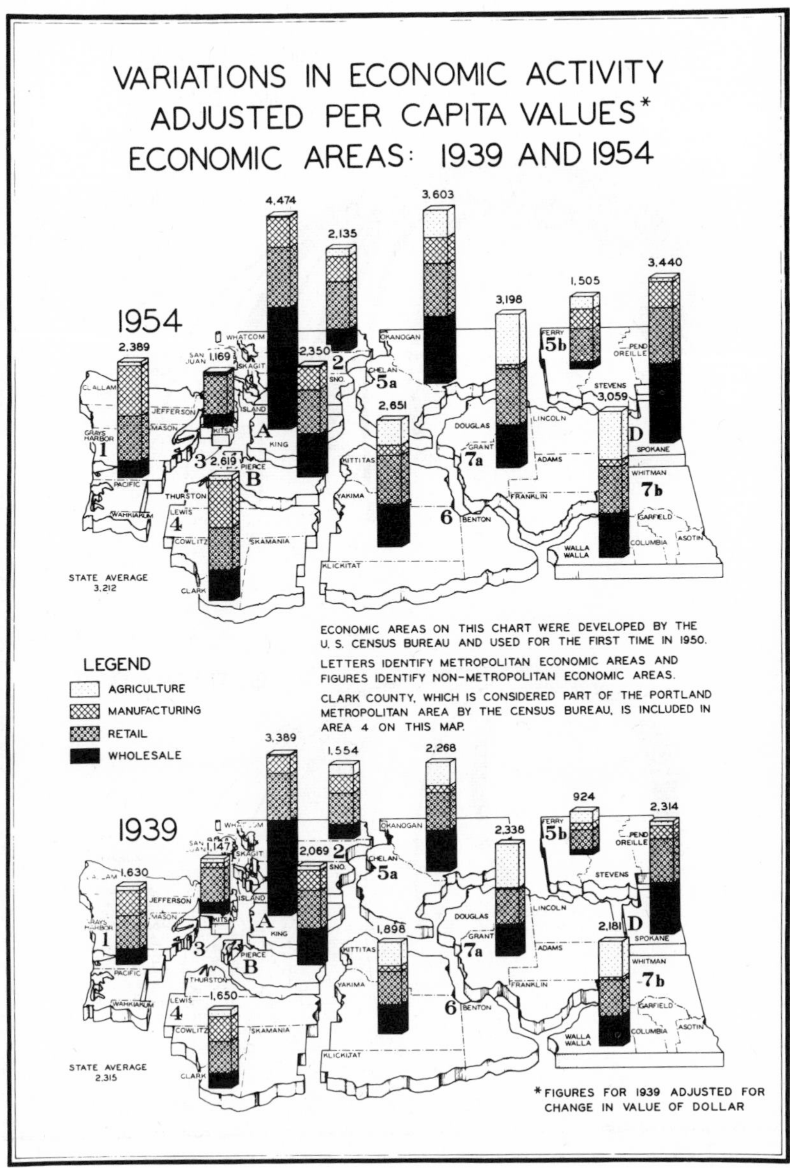

Figure 13.28 Maps with superimposed columns drawn in oblique projection. From Calvin F. Schmid and Vincent A. Miller, *Population Trends and Educational Change*. Seattle: Washington State Census Board, 1960, p. 22.

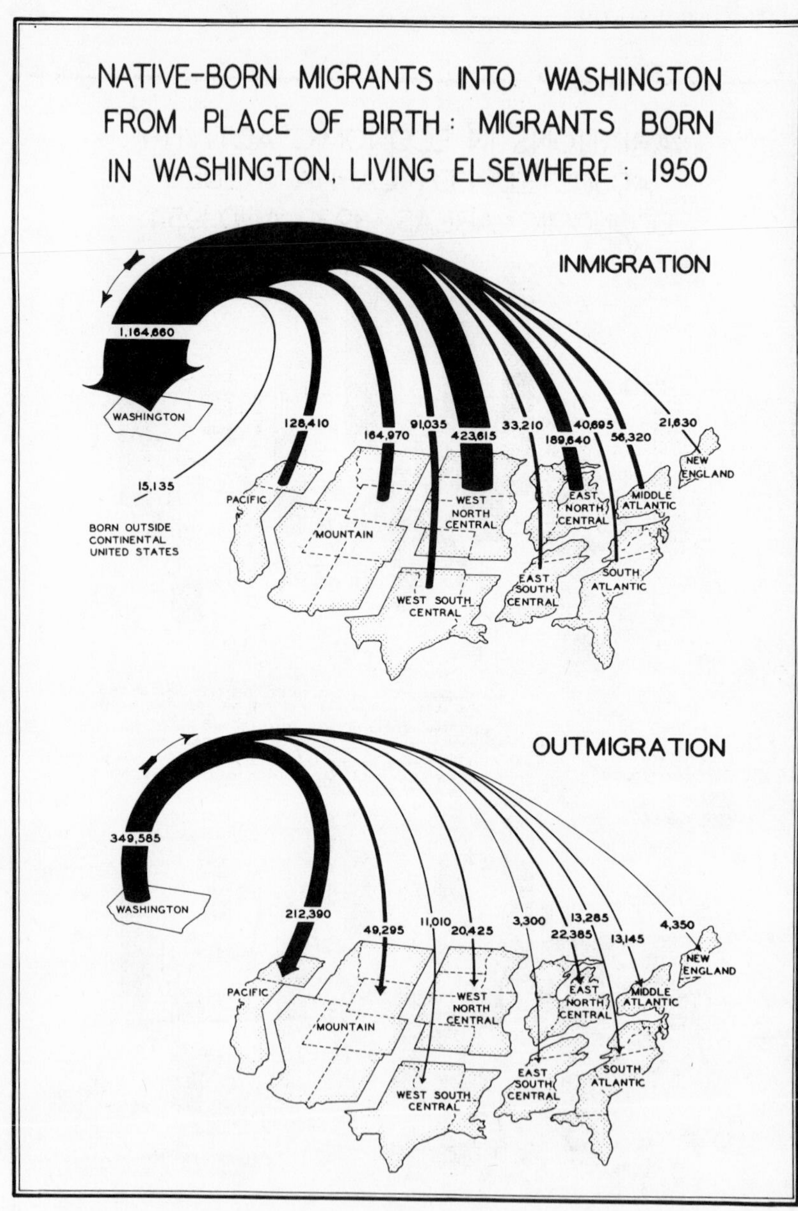

Figure 13.29 Flow map portraying volume and direction of in- and outmigration to Washington. From Calvin F. Schmid, *et al., Population Growth and Distribution, State of Washington*. Seattle: Washington State Census Board, 1955, p. 15.

the land which was included in the highest decile value in 1890 has since depreciated to the third and fourth and even lower deciles at the present time.[11]

Maps with various graphic forms superimposed. The fourth major type of statistical map has various graphic forms superimposed upon it. Sometimes a series of simple bar or column charts or some other graphic form is drawn within the divisions of the map. In such instances the map, of course, provides a more exact and meaningful geographical orientation to the series of graphs (Figure 13.28). Another interesting and significant illustration of this type of map is the flow chart. In the social sciences, for example, the flow map has been widely used to show volume and direction of population movements. Figure 13.29 is an illustration of this type of map.

research techniques in human ecology

By
CALVIN F. SCHMID
University of Washington

Knowledge of the ecological processes is basic to all social sciences, as social and political institutions have a spatial base and arise and function in response to changing conditions of movement and competition.

R. D. MC KENZIE

14

In social research each method shares certain of its procedures with other methods, but each contributes a distinctive approach to the study of human society. The most distinctive characteristic of the ecological approach is its emphasis on the spatial or distributive relationships of human beings and social forms and the principles and factors that determine these relationships.[1]

Because of the limitation of space, only the more fundamental methodological procedures and techniques used in ecological research are considered in this chapter. Although

[1]For more detailed discussions of the subject matter and theory of human ecology see: R. D. McKenzie, "Human Ecology," *Encyclopaedia of the Social Sciences,* V, 314–315. The Macmillan Company, 1931; "The Scope of Human Ecology," in E. W. Burgess, ed., *The Urban Community,* pp. 167–182. University of Chicago Press, 1927; James A. Quinn, *Human Ecology, passim.* Prentice-Hall, Inc., 1950; Amos H. Hawley, *Human Ecology, passim.* Ronald Press, 1950; Otis Dudley Duncan, "Human Ecology and Population Studies," in Philip M. Hauser and Otis Dudley Duncan, *The Study of Population,* Chap. 28, pp. 678–716. University of Chicago Press, 1959; George A. Theodorson, ed., *Studies in Human Ecology, passim.* Harper & Row, Publishers, 1961; Otis Dudley Duncan, "Social Organization and the Ecosystem" in Robert E. L. Faris, ed. *Handbook of Modern Sociology,* Chap. 2, pp. 37–82. Rand McNally and Company, 1964.

quantitative techniques are emphasized, every effort has been made to make the discussion as simple and lucid as possible. Only elementary concepts and skills have been included, so that the main requisite is a knowledge of arithmetic and the ability to substitute in simple formulae.[2]

The Concept of Natural Area

The concept of *natural area* constitutes an important frame of reference for research in human ecology. The fact that every large community is composed of a mosaic of many diverse areas, each with its own type of people, institutional activities, physical characteristics, standards of life, sentiments, and traditions forms a logical basis for compiling data and for conducting research. Sometimes these natural areas are in pronounced contrast with one another; at other times the differences are relatively slight, with the characteristics of one district shading off imperceptibly into those of another.

Natural areas are not the result of plan or design, but come into existence as part of a dynamic, emerging pattern of city growth. During the early stages of city growth the ecological configuration of the community is relatively simple, but as the city increases in size it gradually develops from a relatively small undifferentiated nucleus into a complex of many units all more or less different from one another yet vitally interrelated.

Every large city has a central business district which represents the functional center of the entire urban complex. Here are located the large department stores, smart shops, skyscraper office buildings, large hotels, banks, and theaters. All the main arteries of travel and traffic tend to converge at this center. Surrounding the central business district are usually areas of transition and deterioration—Hobohemias with their sloughed-off buildings and with their services that cater to the wants of the homeless man; the blighted rooming house area and

[2]For a useful and fairly comprehensive selection of readings pertaining to research techniques in urban ecology and demography, see: Jack P. Gibbs, *Urban Research Methods*. D. Van Nostrand and Company, Inc., 1961. For valuable summaries of more than forty research projects documenting the main findings in urban research at the University of Chicago over a period of fifty years, see: Ernest W. Burgess and Donald J. Bogue, *Contributions to Urban Sociology*. University of Chicago Press, 1964. The first 12 chapters, as well as several others, are basically ecological in point of view.

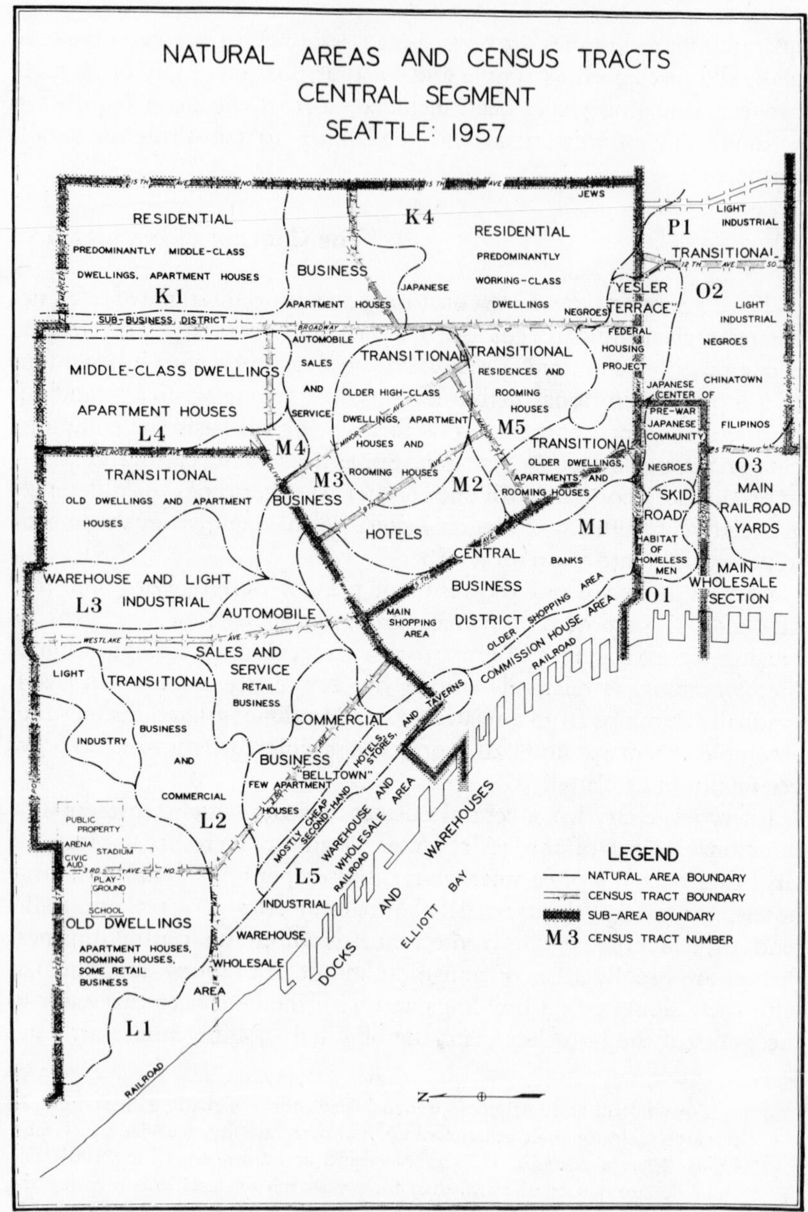

Figure 14.1 Map showing natural areas in central segment of a large urban community. From Calvin F. Schmid, "Urban Crime Areas: Part II," *American Sociological Review,* XXV, 655–678.

residential fringe, once included among the best residential districts in the city; racial colonies such as Negro Black Belts and "Chinatowns" and immigrant communities exemplified by ghettos, "Little Italies," and "Greektowns." Also, relatively close to the central business district are large sections of land devoted to railroads, factories, and warehouses. There are various kinds of apartment house sections and residential communities typified by single-family dwellings representing different socio-economic levels. Figure 14.1 graphically portrays the more important and characteristic natural areas included in the central sector of the city of Seattle.

The term "natural area" is not necessarily limited to a small segment of a city, but may be used to describe a much larger territory. The concept of natural area as it was originally developed by the geographer represented a relatively extensive territory delineated in terms of physiographic and other factors of the natural environment. The modern regional geographer, however, usually includes both physical and human elements as a basis of determining the extent of these larger natural areas. Sociologists and other social scientists also have stressed the value and significance of the regional approach in the study of human relations.

In this connection the terms "metropolitan community," "metropolitan region," and "metropolis" are widely used. As Duncan, *et al.,* point out, these terms represent categories, concepts, or constructs, and are defined differently by different investigators. They are basically classificatory and heuristic in nature and are formulated in different ways to suit the varying objectives and points of view of the investigator.[3] Although similar in many respects, the concepts of metropolitan community formulated by N. S. B. Gras, R. D. McKenzie, and Donald J. Bogue are particularly well-known to the human ecologist.[4]

Bogue states that,

> The metropolitan community thus appears to be an organization of many mutually interdependent and inter-functioning subcommunities oriented about the hinterland cities, which, in turn, are subdominant

[3]Otis Dudley Duncan *et al., Metropolis and Region,* pp. 82–83. The Johns Hopkins Press, 1960.

[4]N. S. B. Gras, *An Introduction to Economic History,* Harper & Row, Publishers, 1922; R. D. McKenzie, *The Metropolitan Community,* McGraw-Hill Book Company, 1933; Donald J. Bogue, *The Structure of the Metropolitan Community: A Study of Dominance and Subdominance.* Horace H. Rackham School of Graduate Studies, University of Michigan, 1959.

to and interdependent with the dominant metropolis, and interfunction with it. The entire community organization appears to be held together by a system of community specialization in, and exchange of, locally produced surpluses to fill those needs which cannot be most efficiently satisfied by local institutions.[5]

An example of metropolitan integration and hierarchical dominance and subdominance is that devised by Rupert B. Vance and Sara Smith. The ranking of southern cities according to their metropolitan status is based on six indices of dominance: 1) wholesale sales, 2) business services receipts, 3) number of branch offices, 4) retail sales, 5) bank clearings, and 6) value added by manufacture.[6] Figure 14.2 portrays

METROPOLITAN ORGANIZATION OF SOUTH
ORDERS OF DOMINANCE AND MAJOR LINES OF INTEGRATION

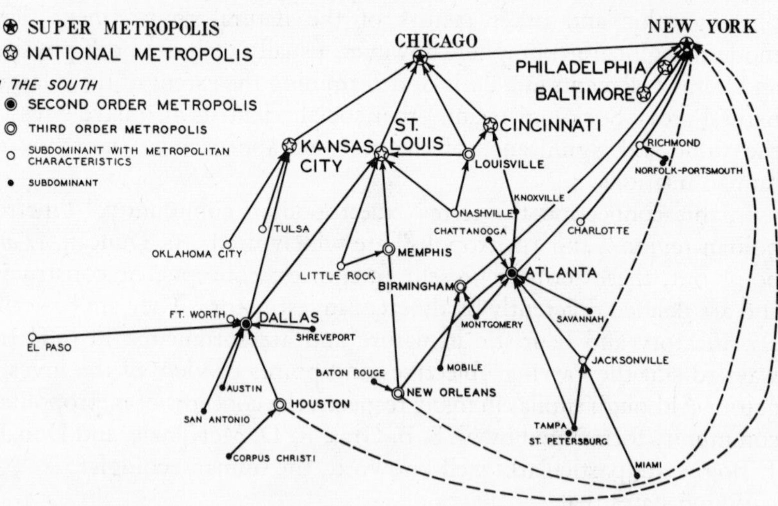

Figure 14.2 The ecological organization of a region is characterized by a constellation of interrelated and integrated metropolitan communities. Some metropolitan communities are characterized by dominance, others by subdominance. Map redrawn by Calvin F. Schmid from Rupert B. Vance and Nicholas J. Demerath (eds.), *The Urban South*. Chapel Hill: The University of North Carolina Press, 1954.

[5]Bogue, *op. cit.*, p. 59.

[6]Rupert B. Vance and Sara Smith, "Metropolitan Dominance and Integration," in Rupert B. Vance and Nicholas J. Demerath, *The Urban South,* Chapter 6, pp. 114–134. The University of North Carolina Press, 1954.

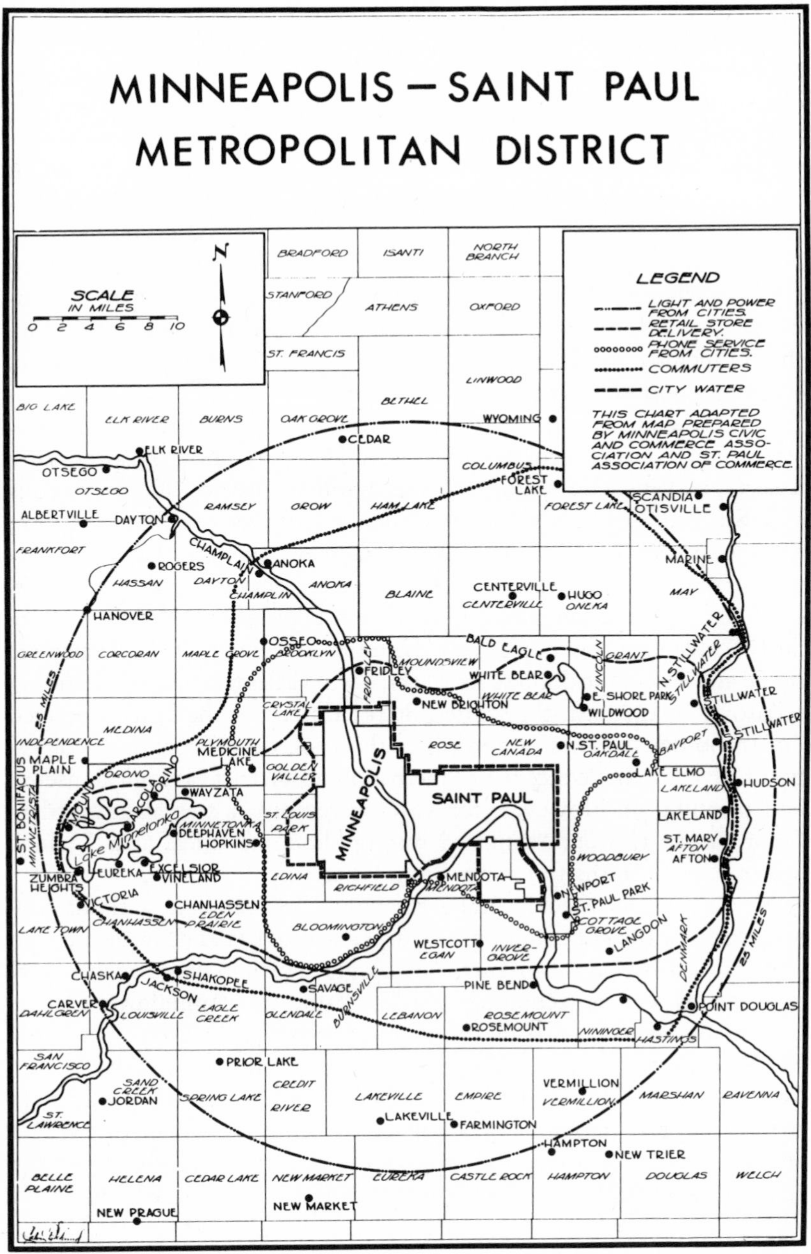

Figure 14.3 Delimitation of a metropolitan district based on certain ecological indices. From Calvin F. Schmid, *Social Saga of Two Cities*, p. 90.

patterns of metropolitan integration in accordance with the scheme developed by Vance and Smith.

In making an ecological study of any large city it will be found that political boundaries are largely meaningless and are generally out of harmony with modern social and economic realities. The city, considered as a political entity, is not identical with the metropolitan area as a social and economic fact. From many points of view the suburbs are as much a part of the city as the area under the municipal government. If we assume, for example, that the larger metropolitan district should include within its natural boundaries a population whose daily economic and social life is predominantly influenced by the central city or cities, it is possible to delimit these boundaries by certain objective criteria or control factors. Figure 14.3 shows how this procedure was applied in determining the metropolitan district of Minneapolis and St. Paul several years ago. Such factors as telephone service, electric power service, retail store delivery, commuting, and city water facilities have been used to delimit this natural area. Of course, these various criteria do not coincide, but taken together they measure fairly realistically and objectively the territorial extent of the immediate social and economic dominance of the Twin Cities over the surrounding territory. In the past, the United States Bureau of the Census defined "metropolitan districts" according to this procedure. From an ecological point of view this concept of "metropolitan district" is logical, useful, and meaningful. However, for various reasons it was abandoned in favor of the concept "standard metropolitan statistical area," which arbitrarily conforms to county boundaries.[7]

No discussion of ecological areas would be complete without consideration of the contributions of rural sociologists. The human ecologist has borrowed from rural sociologists certain basic community concepts as well as techniques for delimiting the community. Charles Galpin pioneered work in this field approximately forty years ago. His studies in Jefferson County, New York, and Walworth County, Wisconsin, represent the prototypes of scores of research projects. In mapping the community of Elkhorn, Wisconsin, Galpin prepared a series of maps indicating spatial patterns of services received by rural families from the town.[8] The spread of these services, particularly the

[7]See *infra* for a discussion of the definition and criteria of "standard metropolitan statistical area."

[8]Charles J. Galpin, *The Social Anatomy of an Agricultural Community,* Bulletin 34, University of Wisconsin Agricultural Experiment Station, 1915, *passim.*

"trade zone," defined the limits of the natural community. A more recent variation of Galpin's technique will be found in Figure 14.4.

SEVEN REPRESENTATIVE SERVICE AREAS
BATAVIA, NEW YORK

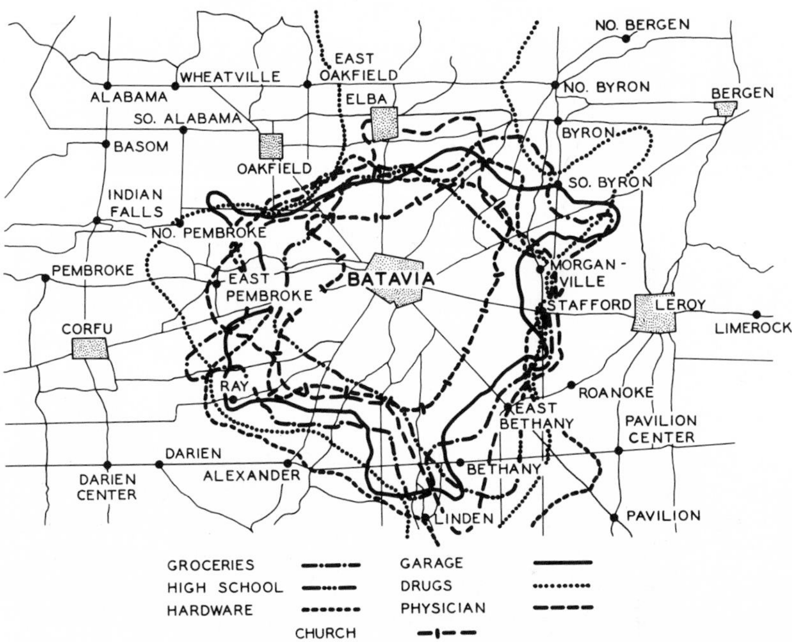

Figure 14.4 A technique for delineating the rural community. Map redrawn from Dwight Sanderson, *Rural Sociology and Rural Social Organization.* New York: John Wiley & Sons, 1942, p. 277. Reproduced by permission of the publisher.

Although the concept of natural area possesses both practical and theoretical significance in ecological research, it should be used with much discrimination and caution. There has been a tendency on the part of many sociologists to think of the concept in a vague and superficial manner. Whether the concept of natural area is applied to a small segment of a city or to a region, the following should be recognized:

1. The concept of natural area should not be applied too rigidly. For example, it would be extremely difficult, if not impossible, to delineate natural areas for an entire city that would serve as a common denominator for all social data. In actual practice it may even

be necessary sometimes to make some unit more or less arbitrarily serve as a basis for compiling data and making analyses.

2. The criteria that are chosen to differentiate natural areas may not be universally applicable. As a general rule it is most satisfactory to select a combination of factors to delineate natural areas. Of course, in human ecology, cultural criteria are stressed more than geographical criteria. The criteria that are chosen will be largely determined by the problem at hand and by the point of view of the investigator.[9]
3. Natural areas are not sharply demarcated from one another. The boundaries are usually indefinite, being zones rather than lines. It is entirely permissible to draw boundaries, but their arbitrary nature should be recognized.[10]
4. Natural areas are not static and fixed but are dynamic and ever changing. The various interrelated factors which differentiate one natural area from another are subject to alteration in the course of time.

Concentric zones. E. W. Burgess has developed a generalized scheme in the form of a series of concentric circles to represent the major ecological patterning and succession of natural areas in the large urban community. The first or inner circle includes the central business section which is characterized by large office buildings, banks, hotels, theaters, department stores, and smart shops. It is the focus of the commercial, social, and civic life of the community. In the second zone—the marginal area or area of transition—is found the largest amount of physical and social deterioration. The prevalence of poor housing, crime, vice, poverty, and disease is indicative of the conditions existing in this second zone. It is also in this area that Black Belts, Chinatowns, Little Italies, ghettos, and other types of racial and immigrant colonies are located. The third zone comprises the neighborhood of second immigrant settlement and of the artisan and office worker. The residents of this zone have escaped the slum areas yet are relatively close to the places of work in the commercial and industrial establishments near the center of the city. The fourth zone contains residential sections consisting of either high-class apartment buildings

[9]W. Wallace Weaver, *West Philadelphia: A Study of Natural Social Areas* (Doctoral Dissertation, University of Pennsylvania, Philadelphia, 1930), pp. 9–21, 160–164; Paul K. Hatt, "The Concept of Natural Area," *American Sociological Review,* XI, 423–427.

[10]National Resources Committee, *Regional Factors in National Planning and Development*, pp. 137-139.

or single-family dwellings. The inhabitants of this zone typify the great middleclass of native-born Americans—small businessmen, professional people, clerks, and salesmen. The fifth or peripheral zone includes the suburban areas of the commuter as well as of satellite cities of various types.

As a generalized theoretical scheme this pattern of *concentric zones* possesses some value in ecological research but its limitations should be clearly recognized. Burgess[11] points out that "it hardly needs to be added that neither Chicago nor any other city fits perfectly into this ideal scheme. Complications are introduced by the lake front, the Chicago River, railroad lines, historical factors in the location of industry, the relative degree of the resistance of communities to invasion, and so on."[12]

The concept of gradient. Closely related to the concept of concentric zones is the concept of *gradient*. In fact, the latter concept seems to be a logical outgrowth of the former. The concept of concentric zones emphasizes the relative universality in the spatial patterning of social phenomena for large American cities and certain other areas, while the term "gradient" stresses the gradation in intensity or rate of change of a variable condition in terms of its distribution over a given area. The conceptual scheme of gradient was first applied in an ecological study of juvenile delinquency by Clifford R. Shaw. After computing juvenile delinquency rates for each of the 181

[11]See Robert E. Park *et al.*, ed., *The City*, pp. 51–52. University of Chicago Press, 1925; James A. Quinn, "The Burgess Zonal Hypothesis and Its Critics," *American Sociological Review*, V, 210–218; Ernest M. Fisher, *Advanced Principles of Real Estate Practice*, pp. 126–127. The Macmillan Company, 1930; Homer Hoyt, *The Structure and Growth of Residential Neighborhoods in American Cities*, pp. 15–26. Federal Housing Administration, 1939; Hans Blumenfeld, "On the Concentric Circle Theory of Urban Growth," *Land Economics*, XXV, 209–212; James A. Quinn, *Human Ecology*, pp. 116–137.

[12]In addition to the hypothesis of concentricity there are other hypotheses of city development and structure. Perhaps the best-known are the "axial," "sector," and "multiple nuclei" hypotheses. Basically all four hypotheses possess some validity and can be considered complementary to one another depending upon the city as well as its particular stage of growth. For further details see: Chauncey D. Harris and Edward L. Ullman, "The Nature of Cities," *Annals of the American Academy of Political and Social Science*, CXLII, 7–17; Arthur M. Weimer and Homer Hoyt, *Principles of Urban Real Estate*, pp. 332–342. The Ronald Press, 1954; Richard M. Hurd, *Principles of City Land Values*, pp. 58–59. Record and Guide, 1911; Homer Hoyt, *op. cit.*, *passim*.

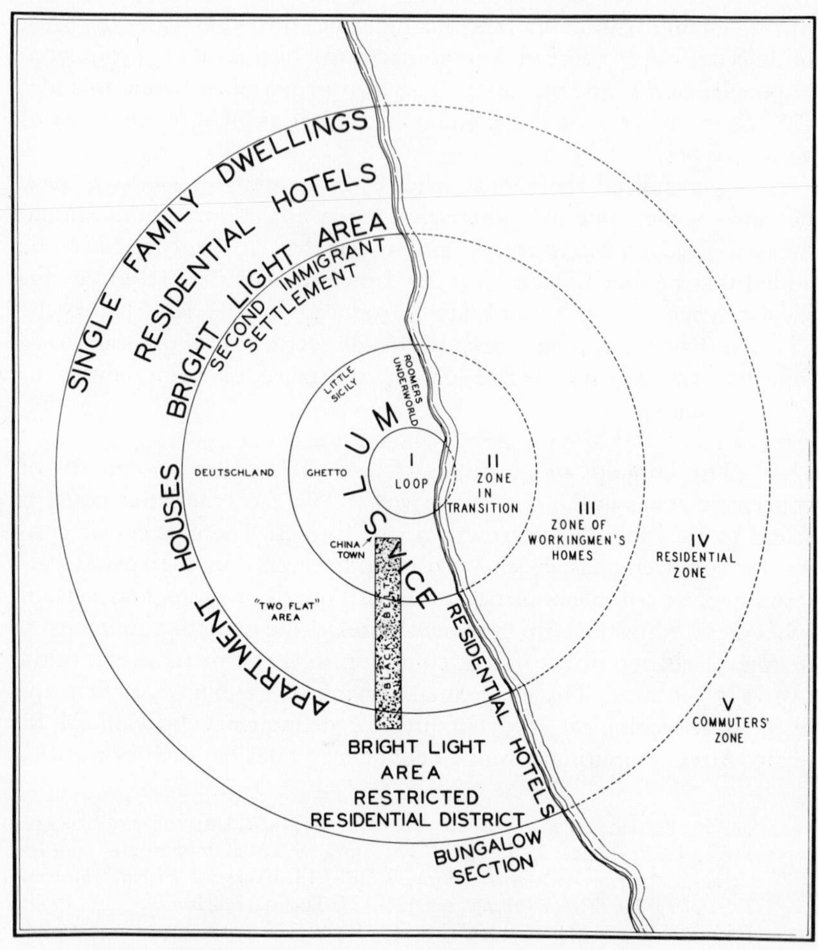

Figure 14.5 Ideal construction of the tendencies of a city or town to expand radially from its central business district. From E. W. Burgess, "The Growth of the City: An Introduction to a Research Project," in Park and Burgess, eds., *The City,* p. 55. Redrawn by Calvin F. Schmid.

mile-square areas of the city of Chicago, Shaw observed that there was a tendency for the rates to manifest a general progressive decline as the distance from the central business district increased.

In corroboration of this observation, a series of radials were drawn upon a map extending from the Loop outward in several directions and the rate within each area crossed was indicated on the radial. It was found that the frequency of delinquency declined as one proceeded from the center toward the periphery of the city, the rates ranging from a maximum of over 35.0 per 100 males between the ages of 10 to 16 to less than 1.0 in certain areas near the city limits.[13] The incidence of delinquency was also relatively high in areas adjacent to such industrial properties as the Union Stockyards and the steel mills of South Chicago.

The concept of gradient has also been applied to many other types of studies. In a study of suicide in Minneapolis, the city was divided into six zones by a series of concentric circles radiating from the center of the Loop—the point of highest land value—and rates were computed for each zone. A tendency was observed for the suicide rates to decrease more or less in direct proportion to the distance from the center of the city, with the apparent exception of the outermost zone, which showed a slight increase over the contiguous zone.[14]

Similarly, there is a tendency for most crimes to decrease more or less in direct proportion to the distance from the center of the city.[15] It will be observed from Figure 14.6 that among a series of "offenses known to the police," embezzlement shows the most pronounced tendency to follow this centrifugal gradient pattern, with shoplifting, theft from person, rape, sodomy, and burglary also exhibiting striking differentials between the central and peripheral zones. For embezzlement the rate for Zone I is 18.7 and for Zone VI only .03. Bicycle theft is the only crime category in Figure 14.6 that shows a higher rate for Zone VI (149.5) than for Zone I (65.3). The differentials between inner and outer zones, however, for peeping tom, obscene telephone calls, indecent liberties, and carnal knowledge are relatively small. All of the remaining 17 crime categories in Figure 14.6 conform to the typical centrifugal crime gradient pattern with relatively high rates in the central zone and low rates toward the periphery.

For the series of gradients based on "arrests," the most pronounced differences between the central and outer zones are shown for bunco

[13]Shaw *et al., Delinquency Areas, passim.*University of Chicago Press, 1929. See also Shaw and Henry D. McKay, *Social Factors in Juvenile Delinquency,* pp. 23–108. Government Printing Office, 1931; Shaw and McKay *et al., Juvenile Delinquency and Urban Areas, passim.* University of Chicago Press, 1942.

[14]Schmid, "Suicide in Minneapolis, Minnesota: 1928–32," *American Journal of Sociology,* XXXIX, 30–48.

[15]Calvin F. Schmid, "Urban Crime Areas: Part II," *American Sociological Review,* XXV, 655–678.

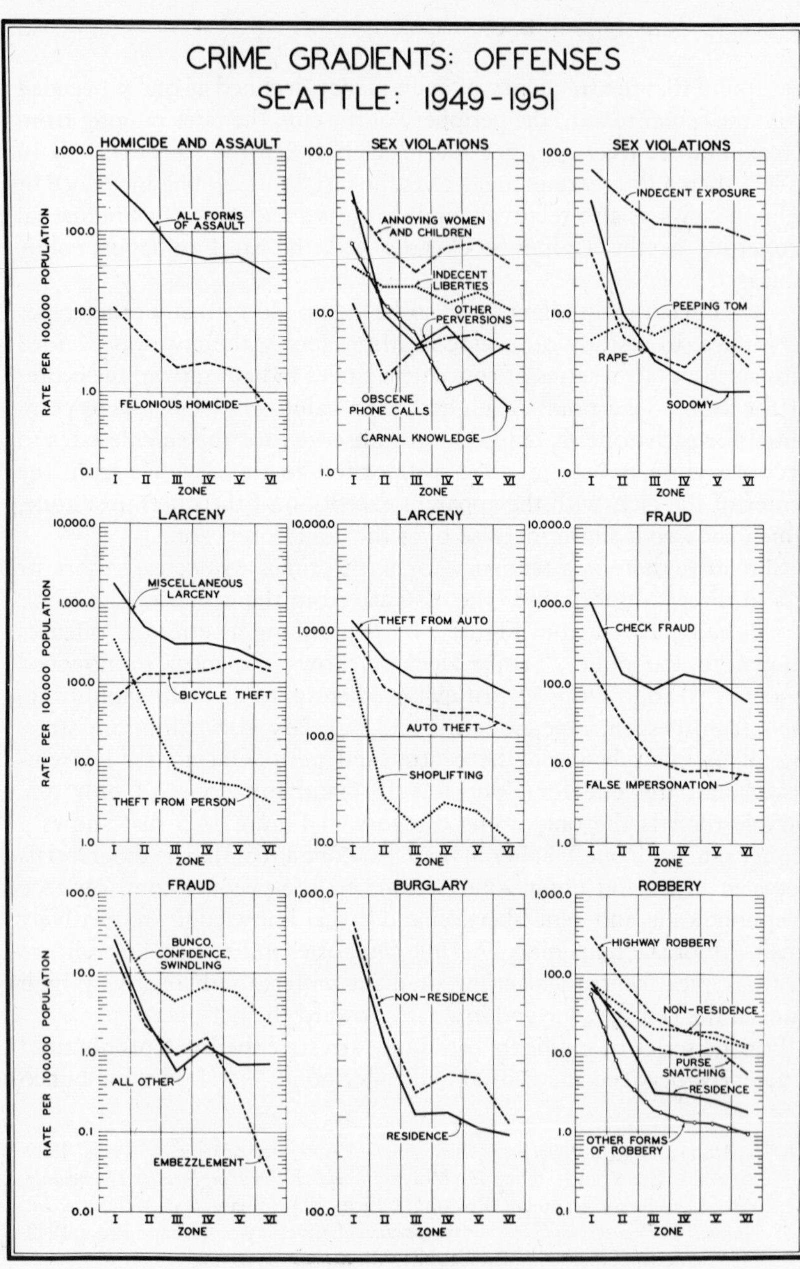

Figure 14.6 An illustration of gradients. From Calvin F. Schmid, "Urban Crime Areas: Part II," *American Sociological Review,* XXV, 655–678.

and other forms of fraud, rape, prostitution, lewdness, robbery, gambling, and common drunkenness. Theft from automobile and indecent exposure indicate the least difference between the innermost and outermost zones. There is not a single category in the arrest series with higher rates in the peripheral zones.

The concept of gradient has been used also in the analysis of social phenomena included in the larger metropolitan community.[16] As an example of this type of study, let us consider briefly an analysis of the non-resident legitimate and illegitimate births in the city of Minneapolis reported during the five-year period 1931 to 1935. The state of Minnesota was divided into 13 zones by a series of concentric circles drawn at 25-mile intervals with Minneapolis as the center, and the exact residence of each mother was plotted on the map. The final rates clearly indicated that there is a pronounced tendency for non-resident mothers who are not married to travel a greater distance for their confinements than married mothers. The crude non-resident birth rates per 100,000 of population varied from 996.0 in Zone I to 3.0 in the peripheral zone for legitimate cases and from 43.0 to 25.0 in the corresponding zones for illegitimate cases. In this connection it was also found that the proportion of illegitimate births among the out-of-state residents was also high. The proportion of illegitimate births in this group ranged from 26.5 per cent for Iowa to 54.3 per cent for South Dakota.[17]

Census Tracts

Census tracts in large cities. From the discussion of natural areas, it is not difficult to see the importance of devising satisfactory spatial units for studying community life. To meet this need, census tract systems have been established in most of the large cities through-

[16]See Robert E. Park, "Urbanization as Measured by Newspaper Circulation," *American Journal of Sociology,* XXXV, 60–79; P. K. Whelpton, "Geographic and Economic Differentials in Fertility," *Annals of the American Academy of Political and Social Science,* CLXXXVIII, 37–55; J. H. Kolb and Edmund de S. Brunner, *A Study of Rural Society,* pp. 355–385. Houghton Mifflin Co., 1946; Mapheus Smith, "Tier Counties and Delinquency in Kansas," *Rural Sociology,* II, 310–322; "Relief Intensity Gradients," *Social Forces,* XVI, 208–223; "An Urban-rural Intellectual Gradient," *Sociology and Social Research,* XXVII, 307–315.

[17]Schmid, *Mortality Trends in the State of Minnesota,* pp. 270–273. University of Minnesota Press, 1937.

out the country.[18] In the past both governmental and private agencies have compiled their data either for the city as a whole or by large political or administrative areas such as wards. But data compiled on this basis are relatively useless for research purposes. From the point of view of scientific diagnosis as well as practical application, it is not enough to know, for example, merely the composition of the population of the city as a whole or of large administrative areas, according to sex, age, race, nativity, or other characteristics. Rather, it is essential to ascertain in detail how these various population groups and classes are distributed within the city if one is to localize problems and gain a larger view of the complexities of urban life. To this end, census tracts include only small segments of the city. In scientific research an object is studied not as a whole but by breaking it up into its parts, which are then described and analyzed in their interrelationships. Census tracts are not only relatively small in size but they are comparable, homogeneous, and permanent. Figure 14.7 is a typical illustration of a census tract layout.[19]

By organizing data of various kinds on the basis of census tracts, it is possible to build up an accurate and detailed picture of social conditions for every part of the city as well as ascertain the changes that are taking place over a period of time. The most fundamental and significant data which have been compiled on the basis of census tracts are the statistics of population and housing of the regular decennial censuses. In addition, in various cities many local governmental, business, social welfare, educational, and religious organizations are compiling

[18]In recent years there has been a marked increase in the number of cities that have established census tract systems. In 1930 when the fifteenth decennial census of population was taken there were 18 census tract cities; by 1940 that number had increased to 60 and by 1950, 64. As the foregoing suggests, tracts were initially established for corporate cities as such; but as the program expanded, tracts were extended to cover heavily settled areas adjacent to cities. In the decade 1950 to 1960, the Bureau of the Census made an effort to encourage local committees in this extension. In 1960, 136 standard metropolitan statistical areas were completely tracted.

[19]For a discussion of the techniques and procedures used in laying out census tracts see Schmid, "The Theory and Practice of Planning Census Tracts," *Sociology and Social Research,* XXII, 228–238; Jerome K. Myers, "A Note on the Homogeneity of Census Tracts: A Methodological Problem in Urban Ecological Research," *Social Forces,* XXXII, 364–366; Robert C. Klove, *Census Tract Manual,* Washington, D. C.: United States Bureau of the Census, (Fourth Ed.) (1958), esp. pp. 6–27.

Figure 14.7 Example of census tract system for a large city. Prepared by Calvin F. Schmid.

their statistics by individual census tracts or combinations of census tracts.

A very essential tool in conducting research based on census tracts is the census tract street index or coding guide. The street index or coding guide is used to facilitate the rapid allocation of street addresses according to census tracts. By means of an index it is possible to locate quickly and accurately large numbers of addresses without resorting to the extremely laborious, expensive, and unreliable procedure of finding numbers on a map. In fact, no map is needed in locating addresses with an index. The index includes all the streets and house numbers in a particular city. Most indexes conform to the basic pattern of listing named streets alphabetically and numbered streets serially, following the named streets. The house number entries for each street indicate the first and last numbers that are contained within a certain specified tract.[20]

The greatest speed and accuracy in coding can be obtained by writing all the addresses on separate slips or cards so that they can be sorted into alphabetical order for the named streets and serially for numbered streets, and then into numerical order of addresses. This will make it possible to code many addresses with only one reference to a given number range, thus eliminating considerable hunting through the index.

Census county divisions. Only in recent years has any tangible progress been made in extending the census tract idea to rural territory. For example, the author completed in the summer of 1949 a state-wide system of census tracts and census divisions for the state of Washington. This project was carried on under the auspices of the Washington State Census Board and the Office of Population Research of the University of Washington in cooperation with the United States Bureaus of the Census and of Agricultural Economics. It is the first system of its kind in the country. In this project the term "census county division" is applied to rural territory and small cities, and the term "census tract" is limited to larger corporate cities and the remainder of standard metropolitan statistical areas. Ecologically, however, there is no basic difference between census tracts and census county divisions. Following the new state-wide census division system in Washington, census county divisions were

[20]For a more detailed description of census tract street index, see Robert C. Klove, *Ibid.*, pp. 19–20.

established by 1960 in 17 other states.[21] These states include Arizona, California, Colorado, Hawaii, Idaho, Montana, New Mexico, Oregon, Utah, Wyoming, Alabama, Florida, Georgia, Kentucky, South Carolina, Tennessee, and Texas.

Heretofore, in rural territory the Census Bureau and other agencies have enumerated and tabulated data on the basis of election precincts and other political areas. The deficiencies of precincts and other similar divisions for research, planning, and administrative purposes have long been recognized, but, unfortunately through inertia and indifference, nothing was done to improve this situation.

Election precincts are subject to manipulation and change. In the State of Washington, for example, there were 2,119 minor civil divisions (almost all were election precincts) in 1940; only 1,154, or a little more than half, are comparable with the 1930 minor civil divisions. This means that every ten years valuable data on population, housing, agriculture, and other subjects are compiled and tabulated at a cost of hundreds of thousands of dollars merely to be discarded because of adherence to the antiquated and useless system of election precincts.

Election precincts are usually laid out for political convenience and without reference to geographic, historic, social, or economic relationships. Census county divisions and census tracts, on the other hand, are carefully planned and possess marked demographic, economic, and social homogeneity. Such units logically tend to become the basic points of reference for fact collecting, administration, and research.

Boundaries of election precincts are difficult, and frequently impossible, to identify in the field. Election precincts in Washington, as in other states, almost invariably follow section lines. Because precinct boundaries are not definitive and readily identifiable, much time and effort are wasted, and omissions and duplications are an inevitable consequence in field enumerating and interviewing. By contrast, census tracts and census county divisions follow clearly identifiable boundaries such as roads, trails, rivers, lakes, canals, railroads, and transmission lines.

Economic areas, standard metropolitan statistical areas, and urbanized areas. In addition to census tracts and census county divisions, other areal divisions have been created for the compilation of data which are useful in ecological research. Such

[21]Schmid, "Washington's State-Wide System of Census Tracts and Census Divisions," in George F. Mair, *Studies in Population,* pp. 39–45. Princeton University Press, 1949.

divisions include "economic areas," "standard metropolitan statistical areas" and "urbanized areas."

Economic areas were an innovation of the 1950 decennial census. Economic areas are relatively homogeneous subdivisions of states. They consist of single counties or groups of counties which have similar economic and social characteristics. The boundaries of these areas have been drawn in such a way that each state is subdivided into a few parts, with each part having certain significant characteristics which distinguish it from other areas which it adjoins.[22] Dr. Donald J. Bogue of the University of Chicago had charge of laying out economic areas for the entire country. With respect to the term "economic area," Bogue points out that it refers to a pattern of economic adaptation, possessing a basic ecological orientation.[23] Figure 14.8 illustrates economic areas for the state of Indiana.

The concept of "Standard Metropolitan Statistical Areas" has been developed to meet the need for the presentation of general-purpose statistics by agencies of the Federal Government, in accordance with specific criteria for defining such areas. On the basis of these criteria, "definitions" of the areas in terms of geographic boundaries are established by the Bureau of the Budget with the advice of the Federal Committee on Standard Metropolitan Statistical Areas, which is composed of representatives of the major Federal statistical agencies.

Standard definitions of metropolitan statistical areas were first issued in 1949 as "Standard Metropolitan Areas." They were developed to replace four different sets of definitions then in use for various statistical series—"metropolitan districts," "metropolitan counties," "industrial areas," and "labor market areas."

The primary objective in establishing standard definitions of metropolitan areas was thus to make it possible for all Federal statistical agencies to utilize the same boundaries in publishing statistical data useful for analyzing metropolitan problems. The term "standard metropolitan area" has been changed to "standard metropolitan statisti-

[22]Donald J. Bogue, *State Economic Areas.* Washington, D.C.: United States Bureau of the Census, 1951, pp. 1–6; Donald J. Bogue and Calvin L. Beale, *Economic Areas of the United States,* pp. xxxix-xc. The Free Press of Glencoe, Inc., 1961.

[23]Donald J. Bogue, "Economic Areas as a Tool for Research and Planning," *American Sociological Review,* XV, 409–416; Rutledge Vining, "Delimitation of Economic Areas: Statistical Conceptions in the Study of the Spatial Structure of an Economic System," *Journal of the American Statistical Association,* XLVIII, 44–64.

Figure 14.8 Map showing state economic areas for Indiana. Map redrawn by Calvin F. Schmid, from chart in Donald J. Bogue and Calvin L. Beale, *Economic Areas of the United States*. New York: The Free Press of Glencoe, Inc., 1961, p. 487.

cal area" in order to describe more accurately the objective of the definitions.

The general concept of a metropolitan area is one of an integrated economic and social unit with a recognized large population nucleus. To serve the statistical purposes for which metropolitan areas are defined, their parts must themselves be areas for which statistics are usually or often collected. Thus, each standard metropolitan statistical area must contain at least one city of at least 50,000 inhabitants. The standard metropolitan statistical area will then include the county of such a central city, and adjacent counties that are found to be metropolitan in character and economically and socially integrated with the county of the central city. In New England the requirement with regard to a central city as a nucleus still holds, but the units comprising the area are the towns rather than counties. The county (or town in New England) is the basic statistical unit. A standard metropolitan statistical area may contain more than one city of 50,000 population. The largest city is considered the nucleus and usually gives the name to the area. The name may include other cities in the area. Standard metropolitan statistical areas may cross state lines. In 1964 there were 219 standard metropolitan statistical areas.[24]

The major objective of the Bureau of the Census in delineating urbanized areas was to provide a better separation of urban and rural population in the vicinity of the larger cities, but individual urbanized areas have proved to be useful statistical areas. They correspond to what are called "conurbations" in some other countries. An urbanized area contains at least one city of 50,000 inhabitants or more in 1960, as well as the surrounding closely settled incorporated places and unincorporated areas that meet certain specific criteria. An urbanized area may be thought of as divided into the central city or cities, and the remainder of the area, or the urban fringe. All persons residing in an urbanized area are included in the urban population.

Units and Indexes

It has already been pointed out (pp. 275–277) that before quantitative methods can be employed, it is necessary to identify and define the objects to be analyzed. Obviously much time can be wasted in laborious measurement if there is no clear conception as to the nature

[24]Excerpted from bulletin, *Standard Metropolitan Statistical Areas,* Office of Statistical Standards, United States Bureau of the Budget, Washington, D.C., 1964.

of the thing being measured. The most refined statistical methods are quite useless if the basic quantitative unit is not well chosen and clearly and rigorously defined.

The human ecologist is concerned with such phenomena as crime, suicide, juvenile delinquency, mobility of population, marriage, divorce, demographic characteristics, land values, residential structures and dwelling units, psychoses, mortality, and morbidity. Sometimes, however, it may be difficult to obtain data pertaining to these phenomena that are based on appropriate, clear, measurable, and comparable statistical units.

For example, in studying juvenile delinquency the most common unit chosen has been the cases that have come to the attention of the juvenile court or of the police department. But data of this kind may be grossly deficient and misleading since there are so many factors of varying importance that determine the actual number of delinquents officially registered even though the behavior of the children may be more or less of a constant from one locality to another. Such factors as race, nativity, economic status, prevailing traditions, and attitudes, which differ so markedly from one section to another, may be of fundamental importance in determining the number of delinquents that come before the police or court officials. If, for example, the unit of juvenile delinquency is defined in terms of cases taken to court, it should be remembered that the following cases are excluded: 1) those that are unapprehended, 2) those that are known but not reported, 3) those that are apprehended but are not taken before the juvenile court, being handled unofficially by psychiatrists, boarding schools, and social agencies. From a qualitative as well as quantitative point of view, a statistical unit may possess serious limitations. Most units of juvenile delinquency have been of a non-specific character, so that truancy, malicious mischief, incorrigibility, robbery, burglary, traffic violations, and many other forms of behavior are lumped together.[25]

Besides providing a basis for comparing the incidence of certain social phenomena, such as juvenile delinquency or family disorgani-

[25]For a methodological analysis and critique of studies in the field of juvenile delinquency see Sophia Moses Robison, *Can Delinquency be Measured? passim*. Columbia University Press, 1936. Cf. the review of this monograph by Samuel A. Stouffer, *American Journal of Sociology,* XLII, 586–590; also the review by C. E. Gehlke, *Journal of the American Statistical Association,* XXXII, 814–817. For a comprehensive, up-to-date, provocative discussion of the problem of measuring the frequency and nature of criminal offenses, see Thorsten Sellin and Marvin E. Wolfgang, *The Measurement of Delinquency*. John Wiley & Sons, 1964.

zation from one area to another, indexes are also indispensable for the identification and measurement of more intricate and fundamental social relationships. To ascertain, for example, the spatial configuration of juvenile delinquency may be illuminating and significant but it does not go far enough in analyzing the problem. It is also important to know how juvenile delinquency is related to other conditions in the community. In order to measure the more elusive and complex social conditions the human ecologist utilizes various kinds of indexes. An index, as we shall use it in the present discussion, is a relatively simple and readily observable phenomenon that is used to measure relatively complex and less readily observable phenomena. The things that are used as measures of the characteristic are either part of the characteristic or things that have some consistent relation to it.[26]

In general, a satisfactory index should be 1) objective, 2) quantitatively expressed, 3) clearly defined, and 4) truly revelatory of community processes. It must measure what it purports to measure. 5) It should have general validity and comparability and should be applicable to various places of different size and type; 6) it should lend itself to the establishment of reasonable norms relative to which the areas measured can be compared; and 7) if more than one index is used, as is generally the case, they should be adequate in number and weighted according to their relative significance among all factors.[27]

In actual practice, however, it will be found that many of the indexes used by the sociologist do not conform to these standards. They are often ambiguous, inadequate, qualitative, and only vaguely indicative of what they are supposed to measure. However, it is only through further study of community processes, experimentation, and the development of more adequate techniques that we can hope actually to measure the more fundamental aspects of social life with a marked degree of refinement.

In order to illustrate the value and application of indexes in ecological research, let us review very briefly a few concrete studies. Is it possible to predict the success or failure of an institution in terms of a few basic indexes of the community in which it happens to be situated? In what ways are the characteristics of an institution determined by its environment? Questions of this kind have very practical significance. The

[26]Carl A. Dawson and Warner E. Gettys, *An Introduction to Sociology,* p. 554. The Ronald Press, 1948; Edward Jackson Baur, "Statistical Indexes of the Social Aspects of Communities," *Social Forces,* XXXIII, 64–75.

[27]Schmid, "Criteria for Judging Community Organization and Disorganization," *Publications of the American Sociological Society,* XXVII, 116–122.

well-known studies of Douglas, Fry, Hallenbeck, Sanderson, and others indicate some of the possibilities in this field.[28]

In many kinds of research problems in human ecology, it is important to know the socio-economic status of the population from one area to another. One of the most satisfactory single indexes of socio-economic status is the mean or median annual income for the families in each area. In addition, such indexes as the following are used to measure socio-economic status: mean or median value of owner-occupied dwelling units, mean or median rent of tenant-occupied dwelling units, median school grade completed, or occupational status.[29] In rural-farm areas a productivity index in terms of farm commodities might also be found useful.[30]

Housing characteristics have sometimes been used as indexes of neighborhood conditions.[31] Studies in the field of juvenile delinquency illustrate some of the possibilities as well as the difficulties and limitations of using a single index such as housing characteristics to explain relatively complex social conditions.[32]

[28]H. Paul Douglas, *1,000 City Churches.* Doubleday & Co., Inc., 1926; Luther Fry, *Diagnosing the Rural Church.* Doubleday & Co., Inc., 1924; R. D. McKenzie, *The Neighborhood: A Study of Local Life in the City of Columbus, Ohio.* University of Chicago Press, 1923; W. C. Hallenbeck, *Minneapolis Churches and Their Comity Problems.* Harper & Row, Publishers, 1929; Ross W. Sanderson, *The Strategy of City Church Planning.* Institute of Social and Religious Research, 1932; Murray H. Leiffer, *Manual for the Study of the City Church.* Willett, Clark and Company, 1938.

[29]Calvin F. Schmid, "Generalizations Concerning the Ecology of the American City," *American Sociological Review,* XV, 264–281; Eshref Shevky and Marilyn Williams, *The Social Areas of Los Angeles, passim.* University of California Press, 1949; Eshref Shevky and Wendell Bell, *Social Area Analysis, passim.* Stanford University Press, 1955.

[30]For a discussion of regional contrasts in economic levels for the entire United States as determined by various indexes see Carter Goodrich *et al., Migration and Economic Opportunity,* pp. 11–61.

[31]For illustrations of housing indexes see Schmid, *Social Saga of Two Cities, op. cit.,* pp. 293–295; and Donald L. Foley, *An Index of the Physical Quality of Dwellings in Chicago Residential Areas* (Unpublished Master's Thesis, University of Chicago, 1942). For an outstanding ecological study based largely on housing data, see Homer Hoyt, *The Structure and Growth of Residential Neighborhoods in American Cities, op. cit., passim.*

[32]See Mildred Hartsough and George Caswell, *The Relation Between Housing and Delinquency* (Housing Division, Federal Emergency Administration of Public Works, Washington, 1936). In this connection, see "Housing and Delinquency" (Chap. II) by Clifford Shaw in the President's Conference of Home Building and Home Ownership, *Housing and the Community;* Bernard

Population characteristics—in addition to educational and occupational status indicated in the foregoing paragraph—such as sex, age, race, nativity, and marital status also have been frequently used as indexes in human ecology.[33] Other indexes which have been used for various purposes in human ecology are: mobility of population,[34] land values,[35] crime and juvenile delinquency,[36] houses of prostitution,[37] various institutions other than those already mentioned,[38] families listed in social registers,[39] psychometric tests,[40] and many others.[41]

Lander, *Towards an Understanding of Juvenile Delinquency*. Columbia University Press, 1954.

[33]Raymond Pearl, "On a Single Numerical Index of the Age Distribution of a Population," *Proceedings of the National Academy of Sciences,* VI, 427–431; Charles Shelton Newcomb, *A Single Numerical Index of Age and Sex Distribution of Population* (Unpublished Master's Thesis, University of Chicago, 1930).

[34]See R. D. McKenzie, *op. cit.,* pp. 157–158; Ernest R. Mowrer, "Family Disorganization and Mobility," *Publications of the American Sociological Society,* XXIII, 134–145; William Albig, "A Comparison of Methods of Recording Urban Residential Mobility," *Sociology and Social Research,* XXII, 226–233.

[35]Schmid, "Land Values as an Ecological Index," *Research Studies of the State College of Washington,* IX, 16–36.

[36]See previous references to studies by Shaw and to Reckless, *Criminal Behavior.*

[37]See Reckless, "The Distribution of Commercialized Vice in the City: A Sociological Analysis," *Proceedings of the American Sociological Society,* XXXII, 168–171; Howard Whipple Green, "Cultural Areas in the City of Cleveland," *American Journal of Sociology,* XXXVIII, 356–367.

[38]See Ernest Hugh Schideler, *The Chain Store: A Study of the Ecological Organization of a Modern City* (Unpublished Doctoral Dissertation, University of Chicago, 1927); Amos H. Hawley, "An Ecological Study of Urban Service Institutions," *American Sociological Review,* VI, 629–639; E. C. Hughes, "The Ecological Aspect of Institutions," *American Sociological Review,* I, 180–189; Harvey W. Zorbaugh, *The Gold Coast and the Slum.* University of Chicago Press, 1937; Anderson, *The Hobo.* University of Chicago Press, 1927.

[39]See Thomas M. Pryor, *Selective Processes in a Blighted Area* (Unpublished Doctoral Dissertation, University of Michigan, 1935); Schmid, *Social Saga of Two Cities, op. cit.,* pp. 86–87.

[40]J. B. Maller, "Vital Indices and Their Relation to Psychological and Social Factors," *Human Biology,* V, 94–121.

[41]Schmid, "Criteria for Judging Community Organization and Disorganization," *op. cit.;* Austin L. Porterfield and Robert H. Talbert, *Crime, Suicide and Social Well-Being in Your State and City.* Texas Christian University; Edward B. Olds, *How Does Your City Rate? Comparison of 57 Metropolitan Areas.* Social Planning Council of St. Louis and St. Louis County, 1952; Douglas H. MacNeil, "The Vulnerability Index," *Survey Midmonthly,* LXXXIV, 3–6; Paul Bates Gillen, *The Distribution of Occupations As a City Yardstick.* King's Crown Press, 1951.

Typological techniques. In recent years urban typologies have been devised mainly to provide analytic frameworks for the study of the social structure of the large American city. The two best known typologies are those constructed by Robert C. Tryon and Eshref Shevky and their collaborators. Both the Tryon and Shevky typologies represent efforts to differentiate with a high degree of specificity the various sub-areas of a city on the basis of certain dimensions or components derived from measures of population and housing characteristics published in decennial census reports.

The Tryon typology is based on cluster analysis (inverse approximation to factor analysis) in which scores for the three dimensions of "Family Life" (F), "Assimilation" (A), and "Socio-economic Independence" (S) are derived for each census tract. These represent weighted mean standardized scores of several population and housing variables. Profiles of F-A-S scores provide the basis for describing configurations of the populations and housing variables among the clusters of census tracts which are sufficiently precise and detailed to identify socially significant sub-areas within a city.

The Shevky typology is a classificatory scheme based on less formalized statistical procedures in which certain patterns are developed in terms of three indexes referred to as "Urbanization," "Segregation," and "Social Rank." The urbanization index is derived from measures of spatially separated ethnic groups; and the social rank index is constructed from equally weighted census tract measures of occupation and education. The configurations derivable from the two typologies are similar but not identical, nor are they, strictly speaking, comparable.[42]

The present writer and his colleagues have developed a third basic procedure for analyzing urban typologies by special application and

[42]Eshref Shevky and Wendell Bell, *Social Area Analysis, Theory, Illustrative Application, and Computational Procedure*. Stanford University Press, 1955; Robert C. Tryon, *Identification of Social Areas by Cluster Analysis*. University of California Press, 1955. For a critical evaluation of "social area analysis" see, Review of *Social Area Analysis* by Otis Dudley Duncan, *American Journal of Sociology,* LX, 84–85, and exchange between Duncan and Bell, *op. cit.,* LXI, 260–262; Amos Hawley and Otis Dudley Duncan, *Land Economics,* XLIII, 337–345; Maurice D. Van Arsdol, Santo F. Camilleri, and Calvin F. Schmid, "An Investigation of the Utility of Urban Typology," *Pacific Sociological Reveiw,* IV, 26–32; and exchange between Wendell Bell and Scott Greer and Van Arsdol *et al.,* "Social Area Analysis and Its Critics," *op. cit.,* V, 3–9; Van Arsdol, Camilleri, and Schmid, "Further Comments on the Utility of Urban Typology," *ibid.,* 9–13; Leo F. Schnore, "Another Comment on Social Area Analysis," *ibid.,* 13–16.

adaptation of the Guttman Technique of Scale Analysis.[43] The results obtainable by these three techniques are very similar.

Vital and social rates. Because of their frequent application, it is very important in social research to possess a thorough mastery of the techniques of computing and interpreting vital and social rates. In order to ascertain, for example, the relative incidence of juvenile delinquency, suicide, infant mortality, or some other social phenomenon for several geographical areas, absolute frequencies will not suffice. Absolute frequencies would be very misleading, since the size as well as the composition of the population for the several areas would undoubtedly show pronounced differences. It is essential to know in addition to the absolute frequencies of occurrence the exact number of people who are "exposed" to the risk of the occurrence. One would naturally expect more suicide in a population of 25,000 than in one of 5,000, or more juvenile delinquents in a population with a high proportion of children between 8 and 16 years of age than in one in which virtually all the people are adults.

To calculate a valid juvenile delinquency rate it is necessary to relate the number of cases of juvenile delinquency recorded during a given period in a particular area to the number of children in the juvenile court age. Similarly, to compute a valid rate of illegitimacy, the number of illegitimate births during a given period is divided by the number of single, widowed, and divorced women in the child-bearing period.

All the rates in this discussion may be expressed in terms of the following basic formula:

$$\text{Rate} = \frac{\text{The number of times a specified kind of event occurs in a given period.}}{\text{The whole number of exposures to the risk of its occurrence.}}$$

It is important to remember that the validity of comparison involved in a rate depends upon a proper choice of both numerator and denominator.[44] The derived ratio is expressed in terms of some base

[43]For a discussion of the Guttman Technique of Scale Analysis, see *infra* pp. 336–341; Calvin F. Schmid, "Generalizations Concerning the Ecology of the American City," *American Sociological Review,* XV, 264–281; Calvin F. Schmid, Charles E. Bowerman, and Fred J. Shanley, "Application of Scale Analysis Techniques in Defining Ecological Areas" (Unpublished ms.).

[44]Raymond Pearl, *Introduction to Medical Biometry and Statistics,* pp. 173–218. W. B. Saunders Co., 1940; Forrest E. Linder and Robert D. Grove, *Vital Statistics Rates in the United States 1900–1940,* pp. 5–91. United States Government Printing Office, 1943; A. J. Jaffe, *Handbook of Statistical Methods for Demographers,* pp. 43–84. United States Government Printing Office, 1951; George W. Barclay, *Techniques of Population Analysis,* pp. 16–202. John Wiley

such as 100 or 1,000 or 100,000, so that it will have one or more integral digits.

One of the most commonly used yet least exact rates is known as a *crude* or *gross* rate. The crude rate is computed in terms of the total population of a given area. There are crude rates of mortality, fertility, marriage, divorce, crime, delinquency, and of other vital and social phenomena. A crude rate is derived according to the following formula:

$$\text{Crude Rate} = \left(\frac{\text{Number of cases during a given period.}}{\text{Total population at median point of period.}}\right)\left(\text{Base.}\right)$$

Because of their deficiencies, crude rates should be avoided wherever possible. The futility of attempting to derive an accurate and comparable measure of the legitimate or nuptial birth rate for several geographical areas by dividing the number of births by the total population is very obvious. All members of the male sex and all single, widowed, and divorced females as well as married women above the child-bearing age should be eliminated from the denominator of the formula, since they would not be "exposed" to the condition which is to be measured.

It should not be overlooked that rates are computed in terms of a given period of time, usually one year, and that the population chosen should represent the median point of the period. In actual practice, in order to obtain a sufficient number of cases a period longer than one year may be chosen. In such cases the mean rate is computed so that the interval will be always expressed on the basis of one year.

In addition to crude rates, many other rates possess varying degrees of refinement. As illustrations of refined rates the formulas for legitimate and illegitimate birth rates have already been discussed. The denominator for a crude marriage or divorce rate would be the total population. A more refined marriage rate would include only the population "exposed" to matrimony, that is, the single of legal marriageable age (generally 15 years and over) along with the divorced and widowed. The denominator for a more refined divorce rate would comprise only the married population. In computing refined rates of juvenile delinquency it is the usual procedure to separate the cases by sex and divide the cases for each group by the respective number of boys or girls included in the juvenile court age, generally from 7 to 16 or 17 years. Since the proportion of juvenile delinquents under the age of 10 is relatively small a further correction can be made to include only

& Sons, 1958; Bernard Benjamin, *Elements of Vital Statistics,* pp. 60–123. Quadrangle Books, Inc., 1959; Evelyn M. Kitagawa, "Standardized Comparisons in Population Research," *Demography,* I, 296–315.

those from 10 to 16 or 10 to 17 years in both the numerator and denominator. Similarly, rates for suicide or insanity based on the population 20 years of age or over would be a more reliable measure of the incidence of these phenomena than rates based on the total population. Further refinements can be made by computing rates by small age groups, sex, race, nationality, and other detailed classes of the population. Rates of this kind are known as *specific* rates.

In the process of refining rates, it may be found expedient to use a denominator other than one based on population. The most satisfactory index of infant mortality is derived by dividing the total number of infant deaths (deaths under one year of age) during a given period by the total number of live births during the same period times a base, which is usually 1,000. Infant death rates based on the population under one year of age are not satisfactory because both the enumerated and estimated population figures for this age period are usually very inaccurate. Again, a mortality rate for automobile accidents based on population is a less reliable measure than one based on the number of automobiles in use or the amount of traveling in automobiles. In a study of automobile accident fatalities in the United States Registration Area for the triennial period from 1929 to 1931, three sets of rates were computed. The first set was based on the total population for each state, the second on automobile registration, and the third on gasoline consumption.[45] The analysis clearly indicated that the rates based on automobile registration and on gasoline consumption were more reliable indexes of automobile accident fatalities than those based on the total population.

One of the most common statistical procedures used in deriving reliable and comparable measures of social conditions for the entire population of several areas is to compute *standardized* or *adjusted* rates. By this technique it is possible to obtain comparable rates regardless of differences in the composition of the population. In mortality rates, birth rates, marriage rates, and other kinds of rates the age factor is of utmost importance. Marked differences in the age composition of the population for several geographic divisions would vitiate any comparisons based on crude rates. Similarly, a series of crude rates covering a period of time may not be comparable if appreciable changes in the composition of the population have occurred. For example, the

[45]Schmid, *Mortality Trends in the State of Minnesota, op. cit.*, pp. 208–212.

Table 14.1

ILLUSTRATION OF PROCEDURE IN ADJUSTING OR STANDARDIZING A DEATH RATE. DATA ARE FOR ORGANIC DISEASES OF THE HEART IN THE STATE OF WASHINGTON FOR THE BIENNIAL PERIOD, 1949–50.

Age	*Number of Deaths*	*Population*	*Mean Rate*	*Standard Population*	*Expected Deaths*
(1)	(2)	(3)	(4)	(5)	(6)
0 to 4..	6	263,326	1.1392	107,258	1.2219
5 to 9..	7	203,786	1.7174	87,591	1.5043
10 to 14..	8	159,695	2.5047	73,785	1.8481
15 to 19..	15	157,695	4.7560	70,450	3.3506
20 to 24..	19	175,619	5.4094	76,191	4.1215
25 to 29..	25	195,087	6.4073	81,237	5.2051
30 to 34..	58	188,636	15.3735	76,425	11.7492
35 to 39..	183	180,749	50.6226	74,629	37.7791
40 to 44..	311	159,090	97.7434	67,712	66.1840
45 to 49..	521	138,714	187.7964	60,190	113.0347
50 to 54..	872	125,939	346.1993	54,873	189.9699
55 to 59..	1,275	115,306	552.8766	48,011	265.4416
60 to 64..	1,918	103,916	922.8607	40,209	371.0731
65 to 69..	2,434	86,551	1,406.1073	33,199	466.8136
70 to 74..	2,608	59,655	2,185.9022	22,641	494.9101
75 and over.	6,102	65,199	4,679.5196	25,579	1,196.9743
Total number of expected deaths					323.11811

crude mean death rates per 100,000 of population from heart diseases in the state of Washington for the periods 1929–31 and 1949–50 were 205.1 and 346.9, respectively, whereas the corresponding adjusted rates were 247.7 and 323.1. In other words, the crude rates indicate an increase of almost 70.0 per cent between 1929–31 and 1949–50, whereas the adjusted rates show an increase of approximately 34.0 per cent during the same 20-year period. Of course, the latter figure is more reliable because the age factor in the population has been held constant by "standardization."

The actual procedure of deriving standardized or adjusted rates is very simple though somewhat laborious. For the sake of simplicity let us take as an illustration the problem in Table 14.1 in which only age differences are considered. The basic data represent mortality from heart diseases in the state of Washington for the two-year period 1949 and 1950.

The first step in deriving an adjusted or standardized rate is to compute age-specific rates according to some suitable class-interval.[46] In Table 14.1 these rates represent means for the two-year period 1949 and 1950. For example, the rate 50.6226 per 100,000 of population for the age group 35 to 39 was computed as follows: the 183 deaths from heart diseases recorded during the two-year period 1949 and 1950 were divided by the population in this age group as enumerated in 1950. The result was 101.2452 per 100,000 of population, but in order to determine the mean rate for the two-year period it was necessary to divide 101.2452 by 2. This step and the preceding one can be done in one operation with a calculating machine. We have, then, 50.6226, which is indicated in column 4 opposite the stub 35 to 39. All of the rates in column 4 were derived according to the same procedure.

The next step is to multiply each age-specific rate by the corresponding standard population in column 5. The results are indicated in column 6. The standard population used in this problem is the population of the entire United States in 1950.

The figures in column 6 are added in order to obtain the total number of expected deaths per 100,000 of population. It will be observed that the total number of expected deaths is 323.1 per 100,000. In comparison, the corresponding crude rate is 346.9.

In allocating data according to geographical areas it is important to adhere to some logical and consistent procedure. The most commonly used basis in allocating data is according to the residence of the case. Deaths, for example, should ordinarily be distributed according to the residence of the decedent and births according to the residence of the mother. Until about fifteen years ago the United States Bureau of the Census allocated deaths and births according to the place where they actually occurred, so that valid comparisons from one relatively small area to another were virtually impossible. In official reports marriages are generally tabulated according to the county in which the license is issued, and divorces according to the county in which the decree is granted.

In allocating cases by census tracts, a rigorous procedure should be

[46]For more detailed discussions of standardized rates see Pearl, *op. cit.*, pp. 269–281; Linder and Grove, *op. cit.*, pp. 60–91; and Jaffe, *loc. cit.*

followed. If one is to compute infant mortality rates by tracts, all non-resident births and infant deaths must of course be excluded. In allocating the resident cases the residence of the mother for both births and infant deaths should be used. For other types of studies, however, it might be much more significant to distribute the cases where they actually occur—not according to residence. If such a procedure is followed, the rates would be relatively unreliable from a statistical point of view, but from a sociological point of view may possess much significance. In the present author's studies of suicide[47] the place of self-destruction was considered just as important as the residence of the suicide. In studies of this kind it would be well to allocate the cases according to both residence and place of occurrence. In ecological studies of major crimes based on offenses known to the police, the primary basis for distributing the cases would of necessity be the place where the crime actually occurred. The address of the criminal would be unknown in most of the cases and the address of the victim would not possess primary significance for studies of this kind. If the index of crime is based on arrests the cases can be allocated according to the residence of the arrestee. The available data as well as the purpose at hand should determine the basis of allocation. In any case, the procedure that is used should be clearly indicated by the investigator.[48]

Mathematical Techniques Pertinent to the Analysis of Spatial and Areal Problems

In recent years there has been an unprecedented development of quantitative techniques relating to the analysis of spatial and areal problems. The major objective is to summarize or reduce large masses

[47] *Suicides in Seattle, 1914 to 1925,* pp. 4–23. University of Washington Press, 1928; *Social Trends in Seattle,* pp. 203–215. University of Washington Press, 1944.

[48] In order to test the reliability of rates for geographic divisions, certain formulas may be applied. See Frank Alexander Ross, "Ecology and the Statistical Method," *American Journal of Sociology,* XXXVIII, 507–522; Chaddock, "Significance of Infant Mortality Rates for Small Geographic Areas," *Journal of the American Statistical Association,* XXIX, 243–249; Frederick F. Stephan, "Sampling Errors and Interpretations of Social Data Ordered in Time and Space," *Journal of the American Statistical Association,* Papers and Proceedings (March, 1934, Supplement), XXIX, N.S., No. 185A, pp. 165–166; and Charles C. Peters, "Note on a Misconception of Statistical Significance," *American Journal of Sociology,* XXXIX, 231–236.

of data into relatively succinct and meaningful measures. These contributions have resulted largely from a convergence of interest in spatial and areal phenomena by students representing such diverse fields as sociology, economic geography, plant ecology, economics, urban planning, statistics, and "regional science." Many of the problems and techniques which in the past might have been considered as part of human ecology have acquired a broad interdisciplinary cast.

The basic interests, perspectives, and emphases in areal differentiation reflect a notable diversity among the various disciplines. There are such interests as the following:

> (a) chorographic interest in areal differentiation, i.e., in the characteristics of area; (b) interest in areal distribution; (c) interest in spatial structure; and (d) concern with the explanation of areal variation. To these "perspectives" must be added (e) the use of areal data for objectives not intrinsically related to areal differentiation or spatial pattern. Though subtle and frequently blurred in actual research, the distinctions among these perspectives are not unimportant.[49]

In examining the many analytical techniques applicable to spatial and areal problems, the student will find them ranging from relatively simple, rudimentary formulas to highly elaborate and complicated mathematical models. Furthermore, some techniques are practical and straightforward, while others are highly theoretical and abstract.

The following are examples of various kinds of statistical techniques that have been developed during the past few decades for analyzing spatial and areal problems.

Centrographical and related techniques. One of the earliest developments of this kind is the "centrographical" method which emphasizes primarily mean centers, median centers, median points and related concepts.[50] Among the various centrographical concepts

[49]Otis Dudley Duncan, Ray P. Cuzzort, and Beverly Duncan, *Statistical Geography,* p. 19. The Free Press of Glencoe, Inc., 1961.

[50]E. E. Sviatlovsky and Walter Crosby Eels, "The Centrographic Method and Regional Analysis," *Geographical Review,* XXVII, 240–254; J. F. Hart, "Central Tendency in Areal Distributions," *Economic Geography,* XXX, 48–59. For excellent summary discussions of the application of statistical techniques to spatial and areal problems see: Roberto Bachi, "Standard Distance Measures and Related Methods for Spatial Analysis," *Regional Science Association, Papers,* X, 83–132; William Warntz and David Neft, "Contributions to a Statistical Methodology for Areal Distribution," *Journal of Regional Science,* II, 47–66.

and tools, the mean center is perhaps the most commonly used for summarizing data as well as for showing trends over a period of time. The mean center represents the center of gravity or center of mean distances of spatial distributions. It has been widely used by the United States Bureau of the Census in computing the center of population from one census to another.[51]

In an attempt to analyze certain processes of city expansion, the present author derived two series of mean centers based on building permits and demolitions for the city of Minneapolis extending back to 1885. Approximately 75,000 cases were used in this analysis. The changes and direction of city expansion were readily observable from the positions of the mean centers of building construction and demolitions for each of the several quinquennial periods.

Indexes and other statistical techniques relating to the spatial distribution of phenomena. In an effort to develop other indexes pertaining to the distribution of population, the author and his colleagues devised several measures of "ecological segregation." Four of these measures were discussed in a published paper.[52] As a basis for testing empirically the four measures of segregation, data on the Negro population for samples of 44 and 25 census tract cities, respectively, were selected for analysis. From this study it was possible to determine the degree of segregation of the Negro population among these cities. Although these indexes were used to measure racial segregation, they also are applicable for measuring the spatial patterning of other phenomena.[53]

Several additional distributional and locational measures and techniques similar to segregation indexes have been devised by Philip M. Hauser, Otis Dudley Duncan and Beverly D. Duncan.[54] The following have been selected for illustrative purposes. The "index of

[51]United States Bureau of the Census, *Census of Population: 1960,* Vol. 1, Part A, p. xi and p. S11.

[52]Julius Jahn, Calvin F. Schmid, and Clarence E. Schrag, "The Measurement of Ecological Segregation," *American Sociological Review,* XII, 293–303.

[53]For subsequent discussions of segregation indexes, see Josephine J. Williams, "Another Commentary on So-Called Segregation Indices," *American Sociological Review,* XIII, 298–303; Wendell Bell, "A Probability Model for the Measurement of Ecological Segregation," *Social Forces,* XXXII, 357–364; Otis Dudley Duncan and Beverly Duncan, "A Methodological Analysis of Segregation Indexes," *American Sociological Review,* XX, 210–217.

[54]*Methods of Urban Analysis: A Summary Report,* Air Force Personnel and Training Research Center, 1956.

population concentration" measures the degree to which a population is distributed unevenly over the area of a city. If a population is distributed evenly throughout the city, the index would be zero. On the other hand, a large index is indicative of a heavy concentration of population in a small part of the city. An "index of centralization" was designed to measure the degree of centralization of various phenomena in the city. Distance from the center of the city is the basic dimension. A high index of centralization indicates that there is a pronounced tendency for the phenomenon in question to locate either in the central area or in contiguous zones.

Correlation and related techniques. Among standard statistical tools in the behavioral sciences, the human ecologist has made extensive use of simple correlation and multivariate analysis. The units of analysis are customarily census tracts or some other area such as precincts or counties. As illustrative of the application of simple correlation, two papers relating to the basic ecological structure of the American city might be cited.[55] Both of these papers emphasize the striking parallelism, as well as certain minor differences, in the ecological patterning of demographic and sociological phenomena in the large American city. In applying correlational techniques to ecological data, the student is cautioned not to make unwarranted inferences concerning the behavior of individuals.[56]

In addition to the utilization of simple correlation in ecological research, extensive use has been made of partial and multiple correlation, factor analysis, and analysis of variance and covariance.[57]

[55]Calvin F. Schmid, "Generalizations Concerning the Ecology of the American City," *American Sociological Review,* XV, 264–281; Calvin F. Schmid, Earle H. MacCannell, and Maurice D. Van Arsdol, "The Ecology of the American City: Further Comparison and Validation of Generalizations," *ibid.,* III, 392–401.

[56]William S. Robinson, "Ecological Correlations and the Behavior of Individuals," *American Sociological Review,* XV, 351–357. In this connection, see also: Leo A. Goodman, "Ecological Regression and Behavior of Individuals," *American Sociological Review,* XVIII, 663–664; Leo A. Goodman, "Some Alternatives to Ecological Correlation," *American Journal of Sociology,* LXIV, 610–625.

[57]See, Donald J. Bogue and Dorothy L. Harris, *Comparative Population and Urban Research Via Multiple Regression and Covariance Analysis.* Scripps Foundation Studies in Population Distribution, 1954; Sultan H. Hashmi, "Factors in Urban Fertility Differences in the United States," in Ernest W. Burgess and Donald J. Bogue, eds., *Contributions to Urban Sociology,* Chapter 4, pp. 42–58. University of Chicago Press, 1964; Nathan Keyfitz, "Analysis of Vari-

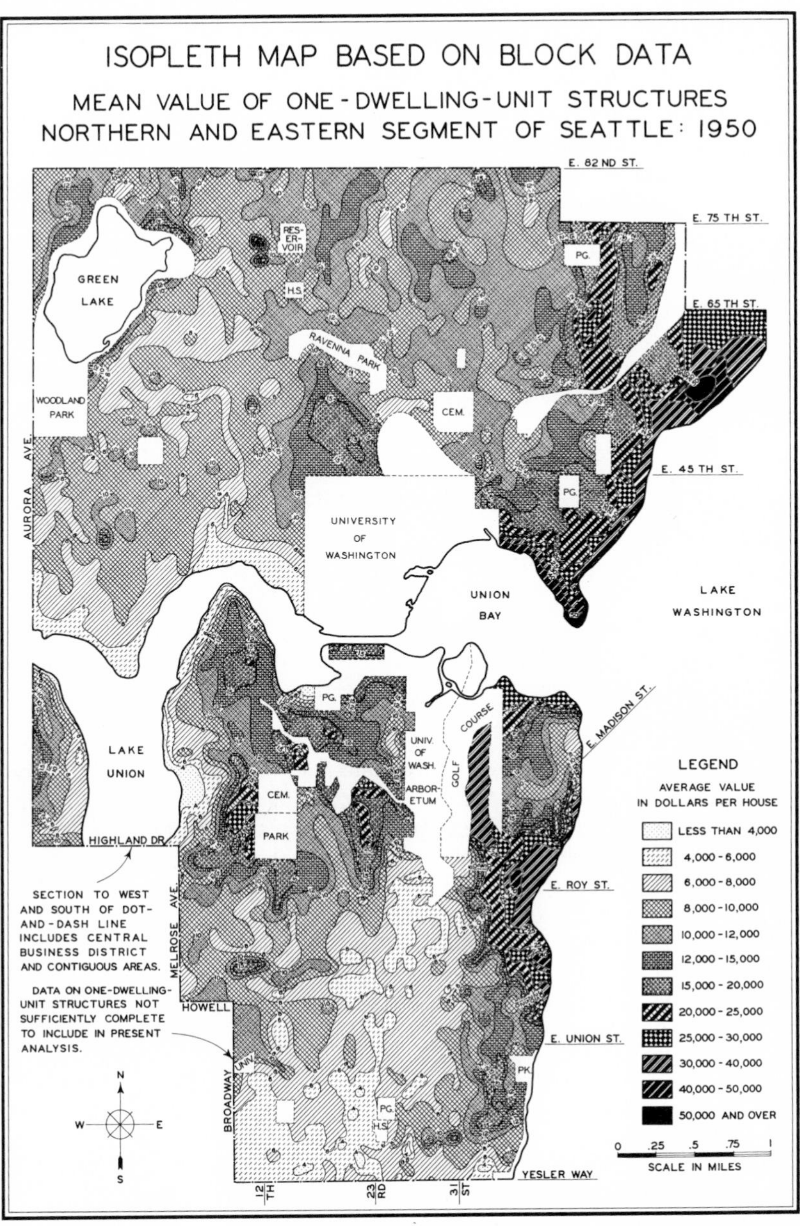

Figure 14.9 An isopleth map based on data for 290 enumeration districts. This portion of Seattle comprises approximately 20 square miles of land area. From Calvin F. Schmid and Earle H. MacCannell, "Basic Problems, Techniques and Theory of Isopleth Mapping," *Journal of the American Statistical Association,* L, 220–239.

Isoline maps. Another technique for analyzing spatial data is represented by lines on a map which are in many ways similar to the contour lines on a topographical map. The generic term for this technique is isoline (from *isos,* meaning "equal") map. In sociology, isoline maps are based almost invariably on rates or percentages for areas such as census tracts, townships, or precincts, rather than on measurements or values for specific points such as are used in developing topographical and weather maps. The type of isoline map derived from rates and percentages for specified areas is referred to as an isopleth map. In constructing an isopleth map, rates or percentages are first computed according to relatively small areas. The isopleth values are then calculated from rates or percentages of the different areal units by means of an interpolation procedure. Figure 14.9 is an illustration of an isopleth map portraying the mean value of residential structures.[58]

Gravity, potential and related concepts, and techniques. During the past two decades gravity and potential models and techniques have enjoyed considerable interest and significance in the analyses of spatial and areal problems. Gravity and potential concepts of human interaction were developed from analogy to Newtonian physics of matter.

> In general terms, the gravity concept of human interaction postulates that an attracting force of interaction between two areas of human activity is created by the population masses of the two areas, and a friction against interaction is caused by the intervening space over which the interaction must take place. That is, interaction between the two centers of population concentration varies directly with some function of the population size of the two centers and inversely

---

ance Procedures in the Study of Ecological Phenomena," Chapter 10, pp. 148–162, *ibid.;* Calvin F. Schmid, "Urban Crime Areas: Part I," *American Sociological Review,* XXV, 527–542; Calvin F. Schmid, *Social Saga of Two Cities, op. cit.,* pp. 293–301.

[58]E.g., Elsa Schneider Longmoor and Erle Fiske Young, "Ecological Interrelationships of Juvenile Delinquency, Dependency, and Population Mobility: A Cartographic Analysis of Data from Long Beach, California," *American Journal of Sociology,* XLI, 598–610. For a more detailed discussion of isoline maps including techniques of construction, see Calvin F. Schmid, *Handbook of Graphic Presentation, op. cit.,* pp. 212–219; Calvin F. Schmid and Earle H. MacCannell, "Basic Problems, Techniques and Theory of Isopleth Mapping," *Journal of American Statistical Association,* L, 220–239.

with some function of the distance between them. In mathematical terms, one way in which the relationship may be expressed is as follows:

$$(1) \qquad I_{ij} = \frac{f(P_{ij}P_j)}{f(D_{ij})}$$

where I_{ij} = interaction between center i and center j;
$P_{ij}P_j$ = population of areas i and j, respectively; and
D_{ij} = distance between center i and center j.[59]

One of George Kingsley Zipf's basic hypotheses is further illustrative of this approach. *The number of persons that move between any two communities in the United States whose respective populations are* P_1 *and* P_2 *and which are separated by the shortest transportation distance, D, will be proportionate to the ratio* $P_1 \cdot P_2/D$, *subject to the effect of modifying factors.* In testing this hypothesis data for passengers by railway, bus, and airplane were used.[60]

John Q. Stewart, an astronomer, also has developed similar formulations. Stewart's principle of "potential of population," originally developed in 1940, has been applied to various kinds of problems relating to population distribution. For example, 1) the drawing power of a college or school on given communities or states tends to be proportionate to the population of a state divided by its distance from the campus, and 2) attendance at the New York World's Fair in 1940 by states is proportionate to the population of a state divided by the distance from Flushing, Long Island. It will be observed that these relationships can be simply expressed by the formula N/D. Stewart

[59]Gerald A. P. Carrothers, "An Historical Review of the Gravity and Potential Concepts of Human Interaction," *Journal of the American Institute of Planners,* XXII, 94–102. For further discussion of gravity and potential models as well as other models and techniques applicable to ecological problems, see: Walter Isard, *Methods of Regional Analysis: An Introduction to Regional Science.* John Wiley & Sons, 1960.

[60]*National Unity and Disunity.* Principia Press, 1941, *passim; Human Behavior and the Principle of Least Effort,* esp. pp. 347–415. Addison-Wesley Press, 1949; "Some Determinants of the Circulation of Information," *American Journal of Psychology,* LIX, 401–421; "The P_1P_2/D Hypothesis: The Case of Railway Express," *Journal of Psychology,* XXII, 3–8; "The P_1P_2/D Hypothesis: On Intercity Movement of Persons," *American Sociological Review,* XI, 677–685; "The Hypothesis of the Minimum Equation as a Unifying Principle: With Attempted Synthesis," *American Sociological Review,* XII, 627–650.

has worked out other formulations as well as the construction of detailed "potential" maps.[61]

Samuel A. Stouffer's papers on "intervening opportunities" are another example of this type of model.[62] Stouffer's basic hypothesis may be stated verbally as follows: *the number of persons going a given distance is directly proportional to the number of opportunities at that distance and inversely proportional to the number of intervening opportunities.*

In mathematical terms the hypothesis is

$$\frac{\Delta_y}{\Delta_s} = \frac{a\Delta_x}{x\Delta_s}$$

where Δ_y = the number of persons moving from an origin to a circular band of width Δ_s, its inner boundary being s − $1/2\Delta_s$ units of distance from the origin or center of the circle and its outer boundary being s + $1/2\Delta_s$ units from the origin. (Distance may be measured in units of space, or even of time or cost.)

X = the number of intervening opportunities, that is, the cumulated number of opportunities between the origin and distance s. (Opportunities must be precisely defined in any employment of the theory. The particular operational definition appropriate will depend on the type of social situation investigated. This is the hardest problem in any practical application. In the main body of the paper a precise definition, appropriate to the concrete study here made, is developed.)

Δ_x = the number of opportunities within the band of width Δ_s.

This hypothesis was empirically tested with intra-city mobility data from the city of Cleveland. Additional tests were made by other investi-

[61]Stewart, "An Inverse Distance Variation for Certain Social Influences," *Science,* XCIII, 89–90; "The 'Gravitation,' or Geographic Drawing Power, of a College," *Bulletin American Association of University Professors,* XXVII, 70–75; "A Measure of the Influence of a Population at a Distance," *Sociometry,* V, 63–71; "Empirical Mathematical Rules Concerning the Distribution and Equilibrium of Population," *Geographical Review,* XXXVII, 461–485; "Suggestion Principles of 'Social Physics'," *Science,* CVI, 179–180; John Q. Stewart and William Warntz, "Physics of Population Distribution," *Journal of Regional Science,* I, 99–123. In recent years the geographer has been giving much more attention to quantitative techniques. The following article contains references which the sociologist will find useful: Robert B. Reynolds, "Mathematical Geography," *The Geographic Review,* XLVI, 129–131.

[62]Samuel A. Stouffer, "Intervening Opportunities: A Theory Relating Mobility and Distance," *American Sociological Review,* V, 845–867; and "Intervening Opportunities and Competing Migrants," *Journal of Regional Science,* II, 1–20.

gators in the field and certain discrepancies were found. The demonstrations, however, were not conclusive, partly because of inadequate data and partly because of needed refinements in Stouffer's hypothesis.[63]

[63]Margaret L. Bright and D. S. Thomas, "Interstate Migration and Intervening Opportunities," *American Sociological Review,* VI, 773–783; Eleanor Collins Isbell, "Internal Migration in Sweden and Intervening Opportunities," *American Sociological Review,* IX, 627–639; Fred L. Strodbeck, "Equal Opportunity Intervals: A Contribution to the Method of Intervening Opportunity Analysis," *American Sociological Review,* XIV, 490–497; Theodore R. Anderson, "Intermetropolitan Migration: A Comparison of the Hypotheses of Zipf and Stouffer," *American Sociological Review,* XX, 287–291; Fred Charles Ikle, "Comment on Theodore R. Anderson's 'Intermetropolitan Migration: A Comparison of the Hypotheses of Zipf and Stouffer'," *ibid.,* 713–714.

15

some guiding considerations in the analysis of research data

Science is built with facts as a house is built with stones, but a collection of facts is no more science than a heap of stones is a house.

JULES HENRI POINCARÉ

"Ideas, facts, ideas, figures, ideas. . . . [With these] you are trying to build a little world containing all the key elements which enter into the work at hand; to put each in its place in a systematic way, continually readjusting the framework around the developments in each part of it. Merely to live in such a world is to know what is needed: ideas, facts, ideas, figures, ideas."[1] So has the late C. Wright Mills succinctly summarized the aims of social analysis.

A social analyst assumes that behind his accumulated data there is something more important and revealing than the facts and figures themselves. He assumes that carefully thought out, well-marshaled facts and figures, when related to the whole body of data, have significant general meaning from which valid generalizations can be drawn. He further assumes that social analysis is a continuous process throughout the entire research undertaking, though rudimentary and tentative at the start. The very determination of what types of data to secure, what techniques to use in securing them, what sources to tap, what hypotheses to formulate and test, and how to test them, necessitates classification and analysis. A student hardly needs to stand in awe of social analysis. He has been involved in it, in a way, since the early beginnings of his research project.

[1]*The Sociological Imagination,* p. 223. Oxford University Press, 1959.

Systematic analysis, however, is a special process used at the time the whole body of the gathered data—facts and ideas, figures and ideas—is at hand. The function of systematic analysis is to build an intellectual edifice in which properly sorted and sifted facts and figures are placed in their appropriate settings and consistent relationships, so that general inferences can be drawn from them—the aim of a mature science.

The aim imposes a number of demands upon the analyst. He must remember that facts and figures, in and by themselves, do not often make scientific sense. And contrary to popular belief, facts and figures do not speak for themselves. Raw and bare, standing in a social vacuum so to speak, unrelated to their historico-cultural context, they can be the prey of the most reckless and treacherous of theorists, as the famed English economist Alfred Marshall observed a long time ago.

It should be remembered also that facts and figures are not free and equal. They have many dependents of varying complexities, sources, and structures. Facts are never simple. They pose many crucial problems, all along the research path. They involve subjective and objective elements in varying degrees and combinations. Two teen-agers, for example, of the same race, nationality, cultural background, even of the same dispositions, mental abilities, and educational achievement, cannot be analyzed on the same level of understanding their personalities, since their experiences and attitudes may differ. Louis Gottschalk[2] tells of two battle-weary, thirsty soldiers who, after hard fighting on the desert, return to their barracks and find a bottle half-filled with water. One exclaims: "God be praised, the bottle is half full." The other cries: "Devil be damned, it's half empty." Facts and figures have to be seen in conjunction with the subjective reactions to them.

Social analysis demands also a thorough knowledge of one's data. Without penetrating, insightful knowledge, analysis is likely to be aimless, if not altogether worthless, representing so much "busy work," interesting and comprehensive as the data might be in other respects.

Scrutiny of the assembled data. A fruitful early step in social analysis is a critical examination of the assembled materials, keeping steadily in mind the purpose of the study and its possible bearing on scientific discovery—the ultimate aim of science.

[2]*The Use of Personal Documents in History, Anthropology, and Sociology,* p. 52. Social Science Research Council, 1945.

It is well to allow one's imagination to roam over "all the key elements" of the study; to dwell on its ramifications, on the contrast, and similarities the data exhibit, on the comparative significances of big and little events which symbolize human behavior. Dr. E. E. Levitt reminds us that a scientist, in his aim to understand his materials fundamentally and realistically, must "play the devil's advocate to his own work. He must constantly be a thorn in his side, ever alert to the possibility of error, always on guard lest he go too far in generalizing from his study . . . or being overly enthusiastic about limited or equivocal data."[3]

The researcher needs to cultivate the habit of asking himself many questions about his project and the collected data—even questions which may appear foolish to him at the time. It is this procedure which stirs his imagination and induces new ways of looking at his problems and his data. Some questions might have been already raised, and perhaps satisfactorily answered, but in view of the total body of materials which may point to broader implications, different and fuller answers may be needed. "The only reasonable thing to do, if one wishes to study a phenomenon, is to put 'a specimen' before one's eye and look at it repeatedly until all essential features sink indelibly into one's mind."[4]

Reading and rereading, examining and re-examining the gathered data is one way of eliminating the thorn from one's side or at least minimizing its discomfort, while accomplishing several other purposes at the same time:

1. "getting a feel" of the intrinsic complexity of the data to be analyzed;
2. perceiving their essential relationships, similarities, and differences;
3. checking and verifying the internal consistency and completeness of the various aspects under consideration;
4. weighing the relative significance of the recorded items;
5. assessing the validity of established categories, codes, and classes to which the data have already been subjected in preliminary form.

(These perceptions and discernments, highly essential to adequate analysis, should be carefully recorded on separate cards or slips of

[3]*Clinical Research Design and Analysis in the Behavioral Sciences,* p. 150. Charles C Thomas, 1961.

[4]Gordon Allport, *The Use of Personal Documents in Psychological Science,* p. 143. Social Science Research Council, 1942.

paper at the time they come to mind. They may never be recaptured for verification or completion of the analysis.)

The following is a specific and detailed, though by no means exhaustive, list of questions suggesting the type of questions which might be profitably raised:

Are the data sufficiently complete to reveal patterns of behavior, sequences, and relationships which might explain the research questions under consideration?

Are the data objectively recorded and are they reproducible? Are they susceptible to quantitative treatment?

Are the sample data representative of the "supply" or the "universe" from which they were chosen? Are they uniform within the same frame of reference?

Are the data still credible in view of different settings, changing conditions, and stages of the investigation? Are they internally consistent?

Is it possible to understand the subjects and objects of study when the data from various sources have been combined into one body?

Do the subjects of study appear as sociopsychological "actors," intricately formed by their cultural contexts? Or do they stand out as isolated beings or systems by themselves?

According to John Dollard and Frank Auld, "sentences [describing human behavior] always have defining emotional and other reactions attached to them."[5]

Do the sentences, especially in the interviews and life history records, carry with them these emotional accompaniments?

Are the data oriented toward the task of understanding the "social structures and the drift, the shaping and meaning" of one's own period of time, to use C. Wright Mills' expression?

If the data were obtained in a contrived social laboratory, can the interplay between milieu and subjects of study be clearly understood?

What essential similarities and differences can be recognized in the phenomena studied?

What significant relationships do the various facts display? What are the bases for the study of cause-and-effect relationships?

Do the established categories still fit? In view of the greater array of facts, what additional categories should be established? Or what old ones revised?

[5] *Scoring Human Motives,* p. 3. Yale University Press, 1959.

How useful are the established categories? (A set of categories is useful to the extent that it is controlled by sound evidence and has reference to concepts, hypotheses, insights, and broader knowledge.) How can the controlling "sound evidence" be demonstrated in the study under consideration?

What new insights can be gained from the total body of data? What new hypotheses can be formulated?

What systematic conclusions can be drawn from the data?

This suggestive list of questions implies the importance of precision, accuracy, and painstaking care in the scrutiny of the data at hand. However, the exercise of these practices should not suggest rigidity and inflexibility. In order to gain any degree of precision, it is necessary to doubt and to experiment with open mind and considerable flexibility. M. J. Moroney maintains that "accuracy of arithmetic" without "accuracy of knowledge" of the whole subject of study, can lead only to "delusions of accuracy," a fatal step which can invalidate any study.[6] And these thoughts come from a master mathematician.

If, on the basis of what has already been said about the analysis of data, the reader anticipates considerable painstaking work, he should remember that such work is not only the basis for scientific discovery but is also extremely fascinating and at times even soul-satisfying. Witness, for example, the words of Roger R. Miller, a social scientist, and Edna Ferber, a highly insightful journalist:

> Analyzing and interpreting the results of a study is exciting business. . . . An otherwise calm and composed individual may begin to act like a gambling addict. He cannot stop if things are breaking well, nor can he quit during a run of bad luck. . . . The investigator has a piece of his life hanging in balance . . . he has made a number of decisions, each of which involves some risk. The die has been set, and all that remains is to learn whether he has won or lost.[7]

> Awake or asleep the story is with you, haunting you, dogging your footsteps. Strange formless bits of material float out of the ether about you and attach themselves to the main body of the story, as though hung there suspended in the air, waiting. [Waiting to be analyzed.][8]

A researcher becomes more than absorbed in his materials. He

[6] *From Facts to Figures,* p. 3. Penguin Books, 1956.

[7] Miller, "Statistical Analysis of Data," in Norman Polanski, *Social Work Research,* 167. The University of Chicago Press, 1960.

[8] Ferber, *A Peculiar Treasure,* p. 224. Lancer Books, 1960.

experiences them. Such a situation, however, may involve some risk to scientific procedure. It may lead a sensitive person, warns Dorwin P. Cartwright, "to insights and conclusions, and these may be, in a certain sense 'correct.' But in the long run, both scientific and practical progress require more than sensitive insight (though both can certainly profit by it.)"[9] Science also requires that the data to be analyzed and interpreted : 1) be reproducible, 2) be readily disposed to quantitative treatment, 3) have significance for some systematic theory, and can serve as a basis for broader generalizations beyond the immediate content of the facts under study.[10]

Preparation of an outline. After thorough review of the materials, it is advisable to prepare an outline—a "blueprint" of the study. An outline is in reality a classification of the major aspects of the assembled facts. For purposes of illustration we present a small section of an outline which might be prepared in a study on the nature and reputed causes of unemployment in a certain district:

A. Introductory remarks
B. Nature of unemployment
    1. Persistent unemployment ascribed to:
        a. incurred industrial injuries
        b. lack of training
        c. excessive labor turnover
        d. consolidations and mergers of industrial plants
        e. high rate of movement from rural to urban centers
        f. age limits in hiring
        g. deterioration in work habits
        ....
    2. Seasonal unemployment ascribed to:
        a. fluctuations and irregularities in production
        b. fluctuations and irregularities in consumption
        ....
    3. Technological unemployment ascribed to:
        a. mechanization in industrial plants
        b. mechanization in agriculture
        c. development of power plants
        ....

[9]Analysis of Quantitative Materials," in Leon Festinger and Daniel Katz, *Research in the Behavioral Sciences,* p. 434. The Dryden Press, 1953.

[10]For a full discussion of these points see D. P. Cartwright, in Festinger and Katz, *op. cit.,* pp. 435–454.

4. Cyclical unemployment ascribed to:
    a. business cycle
    b. maladjustment in exchange
    . . . .

C. Extent of various types of unemployment
    1. Persistent
    2. Seasonal
    3. Technological
    4. Cyclical
    . . . .

D. . . . .

It is obvious that an outline aids in visualizing the whole study as well as the relatedness of its various aspects. The whole range of associated and naturally allied facts comes to view.

A preliminary outline may be prepared on loose sheets—a separate sheet for each of the major topics—to permit additions, reclassification, and other changes which are generally inevitable as the whole body of data is re-examined and insights into it grow. The preliminary outline should be as comprehensive as the data will permit and should focus attention on all major factors in the study. At a later time this outline could be condensed and some detailed items combined into more general groupings.

The sequence in which the various subjects in the outline should be presented is a matter of logical consideration, or of the objectives of the study, or of the need for emphasis of certain factors. At times it may be necessary to begin with trial-and-error techniques, placing the major divisions of the study in the order and relation to each other that seems most expedient and natural in view of the nature of the data. When the trial-and-error techniques are used predominantly, much testing will be necessary before the sequences are arranged in logical order.

The preparation of the outline should not be undertaken when only scattered facts are retained in mind. Under those circumstances, the vital relationships existing between the data may escape us. Neither should an outline be undertaken when we have not sufficient time or energy to devote to it. If it is to be the "blueprint" of the study, it needs attentive thought and care.

In short, a careful outline aids in determining whether the basic facts stand in the proper relationships to each other, whether there are serious gaps in the data, and whether the writer has assimilated his facts.

After a tentative outline has been worked out, it is often advisable to consult with someone who is frank and honest, who has insight into the study, and who will not hesitate to point out omissions, errors in logical arrangement, overemphasis of some points and under-emphasis of others—points the worker himself has not caught. Such critics may be hard to find. At times, even one's best and most competent friends hesitate to say openly what they observe—or they cannot afford the time necessary for the study of the data. However, if the worker has been openminded and has received criticism and suggestions graciously, such hesitancy may be minimized.

It is also valuable to attempt to explain the data and the outline to some intelligent person who knows little or nothing about the subject under consideration. To the extent to which this person gains insight and interest in the material, it may be said that the interpreter has mastery over his subject.

EXTRANEOUS FINDINGS. It was indicated earlier that if unplanned findings crop up and they do not seem to have any relation to the immediate study objectives as far as can be determined at the time, these findings should be set aside for the time being. But they need to be re-examined before the final processing of the data. What may have appeared at first as extraneous information may later become the key to the understanding of a difficult situation. For example, when the Molokans began expounding on the Russian schism which took place in the seventeenth century in central Russia, the information seemed too far removed from the main issues the Molokans were facing in California three hundred years later. Not until a great deal of information had been obtained which shed a great deal of light on the formation of the Molokan personality, did the effects of the schism fall in line. During the schism the dissenters were subjected to many indignities, cruel punishments, excessive and burdensome fines, deprivations, and persecutions—all of which were endured by the dissenters with resolute determination and great pride. The greater the cruelties imposed by the orthodox clergy, the firmer the cohesiveness of the dissenters and the strength of their convictions. The fierce struggle of the schismatics to maintain their religious identity became their very way of life. It influenced their thinking, acting, and feeling, and was passed on from generation to generation, as part of the religious ritual, and was codified in their religious writings. Without a knowledge of the schism, it would not have been possible to understand the bases of the Molokan personality nor to account for the intensity of the Molokans' religious convictions.

Content Analysis

Content analysis is a research technique for the systematic, objective, and quantitative description of the content of research data procured through interviews, questionnaires, schedules, and other linguistic expressions, written or oral. This definition is a slight modification of the one formulated by Bernard Berelson in his famed communication researches.[11] In order to illustrate the technique of content analysis, we will refer back to the life history record of Anna Pavlova, presented in Chapter 10. We note that this record is divided into sentence- or phrase-units which represent fragments of behavior (an attitude, an emotion, or an overt act) to which labels or categories may be assigned. For example, in units marked (5), (14), (15), (16), we discern mobility of Molokan families; in units marked (29), (30), (38), (39), (42), we note occupational mobility of Molokan youth. Keeping in mind the purpose of this study—assimilation processes of a religious sectarian group in the United States—we have assigned such categories to the Anna Pavlova record and to other similar records procured from other Molokan young people in the same study. Behavior which seemed to fall into the following categories was observed again and again in the above records: cultural conflicts, occupational mobility, parents' struggle against the assimilation of youth, youths' assimilation problems, resistence to native heritages, cultural hybridism, and other such concepts. (In scanning the Anna Pavlova record, the reader should attempt, as a special exercise, to fit the above concepts to the marked units in the record.)

Familiarity with social science concepts and theory greatly aids in categorizing research data. Frequently certain categories seem to flow out of the data at hand. Dollard and Auld, as we shall see presently, use a much stronger expression: ". . . the data seem to cry aloud to have a certain sign put upon them. . . ." On the whole, however, the use of concepts and categories requires deliberate thought. The same authors in their attempts to score human motives arrived at another conclusion: "[the analyst] must feel the emotion 'attached' to the sen-

[11]See *Content Analysis in Communication Research,* p. 18. The Free Press of Glencoe, Inc., 1952.

tence as best as the transcript permits him to feel it." They are convinced that the transcript alone will suffice in this endeavor and that the ability to discern emotion is a common and not a rare skill. "If it were not so," they point out, "the emphatic reading of novels or drama would be impossible. Just as sentence and emotion are highly linked in daily life, so are they still linked when the sentence appears in written form."[12] The reader will have little difficulty in feeling the emotion "attached" to many sentences in the Anna Pavlova record.

The complete life history record of Anna Pavlova, from which the illustrative data were excerpted, covers more than 40 typewritten pages. These data were not easy to classify and categorize, chiefly because of the richness and complexity of their content. Only after considerable sorting and resorting and trial-and-error arrangements of the data, was a classification system adopted. It rests on grouping and subgrouping those attributes and simple clusters of traits and happenings which uniformly stand out as relevant to the inquiry. But, with the mere concentration on the content of the cases, they seem to expand in their implications. Complexities and relationships not previously noted seem to emerge. Suddenly a case becomes too complex for the adopted classification. It requires either a new classification system, or at least a new subgrouping of the case data, and a new determination of the relationships of factors which constitute a group or subgroup.[13] In order to avoid the tendency to force certain phenomena into a particular class, rigorous testing is required before a final grouping is made.

In the content analysis of the data on assimilation problems of Molokan sectarians a number of life histories were used, though most of them were not as long as the Anna Pavlova record. Not all of the cases studied exhibited the same behavior patterns, nor the same personality traits, nor social processes. Nor were the factors found in the cases of equal value or intensity. If we wished to ascertain, for example, the extent of occupational mobility among Molokan youth, the classified and categorized data on this item appeared as follows:

Occupational mobility: present______; absent______

Every case in the study on this subject was read and marked accordingly. If we wished also to study cultural conflicts in the group,

[12]Dollard and Auld, *op. cit.*, p. 3.

[13]L. A. Salters, "Cross-Sectional and Case Grouping Procedures in Research Analysis," *Journal of Farm Economics,* XXXV, 801.

we would indicate it by the same code—present and absent, or "yes" and "no," or by any other code which would indicate existence or nonexistence of the factor studied.

In the classification principle adopted above, we used only two categories. These two categories form a *category set*. However, a set may consist of more than two categories. Assuming that we wish to study degree of occupational mobility in a group, we might decide to use five categories: very high, high, medium, low, and very low. Each category set, with whatever number of categories are designated, is subject to certain basic rules.[14] It must be:

1. derived from a single classification principle;
2. sufficiently exhaustive to make inclusion possible of all responses (or marked units) relative to a certain item in one of the categories within a set;
3. mutually exclusive, that is, with responses fitting into one, and only one, category within the set;
4. clearly defined, so that it is understood alike by all investigators who would code the data.

Not all categorizing is as simple as might be inferred from the above illustrations. If we are interested in the varieties of conflicts, for example, which prevail in a group, we might classify and categorize the data as follows:

1. Cultural conflicts (in the Anna Pavlova record units (25), (53), (54), (72- . . .) might be used):
   within the family group: present______; absent______
   between intermingling groups: present______; absent______
   within the person: present______; absent______
2. Economic conflicts . . .
3. Religious conflicts . . .
4. Ideational conflicts . . .

("The sum of the counts in all of the categories in a set should equal the total number of cases; if the [present] as well as the [absent] category is explicitly coded, we can check whether all cases have been accounted for.")[15]

[14]The section on categorizing owes much to discussion in Claire Selltiz, *Research Methods in Social Relations,* pp. 191–196. Holt, Rinehart & Winston, Inc., 1959.

[15]*Ibid.,* pp. 394–395.

Careful deliberation is required in discerning within the data the presence or absence of the items to be coded, in defining each grouping and subgrouping, and in assigning the appropriate code accurately. It should also be stressed that the same data (due to their complexity), may be variously conceptualized. For example, in the Pavlova record, the units marked (29), (30), (38), (42) were assigned the concept of occupational mobility, but these units may also be conceptualized as resourcefulness of Molokan youth. On the whole, a large number of psychological and sociological concepts may be applied to life history documents, depending on the study objectives and the extent to which the reader penetrates into the data.

So far we have stressed chiefly dichotomous categories: present or absent. Although this "either-or" classification may be convenient and expedient, it is highly limited for research purposes. Researchers generally wish to know, in addition to the extent of an occurrence, its intensity. Under these circumstances, they would use some scaling technique. (See Chapter 12.)

Psychologist D. C. McClelland, who regards a written research record as "a piece of frozen behavior,"[16] calls attention to various forms of content analysis to which such records can be subjected: *interaction process analysis* (for an illustration, see Bales's work discussed in Chapter 3); *value analysis,* in which attempts are made to classify and conceptualize the content according to various values referred to in the behavior units; *need-sequence analysis* that attempts to score the changes which occur in the data when the subjects are under the influence of induced need-states; *symbolic analysis,* which is a technique for analyzing " 'latent meaning' behind 'manifest' content," especially in psychoanalytical materials. Other social scientists suggest other forms of social analysis.[17]

Whatever form of analysis to which qualitative data are subjected, an explicit breakdown is required of some totality into the smallest possible units, if the data will be quantified. Since they deal with human behavior which is difficult to fragment, circumscribing small units is not a simple task. The Gestalt psychologists further compound the difficulties by insisting in social analysis on "primacy of form" and "organizational unity," an understanding of which cannot be derived

[16]*Personality,* pp. 31–35. The Dryden Press, 1951.

[17]The reader will be highly repaid by referring to the stimulating discussions, on analysis of various types of research undertakings, by John Madge, a masterful writer and thinker, in *The Origins of Scientific Sociology.*

from viewing their components, any more than the property of wetness can be derived from a knowledge of the hydrogen and oxygen components of water. The Gestaltists' battle cry has been: "The whole is more than the sum of its parts." (It is not our intention to go into the hot controversy between the analytical psychologists and the Gestaltists who, by the way, have greatly modified their viewpoint in recent years. The reader is referred to the bibliography on the subject in McClelland's *Personality*.) Suffice it to say that most social scientists agree that it is possible to define a set of behavior categories, which can be applied to analyses of personal documents and other written records dealing with human behavior.[18] Much can be learned from the experiences of John Dollard and Frank Auld and their attempts to analyze and score human motives. They state:

> In developing our coding system we deliberatly assumed a naive viewpoint. We came, as it were, fresh to the material and tried to see what kind of system of analysis is called for. If the data seemed to be crying aloud for a sign, we grudgingly adopted it, but only on probation; if further experience did not justify the sign, we dropped it. Many variables were suggested by theory and by the work of other investigators. We resisted inventing a sign to meet any theoretical system or adopting one merely because someone else had used it. We believe therefore that our signs are close to the material from which they arose. [Only under such circumstances can strained interpretation of data be avoided.][19]

In short, individual cases of human behavior can become of scientific significance, since it is possible to classify and categorize behavior patterns, social processes, personal traits; to isolate their similarities and differences, and conceptualize them appropriately. But as George Lundberg[20] has stressed, unless the varied data are gathered according to scientific principles, are systematically classified and generalized into specific types of behavior, individual cases are useless for scientific purposes.

Analysis of cause-effect relationships. One of the most difficult tasks in the analysis of data, especially those pertaining to social and personal problems, is the establishment of cause-and-effect

[18]See John Dollard, N. E. Miller, L. W. Doob, O. H. Mowrer, and Robert Sears, *Frustration and Aggression,* especially pp. 1–26. Yale University Press, 1939.

[19]*Scoring Human Motives,* pp. 3–4.

[20]Adapted from personal letter, January 1964.

relationships. A certain problematic situation or bit of behavior owes its origin and process of becoming not to one factor or set of factors but to a complex variety of factors and sequences. The process of disentangling these elements challenges the skill and sociological imagination of researchers. It is easy, but dangerous, to follow a "one-track" explanation which leads to *the* cause. It is imperative to look for a whole battery of causal factors or *syndromes* which generally play a significant role in bringing about complex social situations. Or, as Karl Pearson has aptly observed: "No phenomenon or stage in sequence has only one cause; all antecedent stages are successive causes. . . . When we scientifically state causes we are really describing the successive stages of a routine of experience."[21]

Some scientists hold that human experience is not reducible to cause-effect sequences. Others, particularly those who advance the multiple determination theory of causation, dwell on the almost unsurmountable difficulties involved in detecting spurious factors and on the difficulties in establishing clearly time-sequences of the variables involved. Crime or delinquency, for example, is "assignable to no single cause, nor yet to two or three; [each] springs from a wide variety, and usually from a multiplicity, of alternative and converging influences. . . . The nature of these factors and their varying combinations differ greatly from one individual to another, and offenders, as is amply clear, are far from constituting a homogeneous class,"[22] on which a scientist can base generalizations.

Dr. William Healy, pioneer in the case study technique and proficient in statistical analysis, shows in Figure 15.1 the intricacy in multi-causation. Although the diagrammed group connections of some simple factors bring out sharply the web of their vital interrelationships, the specific cause-effects are obscure for one concerned with general causes of delinquent behavior and for the projection or interpretation of statistics. "We show," says Dr. Healy, "at three different levels—the delinquency, the offender as a member of some general class, and the causal antecedents back of his tendency to delinquency. The combinations are made only from a few of the ascertained facts and types and could, of course, by addition of facts, be infinitely more complex. The combining lines represent either sequence or conjunction of the portrayed elements."[23]

[21]Pearson, *The Grammar of Science,* p. 130.

[22]Cyril Burt, *The Young Offender,* p. 574. Appleton-Century Crofts, Inc., 1925. See also his 4th rev. ed., 1944.

[23]Healy, *The Individual Delinquent,* pp. 164–165. Little, Brown and Co., 1915.

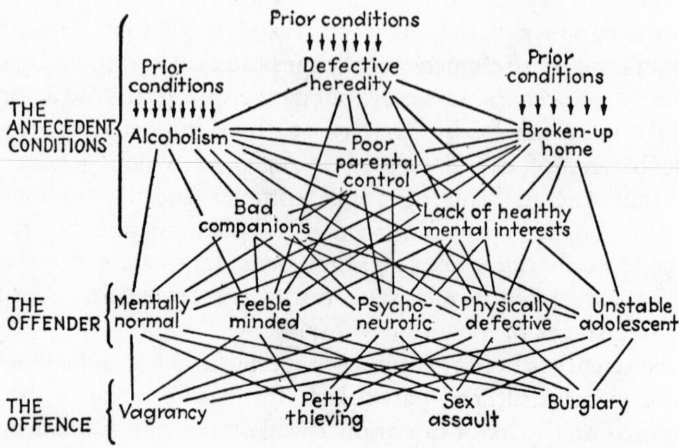

Figure 15.1 Diagram of sequence or conjunction of some simple antecedents and consequents.

> We observe from Figure 15.1 that classification on any level tells little of what is of practical importance on other levels. For example, petty thieving may be committed by any one of the types of offenders on our diagram, who may in turn have been influenced by any of a number of different remotely antecedent or immediately inciting factors. As an instance, the feeble-minded individual, the least difficult of all to group, may be with his deficiency the result of several possible causes, may be directly incited toward crime by inward or outward influences apart from his defect, and may commit any of the diagrammed offenses.
>
> The [delinquent] is not in himself to be grouped according to any logical system, and mere classification of either the antecedent or the consequent of his tendency leads only a short distance along the path of scientific and practical aims. This is the first lesson to be learned from the diagram. The second is that each nucleus of fact cannot, in any fair-minded way, be interpreted as being or having a sole antecedent or a sole consequent. The diagram is worth pondering over with this in mind, before spending time on the estimation of the responsibility of alleged main causes, or the values of even partial panaceas.

Statisticians, as exemplified by the following quotation from one of the oldest, yet still one of the most eminent among them, G. U. Yule, have recognized the fact that statistics "must accept for analysis data subject to the influence of a host of causes, and must try to discover from the data themselves which causes are the important ones and how much of the observed effect is due to the operation of each."[24]

In his "Introduction" to Mirra Komarowsky's *The Unemployed Man and His Family,* Paul Lazarsfeld described a technique, called "discerning," which is used in determining causal relations between two variables.[25] The process of discerning consists of the following procedures:

1. Verifying an alleged occurrence (loss of employment as responsible for alleged loss of man's authority in the family, for example). In order to verify this occurrence, it is necessary to ascertain if the person has actually experienced the alleged situation. If so, how does the occurrence manifest itself and under what conditions in his immediate life? What reasons are advanced for the belief that there is a specific interconnection between unemployment and loss of authority? How correct is the person's reasoning in this particular instance?
2. Attempting to discover whether the alleged condition is consistent with the objective facts of the past life of this person.
3. Testing all alternative explanations for the observed condition.
4. Ruling out those explanations which are not in accord with the pattern of happenings.

The data obtained by Miss Komarowsky in her study of the role of the unemployed man plays in his family are used also as an illustration in our discussion below of theory formulation and scientific generalizations in a research study. (For Komarowsky's findings see our Chapter 3.)

Theoretical formulations and generalizations. (The discussion that follows was prepared by Dr. Herbert Blumer[26] at the request of the present author who took the liberty of infusing a specific example, namely Komarowsky's study. It might also be added that, since considerable discussion on working hypotheses and theorizing appears in our earlier chapters, this discussion should be reviewed, especially what appears on the subject in Chapter 4.)

At the beginning of her study, Dr. Komarowsky, as can be recalled, assumed that unemployment in itself does not materially alter an un-

[24]Yule, jointly with M. G. Kendall, *An Introduction to the Theory of Statistics,* p. xv (14th ed). Charles Griffin, 1950.

[25]Komarowsky, *The Unemployed Man and His Family,* p. ix. The Dryden Press, 1940.

[26]Personal communication, May 14, 1964.

employed man's status in his family, if respect and strong ties existed in the family before his loss of employment. This provisional assumption or working hypothesis helped to set and clarify the problems under study. It suggested lines of connection between the bodies of accumulated data; it sketched the lines of data needed for verification of the hypothesis and ultimately for the interpretation of the relations which appeared among the findings yielded by the inquiry. In other words, the provisional theoretical formulations provided direction for the study, aided in classifying the assembled data and in placing the various classes appropriately alongside of each other.

But the aim of a researcher is more than to make sensitive observations of interesting and relevant occurrences, and to classify them systematically. He seeks also in the interest of analysis to show that his observations point to underlying relations and processes which are initially hidden to the eye. The researcher's task is to identify and disengage such factors and processes. It is in the accomplishment of this task that theory assumes central importance. It is not only a guide, a sensitizer to the underlying factors and processes, but it serves also to confirm propositions initially made in the study or to suggest new and different relations in the empirical observations, which may explain the problems under study. Dr. Komarowsky, for example, found that, when her observations of the role of the unemployed man were classified, verified, and tested, she could formulate some theoretical propositions, among which was: "Unemployment does not so much change the sentiments of the wife toward her husband, as to make explicit the unsatisfactory sentiments that already existed prior to his unemployment."[27] This proposition implies that a researcher assumes that beneath what can be noted in observations in the course of the study, there lies a set of factors and processes which may explain what he has observed about the empirical world.

In the formulation of his theoretical propositions, a researcher is greatly aided by an indispensable knowledge of prevailing theory in the area of his research study (but should not be bound to, or blinded, by it), or he is aided by his own theoretical conceptions.

Ideally, in the course of a research study there should be constant interaction between initial hypothesis, empirical observation, and theoretical conceptions. It is exactly in this area of interaction between theoretical orientation and empirical observation that opportunities for originality and creativity lie.

Finally, after the researcher has moved carefully to refine the cate-

[27]Komarowsky, *op. cit.*, p. 54.

gories or classes in which his concrete facts are grouped, he needs to give reasonable explanations of the relations which he has found. This process again calls for careful theorizing. His task at this point is to interpret the lines of relationship in terms of underlying processes which make the relations understandable and which point to the play of more basic factors operating in the area in which he has been studying. In the above reference to Dr. Komarowsky's work, we may note not only a theoretical proposition but also a theoretical interpretation which serves a double purpose: on the one hand, it gives understanding of the general factors which seem to explain what has been studied; on the other hand, it provides a theoretical conception which can serve in turn as a guide for further research studies. It is in this manner that science comes cumulatively to disengage more successfully the basic processes which shape the portion of the empirical world with which a researcher is concerned.

Frequently after a piece of research is terminated, the statement is made that an array of new questions and problems arises. Some of the new questions constitute the groundwork for new research undertakings and formulations of new theories which will either modify or replace old ones. This is the real meaning of research. "It serves to open anew and more widely the avenues of intellectual adventure and stimulate the quest for yet more knowledge as well as for greater wisdom in its use."[28]

Outline of Report on Research Project

Students-in-training frequently ask what a final report on their research project should include. The following is suggestive of the major topics a report should contain:

A. Introduction:
   1. concise and clear-cut statement as to the nature of the study,
   2. aims,
   3. sources of information (including persons consulted and library materials used),
   4. scope of study.

B. Brief statement of working hypotheses which guided the study.

C. Explicit definitions of units of study.

D. Brief statement of techniques followed in study:

[28]Harold G. Moulton, "Science and Society," *Science,* LXXX VII, 175.

1. types of observation used and conditions under which observations were made;
2. types of schedules formulated and conditions under which information was secured;
3. types of case history data secured, their sources, manner of presentation, and preliminary analysis made;
4. sampling procedures and conditions of selection and testing for appropriateness, representativeness, and errors;
5. statistical procedures, sources of statistical data, conditions under which they were obtained;
6. types of scaling techniques used.

E. Brief description of experimental treatment of data and techniques used in experiments.

F. Major findings of study.

G. Major conclusions reached about findings.

H. Special remarks:

1. problems encountered in gathering the data, classifying them, analyzing them;
2. possible discrepancies in the data collected;
3. suggestions to subsequent investigators on same topics in same context.

I. Bibliographical references found useful in study (with annotations).

J. Appendixes might include sample questionnaires, transcription sheets, sample interviews, and the like.

In summarizing the analytical process we may cite Professor Mills's colorful statement regarding it:

> So you will discover and describe, setting up types for the ordering of what you have found out, focusing and organizing experience by distinguishing items by name. This search for order will cause you to seek patterns and trends and find relations that may be typical and causal. You will search in short, for the meaning of what you have come upon, or what may be interpreted as a visible token of something that seems involved in whatever you are trying to understand; you will pare it down to essentials; then carefully and systematically you will relate these to one another in order to form a sort of working model. . . .
>
> But always, among all the details, you will be searching for indicators that might point to the main drift, to the underlying forms and tendencies of the range of society in [its particular period of time]. For in the end it is this—the human variety—that you are writing about.[29]

[29] Mills, *op. cit.*, p. 223.

suggestive outlines

for the study of:

a culture group

a social institution

an urban and rural

community

In viewing the outlines that follow, it should be kept in mind that there is an essential link between a culture group, a social institution, and the community, even though they are, of necessity, presented as separate units. They all derive their being from various socio-psychological processes that influence them and are, in turn, influenced by them. If viewed as isolated units or independent processes, they give no conception of the life within them.

a study of a culture group

Men are creatures of culture rather than knowledge per se, *creatures of habit rather than reason, and what the individual learns at home and in the streets has much more influence on his behavior than have the facts that he has been told in the schoolroom.*

RICHARD T. LA PIERE

16

What is a Culture Group?[1]

To the sociologist and cultural anthropologist, the term "culture" means the sum total of: 1) inherited artifacts, goods, technical processes, and 2) social heritages, ideas, habits, customs, attitudes, values, morals, law, and art, which have meaning to the group. Culture comprises all the material and the nonmaterial products of common human activity. Culture may be viewed as an exhibit of human achievements in terms of language, artifacts, ideas, ideals, and techniques.

A culture group is a union of persons who have a common material and social heritage, common beliefs, habits, activities, and interests, and who live in the same social environment, whether urban or rural, foreign or native, civilized or primitive.

In a more general sense, any social group which maintains social cohesion and expresses and attains common interests in its own unique manner is a culture group. The "Middletowners" are a culture group, as are the Kentucky mountaineers. The Jews on the East Side of New York are in some respects a culture

[1]See Leonard Broom and Philip Selznick, *Sociology,* pp. 52–92. Harper & Row, Publishers, 1963. See also Edward T. Hall, *The Silent Language.* Chapters 1, 9, 10. Doubleday & Co., 1959.

group distinct from the Jews on Riverside Drive in the same city, and both of these groups are distinct in their culture from a Jewish group in Israel, in spite of the fact that all of these three groups are of the same race, religion, and heritage.

Any large American city has a number of varied culture groups represented by: 1) nationality areas (e.g., Poles, Germans, Italians); 2) racial areas (e.g., Orientals, Negroes, Indians); 3) areas which display marked variations in the prevalent culture of the United States (e.g., hobo groups, rooming-house groups, "gold-coast" groups). The latter are more accurately called subcultural groups.

Any culture group has some social organization, some prescriptions for law and order, some traditions in the pursuit of various life activities, some norms and patterns in carrying on an associated existence, some forms of social control to which members of the group are subjected and which most members recognize and acknowledge. In a word, the culture of the group fairly completely encompasses the activities, the thinking, and feeling of its members. But it should not be assumed that the group is an end in itself. Individual members express and follow to a degree their own purposes, wishes, and aspirations. It should be remembered that individual needs, purposes, and wishes originate and mature in, and are affected by, group activities and relationships. The group is a means for the attainment of individual ends. The researcher is concerned with the extent to which members of the group attain their purposes, the means they use for attaining them, the roles they play in the group, the use the group makes of its members, and the effect each has upon one another. Furthermore, he is concerned with the degree of efficiency of the social organization in extending opportunities for the development of personality and the amplitude of life, both social and individual.[2]

Basic assumptions underlying the study of a culture group. In the study of a culture group we assume that in America, ideally at least, no man is used as a mere tool; that he has freedom of participation in the common life of the group; and that his group does not long remain socially and economically isolated from the surrounding groups and from the wider community. We assume that the necessity of economic participation of the group in urban life has reduced or eliminated

[2]See A. Paul Hare, E. F. Borgatta, and R. F. Bales (Eds.), *Small Groups: Studies in Social Interaction*. Alfred A. Knopf, Inc., 1962.

certain social distances, and a system of new relationships is constantly creating new interests, new standards, and a whole new "apperception mass." We assume that although cultural uniqueness does not disappear, a multiplicity of standards, varying in extent and intensity with the age groupings, is inevitable. With the adoption of new standards, of new habits of thought and action, a certain imbalance tends to occur; tensions and unrest begin to manifest themselves, and social and personal problems begin to develop. We assume that the social processes, social patterns, changes, and trends can be sufficiently recognized and adequately studied and analyzed.

The Content of the Study of a Culture Group

The question frequently arises, "What is important in the study of a culture group?" There is no adequate answer, since the study is highly complex, and the interests of students highly varied. In general, it may be pointed out that most, if not all, students of cultural groups have concerned themselves with culture patterns, the social organization, social control, the observable changes that the culture has undergone, and the influence that it exerts upon the group and upon its members and social institutions. But these statements are in themselves too complex and too general, for one may ask, "What does a study of a culture pattern, or of a social institution, or social control include?" and so on and on.

Obviously the student should have a proper social science background before he undertakes such a complex study as that of a culture group. Only under those circumstances will he be able to select and to relate, to expand and to integrate the major divisions of a study of a culture group. Certain suggestive leads are here presented in outline form, which might be followed in such a study. Although this outline is long and each separate division can easily constitute a separate and lifetime study, it is not exhaustive in any sense of the word. Each student will have to add as well as to subtract, to reorganize, or completely change these suggestive leads according to the nature of his project, his interests, background, and available time.

The following suggestive outlines are useful only insofar as they are thoroughly digested and reshaped before the actual field and library studies begin. A certain logical order is implied in the suggestive outlines. It is not intended that they indicate the order in which the material may be gathered, but they constitute a checklist and suggest a form of organization of the data when the field work is completed. Illustrative examples are included only of those phases of cultural group life which are found to present difficulties in comprehending their complexity.

Some suggested questions apply equally to the study of the entire group as well as to certain aspects of it. For example: "What role does the group play in the life of its members?" may also be raised with respect to the family and the other social organizations maintained by the culture group. Another example: "Do the members experience friendship or tyranny? Conflict, competition, cooperation, and accommodation?" applies also to the culture group as a whole, as well as to its various social organizations and institutions.

The "material outfit" of the group.[3] Each group has some unique artifacts and principles of utilizing them.

What artifacts, crafts, tools, weapons, buildings has the group inherited? What has it added? What use does it make of this material outfit?

What influence does it have on social and economic organization? On personality of the individual?

What mental and moral discipline is required to use and to produce this outfit? What habits has the group formed through the use of this outfit?

What value does it have to neighboring groups? To what extent has it been adopted by, and diffused in, other cultural centers?

What are the forms, uses, degrees of influence, and principles of production and operation of the material outfit of the group under study as compared with those of similar groups? What is the significance of the existing similarities or differences?

To what extent is the material outfit a detriment to the group and a source of disorganization, ill health, and social problems? How may they be eliminated, modified, or improved?

What changes have occurred in the material outfit of the group? What innovations have been introduced? How have these been accepted by the group? What new habits have resulted as a consequence of these changes?

How does the group react to spacecraft? To new technological inventions? What new adaptations has it been necessary to make? In agriculture? In industry? in assembly lines?

[3]See Francis E. Merrill, *Society and Culture,* Part II. Prentice-Hall, Inc., 1961. Also Clark Wissler, *Man and Culture,* Part I. The Crowell-Collier Publishing Co., 1923.

History, tradition, and cultural changes. Every culture group has its history, its origin, development, migrations, conflicts, adjustments. There was a time when the group did not exist, or at least not in the particular habitat in which it is living at present. Few if any members may remember its origin and know its complete history. The accounts of its origin may have been lost in the long development of the social forces which unify as well as isolate groups and institutions. But most social groups will have some accounts, at least fragmentary, which distinguish them from others. There may be a written history of the development, migrations, conflicts, conquests, and unity.

The group's history reveals social relationships, human problems, effects on solidarity of the group. Thus the questions are:

> What is the history of the group in relation to social, communal, and personal life? Under what circumstances is it reviewed and by whom? What effect does this review have on the group? What new history is being developed in the group? Who records this history? How does it coincide with other written accounts of the group?
>
> To what extent are the history and the tradition, and their influences and modes of utilization similar to or different from those of other similar groups? What is the significance of these similarities or differences?
>
> To what extent are traditional behavior and thinking of the group changing? What are the effects of these changes? What social problems arise because of the changes?
>
> To what extent does tradition hinder the social and personal development of the members and the group? Is adherence to tradition a source of conflict within the group? A source of social problems? In what way? How may it be eliminated? Modified?

Every social group develops a certain fund of social values and a set of social attitudes toward these values. The sum total of the attitudes and values which a culture group transplants to foreign soil through immigration and the accompanying sentiments and practices in the new land are called social heritages. These heritages generally condition the life of the group in its new cultural setting. Furthermore, they arouse curiosity or they arouse a feeling of strangeness, shock, or moral disapproval on the part of the new neighbors among or near whom the immigrant group settled. As a result of the elements of strangeness and the emotionally-laden contacts, certain antagonisms arise which further condition the life and the attitudes of the group.

> What are the prevailing social heritages of the group under study? How do they manifest themselves in daily life? How do they control the life of the group? How do they allow for the satisfaction of the

fundamental wishes (for new experience, security, recognition, and response)? How do they control these wishes? How do the heritages affect personal originality and creativeness? What intergroup conflicts arise because of adherence to these heritages?

The immigrant or refugee also attempts to reorganize life when he leaves behind his community which is often the basis of his personality and his self-respect. He has set aside his customary and habitual modes of action and has embarked upon the unknown and at times incongruous forms of acting and thinking. Frequently, new tensions, anxieties, and problems appear.

How do divergent attitudes arise among most members? How widespread are they? How does the group deal with nonconformists? What are the social consequences? What do the nonconformists lose by their divergent behavior? When do they return to the cultural fold?

What are the reactions of outsiders toward the nonconformists? The conformists? Those who attempt to control divergent behavior? When do outside secondary groups and social agencies begin to intervene? What are the consequences of outside intervention?

What differences and similarities are observed between the fund of social heritages, their influences, their changes, their problems of the group and that of other groups? What is the significance of these?

Family organization and control.[4] What form of family life does the group follow? What is the degree of its stability or instability and its effects on the young? What is the divorce rate? What is the status of men, women, and of children? What is the degree of companionship, of common responsibility, and of division of labor?

From what sources do the families derive their income? Their wealth? How adequate are these sources?

What provisions are made for the economically underprivileged? What mutual aid organizations has the group developed?

To what extent is education of the young assumed by the family? What type of education: social, moral, religious, ethical?

What are the sexual practices of the young? How widespread is prenuptial sexual intercourse? What controls are imposed by the group? How effective are these? Does the group observe a single or double standard? What is the attitude toward unmarried mothers? Toward illegitimate children?

What changes has family life undergone? What are the sources of

[4]See Ralph H. Turner, "The Family," in Broom and Selznick, *op. cit.*, pp. 356–395.

change? The effects? What problems are connected with change?

Under what circumstances does family organization or control break down? To what extent is the particular organization obsolete in a dynamic social order? A source of conflict and unrest? Of disorganization? What attempts have been made to strengthen it? Modify it? Outlaw it?

Religious organization.[5] What are the chief beliefs of the group? What are the major sacraments of the group? What social ideals does the religion foster?

What is the role of the religion in the lives of the older and of the younger generations?

What forms of social service and mutual aid has the church developed?

To what extent is the church a unit of social organization? What was the process of growth and development of the church? To what extent is the church a form of social control? To what extent is the religious organization of the group a source of conflict and unrest? To what extent is the church an instrument in power politics?

What changes have religious practices undergone? What changes has the church undergone? Has there been a split in the church? A division into "orthodox" and "reformed" groups? What is the degree of social contact between these groups? Of conflict? Of accommodation?

Who is responsible for the changes? What problems are associated with these changes? What is the effect of these changes on the group?

CEREMONIALS AND RITUALS. What unique ceremonials and rituals are practiced by the group? What effect do these have upon the older generation? Upon the younger generation? Who participates in the ceremonials and rituals? Who is excluded? What is the effect of participation? Of exclusion?

In what respect are the ceremonials and rituals effective means of social control? Are they practiced to the exclusion of other means of control?

What are the ceremonials in illness? In death? In birth, marriage, and burial? In other crises? What is the effect of the ceremonials on the solidarity of the group? Are there any initiation rites inducting the young into the group? If so, what is their effect on "we-feeling" toward the group on the part of the young?

[5]See Gertrude J. Selznick, "Religion," in *ibid.,* pp. 396–442.

To what extent are the rituals and ceremonies a source of conflict and tension among the members?

What changes have the rituals and ceremonies undergone? What are the sources of these changes and their effects on the group?

What superstitions are current in the group? What is their effect on members? Malinowski says that "magic serves not only as an integrative force to the individual but also as an organizing force to society."[6] To what extent is that observable in the group under consideration? How does magic serve as an integrative and organizing force? Is the opposite also true?

Social organization.[7] Malinowski says that "social organization is the standardized manner in which groups behave" and is organized activity through which "human beings are bound together by their connection with a definite portion of environment," and that "the concerted character of their behavior is the result of social rules."[8]

To what extent is this true in the group under study?

What forms of social organization has the group developed? What are their sources? How efficient and effective are they?

What changes have these organizations undergone in view of the changing social situations of the group? How effective are these changes? On what were the changes based? What problems arose because of change?

How well adjusted are the various members of the group to old and new organizations? To what extent is deviation from standardized form tolerated? Who are the deviants? Under what circumstances do they arise?

What effect does standardization have on the social organization? On the group? On the individual member? What effect does deviation have on the general mode of life of the group?

How is the group motivated to follow standard custom? Are members "directed by inner constraints"? Under what cultural conditions are these inner constraints developed?

What sentiments has the group developed? How do these sentiments define behavior? How do these sentiments condition the social wishes?

What problems arise within and because of the particular forms of social organization the group maintains? What is the origin of these problems? Their cause? Their significance? What course do they

[6]Malinowski, "Culture," in *Encyclopedia of the Social Sciences,* Vol. IV, p. 639. The Macmillan Company, 1935.

[7]Broom and Selznick, *op. cit.,* pp. 15–51.

[8]Malinowski, *op. cit.,* p. 622.

follow? By what methods are they curtailed or eliminated? (For a discussion of the economic organization, see pp. 529–553.)

Cooperation within the group.[9] What forms of cooperation has the group developed? On what is cooperation based: on mental sameness, fear of invasion, social habit, or common needs?

Cooperation may mean "sacrifice, effort, subordination of private interests." If this definition is true, does the term continue to be applicable to the group under study? Why? What effect does cooperation have on personality?

Does cooperation tend to eliminate the development of social classes?

Does cooperation tend to eliminate regulation by law?

Is cooperation voluntary or forced? Regulated or "automatic"?

What mutual aid societies, labor unions, guilds, veterans' organizations, and labor services has the group developed? What is the extent of their influence?

What special problems, tensions, and conflicts arise because of the particular principles or practices of group cooperation?

Conflict, accommodation and culture hybridism.[10] Few culture groups living in urban industrial environments can long withstand the corroding influences which penetrate slowly and subtly, but persistently.

To what extent are cultural conflicts in the group clashes between divergent cultural codes? To what extent are these conflicts confined to immigrant groups? To what extent are these conflicts apparent in American-born groups of different ages, social backgrounds, races?

In many culture groups of differing patterns—especially in modern urban centers—the young people are exposed to divergent social environments and consequently tend to create hybrid social attitudes and values. Not infrequently they live simultaneously in two or more cultural worlds without being completely adjusted to any one world. They tend to enter, escape, and re-enter at first one and then the other world under varying conditions of life.

In which of the social worlds does the cultural hybrid of the group under study seek status? Does identification with one world interfere

[9]See Francis E. Merril, *Society and Culture,* pp. 34–43. Prentice-Hall Inc., 1961.

[10]See articles by R.H. Turner and S. Schachter on "Social Disorganization, Deviance, and Social Problems," in S.M. Lipset and N.J. Smelser (Eds.), *Sociology: The Progress of a Decade,* pp. 522–527; 543–560. Prentice-Hall, 1961.

with gaining status in the other? What conflicts does such interference create? What are the specific elements which provoke conflict?

In which of the social worlds does the cultural hybrid seek to satisfy his wishes? What culture patterns does he follow? To what extent are these patterns a mixture of old and new modes of behavior?

How well adjusted is the cultural hybrid to newly adopted patterns? To what patterns of the traditional group does he adhere? What conscience does he tend to develop? What personality traits?

How widespread is assimilation of the older group to American way of life? To what extent is conflict minimized between the assimilated older members and their American-born offspring?

To what social and religious principles, held sacred by the older group, does the cultural hybrid adhere? What common rules of conduct does he observe?

What religious ideals of the group have been replaced by secular pursuits of the cultural hybrid? By what code of moral standards does he abide?

To what extent is he a member of outside groups? Business organizations? Recreational societies? Lodges? What social values does he derive from such associations? How well adjusted is he to them? What status is accorded him in these groups? To what extent is such membership an element in his assuming a multiple role of conduct?

Means of group control.[11] What is the nature of group control? What are the bases for group control? What does the group attempt to control? During war? During peacetime?

How are group control and control by the larger community coordinated?

Is group control in conflict with wider community control? With control by law?

To what extent does group control restrain or stimulate members of the group?

To what extent is control vested in the family group? In the school? In the church? In a special group?

What is the relation between group control and customs of the group? What are the folkways and mores of the group? How powerful are they in influencing the group? What is the power of taboos as a means of group control?

What ideas does the group have in regard to social justice? In regard to civil and criminal law? During national crisis? In war? In peacetime?

[11]See R. L. Sutherland and J. L. Woodward, *Introductory Sociology,* "Process of Social Control." J. B. Lippincott Co., 1963.

What is the role of group opinion? How is it expressed? For or against what is it directed? How does it differ from public opinion? On what is group opinion based: facts, objective analysis of situations, personal judgment of leaders?

What code of ethics has the group developed? What classes within the group have developed such codes? To what extent do these classes adhere to such codes and with what consequences? What role do the business ethics or various codes of professional ethics play in the larger community?

What is the role of leaders in the group? What is the extent of their control? How are leaders selected? How do members respond to group leaders? Under what circumstances do they rebel against leaders? What is the role of the leaders in the larger community? To what extent are the leaders the "group personified"?

Does the group practice control through conscious critical agreement? Through voluntary arbitration and conciliation?

What social reforms has the group advocated? What social reforms has it achieved? By what means were they achieved? What are the influences and consequences of these reforms?

To what extent is art a means of group control? What art patterns has the group developed?

What problems have arisen in relation to group control? What types of members rebel against such control? What conflicts have arisen? How are they met? What are the consequences of such conflicts?

Do conflicts within the group lead to formulation of new means of group control?

To what extent has the group been able to control crime, delinquency, vice, and the environment in which each occurs?

To what extent has the group been able to control dependency? Poverty? Alcoholism?

What attempts have been made to change or modify control by the group?

Social change and the integrity of the group.[12] What social, economic, religious, and political changes have penetrated into the group within the last ten years? During the war and postwar era? Which of the changes have been adopted by members of the group?

What has been the origin and the course of change in the group? With what is such change associated?

What ecological trends have affected the group: growth or mixture

[12]See *ibid.,* Part VI, "Social Change"; F. Stuart Chapin, *Cultural Change.* William C. Brown, 1949.

of population, mobility of population, encroachment and invasion by other groups resulting in cultural diffusion?

Who is the first to respond to such changes? What are the effects of such changes on members of the group? On its institutions? On its means of control? On its mores?

How do the changes affect the philosophy of life of the group?

How do the changes affect the status of the members? Their mode of living?

What is the rate of change in the group? During war? In peacetime? To what extent have rapid changes had a disorganizing effect on the group?

What problems and pathologies have arisen because of social change? What advantages have accrued from social change?

Social reform consciously seeks to improve conditions in the group, chiefly through social legislation, propaganda, and education of the group, frequently on the basis of facts secured through social surveys. Social reorganization is a more natural process occurring because of adequate social change in the natural course of social evolution.

What conscious and deliberate methods have been used to effect social reform movements? What social reforms have been proposed? Accepted? Who is responsible for planning the reforms? How are adherents gained?

What is the nature and role of publicity? Of propaganda? Of leadership?

How are decisions made regarding adoption of reforms? To what extent are coercion, boycott, and violence used?

What are the forms of democratic procedure in making decisions? In instigating change? In adopting change? In wartime? In peacetime?

Has the group undergone a cultural revival? What is the nature of such a revival? Its origin? Its course? Its underlying factors? Its effect upon members? Upon the group?

The preceding brief suggestive outline could be used in a study of a culture group as an aid in understanding how a group in any part of the civilized world carries on its associated life, how the varied behavior patterns are formed, modified, or changed under pressures of social institutions and personal interrelationships. In general and briefly, a few main points—which are not mutually exclusive—may be indicated as being among the social researcher's interests, whether he studies the culture group itself, its social institutions or the communities in which it lives:

> The behavior of persons and groups—including their social attitudes in their respective social worlds and their social roles.
>
> The varied interrelationships between persons and groups and their reactions to themselves, others, and their social milieu.
>
> The modes of life that result as a product of social interactions and the meanings these assume or the definitions of the social situations persons formulate in the process of interaction, whether it is conflict or cooperation.
>
> The types of personalities that are evolved in and through social interaction. The desires, ideas, ideals, skills, norms that spring from social and personal interactions.
>
> The social roles that persons assume or perceive themselves as assuming in meaningful contacts.
>
> The social structures and institutions and social norms that crystallize about human needs, desires, social pressures, conflicts, and accommodations.
>
> The dynamic social changes that occur in the social environment and social relations and the effects of these changes on personalities and social structures.
>
> The social problems that a dynamic group or community produces.
>
> The means of social control that develop in and through social interactions.[13]

[13]Cf. Pauline V. Young, "The Nature of Social Research," in Merrill, *op. cit.*, p. 570 (1961 ed.).

17

a study of a social institution[1]

Social institutions are simply social habits which are systematized, instituted or established by groups, and have still stronger sanctions attached to them than do simple customs. They carry a step further the establishment of the social habit through the exercise of authority or compulsion on the part of a group.

CHARLES A. ELLWOOD

Social institution is a very common term, yet it is difficult to define because of the various emphases which are placed upon it. The range of institutions is as wide as the interests and activities of mankind.

"Arrangements as diverse as the money economy, classical education, the chain store, fundamentalism, and democracy are institutions. . . . Any informal body of usage—the common law, athletics, higher learning, literary criticism, the moral code—is an institution."[2] Such units as a school, a trade union, a church, an asylum, a court, a hospital, a prison are institutions into whose molds are crowded the habits, customs, mores, and procedures of a group.

Sumner's concise definition is of interest: an institution is a concept plus a structure.[3] Law, for example, is an institution. It is based on the concepts of justice and equity. Around these ideas were constructed courts, statutory provisions, systems

[1]See Arnold Rose (Ed.), *The Institutions of Advanced Societies*. University of Minnesota Press, 1958. This is a comparative study of modern social organizations in the United Kingdom, Australia, Finland, Poland, Yugoslavia, Greece, Israel, France, Brazil, and the United States.

[2]Walton H. Hamilton, "Institution," *Encyclopaedia of the Social Sciences,* VIII, 84. The Macmillan Company, 1933.

[3]William Graham Sumner, *Folkways,* p. 53. Ginn & Co., 1906.

of punishment, and the like. Organized relief is a social institution. The concept centers around amelioration, social insurance against unrest and personal disorganization. Around these concepts were built personnel, records, policies, systems of investigation, financial arrangements, and the like.

The student must choose a definition which best suits the purposes of his study. Here the term is used to mean: 1) from the standpoint of the social surveyor: the organization or agency which is the physical and material embodiment of such law or custom which the group has adopted and sanctioned; 2) from the standpoint of the social researcher: "A complex of concepts and attitudes [usages, organizations, instrumental objects] regarding the ordering of a particular class of unavoidable or indispensable human relationships that are involved in satisfying certain elemental individual wants, certain compelling social needs, or other eminently desirable social ends."[4]

Types of social institutions. E. W. Burgess, in his studies of institutions in Chicago, speaks of four major types,[5] each capable of further classification: 1) basic cultural institutions (the family, the church, the school); 2) economic institutions (commercial and economic enterprises, labor unions, real estate boards); 3) recreational institutions (settlements, athletic clubs, art clubs, parks and playgrounds, theaters, cinemas, dance halls, pool halls); 4) institutions of formal social control (governmental and social service agencies, and we might add agencies for promulgation of peace, and of economic development).

To Burgess's fourfold classification might also be added 5) health institutions (hospitals, clinics, convalescent homes, camps—which may or may not be included under social service agencies); and 6) communications institutions (transportation agencies, postal service, wireless service, the telephone, newspapers and periodicals, radio, and television).

Any classification of social institutions can be challenged on the ground that it overlaps another. A classification must be based on the predominant interests and activities of the institutions in question.

[4]Joyce O. Hertzler, *Social Institutions,* p. 67. McGraw-Hill Book Company, 1929. See also his *American Social Institutions*, Allyn and Bacon, 1961.

[5]Burgess, "Studies of Institutions," in T. V. Smith and L. D. White (Eds.), *Chicago: An Experiment in Social Science Research,* pp. 140–141. University of Chicago Press, 1929.

Studies of some institutions are so broad that they "appear as separate sciences in the conventional academic organization of our day."[6]

Content of a Social Research Study of a Social Institution[7]

The nature and role of primary social institutions (the family, church, mutual aid organizations) in the life of a culture group have already been presented in some detail in the preceding chapter. The nature and role of secondary social institutions (public education, public health, correctional institutions, economic institutions) are discussed in the following chapter, in the study of community life in an urban and rural natural area. Here we shall concern ourselves with the role institutional life plays in the social process, with emphasis on the general characteristics of social institutions, their origin, development, and change.

Natural history of the social institution. Under what circumstances did the institution develop? What needs was it designed to meet? What major changes has it undergone? What have been the tempo and direction of change? How adequately has it served the group during periods of change? What methods did it have for recruiting members and for training them to follow its established modes of behavior? Its changes? To participate in its planning, valuation, and propaganda? How amenable to change and transformation was the institutional personnel? Why did the changes occur? In what ways has the institution influenced the life of the group? The life of the individual members? The life of other institutions?

What leaders has the institution created? What followers? What conflicts have arisen because of leadership? Because of membership?

How were the members originally recruited? How are they recruited now? Why did they join? Why do they remain members? What does the institution expect of members? What do the members expect of the institution?

What is the relation between the present needs of the group and the

[6]G. A. Lundberg, *Sociology*. Longmans, Green & Co., 1954, p. 501.

[7]C. H. Cooley, "Case Studies of Small Institutions as a Method of Research," in E. W. Burgess (Ed.), *Personality and the Social Group,* pp. 187–189, is still one of the most provocative statements on the subject. University of Chicago Press, 1929.

present setup and principles of the institution? Has marked institutional lag resulted?

Social institutions as a complex of sanctions and taboos. One of the outstanding features of any institution, formal or informal, rigid or flexible, is the complex of sanctions, taboos, commands, and penalties which it imposes upon its members.

What sanctions and taboos does the institution under study impose? What are the reactions of the group to such sanctions and taboos? In wartime? In peacetime?

How do these sanctions and taboos influence the group? The person? Community life in general?

To what extent do the sanctions and taboos of this institution conflict with those of other established institutions in the group? In other groups? What is the consequence of such conflicts? How and by whom are such conflicts dealt with? What is the result? Have any conflicts arisen during the war? What was the nature of such conflicts?

To what extent do the sanctions and taboos curtail the development of a critical attitude on the part of individual members? To what extent do the restrictive forces cause increased criticism by the members? What is the result of these attitudes?

Many institutions tend to restrict and circumscribe the contacts and activities of their members. But with the widening of social contacts, assimilation with the larger community is inevitable.

To what extent does the institution under consideration restrict the contacts of its members? To what extent does it define their social wishes? To what extent does conflict arise because of restrictions? What is the degree of accommodation to, and assimilation with, the larger community? What are the resulting attitudes? What measures does the institution use to deal with and resist attitudes foreign to it? Incompatible with it in times of national crises?

Dynamic nature of social institutions. Social, political, and economic changes tend to disturb institutional quiet and harmony. In time the conventions tend to disintegrate, authority to become undermined, and exacting demands to become unstable. We seek to learn the factors and social forces that disturb the institution, in peace and war.

What changes occur as a result of national crises? How do the changes affect human personality? The cultural groups? To what extent has the mode of living, of thinking, and of acting changed with innovations?

Specifically, who or what is responsible for the change or the new institutional pattern? Have changes and disorders tended toward reorganization or disorganization?

Are the changes understood by the group? Are they welcomed? Are the changes indigenous to the group—that is, did they emerge from within and were then allowed to develop, or were they introduced or imposed from the outside?

If the changes are desired, what traditions and old usages stand in the way of the performance of new acts and functions, and the creation of new patterns?

Social institutions as assigners of prestige. W. Lloyd Warner sees institutions[8] as channels of vertical circulation that enable persons and families to move upward or downward on the social ladder, regardless of their original social position. A person may gain or lose status and distinction with a particular type of marriage, church affiliation, or club connection, or with the amount of wealth or education he acquires.

How are members of the group affected by social stratification? What is the influence upon them of sudden and rapid advancement? What tensions arise in the individual who is elevated? In the individual who fails to be elevated?

Does the institution select its members and test their abilities adequately? What means does it use for selection? For testing abilities? How does the selection and testing of one institution agree with the selection and testing of others?

To what extent is institutional prestige a safeguard against rapid change? Against "foreign" influences?

To what extent have mutual aid organizations gained prestige for their members? What are the aims of these organizations? To what extent are these aims being realized in the local community?

Social institutions and the allegiance of personnel. An institution is often dominated by its leaders. They may have vested interests in the organization and claim the personal allegiance of its members. They may become solicitous, like feudal lords, about the

[8]*The Social Life of a Modern Community,* Chapters 18–22. Yale University Press, 1941.

maintenance of their authority and ascribe to it almost a divine right in the attempt to maintain the *status quo*.

Are these interests compatible with social needs, with the prestige of the institution, with the services to be performed? Are community leaders aware of these beliefs or of rationalizations?

To what extent have war and postwar activities disturbed such *status quo?* What other activities have tended to minimize or undermine allegiance?

Social unrest and crises as an index to the obsolescence of an institution. As long as the social institution is a harmonious force in the community, its members tend to cooperate with one another and with the community; they accept the time-honored usages uncritically and unreflectively. But if there are accepted changes taking place outside the institution and they are not accompanied by changes within the institution, *institutional lag* sets in.

What changing conditions on the outside have or have not been accompanied by changes in institutional conditions? Why or why not?

What tensions and imbalance occur as a result of institutional lag? How effectively does the institution deal with crises?

How does the institution prevent social unrest? Does it try to rationalize it? To defend it?

To what extent can the institution give new order and direction to a disorganized community?

To what extent can the institution assume control during a period of social unrest?

To what extent does it remain an "alien purpose" in the community?

How does the institution reconcile old and new ideas? Old and new principles? Old and new activities? What are the reactions of the older members to innovations? Of the younger groups? Does the institution hold the respect of both groups?

Does change produce chiefly order or disorder? Satisfaction or frustration of the social wishes? What is the mutual influence of the institution and the group upon each other under the changing conditions?

Development of new social institutions. New social institutions may arise under varying circumstances. Social crises may give birth to them. For example, the depression of the 1930's led to the development of the social security program in this country. When the beliefs, sanctions, tabus, and authority of old institutions continue to persist, with little or no regard for the new needs or without a desire to subordinate their beliefs to some common and general aim, new institutions develop, often alongside the old ones. The Congress of Industrial Organizations is an illustration in point. The American Federation of Labor, in spite of the fact that unskilled groups of laborers continued to increase in this country, did not extend its membership beyond the skilled groups. The unskilled groups then considered the time ripe for a new labor organization, and the CIO sprang up. Not until the middle 1950's were successful efforts made to merge these two labor organizations.

New social institutions, with varied programs, may arise not only in response to local or national needs but to world needs. Local groups often participate in institutions which provide world-wide services (United Nations Association, Women's International League for Peace and Freedom, International Refugee Organization, and numerous other such organizations).

What new institutions were adopted by the local community?

For what specific purpose were new institutions developed? What needs do they fulfill? What were the processes of development? What new social values did they develop? Who opposed development of new institutions? Why?

How much and what aspects of the old structure and of the old ideas were taken over by the new institution? Why?

What new social problems have arisen with the birth of the new institution? How are these problems met?

Has a new group of leaders come to the foreground? What is their function?

How do they translate the role of the institution into the immediate field of fact and action?

Is there conflict between the group and the leaders? If so, what form does this conflict assume?

What pressures, if any, have been exerted upon members to join the new institution? What effect do the pressures have upon the group?

To what extent is the new institution an element in social progress? In growth of public spirit and intelligent solidarity within the group?

Who regards the new institution as "radical"? As "progressive"? What are the bases for these considerations?

How does the community at large react to the new institution? What is its status in the community?

To what extent does the new institution reflect new social trends in the culture of the group?

Can it be forecast when the role of this new institution will need to be redefined?

What branches of national and international organizations have been established locally? How well do they function? What groups of people participate?

What social institutions actively promote the peace movement, integration, medicare, poverty relief, American Field Service, peace corps, economic development? What means are used in their promotion?

What is the role of the local social institutions in meeting world crises?

What are the reactions of the community to institutional activities along above lines of endeavor?

In brief summary it may be stated that a social researcher studies social institutions in all their diversity, complexity, and dynamic nature. He is interested in the origin of social institutions, their structure, functions, goals, role of personnel, and means used in attaining goals and satisfying group needs. The researcher studies also the centers around which social institutions cluster (economic activities, religious beliefs and practices, law and order, social welfare, education). He takes account of the social institutions which, according to Sumner, are *crescive;* that is, they grow up slowly and spontaneously; and those that are *enacted;* that is, they are deliberately planned by the group. The researcher concentrates also on the phases of institutional life which strengthen habits, customs, and mores as well as on those phases which disrupt the life of the group and cause tensions and pressures and which may lead to the necessity to reorganize the existing or establish new institutions.

18

a study of community life in urban and rural natural areas: I

The community, including the family, with its wider interests, its larger purposes, and its more deliberate aims, surrounds us, encloses us, and compels us to conform, not by mere pressure from without, not by the fear of censure merely, but by the sense of our interest in, and responsibility to, certain interests not our own.

ROBERT E. PARK

What is a Community?[1]

In spite of the fact that a large number of social anthropologists, sociologists, social workers, and other students of social life have made comprehensive studies of communities, it is difficult to find agreement even within each of these groups as to what a community is. The term "community," like other concepts taken from common-sense usage, has been used with an abandon reminiscent of poetic license. It is difficult to define a community because of its diversity and complexity.

Community has been used in referring to stable, small, autonomous, largely self-contained units, such as colonies of pioneer settlers, primitive tribes, villages, and immigrant areas. Again the same term has been used to designate large, complex, interdependent urban areas, such as Manhattan or Harlem; or highly specialized and subsidiary areas, such as a "Gold Coast" or a "ghetto community." We also find towns called communities, and cities or "great metropolises" called communities. Professor MacIver refers to the

[1]See especially Otis Dudley Duncan, W. R. Scott, Stanley Lieberson, Beverly Duncan, and H. H. Winsborough, *Metropolis and Region.* Johns Hopkins University Press, 1960. Roland L. Warren. *The Community in America.* Rand McNally & Co., 1963.

"wider community," the "large country-community which seeks to coordinate the whole national life—as . . . in Soviet Russia [where] it establishes a form of economy very different from that of the rest of the civilized world." He visualizes "the country-community" as a "unity which permeates a nation, a sense of its distinctive qualities, traditions, and achievements. . . . There are indeed typical expressions of the character of a nation, revealed in art, literature, and historical event, . . . in such figures as John Bull or Uncle Sam."[2]

Since the postwar era we have been referring to world community, as the destiny of one country affects the destiny of others, even on a global scale, particularly with threatening eruptive crises.

At the other extreme we find small, temporary, diverse personal units designated as communities. A trailer camp has been often referred to as a community on wheels. Conrad Aiken in his *Blue Voyage* referred to a ship as a community, since an "extra-ordinary feeling of kinship, of unity, of solidarity far closer and more binding than that of nations or cities or villages, was swiftly uniting [the travelers]; the ship was making them a community."

Community life means more than common ties and common interests. It means sharing government, school systems, transportation facilities, health care, industrial prosperity and depression, recreational facilities.[3]

In general, whether the local community studied is large or small, complex or simple, incorporated or unincorporated, with definite boundaries or without, it always: 1) occupies a territorial area; 2) is characterized by common interests and 3) common patterns of social and economic relations; 4) derives a common bond of solidarity from the conditions of its abode; 5) has a constellation of social institutions; and 6) is subject to some degree of group control. It should not be assumed that such unity excludes social differentiation and stratification. "The solidarity of a community depends not on the absence of differences within it but rather on the absence of certain barriers to the liberation and the consequent modification or adjustment of these differences."[4]

In view of the diverse conceptions of what a community is, it be-

[2]R. M. MacIver, *Society: A Textbook of Sociology,* pp. 8–11, 157. Farrar, Strauss and Giroux, Inc., 1937.

[3]Jessie Bernard, *American Community Behavior.* Holt, Rinehart & Winston, Inc., 1963, Chapter 1.

[4]R. M. MacIver, *op. cit.,* p. 164.

comes highly important to define and designate carefully the type of community selected for study. If a large urban community is chosen, it should be remembered that—as Park observed—"the urban community turns out, upon closer scrutiny, to be a mosaic of minor communities, many of them strikingly different one from another, but all more or less typical. Every city . . . has its more or less exclusive residential areas or suburbs . . . its slums, its ghettos, its immigrant colonies, . . . its bohemias and hobohemias."[5] These ecological clusters are called natural areas because they are the product of social forces and natural groupings and not of artifice and design. (For the ecology of natural areas see Chapter 14.)

A *natural area* constitutes a social world in itself. It has its unique customs, traditions, social ritual, public opinion, and social organization. It is generally occupied by one or more economic, cultural, and social groupings that have common interests and social ties, and participate in a constellation of social institutions and economic enterprises. Hollywood, or Harlem, or Chinatown, or Hobohemia may serve as illustrations of communities as the concept is used here. They are natural areas within larger communities, but they are also communities by virtue of the fact that they represent a constellation of social classes or cultural groupings, a complement of social and economic institutions, common interests and ties, and a recognition of, and a response to, certain social controls. For this reason the concepts natural area and community are here at times used interchangeably.

The social-philosophical aspects of community living. The local community is an organic and psychical relationship as well as a physical configuration.

The community is the indispensable condition of personal and group life. The community alone, at least in modern life, can promote man's physical, social, and spiritual independence. The community may become an extension of his home. The community is a reciprocal exchange of interests. The members form a "we-interest" group, with the common weal as their goal and ultimate purpose.

In a study of a natural area we assume: 1) that it represents a basic unit by virtue of the relative homogeneity of its members, who have

[5]Robert E. Park, "Sociology," in Wilson Gee, *Research in the Social Sciences,* pp. 27–29. The Macmillan Company, 1929.

strong cultural and traditional ties with the social interests and institutions of the area; 2) that this unit is undergoing certain processes and changes which can be identified and studied; 3) that these changes are occurring in every phase of the community's physical and social life; 4) that changes have created new problems, new social situations, new institutions, and modes of conduct; 5) that a new understanding of these conditions is essential in order to see in what ways they are affecting the life of the group; 6) that it is possible to identify trends of community life and changes; 7) that it is possible to study the forces that direct, organize, and control community change; and 8) that the control can be according to a plan—that is, it can be rational, scientific control by purposive action.

C. Wright Mills[6] stated that many of the old conceptions commonly used by social scientists in their study of community processes pointed to the transition from the old rural mode of life to the urban society of the modern era. Sir Henry Maine's " 'status and contract'; Ferdinand Tönnies' 'community and society'; Max Weber's 'status and class'; . . . Cooley's 'primary and secondary groups' . . . Becker's 'sacred and secular,' are all historically rooted conceptions as they portray historical change."

What Park said about the city as a suitable laboratory for the study of changing social phenomena and for testing social theories may be applied with equal validity to a study of a natural area of any size within the urban community.

> The city always has been a prolific source of clinical material for the study of human nature because it has always been the source and center of social change. In a perfectly stable society where man has achieved a complete biological and social equilibrium, social problems are not likely to arise, and the anxieties, mental conflicts, and ambitions which stimulate the energies of civilized man, and incidentally make him a problem to himself and to society, are lacking. . . .
>
> One thing that makes the city a peculiarly advantageous place in which to study institutions and social life generally is the fact that under the conditions of urban life institutions grow rapidly. They grow under our very eyes, and the processes by which they grow are open to observation and so, eventually, to experimentation.

[6]Mills, *The Sociological Imagination,* pp. 152–153. Oxford University Press, 1959. See also J. P. Gibbs (Ed.), *Urban Research Methods.* D. Van Nostrand Co., 1961.

Another thing that makes the city an advantageous place to study social life and gives it the character of a social laboratory is the fact that in the city every characteristic of human nature is not only visible but is magnified. . . .

The city magnifies, spreads out, and advertises human nature in all its various manifestations. It is this that makes the city interesting, even fascinating. It is this, however, that makes it of all places the one in which to discover the secrets of human hearts, and to study human nature and society.[7]

The Content of a Study of Community Life in an Urban Natural Area

The historical setting of the community. When did the community come into existence? Under what circumstances? Was it ever incorporated? If not, why not?

What groups were the earliest inhabitants of the community? What groups followed? What groups moved away? Why? With what effects on the community?

What industries were established? Why? What changes occurred in industrial organization?

What was the early housing of the community? What changes has it undergone? What is the effect on present housing, on traffic, and on sanitation?

Who were the outstanding personalities? What was their influence on the community?

Which were the outstanding institutions? What is the extent of their influence on the present community life? What changes have occurred in their setup?

Can the history of the community be divided into periods? If so, what are the characteristics of each period? What is the influence of each period?

What are the present trends? What are the factors underlying change? What is the rate of change? What are the turning points in the life of the groups?

What basic social ills are seen to diminish with urban redevelopment? What provisions have been made for dwellers' health and convenience?

What provisions have been made for displaced persons where the

[7]Park, "The City as a Social Laboratory," in T. V. Smith and L. D. White (Eds.), *Chicago: An Experiment in Social Science Research,* pp. 12, 19. University of Chicago Press, 1929.

land has been cleared for urban redevelopment? What are the long-term objectives?

What basic problems preceded, and now accompany, a redevelopment program?

The social influence of the physical configuration of the community. The physical boundaries of a community can generally be determined accurately if the community is staked out by political precincts and administrative districts. But such boundaries are artificial. The student of social life wants to know primarily the natural boundaries of a territorial unit which are determined by evidence of internal cohesiveness. Perhaps W. I. Thomas was the first to call vividly to our attention the fact that the boundaries arbitrarily staked out by official procedure do not determine a community. He said that a community "extends as far as a man's reputation will reach," and implied that common life, common interests, social influence, and cohesiveness encircle a territorial unit and form the base for that community.

It is generally possible to secure maps showing highways and main arteries, bridges, railroad yards, parks, cemeteries, universities, and other main physical structures as well as the natural geographic features such as hills, rivers, and lakes. It should be remembered that these physical aspects of a community—often called nonsocial, since they in themselves have no motive or purpose—exert definite influences nonetheless on the social history, activities, and organization of the group. Furthermore, the physical configuration influences the layout of streets, buildings, physical facilities for transportation and communication—all of which in turn influence the human habitat. All physical mechanisms and technical devices bear a definite relationship to social purposes and problems.

Thus, we want to know how human needs and social organization fit into the structural pattern of the community studied.

How does this structure affect land values? The distribution and nature of the population? Business life and contacts? Free associations with other groups of other areas?

How does the structural pattern affect health and sanitary conditions? What is the significance of these effects?

What changes have occurred in the external form of the community? With what processes are these changes associated? How have they affected land values and rentals? How have they affected the residential district, the business district, and the transitional areas? With a change in land values and rentals, what new groups and social institutions have moved into the district?

TRANSPORTATION SYSTEMS AND COMMUNITY CHANGE. Transportation facilities have a profound effect upon the extent and direction of population movements and community stability and instability. A community within easy reach of main lines of travel will not remain unique, distinctive, and self-contained for any length of time.

What are the means of, and what changes have occurred in, the transportation facilities of the community?

How have they affected its stability? Its rental and land values? Its classes of residents? Its classes of business enterprises? The social institutions of the community?

How is the community affected in case of a transportation tie-up? A strike? A blockade?

How does transportation affect social organization?

What highway towns have sprung up? What freeways?

Social isolation of the community.[8] To what extent is the community socially isolated from surrounding communities? What are the bases of social isolation: physical barriers, religious, racial, cultural differences, occupational differences, different economic levels, different social levels? What is the effect of social isolation on the culture of the group? On its life organization? On the younger generation?

To what extent do isolated groups tend to develop into castes and classes? To what extent does social isolation within the community result in social conflicts?

What are the sources of differences in the community?

What are the manifestations of differences? Do these differences ever threaten to destroy the community? To weaken it? Under what circumstances do they tend to support the unity and solidarity of the community?

Among what classes, groups, generations, and institutions do these differences arise? What course do they run? Do they assume the form of conflict? Of competition?

What social problems do these differences tend to create?

What effect had the war had on the social isolation of the community?

[8]See Richard T. La Piere, *Sociology*. McGraw-Hill Book Company, 1946, Chapter 11, "Transportation," pp. 242–271. See also H. H. Jennings, *Leadership and Isolation*. Longmans, Green & Co., 1950.

Social contacts of the community.[9] What contacts does the community maintain with surrounding communities? What outside influences are most pronounced? What is the nature of influence on the old and young?

What is the effect of social contacts upon group solidarity? Upon the entire culture of the group? To what extent are the outside contacts breaking up the social cohesion of the community? What social and personal problems are created by social contacts?

To what extent do outside contacts enrich the cultural life of the community? To what extent do they bridge or widen social distances?

To what extent do contacts with the outside world promote personal initiative, ambition, individualization of conduct?

What are the manifestations of community solidarity? Are there any evidences of oversolidarity and exaggerated unity?

How does community sentiment manifest itself? What is its bearing on the development of social responsibility? To what extent does it tend to eliminate pursuits for personal gains?

What is the bearing of community sentiment on development of "distinct" community types?

What new contacts has the community made under urban development program? What are the effects of such contacts?

The social influence of economic centers.[10] Generally, business, industrial, and trade centers are influenced by the physical structure of the area. They are also influenced by forces which generate wherever people in any numbers are thrown into close relationships—forces of competition, attraction, struggle for dominance, cooperation for the sake of economy of effort, and so forth.

Does the group live in an economically developed area? Or an undeveloped area? What factors stimulate economic development? New agencies and policies? How is economic development related to social and cultural factors?

Is group economy related to international trade? What are the linkages between foreign and domestic developments?

What is the economic base of the group? What is the commercial structure?

[9]See Jack P. Gibbs (Ed.), *Urban Research Methods,* Parts I-III. D. Van Nostrand Co., 1961.

[10]See Park, "The City: Suggestions for the Investigation of Human Behavior in the Urban Environment," in Park and Burgess, *The City,* pp. 1–46. University of Chicago Press, 1925.

To what extent have technological innovations been introduced into group economy? To what extent have these innovations changed customs of the group? Its social institutions? General way of life?

What economic centers are there in the area? Where are they located? In what way are these centers influencing the social life of the area? That of other areas?

What are the characteristic features of the industrial centers? Of the commercial centers? Of the residential centers? Of the transitional areas?

What role do the economic centers play in creating a local consciousness? A community spirit?

To what extent do the occupational centers provide employment for the group in the area? In other areas?

What relation is there between these centers and the wealth of the area? What is the source of the labor supply?

If the pattern of the community has changed, how have these centers been affected? What is the significance of such effects?

What social and economic problems do these centers create?

What new centers have sprung up? What is their effect on the community? What problems have they created with respect to transportation? Building? Housing?

The social influence of demographic characteristics.[11] Generally, the student of social life is concerned with the distribution of the population not only from the standpoint of a demographer—that is, with regard to population composition in terms of age, sex, nationality, and occupation—but also from the standpoint of *the relation* of demographic characteristics to the life organization of the community and to the struggle for a living. Furthermore, the facts relative to the population should be "correlated with other social data such as home ownership, stability or migration, health, delinquency and crime rates, insanity rates, voting, political and religious affiliation, and other characteristics of population groups."[12]

To what races, nationalities, and occupational and religious groups do the people of the area belong? What groups predominate? Which are increasing or decreasing? Why?

[11]See Philip Hauser and O. D. Duncan, *The Study of Population.* University of Chicago Press, 1959. (See especially Part I, "Demography's Current Status as a Science.")

[12]Louis Wirth, "The Scope and Problems of the Community," *Publications of the American Sociological Society,* XXVII, 68–69.

What is the influence of the population composition on the social life of the area? On the economic life?

What proportion of the people own their homes? What proportion rent? What types of dwellings do they occupy? What is the proportion of new buildings? Of multiple dwellings? Of skyscraper apartments? What types of people are attracted by these dwellings? What mode of life do they maintain? What social relations do they maintain with the community and its social institutions?

What is the rate of population growth? Does it approach "population explosion" dimensions? What is the effect of this growth on the economic structure of the area? On employment of youth? On school provisions?

What provisions exist for the aged: health and welfare programs? part-time employment? retirement programs? What is the role of the aged in the community and its social organizations? What is the impact of the aging population on the social and economic structures of the area?

What social stratification systems[13] have been established and recognized by the population of the area? Have any restrictions been imposed by members of a stratum? Have any distinctive organizations, friendship groups, or occupational clubs been developed? What unique behavior patterns, codes, or etiquette do they impose on members? To what social strata did the parents of the members belong? What social levels do the members expect their offspring to attain?

What is the impact of social stratification on the general mode of life of the entire community? What is the basis of the social stratification of the area: business managerial grouping, professionally elite, socially elite or family elite groupings—the "upper-uppers"? upper-middle class, white-collar groups and labor? Other bases of stratification?

The social influence of population mobility.[14] Generally a high rate of population mobility is associated with instability of local life. Where the rate of mobility is very high, a community which was at one time characterized by a high degree of intimacy and solidarity may become an area where life is lax and devoid of mutual interests. The area under such circumstances is often in the process of becoming a slum where socially inadequate classes tend to congregate and social

[13]See Richard T. Morris, "Social Stratification," in Broom and Selznick, *Sociology,* pp. 176–204. Harper & Row, Publishers, 1963.

[14]See S. M. Miller, "Comparative Mobility," *Current Sociology,* IX (1960), 1–89. S. M. Lipset and R. Bendix, *Social Mobility in Industrial Society*. University of California Press, 1959.

problems multiply. The transition of a community to a slum may be very gradual and may be associated with a variety of changes, of which a change in population composition is only one; the others are changes in land values, in rents, in utilization of land and buildings, in sanitation, in local housekeeping, in social distance, and in social control. On the other hand, it should also be remembered that through mobility new forces, new ideas, and new organizations may penetrate the area.

It is important to learn the nature and the rate of increase or decrease in population as revealed by interschool transfers, by polling lists, by telephone and other directories, and by other suitable means.

What is the extent of mobility among the various economic groups in the community? What is the relation of in-migration to existing community resources: schools, industries, housing, employment?

What are the reasons for migration? Who migrates: upper, middle, white-collar, blue-collar, chronically unemployed groups? What are the effects of migration in these groups?

What changes in their modes of life can be perceived? What new affiliations do they create? What is the effect on the community of in-migration? Out-migration? Who are the out-migrants? Why do they leave? Where do they go?

What is the extent of minority group migration? Of Negroes? Have disruptions occurred? What restrictions have been imposed on minority groups? On Negroes? What tensions have such restrictions created?

Who has taken up "the cause" of the minorities? How intense is the struggle for civil rights? For social equality? For equality before the law? Equality in job opportunities? In educational opportunities?

How does Myrdal's analysis of the American dilemma apply to the Negro-white relations in the community under study? In view of the existing problems in the community, how sound is his proposal that a varied program of education will narrow the discrepancy between practice and creed?

What are the population trends in the community? Any back-to-the-land movements? How many rural people are migrating to the city? What is their method of adjustment to city life?

What were the rates of birth, marriage, divorce, and death after World War II? What are they at present?

Is there a surplus of young women in the community? What population problems did the community face in the postwar era? What steps have been taken to meet these problems? What is their effect on the life of the community?

Which cultural and racial groups have increased or decreased their population most rapidly? What are the growth trends of these groups?

What social conditions bring about variations in the population? How do these changes affect the labor supply? The demand for goods? For housing?

Along what focal points do newcomers settle: areas of high density, industrial, or trading areas? What influences have the newcomers exerted on these points? What influence have these points exerted on newcomers?

How does the change in population affect land values? How does a change in land values affect the type of residents who are subsequently attracted by the district?

Where do the high-income groups live? The low-income groups? The middle-class groups? What contacts are maintained among them? What problems are created?

Does a change in land values mean encroachment by industry? By "under-cover enterprises"?

How does population mobility affect the social institutions in the area?

What kind of problems are created because of population mobility? What has been done to meet these problems?

To what extent has the population preserved its social and cultural identity? To what extent has it adopted new culture traits? What is the effect of a multiplicity of culture traits upon solidarity of the community?

The Community as a Constellation of Social and Cultural Groupings[15]

In addition to a demographic study of an area, we are concerned with the population as a constellation of social and cultural groupings that have unique standards of living, unique social heritages, and a unique organization of life. In Chapter 16, "A Study of a Culture Group," stress was laid on the importance of studying the above aspects. Here the subject is approached from the standpoint of the interrelationships which exist among the various cultural groupings in the area.

What contacts do the various culture groups maintain among themselves? What are the evidences of social solidarity? Of social conflict?

[15]For the content of a study of a culture group, see Chapter 15; La Piere, *op. cit.,* Chapter 4, "The Cultural Basis of Social Life."

Of race or nationality prejudices? What are the effects of such conflicts and prejudices? What are their sources?

What is the status of the racial and culture groups in the larger community? Their reputation as to politics? As to law observance? As to meeting social problems?

To what extent do the various groups participate in local community life? What opportunities are offered for participation by minorities? What leadership do they contribute? How is consensus secured? How are common interests created among the diverse groups?

What changes have these groups undergone as a result of interaction with each other? What social problems have accompanied such changes?

How do the activities, beliefs, and sentiments of the various groups influence the social organization of the community? What is the significance of such influence?

What changes have occurred in the lives of these groups during the last decade. What are their effects on general community organization?

The Community as a Constellation of Social Types[16]

Every community has a variety of social types, but every community may set certain limits to the possibilities for personal development. "In some communities distinctive types of personality may be found which are unique to the area, and are a faithful mirror of its life. The concentration of specific types of personality in specific areas where they find or create for themselves a hospitable culture is one of the factors which has given its distinctive color to the [urban community]."[17]

What distinctive types of personality may be distinguished in the area under consideration? How did these types arise? What are their behavior patterns? What are their traits? Their attitudes? What is the significance of these types in the life of the area? Of the larger community?

What family types may be distinguished: patriarchal, matriarchal democratic?

[16]Based on Erle F. Young (Ed.), *The Case Worker's Desk Manual,* pp. 32–33. Social Work Technique, 1942.

[17]Wirth, *op. cit.,* p. 70.

What occupational types may be observed: businessman, artist, technician, small shopkeeper, professional, clerical?

Among the occupational types, what proportion are Babbitts, promoters, "boosters," shysters? What is their significance? What problems do they create?

What political types may be observed: the political boss, the "ward heeler," the soapbox orator, the agitator, the demagogue, the rebel, the "Pink," the "Red," the reactionary, the liberal?

What high-society types may be found: socialite, climber, club man or woman, debutante, Lady Bountiful?

What cultural types exist? What type does the "greenhorn" display? The partially assimilated? The cultural hybrid?

What are the mobility types in the community: wanderer, joiner, "big-game hunter," explorer, vagrant, hobo, "boomer"?

What criminal types exist in the community: racketeer, "squealer," gambler, gangster, blackmailer, bootlegger, thug?

What parasitic types exist: pauper, beggar, "moocher," faker, grafter, "gold-digger"?

What occupational or cultural types contribute to the Philistine class? To the Bohemian? To the idealistic? To the creative type of personality?

How do these types function? Who are the socially rejected types? Why are they rejected? By whom? What is the consequence of such rejection?

How do the various types influence the solidarity of the community or the disorganization of the community?

What new social types have developed during the war? Since the war? What is the community's reaction to them?

T. W. Adorno[18] lists a cluster of personality traits or syndromes which are associated with social types that betray attitudes of deep-seated prejudices and fascism: surface resentment, conventionality, authoritarianism, rebel, crank, and manipulative syndromes. Have any of these types been studied by civil rights committees? What were their findings and how were these used in attempts to eradicate severe prejudices and limitations on freedom?

What are the social bases of liberal leadership? Of nonliberal and radical leaders? Are the radical members absorbed by a movement and isolated from the community?

What incentives does the community offer liberal groups to engage in political and social action? In the promotion of civil rights?

[18]Adorno *et al.*, *The Authoritarian Personality,* pp. 751–783 and *passim.* Harper & Row, Publishers, 1950.

The Community as a Constellation of Social Institutions[19]

Social institutions of a community include not only such formal and established social structures as schools, churches, courts, business houses, and settlements, but also such phenomena as political parties, rooming houses, clubs, newspapers, recreation centers, and social welfare agencies. The use, development, integration, and coordination of all these institutions depend largely on the consciousness of common objectives, on mutual confidence, and on the formulation of a philosophy of social organization and social welfare.

The local government.[20] What are the nature and significance of the local government? Does the area have an independent governmental unit or is it a part of some other city or town?

What is the governmental unit of the area under study: village, town, or city? Is the unit governed by special charter? Municipal or state law? What is the nature of this charter or the law? What changes have these undergone since World War II? What power of "home rule" are granted the area? What powers are reserved for local government? What powers are withheld?

What are the responsibilities of the executive head of the governmental unit? What powers are delegated to other officials? Are departmental heads elected or appointed? Who determines their responsibilities?

What is the organization of the executive body of the local government? Of the legislative body?

What types of courts are there in the area? What is their organization? Their status?

What major changes have been made in the various branches of the local government in the last ten years? What provisions are made to institute modern administrative practices?

Do any public utilities come under administration of the local government?

[19]See Chapter 16 herein. Also T. B. Bottomore, *Sociology: A Guide to Problems and Literature*. George Allen & Unwin and Prentice-Hall, Inc., 1963.

[20]Some of the above questions are based on R. L. Warren, *Studying Your Community,* pp. 33–55. Russell Sage Foundation, 1955. See also Pendleton Herring, "Research on Government, Politics, and Administration," in *Research for Public Policy*. Brookings Institution, 1961. Maurice Boyd and D. E. Worcester, *American Civilization: An Introduction to Social Science*. Allyn & Bacon, 1963. Chapter 6, "Contemporary American Political Institutions," Chapter 8 ,"The United States and World Affairs."

How are government personnel selected? Promoted? Evaluated? In-service trained? What is their tenure of office?

What are the sources of revenue? What are bases of real property assessment? What is the budget for administration of the area? How are funds obtained?

What is the nature of state or federal grants? What are their purposes? Does the local government run a deficit? What is its amount?

Has the area set up an adequate civil defense program? How have the various governmental units been integrated into this program? What is the role of voluntary citizens' organizations in this program?

What is the party system in the area? How are committee members chosen? Is there a "political boss" in the area? What powers does he exercise? How are they controlled? What problems have resulted from "bossism"?

What is the voting machinery in the area? What is the role of the League of Women Voters? What is the role of the municipal research bureau, if any, in the area?

What do annual governmental reports reveal?

How effectively does the local government control crime? Enforce laws? What provisions exist for improved detention of juvenile and adult offenders? Who are the law enforcement officials? What powers do they exercise? How speedily are criminals brought to trial? What provisions are there for legal counsel? How effective are the probation services? Parole services? Juvenile police services? What is the case load per officer in juvenile police, probation, parole?

What provisions does the local government make for medical and psychiatric care for the needy? For child guidance clinics?

What is the local government's role in desegregation? Have any race riots occurred in area? What action did the government take?

What role does local government assume in world affairs? In world crises?

What support is local government providing for economic planning? For social planning?[21]

Economic and industrial organizations.[22] What are the chief economic organizations of the community?

What economic factors have contributed to technological expansion in the community? What are the social effects of such expansion?

[21]See Georges Gurvitch, "Democracy as a Sociological Problem," *Journal of Legal and Political Sociology,* I (Oct. 1942), 46–71.

[22]See Elton Mayo, *The Human Problems of an Industrial Civilization.* Harvard University Press, 1946.

What are the effects of specialization upon the solidarity of various social classes in the community?

What are the major occupational pursuits? How stable are they? What are some of the outstanding occupational attitudes of members of the group? Are they adjusted to their occupations?

What is the distribution of trades? Of the professions? Of merchants? Of capitalists?

What industries have been permanently closed? What new industries have appeared? From where is the labor supply drawn?

What is the wage rate in each industry? How adequate is it?

What wage disputes have arisen? How were they settled? How often have strikes occurred? How have they been settled?

What responsibility does industry assume toward labor? Toward the unemployed? Toward social welfare programs?

What is the setup for social security?

How do wages and food prices compare? Wages and rents? What are the maximum and minimum wages for men and for women? For skilled and unskilled?

What are the nature and extent of compulsory insurance laws in the industrial organizations?

What are the nature and extent of industrial accidents? In what industries have they occurred? What measures have been taken to prevent them?

What is the nature of the buying behavior of consumers? Of buyers' strikes?

What social controls are used to regulate excessive competition?

Who is responsible for economic planning in depression periods?

Labor organizations.[23] What is the nature of labor organizations in the various industries? What are their functions? What are their internal structures?

What is the relation between the labor organizations and industrial management? Between the labor organizations and the wage earners?

What is the perspective of the union officials?

What labor-management problems have labor organizations been able to wipe out? To minimize?

What is the role of the AFL-CIO, and others? Among wage earners? Among professional groups?

What role do labor organizations play in creating an adequate labor supply? In controlling it? How is the migratory labor supply controlled?

[23]See Florence Peterson, *American Labor Unions: What They Are and How They Work*. New York: Harper & Row, Publishers, 1952.

What is the role of labor organizations in dealing with overexpansion through industrial technology to the detriment of the existing labor supply?

What authority and power do labor organizations exercise? What are the reactions to these powers of the government? The general public? Industry?

What special legislation has been enacted as a result of the efforts by labor organizations? What special legislation has been advocated to curb their authority? What have been the effects of each upon the community?

What are the differences in the wages of organized as compared with unorganized labor?

What age groups, races, nationalities, and wage levels are best organized? Which are least organized?

What is the attitude of labor organizations toward labor legislation?

Who are the leaders of organized labor? What support do the leaders of organized labor get from the community?

What is the community's attitude toward strikes, lockouts, labor problems, and disputes?

What is the leaders' attitude toward industrial democracy? What efforts have been made to attain it?

Who are the leaders of the industrialists? To what extent do they organize? To what extent do they participate in local labor improvements? In social welfare programs? What steps have been taken to socialize these leaders?

How has the steady rise in living costs affected labor? To what extent has labor profited by wage increases?

What extensive alterations in production programs have occurred recently? How did they affect labor? Industry?

What types of small enterprises were forced out of existence through automation? What new types have appeared?

Health organizations.[24] What are the nature and extent of the health organizations in the community? How efficient are they? How are they supported?

What program of public health does the community offer? What is the reaction to medicare as established by law in 1965?

What steps have been taken toward group medicine? Toward socialized medicine? What are the medical profession's attitudes toward these types of medical care?

[24]See E. A. Suchman, *Sociology and the Field of Public Health.* Russell Sage Foundation, 1963.

What are the nature and extent of local public and of private hospitals? Of clinics? Of dispensaries? Of university health centers? Of school health work? Of public health nursing?

To whom are these open? How effective are the services they provide? What is the cost of such care?

What is the cost of medical care in the specialized groups? What problems arise because of such costs?

To what sickness-benefit associations do the groups belong? What provisions exist for compulsory sickness insurance? What groups are insured?

What is the extent of preventive work? Of food, milk, and water supply protection? Of community "house-cleaning"? Of health education for adults and for children?

What trends are observed in mental health care of the area? In institutional management? In development of group and socialized medicine?

Educational system.[25] Education is not a separate part of the culture or organization of an area. Education takes place, at least to some extent, in all social institutions. Formal education, however, is the domain of the educational system, public and private.

What is the nature of local school system? Of its organization and administration? How are the school board members chosen? What are their qualifications? Is the school board politically dominated? How is the superintendent of schools chosen?

What provisions exist for prekindergarteners? For handicapped children? For the mentally retarded? For vocational training?

What is the rate of drop-outs in the area? What is being done about the problem? The rate of daily absences?

What special services do the schools offer: a school nurse and physician, social worker, or guidance counselor? How adequate are their services?

What is the school budget? What is its source? How adequate is it? Who supplements it? How adequate are the physical plants? How are they subsidized? Maintained?

How adequate are teachers' salaries? How are teachers selected? What are their qualifications? What supervision do they receive on the job? Are there pressures on teachers to avoid "controversial

[25]Orville G. Brim, Jr., *Sociology and the Field of Education.* Russell Sage Foundation, 1958.

issues" in the classroom? To introduce materials of special interest groups?[26]

How adequate is classroom instruction? What is its nature? What are diploma requirements? What is the grading system?

What provisions are made for the exceptionally capable students? How adequate are the library facilities? The laboratory? The workshops? What opportunities do schools offer to raise educational standards?

What proportion of the students complete high school? Junior college? University? What provisions are made for adult education?

What relations does the school maintain with the general community? To what extent is the school system geared to "career routes"?

To what extent do social classes permeate the public school system? To what extent do some students feel their unequal statuses? What is the effect of fraternities and sororities in high school? In college?

Have any desegregation problems occurred in the schools in the area? How were these problems met?

Religious organizations.[27] Since the church is a primary group organization, it was considered in relation to the study of a culture group in Chapter 16. Here it should be emphasized that a study of religious organizations of the various social groups needs to be thought of in relation to community life as a whole, with particular reference to the following points:

What influence do the various religious organizations exert on community activities? On the solidarity of the community?

What religious prejudices exist? What rivalries? What is the extent of cooperation among the churches?

What social welfare programs do the churches promote jointly? What legislative programs? What is their role in the civil rights struggle? In integration?

What is the role of the various churches in relation to crime prevention and to civic betterment?

To what extent do religious groups engage in religious activities from personal choice? In deference to tradition? "For the sake of the old folks"?

To what extent has religion created a spiritual one-group? How

[26]Warren, *op. cit.,* p. 101.

[27]See T. B. Bottomore, *op. cit.,* Chapter 13, "Religion and Morality," and D. V. Moberg, *The Church as a Social Institution: The Sociology of American Religion.* Prentice-Hall, Inc., 1962.

frequently do religious leaders and ministers of various denominations exchange visits and services?

What influence do the religious leaders exert on social legislation? On community affairs? On public opinion?

To what extent does religious affiliation reflect social stratification in the community?

What new religious groups have sprung up in the community within the last decade? What is their purpose? What is their rate of growth or decline? What is their influence?

To what extent have the people incorporated the social and moral values of the church into their system of living and communal organization? How well are these moral values understood by the masses of the churchgoing people?

What are the attitudes of the churches toward banning atomic and biological warfare?

To what extent does the church help young people with their moral conflicts over war? What groups, if any, have challenged the position of the church because of its stand against universal military training? In favor of universal military training? Atomic warfare?

What role does the church play in the development of underdeveloped or devastated countries? In the promotion of lasting peace? In UNESCO? World government?

Social welfare organizations.[28] What types of social work activities are carried on in the community?

What is the scope of family casework? Of child welfare work? Of research in social work? Of family counseling? Of correctional institutional work? Of community organization? How are these activities coordinated?

What changes in methods of social work have been adopted?

What is the status of "individualized treatment" in various types of social work?

What specialized services are available: medical social work, psychiatric social work, child guidance and clinical work, industrial welfare work, legal aid service, mental health services, and education?

To what extent is preventive work stressed? What measures are used in preventive work?

What is the status of professional social work in the community?

What is the relation of private social work to expanding public welfare work?

What is the status of the community chest or united crusade? What

[28] *Social Work Encyclopedia*. National Association of Social Workers, 1965.

is its budget? How are funds raised? How are they distributed? On what basis?

What problems are connected with fund raising?

What is the role of the council of social agencies? What are its functions? What research work is carried on by the council of social agencies?

SECTARIAN SOCIAL WORK. What are the various types of sectarian social agencies in the community? To what extent do they cooperate?

What are their objectives? What is their social philosophy of work?

What are their policies and practices with regard to disbursement of funds? To the administration of social service? What types of social agencies do they maintain: medical, children's institutions, family relief, family counseling centers, homes for the aged, destitute, delinquent? What are their standards of work? What proportion of the personnel is composed of laymen? To what extent is the administrative machinery for the welfare activities under religious control and under secular control?

What specialized services do these agencies offer for children? For unmarried mothers? For the aged? For the physically handicapped?

What character-building agencies are maintained? How are they staffed and administered? How efficient are they?

What new services have arisen during the last ten years?

SECULAR PRIVATE SOCIAL WORK. What are the various types of secular social work agencies in the city? How are they coordinated with those under religious auspices? Who constitutes the clientele of the secular agencies?

What are the objectives of the private agencies? What is their philosophy of social work?

Which of the private agencies are national in scope? What is the degree of coordination between the mother agency and the local unit? Between the national agency and the local community?

What is the source of financial support of the private agencies? How adequate is it in relation to the demands of the community at a particular time?

What specialized services do these agencies offer for children? For the aged? For the physically handicapped?

What character-building agencies are maintained? How are they staffed and administered? How efficient are they?

PUBLIC AND TAX-SUPPORTED SOCIAL WORK. What are the various types of public social agencies in the community? To what extent do they cooperate with the secular and sectarian agencies?

What statutory provisions govern the financing of social work? Of relief? Of administrative personnel? How adequate are these provisions?

What is their standard of work and of relief as compared with that of private social work in the same community? With public social work in other well-known communities?

What social security programs meet the needs of families and individuals? In case of unemployment? Illness? Industrial accidents? Death of wage earner? Old-age retirement?

What insurance benefits are available through unions? Employers? Union and employer jointly? Fraternal organizations?

What types of workers qualify for benefits through government agencies? Industrial organizations?

What plans have been made to meet the problem of unemployment?

What relief setup has been organized? What emergency relief setup? For disaster relief?

What industrial plans have been made to meet the problems of the unemployed?

What is the nature of trade union unemployment relief?

What emergency measures have been enacted (breadlines and soup kitchens, newspaper funds, relief by parent-teacher organizations, by citizen groups)?

What degree of cooperation is there between the relief and non-relief organizations? Between public and private relief organizations?

How are transients cared for? By whom? Who assumes responsibility for the care and welfare of transients? Of refugees?

What programs do the social agencies provide for family life education? For the industrially handicapped? For alcoholics? For aliens and foreign-born? For board members? For interracial relations? For social action by volunteer community leaders? For leaders of youth groups? For protection of civil rights?

What social settlements and neighborhood centers exist in the area? What are their objectives? What services do the provide?

What are the current trends in public and private social services? What influences these trends?

19

a study of community life in urban and rural natural areas: II

Living together is by no means an easy job for human beings. . . . We have to compromise, submit to restraints, conform to rules, accept controls. . . . We have to recognize our dependence on others. . . . We have to work with them, compete with them, somehow or other we have to accommodate ourselves to them. And all of this is true in the world community as it is in the family, the playground, the neighborhood, the factory, the town, or the nation.

JESSIE BERNARD

Social Problems of the Community[1]

American community life is greatly complicated by the extraordinary diversity of its ethnic and cultural groupings, by the rapid growth of urban, rurban, and rural areas, by profound changes in social and personal values and in the standard of living. Social problems often arise out of competing and conflicting interests and values between diverse groups and social institutions; out of the failure of groups and institutions to respond to the demands of changing conditions; out of their inability to fit themselves into the larger community; and out of their inability to enact and impose effective social controls.

In the study of community problems it is essential to obtain an accurate account of the nature of the problems, their extent, their sources, their changing patterns, their effects on persons.

[1]See Jessie Bernard, *American Community Behavior*. Holt, Rinehart & Winston, Inc., 1963. See also: E. W. Burgess, "Social Problems and Social Processes, in Arnold Rose, *Human Behavior and Social Processes,* pp. 381–400, Houghton Mifflin Co., 1962; Paul B. Horton and Gerold R. Leslie, *The Sociology of Social Problems,* Appleton-Century-Crofts, Inc., 1960; John J. Kane, *Social Problems: A Situational Value Approach,* Prentice-Hall, Inc., 1962.

What are the economic problems of the community? Are there conflicts of economic interests? Conflicts over methods of production? Methods of distribution? In the means of securing a labor force? Are there conflicts between labor and management? Conflicts in regulating competition? Conflicts within the unions? Conflicts in industrial and economic planning?

What are the problems of "social division"?[2] What problems arise because of caste and class? Because of inequitable social stratification? Rapid social mobility? Marginal groups? What is the "price of prejudice"? Of social and economic discrimination? What problems has desegregation created?

What are the consequences of conflicting ideals, goals, attitudes, and values of various groups in the community?

What problems arise from political controversy? Do those in power determine goals, policies, and group controls? What is the extent of political graft? Of racketeering? Of election frauds? Of violations of civil rights?

What are the major issues at stake in the socioeconomic-political conflicts? What techniques are used by conflicting groups in their struggles to dominate or influence? What means are used to resolve conflicts?

To what extent are the prevailing conflicts constructive? Destructive?

Economic distress and dependency; crime and delinquency; general community disorganization.[3] How extensive is poverty? Dependency? Mental ill-health? Physical disease? Crime? Delinquency? General community disorganization and demoralization?

In what way are rapid social changes responsible for the development and spread of these problems? To what extent have the impersonal social relations within the community contributed to their continued existence? How do community leaders and social engineers account for the persistence of local social problems?

What programs to eradicate poverty locally have been put into operation? How do poverty rates, crime and delinquency rates com-

[2]A. McC. Lee and E. B. Lee, *Social Problems in America: A Source Book,* pp. 549–616. Holt, Rinehart & Winston, Inc., 1949.

[3]See *Monthly Labor Review* (current issues for current labor situations; back issues for historical or comparative factors). U.S. Department of Labor. See also: Mabel A. Elliott and F. E. Merrill, *Social Disorganization,* Harper & Row, 1961; Michael Harrington, *The Other America: Poverty in the United States,* The Free Press of Glencoe, 1962.

pare with those of towns or cities of comparable size and population composition?

What major types of offenses among adults and juveniles prevail?[4] Who are the "overlords of crime"? Is there an upperworld of criminals?[5]

How effective is the police system in crime detection? In crime prevention?

What is the nature of rehabilitative services of punitive and correctional procedures (for men, women, and youth)?

What diagnostic and classificatory centers exist in the community and nearby? What labor camps exist? What "halfway houses" for released offenders are there in the area?

What are conditions in the county jail or town lockup?

What is the extent of drunkenness in the community? Of drug addiction?

What is the extent of the "revolt of youth"? Against what does youth revolt? To what extent is such revolt a factor in delinquency?

What is the extent of cultural conflicts? To what extent is cultural conflict a factor in delinquency? In crime?

What is the extent of sex offenses? Of unmarried mothers? Of illegitimacy? What provisions are made for unmarried mothers?

What is the extent of prostitution? What is the social control of prostitution? The legal control? Control of venereal disease?

COMBATING COMMUNITY PROBLEMS. How are the various community problems being met? By whom? How adequately? What joint action is being taken in meeting these problems? In studying them on a scientific basis? By professional groups? By competent community citizens?

What systems of relief (public and private, local, state, and federal) have been organized for meeting the problems of the totally unemployed? The partially employed? What work-relief systems exist in the community? What is the reaction of the relief recipients to cash relief? To work relief? How adequate are the various systems of relief?

(In the study of crime prevention, the control of disease, and the administration of relief systems, it is necessary to take into account the adequacy of the personnel involved, the structures and policies of the

[4]See Sophia M. Robison, *Juvenile Delinquency: Its Nature and Control*. Holt, Rinehart & Winston, Inc., 1960; Walter C. Reckless, The Crime Problem, Appleton-Centry-Crofts, 1961.

[5]Mabel E. Elliott, *Crime in Modern Society*. Harper & Row, Publishers, 1953. Also, Marshall B. Clinard, *Sociology of Deviant Behavior,* Holt, Rinehart & Winston, Inc., 1963.

organizations concerned with these problems and with the rules and regulations imposed on them by higher governmental units.)

PROLONGED UNEMPLOYMENT. (See studies in Chapter 2.) What is the extent of total unemployment in the community? Of partial unemployment? (See Richard A. Lester, *Providing for Unemployed Workers in the Transition.*)

What is the distribution of the unemployed according to national or racial groupings? According to trades, occupations, professions, and age groupings?

What are the causal factors of unemployment (personal, industrial, automation, fads and fashions, unplanned production)?

What new problems does unemployment create?

What labor demonstrations have been made?

What are the effects of unemployment on the skill of a worker? On his prospects of employment? On his morale? On family morale?

What are the effects of unemployment on young persons who have never been employed? On the chronically underpaid?

What are the effects of unemployment on wage scales? On prices? On the standard of living?

What measures have been taken to combat technological unemployment?[6]

Social control in the community. Social control is the direction of behavior by group influences. These influences may stimulate, or they may inhibit, individual and group action. Social control is effected through the mores of the group, its institutions, public opinion, legislative enactments, police systems, conventions, ceremonials, and the like.[7]

What types of behavior does the community attempt to control? What social controls operate in community life? To what extent are the folkways and mores a means of social control in the community? What are the nature and role of public opinion? How effective are they as a means of social control?

[6] Jerome F. Scott and R. P. Lynton, *The Community Factor in Modern Technology*. The Macmillan Company, 1951. See especially Chapter 10, "The Worker and the Machine."

[7] See Tamotsu Shibutani, *Society and Personality: An Interactionist Approach to Social Psychology,* Part II, "Social Control." Prentice-Hall, Inc., 1961. See also T. B. Bottomore, *op. cit.,* Part IV, "Social Control," Chapters on "Custom and Public Opinion," "Religion and Morality," "Law," and "Education."

What is the relation of the majority and the minority in the community to public opinion? Through what channels is public opinion expressed?

In what different ways does religion control the behavior of groups and individuals in the community?

What is the role of gossip as a means of social control?

In what different ways do the institutions of government operate as formal means of social control?

To what extent is law a means of social control? What is the nature of the law enforcement machinery? How efficient and effective is it?

What is the relation of the mores to common law? To statute law?

Which of the social institutions are the most effective means of social control? Why?

What is the nature of group opinion in the community?

What is the value of group discussion? What opinions are formed and controlled as a result of such discussion?

What are the questions to which public opinion applies?

To what extent does the pulpit promote opinion of the group? Of the community? How does the church form and control public opinion?

To what extent does the press influence public opinion? What means does it use in the formation and control of opinion?

To what extent are TV and radio elements in the formation and control of public opinion?

What groups violate or disregard the social controls of the community? Why? What are the consequences of such violations?

What changes have occurred in social control? What is the significance of such change?

What are the nature and extent of social engineering? To what extent is the social survey a means of social control?

What social problems arise because of social controls? How are these problems met?

The Study of a Rural Community

Dr. Walter C. McKain, Jr., now professor of rural sociology at the University of Connecticut, and formerly social science analyst with the Bureau of Agricultural Economics, U.S. Department of Agriculture, stresses the following points in the study of a rural community:

Comparisons and contrasts of urban and rural studies. Researchers do not necessarily need a new set of tools when they move from an urban to a rural environment. The principles and methods of scientific inquiry described in previous chapters may be applied with assurance in rural areas. Rural America and urban America have been drawn so closely together during the last half-century that the characteristics formerly differentiating them have been considerably dimmed. In fact, rural sociologists are beginning to recognize that the rural-urban dichotomy does not always afford the most useful frame of reference.[8] Nevertheless, social research in rural areas does exhibit some variation from its urban counterpart. The researcher may carry with him the same bag of tools, but he probably will use them in slightly different ways, and he will undoubtedly find that their effectiveness varies in the two situations.

Rural areas are almost always less densely settled than urban areas, and the population of a rural community is usually more homogeneous, less mobile, and not so highly stratified. In general, social interaction in rural areas is more intimate; social control is largely persuasive; behavior is more closely regulated by the mores and the folkways; and status tends to be assigned in relation to the whole personality rather than on the basis of segmented roles. Not all rural communities, of course, possess these traits or hold them in the same degree, but wherever these characteristics do prevail, social research is affected. Rural society poses problems for the investigator but, at the same time, it may simplify some of his tasks and enhance his opportunities.

The field worker who undertakes research in a rural community is judged according to the standards of that community. He soon realizes that he is not anonymous. He may, however, be unaccepted. His behavior on and off the job is carefully observed and the eventual success or failure of his project may depend as much upon his conduct during leisure hours as upon his comportment while on duty. A glance at the methodological notes contained in highly regarded rural studies reveals the importance that the authors attach to the status of the field worker in the communities under observation.

The sources of data in rural areas are usually more limited than in urban areas. Records, reports, and other sources of secondary information are scarce in rural communities, where public and private organizations must depend upon unpaid and often untrained clerical help. Social inquiry in rural areas, therefore, may stress enumeration,

[8]Neal Gross, "Sociological Variation in Contemporary Rural Life," *Rural Sociology,* XIII, 256–273.

interviewing, or some other direct approach with all the advantages and pitfalls that these methods entail.

The U.S. Census has published data by individual townships for 1960 and has unpublished information for each enumeration district. These data are useful in describing the general characteristics of rural communities and in providing the data needed for stratified sampling. Recent census figures also include information on the place of work and means of transportation to work. These data can be especially illuminating as a large part of the contemporary rural population works off the farm.

THE UNIT OF OBSERVATION. In sparsely settled areas the delineation of neighborhoods and communities is especially significant; for in rural places, geographic boundaries and the boundaries of social interaction tend to be coterminous. A rural person, partly because of his relative isolation, is frequently bound to a single locality group by many ties, while an urban person may belong to several special interest groups, the membership lists of which seldom overlap. The territorial community thus becomes a relatively complete area of observation in the rural environment, whereas in the city, the researcher must look for a broader area of observation whenever geographic communities do not coincide with communities of interest.

The U.S. Department of Agriculture, in cooperation with the U.S. Bureau of the Census, has developed a "Master Sample of Agriculture" for area sampling in both the open country and the rural village. This device has greatly facilitated research based on enumeration in rural areas. The "Master Sample of Agriculture" has been used extensively in research on population changes, buying habits, levels of livings, social security, rural health, and many other topics.[9]

The usual statistical techniques, based on probabilities and hence on large numbers, must be applied with caution in rural community analysis where the number of units of observation is small. Ordinary cross-sectional analyses are often unrewarding under these circumstances. Relationships and generalizations based on an examination of the attributes of a few dozen cases are easily computed but hard to defend. Some researchers in rural areas have turned to other techniques

[9]See Everett M. Rogers, *Social Change in Rural Society*. Appleton-Century-Crofts, 1960. Lee Taylor and Arthur R. Jones, Jr., *Rural Life and Urbanized Society*. Oxford University Press, 1964.

of analysis in recent years and their efforts have been singularly successful.[10] They have found that, while the structure of a rural community is far from simple, it can be pieced together and observed as a unit. The same task in an urban community is many times more complex. Rural people may play just as many roles as urban residents but in a rural community the audience (other members of the community) is relatively fixed, while in the city the audience changes as the player moves from one role to another. Thus, the field worker in a rural area is able to grasp rather quickly the essential structure of the community, and he is able to relate the processes of social interaction to this framework. Such an appreciation of the *Gestalt* of a rural community makes the analysis of its separate parts easier and more meaningful.

In many agricultural areas farming is more than a *way of making a living;* it is a *way of life*. The farm home and the farm business are often joint enterprises. The diurnal routine of the farm operator is centered on the farmstead, and farm work is often shared by several members of his family. Rural sociologists have discovered that the social interaction of farm people cannot be analyzed without reference to their economic activities; and agricultural economists have learned that an examination of the farm business invariably calls for an understanding of the noneconomic behavior and aspirations of the farm family.

The content of social research in rural communities also differs in some respects from the subject matter usually analyzed in urban places. Since agriculture is the major industry in rural areas, attention is paid to man-land relationships, farm income, farm labor, tenancy, farm cooperatives, adoption practices, the scale of farm operations, and other topics related to the occupational interests of the population. The level of living enjoyed by a large segment of the rural population, particularly in the South, is relatively low according to urban standards. As a result many investigations are concerned with the problems confronting rural people. The health, diets, and education of rural people, the conservation of their land, decentralization of industry, resettlement, social security for agriculture, and a host of other topics bearing on the problems of rural people are subjects for investigation.

A low density of population poses other problems calling for additional research.[11] Many community facilities, such as schools, churches,

[10]For example, the approach of social anthropology was used by Arthur J. Vidich and Joseph Bensman in *Small Town and Mass Society*. Princeton University Press, 1958.

[11]The population size required to support specific community services is discussed by D. A. Nesmith, "Small Rural Town," *A Place to Live*. U.S. Dep't of Agriculture Yearbook, 1963.

hospitals, utilities, libraries, and ordinary business, professional, and recreational services, cannot be readily furnished to a sparsely settled community. Attempts to improve these services, through rural electrification, bookmobiles, centralized schools, rural hospital plans, and federated churches, require social research.

The task of planning in rural communities has been complicated by the increased diversity of their people and their viewpoints. The power structure has shifted in many rural places and leadership has been diffused through the various segments of the population. Proximity to the city has brought recognition that plans must be part of the larger metropolitan complex.[12]

Despite the persistence of rural values more closely attuned to the self-sufficiency of colonial days than to the commercialization of today's economy, an increasing number of rural people are broadening their economic horizons. They recognize the importance of prices in their general welfare and they realize that progress in the efficiency of production is of little avail if gaps remain in the system of distribution. The growth of cooperatives, the demand for government subsidies, the industrialization of agriculture, and the intensification of rural-urban conflicts are all related to the economic awakening of the American farmer. Research in this field is needed if the economic enlightenment and the political awareness of rural people are to be directed into constructive channels.

The movement of rural people to urban centers has long been a dominant trend in the United States; but the reverse movement of city people to the suburbs and to the fringe areas surrounding the cities has also become an important trend.[13] New communities have sprung up, some almost overnight. Inequities of taxation, zoning difficulties, school needs, family maladjustment, and juvenile delinquency have begun to capture the headlines in these bedroom villages. According to the U.S. Children's Bureau, the largest increase in the number of juvenile delinquents between the late 1950's and the middle 1960's occurred in areas with populations of less than 100,000. The growth of suburbs, particularly those in the last two decades, has created in some instances interstitial areas in which juvenile delinquency is apt to flourish. Often there is conflict between the oldtimers and each succeeding wave of newcomers. When these antipathies are transmitted to the youth, a basis for juvenile delinquency is formed. This situation,

[12]Webb S. Fisher, *The Mastery of the Metropolis*. Prentice-Hall, Inc., 1962.

[13]W. C. McKain, "The Exurbanite: Why He Moved," *A Place to Live, op. cit.*

coupled with the generally uneasy conditions the world over, is a powerful determinant in family and personal maladjustments. The need for research is growing especially in marginal areas—often called the rural-urban fringe.[14]

Closely related to the commercialization of agriculture and to the urbanization of rural people is the plight of one segment of the agricultural population, the hired farm laborers. Their incomes, living and working conditions, and their paths of migration have been recorded moderately well, but only scant attention has been paid to their adjustment in the rural and urban communities where they live, and even less is known concerning their attempts to achieve security.[15] Pioneer social surveys played an important role in improving the lot of urban factory workers, a submerged class for generations following the Industrial Revolution. Similarly, research in the field of farm labor can do much to accelerate the process by which farm laborers will achieve their appropriate share of the privileges and responsibilities of a changed agricultural economy.

Rural communities probably exhibit as many differences as urban communities. A Spanish-American village in New Mexico, a self-sufficing community in the Appalachian highlands, a modern suburb in New England, a farm labor center in California, a village in the Corn Belt, a sprawling farm community in the arid range land, a Mormon village, and a cotton plantation in the South may all be rural communities but they differ from each other in hundreds of ways. Research in rural areas calls for much the same versatility and planning as research in an urban environment, although the research tools are sometimes applied differently.[16]

The Content of Study of a Rural Area

The Bureau of Agricultural Economics of the U.S. Department of Agriculture has worked out an elaborate outline and instructions for studies of rural neighborhoods and communities. The stress of these

[14]"The Sociological Significance of the Rural-Urban Fringe," *Rural Sociology,* XVIII (June, 1953), pp. 101–120; see also recent U.S. Children's Bureau studies.

[15]A noteworthy beginning was made in Walter Goldschmidt's *As Ye Sow.* New York: Harcourt, Brace & World, Inc., 1947.

[16]Statement especially prepared by Professor Walter C. McKain, Jr., for this volume, Mar. 1949 and revised Feb. 1955 and Mar. 1964.

studies falls on rural organizations; the relation of agencies to patterns of organization; the people and the physical environment; salient features and sociological significance.

The social significance of the physical and demographic factors of the rural area.[17] In what respects does configuration of the rural area under study differ from the surrounding urban areas? What are the effects of such differences? What changes have occurred in the structural pattern within the last twenty-five years? What is the social significance of such changes? What are the effects on the people in the area.

What is the density of the population? What are the advantages and disadvantages of living in a sparsely settled community? In what ways are churches, schools, medical services, business establishments, trade areas, employment opportunities, recreation and social life influenced by a low density of population?

What was the original pattern of settlement? How has it been modified by changing agricultural practices? By the advent of paved highways and automobile transportation? By an increasing heterogeneity of the population?

To what extent is the area homogeneous or heterogeneous as to population? What social adjustments have the various groups made to each other? What conflicts have arisen and how have they been met?

What rise or decline in population has been noted in the area since 1900? 1925? 1950, 1965? What are the reasons for increase or decrease? What is the significance of this change in the life of the groups in the area?

What socioeconomic groups occupy the outer fringes of the area? What contacts are maintained by them and urban areas? What is the significance of such contacts?

What trade centers exist in the area? How adequate are they in serving the local groups? What other trade centers are patronized by the group? Why?

What means of transportation are used by the group? How adequate are they? Are some families still using the horse and buggy as a means of transportation? Why?

Social contacts and isolation of the rural community. What psychosocial traits characterize the groups of the area? What social relationships are maintained by their members? By the social

[17]See Jack P. Gibbs, *Urban Research Methods,* Part VI, "Rural-Urban Differences," and Part VII, "Rural-Urban Relations." D. Van Nostrand Co., 1961.

institutions? What changes have occurred in their social contacts since World War I? World War II? What are the effects of such changes?

What social standards are maintained by the rural people? To what extent is there an attempt to imitate urban standards? To develop standards suitable to rural life and practice? What is their degree of rurality?

To what extent have conflicting cultural values arisen? What are the effects of such conflicts?

What are the social attitudes of the younger and older generations toward traditional rural life? Traditional practices of work on the farm? Outside of the farm? Toward new pioneering? Diversification? Hoe-farming? Mechanized farming? Scientific farming? Commercial farming? Subsistence farming? To what extent do these attitudes of various groups conflict? What are the social consequences of such conflicts? How are these conflicts reconciled?

What changes have traditional patterns undergone? Why?

To what extent is the area socially isolated? What factors affect their isolation? To what extent is migration to the city an outgrowth of social isolation?

What occupations prevail in the area? What are the trends in the proportion of agricultural, nonagricultural, and semi-agricultural workers? What is the significance of such trends, if any? What intergroup contacts do these workers maintain?

What types of neighborhoods and villages exist in the area? What are their characteristics? What role does the rural neighborhood play in the socioeconomic life? What informal group relations are maintained by the various population elements? What formal organizations are maintained? What is their significance?

Social control and social institutions in the rural area. To what forms of social control does the area respond: Tradition? Local mores? Eagerness to preserve *status quo?* Work routine? Gossip? Legal pressures?

What are the functions of local governmental agencies in the area? What qualifications for office are required? How adequate are these qualifications? What is the role of the various local governmental units? Of county, state, and federal units?

What are the functions and significance to local groups of the Agricultural Extension Service; Farmers' Home Administration; Rural Electrification Administration? What is the role of the U.S. Department of Agriculture in land planning? In the creation of new agricultural policies? In the conservation of soil? In intergroup cooperation? In promoting the country-life movement?

The rural family. What is the average size of the farm family in the area? In the surrounding rural and semi-rural neighborhoods? In what respects do the modes of life of the urban and rural families differ sharply? What is the significance of such differences?

What patterns of family authority are maintained in the area? To what extent is the authority patriarchal? Democratic? What is the family pattern of religious sectarian groups, if any, in the area? What are the reactions of the young people to existing family authority?

What is the income of the rural families in the area? What is the level of living? What changes has it undergone and what is their significance?

What are the attitudes of the young people toward "life in the country"? Toward their work in the rural area? On the farm? What are the attitudes of their parents? What types of work do the various members perform? What is the influence of such work on family unity? On mobility of the young and migration citywards?

RURAL EDUCATION. How does the educational system in the area compare with that of the nearby urban area? What steps have been taken to improve the country school? What progressive methods of education have been introduced? What special educational programs are maintained for the benefit of the farm youth? The adult farmer? The future farmer? The semi-rural youth and adult?

What subsidies for rural education have been secured? Show how they have been utilized. To what extent is the library an educational agency in the area? How adequate is the local library? What role does the bookmobile play? What role do the university extension services play?

What is the reaction of the rural families to higher education for their young? How many have secured university degrees? What types of work do they follow upon completion of higher education? How many attend agricultural schools?

THE RURAL CHURCH.[18] What is the role of the church in the area? What are its problems? Its trends? What trends can be observed in the religious life of the adults? Of youth? Of sectarian groups in the area, if any?

What are the general characteristics of this church? What is its outlook on the problems affecting rural areas? On problems of youth?

Social problems in rural areas. What social problems prevail in the area? What are their underlying factors?

[18]See David E. Lindstrom, *Rural Life and the Church*. Garrard Press, 1946.

To what extent is migration of young people upsetting the social and occupational balance of the area? What are the trends of urban-to-rural and city-to-farm migrations? What are the motives in such migrations? What are the problems of social adjustment? What are the effects upon the supply of native leadership? Of inexperienced urbanites in rural and farm occupations?

What are the rates of juvenile delinquency and crime in the area as compared with those of surrounding urban areas? What are the underlying causal factors? To what extent do the following factors cause social disorganization: social isolation; limited social participation of youth; ambivalence toward urban mores; unfavorable economic status; extreme conservatism of elders; rural mores-in-flux, and confusion of youth?

To what extent are educational inequalities a social problem? Lack of recreational facilities? Housing inadequacies?

What health problems exist in the area? What is the current volume of illness? What rural medical services are available? How adequate are they? What is the cost of medical care? What hospital facilities exist?

What labor problems have arisen in agricultural districts? Why? How were these problems met? What are the attitudes of farm workers toward their living conditions? Working conditions? Methods of hiring and firing? Importation of foreign labor supply?

Farm tenancy.[19] What is the economic status of the tenant farmer? What is his social position in the area? The social position of his children in the local school? What are his levels of living? His housing conditions?

What social organizations have been created to care for the needs of farm tenants? How adequate are these organizations? What is their significance? What are the tenants' attitudes toward them?

What changes has farm tenure undergone since World War I? World War II? During these crises and depressions? What is the socioeconomic significance of these changes?

How much absentee ownership is there in the area? What are the underlying factors of absentee ownership? What is the proportion of owner-occupiers to tenant-occupiers of the land? How do the agricultural outputs and conditions of the two groups compare? What is the significance of such comparisons?

How many groups in the area display a hunger for land? How many of these groups have lost control of the their land? What effects do economic fluctuations have on tenancy? What are the social effects of tenancy?

[19]See Arthur F. Raper, *Tenants of the Almighty*. The Macmillan Company, 1943.

What role does the migratory worker play in the social economy of the area? What labor problems have arisen in the area since World War I? World War II? What are the effects of mechanization of agriculture?

What crop specialties have been developed in the area? Under what circumstances? By what groups? What problems and successes are associated with such specialties? What is their socioeconomic significance to the group? To outsiders?

What agricultural measures have been adopted to meet the problems of farm laborers? To restore worn-out soil? To conserve and improve agricultural output? What wars have been waged against insect pests? Weeds? Predatory animals?

What is the role of the local Grange? Farmers' Union? Farm Bureau? Farm cooperatives? What are their outlooks on national agricultural policy? On social security? On health insurance; government-sponsored prepayment medical care plans? On migratory labor? On the "lower third" of the rural population? On world peace?

What opposition have the cooperatives met from local entrepreneurs? Why?

What social institutions have arisen to care for the socially inadequate rural groups? Occupationally handicapped persons?

What is the role of rural welfare programs? What are their trends? What effects has the Department of Health, Education and Welfare exerted on the area?

What is the quality of local leadership? Of local initiative in meeting local problems? What evidences of decay can be recognized in the area? Of vigor and regeneration? Of youth participation in problems of youth?

What opportunities exist for creative living? What latent talents can be found among the "grass roots" which express themselves through work, art, social relationships, mutual aid, leadership?

In summary, community life—its complex and diverse phenomena, changes, organization, disorganization, and reorganization—should be viewed as dynamic social processes, closely intertwined not only with the organic life of the immediate area but with the socio-psychological-economic-political phenomena of the larger universe. A community study is thus an exploration of human behavior in vivo, in its natural setting. Such a study should view the community as a constellation of varied social types, groups, social institutions, and social problems which mutually influence each other.[20]

[20]See John Sirjamaki, *The Sociology of Urban Organization*. Random House, 1963.

Selected bibliography[1]

Allport, Gordon W., *The Use of Personal Documents in Psychological Science.* Social Science Research Council, 1942. Still a classic on the use of personal data.

Arthus, Maurice, *Philosophy of Scientific Investigation* (Translated from the French with an introduction by Henry E. Sigerist). Baltimore: John Hopkins University Press, 1943. Some excellent passages presented in a challenging style.

Bales, R. Freed, *Interaction Process Analysis.* Reading, Mass: Addison-Wesley Publishing Co., Inc., 1950. Excellent discussion of use of the laboratory in social science experiments.

Bartlett, F. C. *et al.* (eds.), *The Study of Society: Methods and Problems.* London: Routledge & Keegan Paul, Ltd., 1946. See especially Part IV, "Some Methods of Sociolgy."

Benne, D. D., "Values of the Social Scientist," *Journal of Social Issues,* 1950.

Berelson, Bernard, *Content Analysis in Communication Research.* New York: The Free Press of Glencoe, Inc., 1952.

Bingham, W. V., B. V. Moore, and John Gustad, *How to Interview.* New York: Harper and Row, Publishers, 1959. Good elementary discussion of interviewing techniques in various fields.

Blalock, Jr., Hubert M., *Social Statistics.* New York: McGraw-Hill Book Company, 1960.

Blumer, Herbert, *An Appraisal of Thomas and Znaniecki's The Polish Peasant in Europe and America: Critique of Research in the Social Sciences: I.* Social Science Research Council, 1939.

[1]Supplements to footnote references.

Bogue, Donald J., and Calvin L. Beale, *Economic Areas of the United States*. New York: The Free Press of Glencoe, Inc., 1961.

Borgatta, E. F., and Henry J. Meyer (eds.), *Sociological Theory: Present-Day Sociology from the Past*. New York: Alfred A. Knopf, Inc., 1961.

Bottomore, T. B., *Sociology: A Guide to Problems and Literature*. Englewood Cliffs, N.J.: Prentice-Hall, Inc., 1963. See Part I, "The Scope and Method of Sociology."

Braithwaith, R. B., *Scientific Explanation: A Study of the Function of Theory, Probability and Law in Science*. London: Cambridge University Press, 1955.

Brinton, W. C., *Graphic Presentation*. New York: Brinton Associates, 1939.

Brookings Institution, *Research for Public Policy*. The Institution, 1961. Articles of research on government policy, on economics, and public relations.

Burgess, E. W., "Research Methods in Sociology," *Twentieth Century Sociology*. Georges Gurvitch and Wilbert E. Moore, eds. New York: The Philosophical Library, 1945 and 1949.

———, and Donald Bogue (eds.), *Contributions to Urban Sociology*. Chicago: University of Chicago Press, 1964.

Chapin, F. S., *Experimental Designs in Sociological Research*. New York: Harper & Row, Publishers, 1947. A working manual for research studies in human relations.

Chase, Stuart, *The Proper Study of Mankind: An Inquiry into the Science of Human Relations*. New York: Harper and Row, Publishers, 1958. A stimulating account of the accomplishments of some social scientists, simply written.

Cohen, Morris R., *Reason and Nature*. New York: Harcourt, Brace & World, Inc., 1931. Critical analysis of the significant problems facing the social sciences.

———, and Ernest Nagel, *An Introduction to Logic and Scientific Method*. New York: Harcourt, Brace & World, Inc., 1944.

Dean, Dwight C., and Donald M. Valdes, *Experiment in Sociology*. New York: Appleton-Century-Crofts, 1963.

Dean, John P., and William F. Whyte, "How Do You Know If Informant Is Telling the Truth?" Ithaca, N.Y.: Cornell University Press, 1958. Stimulating 4-page leaflet.

Dewey, John, *Logic: The Theory of Inquiry*. New York: Holt, Rinehart & Winston, Inc., 1949. See especially sections on objectives of research.

Doby, John T., *An Introduction to Social Research*. Harrisburg, Pa.: The Stackpole Co., 1954. See especially Part V, "Principles of Experimentation."

Dodd, Stuart A., "Operational Definitions Operationally Defined," *American Journal of Sociology,* XLVIII (January, 1943), 482–89.

Dornbusch, Sanford M., and Calvin F. Schmid, *A Primer of Social Statistics.* New York: McGraw-Hill Book Company, 1955.

Du Bois, Cora, *The People of Alore.* Cambridge, Mass.: Harvard University Press, 1960. See "Introduction on Techniques of Research." Valuable discussion of studies of a primitive culture.

Edwards, Allen L., *Techniques of Attitude-Scale Construction.* New York: Appleton-Century-Crofts, 1957.

Festinger, Leon, and Daniel Katz (eds.), *Research Methods in the Behavioral Sciences.* New York: Holt, Rinehart & Winston, Inc., 1953. See Part III, "Methods of Data Collection," Part IV, "The Analysis of Data."

Frenkel-Brunswik, Else, "Personality as Revealed Through Clinical Interviews," in T. W. Adorno, *et al., The Authoritarian Personality.* New York: Harper & Row, Publishers, 1950.

Gibbs, Jack P., (ed.), *Urban Research Methods.* Princeton, N.J.: D. Van Nostrand Co., Inc., 1961. Contains excellent bibliography.

Goode, W. J., and P. F. Hatt, *Methods in Social Research.* New York: McGraw-Hill Book Company, 1952. Chap. 11, "Constructing a Questionnaire," pp. 132–69; Chap. 12, "The Mailed Questionnaire," pp. 170–83.

Greenwood, Ernest, *Experimental Sociology: A Study in Method.* New York: Columbia University Press, 1945. See "Is the Controlled Observational Study Experimental?"

Guetzkow, H. (ed.), *Simulation in Social Science Research: Readings.* Englewood Cliffs, N.J.: Prentice-Hall, Inc., 1962. Source materials on use of man/computer and all computer simulations in military and industrial operations and the use of simulation in intergroup and internation relations.

Hagood, Margaret Jarman, and Daniel O. Price, *Statistics for Sociologists.* New York: Holt, Rinehart & Winston, Inc., 1952.

Hare, Paul, *Handbook on Small Group Research.* New York: The Free Press of Glencoe, Inc., 1962. An extensive survey of "all the literature on small groups," listing 1,400 titles.

Hauser, Philip M., and Otis Dudley Duncan (eds.), *The Study of Population.* Chicago: University of Chicago Press, 1959. See "The Data and the Method," pp. 45–74.

Hawley, Amos H., *Human Ecology.* New York: The Ronald Press Company, 1950, passim; Duncan, Otis Dudley, "Human Ecology and Population Studies."

Hempel, Carl G., *Fundamentals of Concept Formation in Empirical Science.* Chicago: University of Chicago Press, 1952.

Herzog, Elizabeth, *Some Guide Lines for Evaluative Research.* U.S. Children's

Bureau, 1959. Good discussion of problems and techniques in evaluative research.

Hyman, Herbert, *Interviewing in Social Research.* Chicago: University of Chicago Press, 1954.

———, *Survey Design and Analysis: Principles, Cases and Procedures.* New York: The Free Press of Glencoe, Inc., 1955.

———, "Interviewing as a Scientific Procedure," in Daniel Lerner, *The Policy Sciences: Recent Developments in Scope and Method.* Stanford, Calif.: Stanford University Press, 1951.

Isard, Walter, *Methods of Regional Analysis: An Introduction to Regional Science.* New York: John Wiley & Sons, Inc., 1960.

Junker, B. H., *Field Work: An Introduction to the Social Sciences.* Chicago: University of Chicago Press, 1960. (Paper ed., 1962.)

Kahn, R. L., and C. F. Cannell, *The Dynamics of Interviewing: Theory, Technique, and Cases.* New York: John Wiley & Sons, Inc., 1959.

Kaplan, Abraham, *The Conduct of Inquiry.* San Francisco: Chandler Publishing Co., 1964.

Kaufman, Felix, *Methodology of the Social Sciences.* New York: Oxford University Press, 1944. See Part II, "Methodological Issues in Social Science."

Kinsey, A. C., *et al., Sexual Behavior in the Human Female.* Philadelphia: W. B. Saunders Co., 1953. See "Case Histories Obtained in Personal Interviews," pp. 58–64; see also pp. 66–83, on "retakes" and validity of data.

———, *Sexual Behavior in the Human Male.* Philadelphia: W. B. Saunders Company, 1948. See "Interviewing" and "Comparisons of Interviewers' Data."

Kornhauser, Arthur, "Questionnaire Construction and Interview Procedure," in Claire Selltiz *et al., Research Methods in Social Relations.* New York: Holt, Rinehart & Winston, Inc., 1959.

Kroeber, A. L. (ed.), *Anthropology Today.* Chicago: University of Chicago Press, 1951. Excellent chapters on interviewing, historical approach, problems of methodology.

Lazarsfeld, Paul, "The Sociology of Empirical Social Research," *American Sociological Review,* XXVII (1962), 757–67.

———, "Problems in Methodology," in *Sociology Today: Problems and Prospects,* eds. R. K. Merton, Leonard Broom, and L. S. Cottrell, Jr. New York: Basic Books, Inc., 1959.

———, and Morris Rosenberg (eds.), *The Language of Social Research.* New York: The Free Press of Glencoe, Inc., 1955.

Lerner, Daniel, and Harold D. Lasswell (eds.), *The Policy Sciences: Recent Developments in Scope and Method.* Stanford, Calif.: Stanford University Press, 1951. See articles by Herbert Hyman on interviewing; H. D.

Lasswell on policy orientation; Rensis Likert on the sample interview survey; R. K. Merton, on social science and research policy; E. A. Shils, on study of the primary group.

Levitt, E. E., *Clinical Research and Analysis in the Behavioral Sciences*. Springfield, Ill.: Charles C Thomas, Publisher, 1961. Brief discussion of problems in research.

Lewin, Kurt, *Field Theory in Social Science,* ed. D. Cartwright. New York: Harper & Row, Publishers, 1951.

Lindgren, E. J., "Field Work in Social Psychology," *British Journal of Psychology,* Part 2, XXVI, 174–82.

Lindzey, Gardner, *Projective Techniques and Cross-Cultural Research*. New York: Appleton-Century-Crofts, 1962.

Maccoby, E.R., and N., "The Interview; A Tool in Social Science Research," in Gardner Lindzey, *Handbook of Social Psychology,* Vol. I. Reading, Mass.: Addison-Wesley Publishing Co., Inc., 1954. One of the best discussions on interviewing.

Macdonald, Mary E., "Social Work Research," in Norman Polansky, *Social Work Research*. Chicago: University of Chicago Press, 1960.

McCollough, Celest, and Loche Van Atta, *Statistical Concepts: A Program for Self-instruction*. New York: McGraw-Hill Book Company, 1963.

McKenzie, R. D., *The Metropolitan Community,* New York: McGraw-Hill Book Company, 1933.

Madge, John, *Tools of Social Science*. New York: Longmans, Green and Co., Inc., 1953.

———, *The Origins of Scientific Sociology*. New York: The Free Press of Glencoe, Inc., 1962. Thorough, stimulating, highly insightful discussion of studies by Emile Durkheim, W. I. Thomas, R. E. Park, the Lynds, Roethlisberger and Dickson, W. F. Whyte, G. Murdal, S. A. Stouffer, A. C. Kinsey, T. W. Adorno, R. F. Bales, R. K. Merton. Considerable stress is laid on planning, method, laboratory experiments, analysis of data.

Mills, C. Wright, *Sociological Imagination*. London: Oxford University Press, 1959. Stimulating and colorful presentation.

Modley, Rudolph, Dyno Lowenstein, *et al., Pictographs and Graphs*. New York: Harper & Row, Publishers, 1952.

Moreno, J. L., *Who Shall Survive?* New York: Beacon House, 1953.

Moreno, J.L., and Helen Jennings (eds.), *The Sociometry Reader*. New York: The Free Press of Glencoe, Inc., 1960.

Moroney, M. J., *Facts from Figures*. Baltimore: Penguin Books, Inc., 1956.

Moser, C. A., *Survey Methods in Social Investigation*. New York: The Macmillan Company, 1958.

Mueller, John A., and Karl F. Schuessler, *Statistical Reasoning in Sociology*. Boston: Houghton Mifflin Company, 1961.

Murdock, G. P., "The Cross-Cultural Survey," *American Sociological Review*, V (June, 1940), 361–70.

Newcomb, T. M., "Theory and Methods: A Brief Overview," in Festinger, Leon, and Daniel Katz, *Research Methods in the Behavioral Sciences*. New York: Holt, Rinehart & Winston, Inc., 1952, pp. 1–12.

Northrop, F. S. C., *Logic of the Sciences and the Humanities*. New York: The Macmillan Company, 1947. See Chap. I, "Initiation of Inquiry," and Chap. III, "Natural History Stage of Inquiry."

Ogburn, W. F., "On Scientific Writing," *American Journal of Sociology*, LII, 283–389.

Oldfield, R. C., *The Psychology of the Interview* (4th ed.). London: Methuen & Co., Ltd., 1951. Elementary discussion of ways of securing data on attitudes.

Palmer, Vivien, *Field Studies in Sociology*. Chicago: University of Chicago Press, 1928.

Parten, Mildred, *Surveys, Polls, and Samples: Practical Procedures*. New York: Harper & Row, Publishers, 1950. See discussion on steps involved in planning a study.

Paul, Benjamin D., "Interview Techniques and Field Relations," in Kroeber, *Anthropology Today*. Chicago: University of Chicago Press, 1951, pp. 430–51. Excellent articles on field procedure.

Pearson, Karl, *The Grammer of Science*. London: J. M. Dent and Sons, Ltd., 1936. A basic book on logical procedure in science.

Polansky, Norman (ed.), *Social Work Research*. Chicago: University of Chicago Press, 1960.

Pool, Ithiel de Sola (ed.), *Trends in Content Analysis*. Urbana, Ill.: University of Illinois Press, 1959.

Popper, K. R., *The Logic of Scientific Discovery*. New York: Basic Books, Inc., 1959.

Quinn, James A., *Human Ecology*. Englewood Cliffs, N.J.: Prentice-Hall, Inc., 1950.

Ray, D. P., (ed.), *Trends in Social Science*. New York: The Philosophical Library, 1961. See chaps. on "Contemporary Research in Education," "Research in Politics, Government, and Law," "Trends in Interdisciplinary Research," "The Funding of Social Science Research."

Riesman, David, and Mark Benny (eds.), "The Interview in Social Science Research," *American Journal of Sociology*, LXII (September, 1956).

Riley, Matilda W., *Sociological Research—I. A Case Approach. II. Exercises and Manual.* New York: Harcourt, Brace & World, Inc., 1963.

Riley, Matilda W. *et al., Sociological Studies in Scale Analysis.* New Brunswick, N.J.: Rutgers University Press, 1954.

Rogers, Carl R., and F. J. Roethlisberger, "Barriers and Gateways to Communication," *Harvard Business Review* (July-August, 1952), pp. 46–52.

Rose, Arnold, *Theory and Method in Social Science.* Minneapolis, Minn.: University of Minnesota Press, 1954.

———, (ed.), *Human Behavior and Social Processes: An Interactionist Approach.* Boston: Houghton Mifflin Company, 1962. See "The Interview and the Professional Relation," pp. 193–206, and "Some Relevant Directions for Research in Juvenile Delinquency," pp. 468–481.

Schmid, Calvin F., *Handbook of Graphic Presentation.* New York: The Ronald Press Company, 1954.

———, *Social Trends in Seattle.* Seattle: University of Washington Press, 1944.

Selltiz, Claire, Marie Jahoda, Morton Deutch, and S. W. Cook, *Research Methods in Social Relations.* New York: Holt, Rinehart & Winston, Inc., 1959.

Shevky, Eshref, and Wendell Bell, *Social Area Analysis, Theory, Illustrative Application, and Computational Procedure.* Palo Alto: Stanford University Press, 1955.

Social Science Research Council, *Theory and Practice in Historical Study: A Report of the Committee on Historiography.* New York: The Council, 1946. Includes extensive bibliography.

———, *The Social Sciences in Historical Study: A Report of the Committee on Historiography.* New York: The Council, 1954.

Sorokin, P. A., *Society, Culture and Personality: Their Structure and Dynamics.* New York: Cooper Square Publishers, Inc., 1962.

Stein, Maurice, and Arthur Vidich (eds.), *Sociology on Trial.* Englewood Cliffs, N.J.: Prentice-Hall, Inc., 1963. A collection of articles of past and present sociologists who question the soundness of sociological theory and the adequacy of approach to studies of social phenomena.

Stephan, Frederick F., and Philip J. McCarthy, *Sampling Opinions.* New York: John Wiley & Sons, Inc., 1963.

Stouffer, S. A., *Social Research to Test Ideas.* New York: The Free Press of Glencoe, Inc., 1962. Selected writings by the late Prof. Stouffer, published posthumously.

———, *et al., Measurement and Prediction.* Princeton: Princeton University Press, 1950. Chap. XII, "Two Case Studies in Prediction," pp. 473–85 and Chap. XIII, "The Screening of Psychoneurotics in the Army," pp. 486–97 and *passim*. See also his *Studies of the American Soldier*.

Sullivan, Harry Stack, *The Psychiatric Interview*. New York: W. W. Norton & Company, Inc., 1954. Clear discussion of problems and processes in interviewing; applicable to interviewers in social research.

Theodorson, George A., *Studies in Human Ecology*. New York: Harper & Row, Publishers, 1961.

Thurstone, L. L., and E. J., Chave, *The Measurement of Attitudes*. Chicago: University of Chicago Press, 1929.

Torgerson, Warren S., *Theory and Methods of Scaling*. New York: John Wiley & Sons, Inc., 1958.

U.S. Bureau of the Census, *Eighteenth Census of the United States: 1960*. Washington: Government Printing Office, 1961, Vol. II, Part A.

U.S. Department of Agriculture, Bureau of Agricultural Economics, *Rural Life Studies*. Washington: Government Printing Office, 1941–1943.

Warner, W. Lloyd, *et al.,* "The Yankee City Series." New Haven: Yale University Press, 1941–1947.

———, and P. S. Lunt, *The Social Life of a Modern Community* and *The Status System of a Modern Community*.

———, and L. Srole, *The Social Systems of American Ethnic Groups*.

———, and J. O. Low, *The Social Life of the Modern Factory*.

Weaver, Warren (ed.), *The Scientists Speak*. New York: Boni and Gaer, 1947. See Chapter I, "Science and Complexity" (by Warren Weaver); Chap. XIII, "The Natural and the Social Sciences" (by Isaiah Bowman); Chap. XV, "The Long-Term Values" (by Arthur H. Compton, *et al.*).

Welford, A. T., M. Argyle, D. V. Glass, J. N. Morris (eds.), *Society: Problems and Methods of Study*. New York: The Philosophical Library, 1962.

Whyte, W. F., *Street Corner Society*. Chicago: University of Chicago Press. 1955 edition has excellent discussion of author's approach and method of study. See Introduction and Chap. I.

———, "Observational Field-Work Methods," in Jahoda, *et al., Research Methods in Social Relations*. New York: Holt, Rinehart & Winston, Inc., 1951. Chap. XIV, pp. 493–513.

Wirth, Louis (ed.), *Eleven Twenty-Six*. Chicago: University of Chicago Press, 1940. Critical review of research studies by social scientists, at the Social Science Building, known on the university campus as 1126; extensive and well-chosen bibliography of historical interest.

Wormser, M. H., and Claire Selltiz, *How to Conduct a Community Self-Survey of Civil Rights*. New York: Association Press, 1951.

Young, Pauline V., *Interviewing and Life Histories* (in preparation).

———, *Scientific Social Surveys and Research* (3rd ed.). Englewood Cliffs, N.J.: Prentice-Hall, Inc., 1956. See Chaps. 1 and 2 on "Historical Background of the Survey Movement," chaps. omitted from 1966 ed.

Zeisel, Hans, *Say It with Figures*. New York: Harper & Row, Publishers, 1957.

Zelditch, Morris, Jr., *Sociological Statistics*. New York: Holt, Rinehart & Winston, Inc., 1959.

Ziskind, Eugene, *Psychophysiologic Medicine*. Philadelphia: Lea and Febiger, 1954. Chap. IV, "The Life History," pp. 55–88 and Chap. VII, "Interview Techniques," pp. 127–155.

Znaniecki, Florian, *The Method of Sociology*. New York: Farrar, Strauss, and Giroux, Inc., 1934. See his discussion on observation in Chap. IV.

index

A

N

Q

R

T

LH 0080593 9

THE SOCIAL ANIMAL

ALSO BY W. G. RUNCIMAN

Relative Deprivation and Social Justice (1966)

A Critique of Max Weber's Philosophy of Social Science (1972)

A Treatise on Social Theory:
Volume I (1983)
Volume II (1989)
Volume III (1997)